STRATEGIC MANAGEMENT

A New View of Business Policy and Planning

STRATEGIC MANAGEMENT

A New View of Business Policy and Planning

EDITED BY

Dan E. Schendel
*Krannert Graduate School
of Management
Purdue University*

Charles W. Hofer
*Visiting Associate Professor
Graduate School of Business
Columbia University*

Little, Brown and Company
BOSTON • TORONTO

To research workers in Strategic Management: past, present, and future

Based on a conference held at the University of Pittsburgh
arranged under the auspices of the Business Policy and Planning Division
of the Academy of Management.

Library of Congress Catalog Card No. 78–73465

First Printing

Published simultaneously in Canada
by Little, Brown & Company (Canada) Limited

Printed in the United States of America

Credits

Exhibit 3.6 Adapted from portrayal of General Electric's "Strategic Business
Planning Grid" ("Corporate Planning: . . . ." 1975) and Michael G. Allen's presentation "Strategic Problems Facing Today's Corporate Planner" at the Academy
of Management, August 1976.

Exhibit 3.7 From Derek Channon, "Strategic Planning Portfolio Models: Practical Progress and Problems in Practice" (Draft, 1976).

Exhibit 3.10 In Derek Channon and R. M. Jalland, *Multinational Strategic Planning.* New York: Macmillan, 1978. Taken from J. Smith's unpublished thesis,
Manchester School of Business.

Exhibit 5.3 Reproduced by permission from *Strategy Implementation: The Role
of Structure and Process* by Jay R. Galbraith and Daniel A. Nathanson. Copyright
© 1978, West Publishing Company. All rights reserved.

Exhibit 5.5 Reproduced by permission from *Strategy Implementation: The Role
of Structure and Process* by Jay R. Galbraith and Daniel A. Nathanson. Copyright
© 1978, West Publishing Company. All rights reserved.

(continued to page 537)

PREFACE

Business Policy has been a required course of instruction in business schools for well over half a century. It has a standing that equals any other course as a prerequisite of the graduate degree in business. Its role in management curricula has been to *integrate* knowledge gained in the so-called functional and tool areas of instruction that, along with business policy, comprise the core curriculum. Conventional wisdom has it that integration takes place simply by exposing the student to the problems of several functions and/or tools at one time, typically through the medium of a complex case, with no further substance required to understand the role of the top manager in a business enterprise.

Recent history of business organizations, especially since World War II, shows that two very significant changes have occurred to elevate the integration problem to one of much greater importance and much more significance than it ever has held before. First, as has been well argued by authors such as Alvin Toffler in *Future Shock*, an enormous, almost calamitous change has taken place in the rate at which technological, social, political, and economic events occur. Under such massive changes, mankind's institutions have been forced to change at unprecedented rates. Business institutions have been no exception.

A second significant change has been the alterations that have occurred in the organizational or structural forms of businesses. Over the past thirty years there has been tremendous growth in the size of firms, as they have expanded into multiple product lines and businesses and even into multinational and multicultural markets. These changes in size and complexity have been accompanied by changes in the administrative structure and processes by which such firms are managed.

These two factors — the increasing rate of environmental change and the increasing size and complexity of organizational structure and processes — have led to important, far-reaching changes in business management practice. Chandler was among the first to recognize the tendency of businesses, and perhaps all organizations, to change under environmental conditions that themselves had changed. Particularly noteworthy is the split that has occurred between "operating" and what has come to be called "strategic" management. Operating management deals with the ongoing conduct of the firm's affairs, with insuring that the day-to-day work of the organization is as efficient as possible. This has been the traditional work of the manager, but with increasingly complex and rapidly changing environments has come the need to change the very direction and nature of the firm. Given ever larger organizations, the twin tasks of efficiently running the firm and of deciding the direction in which it should head proved too much to combine in single administrative positions and in single individuals. Consequently, new organizational forms, new divisions of managerial labor, and new managerial methods were developed which split the directional and character choices from the tasks of insuring operating efficiency.

However, this split between strategic and operating management tasks has not led to the creation of separate positions for strategic managers and operating managers. Rather, the manifestation of these two changes has been the evolution and proliferation of general management positions, which carry responsibilities for both operating and strategic management tasks. Typical of such changes have been the creation of corporate executive offices as well as the creation of corporate, group, division, business, and project general management positions.

At all organizational levels such general managers become involved in both business and corporate strategy formulation, two key tasks of the strategic management process. It is one of the major responsibilities of strategy to insure the integration of functions and businesses across organizational levels and across time. Functional integration takes place at relatively low levels in an organization compared with where that integration once took place, not only because business firms are so much larger today, but also because of a major philosophical shift in managerial practice from cost-based to profit-based control systems.

Underlying this split in management tasks has been the development of the concept of strategy, and more recently, the development of the strategic management process. These two constructs are useful in integrating the firm at three levels: (1) within each functional area of a given business (e.g., marketing strategy); (2) at the business level in integrating various functional areas; and (3) at the corporate level of multi-industry firms in integrating their various businesses.

In management education, the concepts of strategy and strategic management also have emerged as major intellectual platforms of the business policy course because they provide a substantive methodology for integrating the functional and analytical tools learned by the student. Unfortunately, these concepts go well beyond the content of most traditional policy courses. Nevertheless, during the last decade, and especially in the last five years, substantial progress has been made in theory building, research, and teaching in the business policy/strategic management area. Because of this progress, much of which is documented in this book, it can be truly said that the policy area is developing as an academic discipline. To date, this development, which promises to give new direction to the manner in which functional and business integration is taught, researched, and practiced, has gone unrecognized by most academia outside the area.

It was this complex of changes that led to this volume of collected papers and to the conference at which the ideas contained herein were first discussed. In the early 1970s, the first widely attended meetings took place among teachers and researchers of business policy who gathered to talk about their mutual interests and problems in teaching and researching the subject.[1] Subsequent meetings indicated an awareness, although at times a limited one, of the changes that were taking place in management practice and of the significant need to make others in business schools aware of the major upheaval that was occurring in the concepts underlying the field. To those working in the policy field, it was clear that these changes needed to be recognized in the design of policy courses, in research directions in policy, and in the decisions of deans and faculty involving the share of resources devoted to policy. While the American Assembly of Collegiate Schools of Business (AACSB) had long recognized through its accreditation Standard E that a course integrating the functional fields was necessary and that such a course should deal with major uncertainties facing management, it never had been able to achieve consensus regarding the nature and content of that course. Therefore, in recognition of this difficulty and the lack of acceptance of policy as a separate academic field among other business school faculties, some of the leading policy scholars in the early 1970s authored a statement of research needs and priorities in the field as a first step in making others aware of what was needed and to some degree what might be possible.

This early attempt, while useful as a first step, did not provide a definition of the business policy/strategic management area or what it was and where it could and should be going in terms of both teaching and research concepts. This problem was accentuated by the following circumstances: (1) there were no journals exclusively devoted to business policy/strategic management research; (2) there existed no collected body of scholarly works that the student of business policy/strategic management could be pointed toward; (3) there were no concentrated cadres of academics that could be singled out for such students; and (4) there was no independent professional society devoted to the area. Hence, the notion of a conference where leading authorities would gather and present their ideas of what and where business policy/strategic management was and where it was going seemed a useful first step in letting others know what the state of the art in the field really was.

The broad objectives established for the conference were: (1) to define the dimensions and boundaries of this emerging field; (2) to identify opportunities that exist for research in the field; and (3) to help both students and practitioners better understand this new approach to organizational integration. This volume is devoted to aiding that understanding.

[1] Meetings did take place at Harvard University and the University of Manchester, in England, during the 1960s in which selected academics, primarily Harvard Business School professors and D.B.A. students and graduates from Harvard, exchanged their teaching experience and, to a lesser extent, their research ideas.

The conference itself was organized by the editors of this book and was held at the University of Pittsburgh in May 1977. To achieve the above objectives, a set of fourteen research papers was commissioned to: (1) describe and define the field of strategic management by discussing major research findings in the area; (2) critically examine the research methodologies and data sources presently in use in policy and planning research; and (3) suggest directions that seemed particularly fruitful for future research.

In partitioning the field, the editors attempted to identify all the major subtopics in the field which were conceptually distinguishable and on which a reasonable amount of research had accumulated. Our initial list included over twenty such topics. Because of the time constraints imposed by a three-day conference, it was necessary to reduce our list to fourteen topics which could be covered in greater depth. The final choice was our own, and inevitably some important topics, such as social responsibility and boards of directors, were eliminated. In making this reduction, a principal criterion was whether sufficient empirical research had been done on the topic to warrant giving it major attention at the present time. Clearly, our own knowledge of existing research (or lack thereof) influenced these selections.

For each of the fourteen areas included, a leading authority on that topic was invited to prepare a paper describing the topic area in terms of the research that had been done and the most promising directions for future research. For each such major topic area paper, two discussants then were invited to prepare remarks for the conference that would complement the author's observations and, where appropriate, critique the content of the topic paper. Moderators for each area were carefully selected for their knowledge of the area and were asked to insure that the ninety-minute period devoted to their topic involved author, discussants, and audience in an exchange of views. In total, there were fifty-six scholars actively involved in the conference presentations.

In addition to the fourteen topic areas, two separate panels were invited to comment on: (1) the teaching implications of the material being presented and discussed; and (2) the practitioner views and implications of the conference. The latter panel was selected from personnel involved primarily in industrial corporate-planning practice. The full complement of participants is listed, along with the three-day program, in Appendixes 1 and 2.

In addition to the invited authors, discussants, moderators, and panelists, ten other participants were invited from industry, and the remaining places were made available on a first-come, first-served basis to members of the Division of Business Policy and Planning of the Academy of Management.

In all, there were nearly one hundred participants and attendees at the conference, representing more than forty schools, various consulting organizations active in strategic management and planning, and industry practitioners from some of the leading industrial corporations using frontier concepts in strategic management.

All sessions were tape-recorded for the benefit of the authors of the papers and for the later compilation of this volume. While this volume cannot be regarded as a proceedings of the conference, it is fair to say that it represents and extends the substance of the conference. Further, particular efforts have been made to capture the essential conclusions of the intensive discussions that were held over the three days of the meeting.

All of the papers in this volume have been rewritten, most substantially so, since their discussion at the conference in Pittsburgh. Each author has responded to the ideas presented at the conference and has had available for those revisions both the recorded tapes of the conversation surrounding his specific paper and the editors' extensive review comments, which sought to develop ideas the authors did not cover sufficiently as well as to make this an integrated volume rather than just a loose collection of papers. Where further comment seemed necessary to expand each of the papers, we have included such remarks in our introductions to the sections in which the papers appear and we are hopeful that they explain to the reader how each set of papers fits together to form an integrated whole. We have also provided editorial linking comments to connect the various papers and explain their relationships more fully.

Based on our paradigm of the field, the volume is divided into ten sets of papers. This guiding paradigm is developed in the Introduction to the book and presents, we believe, a more complete concept of the field of business policy and planning than has previously been assembled. It is only in the light of this paradigm that the full measure of each paper and our editorial comment can be evaluated and appreciated.

The strategic management paradigm not only represents a new way of viewing the policy and planning field that links the developing substance of the field, but it also can be used as a guide for the direction in which research and teaching in policy and planning is headed. In addition, it can be and is used in management practice to help design the new strategies and organization forms that will be needed to cope with the massive environmental changes business will face in the remainder of this century. Thus, the paradigm deserves study because of its significance to management education and practice and not just because it integrates the papers in this book.

In concluding this preface, we need to acknowledge the efforts of the authors whose work appears in this book. We have not always presented the easiest specifications or deadlines within which to work. To these authors must go special thanks for their patience, tolerance, and willingness to share their experience and expertise. To the participants at the conference who made substantial contributions to the discussions and the subsequent development of everyone else's thought must also go our gratitude, for the conference results exceeded our highest expectations. A note of appreciation must also go to those who provided the funds and material goods that made the conference and this overall effort feasible. In a very real sense, the conference would not have been possible without the support of the Strategic Planning Institute; A. T. Kearney, Inc.; the University of Pittsburgh; and the Division of Business Policy and Planning of the Academy of Management. It was under the auspices of the Division of Business Policy and Planning, with the support of the Academy, that this project had its beginnings.

Our gratitude must also be extended to several individuals who were especially helpful in making the conference a success. Among many, Professor John Grant, who handled the University of Pittsburgh arrangements, was especially successful in providing an ambience in which a fruitful interchange could take place. In addition, Dr. Sidney Schoeffler of the Strategic Planning Institute; Merritt Davoust of A. T. Kearney, Inc.; and Dean H. J. Zoffer of the University of Pittsburgh were helpful in providing their personal and organizational support for this effort.

Whether this volume fulfills the high hopes we have for it should be judged primarily by the influence it has over future thought and practice in the Strategic Management area, as we believe the field will one day be called. If it has the impact we hope for, it will only be due to the efforts of the many different people and organizations who had sufficient faith to devote their time and resources to it. If it fails, it will be due to our failure to convey to others the new directions in which strategic management practice is taking us. The errors and oversights remain with us. All our efforts have been directed at minimizing them and emphasizing the bright future that lies ahead for students of the Strategic Management field.

Finally, a very special note of thanks is owed to Mary Lou Schendel for her patient help with the typing and with the myriad administrative tasks of bringing together into an integrated manuscript a widely diverse set of materials. It would have been impossible to meet our schedules without her support.

DAN SCHENDEL   CHARLES W. HOFER

CONTENTS

xi

SECTION 4   STRATEGY EVALUATION   189

EVALUATION OF STRATEGY: THEORY AND MODELS   196
Richard P. Rumelt

COMMENTARY   212
Bruce A. Kirchhoff

SECTION 5   STRATEGY IMPLEMENTATION   218

FORMAL PLANNING SYSTEMS: THEIR ROLE IN STRATEGY FORMULATION AND IMPLEMENTATION   226
Peter Lorange

COMMENTARY   241
Dale J. Hekhuis

SECTION 7   THEORY BUILDING AND THEORY TESTING
IN STRATEGIC MANAGEMENT   382

SECTION 10   RESEARCH NEEDS AND ISSUES IN STRATEGIC MANAGEMENT   515

STRATEGIC MANAGEMENT

A New View of Business Policy and Planning

INTRODUCTION

DAN SCHENDEL
Purdue University

CHARLES W. HOFER
Columbia University

This book surveys existing research and suggests fruitful directions for further research on the central responsibilities of the firm's leadership. One of the major conclusions that emerges from this survey and its analysis is that a new concept of the general manager's role and responsibilities is developing, a concept we shall call *strategic management*. This book will not only explore the research and theoretical implications of this concept but will also indicate the managerial implications of the concept and the ways that well-managed firms are beginning to use it today. While this work ties to the field more commonly known as Business Policy, the book will indicate why a new view of policy, and its practitioner's counterpart, planning, is not only useful but necessary to further progress in an important aspect of managerial practice, that of top-level management work.

THE VALUE OF NEW PARADIGMS

New concepts or paradigms are important to scientific progress. Kuhn (1970) uses Newton's paradigm of light to show that it was the first "nearly uniformly accepted paradigm for physical optics." Prior to Newton's development, everyone working in optics felt forced to build the field anew from its foundations. This was no longer true in optics after Newton.

Thus, the arrival of the first universally acceptable paradigm is a significant event in any field. Kuhn continues, "History suggests that the road to a firm research consensus is extraordinarily arduous." One reason why, according to Kuhn (1970: 15), is:

> . . . In the absence of a paradigm . . . all of the facts that could possibly pertain to the development of a given science are likely to seem equally relevant. As a result, early fact-gathering is a far more nearly random activity than the one that subsequent scientific development makes familiar. Furthermore, in the absence of a reason for seeking some particular

1

form of more recondite information, early fact-gathering is usually restricted to the wealth of data that lie ready to hand.

This observation seems to characterize very well the history of the policy field. Policy research has consisted mostly of gathering readily available facts, which are usually organized into case studies that are used for comparative research or teaching. Kuhn (1970: 16) suggests why this sort of fact collecting has not been more productive in science:

> But though this sort of fact-collecting has been essential to the origin of many significant sciences, anyone who examines, for example, Pliny's encyclopedic writings or the Baconian natural histories of the seventeenth century will discover that it produces a morass. One somehow hesitates to call the literature that results scientific.

Kuhn's studies of scientific development lead him to conclude that the evidence is overwhelming that such general, uncorrelated fact gathering ends only when an initial, widely accepted paradigm enters the field. Such initial paradigms are never complete, but they always better explain observable events and facts than any existing concepts about the field. The value of paradigms is that they lead to progress and efficiency in the further development of a field. Again we quote Kuhn (1970: 19):

> When the individual scientist can take a paradigm for granted, he need no longer, in his major works, attempt to build his field anew, starting from first principles and justifying the use of each concept introduced.

Today, the policy field is in need of a new paradigm that can end the continual and pointless redefinition of concepts used in both practice and teaching. We believe such a paradigm is at hand, and this book is devoted to developing a better and wider understanding of it.

New is a relative term, of course, and it depends upon your viewpoint. The new paradigm we propose for the policy field is that of "Strategic Management," and it rests squarely on the concept of strategy. Neither of these concepts is new in the sense of being unknown to others, for such terminology has been in use for ten to fifteen years, and the notions represented in these concepts have been utilized in some firms for much longer than that. Nevertheless, for most practitioners, most policy (and management) teachers, and most policy (and management) researchers, the concepts or paradigms of strategy and strategic management offered here are new.

In any field, new paradigms offer an entirely new series of questions, and specific research can be directed toward seeking answers to such questions. Science, art, and politics are replete with examples of new concepts and paradigms that have led to new ways to interpret observed phenomena and ultimately to theories useful in making predictions about these phenomena. Moreover, without such new concepts, progress is not possible and, however comfortable the status quo, it is never a true and long-term friend, for it stifles change and restricts progress.

Sam Walter Foss illustrated the consequences of the blind acceptance of the status quo, and implicitly the value of new paradigms, in the following work:

THE CALF-PATH

One day, through the primeval wood,
A calf walked home, as good calves should;
But made a trail all bent askew,
A crooked trail as all calves do.

Since then two hundred years have fled,
And, I infer, the calf is dead.
But still he left behind his trail,
And thereby hangs my moral tale.

The trail was taken up next day
By a lone dog that passed that way;
And then a wise bell-wether sheep
Pursued the trail o'er vale and steep,
And drew the flock behind him, too,
As good bell-wethers always do.

And from that day, o'er hill and glade,
Through those old woods a path was made;
And many men wound in and out,
And dodged, and turned, and bent about
And uttered words of righteous wrath
Because 'twas such a crooked path.
But still they followed — do not laugh —
The first migrations of that calf,
And through this winding wood-way stalked,
Because he wobbled when he walked.

This forest path became a lane,
That bent, and turned, and turned again;
This crooked lane became a road,
Where many a poor horse with his load
Toiled on beneath the burning sun,
And traveled some three miles in one.
And thus a century and a half
They trod the footsteps of that calf.

The years passed on in swiftness fleet,
The road became a village street;

And this, before men were aware,
A city's crowded thoroughfare;
And soon the central street was this
Of a renowned metropolis;
And men two centuries and a half
Trod in the footsteps of that calf.

Each day a hundred thousand rout
Followed the zigzag calf about;
And o'er his crooked journey went
The traffic of a continent.
A hundred thousand men were led
By one calf near three centuries dead.
They followed still his crooked way,
And lost one hundred years a day;
For thus such reverence is lent
To well-established precedent.

A moral lesson this might teach,
Were I ordained and called to preach;
For men are prone to go it blind
Along the calf-paths of the mind,
And work away from sun to sun
To do what other men have done.
They follow in the beaten track,
And out and in, and forth and back,
And still their devious course pursue,
To keep the path that others do.

But how the wise old wood-gods laugh,
Who saw the first primeval calf!
Ah! many things this tale might teach —
But I am not ordained to preach.

SAM WALTER FOSS

Our purpose in this book is to start some new and straighter calf paths for the field of business policy/strategic management and perhaps along the way kill a sacred cow or two that once started crooked calf paths of their own.

To do this we begin by: (1) defining the field of business policy; (2) tracing its evolution through two basic paradigms that have characterized its history; and (3) presenting a new paradigm for business policy and a new name for it. This introduction then closes with an overview of the remainder of the book and a description of how the strategy and strategic management paradigms have been used to put the volume together.

BUSINESS POLICY AS A FIELD

Schendel and Hatten (1972) observed that "Business Policy is generally thought of as a course, not a field of study or a broader discipline." Unlike the so-called functional areas, which the policy course was originally designed to integrate, policy was not considered to be a field of study with substance of its own. Somehow, the integration of the marketing, financial, production, and other functional fields of management was to be accomplished simply by considering these topics simultaneously. In the Ford Foundation–sponsored study of business schools and their curriculum in the late 1950s, Gordon and Howell (1959: 206) perpetuated this view by stating:

> The capstone of the core curriculum should be a course in "business policy" which will give the students an opportunity to pull together what they have learned in the separate business fields and utilize this knowledge in the analysis of complex business problems.
>
> Without the responsibility of having to transmit some specific body of knowledge, the business policy course can concentrate on integrating what has already been acquired and on developing further the student's skill in using that knowledge. The course can range over the entire curriculum and beyond.

Why a single course simultaneously considering complex business problems in several different functional areas would provide the student "an opportunity to pull together what they have learned" is not so obvious as the statement implies. Could integration really be accomplished without some substantive concept or paradigm for doing it? Without going "beyond" the content of the various functional fields? As important as these questions are, at least as important is the presumption, often fatal when followed in practice, that all there is to managing the total enterprise is the task of coordinating the various functional fields and that this coordination will somehow lead to appropriate choices about the future of the firm. The economic junkyard is filled with managers and firms that thought that way. Inherent in this view of total enterprise management is the idea that the firm can be managed through the collected wisdom of various functional area experts, and all top management must do is pick and choose from what options are brought before them.

Gordon and Howell can be forgiven for such a view, for their calf paths are those of economic theory, where entrepreneurship is accorded mystical properties in enterprise formation, and management technology is accorded no value except to be included in the *ceteris paribus* conditions typical of these theories. But for more serious students of management practice, especially at the general management level, the oversight is not so easily ignored, for it reveals a serious shortcoming in curriculum design and management training, not to mention research priorities and research problems undertaken.

An examination of the evolution of the business firm serves to show that a model that fails to place entrepreneurial choice at the center of the managerial universe is one that is incapable of providing a mechanism for renewing the firm beyond its originally intended purpose.

Any successful business begins with a "key idea" for: (1) supplying a product or service, (2) that will satisfy a consumer need, (3) and in so doing will lead to an excess of revenue over costs, (4) thereby supplying the originator of the idea with an incentive (profit) to continue to provide the supply. This is easily said but very hard to do successfully. If a firm is successful it tends to grow and typically will add other product/market matches[1] that are profitable, reinforcing growth, and so on. But such growth requires, among other things, functional specialization of managerial labor if it is to be maintained.

The "key idea," that product of the entrepreneurial mind, is the central concept that is to be noted. Without it, there is no business, and indeed this same argument can easily be generalized to any type of purposive organization. This entrepreneurial choice is at the heart of the concept of strategy, and it is good strategy that insures the formation, renewal, and survival of the total enterprise, that in turn leads to an integration of the functional areas of the business and not the other way around.

Nonetheless, it is only very recently that strategy has been explicitly recognized as the central concept to business success and thus something to be managed. The reason its importance was not recognized earlier is simple. It stems from the ways most businesses are created. As we have noted, they are created by an entrepreneur with a key idea, that is, a new strategy for a business. Usually, the entrepreneur does not explicitly write out this key idea. Rather, it is kept in the entrepreneur's head where it is used to guide day-to-day decisions. Such day-to-day activities usually demand vast amounts of time and effort, while the strategy/key idea often requires little change for many years. In short, management of strategy is so fundamental and has required such little change that its very importance was overlooked or taken for granted, and therefore not recognized as the force leading and directing the efforts of the various functional areas toward a common end.

So, while there was a recognition that some integration of functional fields was necessary to achieve successful performance, the mechanism (concepts) for achieving such integration tended to be overlooked until recent times. However, since the end of World War II, major changes have occurred in the environment and nature of businesses that have required an explicit identification and understanding of the concept of strategy and its management.

The first of these changes is a significant increase in the rate of change of the environment in which businesses must compete. Moreover, the

---

[1] By product/market matches we mean the joint choice made by a firm of the product to produce and the market(s) in which it will offer the product. Such matches are in fact businesses, and they may or may not be profitable choices.

environment is much more interdependent than it has ever been before, leading to further complexities in the management of the firm. Thus, the birth and death of key ideas, that is of good strategies, must be expected to occur with much greater frequency than it has in the past under these new, dynamic, and interdependent environmental conditions.

The second major force motivating the recognition and use of strategy has been the massive growth in the size and complexity of business organizations themselves. Rumelt (1974) has shown that the majority of *Fortune* 500 firms has shifted from a single-product-line (single key idea) form of organization in 1949 to a multi-industry (multiple key ideas), or even multinational form of organization in 1970. Thus, the problem of integrating different functional areas in a firm such as General Electric now occurs at least four to five levels below the president's office. But there are other integration problems as well. The different businesses in such complex enterprises must also be integrated effectively, as must different cultures in the multinational enterprise, and all of these factors together must be integrated across time. Such integration has required an elaboration of the basic concept of strategy that is at the core of the policy and planning field today.

To better understand the field in its present state, however, it is necessary to examine the two paradigms that have characterized the field over the years and to describe a third, which we have used as the structure for the papers in the field and which we believe is the new paradigm around which the field will develop in the future.

POLICY FORMULATION: THE PRESTRATEGY PARADIGM

Until the early 1960s, the basic paradigm of the business policy area was the one still used in most firms and policy courses today, that of policy formulation. Policy formulation is also the paradigm from which the course and field takes its name, "Business Policy." To understand how this paradigm developed, it is necessary to review the typical evolution of a business in more detail.

As noted earlier, most firms usually offered only one class of products which they sold to one set of customers in a restricted geographic territory. In such circumstances, it was not difficult for the entrepreneur to coordinate all the functional activities of the firm in an informal fashion. However, as such firms added or modified their products and added new markets by serving new groups of customers and/or new geographic territories, it was necessary to provide formal procedures for integrating the various activities of the firm, both within different functional areas as well as across them. Thus, the marketing department needed to have the same concept of the firm's product and its markets as did the production or research departments. Such integration was achieved through the establishment of "policies" that each of the functional areas used in making their day-to-day decisions. In most circumstances, a set of such policies was usually adequate to perform the integration or coordination, since most or all of the products and markets of the firm were closely related and the role of change in the firm's environment was slow.

In both management practice and education, such policymaking came to be considered the principal task of top management. Such policies were made as the need for them became evident. Little attention was paid to anticipating any threats to the current business and its future. All growth was to come from the existing business. "Business Policy" was thus taught from a functional perspective, usually with complex cases that simply recounted the "problems" each functional area was encountering and explored the "policies" necessary to integrate them. As has been stated, this is still a widely used paradigm in many policy courses today, even though it is now a well-worn calf path two generations old.

While this paradigm failed to penetrate to the core of the business, the key idea (strategy) was so seldom threatened that it was seldom worth reexamining, although the perceptive manager was usually able to see that not all failures were the result of inefficient operations; many failures had to do with basic faults in the business' strategy which needed to be changed but were not. With the increasing size and complexity of organizations and the increasing types and magnitudes of environmental changes they faced in the 1950s and early 1960s, however, the policy formulation paradigm proved increasingly unable to deal with the key challenges facing the firm. The "policy paradigm" was simply not rich enough to cope with such massive environmental and organizational changes. Better policies were just not the answer, unless the policies were to sell the business, or to enter a new business. The answer lay instead in rethinking the core concepts of the business and the way it related to its environment, that is, in reformulating its strategy.

THE INITIAL STRATEGY PARADIGM

Recognition of these needs probably came earlier in business firms than it did in academe. One reason for this is that the business policy area had no research tradition. A second, and perhaps more important reason, was at the time there were very few scholars in the policy area throughout the country, and most of these were older faculty who had done their research while younger and in other fields and who had little training in the methods that have since proved useful for policy research. Industry, by contrast, was struggling for its very life with the problems we have noted, as Chandler's (1962) research shows. His research also marked the beginning of interest in the concept of strategy in academe from a teaching and research perspective.

Chandler (1962: 16) defined strategy as:

... the determination of the basic long-term goals and objectives of an enterprise, and the adoption of courses of action and the allocation of resources necessary for carrying out these goals.

This definition of strategy emphasizes *both* formation of goals and objectives (ends) and of action plans and resource commitments (means) utilized to achieve these ends. Also implicit in Chandler's definition of strategy is the search for the key idea, rather than the key idea itself; that is, Chandler really talked more about the *process* for formulating strategy than he did about the *content* of the strategy itself. Also, missing from Chandler's definition is the notion that strategy describes the essential linkage between the firm and its environment. In addition, Chandler's dictum that structure follows strategy turns out to be not the whole truth (see Galbraith and Nathanson, Section 5), for in fact structure also precedes and limits certain strategies in ongoing firms. Nevertheless, Chandler contributed the basic concept of strategy, at least to academe, and from his seminal work has sprung much of the research reported and discussed in this volume.

At about the same time that Chandler was developing his ideas, two other writers were working along similar lines. Both were much more concerned with managerial practice and education than was Chandler, who was a business historian. Ansoff (1965) and Andrews (Learned, Christensen, Andrews, and Guth, 1965)[2] offered other views of the concept of strategy. For Ansoff, strategy was discussed in terms of components, of which there were four: (1) product/market scope, (2) growth vector, (3) competitive advantage, and (4) synergy. Ansoff did not include goals and their determination in his definition. He did, however, distinguish between strategy as a statement and strategy formulation as a process.

Andrews (Learned, Christensen, Andrews, and Guth, 1965: 17) defined strategy as:

... the pattern of objectives, purposes, or goals and major policies and plans for achieving these goals, stated in such a way as to define what business the company is in or is to be in and the kind of company it is or is to be.

This concept was broader than that of either Ansoff or Chandler, as is revealed by this statement (Learned, Christensen, Andrews, and Guth, 1965: 21):

The ability to identify the four components of strategy — (1) market opportunity, (2) corporate competences and resources, (3) personal values and aspirations, and (4) acknowledged obligations to segments of society other than the stockholders — is nothing compared to the art of reconciling their implications in a final choice of purpose.

---

[2] Andrews's ideas were first presented in the text *Business Policy: Text and Cases*, (Homewood, Ill.: Richard D. Irwin, 1965) which he coauthored with Edmund Learned, C. Roland Christensen, and William D. Guth.

Unlike Ansoff, Andrews included goals and policies and plans in his concept of strategy, but like Ansoff he distinguished between strategy content and strategy formulation as a process. Both Andrews and Ansoff were also more concerned with economic opportunities and threats, and their internal managerial implications than was Chandler. Andrews further recognized an environment that was more than just an economic one, and he recognized that internal social and behavioral factors influenced the choice of goals and strategy and their use in the firm. It was in these latter areas that his concept was broader than that of his two contemporaries.

These initial strategy paradigms were incomplete on several counts. First, they did not distinguish between corporate-level and business-level strategy. Thus, the initial strategy model was not capable of differentiating between what has come to be called the portfolio question of what businesses to be in (corporate strategy) and the question of how to compete effectively in a given business (business strategy).

Second, the relationship between policies as a means of integrating functional areas and strategy as a means not only of integrating functional areas, but of integrating the firm with its environment across several organizational levels was not made clear. Later evolution of the concept has shown how strategy can integrate greater organizational complexity amid greater environmental turbulence.

Third, the major differences between Chandler's and Andrews's broad definitions of strategy (strategy includes both means and ends) and Ansoff's narrow definition of strategy (strategy excludes ends) was never explicitly addressed or resolved.

The process of managing strategy was not particularly well developed either. Andrews did make a distinction between strategy formulation and strategy implementation, an important contribution, but neither he, Ansoff, nor Chandler discussed in any detail the problem of managing the strategy formulation and implementation processes.

Nevertheless, over the ten-year period from 1965 to 1975 the concept of strategy came into wide use. Textbooks that once were entitled "Business Policy" or some variant thereof now contained the term "strategy" somewhere in their titles. Other writers offered different definitions of strategy, but none made the insightful forward leap that broadened the initial strategy paradigm offered by Chandler, Ansoff, and Andrews.[3]

Throughout this period, major attention of academics was given to strategy formulation, much less to strategy implementation, almost none to the basic tasks involved in managing strategy, and none to the strategic management tasks of general management work. However, practitioners with the practical problems of directing and managing organizations spent far more time and effort on strategy implementation issues than on the actual work of strategy formulation.

[3] Hofer and Schendel (1978) offer a historical development and content comparison of the strategy concept spanning this period.

In summary, the initial strategy paradigm was incomplete, in terms of: (1) the nature and clarity of the strategy concept itself; (2) the tasks associated with managing and implementing strategy; and (3) the strategic roles of the general manager. Nevertheless, evidence was accumulating that "strategic planning" paid off, but most companies did not know how to make it work for them. What was needed was a better paradigm of top-management work that would not only complete the initial strategy paradigm but also prove useful in dealing with the two major forces pressing on today's complex businesses identified earlier. What was needed was the development of the strategic management paradigm, a subject to which we now turn our attention.

THE STRATEGIC MANAGEMENT PARADIGM

Strategic management is a process that deals with the entrepreneurial work of the organization, with organizational renewal and growth, and more particularly, with developing and utilizing the strategy which is to guide the organization's operations. Before examining the tasks which make up the strategic management process, we must first clarify the nature and meaning of the strategy concept itself.

THE CONCEPT OF STRATEGY

Based on a study of the different definitions and concepts of strategy proposed by leading authors in the field, Hofer and Schendel (1978) have developed a composite definition of strategy built around four components: (1) scope, which may be defined in terms of product/market matches and geographic territories; (2) resource deployments and distinctive competences; (3) competitive advantage; and (4) synergy; and three organizational levels: (1) corporate, (2) business, and (3) functional. While this definition excludes goals and objectives, it recognizes that the achievement of objectives is the aim of strategy and that the combination of objectives, strategy, and policies form a "grand design" or master strategy for the firm. The relationships between the different levels of strategy and the type of "integration" that each deals with is indicated in Exhibit 1.

Exhibit 1 Different Levels of Strategy

Strategy level	Integrates
1. Enterprise	1. Total organization/Society
2. Corporate	2. Businesses/Portfolio
3. Business	3. Functions/Business
4. Functional	4. Subfunctional/Function

ENTERPRISE STRATEGY

Enterprise strategy, as used by Ansoff, encompasses a set of sub-strategies including: a product/market/technology strategy; a capability strategy; a resource strategy; a flexible-response strategy; a limited-growth strategy; a societal strategy; and a legitimacy strategy. Except for the latter two, all of the other sub-strategies are subsumed as components of corporate, business, and functional area strategies. While we have adopted Ansoff's strategy, we have limited its focus to social-legitimacy concerns, which are not explicitly addressed by other levels of strategy.

The increasing interrelationships of governmental units and business enterprises over questions of legitimacy are forcing business firms to reexamine their role in society and to consider whether they can be insular in their decisions and actions. Enterprise strategy attempts to integrate the firm with its broader noncontrollable environment, not in terms of product/market matches in a narrower economic sense, but in the sense of the overall role that business, as one of society's important institutions, should play in the everyday affairs of society. Questions of the governance and function of the firm, and the manner in which it will be allowed to exist, are being raised today, forcing a reexamination of both enterprise strategy and the overall mission of the firm. However, strategy at each of the other three organizational levels must be adapted to their relevant environments. We believe that such broader legitimacy considerations have always been a part of the strategy formulation process. More explicit attention will have to be given to this aspect of strategy in the future, as Ansoff suggests, just as it has been necessary to separate corporate and business strategy considerations from the problems of functional area integration, over the past two decades.

CORPORATE STRATEGY

Corporate strategy addresses the question, "What business(es) should we be in?" It also focuses on the ways that the different businesses a firm chooses to compete in should be integrated into an effective portfolio. During the early 1960s, the principal focus in practice was on the first question, as many organizations added new businesses until they became truly multimission in character. More recently, however, the principal focus in practice has been on the second question as such multimission firms have tried to rationalize the portfolios they developed. In the future both questions will be addressed equally and with more rigor than in the past.

The environment considered in corporate strategy must include not only economic considerations but also the sociopolitical and cultural considerations that Ansoff mentions in connection with enterprise strategy. The focus here is usually on how these factors will influence the future prospects of an industry rather than on the institutional legitimacy of the business organization in society.

BUSINESS STRATEGY

Business strategy deals with the question, "How should a firm compete in a given business?" That is, how should it position itself among its rivals in order to reach its goals? Alternately, how can it allocate its resources to achieve a competitive advantage over its rivals? Clearly, many alternatives are available, and while it is possible to suggest business strategies that work under certain conditions, current research has identified few universals that apply to all circumstances. In addition to answering the question of how to compete, business strategy has the job of integrating the various functional areas that comprise a business, much as functional area policies were once thought to do. In practice, the second task of business strategy (integrating functional area policies) received the major focus during the 1960s, while the first (how to compete) assumed greater importance during the 1970s. And, as at the corporate level, both questions will need to be addressed more rigorously in the future.

FUNCTIONAL AREA STRATEGY

Functional area strategies also address two issues. First, they are intended to integrate the various subfunctional activities in the firm. Second, they are designed to relate the various functional area policies with changes in the functional area environments. For example, in marketing strategy an advertising program is coordinated with personal selling, pricing, packaging, and other marketing decision variables to develop a marketing program that is not only internally consistent but that is also consistent with the other functional areas of the business and with the perceptions and responses of the market to advertising.

THE HIERARCHY OF STRATEGY

Obviously, there is a hierarchical relationship among these strategy levels, just as there is among objectives and environments. As one moves from enterprise strategy to corporate strategy to business strategy to functional strategy, one not only moves down the organizational hierarchy, one moves downward in terms of constraints. Thus, each level of strategy constrains every other level, particularly those below it, in a fashion similar to the hierarchy of objectives noted by Granger (1964). Given this broad overview of the concept of strategy, it is now appropriate to turn to an examination of the various components of the concept of strategic management.

THE CONCEPT OF STRATEGIC MANAGEMENT

There are six major tasks that comprise the strategic management process: (1) goal formation; (2) environmental analysis; (3) strategy formulation; (4) strategy evaluation; (5) strategy implementation; and (6) strategic control. These are shown in Exhibit 2, where the interrelationships of these tasks are indicated. Responsibilities for the process of strategic management, as well as those processes of operating management, are typically shared by all managers rather than being divided by level or function. Thus, no manager is responsible solely for strategic management tasks, and, except at the very lowest levels of operating management, no manager is without some responsibilities in the strategic management process.

ORGANIZATIONAL GOAL FORMULATION

The "first" [4] task in the strategic management process is the formulation of a set of goals for the organization. Goal formulation is a complex process that rests on a coalition based on the relative power of the stakeholders of the organization. This process may be rational in an economic sense; it may involve political processes; it may occur independently of other tasks; or it may be an integral part of other tasks, such as strategy formulation. Goal structures that are put to use in managing organizations invariably involve the use of power in some way, a point which Mintzberg uses in his paper later in this book to identify and classify different types of goal formulation processes found in practice.

The priorities that specific goals are given, and the goal structure ultimately adopted and used in the strategic management process, are influenced by three factors: (1) the power and personal goals of stakeholders; (2) the condition of the organization (e.g., a failing business will have to give priority to economic survival); and (3) the type of organization involved (e.g., a business firm differs greatly in purpose from religious or charitable organizations). The priorities given goals will determine both how goal conflicts will be resolved and the nature of the goal hierarchy that will be used in formulating, evaluating, and implementing strategy.

ENVIRONMENTAL ANALYSIS

The environment in which an organization exists includes all those factors that influence goals, strategy, and structure and which the firm does not directly control. The environmental factors relevant to each strategy level vary, with each lower level constrained by the one above it.

---

[4] It is convenient to order these tasks sequentially. In practice, they are interactive, recycle and repeat themselves and do not move forward in sequence as neatly as described here.

Exhibit 2   An Overview of the Strategic Management Process

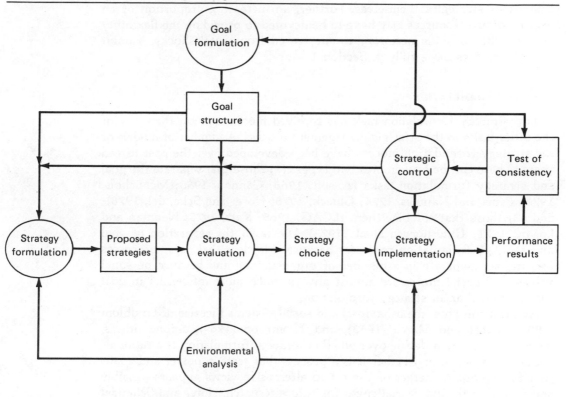

Because an organization cannot control [5] its environment it must make forecasts, not choices, about the environmental conditions it expects to encounter in the future. Such forecasts, really assumptions about the future, are so important that we are highlighting environmental analysis here as a separate strategic management task, even though many would consider it as a part of the strategy formulation task. (We include Utterback's paper and Klein's commentary on environmental analysis, in Section 3 which is devoted to strategy formulation.)

A major problem in environmental analysis, besides the difficulty of accurately forecasting future values of particular variables, is knowing what factors to examine in the first place. Stated differently, it may be a more serious error to overlook a factor than to forecast it inaccurately. Moreover, the magnitude of this problem is increasing as the rate of environmental change increases. Thus, while the purpose of environmental analysis and forecasting is to provide needed input to both the strategy formulation and evaluation tasks, the number and magnitude of major

[5] Even though an organization may not be able to control its environment, this does not mean it cannot influence it. This point will be explored more fully in the commentaries of MacMillan and Child in Section 3.

environmental discontinuities may require major changes in the basic content of strategies themselves. Further, an increasing proportion of an organization's resources may have to be devoted to providing the flexibility and breadth of skills necessary to survive environmental shocks, a point Ansoff explores more fully in Section 1.

STRATEGY FORMULATION

The strategy formulation task has received more attention than any of the other tasks in the strategic management process. A number of models of the strategy formulation process have been developed over the past fifteen years. These can be broken into two types: (1) those that separate the goal and strategy formulation tasks (Ansoff, 1965; Cannon, 1968; McNichols, 1972; Paine and Naumes, 1974; Glueck, 1976; Hofer and Schendel, 1978); and (2) those that combine them (LCAG, 1965; Katz, 1970; Neuman and Logan, 1971; Uyterhoeven et al., 1973). We favor the separation of goal and strategy formulation processes because it is clear that these processes are, in fact, separate in a number of organizations and because personal values and social mores are almost always much more influential in goal formulation than in strategy formulation.

At the same time, the behavioral and social systems theories of Lindblom (1959), Cyert and March (1963), and Thompson (1967), among others, have given rise to a debate over whether strategy formulation is a rational-deductive process, or whether it is a process that rests in power and coalition formation. A merger of these two alternative views appears possible and is one of the major challenges for future research. Hofer and Schendel (1978) suggest how this might be accomplished by developing an iterative process that proceeds analytically and considers personal and social values.

STRATEGY EVALUATION

There are two basic questions to be asked in the strategy evaluation task. First, has the existing strategy been any good? Second, will the existing/proposed strategy be any good in the future? The first question is important to answer because it indicates whether the existing strategy needs to be changed. Also, it can provide valuable information about the direction in which the strategy should be changed. The second question seeks to determine whether the existing or proposed strategy will lead to accomplishment of the firm's objectives in the future given the changes that are anticipated in the firm's environment, its resources, or even its goals and objectives.

Evaluation of the existing strategy requires these steps: (1) an identification of the existing strategy in terms of its components, including its underlying goal structure and environmental assumptions; (2) a comparison of results achieved against those established; (3) a comparison of environmental assumptions made by the strategy with the changes expected based on an analysis and forecast of the future environment; and (4) a determination of whether the strategy appears capable of meeting its goals in light of the existing and expected environment. If that determination is negative, then a new strategy will be required. This evaluation task is compounded by the difficulties of separating the effects of operating inefficiencies from the effects of strategic problems.

The evaluation of the future worth of an existing or proposed strategy can be done using one or more of the following five approaches: (1) an assessment of whether the objectives the strategy is designed to achieve are internally consistent and whether the strategy is consistent with those objectives; (2) an evaluation of the quality of the analysis and organizational processes used to develop the strategy; (3) an evaluation of the content of the strategy; (4) an assessment of the ability of the organization to implement the strategy; and (5) an evaluation of the early performance results under the strategy.

In terms of the strategic management process, the task of strategy evaluation both precedes and follows the strategy formulation task. Thus, while some would include this task as part of the formulation task, its importance, its difficulty, and its relationship to strategic control all suggest that it should be considered as a separate task.

STRATEGY IMPLEMENTATION

Strategy implementation is different from the previous tasks in the strategic management process in several important respects. First, implementation is essentially an administrative task, while goal setting, environmental analysis, strategy formulation, and strategy evaluation can be accomplished analytically and independently of the organization, although that usually is not the best way to do them.

Second, even if the previous four tasks were accomplished in a technical, rational-deductive manner, and were done independently of behavioral and social systems considerations, the implementation task is inherently behavioral in nature. It is this fact that has led a number of researchers to believe that strategy formulation cannot be a rational-deductive process, some because their research does not reveal the earlier tasks being performed at all, and others because they believe that personal goals will always take precedence over organizational goals, even in economically oriented business firms. The reconciliation of social/political processes used in implementation with analytical/rational processes used in strategy formulation and evaluation represents another major research challenge for the strategic management area.

Finally, while implementation has traditionally been viewed as the last step in the strategic management process, and even though Chandler's research suggests that structure follows strategy, in ongoing organizations administrative structure and processes (more broadly conceived than the simple organization hierarchy) [6] also influence strategy. In fact, a case can be made that structure and processes should be considered a component of strategy in order to force attention to the implementation problem.

Strategic Control

The "last" task in the strategic management process is that of strategic control. Strategic control focuses on the dual questions of whether: (1) the strategy is being implemented as planned; and (2) the results produced by the strategy are those intended. The basic criteria used to answer these questions are derived from: (1) the strategy and action plans developed to implement strategy; and (2) the performance results that strategy is expected to produce. If a deviation occurs, then feedback takes place and the strategic management process recycles, as indicated in Exhibit 2.

Strategic control is just emerging conceptually as an important task in the strategic management process. Like other important areas, such as social responsibility, separate consideration was not given to strategic control in terms of an invited paper. Yet there are a number of questions worthy of further investigation and new conceptual thinking concerning strategic control. For example, what criteria should the firm use to assess whether the strategy in use is the one that is intended to be used? Katz (1970) raised this question when he distinguished between an organization's "strategic posture" and its strategy. If performance results do not match established objectives, what part of the variance is attributable to the strategy, and what part to inefficiency or poor execution by operating management? These and other questions remain before us and will make the strategic control task an exciting one for future research.

THE STRUCTURE OF THE BOOK

It was the strategic management paradigm described above that guided our partitioning of the field and led to fourteen invited papers which we have grouped into ten sets or sections of related papers. The sections and authors are shown in Exhibit 3, together with the discussants for each paper.

Section 1 reviews the evolution of the strategic problem and the cor-

---

[6] The terms "structure" and "process" are used here to encompass: (1) the pattern of hierarchical and lateral linkages among decision-making positions in the organization and the information flows associated with these patterns; (2) the informal organizational and interpersonal relationships that exist within the organization; (3) the various organizational systems and processes such as planning, resource allocation, measurement and evaluation, reward, etc. that influence managerial and employee task behavior; (4) the organizational philosophies, management style, and other behavioral functions that together establish the climate and culture of the organization; and (5) the control systems employed by the organization to ensure that desired results are achieved.

Exhibit 3   Topics and Authors Contained in the Book

Section topic	Authors	Commentary
1. Strategy and strategic management	Ansoff	Newman Dill
2. Organizational goals and goal formulation	Mintzberg	Richards Murray
3. Strategy formulation	Grant/King Utterback Bower/Doz	Channon Klein MacMillan Child
4. Strategy evaluation	Rumelt	Kirchhoff
5. Strategy implementation	Lorange Galbraith/Nathanson	Hekhuis Henry Wrigley Miner
6. Strategic management and organization types	Cooper Berg/Pitts Wortman	Susbauer Vesper Brandenburg Spender
7. Theory building and theory testing in strategic management	Steiner Duncan Hatten	Paine Naumes
8. Teaching implications of policy and planning research	Unterman Hegarty	
9. Practitioners' views: policy and planning research	Charan	Aines/Ball Knoepfel/Lancey
10. Research needs and issues in strategic management	Schendel/Hofer	

responding paradigms of strategy and strategic management. It then goes on to suggest some ways that the strategic management paradigm may have to change in the future. The topic paper is authored by H. Igor Ansoff and is discussed by William Newman and William Dill, each of whom have been important contributors to the evolution of the concepts presented in this book.

Section 2 deals with the problem of goals, the ends that strategies are intended to achieve. We have identified goal formulation and goal structures as a separate topic to indicate both their importance and the distinction between goals and strategy, a distinction that is not always made in the literature to date. Henry Mintzberg, in the topic paper, presents a provocative view of the role of power in goal formation. Max Richards and Edwin Murray complement Mintzberg's paper by examining more carefully the goal structure notion and the ways it might be researched.

Strategy formulation is taken up in the third set of papers. First, various analytical, rational-deductive approaches to strategy formulation are taken up in John Grant's and William King's topic paper with commentary by Derek Channon. Then, environmental analysis and forecasting is examined by James Utterback, in his invited paper, as one aspect of the strategy formulation process. Harold Klein offers a commentary that focuses primarily on the problems of incorporating environmental analyses and forecasts into the strategy formulation process. Joseph Bower and Yves Doz then take up some of the internal political and social system aspects of strategy formulation. Ian MacMillan and John Child conclude the section with a discussion of the use of political models in strategic anticipation (a variety of environmental forecasting) and interorganizational strategies.

The fourth set of papers deals with strategy evaluation. Richard Rumelt authors the topic paper in Section 4 and provides a thorough analysis of both contextual and context free models in strategy evaluation. Bruce Kirchhoff then discusses several other types of strategy evaluation approaches and provides a general critique of Rumelt's paper.

Strategy implementation is taken up in the fifth set of papers. Peter Lorange explores the area of formal planning systems and discusses usage of such systems in both strategy formulation and strategy implementation. His observations are elaborated by Dale Hekhuis and Harold Henry. Jay Galbraith and Daniel Nathanson then discuss the structural and process aspects of strategy implementation, with particular attention to research on the relationship of strategy and structure from Chandler's seminal work onward. Leonard Wrigley's and John Miner's papers elaborate and critique Galbraith's and Nathanson's observations in several interesting ways.

The sixth set of papers deals with strategic management in three important organizational typologies. First, Arnold Cooper examines the unique aspects of the strategic management tasks in small businesses where the pure entrepreneurial character of strategic management is perhaps seen best. Jeffrey Susbauer and Karl Vesper offer two interesting supplements to Cooper's views. Next, Norman Berg and Robert Pitts discuss the unique problems of strategic management in the multimission or multiple business organization. Richard Brandenburg extends their observations with a practitioner's view of strategic management in such organizations. Finally, Max Wortman explores the unusual challenge of strategic management in not-for-profit organizations.

Having explored the content and direction of the evolving field of strategic management, our attention turns from the shape of these ideas to their implications for research, teaching, and management practice.

First, Section 7 deals with theory building and theory testing in the strategic management field. This section begins with J-C. Spender's commentary on the philosophy behind theory building and theory testing in strategic management research. Next, George Steiner's paper discusses various contingency views of goal formulation, strategy formulation, strategy content, strategy evaluation, organizational design, leadership, and so on. In particular, Steiner explores four broad streams of contingency theories that have evolved to date and suggests some ways these streams may develop in the future. Frank Paine then shows how the various contingency theories based on behavioral traditions that are identified in Steiner's paper might be combined into a single contingency theory of strategic management. Then, Robert Duncan takes up the subject of qualitative research methodologies such as field research methods as they apply to strategic management research. Next, Kenneth Hatten considers quantitative data analysis tools useful in strategic management research. Finally, William Naumes discusses both the Duncan and the Hatten papers and adds perspective through his development of simulation and gaming approaches.

Section 8 deals with the teaching implications of the previous papers. First, Israel Unterman notes that it is clear that the field of strategic management is indeed a discipline with a substantial content of its own. He then explores the implications of this fact for policy curricula, for the traditional policy course, and for the training of policy faculty. W. Harvey Hegarty then examines various ways that the ideas contained in each of the topic papers might be built into the traditional policy course.

The ninth set of papers examines the implications of the research reviewed in the book for industry practice. Here Ram Charan draws together the views of the industry spokesman in attendance at the conference. In particular, Ronald Aines, Benjamin Ball, Rudolf Knoepfel, and Roderic Lancey offer their comments on the conference papers and discussions from the viewpoint of management practice, which includes the perspectives of both corporate planners and a chief executive officer.

The final section summarizes what we believe are the research implications of the various papers and commentaries and suggests future research needs, opportunities, and priorities for the field. A unique aspect of this discussion is that it is based in part on a Delphi study of the conference participants' thoughts done after their attendance at the conference.

In each section that follows, we provide: an introduction to each section that gives our views as to why the topic(s) was selected; what we believe the highlights of each paper to be; what we believe the discussants have had to say; and finally, to provide our own comments and opinions about significant issues developed in each section. From time to time, we have included appropriate comments on the implications of the papers and commentary for teaching, practice, and research, although for the most part such comments are reserved for later sections of the book specifically devoted to such implications. Above all, understand these comments are our opinions, not all of which the reader or the authors will hold in the same regard we do.

After the comments we make, the topic papers and the commentary papers follow. Hopefully, our remarks will help the reader more quickly isolate the key issues in each paper and otherwise aid the reader in understanding the issues and their significance to strategic management.

The references for each paper are listed at the end of each section, not at the end of each paper, as might be more customary. This was done to avoid unnecessary duplication of individual citations.

References

Ansoff, H. Igor. *Corporate Strategy: An Analytic Approach to Business Policy for Growth and Expansion.* New York: McGraw-Hill, 1965.

Cannon, J. Thomas. *Business Strategy and Policy.* New York: Harcourt, Brace and World, 1968.

Chandler, Alfred D. *Strategy and Structure: Chapters in the History of the American Industrial Enterprise.* Cambridge, Mass.: M.I.T. Press, 1962.

Cyert, Richard M. and James G. March. *A Behavioral Theory of the Firm.* Englewood Cliffs, N.J.: Prentice-Hall, 1963.

Glueck, William F. *Business Policy: Strategy Formation and Management Action.* New York: McGraw-Hill, 1976.

Gordon, Robert A. and James E. Howell. *Higher Education for Business.* New York: Columbia University Press, 1959.

Granger, Charles H. "The Hierarchy of Objectives." *Harvard Business Review,* May–June 1964.

Hofer, Charles W. and Dan E. Schendel. *Strategy Formulation: Analytical Concepts.* St. Paul: West Publishing Co., 1978.

Katz, Robert L. *Cases and Concepts in Corporate Strategy.* Englewood Cliffs, N.J.: Prentice-Hall, 1970.

Kuhn, Thomas S. *The Structure of Scientific Revolutions.* Chicago: University of Chicago Press, 1970.

Learned, Edmund P., C. Roland Christensen, Kenneth R. Andrews and William D. Guth. *Business Policy: Text and Cases.* Homewood, Ill.: Richard D. Irwin, 1965.

Lindblom, Charles E. "The Science of 'Muddling Through.'" *Public Administration Review,* Spring 1959.

McNichols, Thomas J. *Policy Making and Executive Action: Cases on Business Policy.* New York: McGraw-Hill, 1972.

Newman, William H. and James P. Logan. *Strategy, Policy, and Central Management.* Cincinnati, Ohio: South-Western, 1971.

Paine, Frank T. and William Naumes. *Strategy and Policy Formation: An Integrative Approach.* Philadelphia: Saunders, 1974.

Rumelt, Richard P. *Strategy, Structure, and Economic Performance.* Boston: Graduate School of Business Administration, Harvard University, 1974.

Schendel, Dan E. and Kenneth J. Hatten. "Business Policy or Strategic Management: A Broader View for an Emerging Discipline." *Academy of Management Proceedings,* August 1972.

Thompson, James D. *Organizations in Action.* New York: McGraw-Hill, 1967.

Uyterhoeven, Hugo, Robert Ackerman and John Rosenblum. *Strategy and Organization.* Homewood, Ill.: Richard D. Irwin, 1973.

1

STRATEGY AND STRATEGIC MANAGEMENT

The Changing Shape of the Strategic Problem

H. Igor Ansoff
The European Institute for Advanced Studies in Management

Commentary

William H. Newman
Columbia University

William R. Dill
New York University

The evolving strategic management paradigm for the field of business policy and planning is based on the concepts of strategy and of a process for managing strategy. We thought it fitting that the first set of papers should deal with the evolution of these two related concepts and with providing some indication of the future evolution and use of these concepts. What better author is there to do this than Igor Ansoff, who has contributed much to the definitions and refinements of these twin concepts over the past fifteen years! As we have already indicated, there is not yet a wide and clear understanding of the concept of strategy or what it can do, let alone what roles the concept of strategic management can play in the direction and overall management of organizations. Ansoff's paper and the commentaries by Newman and Dill are intended to elaborate on what those roles have been and what they can be in the future.

Ansoff responded to our invitation with the provocative paper he entitled "The Changing Shape of the Strategic Problem." In it, he points out that strategy is a "synthetic concept"; it is "a type of solution to a problem" that managers devised and are using to cope with strategic change "that caught the attention of management in the mid-1950s." According to Ansoff, what gave rise to strategic change in the 1950s was a mismatch between products offered by business and changing needs and demands of the market. This mismatch either no longer exists or its intensity has been lessened. It has been replaced in his view with another mismatch, borne out of a rapidly changing environment just as the original one was, only this time the problem affects what Ansoff calls the interior of the organization, with the very purpose and legitimacy of the business firm in question.

To support this claim, Ansoff devotes a considerable part of his paper to describing the historical and future evolution of the strategic problem. He then argues that the underlying cause of these rapid and significant environmental changes is "society's arrival at a new level of economic affluence." In a macroadaptation of Maslow's (1954) need hierarchy applied to society, globally conceived, Ansoff suggests that the very success of the business institution has caused it to lose its central role in society and that social aspirations have shifted from a "quantity" to a "quality" of life focus, with a corresponding "realignment of social priorities," which is focusing attention on "the negative side-effects of profit-seeking behavior.... Thus, one of the consequences of affluence is the loss of social centrality for the institution that created it." And with this loss comes a shift in the degree of environmental complexity and a much broader strategic problem.

Thus, a concept of strategy that deals only with product/market matches is no longer adequate. Other kinds of strategy are needed, as are changes in several of the assumptions that underlie the strategy concept. For instance, the assumption of growth needs to be modified to accommodate conditions of no- and slow-growth. Similarly, the directional assumption that the strategic problem begins in the marketplace and ends with an adaptation to market needs is no longer sufficient in a world of increasingly scarce and depleting resources. And even the assumption that the strategy concept is a decision heuristic for proactively choosing the organization's external interface with its environment may no longer be useful for an organization facing major environmental discontinuities and strategic surprises. In short, Ansoff's original conception of strategy is no longer responsive in either concept or content to the strategic problems businesses, and presumably other organizations, are facing today.

Instead, aspirations must be lowered, and societal and legitimacy strategies developed to relate the organization to its new sociopolitical environment. *Preparedness strategies* (which deal with flexible resource configurations) will replace historical *action strategies* (which deal with the selection of actions). Resource strategies and capability strategies will also be needed to deal with the problem of scarcity. In general, multiple strategies will be required at multiple levels of tomorrow's complex organizations to deal with the increasingly complex, rapidly changing environments of tomorrow. Ansoff suggests the term "enterprise strategy" for this set of multiple-level, multiple-focus strategies.

Ansoff summarizes these ideas, as is typical of his work, in a series of diagrams that capture the features of his argument, which despite their high symbol density are well worth study, for they reward the student with a visualization of the problem that Ansoff sees. His dire predictions of strategic surprise, of a belligerent, even malevolent environment that takes away the manager's choice and replaces it with a coping enterprise strategy, is an issue to give one pause and hopefully much room for fruitful and rewarding thought and discussion.

Whether Ansoff is right about the current and future state of the environment, and whether it gives rise to a "strategic problem" that cannot be handled by the strategic management process is another question and, in the end, the main point of his paper. In this respect he shares Toffler's (1970) pessimistic view of modern man's dilemma with his progress. He (and business) can no longer cope with what he (it) has wrought.

There are many who would argue with this viewpoint. Among them are those who are struggling with the complex issues of environmental analysis and forecasting. Clearly, there is a long, long way to go, but now is no time to give in to pessimism. A rich area of research lies in trying to better understand the environment, anticipate it, and bring forth at least a managerial accommodation of its complexity, as is well illustrated by the remaining papers in this book and the Newman and Dill commentaries in this section.

Newman makes four points in his commentary on Ansoff's paper. First, he favors Ansoff's extension of the set of environmental variables that influence strategy. However, he also suggests that Ansoff needs to generalize his definitions of the environment even more. Specifically, Newman suggests that an organization's environment should be defined as the total set of external "contributors" with which the organization must deal, rather than being limited to the more specific categories Ansoff depicts in Exhibit 1.8. Newman sees three advantages in such a generalization of the organization's environment: (1) specific groups can be added or discarded as needed in a particular circumstance without altering the validity of the construct; (2) the assessment of the impact of environmental change can be done with respect to specific two-way relationships between the organization and its environment; and (3) the concept of technology is broadened to include marketing and financial skills, managerial processes, and so on, as well as manufacturing and product design considerations.

Second, Newman believes that Ansoff dropped one of the key elements of strategy when he broadened its purview. More specifically, Newman notes that a "cardinal feature of each strategy is the selection of a few relationships upon which the company seeks to distinguish itself" which "become the basis for differential advantage over competitors." Thus, while Newman agrees that the number and complexity of the environmental relationships between the firm and its environment have increased, which may require a broadening of the strategy concept, he also feels that Ansoff has broadened the strategy concept (as opposed to the environment) too far, and in the process lost part of the essence of strategy.

Third, Newman argues that Ansoff's revised view of strategy still maintains one assumption that should be dropped, namely, the assumption that the interactions between an organization and its environment are confined to exchanges at the boundary. Newman suggests instead that strategy needs to go beyond an exchange theory to include interaction methods designed to achieve mutual ends. In this, he is concurring with one of Dill's major points as well as with MacMillan's and Child's later commentaries.

Finally, Newman notes that the historical developments of business enterprise, highlighted by Ansoff in Exhibits 1.1 through 1.7 are too simplistic. He then goes on to sketch a variety of examples which run counter to Ansoff's history.

In general, we would agree with Newman's observations. In particular, we believe further broadening of the environmental concept is necessary, that a focus on competitive advantage is essential, and that political considerations of the mutual interaction variety are worthy of much further study in strategy formulation. However, because of the complex variety of interactions among the organization's external environment, a point that Utterback and Klein give particular emphasis to in their papers, it is less clear that the use of a series of two-party interactions will assist in the environmental analysis and forecasting task.

In addition, in our view, Newman's concern with Ansoff's historical development, while a valid criticism, misses Ansoff's point. Ansoff was simply trying to suggest that the nature of environmental change was changing and was giving rise to strategic surprises, making strategic anticipation and strategic planning of the sort that proceeds in an outside-in, market-to-product development manner no longer useful. Ansoff was not interested in developing a history of industrial organization so much as he was in illustrating the increasing complexity and dynamism of the environment and the relative importance of variables for which management cannot plan.

Dill's commentary is directed more at the business policy field as a whole than at Ansoff's paper specifically. His thesis is quite simple. It is that the concept of strategy is an overworked, ineffective paradigm for dealing with the organization-environment problem. In its place, he suggests the field should return to the inducements-contributions paradigm developed by Barnard (1938), Simon (1957), Homans (1950), which he feels is more useful in coping with a multifaceted environment. Based on this paradigm and the environmental changes Ansoff forecasts, Dill then makes several suggestions for future research, including: (1) the need for better paradigms for describing organizational environments; (2) the need to study the problems of declining organizations; and (3) the need to study the problems of the future rather than those of the past. Clearly this is a provocative view, and one which merits further commentary on our part.

Dill's critique of the strategy concept itself should be examined closely by all strategic management theorists and researchers, since those writing in a field are prone to overemphasize its constructs. It seems to us, however, that Dill has argued from an inaccurate and sometimes inconsistent conception of the strategy construct. Thus, his observation that "strategy pertains to initiative, proclaiming, and leading; and pretending that it stretches to cover activities which involve adaption, listening, and following, simply gets in the way of having your motives accepted as honest ones," reflects a narrow view of strategy that most scholars in the field would not agree with. It is true that strategy has been viewed as a proactive tool of management. This does not mean that all strategies are inflexible and nonadaptive, however. In fact, all strategy formulation models that we know of insist that "good" strategies must accurately reflect the events transpiring in their environments.

Dill also appears to us to set up straw men in his examples of the failure of the strategy concept. Thus, most of the examples he gives appear to us either to deal with nonstrategic issues or to involve poor applications of the strategy concept, and do not deal with failures of the concept. Which of us is correct is for the reader to decide. Such distinctions are important, however, as no paradigm, not even the inducements-contributions one Dill asks us to reexamine, will produce good results if it is applied poorly. Moreover, no social system paradigm can (should) be rejected on the basis of anecdotal evidence, since they will all produce some failures even if applied well because no social system is completely deterministic. Consequently, even if Dill's examples are valid, his argument may not be, since his examples may only represent the "error term" in an otherwise very effective paradigm.

Dill's suggestions that we need to learn more from, and pay more attention to, the "grass-roots" origins of organizations are well founded, as are his suggestions about the need to find ways of cooperating with the environment. Whether an inducements-contributions paradigm is necessary to do this is another matter. Such concerns can be built into the strategy concept, as Ansoff's paper and the later commentaries of MacMillan and Child clearly indicate. The choice between the strategy concept and the inducements-contributions paradigm must therefore be made on the major points of difference. These are: (1) a difference in the environments which these paradigms examine; (2) a difference in the importance attached to different events in their environments and to different organizational-environmental interactions; and (3) a difference in the basic assumptions regarding the ways influenceable organizational-environmental interactions should be handled.

The first difference between the strategy and inducements-contributions paradigms is that the environments which they examine differ. In this regard, the strategy paradigm encompasses a broader environment than the inducements-contributions paradigm. More specifically, the environment of the strategy paradigm includes, at least theoretically, all the elements contained in the environment of the inducement contribution — some of these elements may be given far less attention in the strategy paradigm than in the inducements-contributions paradigm, however, a point that we shall return to shortly — plus some elements not contained in the latter paradigm. The reason for this is that there are some environmental factors that may significantly influence an organization and its strategy that cannot be affected in any way by the organization, that is, they are noncontrollable to the firm. For example, a small plastics firm's raw material availability may be severely affected by an external environmental event, such as an oil crisis, which it cannot possibly influence. Because of the inability of the firm to influence such events (i.e., to offer inducements to the parties causing them), they would not be included in the environmental space of an inducements-contributions paradigm. They must be and are included in the environment space of the strategy paradigm, however.

The strategy and inducements-contributions paradigms also differ in the importance they attach to different events in their environments and to different organizational-environmental interactions. The difference is that the inducements-contributions paradigm attaches no differential importance to the various points in this space, as Newman so eloquently notes. On the other hand, the strategy paradigm effectively discards events and interactions of lesser importance in order to focus on those that are key at a particular point in time. The specific elements that are important at any time may change with changing environmental circumstances, as Ansoff notes so well in his paper. On this point, it seems to us that the strategy paradigm more accurately reflects reality.

With respect to the handling of influenceable organizational-environmental interactions, the strategy paradigm assumes that the organization should *usually* take a proactive stance while the inducements-contributions paradigm assumes a balanced or reactive posture. Neither paradigm assumes a one-way process for such interactions, however; rather, both recognize that the influence process for such interactions will be a two-way street. The difference is that the strategy paradigm suggests that it is better to initiate such interactions when this is possible. Clearly, such initiatives may occasionally produce negative results. Passivity, however, can result in opportunities foregone. While it may only be a matter of style, we would agree with Tennyson that, " 'Tis better to have loved and lost, than never to have loved at all."

Dill's suggestion that more effort needs to be put into developing better paradigms for describing organizational environments is sound advice. The soundness of his corollary suggestion that less effort be placed on developing paradigms for structuring the planning process within firms is less clear, though, since such paradigms are the key to bringing different voices into the strategic management process — a necessary task if the corporate governance process is to be broadened, as Ansoff suggests is happening.

Apart from the critical thinking that Dill's basic thesis requires of all of us, his major contribution, in our view, is his call for future-oriented research in the field, a point echoed by Ansoff. Dill's observation that most policy research has been historical in nature is, unfortunately, all too true. Such research can be of value, however, not only for training of future generations of managers but also to the degree that the future will reflect the past. When done on leading organizations, it can also be of use in the improvement of current practice through the transmission of best practice to average and lagging organizations. As a discipline, however, we should also contribute to the improvement of best practice, and this requires future-oriented research. Developing such research is clearly not an easy task, but Dill provides some useful insights into how it might be done with his suggestions on the need to study the strategic management problems of declining organizations.

SUMMARY

Overall, these papers illustrate very well the need for new and more clearly defined paradigms for the field. They also indicate, as Dill's commentary makes clear, the need for better and more consistent terminology in the field.

In this regard, we suggest that a clear separation must be made between the concepts of: (1) ends, such as goals and objectives; (2) means or strategies for achieving goals; and (3) the noncontrollable environment to which both are subject. A clear separation is also needed between the managerial processes by which an organization formulates, evaluates, implements, and controls the relationships between its goals, its strategies, and its environment. We believe a well-developed concept of strategic management can do that for the field.

The Changing Shape of the Strategic Problem

H. Igor Ansoff
The European Institute for Advanced Studies in Management

Management is the creative and error-correcting activity that gives the firm its purpose, its cohesion, and assures satisfactory return on the investment. Thus, it can be said that the essence of management is creation, adaption, and coping with change. Seen from the viewpoint of general management, there are two basic types of change. One, is the fluctuations in the operating levels and conditions: in sales, profits, inventory, labor force, budgets, productive capacities, etc. This kind of change expands and contracts the activities of the firm, but leaves the nature of the firm intact. The other type transforms the firm: its products, its markets, its technology, its culture, its systems, its structure, its relationships with governmental bodies. I shall refer to this second type as the *strategic change*.

It is the need for strategic change that caught the attention of management in the mid-1950s and led to today's pervasive concern with strategy.

Strategy is a concept which is useful for perceiving the underlying patterns of managerial activity. It is also useful for giving guidance to the enterprise-transforming work. But it is a synthetic concept in the sense that strategies ascribed to organizations are frequently not perceived or made explicit by managers who pursue them.

Strategy is a type of solution to a problem, but not the problem itself. The problem that gave rise to this particular type of solution was a product/technology mismatch between the firm and its newly turbulent markets. But strategy was not the only tool used by firms to extricate themselves from their predicament.

Since the time of the original application of strategy to the task of transforming the firm, the underlying problem has undergone enormous changes. Whereas the original mismatch was at the interface with the environment, today it is the interiors of many enterprises that are mismatched to the surrounding turbulence. Whereas the original external mismatch was with the market environment, today there are additional mismatches with socio-political, ecological and resource environments. Whereas the speed of environmental change was such as to permit a deliberate formulation and execution of strategy, in many situations today strategic surprises do not give sufficient warning to permit advanced strategic planning.

While the problem has been undergoing all these changes, much of the study and research in the field of strategy has been focused on understanding and elaboration of the originally perceived problem. Given the size and the extent of the changes that are taking place, it is necessary to ask to what extent the knowledge gained to date is applicable to the new dimensions of the strategic problem.

This paper suggests that this knowledge is only partially applicable and that further understanding must be sought on several levels. First, on the level of content, in addition to the product/market/technology strategy, content and understanding now must be given to social, political, and resource strategies. Second, the assumption of search for growth, which underlies the original concept of product/market strategy, needs to be modified to accommodate conditions of limited and zero growth. Third, the assumption, ever present in most research on strategy, that the problem starts in the market place, and that all other considerations are derivatives from the product/market strategy (i.e., "structure follows strategy") must be replaced by a question: where does the enterprise-transforming problem start? Does it start with limited external resources, with a particular configuration of internal capabilities; does it start with a zero growth assumption, or with redefining the *raison d'être* of the firm in society? In most cases, we shall probably find that it does not start in any of these places, that it can no longer be solved by a unidirectional flow of logic from the market to technology, to structure, to resources, to social posture. Instead, it needs to be solved by a procedure which involves multidirectional flows and feedbacks.

Finally, on the abstract level, we need to reexamine the usefulness of the concept of strategy as a decision heuristic for choosing the external interface with the environment, formulated through anticipation of trends in the environment. The concept must be reexamined in the context of large multinational firms where it is already evident that the concept of strategy as a style level heuristic is giving way to multiple-level strategy concept. The concept must also be reexamined in situations in which anticipation is impossible and strategic surprise is likely. I would predict that use of the traditional action strategy ("in which direction do we change the firm's position in the environment") will be increasingly supplemented, and sometimes replaced, by a flexible configuration strategy ("how do we configure the resources of the firm for effective response to unanticipated surprises").

To summarize, both the concepts and the content of today's understanding of strategy are now largely responsive to the problem as it existed in the 1950s. Since the problem has changed fundamentally, the concepts must be redefined and enriched.

A useful way to approach this task is to start by tracing the historical evolution of the strategic problem. This is the aim of this paper. We shall proceed in three steps. First, we shall construct a historical scenario of the evolution of the firm's environment. In constructing the scenario we shall try to mirror the complex historical reality, without attempting to organize it. Second, we shall identify several underlying patterns of evolution which are observable in the evolutionary process. Third, we shall combine these patterns to describe the evolution and the future of the strategic problem.

THE INDUSTRIAL REVOLUTION. Modern business history starts in the United States roughly in the 1820–1830s. First, construction of a network of canals, and then of a nationwide railroad system triggered a process of economic unification of the country. A stream of basic inventions: the steam engine, the cotton gin, the Bessemer steel process, the vulcanization of rubber, etc., provided a technological base for a rapid industrial takeoff. Technological invention proceeded alongside the social invention of one of the most successful and influential organizations in history — the business firm.

By 1880–1900 a modern industrial infrastructure was in place. It unified the country into an American common market. The firm emerged as a privileged and central instrument of social progress. This period, which became known as the *Industrial Revolution,* was one of extraordinary strategic turbulence. The early industrial entrepreneurs devoted most of their energies to creating modern production technology, surrounding it with organizational technology, and staking out their market shares. The concept of competition, as it is known today, did not begin to evolve until the 1880s. The earlier concept was to dominate or absorb the competitor rather than meet him head-on in the market place. Thus modern marketing, as we know it today, was yet to be developed.

THE MASS-PRODUCTION ERA. From 1900 on, focus shifted to developing and consolidating the industrial structure created during the Industrial Revolution. This new period which lasted until the 1930s has been named the *Mass-production Era.* As the name suggests, the focus of industrial activity was on elaborating and perfecting the mechanism of mass production which progressively decreased the unit cost of products. The concept of marketing was straightforward and simple: the firm which offered a double standard product at the lowest price was going to win. This was succinctly summarized in the phrase of Henry Ford I, who, in response to a suggestion in favor of product differentiation, responded to his sales people: "Give it [the Model T] to them in any color so long as it is black."

There were many problems to be solved, but worrying about strategic challenges was not one of them. The industrial lines were well drawn and most offered promising growth opportunities. The inducement to diversify into new environments appealed only to the most adventurous firms. A majority were satisfied with their own growth prospects. It was obvious that the steel companies were in the "steel industry," automobile companies in the "automotive industry," etc. As a result, the focus of managerial attention was focused inward on the efficiency of the productive mechanism. The result was a set of managerial perceptions, attitudes and preferences which later came to be known as a "production mentality."

On the political front, the business sector was well protected against outside interference. Political and social controls were minimal. Government "interference" with the free enterprise was infrequent. When needed, the government could be expected to provide a protectionist economic policy. When business flagrantly transgressed social norms, government reacted by limiting freedoms of business action, such as anti-trust or anti-price collusion legislation. But these were occasional events; most of the time the boundary of the business environment remained inviolate. The business of the country was business. It was this sense of the centrality of the business sector that led "Engine Charlie" Wilson, a president of General Motors, to say: "What is good for General Motors is good for the country."

MASS-MARKETING ERA. For the first thirty years of the century, success went to the firm with the lowest price. Products were largely undifferentiated and the ability to produce at the lowest unit cost was the secret to success. But toward the 1930s the demand for basic consumer goods was on the way toward saturation. With "a car in every garage and a chicken in every pot" the increasingly affluent consumer began to look for more than basic performance. Demand for Model-T types of products began to flag.

In the early 1930s, General Motors triggered a shift from production to a market focus. The introduction of the annual model change was symbolic of a shift of emphasis from standard to differentiated products. By contrast to the earlier "production orientation," the new secret to success began to shift to a "marketing orientation." Mr. Ford, having tried to replace a standard Model T with a standard Model A, was forced to follow the multimodel suit of General Motors. Promotion, advertising, selling and other forms of consumer influence became priority concerns of management.

The shift to the marketing orientation meant a shift from an internally focussed, introverted perspective to an open, extroverted one. It also meant a transfer of power from production-minded to marketing-minded managers. Internal conflicts and power struggles were a frequent outcome. But, beyond power struggles, managers resisted the shift because it required costly, time-consuming and psychologically threatening acquisition of new skills and facilities, development of new problem-solving approaches, changes in structure, in systems, and acceptance of new levels of uncertainty about the future.

In process industries and in producer durable industries, the marketing concept was slow to penetrate. When confronted with saturation, firms in such industries frequently settled for stagnating growth under a production orientation, rather than undertake the pains of a shift to the marketing outlook. It was not until after World War II that many of these industries were propelled by new technologies, first into a belated marketing orientation and, soon thereafter, into the higher turbulence of the Post-industrial Era.

Consumer industries and technologically intensive producer industries were early in embracing the marketing orientation. An overswing frequently occurred: marketing began to dominate operations at the expense of the production efficiency. As a compensation for the overswing, a "total marketing concept" emerged which balanced the conflicting demands of marketing and production. Such balanced sharing of priorities gradually emerged and is still to be found in most progressive firms.

The Mass-production Era greatly enhanced the marketing turbulence of the environment. The enterprise-changing strategic activity, which subsided during the mass-production period, was also enhanced but less drastically. In technology-based industries, new product development became an important activity early in the century. An historical milestone was the establishment of intra-firm research and development laboratories in companies such as Du Pont, Bell Telephone, General Electric, a step which institutionalized innovation within the firm.

In low technology consumer industries the advent of the annual model change generated a demand for incremental product improvements, better packaging, cosmetic appeal, etc. But, with significant exceptions, the change in products and markets was evolutionary, rather than revolutionary. Focus on current markets and products dominated the concern with future profit potential.

During the Industrial Era, most of the major changes in the environment originated from leading aggressive firms which established the style and the pace of progress. Thus, with considerable justification, business could claim to control its own destiny. To be sure, business initiative sometimes produced an invisible chain of adverse consequences which led to periodic "loss of control," such as recurring recessions. But these were viewed as the price of competitive freedom well worth paying for "blowing off" of "economic steam" to enable progress to resume. These periodic "surprises" were seen as an exception in an otherwise surprise-free world.

THE POST-INDUSTRIAL ERA. From the mid-1950s, accelerating and cumulating events began to change the boundaries, the structure, and the dynamics of the business environment. Firms were increasingly confronted with novel unexpected challenges which were so far-reaching that Peter Drucker called the new era an *Age of Discontinuity.* Daniel Bell labeled it the *Post-industrial Era* — a term we shall adopt for our discussion. Today change continues at a pace which makes it safe to predict that the current escalation of turbulence will persist for at least another ten to fifteen years. It is harder to predict whether beyond this time horizon, the acceleration will persist or (what is more probable) whether the environment will settle down to absorbing and exploiting the accumulated change.

To an outside observer business problems of the Industrial Era would appear simple by comparison to the new turbulence. The manager's undivided attention was on "the business of business." He had a willing pool of labor (so long as the wage was right), and he catered to a receptive consumer. He was only secondarily troubled by such esoteric problems as

tariffs, monetary exchange rates, differential inflation rates, cultural difference, and political barriers between markets. Research and development was a controllable tool for increased productivity and product improvement. Society and government, though increasingly on guard against monopolistic tendencies and competitive collusion, were essentially friendly partners in promoting economic progress.

But managers inside firms had found the problems of the era very complex, challenging, and demanding. Outside the firm, the manager had to fight constantly for market share, anticipate customers' needs, provide timely delivery, produce superior products, price them competitively, and assure the retention of customer loyalty. Internally, he had to struggle constantly for increased productivity through better planning, more efficient organization of work, and automation of production. Continually, he had to contend with union demands and still maintain the level of productivity, retain his competitive position on the market, pay confidence-inspiring dividends to stockholders, and generate sufficient retained earnings to meet the company's growth needs.

Thus, it was natural for busy managers to treat the early Post-industrial signs in much the same way they had treated periodic economic recessions. Inflation, growing governmental constraints, dissatisfaction of consumers, invasion by foreign competitors, technological breakthroughs, changing work attitudes — each of these changes was at first treated as a distraction from "the business of business," to be weathered and overcome within a basically sound preoccupation with commercial marketing and operations.

Just as in the earlier shift from production to the marketing orientation, the shift to a Post-industrial orientation is still unrecognized or resisted in many firms, because it introduces new uncertainties, threatens a loss of power, and requires new perceptions and new skills. The resistance to change frequently leads to a gap between the behavior of a firm and the imperatives of the environment. The firm continues to focus on marketing and disregards the technological and political changes, continues to rely on past precedents when experience is no longer a reliable guide to the future. Managerial attitudes are well summed up by a popular French saying: "plus ça change, plus c'est la même chose." [1]

But it is not the "même chose." The underlying cause of the new change is society's arrival at a new level of economic affluence. The Mass-production Era was a drive to meet the basic physical comfort and safety needs of the population. The Mass-marketing Era lifted the aspirations from comfort and safety to a drive for affluence. The Post-industrial Era is the arrival of affluence.

Satisfaction of survival needs and growth in discretionary buying power change consumer demand patterns. Industries that served the basic needs in the Industrial Era reach saturation. These industries do not necessarily decline, but their growth slows down. New industries emerge that cater to the affluent consumer — luxury goods, recreation, travel, services, etc.

Technology fundamentally affects both supply and demand. Massive wartime investment in research and development spawns new technology-based industries on the one hand, and brings about obsolescence in others. Internal to the firm, fueled by technological progress, the "R&D Monster" acquires a dynamic of its own, which spawns unasked-for products, increases the technological intensity of the firm and directs the firm's growth thrusts independently and sometimes in spite of the aspirations of the management.

The arrival of affluence casts doubt on economic growth as the main instrument of social progress. Social aspirations shift away from "quantity" to "quality" of life. Industrial bigness increasingly appears as a threat both to economic efficiency through monopolistic practices, and to democracy through "government-industrial" complexes. Large enterprises are challenged on their immoral "profiteering" tendencies, lack of creativity, and their failure to enhance efficiency while increasing size. Acquisition of other firms is challenged because it is seen to destroy competition. Studies are prepared for dismemberment of giant firms. The growth ethic, which had provided a clear guid-

ing light to social behavior, begins to decline. "Zero growth" alternatives are advanced, but without a clear understanding of how social vitality is to be retained when growth stops.

Realignment of social priorities focuses attention on the negative side-effects of profit-seeking behavior: environmental pollution, fluctuations in economic activity, inflation, monopolistic practices, "manipulation" of the consumer through artificial obsolescence, blatant advertising, incomplete disclosure, and low-quality after-sale service. All these effects begin to appear to be too high a price to pay for the laissez-faire conditions of "free enterprise."

The firm is now assumed to be able not only to maintain affluence under stringent constraints (which only twenty years ago would have been considered fundamentally subversive and socially destructive), but also to undertake "social responsibility." Thus, one of the consequences of affluence is the loss of social centrality for the institution that created it.

Having "filled their bellies," individuals begin to aspire to higher levels of personal satisfaction both in their buying and in their working behavior. They become increasingly discriminating — increasingly demanding "full disclosure" about their purchases, demanding "post-sales" responsibility from the manufacturer, unwilling to put up with ecological pollution as a by-product. They begin to lose faith in the wisdom of management and its knowledge of "what is good for the country." They challenge the firm directly through "consumerism" and put pressure on government for increased controls.

Within the firm, the traditional solidarity of the managerial class begins to disintegrate. Middle managers begin to reject the role of working for the exclusive benefit of the shareholders. The traditional aspiration of every manager to become the president of the firm is not shared by the new generation, which wants the firm to become more socially responsive, and to offer opportunities for individual self-fulfillment on the job. Thus managers begin with the interest of technocracy rather than with those of the top management, or the shareholders.

As another result of affluence, developed nations turn their attention to social problems that remained unsolved while the focus was on eco-

[1] The more it changes, the more it is the same.

nomic growth: social justice, poverty, housing, education, public transportation, environmental pollution, and ecological imbalance. The private sector is now called upon to perform a twofold role: (1) to restrain and remove its problem-causing activities (such as pollution), and (2) to take responsibility for positive social progress.

New demands for social services create potential new markets, but they are not easy to serve because they have remained previously unattended precisely because they were inherently unprofitable.

Thus, socio-political transactions with the environment which lay dormant during the Industrial Era acquire a life-or-death importance to the firm. They become important as a source of information and opportunities for new commercial activities, as a source of new social expectations from the firm, and as a source threatening constraints on the commercial activity.

At first glance, the turbulence in the Post-industrial environment may appear as a return to days of the Industrial Revolution. But today's turbulence is much more complex. In the earlier era, creation of marketable products and of the markets was the major concern of the entrepreneurs. They dreamed grandly and had the genius and the energy to convert dreams into reality. But their priorities were almost wholly entrepreneurial. Having created the business sector, they often lacked the motivation and the capability to settle for the job of competitive exploitation of their creations. Other managers, no less talented but less visionary and more pragmatic, replaced them and began to elaborate and perfect the production mechanism of the firm and to realize growth and profit. Later, marketeers injected new vitality in the environment.

Thus, the industrial environment up to the 1950s was a "sequential" one. In succeeding periods the key to success shifted; managerial preoccupation with the previous priority also shifted to the next one.

But in the 1970s, the new priorities do not replace, but rather, add to the previous ones. Competition is not slackening, but intensifying as a result of internationalization of business, scarcities of resources, and acceleration of tech-

nological innovation. Production and distribution problems are growing bigger and more complex. And to these are added concerns with technological breakthroughs, with obsolescence, with structural changes in the economy and in the market, and in the firm's relations to government and society. Thus, entrepreneurial concerns come on top of, and not in exchange for, the historical preoccupation with competition and production.

To summarize briefly, during the past twenty years, a major escalation of environmental turbulence has taken place. For the firm it has meant a change from a familiar world of marketing and production to an unfamiliar world of strange technologies, strange competitors, new consumer attitudes, new dimensions of social control and, above all, a questioning of the firm's role in society.

PATTERNS IN COMPLEXITY

In the preceding sections we have explored, in a discursive fashion, the complex and multi-faceted nature of the changing business environment. In this section we identify several regular patterns in the flow of change.

One such pattern is shown in Exhibit 1.1, which presents a historical perspective of the challenges to the firm, along four dimensions, shown at the left of the exhibit. The upper two are the historically important commercial dimensions, and the lower two are the newly important socio-political dimensions.

As the Exhibit shows, prior to the 1950s the socio-political environment of the firm was quiescent, and the commercial challenges were focused on exploiting the firm's historical market position.

Between 1950 and 1970 the focus began to shift to regeneration of growth potential for the reasons listed in the Exhibit. It is during this period that the problem of strategy was recognized and formulated by a number of business firms.

The solution developed by these firms, which became known as *strategic planning*, was an essentially optimistic one. Confronted, on the one hand, with saturation of growth in their

Exhibit 1.1   Environmental Challenges in a Historical Perspective

Dimensions of challenge \ Time	1900	1930	1950	1970	1990
Products-Markets-Technology	—Basic demand	—Differentiated demand —Product-line expansion —Market expansion —Incremental evolution of technology	—Saturation of demand —Technological turbulence —Multinational markets —Government markets —Leisure markets —Technology created industries	—Loss of control over environment —Socio-political impact on market behavior —Strategic surprises —Constraints on growth —Constraints on resources —Socialist markets —Developing country markets	
Geographic perspective	—Nation-state		—Developed nations	—Socialist and third world	
Internal environment	—"Honest day's work for fair day's pay" —Management by authority		—Enrichment of work —Local participation —Management by consensus	—Redesign of work —Participation in strategic decision —Management by conflict	
External socio-political environment	—*Laissez faire*		—Loss of social immunity —Consumerism —Pressures for social responsibility —Reaction to "pollution" —Reaction to business power	—New ideological *raison d'être:* —Socialism —Neocapitalism	

historical industries, and, on the other hand with new technologies and new growth fields, firms sought to revitalize their historical growth and to diversify into new industries. The optimism of this approach rested on two assumptions. The first was that the initiative in the interaction with the environment belonged to the firm, and that the firm was the master of its own destiny. The second assumption was that the environment was predictable enough to enable the firm to plan its response to change in advance of the event.

These assumptions were consistent with the experience of the previous fifty years of the century. But the right-hand column of the Exibit shows the historical experience no longer applies. The firm is rapidly losing much of its control over the environment. Part of this loss is caused by the increasingly stringent controls and regulations. Another part is due to the new interconnectedness and complexity of environment which make it increasingly difficult for the firm to foresee consequences of its own action, and also to anticipate key events and initiatives by others. Increasingly, positive growth strategies of the firm must be accompanied, and sometimes superseded by defensive *survival strategies* which guard the firm against environmental controls and surprises.

As the lower part of the right-hand column shows, the 1970s also extended the firm's strategic concern beyond its product/technology interface with the markets. The new concerns are with the design of the internal environment of the firm, with assuming a new set of responsibilities with respect to the environment, and with establishing a new basis of social legitimacy for the firm. In response to these concerns, concepts of *capability strategy*, of *social respon-*

sibility strategy, and of *political strategy* have begun to emerge.

Another historical pattern is illustrated in Exhibit 1.2, which shows managerial responses to the challenges of Exhibit 1.1. The transition from the production orientation of the first thirty years of the century to the subsequent marketing orientation was accompanied by a shift of managerial focus from efficiency of internal operations to effective marketing in the environment. After the 1950s the pendulum began to swing back to center, to sharing of managerial attention between internal and external preoccupations.

But as the lower part of the Exhibit shows

Exhibit 1.2 Evolution of Managerial Response

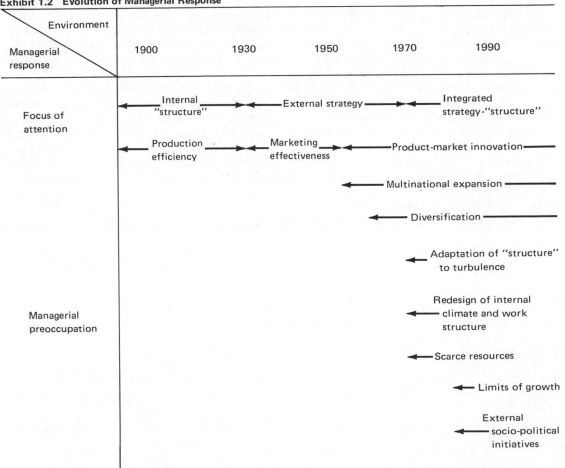

the complexity of the new internal and external concerns is now higher than ever. From concerns with effective marketing, the external concerns have expanded to product innovation, multinational expansion, and diversification into new industries. From a focus on efficient mass production, the internal concerns are shifting to redesign of work, to providing for needs and aspirations of the human beings, and to managing the firm as a political (rather than consensual) environment.

Within the perspective of Exhibits 1.1 and 1.2, the original concept of product/market strategy appears as only one component of a much broader concept. We might call it *enterprise strategy*, which is needed to integrate and relate the new dimensions of the strategic problems.

A third historical pattern is illustrated in Exhibits 1.3 and 1.4 where the evolution of strategies which firms used in their response to changing turbulence is shown. Exhibit 1.3 shows the *competitive strategies* which firms have used to gain success in the market place. It is to be noted that the progression from left to right was not one of replacement, but of proliferation. Today all of the strategies in Exhibit 1.3 can be found in use.

Exhibit 1.4 shows the evolution of the entrepreneurial strategies — the product/market/

technology configuration of the firm. Again the process has been one of proliferation and most of the strategies shown can be found in practice today.

The erosion of the earlier optimistic assumption of predictability of the environment is illustrated in Exhibit 1.5, which shows the historical trend of predictability. The Exhibit shows that there is a growing incidence of events which are novel to the firm (e.g., petroleum scarcity, stagflation, disappearance of the work ethic, etc. etc.), which cannot be predicted in terms specific enough and far enough in advance to permit deliberate "set piece" response through periodic organization-wide strategic planning.

Exhibit 1.6 presents yet another pattern. This is the evolution of formal management systems which firms developed over the years to help them cope with problems of increasing complexity. (The names of most of the systems up to the 1970s will be familiar to the reader.) The newer systems are described briefly in Ansoff (1978).

The three horizontal lines in Exhibit 1.6 represent important barriers in the historical development of systems. The first barrier, crossed early in this century, was a transition from a historical backward-looking to a future-oriented, forward-looking perspective. The series of forward-looking systems that followed this cross-

Exhibit 1.3 Evolution of Competitive Strategy

1900	1930	1950	1970
Price competition			
Market share			
Product differentiation			
Artificial obsolescence			
Consumer manipulation			
Affluence and leisure			
Truth in advertising			
Ecological benefits			
Resource conservation			

Exhibit 1.4 Evolution of Enterpreneurial Strategies

1900	1930	1950	1970	1990

Product rationalization

Backward integration

National expansion

Rounding of product line

Technological evolution

Annual model change

Diversification

Multinational expansion

Technology substitution

Forward integration

Life-cycle balance

Vulnerability balance

Third-world expansion

Resource invulnerability

Recycling

Surprise preparedness

Exhibit 1.5 Decreasing Predictability of the Future

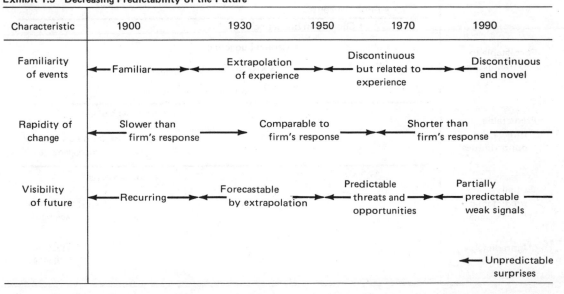

Characteristic	1900	1930	1950	1970	1990
Familiarity of events	←——Familiar——→	←— Extrapolation of experience —→	←— Discontinuous but related to experience —→	←— Discontinuous and novel
Rapidity of change	←— Slower than firm's response —→	←— Comparable to firm's response —→	←— Shorter than firm's response ———
Visibility of future	←—Recurring—→	←— Forecastable by extrapolation —→	←— Predictable threats and opportunities —→	←— Partially predictable weak signals ———
					←— Unpredictable surprises

ing shared an underlying assumption about the environment. This was that the basic structure of the environment remained unchanged and that the variables and the models which adequately explained the past were usable for prediction of the future. In this sense of the word, all of these systems were *extrapolative*.

The second barrier was crossed when past models became inadequate for prediction. The succeeding management systems, such as strategic planning, attempt to analyze the new variables and new relationships which will determine both future demand and the future performance.

The third barrier is presently being crossed in response to the progressive loss of predictability. New systems are emerging which permit the firm to respond rapidly with developing events and to surprises. As such systems emerge, the traditional distinction between systems and structure will disappear, and *preparedness* strategies (which deal with flexible configurations of resources) will replace the historical *action strat-*

egies (which deal with selection of an action response). For an example see Ansoff (1976).

EVOLUTION OF THE STRATEGIC PROBLEM

The previous discussion can be summarized by tracing the evolution of the strategic problem from the middle of this century until the present. As Exhibit 1.7 illustrates, this evolution has been rapid. The problem confronting the firm today is much more complex and richer in content than it was in the 1950s. As Exhibit 1.8 illustrates, the prospects are for a further increase in complexity. (In both figures the word "strategy" is used in a general sense to mean a "solution-guiding heuristic.")

As Exhibit 1.7 shows, the strategic problem of the 1950s was to decide "what business are we in?" This meant finding a profit-producing match between the products/technology of the firm and the needs of the market. Internal capabilities of the firm were seen as important, but

Exhibit 1.6 Evolution of Management Systems

Environment	1900	1930	1950	1970	1990
Recurring	• Systems and procedures manuals				
	• Financial control				
Forcastable by extrapolation		• Short-term budgeting			
		• Capital budgeting			
		• Management by objectives			
		• Long-range planning			
Predictable threats and opportunities			• Periodic strategic planning		
			• Periodic strategic management		
Partially predictable "weak signals"				• Issue analysis	
				• Real time strategic management	
Unpredictable surprises				• Surprise management	

Exhibit 1.7   Evolution of Strategic Problem

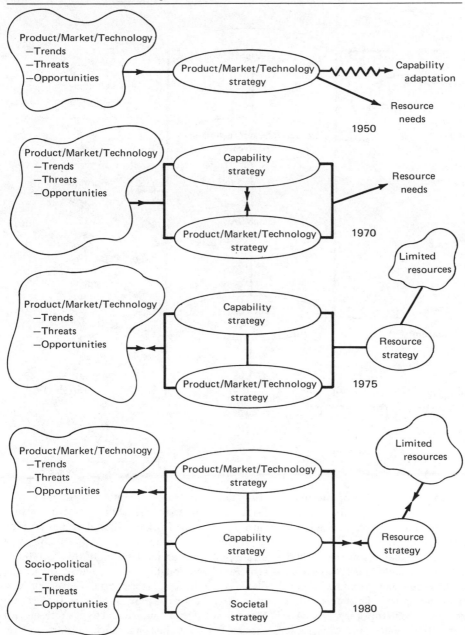

essentially invariant characteristics in this process. The idea was to find a strategy which took advantage of the strengths of the firm and avoided its weaknesses. This reflected the optimism about the environment which was dis-

cussed earlier. The firm perceived itself as the center of a Ptolemean universe which it could understand and control. As the sketch at the top of Exhibit 1.7 shows, changes in strategy generated needs for changes in capabilities, but

Exhibit 1.8 The "Ultimate" Strategic Problem

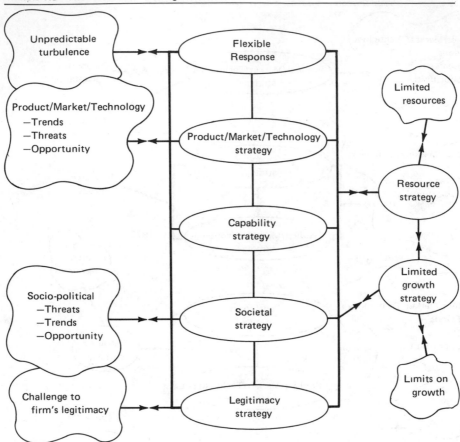

these were largely increases in size of the firm, such as the need for additional capacity, capital, personnel, etc., rather than changes in the basic configuration of the firm.

The Exhibit also shows that resources needed from the external environment were viewed as derivative from strategy; and resource availability was seen as unlimited. This perception was well captured in a contemporary business phrase, "We'll find the money for any right opportunity that comes along."

The second sketch in Exhibit 1.7 shows that capability is becoming a major concern by the 1970s. Many firms have difficulties in finding attractive growth opportunities which match their strengths and weaknesses. Other firms find

that new strategies do not work until the "structure" (managerial skills, rewards, structure, systems, and organizational values and information) was adjusted to support the new strategy. A new understanding of this "strategy-structure" relationship was provided by Chandler (1962) in his classic book, *Strategy and Structure*. This new perception was that transformation of the internal configuration and capabilities was just as much a part of the strategic problem as finding a new viable product/market strategy for the firm. When a firm enters "a new kind of business" it cannot succeed unless it develops an appropriate "new kind of capability." Further, the new perception is that "structure" need not follow strategy;

frequently, the reverse sequence is preferable.

In the mid-1970s another major dimension of complexity surfaces in the strategic problem. This is the increasingly frequent scarcity of strategic resources. Although the particular manifestations come from different directions, such as cost of petroleum, cost of money, or shortage of non-ferrous metals, the underlying phenomenon is a strategic resource scarcity.

Resource scarcity makes it necessary to plan not only the "front" interface with the market but also the "rear" interface with the sources of supply. It also makes problematic the traditional flow of strategic planning from opportunities to the resources. For firms which are severely resource-constrained the reverse flow of planning has become a two-way feedback process in which the "front" and the "rear" strategies must be reconciled.

The lower sketch in Exhibit 1.7 demonstrates the state of the strategic problem which is already a reality in Europe, and which is expected by leading U.S. managers to become an American reality in the 1980s (Barraclough, 1976). It reflects the increasing importance of the socio-political variables in the life of the firm. As the preceding discussion has indicated, two new important dimensions of strategy are added. One is the *strategy* of socio-political relations with the society outside the firm, and the other is the strategy for structuring and managing the internal work within the firm. Both introduce power structure and power dynamics as key determinants of strategic behavior.

Exhibit 1.8 suggests the "ultimate" shape of the strategic problem which includes all of the key variables which have been discussed in the preceding pages. Two new problems are added to the preceding stage. One, shown in the upper left part, is acceleration of change to a point which makes the "conventional" concept of strategy inapplicable in situations in which the speed of change is greater than the speed of strategic response, or, to put this differently, the environment is not sufficiently predictable to permit timely action strategy formulation.

The other new problem is likely to come from society's refusal to continue accepting the historical unlimited "growth ethic" as a legitimate mode of business behavior.

IMPLICATIONS FOR RESEARCH

The general implication from the preceding discussion is that researchers seeking to understand the current and emerging strategic challenges will need to deal with a problem which contains many more variables and has a much more complex structure and dynamics than the problems of the 1950s. Each reader can interpret this general implication for consequences for his own focus of interest. Below several of these consequences are suggested:

1. Whatever aspect of the strategic problems he treats, the researcher needs to check its validity in the light of the 1970s–1980s problem scope. For example, research on goals and objectives has traditionally been based on the assumption that the major influences on goals were to be found within the firm ("control of its own destiny" hypothesis). The 1970–1980s perception suggests that the goals *and* objectives are going to be increasingly influenced by extra-firm influences. Research on goals also has traditionally been based on the assumption of ideological uniformity within the firm. But already, in Europe, the powerful internal constituencies are ideologically polarized, and differences of ideology and realities of power must be taken into account.

2. Much of the research on strategy has focused on logically rational strategic decision-making. The implied hypothesis was that reasonable decisions will induce reasonable compliant response. The introduction of socio-political variables challenges this assumption. As a result, separation of strategic decision-making from strategic implementation becomes artificial. For understanding of strategy we need to shift the focus from the problem of *strategy formulation* to the level of *strategic response*, as evidenced by behavior in the environment.

3. The historical preoccupation with product/market/technology strategies must be broadened to include the other types of "strategy" shown in Exhibits 1.7 and 1.8. Their unique nature needs to be understood, and they must be related to each other. This means the traditional model built on the assumption of one critical contact point with the environment must be

enlarged to handle multiple and distinctive critical contact points. The traditional conception of strategy as one level heuristic problem must be expanded to allow multilevel strategies, hierarchically related to one another.

4. Finally, practically all of literature has focused on strategies of action in the external environment. Concepts of "strategy of structure" now need to be developed.

In recent years, unlike many other fields of inquiry into management, the strategic problem has been unique as a "problem that wouldn't stand still." On the one hand, this has greatly complicated the problems of the researcher and placed him in danger of providing obsolete understanding and obsolete solutions. On the other hand, the rapid change in the shape of the problem gives the researcher an opportunity to develop insights which are new and current to managers, instead of providing a stream of refinements on solutions to well-understood problems, as is done in much of the management science literature.

Commentary

WILLIAM H. NEWMAN
Columbia University

Ansoff lays out a most welcome extension of his earlier concept of corporate strategy. Instead of the narrow focus on growth via diversification, we now are presented with an enriched variety of considerations and options — and even a new banner, "enterprise strategy." As is characteristic of Ansoff's writings, the frameworks presented are pertinent and useful, imaginative yet realistic, stimulating and seductive. Any scholar of business strategy who misses this paper does so at the risk of his professional reputation.

My comments cover three extensions of Ansoff's formulation and one reservation.

GENERALIZING THE APPROACH

The extension of the concept of strategy to embrace a company's resource and social interfaces with its environment does not go quite far enough. It stops just short of a more powerful construct which makes the concept of strategy applicable to a wider array of social enterprises.

Ansoff's new formulation, summarized in his Exhibit 1.8, makes very clear that viewing strategy merely in terms of product/market scope is grossly inadequate. In confronting its environment, each enterprise must also consider the acquisition of resources and winning social-political support; and with respect to each of these interfaces trends, threats, and opportunities will arise much as they do in markets.

Yes, indeed! But why this particular classification of a firm's interfaces with its environment? Let me note just a few of the difficulties with the proposed classification. The social-political forces bear upon not only the company but also on markets and upon resources (as illustrated in Exhibit 1.8 via limits on growth). At the same time, particular features of a social-political system can be treated as a critical "resource" — as anyone who tries to do business in a developing country soon learns. Moreover, especially in capitalistic countries, relations with suppliers of capital may impose even more rigid strategy constraints than do customers. Strategies for interacting with human resources often are complex because that resource has an irresistible proclivity to become entwined with managing — individually and perhaps collectively. And so on.

One can gain flexibility in designing and implementing strategy — and even more in doing research on the strategic process — by generalizing about the interfaces between a company and its environment. For each external group whose cooperation the company needs (customers, stockholders, tax officials, unions, equipment suppliers, etc., etc.), management must obtain a mutually acceptable two-way relationship. And except for one-time projects or deals, this tends to be a continuing relationship. In a dynamic society, however, the wishes and the power of the contributor group change from time to time. So, managing these relationships is a never-ending task.

Strategy deals in a large part, but not entirely, with a configuration of relationships between the company and such external "contributors." They may be called resources, or interest groups, or in systems jargon, "inputs." Since the company benefits from, and is dependent upon, a continuing cooperative exchange relationship with each contributor group, wise strategy formulation and implementation is vital to the company's existence.

The generalized, contributor group formulation of the interactions between a company and sectors of its environment — sketched in the two preceding paragraphs — has several advantages over the more particularized model presented by Ansoff. First, for specific companies, contributor groups studied can be added (or disregarded) as may be warranted by the particular circumstances. This flexibility is especially valuable when one wants to extend the analysis beyond manufacturing firms to service companies and to not-for-profit enterprises. Second, the bearing of environmental changes on a company are easier to sort out: the impact is always felt through the cooperativeness of some contributor group. When changes occur in the environment, one can ask, "Who, if anyone, among the people I interact with will be affected significantly by that change? What should I do now to maintain their continuing cooperation?"

Third, in the generalized model, *technology* takes on a more central role than is implied in Ansoff's diagram. For some reason unclear to me, Ansoff associates technology only with product/market scope. A broader and more useful view of technology is that of an internal system by which the various inputs are *converted* into the diverse outputs (jobs, taxes, and the like, as well as goods and services) promised contributor groups and under restraints imposed by contributor groups (Ouchi and Harns, 1974; Perrow, 1970; Newman and Warren, 1977). The selection of technology, then, is a major element in business strategy because it integrates the diverse flows of goods-services-money in and out of the company. It determines the viability (insofar as the company is concerned) of the totality of arrangements made with contributor groups.

The generalized formulation is represented in the following diagram — Exhibit 1.9.

SELECTING KEY THRUSTS FOR A STRATEGY

Both Ansoff's "ultimate" strategic problem and its more generalized form suggested above have many potential facets. So many resource groups, customer groups, and other special-interest groups are implied in this sort of framework that a chief executive (or a collective "central management") cannot grasp all the

Exhibit 1.9 Generalized Contributor Group Interaction between the Firm and its Environment

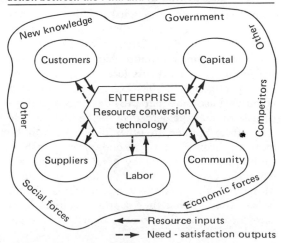

interrelationships. As the model is enriched, its complexity increases exponentially.

This inherent complexity of the total set of external and internal relationships leads us to a second basic feature of company strategy. A cardinal feature of each strategy is the selection of a few relationships upon which the company seeks to distinguish itself. These selected relationships become the basis for differential advantage over other competitors for scarce resources (including customers).

A few examples will highlight this feature of strategy. IBM has always stressed customer service, customer orientation in product design, and liberal treatment of its employees (Watson, 1963). Humble Oil rose to prominence because it gave high priority to acquiring an advantageous crude oil supply. Merck and Boeing stressed building better mousetraps — ethical pharmaceuticals and aircraft, respectively. Conglomerates derive their differential advantage predominantly by the way they raise capital.

Each company singles out perhaps one, but more likely a few areas having synergistic ties. In these areas it tries to develop an unusually favorable resource relationship as compared to that of competitors; typically it pioneers in a new form of relationship with a key contributor group coupled with an internal technology that dovetails with the interaction design in a symbiotic fashion. If the company is wise (or lucky), it selects relationships for emphasis which will be especially important strengths in the future of its industry.

In the numerous external relationships not selected as a source of differential advantage, a company satisfices. Often a company is too small to attempt any more than following general industry practice; its location, history, personal preferences of key executives, or existing resource base may not provide a good springboard; or management may deliberately decide that effort applied in other directions will be more rewarding. These secondary relationships cannot be neglected; they must be adequately maintained — like Herzberg's hygiene factors. Moreover, the secondary relationships should be designed so that they support or are at least compatible with the primary thrusts of the selected strategy.

Of course, over time a company may shift its choice of areas in which it seeks differential advantage. Such changes are crucial elements in company strategy.

In liberating himself from a preoccupation with diversification, Ansoff grasps the breadth of view that strategy should embrace. But the panorama he gives us is not operational. Effective strategy also must be highly selective.

A corollary of the idea that effective strategy is highly selective is doubt about the necessity for the six kinds of strategy shown in Ansoff's Exhibit 1.8. These six categories become options or dimensions, but certainly not elements that every company must elect.

THE POLITICAL REACH OF STRATEGY

The interactions of a company with its environment are not confined to exchanges at the boundary. A company may pursue a strategy that extends well beyond an exchange of dollars for goods or services at the factory gate. Much of our discussion of strategy is deficient in this respect.[1]

The eagerness of a contributor group to cooperate with a specific company, and the terms on which that cooperation is conducted, depend substantially on *other* opportunities and threats which the contributor group faces. So one way a company can build satisfactory relationships for itself is to engage in a bit of active empathy with its resource suppliers.

Well recognized examples include working with a local community to develop schools and other amenities which will help attract competent employees, or using a trade association as a coalition to pressure Congress to provide a subsidy. The feasibility of opening a new coal mine in Kentucky may depend upon inducing a railroad to install service between the mine and a utility customer. An equipment dealer arranges

[1] A notable exception is found in the writing of I. C. MacMillan. See "Business Strategies for Political Action," *Journal of General Management*, Vol. 2, No. 1, Autumn 1974, or I. C. MacMillan, *Strategy Formulation: Political Concepts*, St. Paul, Minn.: West Publishing Co., 1978.

with a local bank to provide his customers with credit. In each of these illustrations, action of the company extends to third parties with whom the company has no direct transaction.

All sorts of indirect help, reciprocity, coalitions, and roundabout pressure may be involved. Some types of coalitions will be frowned upon by the Federal Trade Commission, whereas other joint action may be encouraged. As companies find themselves increasingly the targets of boycotts, environmental protection groups or consumer advocates, the arena and the jousting tools change.

The point here is not to flag a new set of inputs and outputs of sufficient importance to a company to warrant inclusion in its strategy. Rather, the point is concerned with how a company copes. A company may elect to deal with an opportunity or threat in a "political" fashion instead of by means of direct confrontation. Neither Ansoff's paper nor my Exhibit 1.9 catches this political dimension of strategy.

OVERSIMPLIFIED HISTORY

The three suggestions made thus far — generalizing the identification of potential strategic variables, selecting a few variables for strategic emphasis, and recognizing political approaches in dealing with selected variables — can be viewed as extensions of Ansoff's stimulating reformulation of the strategy concept. Before closing I want to note one reservation.

The historical development highlighted in Exhibits 1.1 through 1.7 is too simplistic for my taste. The evolutionary progression, in fact, was not so neat. For example, the description

focuses almost exclusively on manufacturing concerns, neglecting banks, railroads, trade, and extractive ventures. In several of these other kinds of business obtaining resources was an early and dominant feature of company strategy. In fact, history clear back to the Middle Ages is replete with accounts of marshaling resources; think of the early spice trade, sugar plantations in the New World, rubber from the Amazon jungle and then African and Far Eastern plantations, oil exploration in all corners of the earth, to mention only a few. Firms in the 1900's were not solely concerned with production efficiency and internal structure. Resource limitations have been a recurring problem.

The marketing revolution brought on by the vast expansion of railroads during the last part of the nineteenth century probably called for more drastic strategic revisions than did changes in marketing in the mid-twentieth century. A review of the financial history of the United States with its recurring panics, dubious currency, and collapses of financial markets suggests that in some important areas predictability of the future has increased while in other areas it has decreased.

The historical evolution Ansoff describes makes good reading, but let's not take it too literally. Perhaps, like beauty, some of that conceptual growth comes from the eye of the beholder.

Fortunately, an explanation of the nature of strategy by expanding its scope and dimensions is a good exposition technique. And the historical references do lend color. But in our serious research the historical evolution presented must be used with great caution.

Commentary

WILLIAM R. DILL
New York University

Bursk and others (1962) published a four-volume anthology on business which managed to survey 4,000 years of the history of enterprise without making conspicuous reference to the word "strategy." Jim March (1965) compiled a 1,200-page handbook of research on organizations at about the same time and managed to show similar restraint. Even Sloan (1964) found other words to describe what he thought was important at General Motors.

Yet for this conference on research in business policy, ten of the fourteen topics deal explicitly with "strategy" or with "strategic management." This seems a bit much, and the invitation to comment on Ansoff's paper gives me an opportunity to suggest why.

Ansoff has done as much as anyone to build strategy and companion terms like synergy and systems into the managerial and academic vocabularies. At first, Ansoff (1965) offered a relatively simple scheme, built heavily from Chandler (1962) and Sloan (1964):

1. Business, as Sloan argued, should be ambitious for growth and change.

2. Successful managing requires a concept of the business: active exploration of opportunities and challenges in the environment and explicit choices about what the business should become.

3. Strategy is a focused concept for development of the business — a statement of product and market commitments, with implications for technology, structure, and operations.

4. Strategic, active management will win from adaptive, tactical managers.

Over the years, the mix has become richer and the arguments more complex. The environment used to offer prospects for products, technologies, and markets was central. Political, social, and resource issues — as side issues — were treated as relatively stable, often minimal constraints. The environment was uncertain and risky, and Peter Drucker (1969) thought himself bold to argue that it was becoming characterized by "discontinuity." Few people thought the environment malevolent, however; and it was not fashionable to speak of turbulence.

Today, hundreds of charts and diagrams later, Ansoff has introduced many new elements into his master plan for management; but all still hinges on strategy. He now believes that six kinds of strategy must be formulated by the "compleat angler" who becomes the modern corporate leader, and most of these strategies relate to separately labeled sectors of the environment. Off to the northwest in Ansoff's Exhibit 1.8, supposedly the ultimate strategic

diagram, there is even room for the tornado of "unpredictable turbulence."

We are exaggerating the centrality of strategy, just as earlier generations of academics read too much into the concepts of Frederick W. Taylor. Strategic thinking has demonstrably helped many firms stay — or get — out of trouble, but it may be time to ask how strategic thinking creates difficulties of its own.

"Strategy," according to Random House (Stein, 1967), is "generalship . . . a plan, method, or series of maneuvers or stratagems for obtaining a specific goal or result." Strategic management, however, runs the danger of turning into machismo management: the organization plotting and sailing its course through shark-infested seas. Good formulators of strategy are intellectual, inquisitive, activist, confident, and often quite arrogant. Arrogant strategists sometimes get swallowed by the sharks.

Ansoff has embellished his concept of strategy because most of the early heroes of the strategic game have fallen on hard times: General Motors, still supreme in the marketplace, but concerned about ways to rebuild public trust; Lockheed, a business which has known trouble and disgrace; Boise Cascade and Singer, conglomerates that have needed emergency surgery from new management teams; commercial banks, which learned how to diversify into fields like real estate, but not to analyze those diversifications well. Ansoff's answer to failure is always to make the strategy formulation effort more comprehensive. Yet, with less attention to strategy formulation and more to quieter processes of listening and responding to voices in the environment outside the firm, some of these firms might not have gotten into so much trouble.

Too much of the thrust of strategic management neglects the adaptive, "grass-roots" origins of organizational existence. It leaves little room for the "inducement-contributions" model around which people like Barnard (1938), Simon (1957), and Homans (1950) have constructed their views of what makes firms wax and wane. The environment might be less turbulent if managers spent less time splashing their oars in the water.

To the extent that we are still polishing ideas

that were developed in rough form by Sloan and his contemporaries, we need — as Ansoff points out — to recognize how closely tied those ideas were to the necessity of corporate growth. Sloan (1964: xxii) wrote:

> Growth, or striving for it, is, I believe, essential to the good health of an enterprise. Deliberately to stop growth is to suffocate.
> ... Growth and progress are related, for there is no resting place for an enterprise in a competitive economy.

Ansoff also suggests a new kind of strategic activity is needed to deal with problems of limited growth, or in some situations like the universities, with a demand for real shrinkage. Yet the problem in these situations seems usually not to be an absence of strategy, but incapability — given normal dynamics for survival and growth in an organization — to hear signals from the environment that growth is not possible or to manage relations within the organization so that it does not fly apart as various internal and closely related external constituencies fight plans for reduction of investment in areas that affect their personal security and survival.

The concept of strategy is closely tied to assumptions of goals and objectives. Society has been willing to let corporations pursue such goals and objectives, just as they used to allow generals to do so, as long as the messy parts of the operation were off in distant battlefields and the folks at home simply enjoyed the finished product or the glory of the victory. But what we see now, with concerns about environmental protection and conservation of resources for future generations, is what generals have seen in war when the battlefield is the home country. When the real or potential damage begins to sink in, the uncritical acceptance of the glory of enterprise disappears; and business becomes too important to be left to its executives in the same sense that war has become too important to leave to the generals.

This means that what Ansoff touches on briefly, the problem of beating back challenges to the legitimacy of the firm, is growing in importance for managers — and is likely to keep becoming more important. And as long as it is

regarded the way Ansoff seems to regard it, as a problem of fighting off attacks on something which is God-given, the environment is going to seem turbulent, hostile, and intractable. Legitimacy is not really a new concern, and in the view of others like Barnard and Simon, attaining it and keeping it is as close to a central activity of organizations as anything can be.

The success of companies like AT&T, IBM, General Electric, Proctor & Gamble, and Sears Roebuck over the long run has a great deal to do with their concern for building legitimacy and acceptance among key groups on whom they depended, at least as much as it does on their sophistication in preparing product, market, and technology strategies. And a key feature of their efforts to build legitimacy has been their effort to keep listening and to keep hearing what key constituencies expected and wanted from them.

AT&T and General Electric have long studied and analyzed public opinion as it affected their operations and planning. IBM, Proctor & Gamble, and Sears have been distinguished for the genuinely high regard in which they hold customer reaction to their products and services. IBM and Sears have been leaders in creative ways of getting feedback and advice from employees.

Call this strategizing if you like. But others, long before the vogue for discussing active strategizing developed, talked about it as adapting or responding behavior. For the key dimension is the opposite of what strategizing calls for: instead of putting your stamp on the organization, you are really trying to sense and absorb the kind of stamp that others would like to place on it.

There has been less turbulence in the environment for companies which have spent time over the years listening to and assessing what various internal and external constituencies have to say about the powers they are and are not willing to delegate to corporations and corporate management. They are not surprised that a nation affluent enough to buy boats and take to the rivers and lakes for recreation want those rivers and lakes clean enough to sail on and want chemical discharges controlled so that water reserves are safe to drink from. They did not need to wait for Watergate to appreciate that corporate bribes and under-the-table political contributions had the potential for creating severely adverse reactions.

Corporations must also sense that dynamism is not always what the public wants. Companies, like government, must become more subtle about places where they might let some segment of the environment govern their activities so that in turn they can get public acceptance for an activist role in other matters. Ansoff's paper still underplays this view, just as his book did a dozen years ago. Organizational life is some kind of alternation between initiative and adaptation, between proclaiming and listening, between leading and following. Strategy pertains to initiative, proclaiming, and leading; and pretending that it stretches to cover activities which involve adaptation, listening, and following simply gets in the way of having your motives accepted as honest ones.

Ansoff's diagram of the "ultimate," can be redrawn as in Exhibit 1.10 to recognize more clearly that business policy-making is both a base-building and a direction-setting effort.

The diagnosis of who stakeholders are and of how their claims on the organization are evolving is one of several kinds of environ-

mental studies that need to be done. In general, business policy research should put more effort into better paradigms for describing organizational environments, and perhaps less on describing paradigms for structuring the planning process within firms.

Two other areas of research merit attention. The first involves reforms that are being proposed in corporate governance and their interactions with strategic planning and adaptive decision-making within the firm. The second is the special problems of policy formulation in declining, rather than in growing organizations. The shape of the changes in corporate governance is not yet clear, but in various ways they will force more participative reviews of plans and actions with groups outside corporate management. To what extent can and should management give outside groups opportunities to participate in their long-range goal setting and planning activities as a way to anticipate and deflect critical appraisals later by society of corporate results?

The question of decision-making in declining organizations is something familiar today to university administrators, and to leaders of some companies and industries. Studies are needed not only of how planning is done when an

Exhibit 1.10   A Revision of Ansoff's "Ultimate" Diagram

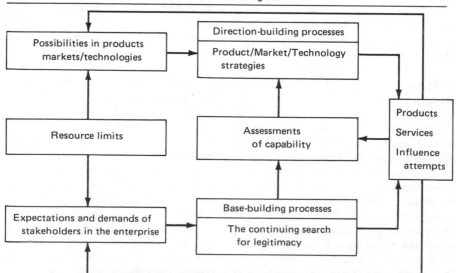

organization must shrink, but of who must participate, if the organization is to hold together and keep the support of those whose help it needs during a period of decline.

Professor Newman's response raises a different kind of issue. He has helped elaborate Ansoff's paper by reminding us of the external constituencies that make up a part of the environment with which the firm must deal. These stakeholders, as they are beginning to be called, are increasingly the focus of attention and research.

Nevertheless, Newman has done what most of us who talk about stakeholders do. He has listed them by category: customers, suppliers, labor, community, sources of capital, etc. A badly-needed piece of conceptualizing and empirical research would analyze the overlap and interaction among categories. Individuals and organizations wear several hats, and speak in different ways depending which one they have on. Peter Drucker, for example, has begun to call our attention to the degree to which employees, through their pension funds, have become important new influences on the flow of capital (Drucker, 1976). For an industrial products company like IBM, its customers are often also suppliers or sources of capital; and for consumer product and service companies, there are often blurred boundaries among customers, labor, and community.

The same executive whose factories pollute air in Pittsburgh or rivers in Alabama may be a rabid environmentalist in opposing efforts to bring oil tankers into harbors near his summer home in Maine. The university professor who cheered legislation which forced openings for blacks and women in corporate management cries foul when HEW applies similar concepts in regulating the way that colleges hire faculty.

We are not dealing with large, separate groups of constituents, each with consistent, stable attitudes. We are dealing with individuals and organizations whose lives are divided among multiple roles, and whose reactions in a particular situation depend on complex combinations of basic beliefs and ways of perceiving with current stimuli. Attitudes and perceptions which dominate in one role, say, as community member, are not only important for themselves, but for the spillover they may have in the playing of other roles, e.g., worker or customer.

Finally, a word of caution for us academics. We fancy ourselves as leaders in building new ideas and concepts for management. In our current fascination with strategy as in other studies of policy-making, we may have become followers and historians, rather than initiators. One thing we should assess is how much of what we are doing still is following up what corporations have already tried and moved beyond. Strategy is clearly the important legacy of Alfred Sloan, and it has been a useful tool for the current generation of managers. It will remain so in the future. But when the history of managerial innovations of the seventies is written, will strategy-related activities dominate? Or will we, as I fear, invent new words to describe processes and practices that none of us yet see clearly enough to capture and translate into a conference paper or a journal article? Let us keep an eye out for prototypes as well as archetypes.

Section 1 References

Ansoff, H. Igor. *Corporate Strategy: An Analytical Approach to Business Policy for Growth and Expansion.* New York: McGraw-Hill, 1965.

Ansoff, H. Igor. "The Concept of Strategic Management." *Journal of Business Policy,* Summer 1972.

Ansoff, H. Igor. "Management in Transition," in *Challenge to Leadership: Managing in a Changing World.* New York: The Conference Board, 1973.

Ansoff, H. Igor. "Managing Strategic Surprise by Response to Weak Signals." *California Management Review,* Winter 1976.

Ansoff, H. Igor. "The State of Practice in Planning Systems." *Sloan Management Review,* Winter 1977.

Ansoff, H. Igor. "Planned Management of Turbulent Change," *Encylopedia of Professional Management.* New York: McGraw-Hill, 1978.

Ansoff, H. Igor. "Theory and Technology for Managing in Turbulent Environments," to be published by the Macmillan Press, Ltd. (England) and Halstead Press (U.S.A.).

Ansoff, H. Igor, Roger P. Declerck and Robert L. Hayes. "From Strategic Planning to Strategic Management," in *From Strategic Planning to Strategic Management*. New York: Wiley, 1976.

Barnard, Chester I. *The Functions of the Executive*. Cambridge, Mass.: Harvard University Press, 1938.

Barraclough, Geoffrey. "Management in a Changing Economy," an AMA Survey Report, 1976.

Bursk, Edward, et al. (editors). *The World of Business*. New York: Simon and Schuster, 1962.

Chandler, Alfred D. *Strategy and Structure: Chapters in the History of the American Industrial Enterprise*. Cambridge, Mass.: M.I.T. Press, 1962.

Drucker, Peter F. *The Age of Discontinuity: Guidelines to Our Changing Society*. New York: Harper and Row, 1969.

Drucker, Peter F. "Pension Fund Socialism." *Public Interest*, No. 42, pp. 3–46, 1976.

Homans, George. *The Human Group*. New York: Harcourt, Brace and World, 1950.

MacMillan, Ian C. "Business Strategies for Political Action." *Journal of General Management*, Autumn 1974.

MacMillan, Ian C. *Strategy Formulation: Political Concepts*. St. Paul, Minn.: West Publishing Co., 1978.

March, James G. (editor). *Handbook of Organizations*. New York: Rand McNally, 1965.

Maslow, Abraham H. *Motivation and Personality*. New York: Harper and Row, 1954.

Newman, William H. and E. Kirby Warren. *The Process of Management*, 4th ed. Englewood Cliffs, N.J.: Prentice-Hall, 1977.

Ouchi, W. G. and R. T. Harns. "Structure, Technology and Environment," in *Organizational Behavior: Research and Issues*. Madison, Wis.: Industrial Relations Research Association, 1974.

Perrow, Charles. *Organizational Analysis: A Sociological View*. Belmont, Calif.: Wadsworth Publishing, 1970.

Simon, Herbert A. *Administrative Behavior*. 2d edition New York: Macmillan, 1957.

Sloan, Alfred P., Jr. *My Years with General Motors*. New York: Doubleday and Co., 1964.

Stein, Jess (editor). *The Random House Dictionary of the English Language*. New York: Random House, 1967.

Toffler, Alvin. *Future Shock*. New York: Bantam Books, 1970.

Watson, T. J., Jr. *A Business and Its Beliefs*. New York: McGraw-Hill, 1963.

2

ORGANIZATIONAL GOALS AND GOAL FORMULATION

Organizational Power and Goals: A Skeletal Theory

HENRY MINTZBERG
McGill University

Commentary

MAX D. RICHARDS
The Pennsylvania State University

EDWIN A. MURRAY, JR.
Northwestern University

Organizations form to accomplish purpose. Without purpose it cannot be said that a group is an organization. It may be a crowd, a throng, a gathering, but not an organization. Purposes can be separated into various classes such as religious, economic, charitable, social, and so on, such classes, in turn, giving rise to what are typically called institutions.

In a very general sense then, purpose, or what has been called mission, implies a goal structure toward which the organization tries to move. As noted in the Introduction to this book, purpose, goals, and objectives are a central part of the strategic management paradigm (see Exhibit 2.1) because they are the names given to the ends strategy is intended to achieve, and because they are an important aspect of strategy implementation and strategic control. Given this central role accorded to the concept of goals and goal structure, those who formulate and implement strategy must recognize some goal structure before it is possible for them to undertake a coordinated set of actions.

The goal structure of an organization as such is important, but goals do not just arise out of thin air. They must have some source if they are to motivate the kind of fundamental action associated with strategy. It is, therefore, fair to ask whether there is some organizational process or processes that might be called goal formulation processes, which correspond

Exhibit 2.1 An Overview of the Strategic Management Process

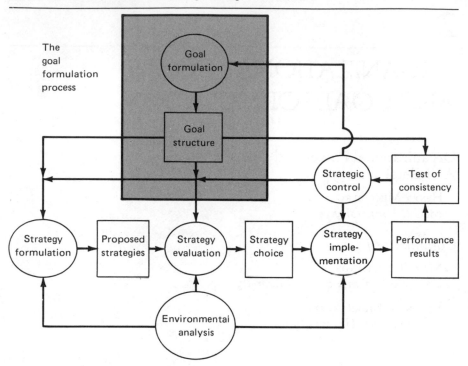

to strategy formulation processes and which might, at times, be intimately intertwined with the organization's strategy formulation processes. Gaining such understanding is not a simple task, however, for as the three papers in this section point out, there exist many unanswered questions about such processes, about the content of the goals they form, and about the role and use of goals in strategy formulation, strategy implementation, and strategic control.

The essence of the problem that any goal formulation process must solve is making sense out of a collection of individual organization member's personal goals, as well as those goals of the parties or actors that can influence the organization. Some consistency among these goals is necessary before effective behavior can result. Such consistency may be achieved through a variety of means, including sequential attention to goals, quasi-reduction of conflict, or by making personal and organizational goals congruent. The premise behind any of these procedures is that goals provide the cues for action, the incentive to act, and a standard against which actions and performance results can be judged. In managerial parlance, goals are instrumental to both planning and control.

There are a number of competing goal formation processes advanced in the literature, as this set of papers points out. Goal formation processes are catalogued by Murray as being of two types: (1) prescriptive, in which goals are viewed as objective statements determined by rational analytical actions, and (2) descriptive, in which goals are subjective statements formed out of political processes. Richards suggests that goals, if not the processes and organizations that determine them, can be divided into three types: (1) approximately rational, in which goals are given and guide behavior (profit maximization may be one type); (2) indirectly rational, in which it is unnecessary to relate individual and organizational goals because a "munificent" environment affords sufficient slack to permit divergent ends to be pursued; and (3) partially rational, in which the degree of slack determines how rational the organization must be.

MINTZBERG'S GOAL FORMULATION MODEL

After reviewing and dismissing the imposed single-goal, rational-actor model of the economist, and the various models of the organizational behavioralists who argue for various coalition models of goal formation based on conflict resolution models, Mintzberg suggests that the root of the issue really lies in power and influence; in the means, the opportunity, and the will to use power; and in the translation of personal goals into organizational decisions and actions. Thus, it is only through understanding the uses of power that an understanding of goal formation and goal content can be gained, according to Mintzberg.

Mintzberg then presents an interesting model of how influence and power can be used to form goals and establish direction for the organization. His model assumes two types of influences, those external to the organization, of which he identifies four main groups (owners, associates, employee associations, and publics), and those influences internal to the organization wielded by five main groups (peak coordinator, middle managers, technical staff, support staff, and operators).

External influencers have power and the means to affect the internal coalition, through what Mintzberg labels an External Coalition (EC), to the extent that these external influencers are *concentrated* and the organization is *dependent* upon them. He then identifies five fundamental external means of influence used: (1) social norms, (2) specific constraints, (3) pressure campaigns, (4) direct controls, and (5) membership on the board of directors. The External Coalition can hold a wide range of power with respect to the Internal Coalition (IC). According to Mintzberg, this range is expressed in three types of External Coalitions: (1) dominated ECs, (2) divided ECs, and (3) passive ECs.

A Formal Coalition (FC) arises around the board of directors in Mintzberg's scheme. The Formal Coalition's power arises through the various roles it plays. There are eight of these, the first three of which are controlling in nature: (1) the selection/dismissal of chief executives (or peak coordinator); (2) the use of authority during periods of change; and (3) the review of performance and major decisions. The next five roles are of a service nature: (4) coopting external influencers; (5) legitimizing the organization; (6) developing contacts; (7) offering specialized advice; and (8) helping raise funds.

The Internal Coalition is where things get done, through the five groups mentioned. Mintzberg identifies explicitly four fundamental systems of influence in the Internal Coalition: (1) a personal control system, (2) a bureaucratic control system, (3) a political control system, and (4) systems of ideology. These are not intended to be mutually exclusive. Combining the five kinds of influencers and these four systems of influence, five kinds, or types, of internal coalitions can be identified: (1) a bureaucratic coalition, the central figure in which is the peak coordinator (PK); (2) an autocratic coalition, also a type where the peak coordinator is dominant; (3) an ideologic coalition, where a shared ideology holds; (4) a meritocratic coalition, where power rests with expertise; and (5) a politicized coalition, where the political system dominates.

The combination of External Coalition and Internal Coalition types along with the sources of their relative influence give rise to fifteen different power configurations into which organizations can be classified, only six of which are observed in practice, according to Mintzberg. Exhibit 2.2 summarizes these six power configurations and suggests the degree of formality that is associated with the goal and strategy formulation processes for each type.

A CRITIQUE OF MINTZBERG'S GOAL FORMULATION MODEL

Mintzberg's model clearly has many strengths. Among the more important of these are: (1) its richness with respect to contingencies, which clearly indicates why organizations may adopt and emphasize goals other than those suggested by traditional economics; and (2) the model provides a paradigm that can be used to design research studies on organizational goals.

On the other hand, several questions can be raised regarding Mintzberg's model. Among the more important of these are the following: (1) is Mintzberg's claim that goals rest on power reasonable? (2) are Mintzberg's power configurations exhaustive? (3) are the linkages between goal formulation and strategy formulation proposed by Mintzberg reasonable? (4) are other linkages possible? For instance, if goal formulation is a political process, does it necessarily follow that strategy formulation has to be a political process too? (5) are the internal workings of the power configurations described by Mintzberg realistic? For instance, is the role of the peak coordinator realistic? (6) are the transitions suggested by Mintzberg among different power configurations reasonable? (7) what kinds of research

Exhibit 2.2 Mintzberg's Classification of Power Configurations, Coalitions, and Formulation Processes

Power configuration	Nature of external coalition	Nature of internal coalition	Principal influence system	Nature of goal formulation process	Nature of strategy formulation process
1. Continuous chain	Dominated	Bureaucratic	Bureaucratic control	Formal, externally imposed	Formal, analytical
2. Closed system	Passive	Bureaucratic	Bureaucratic control	Formal, system determined	Formal, analytical
3. Commander	Passive	Autocratic	Personal control	Internal, entrepreneurial	Internal, entrepreneurial
4. Missionary	Passive	Ideologic	Ideology	Informal, ideologic	Informal, incremental
5. Professional	Divided	Meritocratic	Political (weak)	Informal, sequential, attention to goals	Informal, incremental
6. Conflictive	Divided	Politicized	Political (strong)	No goals, satisfices sequential constraints	None possible

methodologies can be employed to study these questions? Must they be "soft" methods, as Mintzberg claims?

In our view, there are other answers to each of these questions than those implied by Mintzberg's discussion.

Is Mintzberg's Claim that Goals Rest on Power Reasonable? Insofar as it goes, the answer is yes; it is clear that some organizational goals are based on power and its use. However, goals may arise from two other sources. First, goals may sometimes arise from a shared consensus rather than from the use of power or influence. Mintzberg admits this possibility through his discussion of ideology for the internal coalition and through dominated external coalitions. He does not examine the possibility of consensus in internal coalitions through nonideologic means, however. The second, and by far the more important source of organizational goals is the need for organizational survival. Mintzberg assumes away this source of goals when he notes that "customers in straight economic trading relationships are not influencers" and implies that the same is true for competitors. It may be true that some organizations have sufficient excess resources or such strong market positions that they face few threats to their survival and that, as a consequence, power is a more important source of goals than the need to survive — at least in the short term. It is also clear that there are other organizations for whom the problems of survival are sufficiently real that they have a significant impact on the organization's goal structure. This is particularly true for businesses, especially those operating in highly competitive and/or rapidly changing markets.

Are Mintzberg's Power Configurations Exhaustive? Mintzberg develops his power configurations from the three types of external and five types of internal coalitions he describes. While fifteen combinations are theoretically possible, Mintzberg reduces these to six by arguing that "elements, whether they be stars, ants, or characteristics of organizations, tend to cluster into natural groupings, or configurations." He does not discuss the reasons the nine he excludes should or do not occur in practice or offer empirical evidence supporting his exclusion of them. Thus, Richards asks why a passive-politicized configuration is not possible.

Additional configurations can come from two sources: first, from combinations that Mintzberg has excluded; and second, from the addition of different types of internal or external coalitions than those Mintzberg describes. It appears to us that additional configurations of both types are necessary to adequately reflect the diversity of organizations observed in the real world.

Thus, while dominated-ideologic and dominated-politicized configurations do not seem feasible, divided-bureaucratic, divided-autocratic, dominated-autocratic, divided-ideologic, dominated-meritocratic, passive-meritocratic, and passive-politicized configurations appear to be theoretically feasible.[1] Nevertheless, since some of these would appear to have goal formulation and strategy formulation processes similar to Mintzberg's six configurations, it would not be necessary to establish separate categories for each of these configurations. For instance, the divided-bureaucratic configuration would seem to be sufficiently similar to Mintzberg's passive-bureaucratic configuration that these two categories could be combined into one category, which might be more appropriately called a "traditional bureaucracy" than a "closed system." Even after such combinations are made, however, four additional configurations would need to be added to Mintzberg's original six, as indicated in Exhibit 2.3.

Furthermore, it would seem that Mintzberg has assumed away two other types of coalitions, one external and one internal, that would give rise to three other possible configurations. First, Mintzberg has assumed that there are only four types of internal influence systems, (that is, personal control systems, bureaucratic control systems, political systems, and ideologies), that give rise to five types of internal coalitions. (Both meritocratic and politicized coalitions can arise under political influence systems.) While his political and ideology categories seem reasonable, his personal and bureaucratic control system categories stem solely from the nature of the tools they employ rather than from the sources of their power, as is the case with political and ideological influence systems.

Personal and bureaucratic control systems do exist, of course. They derive their power from the sources of influence available to an individual or from the values of the technostructure that actuate the organization's various systems and procedures.

Another source of influence is the demands of the market. When the systems and procedures of the organization are set up to respond to these, it may be more appropriately said to have a strategic control system than a bureaucratic control system. To the extent that strategic control systems exist, they may give rise to an internal coalition that is more responsive to the needs of the market than to the needs of the technostructure. Such an internal coalition might be appropriately labeled a "managerial" coalition. Such coalitions would use control systems that would be similar in organizational form to those used by Mintzberg's bureaucratic coalition. Since the source of influence actuating these systems lies external to the organization (i.e., in the market) rather than internal to the organization

[1] Apparently, Mintzberg has eliminated a number of these categories because he assumed: (1) that the values of the external and internal coalitions are always different; and (2) that a dominant external coalition would have sufficient power vis-à-vis the internal coalition to force its views on the internal coalition. Neither assumption is necessarily true, however. Thus, a dominated-meritocratic organization could exist if the dominant external coalition placed great value on professional work.

Exhibit 2.3 Additional Power Configurations, Coalitions, and Formulation Processes

Revised power configurations	Nature of external coalition	Nature of internal coalition	Principal influence system	Nature of goal formulation process	Nature of strategy formulation process
1. Dominated bureaucracy	Dominated	Bureaucratic	Bureaucratic control	Formal, top down	Formal, incremental
2. Traditional bureaucracy	Passive/Divided	Bureaucratic	Bureaucratic control	Formal, bottom up	Formal, incremental
3. Entrepreneurial leader	Passive	Autocratic	Personal control	Informal, entrepreneurial	Informal, entrepreneurial
4. Charismatic leader	Divided	Autocratic	Personal control	Informal, entrepreneurial	Informal, entrepreneurial
5. Shared dictatorship	Dominated	Autocratic	Personal control	Formal, bargaining	Informal, entrepreneurial
6. Missionary	Passive/Divided	Ideology	Ideology	Informal, ideologic	Informal, incremental
7. Dominated professional	Dominated	Meritocratic	Political (weak)	Informal, adaptive	Formal, incremental
8. Traditional professional	Passive/Divided	Meritocratic	Political (weak)	Internal, sequential attention to goals	Informal, incremental
9. External conflictive	Divided	Politicized	Political (strong)	No goals, sequentially satisfices constraints	None possible
10. Internal conflictive	Passive	Politicized	Political (strong)	No goals, sequentially satisfices constraints	None possible
11. Dominated responsive	Dominated	Managerial	Strategic control	Formal, top down	Formal, analytical market oriented
12. Responsive closed system	Passive/Divided	Managerial	Strategic control	Formal, bottom up	Formal, analytical market oriented
13. Enlightened strategic management	Professional	Managerial	Strategic control	Formal, interactive	Formal, analytical market oriented

(i.e., in the technostructure), it seems appropriate to establish them as a separate category.[2]

These considerations give rise to three additional possible power configurations — dominated-managerial, passive-managerial, and divided-managerial — the latter two of which appear to overlap in their goal formulation and strategy formulation process. Thus, these three possible configurations give rise to two new categories of coalitions which we have labeled "dominated responsive" and "responsive closed system," as indicated in Exhibit. 2.3.

In describing the possible types of external coalitions, Mintzberg has also assumed that the members of the external coalition always look out only for their own interests. This assumption produces quite straightforwardly the three types of external coalitions he has described — dominated, divided, and passive. If, however, one assumes that the members of the external coalition also look out for the values and views of others, then a fourth type of external coalition, which we shall call a professional coalition, is possible. Such a coalition might have one, or a few, or many external influencers. It would differ from the dominant, divided, and passive external coalitions described by Mintzberg in that it would not attempt to maximize its goals while treating those of others as constraints as the dominant EC, or let control revert back to management as the passive EC, or bargain over the goals of the EC members while disregarding others as the divided EC. Rather, it would attempt to develop a composite set of goals that would satisfy both the desires of the existing members of the external coalition and those of parties not currently represented in it. Clearly, this would not always be possible. To the extent that it is, however, such an external coalition would truly be a "professional" external coalition. By its very nature, such a coalition would permit no other type of internal coalition to arise than a managerial one. This would then give rise to one additional power configuration, which we have labeled "Enlightened Strategic Management."

While one can argue for additions to Mintzberg's six configurations, it is not clear that all such additional configurations would be observed empirically. If they are not, or if some could be explained as slight variants of others, then reductions should be made, since the power of any theory is increased to the degree it is more parsimonious.

ARE THE LINKAGES BETWEEN GOAL FORMULATION AND STRATEGY FORMULATION PROPOSED BY MINTZBERG REASONABLE? ARE OTHER LINKAGES POSSIBLE?

The linkages proposed by Mintzberg do appear to be reasonable. Others do seem possible, though, as is indicated in Exhibit 2.3. Whether other combinations are possible for each individual power configuration is a question

[2] Meritocratic coalitions differ from bureaucratic coalitions in that: (1) the source of their influence is external professional standards, not the internal needs of the technostructure; and (2) they use social-political influence systems rather than bureaucratic

(continued)

that could be argued both ways theoretically, given the existing state of knowledge in this area. Its resolution will thus rely primarily on empirical research and on the development of more sophisticated models based on that research.

ARE THE INTERNAL WORKINGS OF THE POWER CONFIGURATIONS DESCRIBED BY MINTZBERG REALISTIC? Most appear to be realistic, although a few seem questionable. The control role attributed to the peak coordinator, for example, seems overdone. Missing seems to be an examination of how compromise is reached and of how the PK really accomplishes this. Again, however, the resolution of this question seems to depend more on new empirical research than on trying to construct more elaborate theoretical arguments, given the limited knowledge currently available.

ARE THE TRANSITIONS SUGGESTED BY MINTZBERG AMONG DIFFERENT POWER CONFIGURATIONS REASONABLE? The transition Mintzberg suggests for business firms, that is, that they start as "Commander Power Configurations," then shift into "Continuous Chain Power Configurations" as they grow and ownership becomes separate from management, and still later shift into "Closed System Power Configurations" as ownership becomes dispersed and systems goals come to the fore is intriguing, especially when compared with the "Stages of Growth" models developed by Scott, Salter et al., that are discussed in Galbraith's and Nathanson's, Cooper's, and Berg's and Pitts's papers. The similarities of these models are great. There are also differences, however. Thus, while large, integrated firms such as steel companies would fit Mintzberg's pattern, the large, diversified majors would not. Scott (1973) made a similar observation regarding the accuracy of the picture painted by John Kenneth Galbraith in *The New Industrial State*. Most of these problems seem to disappear with the addition of the seven new power configurations described in Exhibit 2.3 and the different sequences they make possible.

WHAT RESEARCH QUESTIONS DERIVE FROM MINTZBERG'S PAPER? We know very little about the answers to the above questions about organizational goals and goal formulation in general or about how these factors affect the other aspects of the strategic management process or organizational performance. Richards does note that there is some research evidence to suggest that better goal definition apparently leads to better performance. Such evidence has been accumulated primarily with regard to individual goals either in laboratory settings or at low levels in the organization hier-

---

control systems as the primary method to control behavior. Meritocratic coalitions differ from managerial coalitions in that: (1) their source of influence, while external to the organization, is professional standards, not the needs of the market; and (2) they use weak political influence systems rather than strategic control systems as the primary method to control behavior.

archy. Thus, it badly needs replication at higher levels in the hierarchy and for overall organizational goals.

Richards advocates such empirical research. However, both he and Murray warn that in conducting such research one must be careful to differentiate between "real" and "official" goals if one is to avoid spurious relationships among goals, strategies, and environment.

Richards also advocates studies comparing the differences in goals and goal formulation processes among organizations in the same environment to better isolate the effects of the external and internal coalition structures in goals and goal formulation. Murray not only wishes to know more about the specific goals and goal structures that are associated with each of Mintzberg's power configurations, but he also wants to know what constitutes a "good" goal for each of these configurations. His first question will require in-depth clinical research, and he describes some research designs that might be used for such research. To answer his second question will require normative studies, however.

A final issue on the use of goals in organizations needs to be raised. Arguments exist as to whether organizations have goals, or whether just individuals have them. Many behavioralists argue for the latter. Yet, organizations act and indeed form, and with purpose. Can it be said then that organizations may not have goals or that goals cannot be used in a rational actor sense? Mintzberg does not address this issue directly, but Murray and Richards do.

Murray argues that mixed modes of objective/rational and subjective/descriptive goal formulation processes could exist in the same organization and at the same time. Hall's argument that goal congruency, however achieved, leads to a problem-solving, approximately rational process and to the use of goals, while goal incongruency leads to use of coalition/bargaining/conflict resolution modes to establish goals may be more descriptive, and in the end richer than Mintzberg's model, which emphasizes individual power.

All three authors come to the conclusion that, above everything else, much more research is needed to help us understand not only how goals are formed but also how goals are used to help formulate strategies, how goals are used in strategic control, and so on. Whether Mintzberg's skeletal theory of the relationships between goals and power will provide all these answers will await such further research. At a minimum, however, it has provided a new and different view of organizational goals and goal formulation that can form the base for a host of empirical research studies.

Organizational Power and Goals: A Skeletal Theory*

HENRY MINTZBERG
McGill University

INTRODUCTION: THE EVOLUTION OF GOAL THEORY

The literature on organizational goals has done a complete reversal in this century. Not long ago, the traditional viewpoint of microeconomic theory was widely accepted: that a *single actor*, called the entrepreneur, controlled the organization and that, serving as the agent of the system of pure competition, he imposed a *single goal* on the organization — the maximization of profit. In effect, the organization was his instrument. But this viewpoint came to be attacked on three grounds: whether profit, as opposed to, say, sales, was the one goal that was maximized; whether maximization was indeed possible; and whether it was moral.

Papandreou (1952) sought to save the assumptions of single actor and maximization by discarding that of a single goal. He proposed that *many goals* were imposed on the organization, by a variety of what we shall here call *influencers*, but that these still passed through a single actor, a "peak coordinator" (typically top management), who reconciled them all into a single preference function that was maximized. A decade later, Simon (1964) entered the battle. In suggesting that all goals were really constraints, he sought to do away with the assumption of maximization. On a related front, but much earlier, Barnard (1938) had introduced the notion that the employees too were active participants, who sought to negotiate inducements in return for their contributions. They did not determine the organizational goals per se, but their power to negotiate raised questions about the assumption of a single actor.

That assumption was discarded when Cyert and March (1963) pulled these ideas together into a theory involving *many goals* and *many actors*. A variety of influencers vied for control of the organization, and through the processes of bargaining and coalition formation, they distributed organizational power on the basis of their personal power. But Cyert and March argued that goals did emerge from the bargaining process, although these were inconsistent over time, since the needs of different influencers were attended to sequentially in the continual process of bargaining.

It was left to Georgiou (1973), among others, to complete the story, to take the final step that Cyert and March avoided. The assumption of even many goals was dropped: organizations had *no goals* at all; they were merely political arenas, convenient places for influencers to play power games with each other.

Four sets of questions emerge from this literature on organizational goals: First, how does the organization deal with multiple and often conflicting goals? Does it maximize any one? Can it? If not, how does it reconcile the conflicts? Second, are goals independent or dependent variables? That is to say, are goals given — imposed on the organization to determine decisions and actions — or do they emerge from the bargaining over decisions and actions? Another way to put this is to ask for whom the organization exists. Is it someone's *instrument*? Or is it a *political arena*, in which individuals vie for influence? Or is it perhaps, a *system* unto itself, with its own intrinsic goals? Third, can the organization be said to have goals at all, or only its influencers? Does a distinct "collective intent" really exist? And fourth, the overriding question: How do personal goals, needs, expectations or whatever get translated into organizational decisions and actions?

All of these questions can be answered only by focusing on the last one, on how power is used in the organization. Organization goals — what is sought through the decisions and actions organizations take — if they indeed exist, are the results of the play of power. So our interest in organizational goals must be put aside temporarily. Instead, we must look at power, specifically at: (1) which influencers play the power game in and around the organization, (2) *what means of influence* they use to affect outcomes, that is, decisions and actions, and (3) what kinds of *coalitions* they form to distribute their power. It will be convenient in addressing these three issues to make a fundamental distinction between the *External Coalition* (EC) and the *Internal Coalition* (IC). The former encompasses the *external influencers*, those persons or groups who must vie for power from outside the structure; the latter encompasses the *internal influencers*, those inside the structure, essentially the full-time employees who actually make the decisions and take the actions.

The paper begins with a discussion of the External Coalition — who belongs to it, what means of influence they use to affect outcomes, what basic ways they tend to distribute their power. Then, these same three issues are discussed for the Internal Coalition. Next, these two discussions are put together to present six basic *power configurations* that appear to be common in organizations. Finally, the issue of goals is reexamined, describing the organizational goal system (as well as the strategy formation process) that seems to be dictated by the distribution of power in each of the six configurations.

THE EXTERNAL COALITION

The external influencers of the organization may be thought of as falling into four main groups: the *owners*, who hold legal title to the organization, the *associates*, who trade with it, buying, selling, and working in partnership with it, the *employee associations*, which represent the workers of the organizations, and the various *publics* that surround the organization, including general groups, such as the employee's families and public opinion leaders, and special interest groups and government in its various forms.[1]

How do these influencers, outside the daily decision making process, influence it to get what they want? This same question can be posed in a much more fundamental way, namely: how does society control its organizations?

Influencers have power in the External Coalition to the extent that they are concentrated and that the organization is dependent on them (Jacobs, 1974). Thus the organization is far more responsive to the single monopolist who controls its source of supply than to the one supplier among thousands who does not; the closely held corporation is more responsive to its owners than the widely held one; the hospital is more responsive to the local government that grants its charter than the federal one that does not.

Concentration and dependency provide the potential for power. But that potential must somehow be manifested. Specifically, the external influencers must find some means to influence the decisions and actions of the internal influencers. Five fundamental *external means of influence* can be isolated — social norms, specific constraints, pressure campaigns, direct controls, and membership on the board of directors.

Social Norms

The most general means of external influence is the set of social norms that exist in the environment of every organization. They range from very general values ("Thou shalt not steal") to rather specific guidelines (hospitals should release patient information to relatives first). Social norms impinge on the internal influencers from a variety of sources — their parents and the teachers they had, influential

---

[1] A number of points of clarification are in order. Associates, or any of the others for that matter, are influencers only if they seek to affect outcomes directly. Customers in straight economic trading relationship are not influencers; monopsonists can be. Likewise competitors can be included as associates, for example, when they seek to exert influence through trade associations. The employee associations, as distinct from the employees, are treated as external influencers (at least, like the associates, when they move beyond a pure economic relationship) because they bargain with management outside the usual decision making processes of the organizations, much as suppliers do!

friends, chance encounters, the media, other organizations to which they belong. These norms develop over long periods of time and remain in a perpetual state of transition. Together they vaguely define an n-dimensional space of acceptable organizational behavior. But their perpetual change produces ambiguities for the organization. Can the corporation, for example, always "be efficient" and "keep the environment pollution-free" at the same time?

SPECIFIC CONSTRAINTS

A specific constraint is often a social norm made official. An external influencer defines more precisely some minimum acceptable level of behavior, and couples it with some official sanction to ensure compliance. Many specific constraints are imposed by governments, through laws and regulation, but not all. A union may bargain for a safety regulation in all the firms in one industry, while a supplier may establish a sales quota for a customer, as do the automobile companies for their dealers. The set of specific constraints defines a second n-dimensional space for the organization, within the first, with fewer dimensions, and with better defined boundaries.

PRESSURE CAMPAIGNS

Social norms are vague and unenforceable, while specific constraints are limited to well-defined actions, and even then only establish minimum levels of acceptable behavior. So the external influencers intent on more focused, yet more flexible means of external influence, turn to the pressure campaign. They group around an issue in order to exert pressure on the organization to take some action or change some behavior. The pressure campaign takes a variety of forms. Employee associations use the strike; associates refuse to trade with the organization; governments use moral suasion or threaten legislation (new specific constraints); special interest groups attack through the media, harass at annual meetings, sit down in front of bulldozers, and throw downstream sludge on executive carpets. Pressure campaigns, while they are

often used because social norms and specific constraints fail to control organizational behavior, are also designed to lead these. By focusing on specific cases, such as the dangers of water pollution from a certain factory, they raise the public's consciousness about a general issue, and thereby change its general norms and perhaps also encourage its legislators to introduce new specific constraints.

DIRECT CONTROLS

The most powerful external influencers are able to use two other, much more direct external means of influence. They can rely on a series of direct controls, or they can seek a seat on the board of directors of the organization.

Five kinds of direct controls can be delineated. The first is direct access. Simply having personal access to an internal influencer, as does a spouse, can constitute a significant source of power. Second and more direct is the inclusion of an external influencer in a decision process — in effect the joining temporarily of the Internal Coalition — as when a customer is asked to send a representative to a task force charged with designing a new product. A third and more potent form of direct control occurs when an external group is able to plant one of its own members permanently inside the Internal Coalition, for example, when a parent firm — an owner — names the controller of a subsidiary. A fourth form, and more direct still, occurs when an external influencer retains the power to authorize an organizational decision, sometimes informally, as when a racetrack consults the horse owners on all major decisions because they are key suppliers, and sometimes formally, as when an airline must seek FAA approval on a rate increase.[2] And fifth, direct control is most powerful of all when an external influencer can actually impose a decision on the organization in the first place, as when an owner names the chief executive or a powerful customer dictates what products will be produced.

[2] Such authorization constitutes the power to block or even change a specific decision; in contrast, a specific constraint guides in the same way all the decisions of a given class.

FORMAL COALITION

The final external means of influence is membership on the board of directors of the organization, what I shall call its Formal Coalition (FC). Traditionally such membership has been thought to be restricted to the owners of the organization. In fact, however, representatives of all four groups of external influencers can be found on boards, business and otherwise. Indeed, Chandler (1975) surveyed corporate directorship announcements in the *Wall Street Journal* for three months, and found that less than 1% of the new directors held substantial blocks of shares.

But how much of the organization's power in fact resides with the Formal Coalition? In law, all of it. "The business of a corporation shall be managed by a board of at least three directors," says United States General Corporation law. In fact, however, sometimes none of it resides with a board. The evidence on the power of the board to control decision making (e.g., Zald, 1969; Mace, 1971) suggests a wide range. Some boards are complete facades, powerless bodies set up to satisfy legal requirements. Others are instruments *of* the organization, used by it to provide services to it. And some emerge as more serious controlling devices. It all depends on the type of External Coalition.

Two ambiguities are of interest here. First, to whom are the directors responsible, some external constituency or the organization itself? The National Industrial Conference Board (1967) claims that "The basic legal responsibility of the board is to manage the company in the interests of the stockholders. In carrying out this task, the directors must exercise 'reasonable business judgment' and be 'loyal to the interests of the corporation.' " But what if it is in the interests of the shareholders to liquidate the corporation? Should the board act in the interests of the stockholders or the corporation? In other words, from the directors' point of view is the organization an instrument of outside interests or a system unto itself?

The second ambiguity is that the board is given no *specific* means to control the behavior of the organization; rather it is given *every* means. This provides it with a choice, to manage the corporation itself (in which case the board becomes the executive committee, its chairman, the chief executive officer) or to name a chief executive as its trustee to manage the organization.

The first choice poses some fundamental problems. If board members are part-time, they cannot properly manage the organization, a full-time job. And if they became full-time, they cease to be *external* influencers, to represent external constituencies. To use Selznick's (1949) word, they became "coopted." So boards do not manage corporations at all, or at least, if they do, they leave the External Coalition. (The perfect facade occurs with the so-called "inside board," comprising only full-time executives.)

As for the second choice, of naming a management to run the organization, this causes the board difficulty in keeping itself informed. The evidence is overwhelming that full-time managers are far better informed than part-time directors, typically to the point of being able to manipulate the directors at will. (Curiously, an advantage claimed for the inside board is that it suffers no such information problems [see, for example, Brown and Smith, 1958]. True enough, since it is simply an executive committee by another name. What it suffers is legitimacy problems, since it precludes external influencers — including shareholders — from using this fifth external means of influence.)

With these two ambiguities in mind, the various roles that boards have actually been shown to play in organizations can be considered. Eight in all will be discussed, three of a controlling nature and five of a service nature.

The first control role is the selection (and dismissal) of the chief executive officer, Papandreou's peak coordinator. This constitutes great power — if one believes that the bee has great power by virtue of its sting. For boards cannot hire and fire chief executives frequently; they can sting only once, or at least only once in a while. The second control role of the board is the exercise of authority during periods of difficult change, for example, during a major transformation of strategy or in the event of the incapacitation of the chief executive. During these periods, board members typically spend much more time on the job, insisting that management keep them better informed. Boards can assume great power during such periods, but these are typically short-lived. The third control role is the review of performance and perhaps also major decisions of the management, for example, to acquire a firm or increase the dividend. But here again, management is in charge and is better informed; except for very sensitive decisions, which management may prefer to leave to the board, it typically proposes and the board ratifies. As for performance review, the evidence from Mace and others suggests that it too is often rather cursory.

In effect, the competent chief executive says to the board: "Listen, I am a package. Take it or leave it. You don't understand much about the decisions I have to make. So don't meddle. I will make them. If you don't like them, fire me. Otherwise leave me alone." So while ultimately the board may have power, on a day-to-day basis it is of a rather limited kind. This, of course, assumes it wishes to have power; the evidence of Mace (1971) and others suggests that the directors of widely held business corporations are in effect chosen by the chief executive, and are beholden to him, with little desire to bother him. Mace even claims that these chief executives, upon retirement, select their own successors, and then ask their boards to ratify their choice.

The roles of boards — at least some of them — do not stop with control. Boards also *serve* the organization, in at least five ways. They coopt external influencers, that is, they offer membership to outside groups in order to win favors or support, as when a major customer is given a seat to retain his business. They legitimize the organization by seating high-status members, as when an astronaut joins the board of a cookie company. They develop contacts for it, as does the retired general serving as director of a manufacturer of military hardware (which raises the whole debate about interlocking directorships; Dooley, 1969; Levine, 1972). They provide it with specialized advice, which explains why lawyers and bankers are such prized board members. And finally, they help it to raise funds, another reason why bankers serve on so many boards and businessmen are such popular directors of non-profit institutions.

What emerges from this discussion of the Formal Coalition is an indication that it can vary substantially in the control it exercises over the organization: it may seek to control management, it can serve the organization, or, it can exist as a façade, an entity to satisfy the legal requirements. And this underlies a broader conclusion: that the External Coalition itself can hold a wide range of power with respect to the Internal Coalition. This range can be expressed in terms of three basic types of External Coalitions, or ECs.

THREE BASIC ECs

Most powerful is the *Dominated EC*, where a single individual or cooperating group holds most of the power in the External Coalition. This focus of power facilitates control of the Internal Coalition, either through the Formal Coalition or more likely through the use of direct controls (in which case the Formal Coalition becomes a facade or an instrument of the organization). An external influencer becomes dominant typically because he controls some key organizational dependency. The trustee may be able to dominate the social work agency dependent on him for funds, as can the monopolist, if his customers are dependent on him for supplies.

In the *Divided EC*, power is shared among a few main individuals or groups who seek to impose different goals in the organization. With each of them vying for control of organizational outcomes, every external means of influence is brought to bear, notably pressure campaigns, specific constraints, direct controls where possible, and the Formal Coalition, whose seats are hotly contested (unless, by law, one of the group controls them, in which case the other external influencers rely more extensively on the other means of influence).

When the number of individuals or groups competing for power grows large, an interesting thing happens: the power system reverts back to a form of dominance, but by the management: a *Passive EC* emerges. Shareholders of the widely held corporation, members of the international union, suppliers of the large farm cooperative, customers of the retail chain cooperative — all ostensibly owners — often turn out to be surprisingly passive vis-à-vis the management. As Olson (1968) shows in a mathematical analysis, when power is widely and evenly dispersed, it simply pays no one individual to exert the effort to control the management, or to organize any of the others to do so. Direct controls are little used in the Passive EC, and the Formal Coalition becomes an instrument of the organization or a facade, as Mace describes it in the widely held corporation. However, as in all External Coalitions, some use is inevitably made of social norms, specific constraints, and pressure campaigns as well.

These three basic kinds of External Coalitions form a continuum along a scale of the number of independent external influencers. But, as shown in Exhibit 2.4, it is a continuum that folds back on itself, the Passive EC resembling the Dominated EC. In effect, as the number of independent external influencers increases from one to infinity, the External Coalition metamorphoses from the Dominated to the Divided and then to the Passive form.

THE INTERNAL COALITION

No matter what the External Coalition, it is only through the efforts of the Internal Coalition that actions get taken, and goals emerge. This is the heart of the organizational power system.

The internal influencers can be divided into five groups, as shown in Exhibit 2.5, together with the external influencers already discussed. At the apex is the top management, which shall be referred to (after Papandreou, 1952) as the *Peak Coordinator,* or PK. Below lies the hierarchy of *middle line managers,* which ends up in the "operating core" where the *operators* — those people who do the basic work of the organization — are found. And to either side of the middle line are staff groups. On the left are the analysts of the technostructure, who design the systems by which the organization maintains itself and adapts to its environment (e.g., planning and control systems, work study systems, etc.). And on the right are the *support staff,* who provide indirect support to the rest

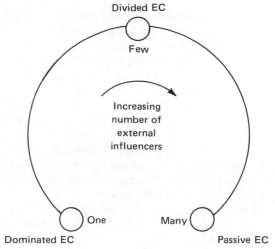

Exhibit 2.4 Three Basic Types of External Coalitions

of the organization (everything from the cafeteria to the legal counsel in the business firm). Power in the Internal Coalition is distributed among these five groups of internal influencers according to the nature of four fundamental systems of influence: the personal control system, the bureaucratic control system, the political system, and the system of ideology.

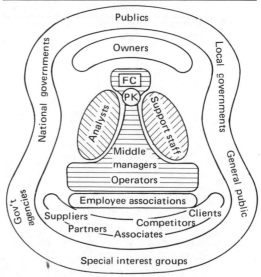

Exhibit 2.5 The Influence in and around the Organization

THE CONTROL SYSTEMS

The Peak Coordinator (PK) inevitably emerges as the single most powerful individual in the organizational power system, for three reasons. First, as noted above, the Formal Coalition cannot manage the organization and so must name the PK as its trustee to do so. Thus all of the formal power of the Formal Coalition passes to the PK in the first instance. This gives rise to a kind of symmetry of formal power, as shown in Exhibit 2.6: the Formal Coalition, representing the formal power of the External Coalition, is mirrored by the PK, representing the formal power of the Internal Coalition.

But as seen above, while the Formal Coalition may hold formal power, a good deal of informal power resides elsewhere in the External Coalition. But this too often leads to considerable PK power. The external influencers do not generally confront each other in face-to-face bargaining to distribute their power. (This can happen, in theory, only in the Formal Coalition, and, as has already been seen, many important external influencers are typically not even represented there.) Rather, as the very term Peak Coordinator implies, they exert a good deal of their power directly on the PK who in turn seeks to reconcile their wishes in the decisions he makes. And in so doing, he gains considerable informal power himself.

Exhibit 2.6 Symmetry of Formal Power between the External and Internal Coalitions

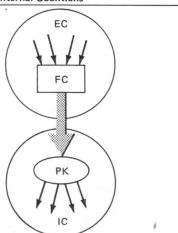

So the PK emerges with considerable informal as well as formal power. But no sooner does he get it than he must delegate it. For in all but the most simple organization, the PK cannot make every decision and take every action himself; he must share his power with others. So he builds a superstructure, a hierarchy of authority through which he delegates some of his formal power, in the first instance to the line managers who form a chain of authority below him, and after that out to the staff members who advise and perform specialized functions and down to the operators who do the basic work.

How then does the PK retain control of organizational decisions? For one thing, he generally has the reward system at his command, wherein the employees are remunerated for their contributions. To quote a Russian proverb, "Whose bread I eat his songs I sing." But how are the employees to know what those songs should be? To let them know — to achieve coordination and control in the organization — the PK, or in turn his subordinate managers, use an array of powers which make up two distinct organizational control systems.

The personal control system includes the issuance of direct orders, the review of the decision of others, and the allocation of the resources that can be used in actions. These powers enable the PK, and his subordinate managers, to exercise their authority in a personal manner.

A second set of powers, which make up the formal or *bureaucratic control system*, establish more clearly defined standards of behavior. These include the control of work content, directly through rules and procedures, and indirectly through training and selection procedures, the control of work outputs through action plans (such as strategic plans and critical path schedules), and the control of work results through performance controls (such as management by objectives and the use of profit centers). The PK can use all of these powers — personal as well as bureaucratic — to try to impose on the rest of the Internal Coalition the goals *he* believes the organization should pursue, what we shall refer to as the *formal goals* of the organization. To take the most pointed example, the PK can use performance controls to operationalize his formal goals. He quantifies them (as "objectives"), and then factors these into a hierarchy of subobjectives which he imposes on each and every unit as the performance standards it must meet. In this way, in theory at least, should all the units achieve their respective subobjectives, the organization will accomplish its formal goals.

THE POLITICAL SYSTEM

But this neat picture of the organization glosses over an important issue. A *political system* arises in the Internal Coalition to "displace" the *formal* goals imposed on it by the PK. This political system arises for a number of reasons. First, there are always ambiguities in the formal goals. Ideally, the PK would like to operationalize them in the hierarchy objectives, since goals are least ambiguous when expressed in quantitative form. It is one thing to be expected to generate profit or knowledge, quite another to be asked to produce a 10% return on investment or publish three articles a year. The problem, however, is that not all goals can be sensibly quantified. (Does the publication of three articles necessarily generate knowledge?) And even for those goals that can, distortions inevitably occur in the process of quantification such that pursuit of the objective is never quite the same as pursuit of the goal. (To achieve a return of 10% this year may necessitate damaging the long-term profit potential.) Moreover, the link between formal goals and specific decisions and actions is always indirect. The internal influencer is supposed to keep the general goals in the back of his mind as he makes specific decisions in the front. But it is not always clear whether a specific decision will actually help achieve a goal or impede its achievement. So formal goals — quantified as objectives or not — inevitably involve ambiguities which leave their appliers discretion to displace them.

A second reason for the displacement of formal goals is the tendency to "suboptimize" inherent in the division of labor of the superstructure. Units are naturally inclined to pursue narrow goals that pertain to their own function at the expense of the broad or formal goals that pertain to the overall organization. Similarly, there is a tendency on the part of internal influencers — each of them specialized in their tasks — to invert means and ends, to focus on their own means of work and forget about the ends these are meant to accomplish. Only if the division of labor is perfect in the organization — and, of course, it never is — do these behaviors not lead to the displacement of formal goals.

Third, group pressures arise within the Internal Coalition which encourage the individual to displace the formal goals in favor of those of the group. Fourth, external influencers sometimes bypass the PK, and use their power on internal influencers directly, encouraging them to give more weight to their demands than the PK saw fit when he developed the formal goals. And finally, the internal influencers have their own personal goals which they seek to pursue in place of those imposed on them by the control systems.

Given the internal influencer's incentive to displace the PK's formal goals, what bases of influence — necessarily informal in nature — are at his disposal to do so? First, he may control a critical function. Research indicates that informal power in the Internal Coalition derives from having a vital and unique expertise, from providing critical resources, or from being uniquely able to cope with an important uncertainty (Mechanic, 1962; Crozier, 1964; Hickson et al., 1971; Thoenig and Friedberg, 1975). Second, he may stand at a junction of important information channels in the organization. By being able to control the information that flows into the different channels, the internal influencer can build an important power base in the Internal Coalition (Hickson et al., 1971; Pettigrew, 1973). A third and very different informal basis of influence is simply the expenditure of effort: power flows to those who have the time, the energy — and the will — to fight the political battles. And finally, political abilities constitute a fourth important basis of influence. Informal power in the Internal Coalition often requires a "constituency." An influencer can generate power by virtue of his personality — "charisma" is the word used to describe natural leaders —

or by virtue of his political skills, such as bargaining and persuasion.

But again, potential power must be manifested somehow. In the Internal Coalition, these bases of influence are used on three prime playing fields. The main one is, of course, the decision making process itself. Internal influencers, particularly the different line managers with formal authority, vie to control the different choices that must be made. But control of choices is not sufficient. Control of the information and advice that feed into the making of these choices constitutes a second major playing field of the Internal Coalition, one used especially by staff personnel. When the decision maker is dependent on his advisors for their specialized knowledge, the latter may come to control the choices he makes. Pettigrew (1973) describes how each of three advisors sought to convince management to buy their favored computer system, the advisor having the best access to management eventually winning the day. And the execution of the choice emerges as the third major playing field of the Internal Coalition, because what counts ultimately is not control of decisions but control of actions, what the organization actually does. A decision is only a commitment to action, an intention to do something. The decision must be executed. And the internal influencers who execute the decisions — in particular the operators — may be able to intervene after the commitment, especially if it contains ambiguities, to deflect it to an action they prefer. Scheff (1961) describes vividly how the attendants of a mental hospital were able to block and distort managerial decisions in the execution phase to serve their own needs.

All kinds of power games arise in the Internal Coalition as the different bases of influence are used on these three playing fields. The operators block formal goals in favor of personal ones in the execution step; battles rage between staff specialists with the informal power of expertise and line managers with the formal authority; alliances push their own strategic candidates through the system; various individuals use whatever formal and informal power they can muster to build empires within the Internal Coalition.

To this point, the control systems and the political system have been developed as independent, and quite opposed, forces in the Internal Coalition. To use the economist's term, the former are "rational": they seek to impose the formal goals on the IC, those that the PK believes should be pursued by the organization. The latter is "irrational": it represents all kinds of private, in a sense clandestine, interests.

But this view can be challenged on two grounds. First, it assumes that the formal goals imposed on the Internal Coalition by the PK — representing his interpretation of the power system — are legitimate, while the informal goals of the other internal influencers, used to displace the formal goals, are not. That is a fair assumption to the extent that formal authority is viewed as valid, specifically to the extent that the organization is viewed as the instrument of the PK, the Formal Coalition, or whoever officially controls these. But as was seen earlier, some theorists view the organization as nobody's instrument, but rather as a political arena, a legitimate place to bring all kinds of power — informal as well as formal — to bear on decisions and actions.

Second, closer study suggests that the dichotomy between the rational and the political is not all that sharp. Especially when the External Coalition does not speak with a clear voice (as in the Divided form), or speaks hardly at all (as in the Passive form), the PK may have considerable discretion to develop formal goals which reflect his own personal ones. In the absence of control by the External Coalition, is he more legitimate an influencer than any other member of the Internal Coalition?

Moreover, the political system often serves the overall needs of the organization, sometimes in spite of control systems which do not. Where the control systems are deficient, it is often the political system that fleshes them out, as when an employee ignores an objective that would lead him to suboptimize in an inappropriate way. The political system also acts in a Darwinian way to bring the strongest elements of the Internal Coalition to the fore — for example, those with inherent leadership or bargaining skills, greatly needed by the organization. In contrast, the control systems often protect weak elements — for example, ineffective managers mistakenly put into positions of authority. The political system also smooths the way for the execution of important organizational change; in fact it is often the only stimulus for such change. Internal influencers who lack formal authority sometimes have to resort to political action to convince those with formal authority of the need for change. Finally, the political system may ensure that both sides of an issue are fully debated, whereas the control systems — with their emphasis on a single chain of authority — may promote only one.

THE SYSTEM OF IDEOLOGY

In some sense, organizations are more than just the sum of their parts; they are living entities with characteristics or "personalities" of their own. I shall refer to these as *ideologies*, the fourth important system in the IC. The existence of these ideologies, above all, leads to the conclusion that organizations can have goals separate from those of their individual members. Ideological goals — for example, the spread of a religious or economic doctrine — become organizational goals. And the members come to accept these organizational goals as their own, and so come to "identify" the organization, to contribute their efforts to it for more than just remuneration.

Ideology arises from a sense of mission, which usually dates back to an early, charismatic leader. It establishes itself through traditions — precedents, habits, myths, what one researcher calls "sagas" (Clark, 1970, 1972). Thereafter it is reinforced through the identifications that new employees develop with the organization, perhaps because they have a natural affinity for the ideology when they join, perhaps because they are socialized or indoctrinated soon after they join (Schein, 1968), perhaps because they calculate that it is in their best interest to identify with the organization.

FIVE BASIC ICs

This discussion can be concluded by describing five basic kinds of Internal Coalitions, or ICs. In the *Bureaucratic IC*, bureaucratic control is the dominant system. Power remains largely with the PK, whom the system is designed to serve. Some also goes to the analysts, who design this control system. But the political system is not dominant here, although some power games do arise as a result of structural rigidities. The decisions of the line managers are resisted by the operators who must execute them, and the line managers with the formal power of authority battle the staff specialists with the informal power of expertise.

In the *Autocratic IC*, the personal control system of the PK is dominant; as a result, the PK gains the lion's share of the power. In this case, he need not share it with analysts, since he runs the control system himself. The political system is minimally developed in this Internal Coalition: formal goals cannot easily be displaced nor can power games easily arise when one individual personally controls all organizational activity.

In the *Ideologic IC*, it is the system of ideology that dominates the Internal Coalition. All the internal influencers share the same ideology and make their decisions in accordance with it. The result is an almost complete absence of political activity. And typically, because the PK embodies the ideology, he tends to have considerable personal power. But only so long as he maintains the support of the other internal influencers. (Should he hold on to his power past this point, the ideological character of the organization will disappear, and it reverts to an Autocratic IC.) But he can share this power, since he can trust all the other internal influencers to pursue the same goals as he when they make decisions and take actions.

In the *Meritocratic IC*, power follows expertise, of which there is a good deal in the organization. Power in these Internal Coalitions is, therefore, widely diffused, a good deal of it resting with the operators at the bottom who do professional work. This is, in effect, the most democratic of the Internal Coalitions. But it is not purely democratic, because power is distributed not evenly on the basis of membership but unevenly on the basis of knowledge. In this IC, the PK holds the least amount of power, although he remains, as always, an important internal influencer (given he has some political skill). So the authority structure of the meritocratic IC is not clearly defined. And in its absence, the political system takes a prominent place, as various experts exploit their critical functions to promote their own strategic candidates and build their own empires.

Finally, in the *Politicized IC*, the political system comes to dominate the Internal Coalition. Power rests not with office, with bureaucratic control, with ideology, or even with expertise, but with the energy and skills that any internal influencer can devote to the playing of power games.

ORGANIZATIONAL POWER CONFIGURATIONS

It remains now to give some life to the elements of our theory of organizational power. The mathematician would say that n elements which can each take on p forms give rise to p^n possible combinations. But reality is not like that. Elements, whether they be stars, ants, or characteristics of organizations, tend to cluster into natural groupings, or *configurations*. In this section, six configurations of organizational power are presented. While these are "pure" types (what Weber called "ideal" types), which stereotype reality, they do seem to capture a

Exhibit 2.7 Six "Pure" Power Configurations

Power configuration	EC	IC
Continuous chain	Dominated	Bureaucratic
Closed system	Passive	Bureaucratic
Commander	Passive	Autocratic
Missionary	Passive	Ideologic
Professional	Divided	Meritocratic
Conflictive	Divided	Politicized

good deal of what the research tells us about real organizations.

The six configurations are listed in Exhibit 2.7 together with the External and Internal Coalition of each. This table suggests a set of hypotheses, linking these two basic Coalitions: a Dominated EC is always found with a Bureaucratic IC; a Divided EC is always found with a Meritocratic or Politicized IC and vice versa; and a Passive EC may be found with a Bureaucratic, Autocratic, or Ideologic IC. It is noteworthy that of all the IC's only the Bureaucratic type is found with more than one type of EC.

Below the influencers and power system of each of the six power configurations are described. Here too, a return is made to the question of organizational goals, describing the goal system that emerges from each of the six power configurations. I also speculate on the conditions that give rise to each power configuration, the kinds of organizations where it seems typically to be found, and the process by which its strategies develop.[3]

The Continuous Chain Power Configuration

This is a classic power arrangement in the organization, shown in Exhibit 2.8. One external influencer, typically an owner (or many who reach a consensus), dominates the External Coalition. Because his goals are clear and operational, the dominant influencer is able to use specific constraints or direct controls (perhaps acting through the Formal Coalition) to control the Internal Coalition, and so to render it his instrument.

Power in the Internal Coalition centralizes around the PK, because he serves as the trustee of the dominant influencer and as the prime channel of communication to him. The bureaucratic control system clearly emerges as the key system in the IC. It is the only one that ensures the dominant influencer that his goals will be

[3] Here, especially, space limitations preclude discussion of the many nuances associated with each of the configurations. Henry Mintzberg, *Power in and around Organizations* (forthcoming).

pursued vigorously. Of course, this is possible only if, as noted earlier, his goals are operational. Operational goals coupled with bureaucratic controls are the only way to assure domination of the Internal Coalition while remaining in the External Coalition (that is, the only way to control the organization without managing it). So a Dominated EC is found only with the Bureaucratic IC.

But the rigidities of a centralized, bureaucratic Internal Coalition inevitably give rise to some power games, as other internal influencers seek to gain advantage in the organization. These, however, do not seriously displace the formal goals of the organization — namely those of the dominant influencer — because the latter are so well-defined.

Finally, the chain of power is complete — continuous — when the Internal Coalition remits the surpluses that arise from its actions to the dominant influencer, in whatever form he favors.

To reiterate, the goals of the Continuous Chain Power Configuration are clear and operational. In fact, this power configuration can maximize a single goal, should the dominant influencer so desire. By maximization is meant showing an obsession with a single goal such as profit, treating all others as constraints.

As for the process of strategy formation, because the organization has clear, operational goals imposed upon it, it is able to generate systematic, integrated strategies to achieve them. In other words, it tends to rely on top down, highly formalized procedures — the planning mode[4] — to develop its strategies.

The conditions that give rise to the Continuous Chain Power Configuration — namely focussed external control and clear, operational goals — are typically associated with stable environments, simple, mass output technical systems, and large, unskilled workforces. Many closely held business corporations and subsidiary organizations meet all these criteria. Typical of Continuous Chain Power Configurations dominated by a consensus of external influencers are fire departments, post offices, coercive

[4] See Mintzberg (1973) for a review of "Strategy-making in Three Modes" — the planning, adaptive, and entrepreneurial.

Exhibit 2.8   The Continuous Chain Power Configuration

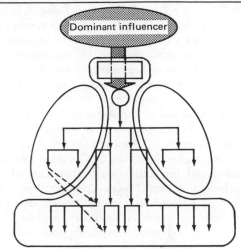

organizations such as custodial prisons, and cooperatives whose owners are organized, such as stock exchanges.

THE CLOSED SYSTEM POWER CONFIGURATION

This power configuration, shown in Exhibit 2.9, exists under all the same conditions as the previous configuration, except one: its External Coalition is Passive, its external influencers

Exhibit 2.9   The Closed System Power Configuration

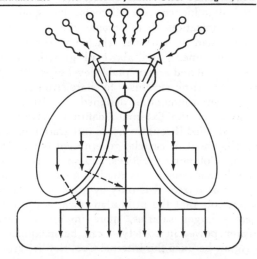

being dispersed and unorganized. With a Passive EC — the Formal Coalition being a façade or serving the organization — power passes into the Internal Coalition, in the first instance to the PK. The conditions of the organization — again a stable environment, mass production operations, and the like — encourage him to rely largely on the bureaucratic control system as his prime means of influence. So we have here a Passive EC coupled with a Bureaucratic IC.

The absence of focussed external control, however, makes this Internal Coalition less centralized and less bureaucratic than that of the Continuous Chain Power Configuration, and, therefore, somewhat more politicized. The empire building game is especially popular. The absence of externally imposed goals coupled with the emphasis on bureaucratic control causes power to flow to those influencers with authority, namely the PK and the middle line managers who operate the control system, as well as, to a lesser extent, the analysts who design it.

The internal influencers of the Closed System Power Configuration are motivated by utilitarian rather than ideologic values. They recognize, moreover, that their rewards are tied directly to the success of the organization. In effect, it is they — not any external influencer — who take the lion's share of the surpluses, in one form or another. And so they come to treat the organization as an end in itself, a system to be protected — and maintained closed to external influence — at all costs. The goals of the organization then become the "systems" goals — namely survival, efficiency, control of the environment, and, above all, growth. Without survival and an acceptable level of efficiency, there can be no surpluses to share. And control of the environment is designed to ensure the passivity of the External Coalition. Associates are controlled through vertical integration or the establishment of cartels, government is pacified through lobbying practices, and so on. But it is growth that emerges as the key goal — the one to be maximized. It is only by growing as large as possible that the utilitarian rewards to managers — larger salaries, more important jobs, greater power in society — can be maximized. Again because the Internal Coalition is rather

centralized and bureaucratic, and the goals (particularly growth) clear and operational, the organization is able to rely largely on the planning mode of strategy formation.

The Closed System Power Configuration is found primarily in large organizations that should be Continuous Chain Power Configurations except that their external influencers, notably their owners, are dispersed and unorganized. It seems to be common in widely-held corporations, especially those with divisionalized structures, as well as in some public service organizations and, more and more, in the totality of large government itself.

THE COMMANDER POWER CONFIGURATION

Here again, as indicated in Exhibit 2.10, the External Coalition is passive. But the conditions of the organization give rise to an organic internal structure, with the PK as the central force in the Internal Coalition, which he dominates through his personal control system. In this case, therefore, a Passive EC is coupled with an Autocratic IC.

The organization is the PK's instrument. It therefore pursues whatever goals he favors, no matter how personal, anything from the maximization of profit or growth to the freeing up of his time to play more golf. Likewise strategy formation assumes the classic entrepreneurial style, in which the PK moves toward his vision of the organization's future, typically in big, bold steps.

The Commander Power Configuration is frequently found in small organizations operating in simple, but dynamic environments, often niches in the market. Many of these are vulnerable organizations with little visibility. Classic examples are young entrepreneurial firms, as well as more mature firms still managed by their owners. The Commander Power Configuration is also found under other conditions, so long as the External Coalition is passive and the Internal Coalition gives rise to strong, autocratic leadership. This often happens, for example, in cooperatives with unorganized owners, such as many trade associations, revolutionary political parties (Michels, 1915), and unions that concentrate on economic instead of ideologic issues. It also tends to happen in young organizations, before the external influencers have been able to organize and while the internal ones still have need of strong leadership to get the organization on its feet. (And when that leadership is especially strong, the organization may stay in the Commander state until the founding PK finally departs.) Likewise, organizations facing severe crises tend to use this power configuration, the external influencers remaining temporarily passive and the internal ones turning to their leaders for direction (Hamblin, 1958). Finally, totalitarian states also represent a variant of the Commander Power Configuration, the population (the External Coalition) remaining passive, the government (the Internal Coalition) being dominated by its leader.

The Missionary Power Configuration

This organization is dominated by its ideology, centered around its mission — converting the heathens, getting everyone to eat health food, or whatever. A charismatic leader, present or past, best embodies the ideology, and so can control the organization's decisions and actions. But that control may be indirect: because the members identify with the ideology, all can be trusted to make decisions and take actions as he would do.

There is almost no political activity in this Internal Coalition, since all members agree on the same basic goal. That one is always tied to the mission (the product/market) of the organization, for example, the spread of the mission or the maximization of product quality. Acting as a unit, however, the Internal Coalition is very aggressive vis-à-vis its environment, pacifying any would-be external influencers. This is indicated in Exhibit 2.11. In effect, the Ideologic IC induces a Passive EC.

The basic strategy of the Missionary Power Configuration tends to be set in the first instance in entrepreneurial fashion by the founding leader. He conceives a bold vision of where the organization should try to go, and thereafter takes aggressive steps to get it there. That strategy tends to rigidify after his departure, so that subsequent efforts tend to be directed at inter-

Exhibit 2.10 The Commander Power Configuration

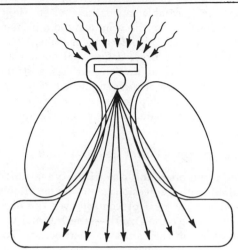

preting the "word" — the strategic vision of that leader — and strategic changes thereafter tend to be incremental.

The Missionary Power Configuration tends to be found where the organization's mission is simple and focussed, unique and attractive, at least to the members. It is usually smaller and younger organizations that use this configuration, although exceptions to both conditions can easily be found. Volunteer organizations with

Exhibit 2.11 The Missionary Power Configuration

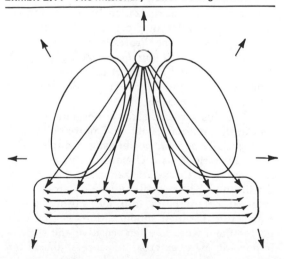

weak utilitarian norms, such as religious orders and certain charitable foundations, often use it, but not those where the volunteers join primarily to satisfy social or power needs (Sills, 1957). Nevertheless, any organization that should use another power configuration but has a strong ideology by virtue of a distinguished history or charismatic leadership tends to emerge, in part at least, as a Missionary Power Configuration.

THE PROFESSIONAL POWER CONFIGURATION

Where the operating core of an organization is staffed with professionals — who inevitably demand a good deal of control over the decisions that affect their work — the Internal Coalition takes on the form of a meritocracy. The analysts cannot regulate the professional operators' work, nor can the managers of the middle line, who are often elected by the professionals in any event. And the PK emerges as the weakest in all the power configurations, although given some political skill, he is never impotent.

The weak control systems — personal as well as bureaucratic — mean weak formal goals. These tend to be expressed in vague missionary terms, such as to "improve health" or "advance knowledge." Such goals cannot be operationalized, and so they are easily displaced by the goals pursued by the professionals. These are often related to the perfection of the practice of their profession (a missionary goal) or the maximization of their remuneration. But this does not mean maximization by the organization, because different professionals pursue different goals. So the Professional Power Configuration tends to pursue a variety of goals sequentially (and inconsistently) over time, much as Cyert and March (1963) described the goal formation process.

All of this gives rise to a strong political system in the Internal Coalition. Empire building is an especially popular power game. Coupled with a Meritocratic IC is a Divided EC, in good part a reaction to the politicization of the Internal Coalition. The internal influencers draw their external counterparts into the various power games to enlist their support. Moreover, because professional work is often sensitive and socially important, many external influencers take a keen interest in the decisions and actions of the organization. And so the whole organization emerges as a political arena, nowhere more clearly than in the Formal Coalition where various influencers — internal as well as external — battle for representation.

Strategy formation is a complex process in the Professional Power Configuration. For one thing, it does not control all of its own strategies. Some are imposed on it by the professional associations, which frequently dictate what types of clients it may serve and what procedures the professionals may use in serving them. Second, as indicated in Exhibit 2.12, the professionals of these organizations often deal with their own clients, and so formulate their own private strategies. That leaves only part of the process of strategy formation to the collectivity of the organization. And given the widespread distribution of power in both the Internal and External Coalitions, that process emerges as a complex one indeed, involving a good deal of bargaining and negotiation. In effect, the Professional Power Configuration uses neither a planning nor an entrepreneurial mode, but rather an adaptive one, in which strategies evolve in small, incremental, disjointed steps, not as clear plans or individual visions spelled out in advance of action taking.

The Professional Power Configuration is

Exhibit 2.12   The Professional Power Configuration

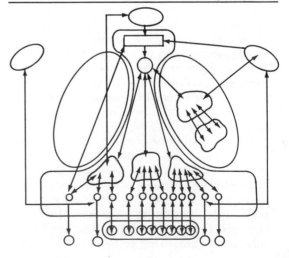

found in organizations where the operating work is complex, requiring the employment of many professionals — hospitals, universities, accounting firms, law offices, social work agencies, research laboratories, and the like. Also, organizations with high degrees of automation tend toward it because they must rely on staff professionals to design, purchase, and maintain their complex technical systems.

THE CONFLICTIVE POWER CONFIGURATION

This organization, shown in Exhibit 2.13, has the highest degree of politicization in both the Internal and External Coalitions. In effect, politicization in one induces or reinforces politicization in the other. Conflicting external demands on the organization create friction in the Internal Coalition. The PK is unable to generate formal goals to satisfy all the external influencers; indeed, making any goals explicit evokes all kinds of conflict. He is better off to keep the formal goals as vague as possible. Moreover, the internal influencers are subjected to all kinds of direct pressures from the external ones. They impose a host of specific constraints, many of them contradictory. Pressure campaigns are frequent and intense. People are often planted in the internal coalition by external influencers. And the external influencers make direct representations to the internal influencers, ones that bypass the PK and the systems of control. Likewise the Internal Coalition divides and politicizes the External Coalition, as in the case of the Professional Power Configuration, when internal influencers enlist the support of external influencers in their power games. So one may conclude that the Politicized IC is inevitably found with the Divided EC.

The Conflictive Power Configuration can pursue no special goals. It is a pure political arena. At best it satisfies a whole set of constraints, attending to these sequentially over time; at worst it spins its wheels endlessly in futile debate. Likewise, at best strategies form over time from the incremental decisions made in an adaptive process; they are never formulated explicitly, for that would involve the kind of cooperation not found in the Conflictive Power Configuration.

The Conflictive Power Configuration tends to appear most commonly in aberrations of the five other power configurations, for example, when a Missionary Power Configuration comes under severe external attack, or a Professional Power Configuration is subjected to excessively tight control from a would-be dominant external influencer. Other common examples are the controversial public agency, often a regulatory one; the corporation politicized by severe external attack; the organization that is excessively regulated by its owner or by government (Frank, 1958–59); the organization with two top managers who share the PK role but are at odds as to strategy; and the one where two major missions conflict, as in the prison that cannot decide on a custodial or rehabilitation orientation (McCleery, 1957).

To summarize, an organization is driven to the Continuous Chain Power Configuration with the introduction of well-defined, focused power in its External Coalition; to the Closed System Power Configuration when a Bureaucratic IC becomes detached from the External Coalition; to the Commander Power Configuration to the extent that any factor puts arbitrary power in the hands of the PK; to the Missionary Power Configuration to the extent that it embraces an ideology; to the Professional Power Configura-

Exhibit 2.13   The Conflictive Power Configuration

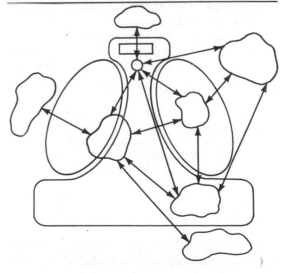

tion to the extent that it must rely on expertise; and to the Conflictive Power Configuration whenever aberrations appear in any of the other power configurations.

TRANSITIONS AMONG POWER CONFIGURATIONS

To illustrate the use of this framework of power configurations, consider the transitions in the power system of the business firm since its earliest times. The business firm typically began its life as a Commander Power Configuration, the instrument of its founding entrepreneur. Later it shifted to the Continuous Chain Power Configuration, as its ownership was separated from its management. But so long as that ownership remained concentrated, the firm remained the owner's instrument. Later, as its ownership became more dispersed and the systems goals came to the fore the firm shifted to the Closed System Power Configuration (Berle and Means, 1968). It now seems to be moving toward a Conflictive Power Configuration, a political arena, as many external influencers seek to jump in to the power vacuum left in the External Coalition by the scattered owners (Blumberg, 1971).

CONCLUSION: THE NEED TO RESEARCH POWER

It is hoped that this paper makes clear the need to understand power in and around the organization in order to appreciate how it pursues goals and develops strategies. The study of power also appears to be important for understanding some major issues facing society, not the least of which is how to control its institutions.

A number of researchable questions are raised as propositions discussed in this paper, for example, how strategy is formed in each of the power configurations. Moreover, the whole framework requires empirical validation. Do organizations in fact adopt power configurations like those described? In other words, will measures of the power of external and internal influencers and the means of influence they use in fact cluster in the ways described? It matters not that this particular typology proves valid; what matters is that we generate a typology that can help us to understand how power is used in and around organizations.

Power is a fuzzy topic. The demand for precision will only impede the researching of it. It seems far more important to research important topics with soft methodologies than marginal topics with elegant methodologies, where these are in fact our options. In the case of power in particular — one is tempted to say Management Policy in general — those do appear to be our options much of the time. A few researchers have managed to study power meaningfully and yet with precision (e.g., Hickson et al., 1971). But most of the real insight has come from studies that used soft methodologies, specifically intensive probes into single organizations (e.g., Clark, 1972; Crozier, 1964; Scheff, 1961; Selznick, 1949). We should not be shy about doing a great deal more of such research, facing the least measurable phenomena, such as ideology, squarely. After all, it is insight, not elegance, that we are after.

Commentary

MAX D. RICHARDS
The Pennsylvania State University

INTRODUCTION

This paper outlines: (1) the general research needs about organizational goals, (2) the contribution of the Mintzberg paper toward these research needs, (3) the relevance of goals toward organizational functioning, (4) the difference between goal research and performance research, and (5) how the dynamic nature of relations may limit cross-sectional research studies upon strategy and goals. Some specific lines of investigation are suggested.

THE GENERAL RESEARCH NEEDS

Ideally, policy researchers engaged in goal research seek knowledge about both: (1) relationships of organizational goal levels and content, and (2) the processes by which goals are formed and the extent that behavior is directed toward goal achievement. More specifically, these needs include:

1. The determination of the relationships of the content and nature of organizational goals to the decisions and behavior of organizational participants or conversely the determination of the relationships of alternate decisions in the form of strategies, structures, and internal contexts of formal organizations to the attainment of alternate sets of possible goals.

2. The line of inquiry into the processes of decision, bargaining, and coalition formation by which organizational goals are formed and through which organizational components do or do not respond.

THE MINTZBERG PAPER

Mintzberg's paper contributes to the process research goal by classifying power configurations of coalitions. He extends prior conceptualizations by sharply distinguishing among five types of internal coalitions. Similarly, he extends former ideas about external groups by introducing three kinds of external coalitions with differing focus of influences upon internal operations. A power configuration is a combination of the internal and external coalitions. Theoretically, there would be fifteen different power configurations. He reduces the number of viable ·combinations by asserting that only six of the fifteen exist in reality. For example, a dominated external and a politicized internal coalition could not exist by definition.

The suggestion by many practicing executives

is that strong regulatory (e.g., E.P.A.) and pressure group (e.g., consumerism) demands have independent and conflicting impact upon them. The Mintzberg model would suggest, however, that the more numerous and diverse the groupings of external interests are, the less influence they would have upon internal structure. It is not clear, however, why divided but powerful external coalitions (e.g., several regulatory groups) would not induce an autocratic (or perhaps a bureaucratic) internal coalition so as to better accommodate external pressures. Are divided external and powerful internal coalitions incompatible? In addition, it would be useful if Mintzberg offered an explanation of why a passive-politicized configuration is not relevant and viable.

In any event, Mintzberg has provided an innovative framework that sharpens, while complicating, the attainment of the second general research objective noted above, i.e., clarifying the processes by which goal formation is influenced by the focus of power in external and internal coalitions.

GOAL DOMINANCE AND RELEVANCE

APPROXIMATELY RATIONAL. The relevance of goals as a factor in organizational operations extends from high to none at all. At the high extreme are a minority of firms (e.g., Lincoln Electric[1]) that establish a single goal or a relatively small set of goals, develop sub-goals, structures, and contexts consistent with the overall organizational goal(s), eliminate strategies and activities that do not fit or contribute directly to achievement, and set levels of goal(s) perceived as difficult to achieve. Firms in this classification can be characterized as approximating (within information and computational constraints) the behavior of the rational model of classical economic theory. The goal content however, might be growth, stock appreciation, or some other end rather than profitability. Nonetheless, maximizing behaviors appear to

[1] See Lincoln Electric Company, Intercollegiate Case Clearing House, #9-376-028, Boston, Mass., 1976.

dominate. In the Mintzberg power configurations, the rational maximizing behaviors could occur in the continuous chain, the closed system (if a powerful leader dominates), the commander, and the missionary configurations. It would appear more likely, however, that the commander and continuous chain configurations could be observed exhibiting these approximately rational behaviors.

INDIRECTLY RATIONAL. At the other extreme are organizations in which formal organization goals have little relevance to behavior, and such goals are not articulated in other than a rhetorical way. No general agreement upon objectives or levels of attainment exists. Participants in the system are relatively free to follow personal and professional objectives. It is rarely if ever necessary to relate individual to organizational goals. Such organizations may require a long-lasting monopoly or munificent environment such as many public universities enjoyed between 1950 and 1970 or as many hospitals have experienced during the decade following 1965. An individual entering such an organization can remain completely ignorant of organizational goals yet achieve personal and organizational success within it by singular attention to professional goals and ethics. Similarly, strategy and resource allocation are decided on the basis of professional norms rather than organizational goals. A planning department is added because that is the norm for other organizations. Structure is realigned because it is fashionable (Rumelt, 1974) rather than because strategy suggests a need for it.

These organizations may be characterized as non-rational from an overall standpoint, but it may be more accurate to label them as indirectly rational because the professional norms followed may contribute to needs as perceived by consumers of the organization's products and services. Thus, exchange between the organization and its environment can remain favorable perhaps over long periods of time. To predict that such organizations will fail or will adapt to a more nearly rational mode as their environments become unfavorable begs the question of attempting to relate organizational goals to environment, strategy, internal context, and struc-

ture. If organizational goals are absent, inoperative, or rhetorical, such relationships will not be found except in long-term longitudinal studies whose results likely will be unclear because of a multitude of non-controlled variables intervening over time.

Furthermore, to contend that professional goals have displaced organizational goals or that professional goals are the "real" (Etzioni, 1964; Thompson, 1967) rather than the stated ones or that there are operative rather than official goals (Perrow, 1961) is just as uncomfortable. In a single organization, there may be hundreds or thousands of conceptions about what ends to direct behavior toward and even more of a variety of behaviors. To conduct goal research upon such indirectly rational organizations appears both impractical and irrelevant to understanding and predicting about organizational goals. If valid organizational goals are absent, how can behaviors be related to them? In terms of Mintzberg's power configurations, the conflictive organization would often appear in this class.

PARTIALLY RATIONAL. The third category of organizations consists of those firms practicing bargaining (Cyert and March, 1963) in attending to goals through organizational coalitions (Thompson, 1967). Since there are multiple goals which are dealt with (although sequentially rather than simultaneously), these firms exhibit a partial rationality. While all goals are not pursued at the same time, resources are, in fact, directed toward some in the set of organizational goals. As slack approaches zero or negative values, the behaviors in the organization tend to approach those of rational firms. Conversely, as slack enlarges, one might hypothesize that behaviors tend to approach those of indirectly rational organizations.

POLICY RESEARCH ON GOALS

There have been few direct policy research studies focusing on the nature of organizational goals and the process of their formulation, with the possible exception of Cyert and March (1963). Policy studies stemming from Chandler

(1962) and organizational-environment studies such as Woodward (1965) and Lawrence and Lorsch (1967) examine the impact of different strategies and structures upon performance. These studies, however, illuminate the relationships among organizational goals, strategies, contexts, and environments *if and only if* the performance measures used coincide with those that the organization is attempting to achieve. It appears unlikely, for example, that firms in the *Fortune* 500 from 1949 to 1969 coincidentally were pursuing only the return on equity or growth measures used by Rumelt (1974). Research on or about goals requires more than the typical studies examining performance. The identification of each organization's goals and the relative contribution of explanation in their variation by (in)dependent variables is called for. This proposed research falls into the third of Hatten's categories. (See Exhibit 7.21).

ORGANIZATIONAL BEHAVIOR RESEARCH ON GOALS

Research upon goals from the field of organizational behavior indicates that goal achievement is enhanced if certain goal characteristics exist: specificity of goal statements (Lawrence and Smith, 1955) rather than generality; difficult, challenging, or hard goals (Locke, 1968; Latham and Baldes, 1975) rather than easy or impossible ones; knowledge of past performance relative to goals (Hundal, 1969) rather than an absence of feedback; and clarity of goal statements rather than ambiguity (Wieland, 1969). In addition to these characteristics of goals, certain characteristics of the processes by which goals are established and administered appear positively related to goal achievement: training in establishing goals rather than relying upon general managerial abilities (Carroll and Tosi, 1971); commitment and belief in the viability of objectives (Steers, 1975); close supervision coupled to a goal-setting process with subordinates (Ronan et al., 1973); performance revision coupled with establishing specific goals; participation in setting objectives (Steers, 1975); and feeding back performance data relative to objectives while supervising and controlling behav-

iors toward goals. The studies generating these results have used samples of individuals drawn from experimental populations and subjects from lower managerial and non-managerial positions. Less data exists to support these findings as propositions relevant to the explanation of goal-setting behavior, achievement, or strategic choices and behaviors at the corporate or business levels of large organizations.

Additional insights on goals is provided by expectancy theory (Vroom, 1964). Expectancy theory has been employed to deduce the goal sets of individuals. These sets have been combined with: (1) the degree to which each goal item in the set is sought by the individual and (2) the likelihood that a given choice will, in fact, enhance the individual's achievement of that item to arrive at the concept of motivational force. The decision alternative eliciting the highest force is the preferred alternative to the individual and is the predicted choice. Supposedly, a similar approach could be used to predict from a given set of organizational goals the nature of internal context if the relative importance of the goal and its perceived contribution from the contextual elements could be estimated.

However, most expectancy theories suffer from the apples and oranges problems. In addition, most expectancy theories have correlations in the .20 to .30 range. It is therefore questionable whether policy research upon goals should use similar procedures until significant improvements are made in the content of expectancy theories and the design and methodology of expectancy theory research.

NEEDS AND PROBLEMS IN GOAL RESEARCH

Since little policy-related research upon organizational goals exists, research priorities are difficult to establish at this time. Several approaches appear useful in future explorations. First, the applicability of the findings of goal research from organizational behavior studies needs to be replicated at higher organization levels. Such a line of study would serve to confirm or disconfirm organizational behavior findings and would illuminate the variations, if any, due to organization level. Second, Mintzberg power configurations could provide a rich source of hypothesizing about: (1) personal vs. rational sources of goals, (2) differences in bargaining, goal content, and levels in different configurations, and (3) whether the Mintzberg model is exhaustive. Third, comparative research among organizations in the same environments espousing different goals ought to reveal differences in strategies, decisions, and behavior, but do they? And to what extent? To what extent do different environments elicit goal variations, if at all? At the same time, the real goals of the organization need to be used in such research instead of (or in addition to) the performance goals selected by the researcher.

SAMPLE PROBLEMS. The need for homogeneity and the consequent partitioning of sample spaces to account for goal differences, rationality differences, culture, industry, and type of strategy may reduce a research sample to such a low level that a unique case study constitutes the sample. In fact, different kinds of studies might be required for indirectly rational firms because they could not be legitimately compared to organizations following partial or approximate rationality. Additional partitioning for differences in structure, incentive systems, planning and control systems, etc., may well leave a number of empty cells in a research design. Moreover, as organizations merge, acquire, or form combinations, relevant data tend to become unavailable to the researcher. Thus, complexity in the environment and within organizations increasingly suggests the practicality and, perhaps, the necessity of case and small sample studies for goal research. Conversely, it is through the reconceptualizing of systems into homogeneous classes as Mintzberg has attempted that policy research can generalize and move the field toward a true discipline.

DYNAMIC CONSIDERATIONS. Relationships among variables in a system can be established through research and confirmed by additional studies. Yet, the history of social science research shows that over a period of time, the relationships among some of the same set of variables that previously held are no longer supported.[2] Because of their intimacy with the environment, policy level goal variables and relations may be particularly subject to dynamic changes. As an example, Rumelt (1974) showed that firms with a dominant product and vertical integration strategy performed relatively poorly during 1949–1969. Yet, during the 1970's, some of these same firms (e.g., the chemicals and oil firms) have had relatively large increases in profitability, partially through the implications that a finite world only has so much abundant raw material. Thus, the relationship previously found between corporate strategy and economic performance was altered. Such change became a factor in General Electric's acquisition of Utah International (Kraar, 1977).

CONCLUSION

If knowledge of policy relationships is subject to rapid decay, what alternatives do the manager and researcher have? The study of policy variables and their shifting relationships is still important since a melding of strategy, structure, and environment are related to goal achievement. To the researcher, the dynamics of changing relationships among variables adds a further dimension for study. To the manager, awareness of potential discontinuity (Ansoff's unpredictable turbulence) would be relevant to strategic choices. But, perhaps discontinuity and awareness of it are a contradiction of terms.

Most normative and descriptive policy and strategy theories assume a set of organization goals. Similarly, the processes of coalition operation presume relations of power and influence. The field is a long way from being able to predict what powers and what goals will dominate. In sum, we teach and consult with a thin empirical base of knowledge in this area. This very fact, however, indicates the vast potential for challenging research in the area.

---

[2] I am indebted to conversations with Ray Bauer of Harvard University, in the spring of 1974, for this idea.

Commentary

Edwin A. Murray, Jr.
Northwestern University

INTRODUCTION

Mintzberg's discussion of organizational power configurations implicitly hypothesizes that certain types of goals and goal-setting processes are characteristic of particular environments, organizations, and — most importantly — power configurations. How can these hypotheses be tested? Mintzberg does not indicate in any detail how this might be done, but it seems appropriate here to discuss research designs and methodologies which could be effective in the testing of his hypotheses. In addition, some of the issues identified by Richards in his discussion of the problems of goal research will be addressed.

After a brief overview of the prerequisites for meaningful goal theory and research, this paper will describe the two dominant theoretical schools of thought regarding goals and their formation: prescriptive theory, which views goals as "objective" phenomena arrived at through rational, analytical processes; and descriptive theory, which sees goals as "subjective" phenomena arrived at through political processes. Mintzberg's contingency approach will then be explored and critiqued with special emphasis on appropriate research methods to test his theory.

PRE-REQUISITES FOR THEORY AND RESEARCH ON GOALS

As noted by Richards, policy researchers engaged in goal research need to focus their efforts on understanding the substantive content of organizational goals and the processes by which those goals are formulated. Two fundamental research questions need to be answered:

1. What constitutes a "good" organizational goal?
2. How can the organization arrive at (develop) such "good" goals?

Presumably, "better" goals are instrumental in achieving better organizational performance, but this is an empirical issue which can and should be tested. To this writer's knowledge, there has been no policy research on the question of whether organizational performance varies systematically with respect to different levels of aspiration as expressed in organizational goals, although the research of Ansoff et al. (1971) suggests indirectly that it does.

Similarly, there are no doubt a number of ways in which organizational goals can be formulated. The relevant question is whether some of these approaches are better than others. So often, we assume that organizations have goals, but we have little understanding of how those goals actually were determined or whether an alternate goal-setting process would have generated preferable goals. If different degrees of effectiveness can be ascribed to various goal-setting processes, this would be of interest to students of management policy and of considerable value to practicing managers. Again, this appears to be an empirical question appropriate for policy research.

THE NATURE OF GOALS: A THEORETICAL DICHOTOMY

Organizational goals are viewed by prescriptive theorists as collective aspiration levels arrived at through a logical and relatively "objective" form of analysis. Thus, the planning literature asserts that goals are of central importance to top management. Andrews, for example, assumes that there is value in rationality and the structuring of choice through the establishment of goals (1971: 23):

Our theory begins with the simple proposition that every business organization, every subunit of organization, and even every individual should have a clearly defined set of purposes or goals which keeps it moving in a deliberately chosen direction and prevents its drifting in undesired directions.

Ansoff (1965) also assumes that the business firm has goals or objectives that are distinct and different from those of individual participants within the firm. He further notes that, "In our main area of interest, the strategic problem, objectives are used as yardsticks for decisions on changes, deletions, and additions to the firm's product/market posture."

Moreover, these objectives, according to Ansoff, can take the form of a "threshold objective" (the minimum acceptable level of achievement) or a "goal" (the desired outcome or level of aspiration) and they should be ranked to form a hierarchy, a notion to which Granger (1964) also subscribes.

The question of what constitutes a genuine, meaningful goal still remains. Of crucial importance in understanding goal structures is a way of separating "real," or operational, goals from those which are formally stated, but in fact less directly relevant to the guidance of an organization. Perrow (1961) makes such a distinction between what he calls "official" and "operative" goals. He furthermore asserts that the tasks an organization must perform determine what groups or type of people will be dominant, and that these in turn will strongly influence the choice of operative goals for the organization.

Thus, the way is paved for descriptive theory which views organizational goals as relatively "subjective" in nature and the resultant of a political process. Cyert and March (1963) argue that any organization is in fact a coalition of individuals and subcoalitions, and that these various coalitions have their own objectives and agendas. As a consequence, there exists a bargaining process by which organizational goals are determined. However, this bargaining leads to goals with the following deficiencies:

1. The goals are imperfectly rationalized.
2. Some are stated in the form of aspiration level constraints rather than genuine goals to be achieved.
3. Some are stated in non-operational form.

The research question to be raised at this point is whether any or all of the several propositions set forth above can be supported through empirical research. Neither the prescriptive nor the descriptive theorists offer supporting evidence of a convincing nature. Moreover, each approach implies a universal applicability which, upon reflection, is highly implausible. At least in Mintzberg's theory, there is postulated a variation in the types of goals which is contingent upon the power configuration characterizing the organization. As a consequence, Mintzberg's model usefully suggests that the type, number, and specific content of organizational goals will differ according to the situation. Thus a new venture dominated by its founding entrepreneur and exhibiting what Mintzberg terms the Commander Power Configuration could be expected to have goals (such as maximization of sales growth and stock price appreciation) quite different from the several goals which might characterize a larger, more mature company with a Closed System Power Configuration. This latter organization's goals might include the achievement of some minimum acceptable level of growth, efficiency, and control of the environment. To say that either one (or both) of these organizations has only "rationally objective" or "politically subjective" goals oversimplifies and to no particular advantage.

THE NATURE OF GOAL FORMULATION PROCESSES: TWO VIEWS

Likewise, the goal formulation process is viewed as either an objectively rational or subjectively political phenomenon. Granger (1964) states that goals should be formulated through a logical process which starts with a statement of the broad objective. (How that broad objective is first developed is not made clear.) Then increasingly more specific subobjectives are developed in support of the broad objective. Ansoff (1965) prescribes a similar, iterative process designed to narrow and ultimately close any gap between current objectives (both short- and long-term) and future prospects for the organization. To deal with multiple (and possibly inherently conflicting) goals, modeling and goal programming has been undertaken with some success by Kahalas and Satterwaite (1975) and Gleason and Lilly (1977).

Such approaches by prescriptive theorists have in common an emphasis on the need for rationality, logic, and comprehensiveness in the development of goal structures. However, Simon (1964) cites the bounded rationality of decision makers and notes that goals generally consist of a set of constraints; Cyert and March (1963) contend that organizational goals are arrived at by bargaining among coalitions to the organization; Thompson and McEwen (1958) stress that goals are dynamic variables subject to review and adjustment — particularly in response to pressures from the external environment; and Braybrooke and Lindblom (1963) offer the view that policy choices (including the selection of goals) are often disjointed and incremental rather than integrated and large. Empirical policy research by Mintzberg, Raisinghani, and Theoret (1976) and Murray (1976), while not exclusively on goals and goal-setting processes, offer supporting evidence for these approaches.

Allison (1971) sees a complementarity in his three alternate paradigms of policy analysis (and formation). In addition to his "rational actor" model, there is an "organizational process" model in which hard choices among goals are avoided and incompatible constraints are attended to sequentially. This would most closely resemble Mintzberg's Closed System Power Configuration. In his "bureaucratic politics" model individual players seek to exert power within the rules of the game to yield goals acceptable to them as individuals — a situation analogous to Mintzberg's Professional Power Configuration. Allison thus helps lead us away from an approach to goal-setting processes which is simply "either" analytical "or" political.

Taking us one step further is Hall (1975) who in a synthesis of theory and research on organizational goals, argues that appropriate goal-setting modes should be selected according to circumstances. This contingency approach yields three major alternate processes in goal-setting. Problem solving is appropriate when power is concentrated among the policy-makers and the individual goals of policy makers and other parties are similar or can be ranked. Coalition formation is called for when power is dispersed among policy-makers and other parties and the individual goals of policy-makers and other parties are in conflict. Bargaining would be preferable when power is balanced between policy-makers and other active parties and the individual goals of policy-makers and other parties are conflicting. One or more of the processes may be used by the same organization according to the situation.

MINTZBERG'S THEORY: A CRITIQUE

Mintzberg also offers a contingency theory which, by virtue of its six power configurations, promises an even richer framework within which to conduct management policy research. After a brief review of the literature on goals and goal-setting, he concludes that an understanding of organizational goals must be preceded by an understanding of how power and its exercise leads to the formation of goals. The importance of power relationships in most organizations leads Mintzberg to posit the existence of six major power configurations which characterize the bulk of "real world" organizations. These power configurations are then presented so as to suggest a set of hypotheses about the types of environment, "external coalition," "internal coalition," organizations, goals, and strategy-making processes associated with each.

Of particular value to the student and researcher of management policy is Mintzberg's establishment of power configuration categories within which there are hypothesized to be particular goals and goal-setting processes associated with particular types of organizations and environments. The researcher thereby has a theoretical basis for focusing his or her efforts on the investigation and comparative analysis of goals and goal-setting processes within different types of organizations. For example, the researcher would expect to find different kinds of goals and goal-setting processes in a small, fast-growing electronics company recently launched by an entrepreneur (Mintzberg's Commander Power Configuration), and a large, stable and traditional university, experiencing slow growth (Mintzberg's Professional Power Configuration).

Less clear — to at least this writer — are the differences one might find between Mintzberg's Continuous Chain Power Configuration and his Closed System Power Configuration. He hypothesizes that in both situations the goals will be clear and operational and that the planning mode of strategy formation (and presumably goal-setting) will be found. It is therefore probably safe to infer that the two power configurations will differ chiefly in the substantive content of their respective goals. However, Mintzberg does not spell out in sufficient detail the types of goals, or for that matter the goal-setting processes, associated with each power configuration. It is even doubtful that his typology is complete in its enumeration of categories. Would there not, for example, be differences in goals and goal-setting processes associated with a new versus a long-established planning system in a Closed System Power Configuration as posited by Lorange and Vancil (1976)? But these are empirical questions which can and should be answered in the course of future policy research. The question is, how?

RESEARCHING MINTZBERG'S MODEL

A beginning could be made by surveying the established goals of a large number of diverse organizations and then cross tabulating the types of goals with Mintzberg's six power configuration categories. The data could be arranged in a matrix such as that shown in Exhibit 2.14. At the very least, this approach would shed light on the degree to which goals do differ among different power configurations and perhaps even organizations *within* power configuration groupings. (This would then be a basis for extending and refining Mintzberg's typology.)

Less accessible via this survey would be the goal-setting processes themselves and the "operational" or "real" goals as and if distinct from the organization's "formal" (Perrow's "official") goals. Because goal structures and power relationships (which Mintzberg asserts are central to the determination of goals) are so intimately involved in the broader and more complex phenomenon of organizational "decision making," longitudinal case studies of single incidents of major importance to management are appropriate (if not inevitable). The works of Allison

Exhibit 2.14   Types of Goals Found in Different Types of Organizations

Mintzberg's power configuration category:	Continuous chain	Closed system	Etc.
Specific types of organizations:	Evanston Post Office	General Electric	Etc.
	Chicago Fire Department	Textron	
Goals: Growth:			
—Revenues	Not articulated	10–15%/year	
—Physical size	"Moderate"	10–12%/year	
Efficiency:			
—Profits	Deficit containment	10% PBT increase	
—Costs	5–10% reduction/year	Not applicable	
—Return on investment	Not applicable	12–15% ROE	
Flexibility:			
—Financial slack	Not applicable	$X reserve lines of credit	
—Organizational slack	Not articulated	Not articulated	

(1971), Steinbruner (1974), and Bower (1970) are illustrative of this approach.

Also needed, however, is enough parallelism in such clinical research to result in genuinely comparative data. As a starting point, it is recommended that one "stereotypical" organi- zation from each of Mintzberg's six categories be selected for an in-depth study of its "goal formulation" and "planning process" (whether formal or informal) over the course of two years. Particular attention should be devoted to care- fully describing how "operational" goals are

Exhibit 2.15 Goal-setting Processes in Different Types of Organizations

Mintzberg's power configuration category:	Continuous chain	Closed system	Etc.
Specific organization:	Chicago Fire Department	Textron	Etc.
Formal goals per 1978 annual plan			
"Formal" planning process (procedures, dates, responsibilities, etc.)			
Major subunits/individuals (coalitions) with inputs or analyses			
Initially proposed goals for 1979 annual plan			
Chronology of major discussions of, analyses of, and modifications of 1979 goals			
"Formal" 1979 annual plan goals			
"Operational" goals per observed behavior in 1978			
Prediction of 1979's "operational" goals per observed differences in 1978's "formal" and "operational" goals			
"Operational" goals per observed behavior in 1979			
Observed differences in 1979's "formal" and "operational" goals —compare with predictions			

perceived to differ from "formal" goals. Such differences will probably vary by organizational subunits and individuals, but at a minimum, such knowledge should help demarcate the relevant coalitions within each organization. Similarly, a detailed account of exactly who contributed to the conceptualization, articulation, and achievement of specific major goals should reveal much about the goal-setting processes of such organizations and how they may differ from one another.

The structure of such parallel clinical research could take the form shown in Exhibit 2.15.

CONCLUSION

The key, of course, is to actually do empirical research on goals and goal-setting processes. One of management policy's central tenets is the importance of and need for collective purpose as expressed in organizational goals, and yet we still know relatively little about them.

Mintzberg has argued persuasively that power relationships between external and internal coalitions have important impacts on the types of goals and goal-setting processes. He has developed a useful set of categories and hypotheses which now await the use of empirical researchers.

The research will not be easy because in several respects Mintzberg's theory is just what he says it is — skeletal. It is not complete, nor is it as explicit as it could be, but it should be tried and, if found wanting, modified. After all, management policy is virtually by definition an uncompromisingly vast and complex field, and when you're trying to eat an elephant it doesn't much matter where you take your first bite.

Section 2 References

Allison, Graham T. *Essence of Decision: Explaining the Cuban Missile Crisis.* Boston: Little, Brown, 1971.

Andrews, Kenneth R. *The Concept of Corporate Strategy.* Homewood, Ill.: Dow Jones–Irwin, 1971.

Ansoff, H. Igor. *Corporate Strategy: An Analytic Approach to Business Policy for Growth and Expansion.* New York: McGraw-Hill, 1965.

Ansoff, H. Igor, Richard G. Brandenburg, Fred E. Porter and Raymond Radosevich. *Acquisition Behavior of U. S. Manufacturing Firms: 1946–1965.* Nashville, Tenn.: Vanderbilt University Press, 1971.

Barnard, Chester I. *The Functions of the Executive.* Cambridge, Mass.: Harvard University Press, 1938.

Berle, A. A. and G. C. Means. *The Modern Corporation and Private Property* (revised edition). New York: Harcourt, Brace, and World, 1968.

Blumberg, P. I. "The Politicalization of the Corporation." *The Business Lawyer,* July 1971.

Bower, Joseph L. *Managing the Resource Allocation Process: A Study of Corporate Planning and Investment.* Boston: Graduate School of Business Administration, Harvard University, 1970.

Braybrooke, David and Charles E. Lindblom. *A Strategy of Decision.* New York: Free Press, 1963.

Brown, C. C. and E. E. Smith (editors). *The Director Looks at His Job.* New York: Columbia University Press, 1958.

Carroll, Stephen J., Jr., and Henry L. Tosi, Jr. "Relationship of Characteristics of the Review Process to the Success of the MBO Approach." *Journal of Business,* July 1971.

Chandler, Alfred D. *Strategy and Structure: Chapters in the History of the American Industrial Enterprise.* Cambridge, Mass.: M.I.T. Press, 1962.

Chandler, M. "It's Time to Clean Up the Boardroom." *Harvard Business Review,* September–October 1975.

Clark, B. R. *The Distinctive College.* Chicago: Aldine, 1970.

Clark, B. R. "The Organizational Saga in Higher Education." *Administrative Science Quarterly,* June 1972.

Crozier, M. *The Bureaucratic Phenomenon.* Chicago: University of Chicago Press, 1964.

Cyert, Richard M. and James G. March. *A Behavioral Theory of the Firm.* Englewood Cliffs, N.J.: Prentice-Hall, 1963.

Dooley, P. C. "The Interlocking Directorate." *American Economic Review*, June 1969.

Etzioni, Amitai. *Modern Organizations*. Englewood Cliffs, N.J.: Prentice-Hall, 1964.

Frank, A. G. "Goal Ambiguity and Conflicting Standards: An Approach to the Study of Organization." *Human Organization*, Winter 1958–59.

Georgiou, P. "The Goal Paradigm and Notes Towards a Counter Paradigm." *Administrative Science Quarterly*, September 1973.

Gleason, John M. and Claude C. Lilly. "A Goal Programming Model for Insurance Agency Management." *Decision Sciences*, January 1977.

Granger, Charles H. "The Hierarchy of Objectives." *Harvard Business Review*, May–June 1964.

Hall, Francine S. "Organizational Goals: The Status of Theory and Research," in Livingston, Leslie J. (editor), *Managerial Accounting: The Behavioral Foundations*. Columbus, Ohio: Grid Press, 1975.

Hamblin, R. L. "Leadership and Crises." *Sociometry*, Vol. 21, 1958.

Hatten, Kenneth J. and Dan E. Schendel. "Heterogeneity Within an Industry: Firm Conduct in the U. S. Brewing Industry 1952–1971." *Journal of Industrial Economics*, December 1977.

Hickson, D. J., C. R. Hinings, C. A. Lee, R. E. Schneck and J. M. Pennings. "A Strategic Contingencies' Theory of Intraorganization Power." *Administrative Science Quarterly*, June 1971.

Hill, Walter. "The Goal Formation Process in Complex Organizations." *Journal of Management Studies*, 1969.

Hundal, P. S. "Knowledge of Performance as Our Incentive in Repetitive Industrial Work." *Journal of Applied Psychology*, June 1969.

Jacobs, D. "Dependency and Vulnerability: An Exchange Approach to the Control of Organizations." *Administrative Science Quarterly*, March 1974.

Kahalas, Harvey and Walter Satterwaite. "Social Responsibility in the Utility Industry: A Quantitative Case Study." *Academy of Management Proceedings*, New Orleans, August 1975.

Kraar, L. "General Electric's Very Personal Merger." *Fortune*, August 1977.

Latham, Gary P. and J. James Baldes. "The 'Practical Significance' of Locke's Theory of Goal Setting." *Journal of Applied Psychology*, February 1975.

Lawrence, L. C. and P. C. Smith. "Group Decision and Employee Participation." *Journal of Applied Psychology*, Vol. 39, 1955.

Lawrence, Paul R. and Jay W. Lorsch. *Organization and Environment: Managing Differentiation and Integration*. Boston: Graduate School of Business Administration, Harvard University, 1967.

Levine, J. H. "The Sphere of Influence." *American Sociological Review*, pp. 14–27, 1972.

Locke, Edwin A. "Toward a Theory of Task Motivation and Incentives." *Organizational Behavior and Human Performance*, Vol. 3, 1968.

Lorange, Peter and Richard F. Vancil. "How to Design a Strategic Planning System." *Harvard Business Review*. September–October 1976.

Mace, Myles L. *Directors: Myth and Reality*. Boston: Graduate School of Business Administration, Harvard University, 1971.

McCleery, R. H. *Policy Change in Prison Management*. East Lansing, Mich.: Michigan State University, 1957.

Mechanic, D. "Sources of Power of Lower Participants in Complex Organizations." *Administrative Science Quarterly*, December 1962.

Michels, R. *Political Parties, A Sociological Study of the Oligarchical Tendencies of Modern Democracy* (translated from Italian). Glencoe, Ill.: The Free Press, 1958 (also, Jarrold and Sons, 1915).

Mintzberg, Henry. "Strategy-making in Three Modes." *California Management Review*, Winter 1973.

Mintzberg, Henry, D. Raisinghani and A. Theoret. "The Structure of 'Unstructured' Decision Processes." *Administrative Science Quarterly*, June 1976.

Murray, Edwin A., Jr. "Limitations on Strategic Choice." *Academy of Management Proceedings*, Kansas City, Mo., 1976.

National Industrial Conference Board. *Corporate Directorship Practices. Studies in Business Policy*, No. 125, 1967.

Olson, Mancur, Jr. "A Theory of Groups and Organizations," in Russett, Bruce M., *Economic Theories of International Politics*. Chicago: Markham, 1968.

Papandreou, A. G. "Some Basic Problems in the Theory of the Firm," in Haley, B. F. (editor), *A Survey of Contemporary Economics*, Vol. 2. Homewood, Ill.: Richard D. Irwin, 1952.

Perrow, Charles. "The Analysis of Goals in Complex Organizations." *American Sociological Review*, December 1961.

Pettigrew, A. M. *The Politics of Organizational Decision-Making*. London: Tavistock Publications, 1973.

Raia, Anthony P. "Goal Setting and Self-Control: An Empirical Study." *Journal of Management Studies*, February 1965.

Ronan, W. N., G. P. Latham and S. B. Kinne. "Effects of Goal Setting and Supervision on Worker

Behavior in an Industrial Situation." *Journal of Applied Psychology*, December 1973.

Rumelt, Richard P. *Strategy, Structure, and Economic Performance*. Boston: Graduate School of Business Administration, Harvard University, 1974.

Scheff, T. J. "Control Over Policy by Attendants in a Mental Hospital." *Journal of Health and Human Behavior*, pp. 93–105, 1961.

Schein, E. "Organizational Socialization and the Profession of Management." *Industrial Management Review*, Winter 1968.

Scott, Bruce R. "The Industrial State: Old Myths and New Realities." *Harvard Business Review*, March–April 1973.

Selznick, P. *TVA and the Grass Roots*. Berkeley: University of California Press, 1949.

Sills, D. L. *The Volunteers*. New York: The Free Press, 1957.

Simon, Herbert A. *Administrative Behavior*. New York: Macmillan, 1957.

Simon, Herbert A. "On the Concept of Organizational Goal." *Administrative Science Quarterly*, June 1964.

Steers, R. M. "Task-Goal Attributes, Achievement, and Supervisory Performance." *Organizational Behavior and Human Performance*, Vol. 13, pp. 392–403, 1975.

Steinbruner, John D. *The Cybernetic Theory of Decision*. Princeton, N.J.: Princeton University Press, 1974.

Thoenig, J. C. and E. Friedberg. "The Power of the Field Staff: The Case of the Ministry of Public Works, Urban Affairs and Housing in France," in Leemans, A. F. (editor), *The Management of Change in Government*. The Hague: Mortimus Hijoff, 1975.

Thompson, James D. *Organizations in Action*. New York: McGraw-Hill, 1967.

Thompson, James D. and William J. McEwen. "Organizational Goals and Environment: Goal-Setting as an Interaction Process." *American Sociological Review*, February 1958.

Vroom, Victor. *Work and Motivation*. New York: Wiley, 1964.

Wieland, G. F. "The Determinants of Clarity in Organization Goals." *Human Relations*, April 1969.

Woodward, Joan. *Industrial Organization: Theory and Practice*. London: Oxford University Press, 1965.

Zald, M. N. "The Power and Functions of Boards of Directors: A Theoretical Synthesis." *American Journal of Sociology*, pp. 97–111, 1969.

3

STRATEGY FORMULATION

Strategy Formulation: Analytical and Normative Models

JOHN H. GRANT
University of Pittsburgh

WILLIAM R. KING
University of Pittsburgh

Commentary

DEREK F. CHANNON
University of Manchester

Environmental Analysis and Forecasting

JAMES M. UTTERBACK
Massachusetts Institute of Technology

Commentary

HAROLD E. KLEIN
Temple University

Strategy Formulation: A Social and Political Process

JOSEPH L. BOWER
Harvard University

YVES DOZ
Harvard University

Commentary

IAN C. MACMILLAN
Columbia University

JOHN CHILD
University of Aston Management Centre

As noted in the introduction, there is disagreement both as to the definition of the strategy construct and the processes by which strategy is formulated. On the purpose served by strategy, however, there seems to be agreement. Strategy links an organization to its environment in ways that lead to achievement of its goals and objectives. This linkage occurs at three levels of organization: the corporate, the business, and the functional area.[1] Thus, just as an organization may have a hierarchy of objectives, there exists a hierarchy of environments and a hierarchy of strategies.

At whatever organization level it exists, a given strategy can be described in terms of four common components, the mix and importance of which will differ by level. In this regard, an effective strategy will usually describe the present and planned: (1) scope or domain of action within which the organization will try to achieve its objectives; (2) skills and resources, sometimes referred to as the distinctive competences, that the organization will use to achieve its objectives; (3) advantages the organization expects to achieve vis-à-vis its competitors through its skills and resource deployments; and (4) synergies that will result from the ways the organization deploys its skills and resources. Since strategy provides directional guidance to the entire organization, effective strategies will usually specify a time-sequenced series of current and future choices for each strategy component rather than just the present state.

Although this definition seems to imply that strategies are *explicit* statements of the fundamental means organizations will use to achieve their goals and objectives, such need not be the case. Strategies can also be implicit. For example, they usually are implicit in the case of small organizations led by charismatic entrepreneurs. In such instances, the implicit strategy of the organization is usually developed solely by the entrepreneur based on the totality of knowledge he has about his organization and its environment. Sometimes this knowledge and strategy will be the result of an explicit analytical process, but more often than not in smaller organizations such thinking is done informally and perhaps even unconsciously as the entrepreneur reacts to and anticipates various developments in the environment.

By contrast, large, complex organizations such as General Electric and IBM have developed rather formal and complex procedures for developing the various types of strategies they need to survive and grow in a changing and complex environment. There is, moreover, some evidence to suggest that such formal procedures produce superior results, and presumably superior strategies, for medium and large businesses (Thune and House, 1970; Herold, 1972; Rue and Fulmer, 1973; Karger and Malik, 1975; and Ansoff et al., 1971).

Whether simple and informal, or complex and formal, the process by

[1] Of course, these three levels are usually separate and distinct only in large businesses. In small firms all three levels may be combined.

which an organization develops a strategy to achieve its objectives is called its strategy formulation process. As indicated in Exhibit 3.1, these processes are usually visualized as taking place after the organization's goal formulation processes and before its strategy implementation processes.

As noted later by Rumelt, one of the purposes of such strategy formulation processes (and of strategy itself) is to help structure the unstructured problems the organization faces. As a paradigm for "solving" such unstructured problems, the strategy formulation process contains all of the substeps of any general problem-solving process: (1) problem (issue) identification, (2) problem (issue) analysis, (3) alternative generation, (4) alternative evaluation, and (5) choice.

Since we wanted to give particular attention to some aspects of the strategy evaluation task, we have separated the issue identification, issue analysis, and alternative generation steps of the strategy formulation process from those of evaluation and choice to form a narrower concept of the strategy formulation task. One result of this classification system is that some overlap has been created between the discussion of Grant and King and that of Rumelt, since some analytical concepts are used both to identify issues and alternatives and to evaluate them. It also means that Channon's critique of the narrowness of Grant's and King's paper is more appropriately directed at us and the choice we made rather than at

Exhibit 3.1 An Overview of the Strategic Management Process

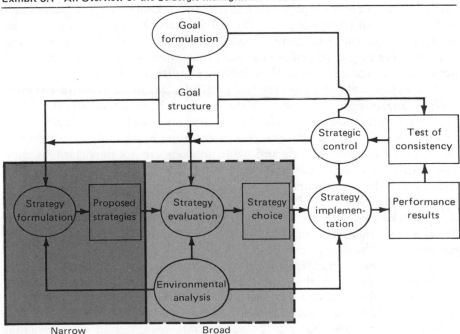

The strategy formulation process

Grant and King. Nonetheless, we still feel this separation is useful, for several reasons.

One of the most important reasons is the attention such separation gives to strategy evaluation. In some ways, evaluation is one of the least important steps in the strategy formulation process, since it can only reject poor alternatives, that is, it cannot create good ones. However, because strategy content significantly influences overall organizational performance, it is critically important to reject poor alternatives, even if better options are not immediately apparent. A second reason for separating the steps of the strategy formulation process is that research on structured problem-solving and decision-making indicates that superior performance occurs when the steps in these processes are explicitly separated. The work of Mintzberg et al. (1976), while limited in scope, seems to indicate that the same principle applies to unstructured problem-solving and decision-making. Such separation should also indicate more clearly the range of applicability of various tools and techniques in the strategy formulation process. Ideas such as portfolio matrices, life cycles, and experience curves are thus seen to be useful to both formulation (issue identification, analysis, and alternative generation) and evaluation, while concepts such as brainstorming and policy Delphi are seen to apply primarily to formulation.

The strategy formulation process contains at least three subprocesses: (1) environmental analysis, which is shown explicitly in Exhibit 3.1 and which is used in several different tasks in the strategic management process; (2) resource analysis, which deals with an assessment of the financial, technological, physical, human, and organizational resources and skills of the organization; and (3) value analysis, which deals with an analysis of external and internal coalition values in terms of goals involving such matters as growth, efficiency, asset utilization, and other economic and noneconomic considerations that influence strategy selection.

It is appropriate to note here the particular attention given to environmental analysis in our model of the strategy formulation process. Most strategy formulation models emphasize environmental, resource, and value analysis equally. By giving priority to environmental analysis, we do not mean to imply that resource and value analysis are not important, as they are. Rather, our emphasis on environmental analysis stems from the fact that of the three elements that can influence strategy, the environment is the one over which the firm normally has the least control. Even though it may take great effort and a long time, both resources and values can be changed relatively directly by the organization's management. The environment, however, cannot be. Because of this fact and because the response times to major environmental changes can be very long, it is of crucial importance that the organization take steps to anticipate and prepare for the changes that are likely to occur in its environment. In this regard, Utterback has proposed several hypotheses about the types of forecasting methods that may be appropriate for different environmental circumstances, while Klein and Channon have noted some techniques that are actually used by organizations today, especially in the areas of social/cultural and political/legal forecasting. Klein has also examined some of the problems involved in trying to overcome the value-infused nature of many forecasts and in incorporating such forecasts in the strategy formulation processes of firms. Clearly, more research needs to be done in this vital area.

THE STRATEGY CONCEPT AND STRATEGY FORMULATION PROCESSES: SOME DIFFERENT PERSPECTIVES

One of the major dichotomies in the business policy field today involves the breadth of the definition of strategy and the scope of the strategy formulation process. Specifically, the question is whether the strategy concept should encompass statements of both means and ends, which is the approach followed by Bower and Doz and Rumelt in this text as well as by Chandler (1962), Andrews (1971), and others, or whether it should encompass statements of means only, which is the approach followed by Grant and King in this text as well as by Ansoff (1965), Cannon (1968), Katz (1970), and others.

If the former approach is adopted, then the goal formulation and strategy formulation processes are identical, since the strategy formulation process would, by definition, produce a statement of ends as well as a statement of means. If the latter approach is adopted, then the goal formulation and strategy formulation processes are distinct, even though they may be interrelated.

We have adopted the second approach and have developed separate sections on goal formulation and strategy formulation. This separation was made for three reasons. First, it is clear that ends and means are distinct concepts. Since the terms "goals" and "objectives" have been used to describe the former concept, it would be redundant to use the term "strategy" to apply to both. Also, if the term "strategy" were applied to both, then it would be necessary to coin a new term to apply to means alone. Second, it is clear that some organizations do formulate their desired ends (goals and objectives) separately from the means (strategy) they will use to achieve these ends. It makes more sense to us to attach different labels to these processes than it does to apply a single label to phenomena that are often distinctly different, even though in some instances they may be intimately intertwined. Finally, as noted above, research on structured problem solving and decision making indicates that superior performance occurs when the different steps of problem solving and decision making processes are considered separately. The work of Mintzberg et al. (1976) seems to indicate that the same principle applies to unstructured problem solving and decision making.

We do not expect that these arguments will settle this question of separating goal formulation and strategy formulation even though the separation clarifies exposition. However, by explicitly focusing attention on the dichotomy, some resolution of the issue may be possible in the future. It is also clear that such separation is often easier to accomplish when the parties involved have some substantial commonality of goals than when they do not, since in the latter case it may not be possible to reach an agreement on a joint goal set.[2] It was such difficulties that led Lindblom (1959) to suggest that in such circumstances the parties involved should seek agreement on means rather than ends. While his observation is probably correct, it is more pertinent to note here that if agreement on a joint goal set is not possible, then the group of parties cannot be said to be an organization, since an organization is, by definition, a collection of parties who have joined together to accomplish some common purpose.

A second major dichotomy in the business policy field today involves the question of whether the strategy formulation process is (should be) primarily an analytical/conceptual process or whether it is (should be) primarily a social/political process or whether it is (should be) some balanced combination of both.

The nature of this dichotomy is made clearer by reference to Exhibit 3.2. As noted earlier, most strategy formulation processes include three broad subprocesses: (1) environmental analysis, (2) resource analysis, and (3) value analysis. The dichotomy occurs with respect to the relative importance and the sequencing of these subprocesses. Those who argue that strategy formulation is (should be) an analytical/conceptual process place greater importance on the environmental analysis and resource analysis steps and make these the start of the process. Only after a set of feasible economic strategies is identified are the values of the external and internal coalitions allowed to enter the process to influence the strategy choice. Moreover, the final choice usually maximizes economic performance subject to value constraints. By contrast, those who argue that strategy formulation is (should be) a social/political process place greater importance on the value analysis step and place it at the start of the strategy formulation process. Such models then identify a set of desired strategies, which, because of the stability of value structures and organizational coalitions, are usually modifications of the existing strategy. These desired strategies are then checked to see whether they are consistent with environmental opportunities and risks and organizational skills and resources. The final choice usually maximizes values subject to economic constraints rather than the other way around. Under the balanced approaches, the environ-

---

[2] Goal commonality may be much easier to achieve in business firms than in other types of institutions because the primacy of economic goals often forces other goals to a secondary position. This observation may be generally true for all organizations where "economic slack" does not exist. This point may also explain why researchers who study nonbusiness organizations do not observe the same phenomena as do researchers concentrating on business firms.

Exhibit 3.2 The Nature of the Strategy Formulation Process

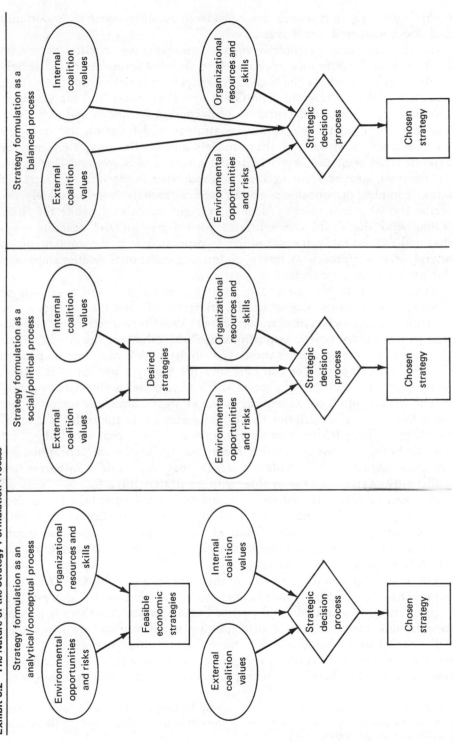

ment, resources, and values are considered roughly equal in importance and are considered simultaneously.[3]

To provide some perspective on this question, we solicited papers on both analytical/conceptual approaches to strategy formulation and social/political approaches to the topic. The papers themselves approach their tasks somewhat differently. The Grant and King paper and the Channon commentary describe different analytical/conceptual models and techniques that may be used to help formulate strategy and focus on the strengths and weaknesses of each of these models and on the ways they may be extended and their use improved in the future. The Bower and Doz paper, by contrast, argues from existing research and theory that, at least for large, complex organizations, social/political models more accurately describe the way that strategy does in fact get formulated, while the MacMillan and the Child commentaries both argue for and describe ways that political considerations can be incorporated into the content of an organization's strategy in terms of interorganizational relationships and the anticipation of competitive responses.

Examples of all three types of strategy formulation processes can be observed in practice. Consequently, in terms of descriptive theory, the principal questions worth attention are: (1) What type of strategy formulation processes do most organizations use? (2) What are the conditions or situations, including organization type, under which one type of process is used or preferred over another? and (3) Given a particular condition or situation, which types of process will lead to better performance results?

The major points of contention in the strategy formulation area do not lie in the realm of descriptive theory, however, but in the realm of normative theory. That is, the major arguments are over "what should be," not over "what is." Those advocating the primacy of analytical/conceptual approaches to strategy formulation argue that the world's resources are sufficiently scarce and the problems to be dealt with sufficiently difficult that organizational survival and economic efficiency must take precedence over the social needs and the political aspirations of particular individuals and groups. Moreover, they would argue that any other premise would relegate research and teaching to the bleak position of not being able to contribute beyond what currently exists.

On the other hand, those advocating the primacy of social/political approaches to strategy formulation argue: (1) that social and political factors are such a fundamental part of human nature that there is no way to eliminate them, that is, if attempts are made to eliminate them, they will at most only change the way these factors enter the process; (2) that most social/political processes will produce at least survival-level economic results; and (3) therefore, such procedures are superior to analytical/

---

[3] If time and resources were not constraining factors, the differences between these approaches should be minimal because all three procedures should eventually produce similar sets of strategies.

conceptual ones, since the latter may produce more failures because of the social disharmony and political infighting they may cause. Those advocating analytical/conceptual approaches would dispute the third point, arguing that, while social and political factors will always be present, these can be channeled in productive directions by altering the organization's measurement and evaluation, and reward and sanction systems so that better than survival levels of results will be produced.

Based on the theories and research cited by authors in this section, several conclusions seem possible and reasonable. First, it is clear that both points of view have major supporting arguments. Second, it also seems clear, at least to us, that an integrated view is possible. However, it also seems likely that such an integrated view will not consist of the adoption of a "balanced process," but rather that a contingency approach will be needed that will suggest that the kind of process adopted by an organization will depend on factors such as: (1) the type of organization involved; (2) the nature of the environmental threats and opportunities that the organization faces; (3) the size and level of the organization involved; and (4) the history and culture of the organization involved.

It is worthwhile considering possible hypotheses that would stem from such a contingency approach. Before presenting these, however, we should note that an organization may adapt one of four different types of strategy formulation processes: (1) an analytical/conceptual process, (2) a social/political process, (3) a balanced process, or (4) no formal process. Each of the following hypotheses, except H_6, relates some variable (e.g., organizational size) with the probability of occurrence of one of these four types of processes (e.g., social/political processes). Each hypothesis is silent, however, on the probability of occurrence of the other three types of processes individually, although each does of course imply either an increase or a decrease in the sum of the joint probability of the other three processes being used.

— H_1: The greater the degree to which the organization focuses on a single objective or a small set of similar objectives, the greater the likelihood that it will use an analytical/conceptual strategy formulation process.

— H_2: The greater the degree of environmental risk/threat the organization faces, the greater the likelihood it will use an analytical/conceptual strategy formulation process.

— H_3: The smaller the organization, the lower the probability that it will use a social/political strategy formulation process.

— H_4: The lower the level of the organization (i.e., the lower the strategy is in the corporate, business, functional area hierarchy), the greater the probability that an analytical/conceptual strategy formulation will be used.

— H_5: The younger the organization, the lower the probability that it will use a social/political strategy formulation process.

— H_6: Unless there is a crisis threatening the very survival of the organization, the strategy formulation process that an organization will use is most likely to be the same type of process that it has used in the past.

— H$_7$: If the survival of the organization is seriously threatened, it is most likely that an analytical/conceptual strategy formulation process will be used to respond to the crisis.

Clearly, additional research will be needed to shed light on each of these hypotheses as well as on the various more specific hypotheses and questions raised by the individual papers. Whenever possible, such research should be of a hypothesis-testing rather than a hypothesis-generating character and more normative than descriptive in character. This is not to suggest that additional descriptive research such as that of Bower (1970) or Mintzberg et al. (1976) is not needed, since it is. However, descriptive research is not sufficient, for it makes no attempt to distinguish between good and bad practice. Thus, while it may be true that one cannot prescribe effectively until one knows "what is," to have a complete understanding of "typical" practice may not advance knowledge nearly as much as to know what constitutes "good" practice and how that differs from both "typical" and "poor" practice. Moreover, even a knowledge of current practice may not fully reveal what can be, since even the best-managed organizations are always in the process of "becoming," that is, of improving what they are.

Perhaps most importantly, until good practice is studied, one cannot know whether the conclusions drawn from purely descriptive studies will have any major significance for the improvement of management practice. For instance, the research of Mintzberg et al. (1976) revealed many common patterns in the ways in which different organizations made the same type of decision. Mintzberg also noted elsewhere that he was able to use the knowledge of such patterns to improve the practices of other organizations faced with similar problems. While this may be true, it is likely that the empirical patterns noted by Mintzberg et al. (1976) were those of "average" or "typical" practice, not those of "best" practice, since no attempt was made initially to select those organizations employing "best" practice, or to evaluate the practice found against criteria that revealed its relative quality. Thus, while Mintzberg's observations of "average" practice may permit him to suggest improvements in that practice, it may well be that "best" practice utilizes methods entirely different from those observed by Mintzberg and that the application of these methods would result in improvements far more substantial than those derived from the observation of "average" practice. It is also possible, of course, that this may not be true. The point is not whether deductions based on "average" practice will be superior or inferior to those based on "best" practice in any individual instance, but rather that in general, deductions based on the observation of "best," "average," and "inferior" practice will be better than those based only on the observation of "average" or undifferentiated practice.

In closing this introduction to the strategy formulation section, we should make one final observation. It is that there is no discussion in this section of the organizational systems and procedures variously referred to as formal planning systems, long-range planning systems, or strategic planning systems. Such planning systems and procedures are used by organizations, especially large, complex ones, to perform the various analytical and conceptual analyses that comprise the strategy formulation process. They are also the territory in which the various social and political activities described by Bower and Doz, MacMillan, and Child occur. These planning systems and procedures are described in a later paper by Lorange, with commentaries by Henry and Hekhuis. These methods have been deliberately placed in Section 5, which discusses strategy implementation, to emphasize that in practice such systems link both formulation *and* implementation.

Strategy Formulation: Analytical and Normative Models

JOHN H. GRANT
University of Pittsburgh

WILLIAM R. KING
University of Pittsburgh

The objectives of this paper are to identify and analyze analytical and normative models which deal with the strategy formulation process. After delineating the arena of interest, several models of non-behavioral aspects of strategy formulation are discussed and evaluated. Finally, some potentially fruitful directions for future research are suggested.

Our approach to the literature will be one of attempting to cluster the conceptual models or frameworks and the related empirical research in a manner which will permit the reader to evaluate which concepts have been supported, which seem to have been rejected, and which remain essentially untested. This approach should permit an evaluation of the most promising avenues for future research.

BASIC DEFINITIONS

STRATEGY FORMULATION

For the purposes of this paper, strategy is considered to be a conditional sequence of internally consistent resource allocations which defines an organization's relationship with its environment over time. Resources are specifically taken to include non-financial as well as financial dimensions, and a strategy may well be expressed in terms of such a complex array. *Strategy formulation* then refers to the sequence of steps taken between the time at which resources, the operating environment, and a set of goals are preliminarily identified and the time at which a proposed strategy is subjected to formal evaluation. Although the strategic alternatives developed may include changing the size of the resource base or a portion of the

operating environment, the formulation process is seen as following that of goal formation and preceding those of evaluation, selection, implementation, and control. As such, strategy formulation involves two essential elements:

(1) the identification or delineation of the factors which comprise an appropriate strategy for the enterprise, and
(2) the specification of alternative strategies for subsequent consideration in the evaluation and selection phase.

Because management literature generally defines strategy formulation in broader terms than are used in this paper — e.g., to include the evaluation phase — it may be useful to paraphrase our territory as consisting of "analytical techniques for structuring strategic alternatives." [1]

ANALYTICAL AND NORMATIVE MODELS

Although the goal hierarchy of an enterprise may be varied and complex, it is assumed there is a profitability threshold which must be attained in order to ensure survival and to permit the pursuit of other goals. Therefore, the analytical models or techniques which are discussed here are biased toward those which are grounded in disciplines such as economics and

---

[1] The selection of this phrase is the outgrowth of many comments made during the discussion of this paper at the Conference. One participant went so far as to note the field has many broad conceptual schemes for corporate strategy and a few techniques for evaluation, but that the area described as "models for formulation" is almost devoid of content.

mathematics and applied areas such as marketing and finance. Such models are typically designed to aid the pursuit of long-term profit satisfaction.

It is clear that our definition of analytical is both restricted and narrow. For instance, someone familiar with Allison's *Essence of Decision* (1971) might describe it as analytical, but it is excluded here because it draws more upon organizational, behavioral, and political theory. Our use of the word *normative* is the conventional one which suggests the prescription of a path to be followed, but it includes the implicit contingency, "if you want to improve economic performance." *Model* is a word with a wide variety of denotations and connotations, but we will use it in a very broad sense to refer to any simplified abstraction of reality. Some readers will be more comfortable in substituting "framework" or "technique" where we will use the term "model."

A FRAMEWORK FOR ANALYSIS

As portrayed in Exhibit 3.3, our framework divides the corporate strategic process into five phases which can be visualized as occurring over at least three distinctive hierarchical levels within the modern diversified enterprise. Within this broad context, our primary interest is in the "corporate level" and the "product/market level" activities within the "structuring of alternatives" phase. Some of the models which are included also have applicability in the arena described as being of secondary interest, but those which have applications *only* in the secondary area have been excluded. The other cells of the matrix are included as a means of convenient reference when addressing concepts or models which extend into still other phases or levels of the overall strategic process.

Although the corporate level and product/market level decision process may be inex-

Exhibit 3.3 Framework for Corporate Strategy Concepts

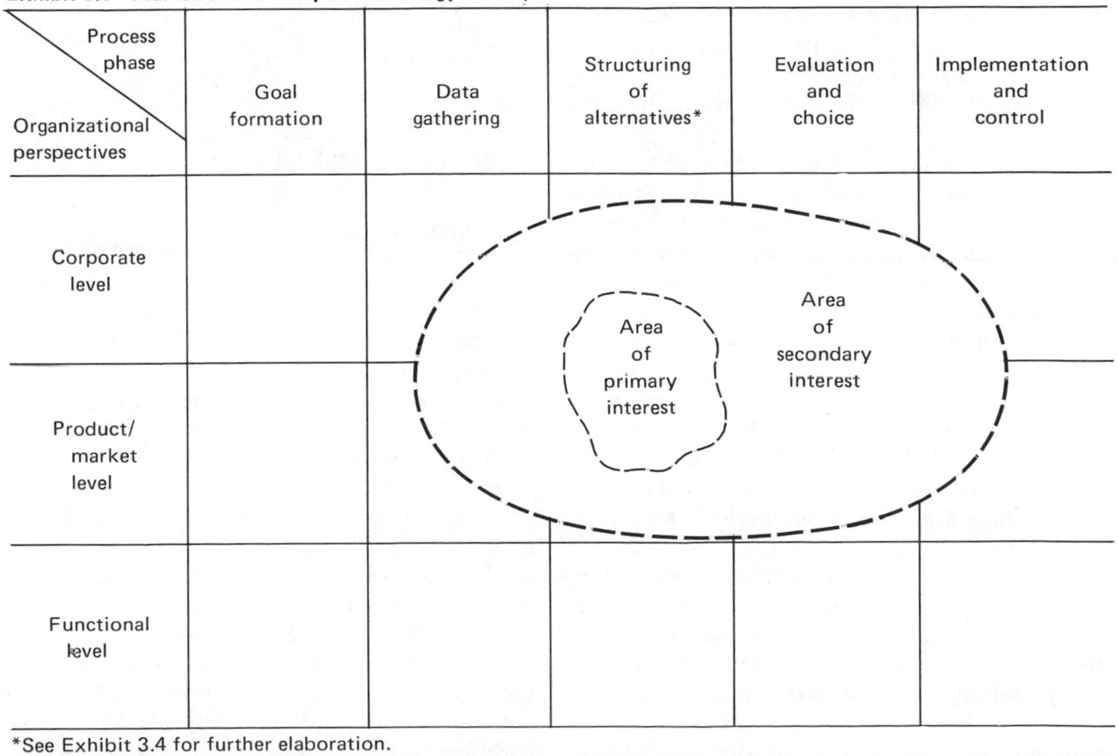

Process phase / Organizational perspectives	Goal formation	Data gathering	Structuring of alternatives*	Evaluation and choice	Implementation and control
Corporate level					
Product/ market level					
Functional level					

*See Exhibit 3.4 for further elaboration.

tricably intertwined in small firms or in large vertically integrated ones (Ackerman, 1970), there seems to be ample evidence to suggest that, within diversified firms, the nature of the strategic problem is different at these two levels (Berg, 1965; Bower, 1970). Therefore, an attempt will be made to distinguish the analytical models according to types of questions they seek to answer. Those techniques and models whose application seems to be limited to problems at the functional area level of the organization, however, will be largely ignored. In Exhibit 3.4, several analytical models which seem to have research applicability are identified and classified according to applicability to organizational level.

Those concepts which seem to have their primary application to corporate-level decisions have been grouped together at the top. The second group of models consists of those which have potential applicability to the structuring of both corporate and product/market level alternatives. (The dotted lines are intended to suggest the rather arbitrary classification of some of the models within this taxonomy.) Concepts which have found their primary application in answering the question "How shall we compete in market X?" have been placed in the third cell.

Because the intended application of a given model can vary so significantly depending upon the perspective of the user, it is worth citing one example of what is meant by arbitrary classification. "Scenarios" are included within the "dual level" cell because such models have been useful in helping managers and researchers structure and analyze expected competitive behavior under different sets of assumptions within a defined industry sector. In addition, scenarios have been used at the "corporate level" to help managers choose *which* business units or sectors should receive given levels of resources. In other words, scenarios appear to be useful for structuring strategic alternatives in response to questions at both hierarchical levels. Our taxonomy is intended to facilitate discussion and analysis; it is not intended to constrain creativity. Indeed, one of the most important sources of future advances in the area of strategy formulation may lie in the transfer of concepts

from other areas and levels of application to those of strategy formulation.

It is now time to direct our attention to a discussion of the analytical models which have been offered or developed to help managers and strategy researchers bridge the gaps between the abstractions of economic theory and the vagaries of much normative management theory. These models may be viewed as a series of weapons with which to attack the weaknesses that Mintzberg (1977) saw when he noted that:

> generally the softer side of the strategic decision process has been least studied — for example, diagnosis of the situation and design of the solution, as opposed to evaluation and choice of alternatives.

Our discussion begins with a review of the more comprehensive models which have contributed to strategy formulation at both the corporate and product/market levels. The next section will focus on models which have had their greatest impact at the product/market level, and the final section will take us to the multiple market analyses which face corporate-level officials.

DUAL LEVEL MODELS

Capital Investment Theory

An appropriate point of departure for this inquiry is that field of microeconomics known as capital investment theory. Although the limitations of the essential elements of this theory have been ably critiqued before (Ansoff, 1965; Bower, 1968), some of its characteristics which are more salient to strategy formulation are worth noting. The theory contains a general presumption of competition for resources (largely money or capital) based upon "rates of return," so the long-run size of the firm is constrained by its relative efficiency as evaluated by investors. The firm has a built-in stimulus for cost-effective search techniques which will reveal potentially high return investment opportunities because such opportunities influence both the firm's growth and its cost of capital.

Exhibit 3.4 Analytical and Normative Models for Structuring Strategic Alternatives

Organizational perspective	Model or concept	Research source	
		Conceptual	Empirical
Corporate level models —What kind of a firm are we? —In *which* markets should we compete?	Directional policy matrix Business planning matrix Frontier curve Portfolio theory	Royal Dutch Shell Oil Company General Electric Company Moose & Zakon Lintner; Mason & Goudzwaard; Carter & Cohen; Ansoff & Leontiades	Kitching; Rumelt; Jauch
Dual level models —Pertaining to *both* corporate and product/market questions	Capital investment theory Comprehensive planning models Corporate simulation and financial planning models Mathematical strategy models Scenarios Policy Delphi Dialectical policy analysis Brainstorming	Scherer Learned; Ansoff; Cohen & Cyert; Denning Forrester; Gershefski; Coyle Schendel; Schoeffler; Kirchhoff; Macintosh Kahn & Weiner Turoff Churchman; Mason Rosenstein	Baumol Scott; Berg; Hanna; Bower; Ackerman; Lupton; Guth Naylor & Schauland; Hall; Hatten; Patton; Schoeffler Zentner; Noland Turoff Mason
Product/Market level models —*How* shall we compete in our selected markets?	Game theory Meta-game theory Strategic data base Growth-share matrix Product life cycle Experience curves	McKinsey; Schelling; von Neumann Howard Vancil; King & Cleland Henderson A. Patton; Kotler; Levitt; Hofer; Rink Henderson; Hedley; Rutenberg	Rao & Rutenburg Dutta Rodriguez Chevalier; Fruhan Cunningham; Wasson; Metzner; Dhalla & Yuspeh BCG; Abernathy
Functional level models —Which techniques will yield effectiveness with efficiency?		Outside the domain of this paper	

Models of strategy formulation should thus seek to configure resources for efficiency and to institutionalize scanning procedures for detecting changes in comparative advantages vis-à-vis competitors.

Although the economic theory is rigorous, its applicability in *strategy* formulation has been quite limited because of its heavy reliance on quantitative measures and its restrictive underlying assumptions regarding information availability. Baumol (1968) perhaps summarized economists' frustrations best when he noted that "our body of theory offers us no promise of being able to deal effectively with a description and analysis of the entrepreneurial function." The most promising areas of application for this synoptic methodology, however, will be those where the strategist seeks incremental change in contexts where information is available and knowledge is quite high (Braybrooke and Lindblom, 1963). Further, many concepts have been borrowed from economic theory and explicitly or implicitly applied under the rubric of many of the models to be subsequently discussed.

Comprehensive Planning Models

In response to the perceived limitations of economic theory, a number of different authors have proposed comprehensive models of strategy formulation which relax some of the behavioral and value-oriented management issues which capital investment theory omits.

The strategy formulation model proposed and refined by Learned, Christensen, Andrews, and Guth (LCAG, 1965) places heavy emphasis on the strategist's ability to integrate the values of the top management group with the resources of the organization in a rivalrous environment (LCAG, 1965). This model was stated somewhat more formally by Bower (1967), but still contained the essential elements of a quasi-rational decision process to be pursued, typically, by a single individual. Emphasis was placed upon the internal consistency (efficiency seeking) of the strategy and the uniqueness (comparative advantage) of the relationship between the firm and its environment. Further, Bower sought to make explicit the notion that strategy formulation is a dynamic concept for addressing evolving managerial difficulties rather than an approach to static puzzle solving.

The open-system dimension of the LCAG model was supported by Scott (1963) and the interrelationships among the variables tested in the "stages of corporate development" models of Salter (1970), Scott (1971), and Grant (1972). However, the unitary or congruent goal(s) assumption was rejected in research of Berg (1965) and Hanna (1968) when the LCAG model was tested in large diversified firms. Additional behavioral and political dimensions were revealed by the research of Bower (1970) and Ackerman (1970) as they studied strategy formulation in large, complex firms. In spite of the fact that the LCAG model has stimulated research in several different directions, its normative view of the strategy formulation process is so abstract that it would be difficult to test; thus, it has made little contribution to furthering research with analytical models.

In 1965, Ansoff proposed a normative model for strategy formulation based upon an adaptive search methodology. Although the initial model contained a distinct bias in the direction of growth and diversification, it placed a valuable emphasis upon the "gap reducing" potential of options identified during the search process. Further, the model encouraged the systematic structuring of variables in the formulation process, particularly those contributing to potential synergy. The complexity of the proposed model did much to stifle efforts at comprehensive testing, but it must be viewed as a major conceptual contribution to work on strategy formulation because it demanded more specification and elaboration of variables than most comparable models, and, by placing emphasis on the role of information feedback, encouraged the recognition of the dynamic nature of the strategy formulation process.

Cohen and Cyert (1973) built upon earlier work regarding the behavioral theory of resource allocation and some of Ansoff's concepts to specify three formulation steps between goal quantification and portfolio selection, namely: (1) the microprocess of strategy formulation; (2) the gap analysis; and (3) strategic search. Although their model addressed the relationships between the corporate level and business units, it placed heavy emphasis upon local search as a means of reducing the gaps in quantified goals. It thus sought to solve strategic problems through modifications in existing relationships rather than through major reconceptualizations of product/market positions. The importance of the need for occasional in-depth reviews of product/market level strategies has since been highlighted by Schendel and Patton's (1976) research regarding stagnation and turnaround, but the problems of transferring resources to distinct new market arenas remain significant (Biggadike, 1976).

Denning's model (1968) of strategy formulation implies that from given values, objectives, strategies and policies, the appropriate action will follow if the organizational structure is designed properly, managers are motivated and incentives are established for workers. Some preliminary tests based on case examples were cited, but later research efforts by others tended to reject the model as overly simplified. Later, a group of seminar participants at the Manchester Business School proposed a model of strategy formulation which was predicated on the concept of management coalitions, made allowances for imperfect information, recognized delays in response to external stimuli, and incorporated the notion that subunits transact independently with the environment (Lupton *et al.*, 1969).

Many of the factors which others have identified as being important to the strategy formulation process were given further structure in conceptual work by Guth (1972). Although his general relationships were based upon the analysis of over sixty American and European firms, he offered no contingency statements indicating the classes of circumstances which should serve to focus attention and analysis on more limited sets of variables. Nonetheless, work such as Guth's stands as an example that specific factors and proposed directional relationships can be developed for later testing and refinement.

Because most comprehensive strategy models have applicability in a number of the cells in Exhibit 3.3, they have been able to directly stimulate relatively few of the sort of contingent statements which form the basis for empirically testable hypotheses even though such hypotheses are necessary for testing and validating the global models (Hofer, 1975).

CORPORATE SIMULATION AND FINANCIAL PLANNING MODELS

Like many other mathematical and simulation models, financial planning models and total corporate models[2] provide relatively little assistance in the analytical aspects of strategy formulation. Much of the early enthusiasm for the potential of such models (Gershefski, 1969) has waned because of the complexities of developing the causal relationships among variables and the behavioral patterns of managers who often are not "maximizers" (Hall, 1973b). In fact, a recent survey was able to identify only three corporations which have implemented total corporate simulation models (Naylor and Schauland, 1976). The implicit conclusion here, however, is too strong; a firm does not need a "total corporate simulation model" in order to have a tool useful for strategy formulation.

Systems dynamics, an extension of the industrial dynamics concept developed by Forrester (1961), has been proposed as a means of helping to cope with certain aspects of strategy formulation (Coyle, 1973). The discipline required in problem definition, "influence diagram" development, and equation structuring demands a high degree of analytical attention. Although the mathematical simulation methodology can be extended and applied to strategy evaluation and selection, the initial three steps seem to be worth considerable testing as means of determining the thoroughness or completeness of proposed alternatives. Moreover, as with any simulation model, the systems dynamics approach permits the testing of proposed strategies on a "what if?" basis. This capability, if used in the context of a structured experimental design, gives insights into the relative importance of various strategy components. For in-

---

[2] Corporate models are grouped with financial planning models because most "total corporate" models are heavily biased toward financial measures and because most models of both varieties utilize simulation methodologies.

stance, an early application by Forrester (1961) demonstrated the importance of the *timing* of production decisions on market performance.

As large diversified firms seek to pursue multiple objectives through a portfolio of product/market entries, future research should probably focus on the development of probabilistic models which more adequately capture the economic interdependencies among subunit cash flows and profits and changes in competitive and environmental forces. When linked to a business planning matrix, a financial planning model can serve as a valuable feedback loop to the formulation phase, which may tend to omit critical resource relationships as the scope of the analysis broadens.

MATHEMATICAL STRATEGY MODELS

Several mathematical modeling thrusts have extended the earlier and more rudimentary financial models in an effort to capture more strategic factors directly. The most ambitious project to date involves the Strategic Planning Institute's (SPI) use of the Profit Impact of Market Strategy (PIMS) data base (Schoeffler *et al.*, 1974; Buzzell *et al.*, 1975). Researchers at SPI have developed a series of cross sectional multiple regression models, based upon data drawn from several hundred business units of large manufacturing firms, which have utilized more than two dozen variables to explain up to eighty percent of the historical variability in business unit profitability.

The PIMS "par" reports for return on investment (ROI) and cash flow can be particularly useful in the diagnostic and search facets of strategy formulation. One corporation, for example, was provided with four major factors that negatively affected one business area's ROI as compared with a "par" ROI for all businesses in the PIMS data bank. These factors were numerically scaled in terms of their relative impact:

— Vertical Integration	−7.9
— Market Position	−7.4
— Product Quality	−3.9
— Sales Direct to End Users	−2.2

In addition to identifying these factors as sources of potential "weaknesses," the PIMS analyses for the firm in question showed that, on the basis of their position vis-à-vis other firms in the data bank, one could conclude that ROI is highest at the beginning and end of the product life cycle (for businesses such as this one, which had low relative market shares). This understanding led the firm to new consideration of the *timing* of the product's R&D investment level as well as to reconsideration of the pricing policies for products that were then in the early and late phases of the product life cycle. Current research with the PIMS data base is also beginning to shed light on the role of various functional elements of strategy across a portfolio of business areas (SPI, 1977). Although many of the causal links in the relationships among strategic factors have not as yet been answered by PIMS, the fact that their findings are consistent with some descriptive research (Chevalier, 1972) suggests that further use of the data base by other researchers may yield many fruitful results.[3]

Another path of inquiry which holds promise of contributing to our understanding of analyses underlying the normative strategy formulation process can be found in the work of Schendel et al., (1975), Schendel and Patton (1976), Hatten (1974) and Patton (1976). Hatten used time series data and developed a linear regression model relating market share, product price, plant proliferation, and other factors to return on equity in the brewing industry. He was able to demonstrate that the beer industry, broadly defined, could be clustered into five subindustries with different interrelationships among the selected strategic factors. Subsequently, Patton fitted simultaneous equation models to three clusters of firms within the brewing industry and noted different combinations of factors leading to successful economic performance in each cluster. Such approaches are currently limited in terms of the strategic factors which they can accommodate. However, there is strong evidence

---

[3] For a more complete critique of the analyses of PIMS data, see Channon (1976), Anderson and Paine (1977), and King and Cleland (1977b).

that mathematical methodologies will aid analysts in understanding industry structure at the product/market level and that they will focus attention during the formulation phase on those competitive factors which have had significant historical roles in successful performance within the industry subsegment.

Additional investigation of the relationships among internal variables and their impact on divisional performance has been undertaken by Kirchhoff (1975). Although his initial regression analyses of cross sectional data did not provide as strong a set of inferences as might be desired, they did serve to demonstrate the importance of internal consistency among the elements included during the formulation of strategy.

Econometric modeling has also been proposed as a technique which may become increasingly useful in strategy formulation. Through their analysis of the Canadian meatpacking industry, three researchers (Macintosh *et al.,* 1973) were able to effectively link individual firms to broader macroeconomic indicators. They found the econometric model to be helpful in isolating key variables in the economy and limiting the range of viable strategic options during the formulation phase. For example, an earlier series of five consulting firms' reports stressing the importance of advertising could have been rejected *a priori* given the econometric model.

As with most other quantitative modeling techniques, econometric analyses presently offer the greatest potential for strategy formulation within familiar and relatively mature industries. Through the simulation of possible future outcomes, the technique can serve to stimulate search processes with other techniques and thus also make a significant indirect contribution to formulation efforts.

Most mathematical modeling research efforts which show promise of contributing to strategy formulation are of relatively recent origin. Because of the voracious demand for quantitative data found in most of these models, research efforts will probably be limited to rather mature product lines sold by single product firms. It remains to be seen whether the Security and Exchange Commission's new product line or segment reporting requirements will yield enough public data to permit mathematical modeling research in markets inhabited by several multi-divisional firms.

SCENARIOS

In response to the difficulties often·encountered in trying to secure the large volume of relevant quantitative data typically required for mathematical and simulation modeling, many firms have turned to the process of scenario development as a means of addressing some of the less well structured aspects of strategy formulation.

Scenarios are attempts to describe in detail a sequence of events which could plausibly lead to a prescribed end state, or alternately, to consider the possible outcomes of present choices. Although scenarios are usually rather qualitative, they are nonetheless detailed. Their particular advantage is to permit the integrated consideration of many diverse factors. For instance, a specific corporate mission and its associated strategy and programs may be explored in terms of a scenario involving societal change, competitive reactions, regulatory change, etc. The scenario thus becomes a structured way of considering the overall system in a way that few abstract techniques can hope to do.

The best-known use of scenarios is undoubtedly the work of Kahn and Wiener (1967) who applied them on a worldwide scope. Scenarios have been used in organizational planning to explore the consequences of current choices of missions, objectives, strategies and programs as they will impact on, and be impacted by, a complex environment. Zentner (1975) summarized more than thirty articles in the literature which discussed the use of scenarios in a variety of applications pertaining to the role of management in dealing with governmental intervention, the seizure of Arab oil, bank assets and liabilities, the pulp and paper industry, and world energy systems, etc. Since most uses of scenarios by business firms are proprietary in nature,[4] they appear less fre-

---

[4] One of the most comprehensive sets of scenarios available for public scrutiny was prepared by the Stanford Research Institute (SRI) for the Environmental Protection Agency (EPA) in the early 1970s.

quently in public literature, but firms such as General Electric, Monsanto, Shell Oil (Noland, 1974), and Atlantic Richfield (*Long Range Planning*, 1976) have been known to use the approach in strategy formulation.

Although the reported empirical research pertaining to the use of scenarios in strategy formulation is very sparse, corporations have utilized the concept internally to analyze the expected behavior of critical strategic elements across several alternative paths. The variety of factors and interdependencies which can be examined through comparative scenarios can thus be expected to stimulate more comprehensive analyses of strategic alternatives in future research.

An extension of the scenario concept as it applies to external factors is often referred to as the study of "alternative futures." Through a process of positing significantly different alternative future operating environs, analysts are stimulated to think more openly and creatively about possible strategic roles for a corporation in question. Although research in this area is at an early stage of development, much of the private and public sector work is being synthesized and extended by Nanus (1976) and others at the Center for Futures Research.

POLICY DELPHI

One means of refining analyses which often develop from comparisons of alternative scenarios is the Policy Delphi (Turoff, 1970). In situations where no single optimal solution can be found, the Policy Delphi seeks to explore opposing personal interpretations of data by developing the strongest possible opposite points of view on policy issues.

Policy Delphis have been reported in conjunction with analyses of several public sector issues (Turoff, 1970), but none is known to have been reported in a business context.

Research designed to test the Policy Delphi methodology in strategy formulation will be extremely difficult to execute because of the need for cooperation from managers who may perceive high personal stakes in a conflict laden situation. Nonetheless, a methodology which

may be useful for grappling with the formulation or structuring of either corporate or product/market level alternatives should not be discarded prematurely.

DIALECTIC POLICY ANALYSIS

Another potentially valuable approach to strategy formulation which makes use of opposing viewpoints is that of Mason (1969). Unlike the Policy Delphi which, like all Delphis, relies on non-face-to-face communication, Mason has used a face-to-face communication technique to analyze the different assumptions which must prove to be valid if each of two opposing strategies is to be effective. He, acting as a consultant to the "RMK Abrasives" company, took opposing strategies and analyzed them with respect to their underlying assumptions. In doing so, he reportedly produced a level of understanding which could not have otherwise been achieved.

Although the dialectic approach is not known to have been replicated in a similar environment or formally evaluated in a research context, it does show promise since it directly addresses the strategy formulation problem.

BRAINSTORMING

Standing in marked contrast to the structured process of the Policy Delphi is the free-form communications procedure known as brainstorming. As a means of stimulating new ideas at an early point in the strategy formulation process, brainstorming can be viewed as being analytical in only the most liberal definition of the term. However, in spite of this and in the absence of research supporting the validity (or even utility) of this methodology, it is a "named" and recognized approach which is directed toward strategy formulation rather than evaluation. Some firms have been using it for over a decade, and Hall's research (1973a) regarding new venture initiation showed that most large corporations use some form of brainstorming as a means of stimulating ideas early in the strategy formulation process.

In the context of strategy formulation, brainstorming represents one model which can be used for group "invention" of alternative organizational strategies. If it is complemented with subsequent evaluation sessions, it can serve as a vehicle for introducing strategy-oriented debate into the organization (Rosenstein, 1976). Only future research efforts, however, will determine whether or not the early search processes in strategy formulation can be executed more effectively through systematic economic analysis or some variant of brainstorming or synectic analysis (Gordon, 1968). The value of such techniques in a given organization obviously may lie in the nature of the "solution" being sought; perhaps brainstorming is as good as any other method for coping with problems requiring "large change" under conditions of "low understanding," e.g., Braybrooke and Lindblom's quadrant 4 (1963).

Future Directions

In this section, a variety of models have been identified with differing degrees of structure which seem to have continuity value in the analytical aspects of strategy formulation at both the corporate and product/market levels. Those models directed toward the strategy formulation phase, as opposed to the evaluation phase, tend to be less structured, less applied and less frequently tested. Those which contribute to formulation in an ancillary fashion are more widely understood and practiced, if not empirically evaluated. Thus, such approaches as comprehensive planning models and Policy Delphi promise to continually ensure that an open-system view is maintained, while capital investment theory and mathematical models provide greater structure and specificity of variables. The challenge for managers and applied analysts will be to see that judicious trade-offs are made between specificity and rigor on one hand and creativity on the other — for both are important to strategic success. The challenge to researchers is to devise ways of validating and testing, particularly in the case of some of the less structured and more open approaches.

PRODUCT/MARKET LEVEL MODELS

The models presented in this section are ones which appear most applicable in guiding the manager's choice of *how* to compete within a given product arena. Again, it is necessary to recognize that some of these concepts may also be viewed by others as having applicability at other levels as well.

Game Theory

Game theory, in its extensive form (as opposed to the "normal" form which is usually discussed in most basic texts), deals with the strategy formulation process in terms of both the strategy set from which a choice is to be made and the constituent elements of individual strategies, but in the limited domain of the competitive environment. In converting a game in extensive form into one in normal form, one must identify the constituent elements which make up a generic strategy and then identify all of the possible combinations of those elements so as to enumerate the set of available strategies (McKinsey, 1952). Although game theory has some conceptual appeal for strategy formulation because of its "focus on the interdependence of adversaries' decisions" (Schelling, 1960), it also contains a conceptual weakness because "there is logically no simple extension of the concept of individual rational behavior to groups of individuals in general" (Shubik, 1972). Because of this difficulty, it is not surprising that there is little evidence of empirical research regarding the use of game theory in strategy formulation. Rao and Rutenburg (1977), however, have combined product life cycle and cash flow analyses with game theory concepts to study the conceptual relationships among two firms competing for market position in a new geographical region.

Meta-Game Analysis

An innovative extension of game theory to strategy formulation is that involved in meta-game analysis (Howard, 1971). This approach emphasizes the general concept of competitive equilibrium as derived from that of the better-known *Theory and Games* of von Neumann and Morgenstern (1947). However, because meta-game analysis involves the process of mutual anticipation of competitors' strategy choices, an element which is omitted from classical game theory, and because it does not require the assumption of a simple utility function for payoff, it has greater potential applicability to business situations. Moreover, whereas game theory is primarily a strategy evaluation approach, meta-game analysis is inherently part of the formulation process since it:

(1) Seeks to discover stable scenarios — those scenarios from which all competitors will find no reason to depart, and

(2) Suggests strategies to the user which have been identified by the model as potentially "better" than the one that he is preliminarily considering.

Initial research in a business context by Dutta (1977) has shown that an interactive computer system can be developed to integrate the complex "mutual anticipation" process with Howard's meta-game algorithm and mathematical market models to produce predictions of the outcomes of the complex strategy choices made by two competitors. This system allows strategies to be defined in terms of a number of variables and outcomes are predicted in multi-dimensional form. The meta-game model identifies possible "sanctions" which may be taken by each competitor against a proposed strategy and evaluates alternative strategies which are generated through a combinational algorithm.

The system developed by Dutta is one which addresses the formulation phase in much of its complexity. Yet, it does so in a structured way using the power of the computer. Although unevaluated, except for one corporate demonstration, the approach shows promise as a means of structuring the inherent complexity of the strategy formulation phase.

Strategic Data Bases

Because of the apparent significance of highly personalized factors in the strategy formulation process, one of the key elements of a normative formulation model should be a systematic data collection and structuring procedure which could protect the organization from arbitrary and unwarranted constraints imposed by analysts (Vancil, 1976; King and Cleland, 1977b).

The strategic data base concept has been introduced by King and Cleland (1977a) as a set of concise statements of the most significant strategic items related to various clientele or environments which affect an organization's strategic alternatives. The statements are thus the mechanisms through which the current situation and future opportunities are assessed, and strategies are formulated. Strategic data bases which may be developed include:

— Business and Industry Criteria (what it takes to be successful in this business and industry)
— Organizational Strengths and Weaknesses
— Competitive Profiles
— Environmental Opportunities and Risks
— Management Viewpoints and Values

In order to determine the list of strategic factors, a team of managers is charged with responsibility for identifying the ten or fifteen most important factors affecting the future of the organization in a specified product/market area.[5] Thus, managers are made to separate those things that are very important from those that are not. This process of selecting the most relevant factors and data from the myriad of potential elements and information is logically equivalent to the qualitative modeling of a preliminary strategy.

Strategic data bases can be used in strategy formulation to determine relationships among the strategic factors and the basic elements of an organization's strategy space. From these analyses, initial strategic alternatives can be outlined which highlight the comparative strengths to be emphasized or the weaknesses to be protected. Although this framework has not yet

[5] The development of this limited list of critical strengths and weaknesses is somewhat similar to the "multi-factor assessment" recently attributed to General Electric's managers in their assessment of business unit positioning (Allen, 1976).

been subjected to systematic empirical testing, it has been used in a number of firms with considerable success.

GROWTH-SHARE MATRIX

The growth-share matrix is a framework designed to focus the analyst's attention on market forecasting and comparative analysis in the strategy formulation phase (Henderson, 1974). By plotting businesses on a four-cell matrix according to expected growth rates and relative market dominance, one can classify businesses as "stars," "cash cows," "dogs," or "wildcats." As suggested by Exhibit 3.5, the normative resource allocation model encourages one to transfer cash from "cows" to "wildcats" in the hope that some will develop into "stars," while "dogs" should be liquidated.

As Rutenberg (1976) has noted, most corporate-level strategic decisions concern the growth of "wildcats" and liquidation of "dogs," but the "cows" have the data which permit sophisticated, quantitative analyses for strategy formulation. In addition to providing guidance for one's preliminary strategy formulation, the growth-share matrix can also be used to help predict the behavior of competitors' product/market units. The popularity of this model with consulting firms and authors attests to its intuitive appeal, but there is little available research to support the contention that the model yields improved performance. As a matter of fact, the hypothesized results from the matrix or from its extension in the form of frontier curve analysis are dependent upon efficient strategy implementation at the proper stage of the product life cycle. Some of the limitations of this bivariate model are overcome in the broader format, referred to as the business planning matrix.

PRODUCT LIFE CYCLE

The product life cycle (PLC) concept has held considerable interest for researchers and practitioners in the marketing and strategy areas for many years (A. Patton, 1959; Kotler, 1965; Levitt, 1965). Although the applications of the concept have been more limited than might have

Exhibit 3.5 Growth-Share Matrix

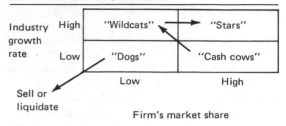

been expected (Polli and Cook, 1969), the linking of additional contingencies to the theory (Hofer, 1975) and more sophisticated pricing concepts (Rink, 1977) promise to yield greater leverage for strategy formulation.

Analyses of product life cycles at the business unit level, however, have provided some normative statements regarding relationships to be considered in strategy formulation. Building on the work of Gutmann (1964), Cunningham (1969), Wasson (1974), and others, Hofer (1975) developed examples of general contingency statements governing factors which should be considered in conjunction with the product life cycle while formulating given strategies. However, in spite of the progress which has been made in understanding the strategic implications of the product life cycle, it is important to remember that there is great difficulty in predicting market segmentation relationships which markedly influence the shape of life cycle curves. Perhaps as a result, recent research by Metzner *et al.* (1975) and Dhalla and Yuspeh (1976) has begun to seriously question the utility of the product life cycle (PLC) concept as a guide to profit-oriented strategic analyses.

EXPERIENCE CURVES

Experience curve effects are receiving significant attention in the strategy formulation process because they often permit quantitative estimates of cost relationships among competitors in an industry segment (Allan and Hammond, 1975; Hedley, 1976). The Boston Consulting Group and others have identified several historical examples which support the proposed relationships between the cumulative volume of output and the declining cost curves. Nonetheless, analysts must be very careful that the combination of factors comprising "experience" be specified so they do not deceive themselves regarding relevant and transferable experience in various businesses (Rutenberg, 1976). Research by Rumelt (1977) in which he identified relatively high profits at the intersection of extensible core skills and market segmentation suggests that further study of transferable experience effects may well be warranted in the manufacturing sector.

Most experience curve applications are still being found in the manufacturing sector, but increasing opportunities for price competition within the professional segment of the service sector, which have resulted from recent Federal Trade Commission rulings, promise to provide strong incentives to engineers, architects, accountants, attorneys, consultants, etc., to try to extend the concept into service dimensions as well.

FUTURE DIRECTIONS

The significant deficiency in product/market level models is their lack of validation. Various ideas and approaches are invented, applied and become faddishly popular without stringent evaluation being applied.

Another major weakness in this set of models is one common to many formal modeling approaches — that the models are not well integrated into the policy making process. Thus, such models often have limited impact, even if their potential value is great. Such problems are being addressed in the "implementation" literature of management science (Schultz and Slevin, 1975). Research, such as that by Rodriguez (1977) and Dutta (1977), in assessing the impact of a model on a system as it is being developed and implemented shows promise of alleviating some of these difficulties.

CORPORATE-LEVEL MODELS

PORTFOLIO THEORY

The conceptual foundation for much of the work with corporate-level analytical models of strategy formulation has been borrowed from the portfolio management literature of finance (Lintner, 1965; Mason and Goudzwaard, 1976). The translation from investment theory of the importance of considering multiple dimensions of various product/market entries has been provided by Carter and Cohen (1972) and Ansoff and Leontiades (1976). These reflect the "mission slice" concept popularized in the Department of Defense in the 1960s. The basic portfolio concept has been elaborated and developed to assist in strategy formulation by focusing attention on the interdependence of such diverse elements as phases of the product life cycle, cash flow patterns and raw material sourcing relationships which are apt to influence the overall strength and performance of multiproduct firms.

In spite of the theoretical appeal of portfolio theory to the process of strategy formulation, there has been little direct testing of the construct in the corporate strategy literature. Some indirect empirical tests by Kitching (1967), Rumelt (1974, 1977), and Jauch *et al.* (1977) strongly suggest that the *process* by which a corporation pursues a balanced portfolio may be as critical as the economic "balance" among the product/market elements of the portfolio in determining the level of performance.

FRONTIER CURVES

Based upon their experiences with the Boston Consulting Group (BCG), Moose and Zakon (1972) developed the concept of frontier curve analysis as a means of linking the growth-share matrix into the financial resource allocation process. By plotting the annual "growth rate in income after-tax (IAT)" against "cash use as a percentage of cash generation," with circles representing the relative dollar size of the various product/market units, they are able to illustrate the direction of investment (implicitly, the general product/market strategy) for the business units under different corporate growth rate goals.

The frontier curve concept seems to be particularly useful for structuring the corporate-level trade-offs between higher overall growth rates and the cash demands of "star" products in capital intensive industry structures. Unfortunately, there is no available empirical evidence of the application of this concept, but it seems like a potentially powerful framework if it is linked with a financially-oriented simulation model. The primary limitations are the same as those which haunt other future-oriented analytical models, i.e., how tight are the distributions of estimates regarding industry sector growth rates, competition, and resulting cash needs?

Business Planning Matrix

Limitations in the quantification of many factors influencing the analysis of product/market interrelationships led firms such as General Electric and McKinsey & Company to a somewhat qualitative analytical framework in matrix form. The business planning matrix is an attempt to explicitly relate the multiple factors comprising a firm's "strengths and weaknesses" to the environmental characteristics which yield business "risks and opportunities." Industry attractiveness includes such factors as size, growth rate, price sensitivity, competitive structure, technology, social governmental interest, labor market, and industry profitability. Business strengths for a given firm encompass factors such as technology, market share, financing ability, human talent, product image, and margins.

Exhibit 3.6 includes some rough "rules of thumb" which might be associated with each cell in the matrix.

A business planning matrix, as employed at General Electric, has apparently provided a stimulus for closer monitoring of industry characteristics comprising "attractiveness." It has encouraged careful tests of internal consistency across functional areas, and it has served to "protect" developing business units which were marked for growth from cutbacks during economic downturns. Elaboration of this model through the specification of functional area postures and management structures/styles for each of the three main strategic alternatives provides a set of contingencies which will help focus strategy formulation activities (Channon, 1976). Although there is little rigorous empirical research available which supports this model, the fact that some of the most sophisticated indus-

Exhibit 3.6 Business Planning Matrix

High	E	I	I
Medium	D	E	I
Low	D	D	E
	Low	Medium	High

(Industry attractiveness — vertical axis; Firm's business strengths — horizontal axis)

Firm's business strengths

I = Invest ("grow")
E = Evaluate ("manage selectively")
D = Disinvest ("harvest")

trial and consulting firms subscribe to the basic outline strongly suggests that it provides a comfortable mix of quantitative and qualitative elements which have been found to be useful in practice.

Directional Policy Matrix

In order to provide more specificity to the strategic alternatives posed by the business planning matrix without abandoning the multivariate aspects of the model, the Royal Dutch Shell Group, working in conjunction with a major consulting firm, developed what has been labeled the directional policy matrix (DPM) (Channon, 1976). This model, as reflected in Exhibit 3.7, requires the positioning of one's product/market unit within a nine-cell matrix along with the firm's best estimates of competitors' positions. The process of articulating the quantitative and qualitative factors for several competitors seems to provide a useful mechanism for ensuring that a maximum number of the significant strategic elements will be included in the formulation of alternative moves.

It seems possible that researchers with an interest in game theory might want to experi-

Exhibit 3.7 Directional Policy Matrix

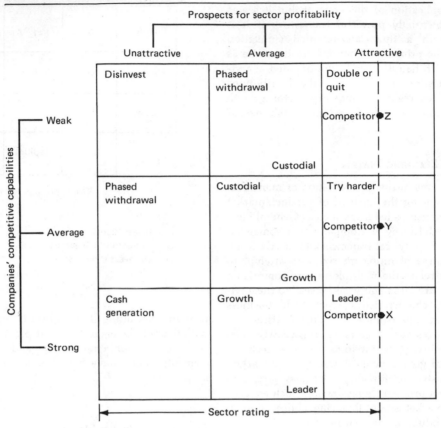

ment with various gaming structures for different levels of competition across alternative cells of the matrix. Concepts from industrial organization theory (Scherer, 1970b) combined with evolving notions of the process of successful market entry (Biggadike, 1976; Rumelt, 1977) may provide a basis for the development of explicit hypotheses regarding at least the normative behavior patterns of present and potential competitors within particular market sectors. As our knowledge is extended of the roles of differing goal structures and performance criteria in strategic choice, further extensions of the directional policy matrices (DPM) may be found to be very useful in narrowing the set of rational alternatives from which the rivals in a given arena might choose.

FUTURE DIRECTIONS

Most of the corporate-level portfolio management models which have been discussed in this section have the objective — either implicitly or explicitly — of constraining the perceived risk associated with the corporation's economic performance (or security prices). Although no research studies have been identified which directly link product/market portfolio changes to changes in corporate beta coefficients, the research of Kudla (1977) represents one step in this direction. His study of the impact of formal planning systems on changes in stock price performance over several years showed very little effect; however, his work did again highlight many of the research problems associated with linking new strategic planning models to changes in resource allocation patterns which will be responded to in a detectable way by the stock market (Mandelker, 1974).

Significant progress has been made in recent years in the refinement of analytically-based corporate-level models for strategy formulation. As these developments are more widely publicized, both theoretical and empirical researchers can be expected to develop and test the models more fully. However, as these are more sophisticated and complex, the implementation process will itself become a more challenging task.

CONCLUSIONS

There is substantial evidence to demonstrate that researchers and practitioners have made real progress in their development of analytical tools for strategy formulation since Miller's (1971) survey only a few years ago. Conceptual efforts have been advanced (Channon, 1977) and hypotheses have been developed (Hofer, 1975; Abell, 1975). The major challenges seem to lie in a number of areas. First, there is a need for improved definition and operationalization of variables in a manner which will permit more efficient communication among researchers. Second, the testing of more complex hypotheses and the development of increasingly sophisticated models increases researchers' demands for comparable data, so that access to useful data becomes a real issue. Fortunately, organizations such as the Strategic Planning Institute have begun to accumulate substantial quantities of data which are being used both for hypothesis generation and testing.

In spite of the progress which has been made in the development and refinement of several analytical models, many research questions remain. Exhibit 3.8 summarizes our judgmental assessment of the opportunity for research progress in strategy formulation with analytical models at various organizational levels. It should be emphasized that these are the combined judgments of the authors, made on a subjective basis after reviewing the literature pertaining to the various models and approaches. The

classifications in Exhibit 3.8 are only intended to be suggestive of possible research directions; they should not, in and of themselves, be used to constrain research or inquiry in any way.

FUTURE RESEARCH OPPORTUNITIES

The urgent need for improved research regarding the analytical aspects of the strategy formulation process has been noted by several authors during the past decade (Ansoff and Brandenburg, 1967; Grinyer, 1972; Anshen and Guth, 1973; Spender, 1976). The purpose here is to identify problems and topical areas which require increased research attention if understanding of the role of analytical models in strategy formulation is to be enhanced in the years ahead. The sequence of the following list is not intended to suggest relative significance or urgency.

Specific Topical Issues

1. Experience curves have proven to be useful analytical tools. How can our understanding of what constitutes "transferable experience" be further refined? How can concepts from the manufacturing sector be operationalized in service industries?

2. If "experience" is important to industry leadership, what factors or circumstances explain the erosion of a leader's position? Industries as diverse as steel, automotive, appliances, chemicals and television have experienced significant shifts in the leader's strength and position. Why?

3. Closely related to the above point is the question of whether the relative usefulness of various analytical models differs among firms of different relative stature or ranking within an industry sector. Although it is widely recognized that most industries contain so many divisions of large diversified firms as to make such analysis very difficult, Rutenberg (1976) suggested that the brewing and aluminum industries might be instances where such research could be fruitfully executed.

4. How can analytical models be linked and tested in ways which will strengthen our pre-

Exhibit 3.8 Future Research Potential of Analytical Models by Level of Strategy Formulation

Organizational perspective / Model or concept	Corporate level	Product/market level
	Potential for progress	
Directional policy matrix	High	Moderate
Business planning matrix	High	Moderate
Frontier curves	Moderate	Low
Portfolio theory	Moderate	Low
Capital investment theory	Low	Low
Comprehensive planning models	Moderate	Low
Corporate simulation and financial planning models	Moderate	Moderate
Mathematical strategy models	Moderate	High
Scenarios	Moderate	High
Policy Delphi	Low	Moderate
Dialectical policy analysis	Low	Moderate
Brainstorming	Low	Moderate
Game theory	Low	Low
Meta-game	Low	Moderate
Strategic data base	Moderate	High
Growth-share matrix	Moderate	Moderate
Product life cycle	Low	Moderate
Experience curves	Moderate	High

dictive skills? The combined use of experience curves, product life cycle analyses, and game theory is one example. Tests of the influence of product life cycles across stages of corporate development is another. Further efforts to link growth-share matrices with portfolio theory or frontier curve analysis should also prove useful for corporate-level strategy research.

5. The role of analytical models in relating corporations' strategies to their beta coefficients (as measured in finance) was proposed as a topic for further study by Rutenberg. If a direct linkage between corporate strategies and changes in beta coefficients could be established, such analysis would seem to be particularly appro-

priate during the strategic evaluation and choice process.

6. How can strategy formulation concepts which have often focused primary attention on internally-oriented variables or competition with known rivals be expanded to include a broader set of influences or constraints? It seems as though the extensions of econometric modeling initiated by Macintosh (1973) deserve further research attention in this regard.

7. If, as some have asserted, increased speed and flexibility are needed in the strategy formulation process, should more research emphasis be placed upon computer-based scanning and simulation models which will permit faster re-

sponse to the simultaneous occurrence of seemingly independent factors in the competitive environment? Admittedly, the strategy formulation process needs better structure in many instances if it is to be amenable to computer support, but the search and evaluation of options under different contingencies can seemingly be aided by such technology (Hammond, 1974; Simmons, 1976; Dutta, 1977).

8. It has been noted by both Hamermesh and Hatten that most of the current analytical models are designed to deal with existing product/market relationships, not with significant changes in corporate direction. Research questions directed toward the selection of appropriate analytical models for significant new product/market positioning seem worthy of further pursuit. At the product/market level, "how can Corporation X convert Product Q from a 'dog' to a 'star?' Is the result economically justifiable?" At the corporate level, the question becomes, "what characteristics should a new product line possess in order to balance our portfolio?"

9. What data, abilities, modes of thinking, etc., serve to stimulate the recognition of creative new relationships among corporate resources and between firms? What roles are played by people versus organizational context (or structure or climate)? Further research designed to study both the origin (invention) of new strategies and the means of successful application (innovation) seem to be warranted.

GENERAL ISSUES AND IMPLICATIONS

10. It has been noted in several places that existing sophisticated models require larger quantities of more accurate data than are now available. Therefore, it is important that empirically-oriented researchers seek to identify, access, and share relevant data bases which may exist in government agencies, trade associations, or research institutes. Without access to such data, researchers will be condemned to endless repetition of prior "experiments" with relatively little accumulation of empirically tested theory.

11. For those analytical models tied to market definitions, there remain some very serious problems of boundary definitions to which our colleagues in marketing research are devoting increasing attention. As strategists seek to gain competitive advantage through innovative acts which modify existing market relationships, they will be well advised to review recent research focusing on market definition problems (Day and Shocker, 1976; Shocker, 1978). Research themes involving experience curves, product life cycles, and diversification process should all be useful in such research.

12. Although the rather limited rigorous testing of many extant analytical models has proven troublesome to some researchers, Bowman suggested that perhaps most of the models will find more use as heuristics than as literally applied models. It thus seems appropriate to suggest that some research be pursued which would seek to address the question of which analytical models noted in this paper will have their best potential application in formal use and which can only be used efficiently as heuristic devices.

13. In economies characterized by significant inflationary and nationalistic tendencies, strategists and researchers studying strategy formulation will have to be increasingly critical of the performance measures which they choose to utilize in their analytical models. Channon and Parker both urged caution in the use of ROI measures, and they emphasized the growing importance of discounted cash flow (DCF) analyses in Britain and Canada. Mintzberg cited Eastern Europe and Canada as examples of areas where nationalistic concerns might dominate economic factors in a strategic sense. The application and testing of many portfolio concepts obviously becomes even more difficult when multiple qualitative performance measures must be satisfied, so efforts to test such models should clearly be executed in contexts where such difficulties are minimized.

14. On a somewhat broader plane, Channon raised an important question with respect to the possible long-term implications of increasingly sophisticated analytical models for the degree of decentralization within large, diversified firms. It is conceivable, for example, that decentralization might continue in the areas of environmental surveillance and strategy implementation, but the analytical and choice phases might be significantly recentralized, as they have been

in the area of international cash management during the recent turbulent times in foreign currency markets.

Although the development and testing of analytical and normative models for strategy formulation is still in a rather embryonic state, a large number of researchers and practitioners have made significant contributions to the field in the last decade. A critical mass of concepts and data now seem to exist, so further research in the field should proceed somewhat more efficiently than in the past. Hopefully, this analysis of portions of the existing literature will both stimulate and assist the development of such research.

Commentary

DEREK F. CHANNON
University of Manchester

INTRODUCTION

The use of analytical techniques in the process of strategic decision making has grown rapidly over the past decade. In their review paper Grant and King have endeavored to catalogue and categorize the main techniques which have emerged. In discussing their paper, I find myself taking issue with their framework in several ways.

First, while Grant and King acknowledge that some of the techniques they discuss may be used for other parts of the strategic management process, their classification system seems to imply that these techniques are used primarily for structuring strategic alternatives, only secondarily for data gathering or evaluation, and not at all for strategy implementation and control. However, it is clear from practice that many of these techniques are in fact being used as integral components of the strategy evaluation and choice processes, while others are even used extensively in strategy implementation and control. Thus, their framework appears restrictive in its classification of several techniques.

Second, although they do not say so explicitly, their paper seems to imply that the models are alternates to one another. In fact, however, most of these models are rarely used on their own, but rather as a component in the overall process of strategy making, and often in conjunction with one another.

Third, their paper tends to treat the analytical models as if they were equal in importance. This is clearly not so, and some have much greater significance than others in their influence on corporate practice.

Finally, this paper does little to illustrate the limitations or actual practical usages of these techniques. It seems important to realize that the bulk of the development of successful techniques has come from practitioners rather than academicians, and the principal measure of any technique must be its usefulness in practice.

This commentary, therefore, endeavors to deal with these points of criticism. First, it tries to show where and how strategic decision makers are making increased use of analytical methods and in particular how these techniques are being used more widely than as a means of structuring alternatives. Second, it endeavors to illustrate how new techniques are being developed to help resolve a number of particular business problems that are pressing. Third, it expands upon the Grant and King discussion of portfolio and business models. Fourth, this commentary also tries to show some of the particular limitations which have still to be resolved in the use of these models. Finally, it points to a number of further research topics which could usefully be explored which might help resolve some of these problems.

THE IMPACT OF ENVIRONMENTAL CHANGE AND CORPORATE EVOLUTION

The increased use of analytical techniques in large measure stems from changes that have taken place in the environment which have tended to increase the relative complexities and uncertainties facing top management. It is useful therefore to briefly examine these environmental changes and the resulting effects they have produced in strategic planning and control techniques since these illustrate the much more widespread usage of analytical techniques in the strategic decision making process than that suggested by Grant and King.

The environment for the business firm from 1950 to the mid 1970's was rich in opportunities. The period following the Second World War was characterized by general stability and only gradual change in global political terms. Inflation was not considered a major problem, increased levels of disposable income were expected, business growth was perceived as desirable for all businesses within a group and investment funds were seen as being readily available from borrowing. As a result of this favorable climate, many firms grew rapidly and in so doing many became diversified both by product line and by geography.

The favorable environment of the period to the mid 1970's has become transformed more recently, primarily as a result of the traumatic shock of the oil crisis and similar environmental discontinuities. These events have brought about major change in the expectations and attitudes of managers. Thus, for now and the future there is a widespread expectation that overall real economic growth is likely to be slow or even negative; that there will be reduced availability of discretionary income; that resources are finite and often scarce, making supply considerations an important strategic issue; that high levels of debt may be positively dangerous; that inflation is a major problem and coupled with variations in foreign exchange rates can have a major impact on corporate profitability; that the past is no longer necessarily an adequate guide for the future; that increasing intervention into business by governments is to be expected; that growth can be bad

and selectivity is therefore important; that earnings per share are not necessarily the primary determinant of share prices which themselves are not the hedge against inflation once expected; and finally that cash flow and liquidity are vital to corporate survival and must be taken into account in addition to any return on investment criteria.

THE CHANGING PATTERN OF STRATEGIC DECISION MAKING SYSTEMS

This brief digression into the changing environment of business helps to show why widespread changes have been made in strategic decision making, planning, and control techniques. The types of changes which are occurring are summarized in Exhibit 3.9. The rapid rate of change in the external environment has led many companies to develop a range of strategic plans with shorter time horizons, at least for quantitative projections, rather than the simple forward extrapolation of existing financial positions. For the longer term, managements are increasingly planning their business under a series of alternative future environmental scenarios. These scenarios may in turn contain built-in trigger points which call into action predetermined contingency plans. Such systems thus go much further than the identifying and structuring alternatives implied by in Grant's and King's framework. They find usage as an integral part of the processes of evaluation and choice and also of implementation and control. Further, such techniques can apply at all levels within the firm, functional, product, and corporate (we would also add geographic to these organizational perspectives).

The development of plans for future strategic action may itself involve many specific techniques. For example, in scenario building some variables are relatively stable, others may be changing slowly and can be assessed with trend curve analysis, while others are more uncertain or even random and require techniques such as Delphi and Cross Impact analysis for their assessment. In the development of the base scenarios at General Electric, for example, most of these techniques are used to produce domino

Exhibit 3.9 Changes in Planning and MICS Systems

Third quarter century 1950–early 1970s	Fourth quarter century late 1970s–2000
1. Annual plans for around 5 years ahead, prepared annually.	Annual plans with shorter horizons, modified quarterly.
2. Single point estimates based on a single set of assumptions.	Multiple scenarios of possible outcomes with built-in decision points.
3. Little evaluation of risk or alternative courses of action.	Extensive sensitivity analysis coupled with contingency plans.
4. New investment planning only, including diversification.	Corporate portfolios analysis with selective investment and divestment.
5. Little evaluation of competitive strategies.	Detailed competitive analysis.
6. Little evaluation of political and social environment.	Development of socio-political reaction models.
7. Little account of inflation and currency fluctuation in capital investments.	Focus on cash flow, exchange risk.
8. Capital investments evaluated pretax.	Tax planning for capital investment and operations.
9. Plans based on monetary measures and monetary volume.	Plans take account of exchange risks and physical unit measures.
10. Periodic reporting, usually monthly decentralized cash management.	Faster feedback, some financial monitoring weekly, some cash daily and control centralized.
11. Simple measures with few variables.	Composite, comprehensive measures, concentration on critical factors like cash and exchange risk.
12. Performance appraisal over time.	Comparison of actual or adjusted standards; focus on activities with built-in action trigger points.
13. Focus on measurement of historic results.	Focus on future actions.
14. Broad, across-the-board controls.	Provide close, detailed controls from the center when possible.
15. Planning assumptions and responses modified annually to environmental changes.	Fast responses to short term environmental changes.
16. Plan for maximum EPS growth.	Plan for balanced cash flow.
17. Planning essentially a manual process.	Widespread adoption of modular "what if" type corporate models.

event chains where the occurrence of one event triggers another in order to construct internally consistent scenarios. Against the backdrop of each scenario, the implications for each organizational perspective can be assessed and contingency plans made for future strategic changes to be introduced according to which scenario turns out to be reality (Wilson, 1974). Such contingency plans themselves are primarily concerned with implementation, for example, what should be done if a particular event occurs such as a 20 per cent reduction in sales volume.

Today strategic plans themselves are reviewed much more frequently. Instead of being updated annually, the widespread adoption of corporate models capable of responding to "what if" questions allows plans to be updated more frequently on a regular basis or in response to unexpected external changes. In a recent survey of 346 U.S. firms, for example, 73 per cent were already using or developing corporate planning models (*Business Week*, April 28, 1975). These tools are not only used for structuring alternatives but also serve as a vital element in the ongoing strategic management and operating control of the organization allowing a much closer central office involvement into operations. At Ralston Purina, for example, a one per cent change in the price of a prime commodity triggers a change in the company's cost models and the whole corporate plan may change accordingly (*Business Week*, April 28, 1975).

The impact of computer technology which links the strategic and operational control aspects of a business on a global scale is well illustrated by the systems developed by a number of the leading U.S. commercial banks which have established or are building on line computer based networks capable of assessing the bank's global position by currency type, by country, by industry, by company and the like. With this type of information immediately available the ability of central management to rapidly intervene in a policy sense in remote operations is clearly apparent. The growing multinational interests of large manufacturing corporations are resulting in the increased use of such systems outside the banking system as well, and in a strategic sense leads to an increasing central involvement in short-run operating decisions,

since the management of the international treasury function can be of a vital significance in the determination of corporate profitability. This involvement tends to reduce the autonomy of local operating units and distorts the validity of simple performance measures such as return on investment for individual business units — a problem that can significantly affect the usefulness of certain of the portfolio planning techniques. There are also other organizational consequences from the increased use of such global financial optimization systems in that much closer linkages need to be forged between strategic planning and business unit managers and financial and taxation planners.

It is certainly true that analytical techniques are being increasingly used in structuring and ranking strategic alternatives as Grant and King acknowledge. Thus, traditionally capital investment planning centered upon economic evaluations using techniques such as discounted cash flow to measure pretax rates of return. Usually there was little evaluation of risk or alternatives while each capital request was considered on its merits and irrespective of any corporate view on the business unit the investment formed part of. Today while discounted cash flow techniques are still used, payback has returned as an important additional criterion to allow for high inflation and interest rates. Similarly, cash flow and exchange exposure considerations are taken into account together with factors such as international tax, financial resources and remittance considerations. For major projects a full risk sensitivity appraisal is also usually conducted.

In addition to the use of financial techniques for appraising resource allocation, however, there is an increasing need today to take into account much less quantifiable socio-political variables which are taking on increasing strategic importance. A number of techniques are emerging which have been used for predicting socio-political reactions and investment climates for both the long term and more short term. These extend from relatively simple check lists to complex decision theory based systems coupled with sensitivity analysis (Channon and Jalland, 1978). In practice, the more complex techniques have so far not found widespread acceptance, but managers are being forced to pay increasing attention to the impact of societal variables, and are developing new tools to cope with them. For example, the General Electric Company has endeavored to identify future trends in social pressures which have been translated into their expected effect on individual businesses and the corporation as a whole together with the development of plans to defuse any such negative effects (Wilson, 1974).

More directly appropriate for individual investment analysis is the social response matrix developed by a major multinational oil company and illustrated in Exhibit 3.10. This matrix has two dimensions, the first listing issues of concern to the company and interested parties or constituents and the second the constituencies seen as potentially important influences on the success of a particular project or plan. The concerns are then assessed from the point of view of each constituency and their expected reaction ranked as one of three categories, namely supportive, neutral but interested, or hostile. By highlighting possible responses in this way, it is possible to modify project proposals to reduce possible hostile reactions and even to eliminate proposals if important hostility appears intransigent (Smith, 1977).

THE USE OF CORPORATE PORTFOLIO MODELS

Perhaps, the most significant change in resource allocation techniques, however, concerns the widespread adoption of corporate portfolio planning techniques, which means that resources are increasingly being allocated according to a corporate strategic perspective of each business within the total portfolio. Grant and King have briefly reviewed the main portfolio models presently available, but do perhaps not give as much weight to these as they might. These models are the first major advances in systematically identifying the main underlying, strategic characteristics of specific individual businesses, and deserve to be developed in greater detail.

The most simplistic of the models is the bivariate growth share model developed by Boston Consulting Group (BCG). The model is based on the underlying concept of the experience curve which assumes that under normal circumstances each time the accumulated experience of manufacturing a particular product doubles, the total per unit cost tends to decline by a characteristic percentage when measured in real terms. From the experience curve effect, BCG concludes that, irrespective of relative changes in the economic environment, the competitor with the highest market share or relative competitive dominance should be able to develop the lowest cost position within an industry and hence the highest and most stable profits.

Using the experience curve concept, therefore, the most successful competitive strategy is to achieve and hold a dominant market position either through pricing tactics or by segmenting the market into discrete sectors which can be dominated and defended. If market dominance cannot be obtained, then it is argued that an orderly withdrawal may represent the optimal strategy.

For most businesses it is not possible for any one firm to obtain full market dominance on a global scale. It is often possible, however, to subdivide a market into a series of defendable strategic market segments in which a company can obtain a sustainable economic advantage if it concentrates on servicing the segment needs. Such segments may be identified from a careful analysis of the underlying cost structure for any business on the expectation that the experience effects will normally be different for different cost areas. Coupled with a similar analysis of competitive positions, BCG claims it is usually possible to identify the most appropriate dimensions for segmentation and to estimate the value of "barriers" between such segments. These barriers represent the level of investment required to go from one segment to another.

Once strategic market segments have been identified, they should be dominated to gain the advantage of the experience curve effect. This dominance should be developed during the growth phase of the product life cycle since at this time increased market share can be obtained by gaining a disproportionate share of market growth rather than attempting what BCG considers to be the much more expensive

Exhibit 3.10 Societal Response Profile Assessment Matrix

Concerns	Economic concerns		Adequate compensation	Reliability of SBM	Societal concerns			Involvement		
Constituents	Local employment opportunities & contribution to revenue	Adverse effect on tourism			Pipeline safety (submarine and land)	Visual disamenity & noises, smells	Fear for further industrial development	Subsequent plan alterations	Information disclosure	Project legitimacy

Stakeholders

- Amlwch Community Council
- Anglesey County Council
- Anglesey Residents Association
- Country Landowners Association
- Tourists Association
- Farmers Union of Wales

Closely Involved Parties

- Dept. of Trade & Industry
- The National Farmers' Union
- Liverpool Pilotage Authority
- Council for Preservation of Rural Wales
- Welsh Nationalists
- Mass Media

Legend:

☐ = Positive, supportive   ▨ = Concerned, but Neutral   ▨ (dotted) = Negative   ⊠ = Not concerned route of seizing share from competitors in mature markets. Once dominance has been achieved, however, prices should be reduced in line with experience to deter competitors from adding capacity and gaining share thereby nullifying the effect of a dominant market position. The securing and holding of a dominant position is then expected to ultimately yield the best profits. During the growth phase of the life cycle, however, the cash flow effect of a dominant market position is unlikely to be largely positive since increased investment will be needed constantly in order to maintain dominance and it is only at the mature stage of the life cycle that a dominant position pays off in terms of a large positive cash flow which can be redeployed into development businesses.

It is the interplay between these two variables of market growth rate and market share that gives rise to the concept that any successful corporation needs a balanced portfolio of products or businesses. The BCG mode of analysis thus focuses first upon the individual business unit and then upon the development of a corporate portfolio in which each of the corporation's businesses can be mapped and which can be used as a guide to the deployment of overall resources to ensure strategic balance.

Models such as the Shell Directional Policy Matrix allow for the introduction of greater complexity than the bivariate BCG model by the use of weighted multivariate analysis to strategically position a business on a three by three matrix of competitive capability versus industry attractiveness. In so doing, the approach avoids the simplifications made by the BCG approach, but sacrifices some rigor in terms of quantification. The Shell technique has also been usefully extended to the development of a series of second order transition matrices which permit a reconciliation between business and more qualitative variables such as socio-political objectives. Such a matrix is shown in Exhibit 3.11 which illustrates business attractiveness on one axis and corporate geographic priorities on the other. The investment possibilities for each business are indicated by Xs. Using such a matrix, it is possible to produce a relatively optimal allocation of investments so as to fund those businesses which are most attractive while at the same time fulfilling geopolitical objectives.

The PIMS program offers perhaps the most important single strategic decision making tool developed to date. Like the BCG approach, PIMS offers the opportunity for real quantification but over the full spectrum of strategic variables such as that used in the directional policy matrix system. In addition, however, PIMS is not one but a series of models. Among these are facilities which: (1) permit the underlying strategic impacts of various variables on both the ROI and cash flow for each business to be evaluated, (2) provide a forward prediction for the impact of different strategic changes on the individual business, and (3) permit the development of overall forward optimization programs across the entire corporate portfolio.

A number of the general findings which have been identified from analysis of the PIMS data base of over 1500 businesses have been published (Schoeffler et al., 1974, 1977; Buzzell et al., 1975). While these have supported the importance of market share as a determinant of profitability and of market share and growth rate as determinants of cash flow, the main variables used in the BCG model, they have also pointed out the importance of other variables, most notably investment intensity, which are ignored in the BCG analysis. Further PIMS points to the possibility of alternative com-

Exhibit 3.11 Product/Geography Second Order Directional Policy Matrix

Corporate geographic priority (Low → High)	Business attractiveness Low → High					
	Business 1	Business 2	Business 3	Business 4	Business 5	Business 6
Increase employment in UK		X			X	
Absorb surplus cruzeiro funds			X			X
Increase operations in Japan				X		X
Utilize excess German feedstock		X	X			
Increase dollar cash flow	X				X	
Increase investment in France (political)				X	X	X

Exhibit 3.12 PIMS Indicated Cross Impact Relationship Effects of Market Share and Investment Intensity on ROI

Impact of High	Given market share		Impact of high	Given investment intensity	
	Low	High		Low	High
Product quality	Vital	Helpful	Marketing expense level	Indifferent	Avoid high
Purchase frequency	High best	Med/low best	R&D effort	Favorable	Favorable
Manufacturing intensity	Avoid desparately	Avoid strongly	Capacity utilization	Favorable	Vital
Relative price	Average	High	Market share	Favorable	Vital
			Sales per employee	Favorable	Vital

binations of variables which could provide viable attractive strategies which might be in direct contradiction to a conclusion reached by the BCG approach. Thus, for example, it is conceivable that a low market share business in a low growth market could be extremely attractive in cash flow terms if it was also low in capital intensity, while such a "dog" business in BCG terms could well be a candidate for divestment. A number of these main cross impact relationship effects identified from the PIMS data base for return on investment are shown in Exhibit 3.12, while the key determinants of cash flow and the direction in which they affect it are shown in Exhibit 3.13.

PRACTICAL PROBLEMS WITH PORTFOLIO PLANNING MODELS [1]

There is no doubt that for the central management of large diversified corporations, strategic portfolio planning provides a useful tool for decision making both at the business unit and the corporate level. In use, however, a number of problems have emerged some of which can be fairly readily overcome, but others are more difficult to overcome. These problems apply to different degrees to the various models, but must always be borne in mind by managers.

[1] See Channon (1976) for further discussion of this topic.

Exhibit 3.13 Effect of Increases in Major Determinants of Business Cash Flow

Factor	Effect on cash flow
Percentage point change investment/sales	(−)
Real market growth, short run	(−)
Market share growth rate	(−)
Investment/sales	(−)
Selling price growth rate	(−)
Market share	(+)
Vertical integration	(+)
New product sales (% of total sales)	(−)
Marketing expense/sales	(−)
Marketing expense growth rate	(−)

Exhibit 3.14 Importance of Market Segment Identification for Business Analysis

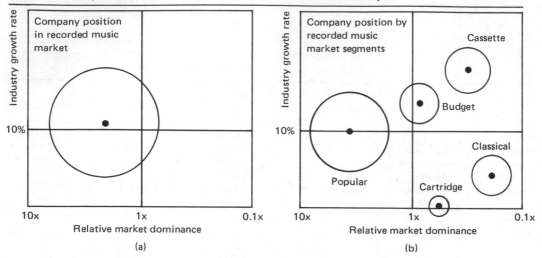

The Problem of Market Definition

The first and one of the most serious problems which potentially affects all the techniques is that of market definition, which if incorrectly done, makes the measurement of market share and/or market growth rate unreliable. It is difficult to determine the precise boundaries of any market and mistakes can and do often occur. This is a problem which is especially important for multinational corporations where the identification of geographic market boundaries can be particularly difficult.

Similarly there is often a serious problem of accurate market segmentation. This is illustrated in Exhibit 3.14, which shows the growth/share matrix position of a particular company in the recorded music market. In Exhibit 3.14a, the company's position appears to be that of a major distributor with an overall dominant position in a high growth market. In Exhibit 3.14b, the market has been segmented into a series of smaller units and it can be seen that the company's position varies widely into terms of market share in the individual segments which themselves have significantly different growth rates. Further, apart from problems of accurately identifying market segments, there is also

that of distinguishing between product differentiation and segmentation.

The Problem of Inflation

In recent years, high rates of inflation have had a serious effect on the cash flow and profit characteristics of any business. The effect of inflation is felt in several ways. First, under inflationary conditions, price and cost changes can affect different businesses in different ways. One general effect of high inflation is that it tends to make even low growth businesses into apparent high growth operations. As a result, the working capital requirements of even low real growth businesses tend to escalate rapidly and cash generators can become cash users. The effect of inflation is not uniform, however, and a significant change in the structure of the corporate portfolio can take place under such conditions.

In addition, high inflation can have a different effect on businesses with varying levels of capital intensity. Generally speaking, under high inflation many capital intensive businesses move into a loss position due to the escalating cost of replacing capital assets and the like, while firms engaged in low capital intensity businesses such as retailing are largely unaffected.

THE PROBLEMS OF ECONOMIC GROWTH

While the differences between real and inflationary growth rates represents a problem, a further difficulty can occur in identifying the actual underlying growth rate of a business. Many businesses, for example, are cyclical and unless such a cycle is clearly understood and a long enough time span used in assessing growth rate, all the systems can give potentially misleading positioning. Even with non-cyclical businesses, it is extremely difficult to identify growth rates accurately. There are relatively few businesses where a sufficiently long demand history exists to provide a satisfactory basis for forecasting. As a result, attempts to fit trend curves can give similar correlation coefficients for significantly differing functions, which when used to forecast ahead, yield results which can show widespread variations. Moreover, there is still no guarantee that historic trends will continue into the future. In practice, therefore, it is not unusual for external consultants to incorrectly identify the real growth position of specialized cyclical businesses. This problem is especially important for the BCG system where growth rate is a primary variable in deciding future policies toward a particular business. The difficulty of predicting future growth also affects the other models, but in the case of PIMS a built-in sensitivity feature permits users to assess how important accuracy in growth rate projections is for deciding upon optimal strategy.

THE PROBLEMS OF FOREIGN EXCHANGE VARIATION

One problem that has become increasingly important with the growth of multinational operations has been that of exchange risk exposure. The effect of foreign exchange rate variation can totally transform the experience curve effect when translated into another currency. Thus, for example, the slope of experience curves measured in yen might well be reversed when the yen values were translated into a weaker currency such as sterling at prevailing rates of exchange over the time of the development of accumulative experience. For markets where global relative cost positions are important, therefore, experience curves need to be modified to account for exchange rate variation in order to assess relative cost advantage.

Foreign exchange rates also have a similar effect to inflation on relative capital intensities. Further, the performance of individual businesses is often distorted by cross border product movements which result in tax planning and central treasury intervention to maximize post tax profitability and minimize foreign exchange exposure.

THE PROBLEMS OF ORGANIZATION AND MOTIVATION

Although significant technical problems do occur in practice with portfolio planning, the most serious area of difficulty emerges when the implementation of a portfolio strategy is attempted. Such problems surface in a number of ways. First, it is rare that the division of a company into strategic business units will conform to its existing formal organization structure. Thus it is often possible to find elements of an SBU located in two or more product or geographic divisions of a multimarket firm. Moreover, there is a tendency for top management to endeavor to implement strategy in conjunction with the existing formal structure rather than reorganizing around the dimensions of the business units. As a result dysfunctional behavior can and often does occur.

A second problem of implementation occurs when companies fail to have adequate cash control systems to ensure cash resources are collected from those businesses to be harvested so they may be redeployed to other businesses which are cash users. Successful redeployment of cash resources usually requires the presence of such features as central bank accounts, global or regional cash pools, and capital charge systems on managed assets.

Exhibit 3.15 **Alternative Organization Structures and Management Styles for Different Portfolio Positions**

Stategy	Invest/Grow	Selectivity/Earnings	Harvest/Divest
Objective	Growth	Earnings	Cash flow
Strategy characteristics	– Intensive pursuit of market share – Earnings generation subordinate to building dominant position – Focus predominantly on long term results and payout – Emphasis on technical innovation and market development	– Intensive pursuit of maximum earnings – Focus balanced between long and short term – Emphasis on complex analysis and clear plans – Emphasis on increased productivity, cost improvement, strategic pricing	– Intensive pursuit of maximum positive cash flow – Sell market share to maximize profitability – Intensive pruning of less profitable products/segments – Emphasis only on short term
Organization characteristics	– Must enable future growth – Product or venture operations – Separate "futures" from operations – Build technical competence – Strong international focus – Highly competent staff functions	– Must provide flexibility at moderate cost – Matrix organization (balance cost & people development) – Centralized product planning – Overseas sourcing operations – Pooled sales & distribution utilization – Centralized finance	– Must be low cost/no frills – Functional structure (lowest cost) – Collapse product departments into functionally organized division – Reduce/eliminate R&D labs and forward engineering – Maximum pooling where cost effective – Combine manufacturing/engineering operations
Management characteristics	– Emphasis on entrepreneurs – Young, ambitious, aggressive – Strong development & growth potential – High risk tolerance – Highly competitive by nature	– Emphasis on "solid businessman" – Tolerates risk, but doesn't seek it – Comfortable with variety and flexibility – Careful, but not conservative – Trades off short term, long term risk/reward	– Emphasis on "hard nosed" operators – Seasoned and experienced – Seeks high efficiency – Low change tolerance – Wants instant results, doesn't look ahead

A third problem occurs when a business is identified as a cash generator or placed in the harvest/divest category. For most organizations there is a fairly common value system among managers that growth and progress is normal to all businesses. Where a business is therefore identified as one to be run down for cash generation, this is alien to accepted management values. Moreover, the harvest position is soon recognized by the workforce who tend to become demotivated and resistant to management policies. Industrial relations problems often accumulate in a bid to maintain jobs and pressure mounts for reinvestment in the cash generating business which may be exactly the reverse of intended strategy. One mechanism which has been used in an attempt to overcome the problem of management motivation is to employ management teams with varying characteristics to operate different types of business as shown in Exhibit 3.15.

QUESTIONS FOR FUTURE RESEARCH

There are many areas where further research could be usefully conducted to improve the usefulness of analytical models. Close examination of the different corporate portfolio approaches, for example, reveals some interesting inconsistencies which merit further research. Thus, the BCG model relies for its conceptual base upon the experience curve which is an empirical device found to operate principally in relatively high capital intensity manufacturing industries. How well then does the BCG principle hold up under varying conditions of capital intensity or when applied to service based businesses where there is often not only no manufacturing process, and also no physical product and hence no inventory?

Second, all the portfolio models feature industry growth rate as an important positive determinant of business attractiveness, and conclude that new investments should be made primarily into high growth markets. Is this realistic, however, since such industries may actually be highly competitive and cash absorbing by comparison with low capital intensity mature industries? Some research, therefore, to assess the tradeoff between industry growth and variables such as capital intensity, attractiveness under conditions of high inflation or low exchange risk and the like might well be useful.

Third, despite the theory that relative dominance should make it difficult if not impossible to attack an entrenched market share position in mature markets there are many examples of where this has been successfully accomplished even by firms with very limited financial resources. Why should this be, and what, if anything, do such successful giant killers have in common in their approach?

Fourth, despite the substantial relative revaluation of currencies such as the mark or the yen and the loss of some relative advantage in experience curve effect, the main export industries of these countries do not seem to have been noticeably impeded. Some research which attempts to establish why this should be would also be useful in understanding further the value of the experience curve effect.

Finally, some work seems clearly necessary to try and gain a better understanding of the behavioral and motivational problems associated with the introduction of a portfolio planning system in an attempt to isolate successful methods of introducing possibly radical changes, especially in businesses which are recommended for harvesting or divestment.

Environmental Analysis and Forecasting [1]

JAMES M. UTTERBACK
Massachusetts Institute of Technology

The focus of this paper is on the firm's environment, the economic, technological, social, political, and institutional context within which the firm operates, and on the ways in which firms have attempted to analyze their environments as an input to the process of accommodation between the firm and change in the world outside. To explore the topic fully, several questions are addressed in turn.

— What problems are created for the firm by changes in its environment?

— What can be known about changes in the environment, and how can such knowledge about change be acquired as an aid in strategy formulation and planning?

— What methods have been used to forecast environmental changes?

— Are particular methods of analysis and forecasting better suited for some types of environments than others?

— How should the firm integrate environmental assessments into its strategic planning process?

— What topics are suggested for further research in this area?

A large amount of work has been done in the development and use of forecasts of specific economic and market variables. A growing body of work has emerged in attempts to forecast technological change. Much less research has appeared in the literature reviewed related to forecasting social, political, and institutional changes which affect the firm. Often attempts to an-

ticipate change in these areas are based on generalizations of methods tried in the economic, market or technological contexts. Economic and market forecasting are not dealt with extensively, because work in these dimensions is so widely accepted and known (Aguilar, 1967; Wheelwright and Makridakis, 1977). Rather, this paper stresses work on dimensions of the environment which are usually treated in more qualitative terms (Dunckel, Reed, and Wilson, 1970). No attempt is made to be encyclopedic or to discuss specific forecasts of the business environment, as this has been done well by others (Martino, 1972; Morris, 1970; Robinson, 1974; also see Daniells, 1970; and Padbury and Wilkins, 1972, for bibliographies).

WHAT PROBLEMS ARE CREATED FOR THE FIRM BY CHANGES IN ITS ENVIRONMENT?

Are there ever greater risks and constraints associated with environmental change as some claim, or is the pace of change increasing at an ever increasing rate as claimed by others? Could both be true, and if so, with what consequences?

Perhaps the resolution of this dilemma lies in one's point of view. Change may be more difficult for any one organization. But if there are many more potential *sources* of change than in the past, then the pace of change and its attendant uncertainty could indeed be increasing. Worse, the environment would essentially be a turbulent field with changing *sets* of variables to contend with and changing relationships among them (Emery and Trist, 1965). Margaret Mead (1976) in a cogent analysis of the problems that such situations pose concluded that they are inherently unstable, and that small changes can lead to large effects. Lorange (1977) argued that such changes in the structure of an organization's environment are the most difficult to cope

[1] Many of the ideas expressed in this paper were developed in earlier field work with Elmer Burack. I am deeply indebted to him not only for contributions to the substance of this work, but also for his encouragement and advice in our earlier research. The sections on methods, on use of methods in different environments, and on integration of forecasting in the firm are an expanded version of parts of our earlier work (Utterback and Burack, 1975).

with, because they require more fundamental and permanent organizational responses.

In such a case, peripheral information on changes in their nascent stages may be crucial to creative solutions (Utterback, 1971). The fact that change often takes a number of years to implement or to have significant effects is an advantage if one is attempting to anticipate change (Utterback and Brown, 1972), but a difficulty if one is participating in the change process. A late start reduces one's chances of getting into the game in a timely way, and the length of time and durability of the commitment required to introduce a change increases one's exposure to the introduction of alternatives by competitors. Changes that can revolutionize a firm's business and strategy will tend to come from unexpected directions and to be viewed as disruptive. These include functional competition from new technologies often introduced by new firms or existing businesses entering a new market. Functional competitors may offer qualitatively higher product performance which dominates the older technology in some or all segments of the market as well (Utterback and Abernathy, 1975; Cooper and Schendel, 1976). Greater competition across national boundaries also expands the number of potential sources of disruptive change. Introduction of process equipment which produces standard products for much lower costs may promote entry of new competitors as well as changing the existing structure of competitive relationships. Unexpected changes in prices of energy and materials may alter the attractiveness of particular products, processes, plant locations and investments. And increasing regulation of product and process technologies as well as firms' other activities also creates the need to search in new directions for solutions (Allen *et al.*, forthcoming).

The firm must accommodate itself to changes in its environment which are often beyond its control or influence. To do so may involve changes in products, policies, organization structure and procedures. This requires a degree of flexibility and time for effective responses and consequently a need to anticipate important environmental changes. Our focus will be primarily on the ways in which firms gather and analyze information about the environment; accommodation to change will be treated only in the sense that firms' efforts to anticipate change are in themselves a response to environmental uncertainty.

WHAT CAN BE KNOWN ABOUT CHANGES IN THE ENVIRONMENT, AND HOW CAN SUCH KNOWLEDGE ABOUT CHANGE AS AN AID IN STRATEGY FORMULATION AND PLANNING BE ACQUIRED?

Remarkably, our ability to assess single future trends and changes is quite accurate and comprehensive. Methods for generating forecasts are growing rapidly in number, and projections of specific trends and events are growing even more rapidly. The expansion of the futures field has been characterized as a new discipline striving for professional recognition on the one hand and as a social movement, attracting a degree of involvement similar to that of the civil rights movement, ecology, or consumerism on the other (McHale and McHale, 1976).

Despite the burgeoning popularity and growth of environmental analysis and forecasting and its enthusiastic reception by policy makers in business and government, both in the United States and abroad, its usefulness is severely constrained in practice. The reason is that predictions of the *effects* of trends and events are much more difficult than foreseeing the primary changes themselves (Gilfillan, 1937; Farmer, 1973; Wise, 1976). This is even more problematic in an organizational context of limited resources and established interests and programs, where potential changes and effects must be linked to corporate, agency, or institutional strategy and plans. And there are also some general problems noted below with the use of popular methods for environmental analysis and forecasting.

For instance, forecasts of future trends and potentials are seldom value free. Indeed, forecasts are often meant to be self-fulfilling, to marshal resources and efforts toward some goal, or self-defeating, to create action to avoid some negative consequences of continuing the status quo. In some cases, it is appropriate to look for a converging set of forces or trends, but in others conflict over alternative assumptions and their consequences may be crucial. Often the underlying philosophy of a method of analysis is unrecognized, and it is generalized to too great an extent or is misapplied (Mitroff and Turoff, 1973). But futures research has tended to ignore the intellectual roots of systematic conjecture, concentrating instead on specific techniques and specific forecasts. Application of the principles of value free science to forecasting may at best be a self-deception and at worst a limitation of the range of human possibility (Encel, Marstrand, and Page, 1976).

Another problem arises in the fact that attempts to forecast often involve rich and diverse collection of data with little attempt made to relate them in a formal way, or involve elaborate manipulation of narrow and subjectively derived data (Roberts, 1969). There is also a tendency to be sophisticated about model building without being equally sophisticated about data gathering or the use of results. This can be particularly limiting since peripheral information and data from diverse sources are often crucial to the validity of a forecast. Development of measurements and means for gathering data may make the most significant contribution to futures research according to Miles (1976).

In Section 5, Lorange points out the danger that arises when a firm behaves as though it can dominate its environment and completely predict outside developments. The consequence is an attempt to "plan" uncertainty away, reducing the firm's sensitivity to unexpected developments and its flexibility to deal with them. A related problem is that the firm may selectively perceive much of the environmental information available to it. But as noted above, environmental change often comes from unexpected directions, and the "peripheral" information which is discarded may be the very information which is most crucial. Klein (1973) has addressed this problem by devising a prescriptive method for directing management's attention to a broader range of interactions with the environment as they are related to a particular firm's products and resources.

With these concerns in mind, the basic techniques which are widely used for environmental

analysis and forecasting will be summarized briefly. Then it will be argued that different approaches for analysis and forecasting will be better suited to different environments. The integration and use of forecasts in corporate strategic planning, and the effectiveness with which information is obtained for analysis are key concerns, and research in these areas will then be treated briefly.

WHAT METHODS HAVE BEEN USED TO FORECAST ENVIRONMENTAL CHANGES?

A number of methods and approaches have been developed in attempts to anticipate the nature and direction of change and its impact on the firm. These include various means for quantification of expert opinion, constrained extrapolation of past trends, scanning or monitoring the environment, and simulation of the interaction of changes in environmental variables and constraints. These have been described and explained in several comprehensive texts. Martino (1972), for one, provides an excellent broad coverage of techniques. A burgeoning literature has developed covering refinements, critiques, tests and applications of many different methods. Only a brief summary of this work will be possible here.

Quantification of expert opinion is usually based on questions about either the estimated probability of the occurrence of a given event before some time or conversely about the estimated time by which the expert thinks the event may have occurred with a given (usually 0.50) probability. Fusfeld and Foster (1971) review the elements of the "Delphi" technique in which such questions are asked of an anonymous panel of experts. Each member of the panel is given several opportunities to revise his estimate after being given feedback on the distribution of the panel's estimates and individuals' reasons for extreme positions. Versions using a computer to increase interaction and feedback among the panelists have been developed (North and Pyke, 1969), and research has been done on the reliability (Dalkey and Rourke, 1971) and validity (Ament, 1970) of this concept. Recent research and applications (Delbecq *et al.*, 1975) have focused on the interpersonal dynamics of the Delphi approach and on ways to improve the process through discussion with other members of the panel while still raising and resolving conflicting points of view. Delphi has been widely used to highlight social (Gordon *et al.*, 1971), demographic (George, 1971), and political (Morris, 1970) shifts which may affect the firms, though reading these studies leaves the strong impression that the panels reflect business' views of the changing environment rather than more diverse views. The use of the Delphi technique, which originated at RAND, for policy and strategy analysis has been sharply criticized in a recent extensive study from the same source (Sackman, 1975), and the popularity of this approach has resulted in many poorly designed and inappropriate studies.

Extrapolation of trends in technological parameters and capabilities was one of the earliest methods attempted to forecast technological change. Various equations based on both theoretical and empirical results have been used to derive projections from available data. A recent example is provided by efforts to determine the future course of substitution of one product for another based on the current proportion and rate of substitution (Mansfield, 1961; Lenz and Lanford, 1972). Terleckyj (1975) has recently made near term estimates of possibilities for improvements in the quality of life in the United States, while Robinson (1974) and others have conducted a broader, international extrapolation of trends in the business environment over the coming decade. Consistent projection of logically related trends is an important consideration in the use of extrapolation and the focus of several recent publications (MacNulty, 1977).

Monitoring or scanning the environment is closely related to the ideas of statistical decision theory in that the prior probabilities assigned to a set of competing hypotheses are revised as more tangible early evidence of changes becomes available. The idea of monitoring different dimensions of the environment and its relationship to the process of innovation has been stated by Bright (1970). Monitoring involves searching the environment for signals that may be the forerunners of significant change, identifying the possible consequences assuming that the indications persist, and choosing the events

and decisions that should be observed and followed in order to verify the speed and timing of the anticipated change. This method is predicated on the idea that change will be visible in increasingly tangible forms over a period of time before it assumes economic, social or strategic importance (Utterback and Brown, 1972). An example of General Electric's initial attempts to monitor its environment is given by Dunckel, Reed, and Wilson (1970), and other examples are cited by Utterback and Burack (1975). One of the most interesting monitoring applications is the Trend Analysis Program of the Institute of Life Insurance (various dates). Members of the Institute monitor different areas of change and contribute to a series of occasional reports on trends which might affect the industry, but which are of much more general interest as well.

Simulation of the interactions of environmental variables and constraints has been attempted at the level of the firm and its products (Blackman, 1971) for housing choices in an urban area (Birch, 1970), at the level of a region and its resources and industries (Watt, 1969), and on a global basis for particular resources and pollutants (Meadows *et al.*, 1973). The use of simulation for forecasting to date has been largely an exploratory effort due to measurement problems and a lack of understanding of underlying relationships. The simplification of known relationships in an operational model structure also requires careful attention (McLean and Shepard, 1976), as does the level of aggregation at which relationships are modeled (Pestel and Mesarovic, 1974). An application of great interest is Forrester's (1976) attempt to model the dynamics of the United States economy. With relationships and data being reasonably well known and available, he has shown that the economy may be less responsive to monetary and fiscal policies than currently assumed, with the underlying structure of the system of production having a greater long term influence on its dynamics than generally expected.

While each of the basic approaches to anticipating change has been treated separately, they are logically related in the order presented. For example, expert opinion has been used to establish "confidence" intervals for projected trends. Both expert opinion and trend extrapolation provide useful data for establishing hypotheses in monitoring, while developing a simulation model requires each of the preceding types of inputs to establish relationships, initial conditions, reasonable ranges for the variables, and so forth.

Two fascinating papers have recently examined how well past forecasts passed the test of time. Most of the forecasts examined were based essentially on expert opinion, but often were quite detailed, comprehensive, and sophisticated in their approach. Wise (1976) constructed a sample of more than 1500 specific predictions made in 18 specified areas of technology from 1890 to 1940, and predictions of the effects, economic, social or political to be expected from changes in these fields. Forty percent of these predictions were either fulfilled or in progress while one third (33 percent) have been refuted. Experts had a better record of prediction, but not significantly so, and batting averages appeared to improve with increases in the experts' age and experience. No individuals were remarkably better than average, but a number had success rates of better than half. Predictions of continuation of the status quo were no more accurate than predictions of change. Most interesting from our point of view is Wise's finding that predictions of the effects of the changes which were accurately foreseen were woefully inadequate. This point is strongly emphasized in a study by Farmer (1973), who examined forecasts published in *Fortune* from 1933 to 1950. He found that authors were not only able to hit the mark more often than they missed, but to predict in considerable detail. Gilfillan (1937) in a seminal study also reports a better than average success rate for forecasts of major technical change. Forecasts of general trends, structural change and performance of the economy reviewed by Farmer were also quite accurate. However, he reports that changes in key political and legal constraints were most difficult to anticipate and also strongly affected accuracy in other areas. While the economic trends were clear, their impacts on individual choices were not. Nor were the impacts of technological change foreseen. Farmer concludes that even the most radical of *Fortune's* forecasts were too conservative when compared with the actual trends which have occurred.

The most serious flaw evident in past and current forecasts is their inconsistency and an inability to fathom the impact of several changes taken together. Mitroff and Turoff (1973) noted that many of the techniques of forecasting attempt essentially to simplify and highlight significant interactions. When a well understood structure exists with few interactions, then a network or tree structure is often used. But when interactions are more complex and less well known, matrix methods such as cross impact or morphological analysis may be used. Most of these techniques are unsatisfactory on grounds both of substance and method. This brings us back full circle to the need to understand underlying relationships before the meaning of clearly envisioned changes can be imagined, especially changes in social and political relationships.

ARE PARTICULAR METHODS OF ANALYSIS AND FORECASTING BETTER SUITED FOR SOME TYPES OF ENVIRONMENTS THAN OTHERS?

Based on the above analysis, one can hypothesize that the emergence of formal efforts to forecast change will depend on the degree of uncertainty and complexity of the firm's environment and the differing salience of economic, technological, social and political factors in the firm's strategy for competition and growth. The effectiveness of a firm's forecasting effort in terms of integration of its outputs into the planning process is expected to be mainly related to internal factors such as formal and informal communication, and the organization's structure and support given to the forecasting and planning functions. One could further hypothesize that those firms with formal forecasting efforts will experience greater sales growth and profitability than comparable firms that carry on these activities on an informal or ad hoc basis.

Gerstenfeld (1971) reported results from 162 responding firms that are compatible with these hypotheses. He found that there was a positive relationship between an industry's growth rate and its use of technology forecasting techniques. Five of six higher growth industries also had a majority of firms using some technology forecasting techniques, while this was true of only one industry with a lower rate of growth. Gerstenfeld (1971) speculated that more rapidly growing industries "are faced with such rapid technological change that they are forced to use forecasting techniques." One would expect this hypothesis to hold for other types of changes as well.

The essence of the argument to follow is that a firm's environment largely determines its strategy and other responses such as policy, organization structure, and planning process. The appropriateness of these responses, both in the context of the environment and with respect to one another largely determines the effectiveness of its performance. Formal environmental analysis and forecasting efforts are one possible response to more complex and changing environments.

Firms in a simple-static environment will probably not use formal methods in forecasting, or will use the simpler (expert opinion) of the approaches outlined above as shown in Exhibit 3.16. Those facing a complex-static environment could be expected to use monitoring, perhaps in a less formal manner than described above, because it seems well suited to handling complexity and is based on the premise that change will occur gradually with increasingly tangible and

unambiguous signals. Firms in a simple-dynamic environment would probably use trend-extrapolation, computer based interaction of expert panels, and other means suited to a limited, but rapidly changing data base. Only those firms in the most complex and dynamic environments would be expected to undertake simulation, quantification of environmental scanning or other approaches designed to deal with both a large and rapidly changing set of variables. Further, the planning process may be expected to be more dynamic (to involve more iterations and more frequent iterations) in this type of environment than in the less difficult ones. A firm using any of the forecasting approaches that are more complex and require more data and computation would probably also use some of the simpler approaches to developing forecasts.

Environmental uncertainties are likely to transcend firm and often traditional industry boundaries. But our particular interest here is in predicting differences in the use of forecasting models among firms in differing environments. It seems logical to propose that a given firm's approach to its environment, that is its competitive strategy, is likely to have a major influence on differences between it and other firms with which it competes. For example, Ayres (1969) has suggested that explicit competitive strategy probably has as great an impact on the types of accommodations to environmental changes undertaken by a firm as the types of opportunities

Exhibit 3.16 Types of Environment Related to Forecasting Methods

Complexity	Change	
	Static	Dynamic
Simple	No formal methods, or expert opinion	Expert opinion, monitoring, and trend extrapolation
Complex	Expert opinion, monitoring	As above and simulation, quantitative models, probabilistic information processing

and needs available have on the evolution of strategy. He suggests that three distinct strategies can be described as "performance-maximizing," "sales-maximizing," and "cost-minimizing" (based on Charpie, 1967). Simmonds (1973) has developed this idea further and provided a gross classification of industries by dominant strategy.

These categories of types of strategies are highly oversimplified and surely need to be differentiated into more dimensions than performance, sales, and cost. Nor is there any empirical basis for such a taxonomy. It is simply suggested here as an exploratory hypothesis which does have appeal through its tie to characteristics of the environment as noted below.

The importance of a firm's competitive strategy is that we expect that performance-maximizing firms will clearly be more likely to employ formal and sophisticated models for forecasting and planning than will those with other strategies as shown in Exhibit 3.17. Sales-maximizing firms would likely concentrate on product improvements and components and perhaps use extrapolation or monitoring with respect to these. Cost-minimizing firms would be least likely to adopt technology forecasting effects or techniques with the exception of attempts to anticipate changes in a few variables or technologies that might lead to major cost reductions in competitors' operations.

There is some evidence for these hypotheses from previous research. Litschert (1971), in a study of 35 firms in the paint industry, noted that the 14 which were research (product performance) oriented used the most sophisticated planning techniques of those in the sample. The 21 firms which were market oriented focused on existing products and were generally less sophisticated in their planning approaches. He also found that the greater the change in the firm's area of product technology, the greater the focus on research oriented strategies, while the more stable the technological environment, the greater the use of market oriented strategies.

A complex-dynamic environment as described above would be characterized by diverse products and rapid product change. One would expect a majority of firms in this type of environment to follow a performance-maximizing strategy and to emphasize product technical performance. Flexible, uncoordinated types of production technology would be typical (Abernathy and Townsend, 1975). Conversely, a simple-static environment would be characterized by few highly standardized products and relatively slow, incremental product change. One would expect a majority of firms in this type of environment to follow a cost-minimizing strategy and to emphasize highly automated, large scale production facilities, minimum factor and trans-

Exhibit 3.17 Environmental Characteristics and Firm Strategy Related to Forecasting Methods

Environmental change	Environmental complexity	Type of strategy	Forecasting methods
Static	Simple	Cost-minimizing	No methods, or expert opinion
Static	Complex	Mixed and sales-maximizing	Expert opinion, monitoring, and trend extrapolation
Dynamic	Simple	Mixed and sales-maximizing	Expert opinion, monitoring, and trend extrapolation
Dynamic	Complex	Performance-maximizing	Above and simulation, quantitative and probabilistic models

portation costs. Firms in environments with intermediate levels of uncertainty and complexity might follow sales-maximizing and mixed strategies with emphasis on product differentiation and using varying degrees of automation and subcontracting in the production process. It follows that a firm in a complex-dynamic environment with a performance-maximizing strategy for competition would be most likely to use formal methods to anticipate change, and firms in a simple-static environment following a cost-minimizing strategy, least likely to do so, as shown in Exhibit 3.17.

Complexity may be viewed as a function of both the number of environmental variables and constraints of importance to the firm and as a function of the diversity, or number of different components of the environment (technological, political, legal, etc.) containing important variables or constraints (Duncan, 1972). One might extend this view to argue that it is not simply the number or diversity of variables and constraints that contribute to complexity, but fundamentally the number of relationships that exist among important variables. For example, the formation of organized groups to contest utilities' decisions on the location of nuclear generating plants (Jopling *et al.*, 1973) poses a new relationship, but not additional variables in the environments of these firms. An extreme case of the complex-dynamic type of environment is one in which *relationships* among different variables and sets of variables are changing. That is to say, cases in which the structure of the environment is changing. The term "turbulent" was used earlier to apply to this special case.

None of the approaches for environmental analysis and forecasting discussed above seems suited for dealing with turbulent environments. Current mathematics and ways of formal thinking about the environment may be reasonably well tailored to deal with change and complexity, but not with moving structure and relationships. Systems for this setting will need to be adaptive and to be flexible in their approach. Means must be available to include crucial informal communication and seemingly peripheral information. One idea which might prove a fruitful avenue for development has been originated by

Edwards (1968). It essentially takes a rigorous approach to the monitoring concept already discussed. A panel of judges establishes the hypotheses to be tested, while a similar panel estimates the impacts of individual data on the prior probabilities for each hypothesis. A computer display is used to revise and graphically portray the resulting probabilities of different potential threats for the panel. Such a probabilistic information processing system can deal with a changing structure of relationships and includes informal and subjective information in a rigorous manner. But on the whole, if we are ill equipped to anticipate change in changing and complex environments, we are even less well equipped to do so in turbulent ones.

In sum, we are suggesting that a firm's environment largely conditions its strategy and that its use of formal methods in anticipating change is largely a response to both its environment and strategy.

HOW SHOULD THE FIRM INTEGRATE ENVIRONMENTAL ASSESSMENTS INTO ITS STRATEGIC PLANNING PROCESS?

Studies of the actual use of formal methods for environmental analysis and forecasting show that few firms are using the methods discussed and fewer still to the degree suggested in the previous section. Aguilar (1967) stresses the essentially informal nature of environmental scanning as does Collings (1968). Keegan (1974) concluded from a study of executives responsible for multinational operations headquartered in the United States that they rely little on systematic monitoring methods. Similar results are reported by Kefalas and Schoderbek (1973) and Fahey and King (1977).

An exploratory study by Utterback and Burack (1975) yielded a number of cases in which formal forecasting efforts or methods had been initiated only to be discarded later or continued in use in an isolated or ineffective manner. It is clearly not sufficient for a firm simply to adopt such techniques. To be used effectively the techniques must be integrated into the normal routine of the firm's planning and decision-making processes. In general, we hypothesize that integration requires development of a network of informal communications both inside and outside the organization.

The difficult problem of integration in uncertain environments may be met in several ways. It requires among other things more fully developed informal relationships, boundary roles and lateral relationships, or a more "organic" form of organization (Burns and Stalker, 1961). Additional alternatives include increasing slack resources, simplifying organization structure, or increasing the amount of redundancy in the structure, and greater definition of formal integrative devices such as staff groups and management information systems (Galbraith, 1969). Our argument is that the use of formal methods or procedures for forecasting will be one of the types of specialization encountered under conditions of increasing environmental uncertainty and complexity, and effective use of forecasting will require integration with the firm's strategic planning effort.

In some respects, an environmental analysis and forecasting department might be thought of as an integrating unit. Respondents in Utterback and Burack's study (1975) stressed the role of forecasting in stimulating ideas and communication among management and technical personnel. Lawrence and Lorsch (1967) claimed that to be successful, integrating units must be viewed as legitimate in terms of both formal and informal criteria. This requires a position in the formal organization intermediate between the functions to be integrated and a broad base of technical and managerial skills to assist in developing informal relationships.

Similarly, we expect that analogous formal linkages between groups and the formal status and support given the firm's forecasting effort will influence its integration into the planning and decision-making process. Recent evidence on this point has been reported by Regan (1971). His study involved comparison of seven successful and seven less successful (in terms of their exploration efforts) metals mining firms. Regan found that the more successful companies considered long range corporate and exploration planning (including the coordination of exploration with total corporate goals and objectives) of greater importance than did less successful

firms. Long range plans had a greater effect on the size of the exploration budget in more successful companies, while short range factors had more influence in the less successful firms. Regan also notes that five of the more successful firms had a formal integrating group functioning to transfer discoveries from exploration to operations, while this was true in only one of the less successful cases.

Environmental uncertainty may be expected to affect patterns of informal communication, and firms' competitive strategy may be expected to affect formal relationships and the support given the use of forecasting. The finding that firms in less certain environments tend to have more extensive informal and lateral relationships was mentioned above. Aguilar (1967) shows that most of the critical information for strategy formulation comes to the firm from informal and unstructured contacts with its environment. Connolly (1972) has addressed this question directly in the context of technology planning decisions in four NASA laboratories. He found that individuals' communication activities are systematically related to perceived uncertainty and lead to uncertainty reduction. Further, nets facing high uncertainty tend to develop a decentralized decision making structure, while nets facing low uncertainty tend to develop centralized decision making structures. (A net is defined as a diffuse group participating in the planning-budgeting process.) Litschert (1971) has reported a similar finding for planning groups in four industries ranging from two with numerous product changes and innovations (electronics, chemicals) to two with few such changes (oil refining, utilities). He concluded that groups operating under conditions of rapid technological change possessed little formal structure, while in the more stable environments planning groups were formally structured and divided into subunits. Most recently, Brown (1976) has shown from a study of technical communication in six firms in three industries that those in more complex and changing environments had a greater degree of external communication than those in more simple and static contexts. He also showed that some individuals mediated the flow of outside information and thus served to buffer others from high levels of perceived uncertainty.

In sum, we expect that formal efforts for environmental analysis and forecasting will be less frequently encountered in simple and static environments. When such efforts are undertaken, we would expect them to be highly structured, more centralized, and more formally integrated into the existing line organization. Simple techniques would be used on a relatively continuous basis to reveal possibly disruptive longer run trends. In contrast, we expect conscious efforts by firms to analyze and forecast outside changes will be more necessary and much more frequently encountered in complex and changing environments. But to be effective such efforts would involve a more decentralized structure, greater participation by various elements of management including top management, a more informal and flexible organization, and greater use of informal integrating devices such as liaison groups, parallel assignments and so on. More diverse techniques might be used, but on an ad hoc basis to detect immediate opportunities and threats.

WHAT TOPICS ARE SUGGESTED FOR FURTHER RESEARCH IN THIS AREA?

The findings and hypotheses above suggest many topics for research, the majority of which and the most important of which link various topics discussed in this volume rather than falling strictly within the area of environmental analysis and forecasting. For example, the most critical issue, at least in the author's view, is understanding the process through which organizations can accommodate themselves to changes in their environment. Various ideas about constraints to change and flexibility to allow change were mentioned at the outset. If a firm clearly knows that it is threatened by change, will it have the resources, perception and creativity to respond? Aren't its incentives and options quite different from those say of others invading its business? What of the conflicts and power shifts that such knowledge would generate? How can needs for productivity and efficiency be balanced against needs for

slack resources required to respond flexibly? How can a highly structured and previously successful firm change to meet an unexpected threat resulting from change in its environment? Conversely, if presented with a major opportunity would such a firm recognize it, and if so would it respond rapidly enough to realize its full potential?

Another class of problems centers on environmental analysis and forecasting as a problem of information and communication. How can information about change in the environment be presented in ways which facilitate accommodation? How can the problem of selective perception of too narrow a part of the environment be overcome? What ways can be devised to avoid the pitfall of treating forecasts as deterministic? How can "peripheral" and subjective sources of information critical for successful accommodation to change be captured? How can consistent sets of measurements and data about the environment be generated, especially about the more general or non-proximate aspects of the environment, political, social, and institutional changes? How can the firm create and maintain a viable network of contacts and channels of communication with its environment?

Clearly, designing new techniques for forecasting and adding nuances to existing techniques are research directions with little potential. Nor will another Delphi study, extrapolated trend, etc., add much of any value. Research on the reliability, validity, and generalizability of different methods might be productive. More comprehensive approaches to environmental analysis which are compatible with the regular activities of management would offer real promise. This lends importance to processes for creatively drawing on the resources of groups of managers, such as the nominal group technique (Delbecq et al., 1975) and probabilistic information processing (Edwards et al., 1968). Research on the usefulness of monitoring approaches such as that of the Institute of Life Insurance would be of immediate interest for the same reason. A more differentiated approach for selecting techniques which fit the demands of given environments and corporate strategies should hold promise. This might be extended to the case where different divisions of the same firm require quite different approaches to their different arenas of business. And much needs to be done toward better understanding the ways in which environmental analysis and forecasting can be implemented and linked to firms' strategic planning processes.

Finally, the idea that predictions of the effects of trends and events are much more difficult than seeing the primary changes themselves was repeatedly stressed above. Perhaps the reason for this finding is that there are so many influences shaping outcomes for a particular firm. Other environmental changes, internal resources and capabilities, established interests, and so on, must be considered as they interact. How can we understand the implications of important interactions? How can we deal with the difficulties involved in accommodations to structural changes in the firm's environment? Surely the above agenda is incomplete and represents the author's biases, but it includes many of the important and immediate challenges for research.

Commentary

HAROLD E. KLEIN
Temple University

INTRODUCTION

There is little doubt that all organizations today are confronted by an increasingly changing environment. Some researchers, including Utterback, would suggest that this environment is "turbulent," i.e., an environment characterized by an increasing number of environmental variables that impact corporate performance, instability in the kind and degree of interrelatedness among these variables, and even uncertainty as to their very identity at any point in time (Terreberry, 1968). How does one deal with this state of affairs? How does one even know what *is* the state of affairs?

Normative theorists suggest that it is in the environmental analysis step within the strategy formulation process that the external states of the corporation are filtered and processed, leaving that residuum of stimuli relevant to objective and strategy reformulation.[1] The key problems that need to be addressed by policy research in the environmental analysis and forecasting area, then, might well be reduced to three sets of issues: (1) What is the role of environmental analysis and forecasting within the strategic planning process? More specifically, what functions does environmental analysis play within the strategy formulation process? What types of environmental forecasts are most useful within the strategy formulation process? (2) What are the major types of forecasting techniques and approaches that are most appropriate in fulfilling the environmental analysis role? and, (3) What is the process whereby the environmental analysis step is accomplished within the strategy formulation and planning process?

This paper addresses itself to these issues with major focus on: (1) the identification of

---

[1] It should be emphasized here that the types of environmental assessments referred to are not market, sales, and economic forecasts which are routinely included in long-range plans and with which business decision makers have a great deal of familiarity. Reference here is to such environmental factors as technological changes, social, political, cultural, and ecological conditions which heretofore may not have been systematically included or even identified as relating to the strategy formulation process.

the contribution of existing conceptual frameworks and research to the further development of each of the above areas, and (2) the identification of the types of future research efforts that might profitably be undertaken in the area.

Utterback addresses himself to a set of questions which deals in part with these issues, but from different perspectives. The difference in orientation is important, since alternative research directions may well be indicated by such a change in perspective. These other directions are identified below.

THE LACK OF ATTENTION GIVEN TO ENVIRONMENTAL ANALYSIS IN THE PAST

When reviewing the textual literature on formal planning systems, what must strike the student of formal planning processes immediately is the almost total lack of elaboration of the environmental analysis step in the process. More specifically, environmental assessment is invariably defined much in the manner given above; then, the subsequent planning process steps that utilize the environmental examination results are identified and elaborated. Often, the types of environmental factors that impinge upon most corporations are suggested and lists are provided of environmental factors that might be considered relevant. Some examples are also usually given and, possibly, some alternative methods for forecasting (Ackoff, 1970, 1974; Lorange and Vancil, 1977; Steiner, 1969).

However, neither of the questions posed at the outset of Utterback's paper, nor the three mentioned above are explicitly addressed in such models. In short, otherwise exemplary treatments of strategy formulation and planning processes consider the environmental assessment step more in terms of the results it yields than in the process whereby such results are obtained. This omission may well result from a lack of conceptual perspective which may reflect, in turn, indifferent managerial attitudes toward this activity. Thus, empirical research on corporate practice does indicate that environmental assessment is a process that, in the past, had been accomplished in an informal and, perhaps,

casual manner (Aguilar, 1967; Keegan, 1974) and, currently, is not performed effectively. The twelve large firms recently studied by Fahey and King (1977) all assessed their own environmental scanning activities as "a bad job." At least, in the latter case, the corporate managements explicitly recognized their inadequacies in the performance of the environmental scanning activity and, implicitly, thereby recognized its importance.

However, as Utterback suggests, it is reasonable to expect that under conditions of greater environmental uncertainty and turbulence, corporate managers will pay greater attention to environmental assessment and reflect this attention through greater formalization of environment-coping activities, whether these be in adoption of novel procedures and/or organization structural change. Thus, the rather casual nature with which environmental information was picked up by executives in those companies studied by Aguilar (1967) in the mid-1960s may well bear little relevance to the techniques and practices of such executives in their companies today, operating under radically different environmental circumstances. For instance, Klein and Linneman (1978) found high adoption rates of speculative or conceptual forecasting techniques in the very industries studied by Aguilar more than a decade ago. Moreover, their study showed that corporate managements were themselves participating directly in the forecasting process, particularly in the specification of types of environmental variables that were relevant to them.

THE ROLE OF ENVIRONMENTAL ANALYSIS AND FORECASTING IN THE STRATEGIC PLANNING PROCESS

Utterback poses the question, "How should the firm integrate environmental assessments into its strategic planning process?" However, it would seem that before this question can be addressed another ought to be answered: What is the purpose or function of the environmental assessment step itself, within the strategic planning process? The latter question may seem at first self-evident. Environmental assessment should provide "assessments," "forecasts," or "predictions" of that portion of the environment relevant to corporate designs. Nonetheless, despite large-scale commitments to the development and refinement of environmental forecasting techniques, the application results of these developmental efforts have been curiously ineffectual in significantly influencing the strategic planning processes of most businesses. For instance, large numbers of companies instituted formalized forecasting exercises almost a decade ago, especially after the broad exposure of the business public to the Delphi technique (*Business Week*, 1970). Much of this forecasting effort concentrated on the selection of potential technical research projects and resource allocation issues. Yet, a survey of corporate planning practice, at the time, found that the results of such forecasting studies were ineffectual in affecting decision making (Dory and Lord, 1970). Thus, forecasting efforts were found to be in some cases irrelevant or incommunicable to management. Dory and Lord concluded that forecasting efforts must be included in or linked explicitly to the planning process, if technological forecasting results are to meaningfully influence corporate decision making. Thurston (1971) reached similar conclusions in a study conducted about the same time. More recently, Utterback and Burack (1975) diagnosed the same problem. Clearly, the availability of a forecast or set of predictions does not in and of itself assure its believability or adoption.

Moreover, research into the use of environmental forecasting in strategy formulation has not dealt with the conditions under which alternative forecasting approaches are acceptable within the strategic planning process or, alternatively, whether variations in strategy formulation/planning processes (e.g., alternative sequencing of process steps or alterations in the functional role of planners and managers in the performance of these steps) allow for the incorporation and utilization of novel environmental forecasting approaches. The question, then, of just how this introduction ought to take place in any manner different from what conventional strategic planning methodology suggests is not at all clear. Utterback proposes something close to a mediating role for "an

environmental analysis and forecasting department," which would serve as "an integrating unit" between management on one side and technical personnel on the other. He further suggests the need for improving informal communications channels among the three interest groups, as well as increasing "formal status and support" for the forecasting unit.

The formalization of the environmental analysis function might well increase its stature; concurrently, however, any possible role for management's participation in the environmental analysis probably would be diminished by such formalization. In this regard, Klein and Linneman's (1978) recent survey of the use of alternate scenario techniques for environmental examination among corporations found high correlations between adoption of these techniques and the understanding of these techniques by corporate management. Furthermore, the companies which indicated that these techniques were "most helpful" within the strategic planning process were those in which managers themselves participated in the scenario generating process, and had no formal environmental assessment units. In these instances, it appears that the role of the environmental assessment step is somewhat different from that found in other surveys of corporate practice.

Theorists also differ with respect to whether managerial stance or strategic orientation can influence the role and content of environmental assessment in strategic planning processes. Some theorize that the strategic orientation (whether a firm holds to reactive or adaptive positions) is a function of organizational and environmental characteristics (Schendel, 1977); others would argue that the nature of managerial stance is independent of environmental factors (Ackoff, 1970). (Ackoff suggests that it is possible for comparable organizations within the same environment to address these environments in different fashions: one, say in reactive fashion and the other in an adaptive posture.)

In either case, systematic research on the relationship between strategic orientation and the role of environmental examination is needed. Some of the more important issues that need to be dealt with are as follows:

(1) What is the relationship, if any, between a corporation's strategic orientation and the characteristics of its environmental assessment processes?

(2) Do different types of environmental assessment processes result in different degrees of usefulness or effectiveness under alternative strategic orientations?

(3) Do different environmental assessment processes either tend to reinforce or change in any way existing strategic orientation in companies?

THE SELECTION OF APPROPRIATE FORECASTING APPROACHES FOR ENVIRONMENTAL ASSESSMENT

The question of selection of appropriate forecasting techniques for business planning situations has been treated in both normative and descriptive fashion (Chambers, Mullick, and Smith, 1971; Naylor and Schauland, 1976; Wheelright and Clarke, 1976; Lebell and Krasner, 1977; Wheelright and Makridakis, 1977). While normative discussion indicates the various technical conditions which might indicate utilization of causal, trend extrapolation or qualitative (i.e., speculative, conjectural) forecasting approaches, empirical research on corporate practice has focused mainly on utilization characteristics of such analytical techniques.

There is much less cross-sectional data on the extent and quality of utilization of conjectural or speculative forecasting techniques, the types most closely identified with forecasting within turbulent states. A few such studies have been recently published though. For example, Linneman and Klein (1978) surveyed a cross-section of large U.S. corporations to learn the extent of usage of multiple (or alternative) scenario analysis techniques within their strategic planning processes. Similarly, The Conference Board (1978) examined the manner in which fifty-eight corporations "sought to account for the uncertain future in planning." The focus in The Conference Board study was also on the use of alternate scenario approaches. It would seem that the principal reason for the limited number of such surveys is the nascent stage of development of the forecasting techniques themselves and the limited degree to which they have been adopted by major corporations.

CONTINGENCY THEORIES FOR SELECTING ENVIRONMENTAL FORECASTING APPROACHES

Utterback identifies a classification system for appropriateness of forecasting methods based on the static/dynamic-simple/complex taxonomy of the environment, a descendant of the Emery and Trist (1965) four-type causal texture continuum. The selection of this classification scheme is predicated upon the notion that the firm's environment is the major determinant in its strategy selection. The selection, then, of a particular forecasting approach is predicated upon an identification of just where on the static/dynamic-simple/complex grid one finds oneself. The difficulty with this approach is that such a determination can be made in an objective fashion only after the fact. Stated differently, at any point in time, the categorization of a firm's present environment as one type or another is purely subjective on the part of the corporate manager, i.e., what may be perceived as a static and stable environment to one firm's management might appear highly dynamic and complex to another's. Moreover, the manner in which any individual management perceives the environment (simple/complex, static/dynamic, etc.) is influenced by its own managerial stance or strategic orientation (e.g., whether the firm intends to be reactive, inactive, preactive, or interactive in its relationship with the environment) (Jurkovich, 1974). Thus, a large firm which takes an interactive role with its environment may be faced, due to its size and industry position, with many and more complex environmental factors than another smaller firm which might interact with the same broad environment through a reactive posture (Ansoff et al., 1976). Yet another order of complexity is possible: a firm may change its managerial stance or strategic orientation in light of a new perception of its environment. Consequently, some have concluded that this type of taxonomy, however insightful, may not be very helpful in assisting managers in the problem of strategic choice since the organization is treated as a "static entity," not responding and adjusting to environmental change over time (Miles, Snow, and Peffer, 1974).

Another difficulty with the use of a complexity/dynamism taxonomy in classifying forecasting techniques is the implication that for each category within the classification there is some appropriate forecasting approach(es). Utterback identifies "forecasting methods" appropriate for various specified environments with one exception, the "complex-dynamic type." He defines turbulence in this environmental context as "one in which relationships among different variables and sets of variables are changing." In this case, environmental forecasting is even more complicated, since the identification of relevant environmental factors and the assessment of their impact on corporate performance may itself be difficult. Rigorous analytic forecasting techniques are of little use under such circumstances, since they require the variables of interest and their causal relationships with other variables to be clearly stated. Thus, such techniques cannot deal with "historyless" situations. More to the point, the critical question in such turbulent arenas is not one of *how* to forecast, but *what* to forecast. It is exactly at this point where the "relevant uncertainty" is greatest, that the selection of those environmental issues and factors which bear upon a corporation during some prospective time horizon becomes the critical determinant of the utility of environmental analysis in the strategic planning process. However, this issue has received little research attention.

For all the reasons noted above, it would appear that an alternate taxonomy of environmental forecasting approaches might have more potential for conversion to normative theory. The author prefers a taxonomy of forecasting methods determined by the strategic orientation or managerial stance of the firm, since these factors determine to a great extent the use to which such environmental forecasts are put and the most useful attributes of such forecast results. Using a similar approach, Jantsch (1973) has established a conceptual framework for classifying forecasting tasks predicated on the planning level at which the forecast is made and the "task" internal to the system to which the forecast will be applied. Jantsch suggests three questions that need to be addressed in order to establish a "framework of reference" for the identification of forecasting approaches:

(1) What are the assumed behavioral characteristics of the system: (a) internally, in the modes of generation and utilization of information, and (b) externally, in the modes of interaction with the environment?

(2) What is the dimensionality of the system and its degree of dimensional integration?

(3) What are the criteria and measures assumed to be applicable in the pursuit and measurement of system improvement?

Thus, using either classification, an interactive stance (or "mode of interaction") argues for an interventionist role by the corporation with the environment itself (Ackoff, 1974). The firm not only attempts to anticipate future states, but to participate in processes that may very well change ultimate "futures." Clearly, the firm adopting such a posture needs to understand the intermediate dynamics and conditions that presage any future state, desirable or undesirable. The types of forecasting approaches that need to be employed must deal with environmental dynamics — issues of causality under changed conditions — where conventional analytic, causal models are inapplicable. Similar conclusions can be derived for the other possible orientations the corporation might adopt.

THE STRUCTURING OF RELEVANT ENVIRONMENTAL FORECASTING MODELS

The key initial task within any strategically-oriented forecasting system is the selection of variables to forecast. This task and the generation of forecasts for planning purposes for the most part have been a staff function. In fact, of all the sequential steps in the strategic planning process, the environmental assessment step has the least input from or participation by line management. Nevertheless, this particular issue has not been studied extensively.

Any forecasting approach that incorporates the task of environmental variable selection will be based more on the formalization of models of perception and conjecture — what might be called mental models (Coates, 1976) — than on conventional analytic techniques. It is in the formalization of such mental or heuristic models that line managers can play a meaningful role (Klein and Linneman, 1978).

Some approaches which appear to hold promise deal with attempts to formalize and make explicit management perceptions of potentially critical environmental impacts on the firm. An example of such an approach is Mitroff's (1971) work on the development of dialectical inquiring systems. He has attempted to develop a management information system that provides for formalized pro and con arguments concerning specific issues of importance to a decision maker. Mitroff premises his approach on the belief that most management information systems do not inspect the user's underlying images of the world. As a result, they are unable to examine how all the user's unstated and unconscious assumptions profoundly affect the user's conception of his own problem.

An approach that Klein (1973) has followed is the development of a systematic procedure which allows both planners and management through a series of simple individual steps to define an environmental structure that has specific relevance to corporate areas of strategic planning concern. The steps attempt to replicate the thought processes whereby complex theory is generated. In effect, the result of the approach is a formalized environmental paradigm that denotes the individual environmental factors and issues and their interrelationships which have impacts on individual parts of the company that could influence the achievement of at least one of the firm's specific strategic objectives. This paradigm-like environmental structure then becomes a specification for a forecasting model.

Hammond et al. (1975), by contrast, have developed theories of judgment and applied them to problems of causal ambiguity, particularly those in which the individual or firm interacts with the environment in such a way that, because of uncertainty and complexity, perception, learning, and thinking must be brought into play.

There are several common threads that run through these three approaches. First, they all attempt to make explicit underlying hypotheses, values, beliefs and perceptions about environmental behavior and its relationship to the organization in a systematically recursive fashion. Second, in each, the problem of identifying managerial stance is subsumed and need not be addressed overtly, since the relevant environment is evoked notwithstanding. In addition, in the Klein and Hammond approaches, visual display of environmental/organizational interactions is employed to allow for wholistic inspection of formalized environmental paradigms and facilitates their possible revision.

Given the above developments, this author does not share Utterback's pessimism about the lack of methodology for dealing with turbulent environmental conditions. In such conditions, one can expect greater reliance to be placed on formalized conjectural techniques such as scenarios, systems dynamics and mental (or heuristic) models — methods which allow for the development of forecasting models which one typology characterizes as models of "prospective causality" (Evered, 1976).

Nonetheless, one does not propose the foregoing as viable candidates for research or for corporate adoption without some trepidation. Any researcher in the field cannot help but be mindful of the lengthy and continuing acrimonious debate raging both in and out of academic circles on the issue of validation of systems simulations (particularly the systems dynamics approach used in the Club of Rome study) versus that possible for econometric models. The debate has been documented extensively and very well by Greenberger (1976) and others.

A second critique that is made of most conjectural forecasting approaches, both in concept and application extent, is that they lack a methodology or systematic approach for specifying variables and their interrelationships. Indeed, most scenarios are presented without any rationale given for the inclusion of the variables they contain or the interrelationships postulated among them. However, this weakness can be overcome through the introduction of procedures for defining the prospectively relevant environmental variable set using methodological approaches of the types developed by Mitroff, Klein and Hammond. Moreover, it is through such approaches that the perceptions of management can be elicited and formalized to a sufficient degree so as to become the specification for forecasting models whose relevance, therefore, has been determined in some *a priori* fashion.[2]

There is great prospect for much descriptive research concerning the practical utility of various conjectural forecasting approaches. Different types of forecasting models appear to have different potential applicability in formal planning processes, particularly under alternative strategic orientations. Explicative models as a class, for example, may well be far more important in a strategic planning context than purely predictive models. The role of just how differences in a forecasting approach in and of itself affects the utilization of a forecast has not been systematically explored. Nor has much attention been given to the role that the forecasting approach taken might have on the sequence of steps in the planning process.

THE ENVIRONMENTAL ASSESSMENT PROCESS

It is clear that the administrative process whereby environmental examination is accomplished should be linked to its role or function in the planning process and to the forecasting techniques employed. However, except for individual company case studies, no empirical research has been performed attempting to examine this three-way interrelationship, nor how these relate to the strategic planning process itself.

On the other hand, recent experiments in the development of formal procedures for identify-

ing and organizing relevant environmental issues for forecasting purposes all involve managers in roles not usually assigned to them; i.e., they involve different approaches for assimilating environmental assessment into the strategy formulation process itself. Thus, Mitroff, Barabba, and Kilmann (1977) report an attempt at effecting interactive planning in a large-scale organization, the Bureau of the Census. Their methodology employed inquiring system technologies (Churchman, 1971) and Jungian psychological principles in designing a strategic-level planning exercise involving "all job levels" within the Bureau. In this process, "futures" forecasting was conducted within the framework of alternative strategy formulation — and the same personnel did both types of tasks. Similarly, Linneman and Kennell (1977) suggest an elemental procedure for using multiple scenario analysis as an integrative framework for designing environmentally-responsive strategies. In both cases, the strategic planning "process" is materially compressed, and functional roles altered.

Substantially more empirical research needs to be conducted on how companies adapt their strategic planning processes in light of greater recognition of the importance of environmental impacts:

1. To what degree and under what environmental circumstances are companies experimenting with novel "compressed" approaches to strategy formulation (i.e., integration of environmental assessment and alternative strategy formulation)? Other approaches?

2. What role does corporate management play in this process (e.g., assist in specifying environmental variables; structuring alternative futures; evaluating alternative futures)?

3. How does managerial stance affect environmental assessment process characteristics?

SOME CONCLUDING OBSERVATIONS

There is little doubt in this author's view that more research emphasis will be placed on environmental analysis within the strategy formulation/strategic planning process. Researchers will take note as corporate management becomes more cognizant of this activity's importance and,

---

[2] Those interested in the development of forecast model methodology might also consider this issue, although some attempts at formalization of variable selection procedures for environmental forecasting purposes already have surfaced (Palmer and Schmid, 1976; McLean and Shepard, 1976; Abt et al., 1973).

at the same time, becomes more dissatisfied with their current practices. The research questions posed above mainly suggest guidelines for prospective descriptive research in corporate practice. Although such research is necessary, it is not by any means sufficient. Indeed, empirical research of corporate practice in this area to date has not contributed substantively to normative concept development (i.e., to just how environmental analysis ought to be performed within the strategy formulation/planning process in different organizational settings). Rather, a more fruitful direction seems indicated by experimental research of the development and testing of novel approaches to the conduct of the environmental analysis task itself. In this author's view, those examples of experimental research cited above which hold promise are based on theoretical developments in other disciplines such as psychology, learning and inquiry theory, and the more recently established field of policy science. Future modifications in corporate practice as well as maturation of normative theory may derive more from these latter fields than from descriptive research of current corporate practice.

Strategy Formulation: A Social and Political Process

JOSEPH L. BOWER
Harvard University
YVES DOZ
Harvard University

The task of a chief executive officer (CEO) in formulating company strategy is twofold. First, the CEO must develop a broad vision of what to achieve — a desired future position for the company in its environment. Second, the CEO must manage a network of organizational forces that lead to the discovery, evolution, and enrichment of that vision. Daily activities of the CEO involve using his or her time, presence, and influence to act upon that network of forces.

Perhaps one of the clearest examples of this mix of task and activity vision is available in the case of Dennison Manufacturing Company.[1] In the key incident described in the case, the president of Dennison is faced with a dispute between two divisions over transfer price. A new product has been invented in one division, but its principal markets are being developed in a second. The two division managers are arguing over the price at which the product should be transferred, and the way in which development costs should be reimbursed. The question looks particularly important to the managers involved because an incentive bonus is tied to division profitability.

An initial analysis reveals that any number of transfer prices can be justified. The problem for the president is more complicated. He has envisioned a more rapidly growing and more profitable company than the present one. In order to generate a more energetic approach to the development of markets, he has reorganized his company in product divisions. He has also created an incentive compensation system to

reward divisional profit. This particular incident will have a great deal to do with how his system is regarded by his managers. Moreover, the contenders are not without importance. On the one hand, the division providing the new product is led by a 65-year-old officer who also sits on the board of directors. His division has been a source of creativity and strength throughout the life of the company, although according to the accounting system under the new organizational form, it is not particularly profitable. On the other hand, the contending division under the leadership of a 49-year-old vice president shows dynamic marketing. It is the second manager and his division that are expected to help the company achieve a more rapid rate of growth in the future. *How* Mr. Hamilton goes about resolving the transfer price question will determine how the outcome of the dispute between the two divisions is perceived by the members of the organization. Who "won"?, Who "lost"?, and Why? are the questions of interest. The organization members' *perception* of patterns of decision making to answer questions like this will determine how they interpret the strategy of rapid growth.

It is easy to decide that profit should be earned in the division expected to grow in a dynamic fashion. But how should this decision be communicated? The seriousness of the problem can be understood from the fact that the contending positions are already in writing on the president's desk. Should he respond in writing? If not in writing, to whom should he communicate first? What face should he put on his decision? Should it be an outright victory for the younger man, or should it be a victory for the older man in every aspect, save the substance of the decision? In other words, how the

---

[1] In Christensen, Andrews, and Bower (1973); also see *Dennison Manufacturing Company*, Intercollegiate Case Clearing House, Boston, Mass., ICCH #9-371-284.

CEO carries out his actions constitutes communication. It is the sequencing of the phone calls or meetings that will communicate the president's decision, that will shape the future of his reorganization, and that in turn will have a great deal to do with whether his vision of more rapid growth into new markets can be achieved.

The incident summarized above evidences the intertwined and complementary nature of the *positional* and *managerial* aspects of the chief executive officer's function. Most of the literature of general management has separated the positional aspects from the managerial ones. In positional frameworks, the problem of managing is described in terms of getting the firm from one position to another. Dennison seeks more rapid growth and profit. Those goals are considered to be a fundamental guide, shaping the actions to be undertaken in the company. In contrast, we can distinguish frameworks which describe how the firm is managed. Dennison will be managed in a more decentralized fashion. In the managerial framework, attention is focused on how goals are developed, on how resources are allocated, and on how the efforts of individuals are coordinated to achieve particular goals and patterns of allocation. Managerial frameworks focus on the *process* of management more than on the overall direction followed by the company.

We argue here that the principal difficulty in formulating a strategy for a large, complex corporation derives from the need to integrate both the positional and the managerial aspects of the management task. Our motivation in this paper is: (1) to explore the critical interaction between positional and managerial concepts, (2) to consider the possibility of integrating these two approaches into a single strategic management process, and (3) to review what social and political models of strategy formulation contribute to an integrated view of strategic management.

POSITIONAL AND MANAGERIAL VIEWS OF STRATEGY

The emergence, evolution, and refinement of the strategy of a firm in positional terms, but through an administrative process, was well recognized by Barnard and Chandler long ago. Barnard (1938: 235) captured the links between executive functions:

> The executive functions which have been distinguished for the purpose of exposition and which are the basis for much functional specialization in organizations, have no separate concrete existence. They are parts or aspects of a process of organization as a whole. This process in the more complex organizations, and usually even in simple unit organizations, is made the subject of specialized responsibility of executives or leaders. The means utilized are to a considerable extent concrete acts logically determined; but the essential aspect of the process is the sensing of the organization as a whole and the total situation relevant to it.

Barnard pointed out the interactions between the formulation of purpose, communication within the organization, and the sum of executive functions. Similarly, Chandler (1962: 13) considered strategy as a process:

> Strategy can be defined as the determination of the basic long-term goals and objectives of an enterprise and the adoption of courses of action and the allocation of resources necessary for carrying out these goals.

Clearly the emphasis on determination of goals, adoption of courses of action, and allocation of resources connotes a process view. But in *Strategy and Structure*, Chandler viewed the CEO as a leader who carries out most of this process himself in formulating strategy. It is only when the strategy is being implemented that a complex administrative process takes place. As Chandler analyzed the transition from functionally integrated structures toward divisional structures, he tended to view the work of top management in positional terms, and gave a somewhat lesser importance to managerial aspects in the emergence of a new strategy.[2]

---

[2] It is important to note that Chandler studied in most detail companies whose structure still reflected single industry operations, where managerial elements are less visible and less important because they are handled by a small, tight-knit group of executives or are entirely within the purview of a

Most authors on strategy have not even gone as far as Chandler in stressing the managerial aspects of strategy formulation. They choose instead to postpone considering managerial issues when discussing strategy. In their view, strategy is an output and its formulation an analytical process. Thus as most often interpreted, the concept of corporate strategy is a sophisticated version of positional analysis, concerned with the present and future status of the organization, relative to competition and other aspects of the external environment. Scott (1971), for example, emphasized a series of conditional moves:

> [Corporate strategy involves] several elements, including a concept of how to compete in the environment, a set of specific, operational, company objectives, and a timed sequence of conditional moves for deploying corporate resources with a view toward obtaining these objectives. . . .

In this positional view, strategy is the pattern of resource generation and allocation in a planned sequence over time to achieve explicitly defined desired objectives. It is expressed as if it were a means of defining and guiding the transactions of the firm with its environment.

Although considering strategy as the output of a positional approach to management does not rule out social and political factors as influences on the formulation of strategy, many authors do not consider those factors when analyzing the behavior of a company. Most early authors[3] did not delve much into how

purpose or objectives are determined, but focused on how the environment is searched in looking for economic opportunities to enable the firm to meet its objectives. Since strategic planning was thought to be the intellectual designing of the pattern of resource generation and allocation that would lead to the desired objectives, strategy formulation was reduced to a planning analysis. The problem of setting objectives was tackled only by Ansoff (1965) among the early authors. He saw setting objectives as obtaining a consensus among members of the power structure of the firm to pursue a set of agreed upon objectives. Mostly economic, the objectives were usually defined as minimum levels of achievement which could serve as constraints in a strategic planning analysis.

Andrews and his colleagues, although principally developing the positional aspects of strategy and stressing the usefulness of an explicit strategy, have grounded the task of strategy formulation in an assessment of organizational competences (Christensen, Andrews, and Bower, 1973: 619):

> In real life the process of formulation and implementation are intertwined. Feedback from operations gives notice of changing environmental factors to which strategy should be adjusted. The formulation of strategy is not finished when implementation begins. A business organization is always changing in response to its own makeup and past development.

By recognizing the evolution of strategy through administrative feedback, the policy approach overcomes some of the difficulties of purely positional approaches, such as that of the "corporate planning" proponents, who often tend to overlook the relationships between analysis and action. In fact, it is not possible to deal sensibly with the analytical problem of formulating a strategy for a company without basing it on an assessment of the current posture of the company and of its possible moves. Because the processes that determine and constrain the company's economic and financial posture are administrative in nature, a feasible strategy can be formulated only on the basis of an administrative understanding of what the company is and what the leverage points are

---

chief executive officer. Ackerman (1970), in his study of resource allocation in integrated companies, also stressed the concentration of the strategic process in the hands of a few people. This suggests that the argument presented in this paper is mostly applicable to large, complex, diversified companies. Smaller, simpler, one product line companies may not raise the same issues in terms of strategic management.

[3] For instance, Steiner (1963). Steiner himself (1966) later pointed out that "a major roadblock exists because the theory of planning is not adequate to meet today's needs." Ewing (1967) stressed the lack of impact because of a failure to incorporate motivational and behavioral aspects.

within it. By assuming complete plasticity of the organization in terms of transfer of resources, corporate planning models may be a useful analytical tool. But they do not allow the development of an overall workable strategy grounded in reality.

All positional views of strategy raise an obvious question. Though they capture the intellectual substance of strategy formulation, they tell us little of how strategy is developed socially in an organization. Moreover, the more comprehensive a view of strategy from a positional perspective (for instance, Scott's explicit integration of competitive and time dimensions), the more questions it raises from a managerial perspective. The more detailed and far reaching the "grand strategy," the more administrative consistency is implicitly assumed in its design. How much consistency can be expected if strategy is the outcome of a social process? The business policy approach recognizes that strategy formulation is a social process, at least in complex organizations (Christensen, Andrews, and Bower, 1973: 863):

Strategy formulation is itself a process of organization, rather than the masterly conception of a single mind ... the sheer difficulty of reconciling uncertain environmental opportunity, unclear corporate capability and limited resources, submerged personal values, and emerging aspirations to social responsibility suggests that at least in complicated organizations strategy must be an organizational achievement and may often be unfinished.

Contrary to this conclusion is one reached by many researchers who have observed organizational decision-making processes, convincingly concluding that a consistent strategy as an output of a social process is, at best, unlikely. Briefly, their view of strategy is one of disjointed, incremental decisions made in reaction to pressing problems without overall integration among decisions over time. The foremost proponents of this view have been Cyert and March (1963), who consider the firm as a behavioral entity, the goals of which are the results of coalitions among individuals who have specific objectives and can agree on specific actions without sharing common personal goals.

That process of group decision making leads the firm to display a series of traits in its behavior (uncertainty avoidance, problemistic search, quasi-resolution of conflicts and organizational learning) that practically rule out the existence of an overall strategy. Cyert and March focus on short- to medium-term decisions in response to immediate problems. Longer-term change is achieved by organizational learning, i.e., adaptation of goals, attention rules, and search rules. Combined with uncertainty avoidance, problemistic search, and quasi-resolution of conflict, the process of adaptive learning leads to reactive behavior, not to the foresight and overall design implicit in a manager's vision of the future of his company. Similar conclusions were reached by Lindblom (1959: 27) in studying public policy making:

Policy making is typically a never ending process of successive steps in which continual nibbling is a substitute for a good bite.

The cure for such fragmentation is to find a balance between uniformity and diversity. Uniform rules and procedures are needed for everyday activities, yet strategic decisions require controlled departures from these rules and procedures. Departure from the rules may cause each strategic decision to be treated separately with little attention to its administrative implications and to its integration into an overall stragegic vision. How to provide consistency in incremental changes was left unclear by Lindblom.

Simon, and later the proponents of the conventional planning approach, assumed that such consistency is achieved by separating policy making from administration and by designing an organization which implements a hierarchically organized cascade of means-end relationships which guide every decision (Simon, 1945). This simplification was challenged by Selznick (1957), who recognized that decisions are subjective judgments made by individuals and not just the outcome of the manipulation of premises in which a neutral individual makes "boundedly" rational decisions. Personal and motivational aspects thus make strategy formulation substantially more complex.

Even if we assume that Simon was right and that coalitional formation at the top does not prevent consistent sets of goals from being developed, the question of how managers integrate positional and managerial aspects remains. Mintzberg (1973) studied how the activities of top managers fall into a role set that spans both managerial and positional aspects, and concluded that strategy formulation does not take place in a positional mode that is explicit. The closest to such a mode is a set of "semi-articulated 'what if' structures" the manager has in his or her own mind. Mintzberg (1973: 163) concluded:

> Current practice, largely in accord with the incremental view of strategy making presented in the literature, is becoming more and more inadequate because of time constraints on the manager, the increased complexity of organizational decisions and the difficulty of integrating decisions made incrementally.

Mintzberg also stressed the usefulness of policy analysts to structure decisions (in a positional sense). Subsequently he and others developed a systematic comparison of strategic decision making in different organizations. They described the particular character of strategic decision making (Mintzberg, Raisinghani, and Theoret, 1976: 263):

> There is not a steady undisturbed progression from one routine to another; rather the process is dynamic, operating in an open system where it is subjected to interferences, feedback loops, dead end and other factors. These dynamic factors are perhaps the most characteristic and distinguishing features of decision processes that are strategic.

Mintzberg et al. tracked the processes leading to significant decisions in the organizations studied through a set of phases during which specific routines are activated. By reviewing original stimuli, the decision track, and the decisions finally reached, they succeeded in building crude categories of strategic decision processes. Unfortunately, by selecting different decisions in a wide range of organizations, they made meaningful comparison difficult. Another limitation of their research is that it does not really explore the strategic management process over

time. If strategy has any meaning, it is about time-critical decisions. Nonetheless, Mintzberg et al. have not ruled out the CEO as a figure who would consistently operate on individual decision processes so as to implement an all-encompassing strategic vision over time.

Managing the decisions that shape the implementation of a long-term strategic vision for a firm is, in fact, the central task of the CEO as illustrated by the Dennison example. For the CEO who has to integrate the positional and managerial approaches in order to provide direction to a corporation, the concepts of strategy formulation reviewed above all raise obvious problems.

The managerial view of strategy as exemplified by Mintzberg makes full recognition of this difficulty. But, the conceptual and methodological problems of linking the significant individual decisions studied to the overall evolution of their pattern over time and to the management of the major decision processes have prevented much real progress from being made in the analysis of strategy formulation. Despite the difficulty of doing so, as evidenced by Allison's (1971) explanatory analyses of the decision-making process of the United States government in the Cuban missile crisis, positional and managerial elements need to be considered simultaneously in order to comprehend a reality substantially more complex than that which a single framework can capture.

From a top management perspective, managing the processes which lead to strategy formulation and implementation in complex organizations becomes different from carrying out the actual formulation and implementation. The two activities are closely related, and a manager concerned only about either the management of the process, i.e., the managerial approach, or its performance, i.e., the positional approach, would *not* be well equipped to face extensive environmental change. Similarly, an analyst who only looked at separate instances of managing the process (individual decisions) or confined his or her view of strategy to analytic positional concepts would miss a large part of reality.

The following section explores systematically the difference between strategy as a pattern of administrative and positional outputs in the relationship of the organization to its environment, and strategic management which operates on the process which generates this pattern of output.

STRATEGIC MANAGEMENT

If strategy deals with the long term, the precedent setting, and the commitment of critical resources, then the process of developing strategy is the nonroutine activity of altering normal patterns of planning and operations. For the general manager, exploiting the firm's "distinctive competence" must mean identifying and carrying out those nonroutine social and political shifts that he or she knows how to manage.

The positional theories are concerned with outputs, or the history of outputs, of a social process. By focusing on the chief executive as if his or her "decisions" alone produce the output, or even the plan or program, leading to the output, the theories help us to understand the firm, but not how it is managed. In fact, the decisions — in the sense of individual commitments of resources — are distributed throughout the organization, as Barnard (1938: 187) noticed long ago:

> The formulation of organization purposes and objectives and the more general decisions involved in this process and in those of actions to carry them into effect are distributed in organizations, and are not, nor can they be, concentrated or specialized to individuals, except in minor degree.

Far from the heroic view of the chief executive as the source of dicta, what emerges is a view of the CEO as a shaper of the premises of other executives' thoughts and the source of balance in the personal interactions of others. His or her contributions to strategy may be more than anything else, an effective call for change. Direction or purpose for a complex, diversified company may take the form of an expressed need for the company to be more "technology intensive" as at Philips or "more international" as at Nippon in the early 1970s (Bower and Prahalad, 1978). Even in the large, complex, dominant product company, the chief executive's contribution to strategy formulation is often more likely to be a higher level of aspiration or a new sense of what voices should contribute to the debate. This certainly seems to be the role Thomas Watson, Jr., played in IBM.[4]

For the complex modern firm then, purpose is a sense of what the distributor of rewards wishes the organization to become. The purpose may be embodied in an incentive compensation system,[5] the personnel practices and behavior of the managers,[6] or an explicit statement of strategy.[7] Whatever the embodiment of purpose, the chief executive's role in establishing it is to focus the attention of independent social activity so that the objectives being pursued are limited relative to the resources being brought to bear.

An understanding of the social and political content of strategic management seems to be the objective of the so-called process school of research.

THE PROCESS SCHOOL OF RESEARCH

The conceptual underpinnings of what has become the process school of research are old. Barnard (1938) provided the overall framework and Simon (1945) the articulation of the operative principles. It remains hard to discuss the process school because it lacks integration: the authors who might be qualified to discuss it, though familiar with each other's work, have seldom interacted for research in groups larger than two.

The context of the development of the process school is important. At a time when simple cognitive models were widely hailed (predominantly Cyert and March, 1963), the complexity revealed by exploratory field observations of large, complex companies defied easy explanations. For instance, the first policy cases written

---

[4] As reported in the *Fortune* story of the development of the 360 series (T. A. Wise, 1966).

[5] For an illustration see, for instance, *Adams Corporation*, Intercollegiate Case Clearing House, Boston, Mass., #6-372-263.

[6] For an illustration see, for instance, *Marks & Spencer*, Intercollegiate Case Clearing House, Boston, Mass., #9-375-358.

[7] For example, Ruckelshaus at the U.S. Environmental Protection Agency.

about the management of large, complex companies such as Hilton[8] or IMC [9] (the world's largest sewing machine manufacturer) did not fit into the simple models then available. Berg's study of Westinghouse (1964) and his subsequent articles (1965, 1969) laid out the framework of levels and systems characteristic of large, diversified corporations. But a mere comparison of a small, one-product company such as Compagnie Chillon Electronique,[10] with a large, one-product company such as American Motors,[11] and then a General Motors[12] would have led a student of management to discover what Bruce Scott (1971), following Chandler (1962), later described as stages of corporate development.

Once one moved beyond the entrepreneurial unit, purpose was largely a social output. If a straightforward application of Cyert and March could not be used to explain something as complex as corporate strategy, Simon's early work on administrative behavior provided a richer language. Subunit behavior could be explained in terms of the premises that subunit managers brought to their decisions. The division of tasks and information could account for behavior. Simon saw these explanatory factors as solely cognitive; he did not assess there to be a need for a more complex explanation. Nonetheless, it was too apparent from field observation and the clinical analyses of large companies that nonintellectual factors were important as well. It was natural to express these findings in the language of an open system model of the firm as Bruce Scott did (1962). In his view the organization, measurement and information systems, and reward and punishment systems shaped the organization's subunits' behaviors. These behav-

iors, in turn, in their strategic dimensions, shaped strategy. Thus, the process school came to focus on the way structure, or structural context, as Bower (1970) called it, could be managed to shape strategy.

In this emergent system of description, Berg's analysis (1965) of parochial subunits could be reinterpreted as a structural context that, through its measures and rewards, focused attention on the short term. One could observe the same sort of behavior in the transfer price disputes and the apparent dilemma of the product manager in Texas Instruments[13] as well as in the Dennison example.

Bower's research (1970) used the rich data from four studies of how resources were being allocated to construct a somewhat more elaborate framework for viewing that process. Different people were involved in the development of the substantive content of strategy, on the one hand, and the commitment of resources to major projects, on the other. Still others shaped the structural context. One could identify different general management tasks being performed by differentiable classes of generalists.

Thus, in contrast to strategy formulation as the critical direction-setting general management activity, this new process school of research suggested an alternate, that is, managing the strategic process. The strategic process was defined as "the evolution of a crude concept of corporate purpose, sometimes in response to administrative intent but also in reaction to competitive moves and broad environmental change" (Trevelyan, 1974). The differentiated generalists observed, play different roles in the process. Within large, complex organizations, each unit's general manager is held responsible for the planning and coordinating that are traditional tasks of the owner of a single product business, except that control of the capital budget, and much of the personnel system lie outside the purview of this role. If there is entrepreneurship in product/market terms, it rests with this business oriented generalist. Another general management role involves responsibility for the corporate whole in all its

---

[8] *Hilton*, Intercollegiate Case Clearing House, Boston, Mass., #9-302-089.

[9] *IMC*, Intercollegiate Case Clearing House, Boston, Mass., #9-309-249 — 9-309-258.

[10] *Compagnie Chillon Electronique*, Intercollegiate Case Clearing House, Boston, Mass., #9-307-143.

[11] *American Motors*, Intercollegiate Case Clearing House, Boston, Mass., #9-364-001, BP-765, #9-372-350.

[12] *General Motors*, Michael Lovdal and Kirk Hanson, Intercollegiate Case Clearing House, Boston, Mass. (Forthcoming, 1978.)

[13] *Texas Instruments*, Intercollegiate Case Clearing House, Boston, Mass., #6-312-030.

variety, including most importantly its relation with external suppliers of resources — not only the owners and lenders, but also governments and interest groups. In between is a third role in which a general manager is responsible for managing the relationship between the operators and entrepreneurs and the corporate architects. These managers in the middle are the last level of management to understand the critical substance of subunit plans, personnel, and operations, and the first to have frequent interaction with top management. They are the critical link in the part-whole relationship.

In some corporations, the general management roles are clearly identified with different levels of organization. In others, particularly where the product line is relatively simple (for instance, General Motors) or where the chief executive wants to work very hard (for instance, Geneen at ITT), the roles tend to overlap.

Explicit recognition of these different management roles vastly increases the problem of organizational design. Designing a structural context that suits the demands of operating activities, but does not interfere with the development of strategy, taxes most companies. The short-sightedness earlier observed (for instance, by Berg, 1965) seems to be a reflection of the fact that the overwhelming force of incentives tied to the operating budget makes a long-term view a luxury for subordinates.

Still another difficulty emerged when researchers turned to consider how the chief executive officer deals with what has been called the "corporate phase" of the process, that is, setting broad goals, confirming resource commitments, and designing context. If structure is to shape strategy, what vision shapes structure and how is that vision to be developed? Who has a say in the process? More research is needed.

Finally, it has also become clear that where the product of subunit businesses is technologically complex, or where there is great variety in products or markets, the process of shaping the structural context and controlling the strategic management process is made even more difficult. Top management must find a way to make sensible commitments based on abstractions and other substitutes for substantive understanding. The problem was highlighted at a recent senior managers' conference when one group reported their findings on successful matrix management. A key "rule" was that "knowledgeable" members of a matrix planning team must be able to make commitments. One colleague commented, "The key people who have the knowledge do not have the power to commit."

This concise summary of some key findings of the process school of research also introduces the concept of power. Often, process research has described behavior that is more easily understood in political terms than it is in the simple language of apparent material self-interest. As a consequence, much insight that has been gathered in recent years on the management of complex organizations comes from work in sociology and political science as well as from specific studies of the strategic process.[14]

In fact, the management of the strategic process raises a set of questions that are familiar to social scientists and political analysts. In their language, process research has adopted a simple systems view that recognizes the existence of interactions among:

1. The cognitive processes of individuals on which understandings of the environment of strategy are based;

2. The social and organizational processes by which perceptions are channelled and commitments developed; and

3. The political processes by which the power to influence purpose and resources is shifted.

Strategy is viewed as an outcome of these processes and the task of the chief executive is viewed as the administration of these processes. Each dimension of the strategic process raises different issues:

1. Whereas the cognitive dimension has been researched extensively for individual decision making and simple trade-offs, it raises more difficult questions when applied to collective nonrecurrent decisions under conditions of high complexity and uncertainty (multiple value

[14] Some of the most significant of these contributions are presented in the next section.

trade-offs, partly unknown outcomes, different perceptions of environment, and group decision making).

2. Once we cease assuming a heroic view of top management, and accept that "decisions are distributed" (in Barnard's sense), we need to separate actual power from hierarchical authority and to recognize the management of power as an explicit CEO function.

3. We also need to recognize that the configuration of the pattern of exchanges between the firm and its environment is not controlled from a single office, but that consistency among the several components of the strategic process needs to be maintained through an extensive array of administrative procedures: communication channels, information and planning systems, and rewards and motivation systems.

CONCEPTUAL BUILDING BLOCKS

To help clarify and expand our understanding of each of these three difficulties we can draw extensively on the research of political scientists and sociologists in trying to reconcile different models of decision making under uncertainty and complexity. One of the most careful attempts to reconcile different models was made by Steinbruner (1974). He built upon Simon's work to show how the cognitive mechanisms of the mind use already existing sets of beliefs to simplify and structure the context of even the most complex and uncertain decisions far enough so as to make them amenable to simple cybernetic decision processes. In reviewing the implications of these cognitive mechanisms for strategic decision making by organizations, Steinbruner raised the dilemma of organizational adaptive capacity versus internal structural simplicity. He also stressed the need to consciously decompose complex problems into segments that can then be treated through a simple cybernetic decision process.[15] The adoption of simplifying premises by decision makers grounded in their own personal sets of beliefs,

creates the need and opportunity for manipulation of these premises. Simon had described establishing premises as a kind of top-down, mechanistic, almost Weberian, factoring process, necessitated by the limited rationality of the individual. Instead, Steinbruner argued that actors in situations involving substantial risk and complex trade-offs will, by themselves, simplify their perceptions so as to produce a kind of psychological peace that makes decision making tolerable. For organizations, a system of beliefs is necessary to make the simplifications of its general managers congruent.

Zysman (1973), researching top management's role in the resource allocation process in large, diversified companies, developed findings which lend support to Steinbruner's and extend their applicability to the top management of corporations. Briefly, Zysman found that in evaluating long-term capital investment opportunities, top management relied on information and personal beliefs developed in their short-term (earnings per share oriented) control function. They did not try to develop alternate channels of information more fitted to the content of strategic plans and investment proposals, but relied on analogy to develop an understanding of their businesses (analogy is one of the simplifying mechanisms identified by Steinbruner).

Steinbruner's analysis left two major questions open: (1) How do organizations adapt to environmental variety? and (2) How do they carry out internally the complex value trade-offs inherent in reflecting the external variety? If the concept of power is introduced, both in the transactions of the organization with its environment, and in the internal decision processes, these questions are illuminated.

In an effort to explore systematically the implications of considering corporations as open systems, Rhenman (1973) developed terminology to describe strategy formulation in a system theory framework. In a straightforward adaptation of Ashby (1960) and Buckley (1967), Rhenman stressed the need for consonance between the value system of the firm (internal structure of meanings) and its value environment (what other subsystems in the environment expect and need from the firm). In Rhenman's view, "corporations must dominate their environment if

---

[15] For a treatment of the cybernetic theory applied to social systems see Buckley (1967). For a simple treatment of cybernetics applied to individual thought processes, see Ashby (1960).

they are to be able to fulfill their own internal strategic planning," and dominance is achieved by "transforming the uncertainty of forecasts into the certainty of planning by requisite variety of countermeasures" [16] or by "introducing into the environment a new and powerful systemic solution." [17] Organizations that cannot dominate can still "map" (survive by adapting to environmental demands), but cannot develop their own strategic goals and autonomous strategic plans. In Rhenman's view, the value system of the firm emerges from the stabilization of a small group of critical actors' demands on the firm in a guise very similar to Cyert and March's "dominant coalition."

Crozier's (1964) research on the sociology of public bureaucracies and state monopolies can be useful for understanding the relationship between the uncertainty of environmental expectations and the stabilization of power within the organization. Crozier's basic argument was that the control of sources of uncertainty yields power within the organization (Crozier, 1964: 164)

> Comparing the competing claims of the different individuals and groups within an organization, one can state that in the long run, power will tend to be closely related to the kind of uncertainty upon which depends the life of the organization.

By stressing the importance of power relationships in the organizations, and the rigidities that develop when they are not explicitly recognized and managed, Crozier made an important contribution to the managerial view of strategy. In particular, he clarified the relationship between variety matching and administrative power by showing that internal power hinges largely on knowledge useful to uncertainty reduction. Rhenman showed that uncertainty can be eliminated by dominating the environment with sufficient resources (requisite variety). But

Crozier shows that power in an organization flows to those who can reduce the uncertainty to which individuals are subjected. He thereby revealed the *sources* of power inherent in strategy formulation.

A more comprehensive approach viewing the organization as a set of subsystems, some of which need to match environmental variety (boundary spanning), and some of which need to be buffered from environmental variety (technical core), was developed by Thompson (1967). He first unfolded a logicodeductive construct of analytical propositions which provides a language system and a framework to conceptualize complex organizations. Thompson then stressed that the basic administrative function is the maintenance of "coalignment" between the positional (domain and task environment) considerations and managerial (organization design and structure, and strategic variables) considerations (Thompson, 1967: 147,8):

> Survival rests on the coalignment of technology and task environment with a viable domain, and of organization design and structure appropriate to that domain.... The configuration necessary for survival comes neither from yielding to any and all pressures nor from manipulating all variables, but from finding among the *strategic variables* (Barnard 1938) those which are available to the organization and can be manipulated in such a way that interactions with other elements will result in a viable coalignment.[18]

Comparable conclusions were reached by political analysts in the study of leadership in government. A central conclusion by Thompson was that "the key function of administration is to keep the organization at the nexus of several necessary streams of actions." This conclusion applies very well to the examples developed in Neustadt's study of presidential power (1960). It applies, for example, to Neustadt's description of the web of forces that led to the Marshall Plan.

As an analytical pendant to the process school of research, Thompson's work was most com-

---

[16] The extensive "resilient" planning scenarios currently developed by large, sophisticated firms and proposed by management consultants try to fulfill that condition.

[17] Not very dissimilar from Cyert and March's reduction of uncertainty by negotiating with the environment.

[18] Note here that Rhenman's "dominance" is required for the firm to be able to manipulate strategic variables.

prehensive. However, because of its logico-deductive nature it did not offer a sufficiently detailed view of actions by individuals. Its treatment of "the human variable" added little to the work of Barnard and Simon, whereas the works of Steinbruner and Crozier have provided strong evidence for the key importance of cognitive and power aspects in strategic decision processes. However, by relating the degree of uncertainty in the environment to the nature of interdependence within the organization, Thompson did establish a critical link between positional and managerial concepts.

Schwartz's study (1973) of strategic innovation and resource allocation in a high technology industry provided a specific, detailed example of the links between uncertainty and strategic management. His major finding was that the context can be designed to encourage more risk taking. In particular, rewards for success are very important; and risks must be negotiated and shared, as well as reduced by factoring, with middle managers acting as risk-brokers. Schwartz also stressed the importance of a "consistent context" provided by ad hoc groups (for communications and commitments), planning systems, and rewards systems.

Schwartz's work on innovation also has broader implications. It pointed a way toward making the individual managerial risk associated with strategic decisions more bearable. Size and diversity make large companies less sensitive to the risks involved in individual decisions, but for particular managers involved, the odds and costs of "losing big" on a particular decision result in extreme conservatism. Losing power is often the most dreary prospect to managers.

Building upon Cyert and March (1963), Aharoni (1966), and Bower (1970), Gilmour (1973) has shown how the importance of the personal commitment of general managers to particular businesses and subordinates can prevent them from acting in the face of discrepancies. Hamermesh (1976) complemented Gilmour's findings with new evidence of how the outputs of the cognitive processes described by Steinbruner are stabilized into commitments, which in turn are frozen by the power structure within the organization. In other words, changes in strategic orientation must be preceded by cognitive

changes. But early commitments congeal individual views so that cognitive changes for the organization only occur through changes in power.

Cognitive premises of managers are usually shaped over time by the interaction between the manager's personality and the dominant structural lines of the organization, which normally reflect the demands of operating tasks. As they climb in the hierarchy and face increasingly nonroutine uncertain decisions, various managers will define the same problems differently and be committed to different types of solutions, their preferences having been set by their previous experience.[19]

The organizational implications of this phenomenon have been researched in depth by Lawrence and Lorsch (1967) in a comparative study of differentiation and integration between functional managers in several businesses. Though they did not address the strategy formulation process, their discussion of conflict resolution is relevant to the management of the strategic process. Lawrence and Lorsch suggested that in a diverse and dynamic environment, organizations have to be highly differentiated to match the environmental variety; organizations also have to be highly integrated, that is, have collaboration between departments. Effective differentiation inevitably creates conflicts; effective integration "means that these conflicts must be resolved to the approximate satisfaction of all parties and to the general good of the enterprise."

Thus, conflict is unavoidable if it results from effective differentiation, but it can also be exploited by the CEO to enrich the strategic management process. Conflict can be used to broaden the frame of reference within which strategic issues are considered. The dominant frame of reference is likely to reflect narrow short-term operational needs and the choices of a dominant coalition brought to power by a particularly successful fit with the current (or past) environment. Managers who are not part of the dominant coalition are likely to be on the lookout for environmental evolution which could challenge the dominant coalition and in-

[19] See, for example, Zaleznik (1975).

crease their own power. A CEO should not want to leave them out of the strategic process. As they seek an environment that fits their premises, they can act as "feelers" and "early warners" of change. Moreover, assuming that strategy is the art of imbalance, the CEO of a complex organization will want to keep a nucleus of dissenters who could rapidly become catalysts of strategic reorientations. Particularly when dominance cannot be achieved (in systemic terms), tensions with parts of the environment provide the conditions that make structural change possible. Misfits and negative feedback will be acted upon more rapidly. It is for this reason that crises are so useful as a premise for change that they are sometimes manufactured.

Learning takes place where knowledge is confronted with different knowledge. By managing conflict and letting executives compete for knowledge-based influence, the CEO improves the odds that strategic decisions will benefit from thorough examination and be based on creative solutions. Although the context within which particular managers operate benefits from consistency, there is also a case for allowing different networks of influence contexts to coexist within the organization. Selznick (1957) argued that protecting divergent values is needed to preserve the possibility of strategic change.

A question remains as to what motivates or shapes top management's substantive interventions. We now can understand how a CEO's strategic charge that "we need to become more multinational" might provide an effective discrepancy to drive problem solving and reorient coalitions in his or her company. We can also recognize that at IBM, Learson's selection of Evans' "product proliferation" diagnosis as well as his management of an adversary process of elaboration of the business idea of "a new compatible line" provided the premise for a new structure and a new strategy.[20] But more generally the processes of shifting from an "uncommitted" posture (see Steinbruner) to a committed posture are poorly understood.

The coexistence of several different ways of thinking and their conflict over specific decisions

may facilitate the CEO's overall vision of a desirable direction of evolution, and provide him or her with alternate vantage points on the strategic process. But as Cyrus the Great noted, "Diversity in counsel, unity in command."

Taken together, the works of the several authors reviewed in this section provide a basis for understanding and conceptualizing the behavior observed around streams of strategic decisions in the complex organization. These authors also document the political role of the CEO of such an organization as the governor of a complex strategic process.

The common threads which provide a unity in this body of knowledge are spun from a few simple underlying theories. The vision of the strategic process that emerges from a review of these works is rooted in cognitive psychology, in simple models of power, and the conceptualization of the firm as an open system.

In a wide variety of settings (both corporation and governmental organization), the language developed by the authors reviewed in this section has been remarkably useful for describing and explaining the behavior of groups of managers in developing strategy. Still the outputs of their research and conceptualization efforts have not yet been combined into a theory that would provide a critical observer with a view of the totality of the firm's strategic process. Though academics and consultants involved in studying the strategic process can integrate these concepts around specific cases, a convincing presentation (for those who reject case studies as a method or are not familiar with top management consulting) remains to be found. Practice being the only relevant test for a theory of practice, a convincing presentation is the only possible advancement of a general theory of the strategic process. Differences in the strategic process according to various conditions can be researched in a positivistic paradigm with testable hypotheses, but the overall conceptualization itself cannot, nor can its usefulness be measured.[21] These are the major

---

[20] As described in T. A. Wise (1966).

[21] It can only be approximated in a very crude way by assessing the extent to which ideas developed from it are used by practitioners, thus providing an amount of "face" validity.

methodological and expository challenges facing the integration of positional and managerial concepts into a single administrative theory.

CURRENT WORKS AND CHALLENGES FOR FUTURE RESEARCH

The complex task of managing a large, complex firm has been shown to be a delicate art of mixing substantive, organizational, and interpersonal considerations. Recent research on the problem of managing a multinational corporation has indicated, however, that this task is even more demanding (Prahalad, 1975). The many conflicting demands of the task make it possible to outline more clearly the strategic aspects of the general manager's job. Finally, in the work of Doz (1976), we have had an opportunity to see how the demands of host governments to influence the behavior of large corporations made the top management task still more difficult.

Perhaps the most insightful glimpse yet put forward of the workings of the management of the multinational corporation has been provided by Prahalad. He asked an obvious question: What possible meaning can be given to the concept of strategy in a company whose businesses participate in multiple industries and scores of countries? What does purpose mean in this context? Recognizing that a product-area matrix organization is the natural form to use in managing such a corporation, Prahalad sought to understand how a business comprising such a variety of activities could be said to have a corporate strategy.

As an approach to understanding the problem facing the large company's top management, Prahalad drew on Crozier's dynamic notion of power defined in terms of relative influence. He coined the term "relative power," explaining, "Power in a matrix is the extent of influence of an individual or group in formulating important decisions," and the individual or group with the most influence is considered to have "relative power." The locus of relative power is key to the behavior of the lower levels of general management responsible for areas and products in the following ways: [22]

1. The locus of relative power changes the concept of risk associated with projects as well as their content. An area-responsive organization spreads risk over a portfolio of products. It may not see the need to achieve worldwide dominance in a particular product line since investments of this sort unbalance the portfolio. A shift in the locus of power toward emphasis on worldwide coordination by product group will change the concept of risk so that it is viewed in terms of a portfolio of countries. In the long run, strategy is changed.

2. The locus of relative power influences the corporate capability to manage foreign exchange exposure risk. An area-predominant organization is likely to have very little interest in, or capability for, foreign exchange risk management. Only the cross-border flows of the sort managed by a worldwide product group can create real opportunities for foreign exchange gains or even avoid losses.

3. The locus of relative power determines the extent of stress in relationships with joint venture partners. A centrally led worldwide product organization has a very hard time coping with joint ventures. IBM has none for this reason and withdrew from India rather than tolerate one. Conversely, General Motors created an area firm to help manage their Japanese joint venture.

4. The locus of relative power influences the development of managers in terms of their career progression and mobility. Area predominance leads to area-bound generalists. Product dominance leads to product or functional specialists. In short, the locus of relative power influences strategic orientation and the process by which resources are allocated.

Prahalad then raised two questions: How should a management decide on the appropriate locus of relative power, and how can the base of power be moved? The answers can be found by examining the dilemma of the apparent either-or choices presented by area or product dominance in a multinational matrix. The ten-

---

[22] The list is paraphrased from Prahalad (1975).

sion derives from the desire to respond (in the contingent sense of Lawrence and Lorsch) to the variety of regional markets on the one hand, and to achieve the global benefits of inter-country coordination on the other. The great problems for top management come from the contradictory demands inherent in managing variety on the one hand and interdependence on the other.

In the present usage, variety and interdependence are not extremes on the same linear scale. Rather, they are orthogonal notions. A firm may perceive a need to respond to high or low variety in its markets, in the pattern of competition (fragmented in some places, oligopolistic elsewhere), in manufacturing (advanced or primitive), in technology, or in the executive group (local nationals or homogeneous). At the same time it may seek the benefits of interdependence in strategy, marketing (prices, packaging, products, or customers), manufacturing (local or global scale facilities), technology, and in control systems.

A management seeking to achieve a high degree of managerial variety will seek to have relative power reside in the area components of the matrix. An effort to achieve a high degree of interdependence will result in an emphasis on the product divisions.

Having decided on the appropriate locus of relative power, management must still decide how the locus can be moved. With structure given in the form of the matrix, what other sources of managerial influence are available? The answers are people, technology, procedure and the pattern of information flow.

1. *People.* Executives in an organization are seldom even in capability or temperament. By putting more capable or more aggressive managers in one part of the matrix, the locus of power can be altered.

2. *Technology.* In most multinationals, the source of technology is laboratories in the parent country. Where standardization of technology is imposed (either to achieve benefits of scale or with proprietary knowledge) a considerable shift toward worldwide coordination can be effected.

3. *Procedure.* Where a common language system, a reporting format, a training process, or a common socialization is provided, it is possible to move the locus of power so as to achieve more interdependence.

4. *Information flow.* Worldwide planning systems, change in reporting relationships, worldwide functional directors or coordinators, or other forms of organizational overlays can all be used to shift the locus of power.

While Prahalad confined his conclusions to the multinational, the logic of his analysis and the power of his analysis would seem to provide insight into the problem of altering the direction of the strategic process in any large, complex organization in which the key people with the power to commit do not understand the critical substance of most issues. In sum, the task for the top management of a multinational is not fundamentally different from that which Barnard (1938) described as the executive's key function: the establishment of a balance between competition and cooperation within the organization. Managerial differentiation enables the firm to cope with variety, but leads to internal competition. Interdependence through cooperation may suppress the ability to handle variety. Thus the modern executive faces what Arthur D. Little's Robert Wright calls "the ultimate matrix game." Managers of today's multinationals are not so much economic decision makers as they are governors of a social and political strategic management process. Managing the locus of relative power in that process shifts strategic direction. Put more sharply: in large, complex organizations we cannot talk about the process of strategy formulation except in social and political terms.

The task we have described thus far more than suffices to challenge company managements. Few firms are satisfied with their management capability. A delicate balance is barely established before a shift in the world economy or new competition forces some sort of structural, procedural, or executive change. But aggravating the difficulty facing top management is the desire of virtually all governments in the world to sit at the managing committee table and influence the locus of power. In almost every situation, the desired balance of administrative rationality contradicts the demands of political acceptability. Or, if for purposes of analysis here we can separate economic effects in a country from that country's political objectives, the problem of achieving political acceptability may add a third dimension to the task of balancing variety and interdependence.

How multinationals respond to such political pressures is a question that has been investigated and reported elsewhere by Doz (1976). Briefly, a major finding was that to the extent they were able, top managers did not reallocate relative power globally, but instead sought to vary its locus between products and between countries and even between individual strategic decisions, largely as a function of governments' demands and of the bargaining position of the firm in responding to these demands. Functional management was used to regulate more precisely the exercise of power by area and product group managers, so that relative power remained ambiguous and top management could intervene substantively into decisions on an ad hoc basis. Both area and product group managers were competing to find the sources of influence that would make their cognitive orientation become predominant. Careful design of communication lines and reward systems allowed top management to orient the internal competition toward the search for solutions useful for the organization as a whole. The constant interface between external and internal environments was a critical basis for teamwork. The external and internal environments were directly reflected in the strategic process.

For our present purposes it is sufficient to recognize that strategic intent as well as the management of the strategic process takes on a political character. Many questions which were easy to ignore in the past now emerge as central:

1. Which stake-holders will have "executive roles" in Barnard's sense of that word?
2. If some managers of the strategic process are "outsiders," how should efficiency be measured?
3. Will corporate managers be "elected"? Should they be?
4. What does corporate strategy mean if it is shaped by opposing political forces?
5. Or, what does it mean to be the private manager of a public multinational organization?

These questions are proposed as an agenda for future research.

Commentary

Ian C. MacMillan
Columbia University

INTRODUCTION

There are two topics of organizational/political behavior which appear to have direct relevance for corporation strategy and policy formulation, which have not received direct attention in the Bower/Doz paper. The purpose here is to briefly discuss these topics and make a plea for more sustained research efforts on the role of organizational/political behavior in strategy formulation.

The first topic is Interorganizational Strategy — that aspect of strategy which explicitly recognizes the fact that organizations (and in particular, businesses) should take into account opportunities for restructuring their environments in the pursuit of their objectives. While Bower and Doz speak of the need for dominance over, or at least a need for coalignment with, the task environment, they do not go into a detailed analysis of the process by which this can be done.

The second topic is concerned with Strategic Anticipation — that aspect of strategy which concerns itself with strategy formulation in the expectation that competitive organizations will respond to the corporate strategy with counter strategies, instead of passively accepting the moves of the strategist.

Both of these areas can be considerably enriched by making use of organization theory which is now extant, and by applying concepts which have been explored by behavioral scientists specifically to the strategy formulation problem.

INTERORGANIZATIONAL STRATEGY

Cyert and March (1963) and Thompson (1967), among others, have been eloquent in their pleas to recognize that organizations need to negotiate a viable domain in their environment if they are to survive.

If the plea is heeded, then it would appear that the topic of negotiated environments is of direct relevance to scholars concerned with the process of strategy formulation or policy formulation in an enterprise. Emery and Trist (1965) argue that in "turbulent field" type environments "the individual organization . . . cannot expect to adapt successfully simply through their own direct action." One can argue that even organizations in simple environments *should* not adapt through their own direct action, if willing and able allies can be found to assist them (MacMillan, 1974). Aiken and Hage (1968) argue that organizations are pushed into joint activities because of lack of resources. One can correspondingly argue that the strategist is guilty of squandering resources by deliberately ignoring joint activities as strategic options. Strategy formulation then comes clearly and firmly into the conceptual realm of a political economy (Zald, 1970) and attention should be given to the options available to the strategist on a broader set of dimensions, including political ones, than is traditionally the case in works on strategy.

Furthermore, if the arguments of Schumpeter (1942) and Marchal (1951) are to be heard, the organization should be attempting to secure a monopoly (albeit temporary) which will in effect "guarantee" environmental support until competitors can retaliate with counter strategies to dislodge them. In fact, if one accepts the data of Osborn and Hunt (1974), then the manner in which the organization tries to link itself with the environment has an important influence on effectiveness.[1]

The thrust of the argument here is that strategy formulation should take place in the context of an environment in which it is possible to undertake "political" actions which enhance the probabilities of strategic success, and that research is necessary to determine how firms go about selecting these actions.

To continue the argument, it is convenient to develop a taxonomy of generic options which are available to the organization contemplating such interorganizational actions.

The first useful option is the decision as to whether to act on the symbiont or the commensal. Chamberlain (1955) discusses the relationship between the firm and elements in its environment in terms of whether the element is providing some necessary input for the organization (funds, labor, information, material resources, and so on), which elements he terms *symbiont*, or whether the element is competing for these inputs, which elements he terms *commensal*. The usefulness of these terms is that they obviate the narrow focus which terms such as competitor and customer instigate. Pfeffer (1972b), and Pfeffer and Nowak (1976) in their investigations of merger activity and joint venture activity appear also to have found the term "symbiotic" useful in this regard. While economists have long recognized the "two-dimensionality" of environments (in terms such as oligopoly, oligopsony, etc.), this two-dimensionality of environmental complexity tends to have been disregarded in many policy and behavioral science studies.

The second generic option available, discussed by Thompson (1967), is concerned with whether the organization elects to use a competitive

---

[1] Unfortunately, their results are based on data for small, rigidly structured social service agencies, raising problems of generalizations to larger, more loosely structured profit seeking organizations.

(manipulative) strategy or a cooperative (accommodative) strategy. The manipulative mode would be concerned with the role the use of power and influence plays to convince the target environmental element to act as desired, while the accommodative mode would involve attempts to reach agreement with it. This dimension of the options available was implicitly considered by Benson (1975) in discussing the various strategies which could be employed to change interorganizational networks.

A third generic option available is whether the organization elects to confine itself to the *existing* domain of action or decides to alter its domain and enter into *new* interactions with its environment. Pfeffer (1972b) compresses this dimension by treating it as a third alternative to competitive or symbiotic mergers. It is conceptually more convenient to think in terms of an additional dimension, since the focus and effect of analysis is distinctly broader if one is exploring options for new domains rather than old ones.

Finally it is important to recognize that the firm contemplating interorganizational action has the option of *direct action* on the element targeted or of *indirect action*, in which the firm operates via a third element in its attempt to elicit the desired action by the target element.

Obviously, in a real life situation the firm may elect to use a combination of these options. However, it appears that the major options available to the firm can be conceived along the generic dimensions discussed above. These are depicted in Exhibit 3.18.

To summarize, then, there appear to be four major dichotomous dimensions along which the firm can undertake interorganizational strategy to restructure its environment to achieve its ends: namely (Direct or Indirect), (Manipulative or Accommodative) action aimed at (Symbionts or Commensals) in (Existing or New) domains. To illustrate the variety of these options, consider the following two examples:

A truck seat manufacturer, unable to sell his "physiologically designed" seat to certain truck assemblers, resorted to persuading (manipulation) a truckers union (indirect action) to demand his seats, thus causing customers of the assemblers to put pressure on these assemblers (symbionts in the existing domain).

In contrast, a travel company in deciding to reduce a certain shipping company's power in the market place negotiated (accommodation) with other travel companies (commensals) the formation of a travel agent's association (direct action) which would negotiate fare structures for all shipping companies in-

Exhibit 3.18   Four Dimensions of Interorganizational Strategic Action

Symbionts	Direct	Accommodate	New
			Existing
		Manipulate	New
			Existing
	Indirect	Accommodate	New
			Existing
		Manipulate	New
			Existing
Commensals	Direct	Accommodate	New
			Existing
		Manipulate	New
			Existing
	Indirect	Accommodate	New
			Existing
		Manipulate	New
			Existing

cluding ones that the travel company did not use (new domain).

One could argue that it is wasteful of resources and decreases the probability of strategic success, if the options opened by interorganizational action are not explicitly considered in formulating corporate strategy.

Moreover, there is ample evidence from existing research that such interorganizational strategies *are* employed and therefore warrant the serious attention of organization and policy/strategy researchers. Some of the evidence from existing research will be quoted below.

Scherer (1970) documents many cases of accommodative interorganizational action in his extensive discussion of industrial pricing, particularly "oligopolistic coordination." He quotes cases of overt and covert pricing and production agreements, price leadership strategies, tacit coordination via focal point pricing and various forms of pricing discrimination employed to secure greater profits via interorganizational action.[2]

Starbuck (1976), in his extensive review of organization environments, lists many publications which have been addressed to such topics as interorganizational coalitions, influence exerted on governmental politics, control of criteria by which organizations are evaluated externally, and discrimination among symbionts.

Pfeffer (1972a) in his study of size and composition of boards of directors was able to gather evidence of cooptation of board members who represented significant contingencies for the hospitals in this study. (Cooptation is one of the cooperative or accommodative strategies suggested by Thompson [1967].) Pfeffer also showed evidence that the function and composition of the board was positively correlated with ability to obtain community support and to attract resources, both to some extent measures of organizational effectiveness.

In another study, Pfeffer (1972b) showed that there is a significant relation between mergers and total transactions between the merging companies. He argued that this is a way of securing a negotiated environment (in this case

via coalescence, another accommodative strategy proposed by Thompson). In the same article, Pfeffer also found a correlation between mergers aimed at diversification and amount of government business done by the merging firm, showing some empirical support for the concept of domain *innovation* as an interorganizational strategy to reduce dependence (in this case, on government business).

So it would seem that organizations themselves see the viability of interorganization strategies, and it appears that organization behavior studies which focus on interorganizational strategies could provide useful insights for the corporate strategy theorist grappling with the task of studying strategy formulation process and major policy decisions in business organizations.

Of course, the strategy formulation task could be considerably lightened if the strategist had empirical research results on which to draw in deciding which of the generic options that are available in the decision circumstances will produce the best results.

Certain conditions would seem to preclude some options, or at least reduce their probability of success. Pfeffer (1972b) argued in his research that in mergers between commensals the benefits were an "inverted-U" function of the number of commensals in the industry. Very high or very low concentrations of firms tended to preclude such merger activity.

Pfeffer and Nowak (1976) reached the same conclusions for joint venture activity. Moreover, the numbers of symbionts and commensals in an industry have long been acknowledged by economists as being important determinants of competitive action. Presumably these will also influence the success of interorganizational strategy (MacMillan, 1972).

Staw and Szwajkowski (1975) argue that scarcity (munificence) in the environment of the organization encourages (discourages) legally questionable activities and present evidence to support the argument. Thus, resource scarcity may also be a factor which could influence the degree to which firms will undertake interorganizational action, and warrants further research.

The form which interorganizational coordination will take is another topic of potential research interest. Warren (1967) identifies a ty-

---

[2] Ethics, morality, and legality of such strategies are not discussed here.

pology of contexts within which organizations interrelate ranging from highly structured to highly unstructured systems in which inclusive goals are sought. Research could be directed towards determining the conditions which would give rise to, or create a demand for a highly structured interorganizational system, such as a manufacturers association, or a less structured one.

Litwak and Hylton (1961) and Van de Ven (1976) specify dimensions which influence interorganizational relationships, citing situational factors, process dimensions, structural dimensions and outcome dimensions as being major determinants of interorganizational systems. However, these are advanced in the context of service agencies, and we need to ask whether similar arguments can be applied to businesses. "Under what circumstances is it useful to form an industry association? an employers' association?" are questions with which the policy theorist could be assisted by research input.

Turk (1973) has indicated that two important factors which give rise to a need and a demand for more formal interorganizational relations in municipal government are scale and diversity. He argued that the larger the municipal organization and the more diversified its activities, the greater the need, and demand, for formal interorganizational relations. Does this apply to industries in the business sphere?

If research issues such as these could be pursued in the business arena, the results of the efforts would provide valuable guidelines for the selection by business strategists of generic options appropriate to the circumstances in which the strategy must be formulated, and thus provide some systematic structure by which to explore these possibilities, instead of relying on intuition, as is done at present.

STRATEGIC ANTICIPATION

The second topic which Bower and Doz do not address, but in which a consideration of behavioral and political variables could provide useful inputs to the theory of policy formulation processes, is that of strategic anticipation, by which is meant the anticipation of competi-

tive response to contemplated strategic moves.

Instead of implicitly assuming that unilateral action will be passively accepted in a competitive environment, it is important to consider the possibility of aggressive reaction by competitors.

It is felt that the application of existing organizational theory can provide valuable insights into the likelihood of certain responses. In this regard, the work of Allison (1971) cannot go unmentioned. Allison's work is discussed by Bower and Doz, but not in an *anticipatory* context. Allison's use of three models: rational actor, bureaucratic process, and organizational politics models proved useful in explaining many facets of the Cuban missile crisis and his work provides useful guidelines for policy research into the types of decision-making which incorporates strategic anticipation. A great deal of insight into the strategic moves of businesses could be developed by replicating his work in a number of business contexts, to determine under what circumstances and to what extent Allison's models are applicable.

As far as prediction of organization response is concerned, it is important to recognize that a firm's action is constrained by the fact that it must deliver certain results which are demanded by constituents of the organization, as Bower and Doz have aptly discussed in their paper. Yet equally important in strategy formulation is recognition that these phenomena constrain *competitors* as well.

In this regard, Thompson's (1967) thoughts on organization evaluation could be extremely useful. If the target organization's behavior in response to how it is being evaluated by constituents is taken into account, the strategist will be in a better position to judge the responses which the target will make to the strategist's action.

To use a simple example, Thompson states the following proposition:

> Under norms of rationality, organizations facing dynamic task environments seek to score favorably in relation to comparable organizations.

The point is that if one can be fairly sure that under specified conditions most organizations will act in a certain way, this provides a tool for "predicting" a response that the target does not even know it will make until it occurs!

This specific proposition proved useful to a travel company during the 1973 oil crisis. Airlines were rapidly increasing prices and throwing most travel companies into complete disarray. A particular travel company was able to determine their customer responses to price increases, and being in the luxury travel business found that their client base was actually expecting increases to be passed on. The issue was whether to move ahead of airline price increases or not. At a trade association meeting it became apparent that under these new dynamic conditions the competitors were attempting to hold down prices. It was decided that the company would apply Thompson's proposition and hold itself up in the trade as the "comparable organization," and that the standard of comparison was to be price. The company complained bitterly that the price increases of the airlines were driving it to push its own prices up or squeeze its profits down. The competitors duly fell in line and tried to hold their prices below that of the company, which then pushed its prices up until volume started to be affected. In this way, it developed sustained cash flow increases which provided it with much needed capital to secure charter contracts (which it could not afford before) and come in at a lower price which gained market share in the non-luxury market.

The point which is being made by this example is that existing theory from the behavioral science area has direct relevance to policy theory and policy research and can be used in an aggressive sense in policy formulation. There are thus a wealth of opportunities available to the strategist or policy theorist which can be tapped if existing behavioral theory is used in a *competitive* context. Schramm (1975) has done some empirical testing of Thompson's propositions concerning organizational assessment for universities and found support for Thompson's proposition concerning the tendency for organizations to demonstrate their fitness for the future by demonstrating historical improvement and by attempting to serve formally with comparable institutions. Perhaps it is important that similar research be done for firms' behavior.

The second area where organization theory can be useful in strategic anticipation is for use in "predicting" behavior of decision-making within target organizations.

Here again some of the work by Thompson on organization discretion is of relevance. If one can be fairly sure of the way in which discretion will be used by competitors in a set of circumstances then one is in a far better position to anticipate competitive response to a strategic move.

For illustrative purposes again, consider the following proposition from Thompson:

"The more serious the individual believes the consequences of error to be, the more he/she will seek to evade discretion."

One firm took explicit note of this proposition and used it by waiting until a certain competitor's marketing manager went on an extended business trip/vacation before making a move to launch and secure a dominant position in the market with a new product. The competitor was literally paralysed while the manager's replacement procrastinated the decision to respond. By the time he did so it was too late.

Discretion and its use could thus prove an invaluable help in understanding strategic anticipation. Policy theorists should investigate its use in business firms to gain better understanding of the phenomenon.

Starbuck (1976) argues that the selection of environments is a function of the perceptions of organization members, and that implicit criteria for selection of alternatives are determined by the organization set in which the organization is embedded, which set in turn biases the data which they supply to the organization for evaluation of these strategic alternatives. Duncan (1972), in his study of environments, also suggests that attention should be given to the individual *perceptions* of uncertainty, rather than just some absolute organizational uncertainty. To paraphrase Cyert and March (1963), ultimately it is *individuals* who make decisions in terms of their *perceptions* and not *organizations*, which make decisions in terms of *reality*. The strategic anticipation implications of these arguments are obvious. We need to try to learn via research what perceptions, of which individuals, under what conditions will tend to lead to certain strategic responses.

If this type of thinking is extended to include the work of Hage and Dewar (1973), some useful insights for strategic anticipation result. Hage and Dewar argued that elite values[3] were useful predictors of innovation. Extending this idea to strategic anticipation, one can ask whether elite values might not also be useful predictors of strategic responses. Research in this area will do much to build up a theory of strategic anticipation and hence enhance the whole of policy theory.

CONCLUSION

It is hoped that the above arguments have demonstrated a need for policy researchers to

[3] That is, the values held by the elite or dominant group in the organization.

give attention to two areas in which there are gaps in the current theory of strategy formulation. These are interorganizational action and strategic anticipation. Work related to these areas is already being done, but most of it is confined to non-business areas and is being investigated by organization theory and organization behavior researchers.

If these concepts can be transferred to the business context then current theories of corporate strategy should be considerably enhanced by producing models which better reflect the more aggressive strategy formulated by many corporate leaders in industry.

At the same time, the internal political phenomena, which are the main focus of the arguments by Bower and Doz, warrant further research if models are to be developed which reflect the full complexity of the strategy and policy formulation task.

Commentary

JOHN CHILD
University of Aston Management Centre

The main theme of Bower and Doz's paper is that the development and implementation of a firm's strategic vision — "a desired future position of the company in its environment" — depends upon the successful management of a network of organizational forces which create and foster that vision. The management of these forces is a social and political process.

This is a timely reminder that strategy formulation cannot proceed simply by appeal to a rationality, or "law of the situation," which top management defines. Nor can it then be embodied into a plan which all will accept equally as specifying objectively necessary action. For top management is dealing with people and interest groups who hold different expectations of the firm. Management may not be able fully to reconcile or satisfy such expectations. There may at best be an uneasy equilibrium in which con-

flicting demands are temporarily accommodated (Cyert and March, 1963). Various interests within the firm, corresponding to different subsidiaries, professional groups, union locals and so forth, may well be in a position to influence its strategic vision through their control of information, shaping of decision options, and even potential veto. Politics by one definition is the exercise of power, but when power within large, complex corporations cannot be exclusively concentrated into the hands of the chief executive or his corporate team, then an alternative definition — that politics is the art of the possible — becomes a more appropriate description of strategy formulation.

A precondition for business success is that possibilities are created for planned future developments to be realized. This means that the maintenance of social and political legitimacy for the corporation's activities is a prime strategic requisite. Bower and Doz analyze the internal, intra-organizational dimension to this problem. This consists of generating a sufficient consensus between departments, functions and/or divisions, and a synergy in their contributions, around a strategic objective and policy. In this perspective, the chief executive emerges as "a shaper of the premises of other executives' thoughts and the source of balance in the personal interactions of others."

In a European context, the analysis would require extension to include lower level employees. In some industries particularly, organized employee resistance to managerial plans has long been a condition of business operation — newspaper publishing, automobile manufacture and coal mining are examples. Today, some European countries are witnessing a demand from labor that it should participate in the very formulation of strategic plans.

Labor is organized partly from outside most corporations, and European management is therefore moving into the problem of how relations with outside organizations can be managed so as to secure conditions supportive of the company's "strategic vision." This is the side of the social and political process which Bower and Doz largely ignore. They are at one in so doing with much of the teaching and analysis of business policy which has been available to date. In a recent attempt to re-orient the subject towards a recognition of the significance of the external sociopolitical dimension, Kempner, Macmillan, and Hawkins (1976) emphasize "that the businessman's view of the opportunities and constraints open to his firm (and hence his judgements of the firm's strengths and weaknesses), is dependent on his analysis of the relationships between his business and the economic, political and social system ... this relationship tends to be modified as the activity and the structure of the economy and society changes. In particular, societal expectations and judgements of business enterprise are liable to be amended."

Historically, external support for business policies has always been conditional and judgments have continually been made of business enterprise. Government agencies such as the Antitrust Division of the U.S. Department of Justice have been active for a long time now. However, in recent years the degree of close interdependence of businss corporations both with government and other outside organizations has been growing. This lends a greater strategic significance to the quality of a corporation's external relations, which as MacMillan points out in his Commentary are primarily inter-organizational relations. As the market place is replaced by direct inter-corporate arrangements and as the intervention of government increases, so a carefully thought-out *management* of these relations is required.

This commentary will concentrate on the external social and political side to strategy formulation in view of the limited attention it receives from Bower and Doz. It also briefly reviews relevant concepts and research on the management of external relations.

THE STRATEGIC IMPORTANCE OF EXTERNAL SOCIAL AND POLITICAL RELATIONS

Mintzberg (1973) found, when observing five chief executives ten years ago, that they spent 38% of their working time away from their organizations. John Fidler (1977) who has recently interviewed 110 chief executives of British companies for his doctoral research in process at the University of Aston suggests that when they reach the top, these men turn outwards and attach considerable importance to relationships with leading shareholders (usually institutional), financial analysts, senior government officials and politicians. As one chief executive put it with reference to the latter two groups: "nowadays politics enters into business a great deal ... we spend ten percent of our time on the political side."

This kind of research evidence, and personal observation in addition, suggests that chief executives tend to spend a significant portion of their time on managing strategic external relationships. One would predict that these relationships will occupy the attention of executives concerned with strategic issues to an increasing extent as business corporations enter into greater interdependencies among themselves and with governmental and community bodies.

Attempts to manage the external environment through collaborative relationships with other corporations were observed by Adam Smith to be characteristic socio-political processes among businessmen two hundred years ago (Smith, 1776). Smith was referring, of course, to restrictive practices! As MacMillan notes in his Commentary, there is ample evidence from more recent research that strategies aimed at securing and defining a domain of operation, or at entering a new field through non-competitive means, are employed frequently by many organizations today. The range includes agreements to regulate prices and production levels and to define market segments; joint programs and ventures; cooptation of key external resource providers and, at one extreme, actual mergers. Each of these forms of interdependence between corporations can significantly affect the strategic opportunities available to the partners and considerably increase their certainty about the environments in which they operate. Such arrangements, however, require negotiation and maintenance. Their negotiation demands senior executive time and is a significant top management process. Their maintenance, judging by research on joint programs (Aiken and Hage, 1968; Broden, 1976), requires modifications to the internal management structure so that specialist roles can be created to deal on a continuing basis with counterparts in the collaborating organization(s), and so that the additional load of intensive communications can be adequately handled.

Back in the 1960s, the costs and demands of technological innovation were the prime movers behind growing interdependence between business and government (Child, 1969). In advanced industrial societies, government is a significant provider of funds for new developments, and, in instances such as the space program, government agencies went so far as to impose specific requirements concerning the internal organization of contractor companies. Today, the grounds for interdependence between business and government are extending. It is no longer simply a question of defining the performance conditions under which corporations are to receive public finance, or maintaining basic rules of the game governing traditional areas of public concern such as competition, health and welfare at work, and industrial relations. Expectations are being placed upon business corporations that draw them far closer to being instruments of government economic and social policy. Events have moved particularly far down this road in some European countries. The chief executive of a major British food manufacturing company has listed the examples of specific issues "which represent the changed terms which society is demanding of business" (Cadbury, 1977). These include adopting pricing, profit, and pay policies in support of government actions to counter inflation; investment in non-productive equipment to reduce pollution and to improve working conditions; releasing managers to take on non-business assignments and encouraging employees to take up public service; and providing for board representation of the views of employees, consumers and the public interest.

Several long-term developments appear to have contributed to the placing of these new demands and constraints upon business. Along with a questioning of economic growth as a viable objective of social policy, there is more reluctance today to accept the idea that business's record as the vehicle of economic progress constitutes a sufficient justification for its power within society. Giant corporations dominate in many industries and within many developing economies. This has generated an awareness of business power, and has lent a sense of urgency to the task of controlling such power. Relations with host governments are for this reason becoming more sensitive for strategists within multinationals (Vernon, 1973; Negandhi and Prasad, 1975). Interdependence with government is further promoted because a relatively small collection of dominant corporations lend themselves as manageable instruments through which national indicative economic planning and policy guidelines can be implemented. They are the commanding heights of modern economies which governments are learning how to control without having to own or operate directly. Recently, for instance, the British government has successfully pressured the Heinz Corporation to rescind a remuneration agreement in order to have this conform to entirely non-statutory national wage and salary "guidelines."

Another force behind the growing significance of government and community organizations lies in evolving attitudes toward social criteria of business performance. A low quality of urban life, dissatisfaction at work, energy wastage, poor product quality and reliability, pollution and waste disposal — all these are problems for which business has in recent years been asked to accept some share of the blame. Pressure groups for the protection of public interests in these fields have proliferated, while governmental responses can be seen in a spate of legislation on matters ranging from product liability to health and safety at work. Action taken by government agencies on the basis of such legislation can easily become of strategic significance to a corporation which is affected. A measure of the changing environment created for business by recent legislation in the United States is the increase in agencies with which business now has to deal (*Business Week*, 1977).

The trend towards growing interdependence with other organizations, especially those of government, is evident throughout the industrialized world, though it clearly varies in degree and in detail. Looking ahead such interdependencies raise the question of how far business strategy will continue to be formulated *by* the management of corporations rather than being formulated *for* management. Even in the American context, if one asks what will be the most significant strategic development for General Motors over the next five years, the answer could be the demise of American Motors and even Chrysler. This would be significant not so much because it changed GM's economic competitive environment, where the difference would be relatively limited, but because it could be the trigger for anti-trust action aimed at breaking up GM itself. Moreover, it may not be wise simply to dismiss the increasing level of intervention being placed upon business in the European "social democracies" as aberrant to the normal course of capitalist development. If one's analysis is that growing intervention is a product not entirely of political ideology, but also

of structural factors such as the size and scope of big business relative to the total economy, and the emergence of a better educated and more demanding population, then what is happening now in Europe may well come to America some years later.

MANAGING EXTERNAL RELATIONS — CONCEPTS AND RESEARCH

Organizations outside the corporation are today extremely significant for the formulation of business strategy. Governmental actions pursued through a growing number of public agencies have come to impinge particularly strongly on business in recent years. For students of business policy, then, the management of external relations should clearly be an issue of major concern. But what framework of analysis can they begin to apply here? Are some relevant concepts already available as theoretical building blocks and does some existing research point the way to fruitful future enquiry?

There has, perhaps, been too much of a tendency to view external institutions exclusively as sources of constraint upon business actions. Nostalgia for the "free market" of the independent self-financing entrepreneur encourages the opinion that the complexity of interdependencies with other organizations which corporations have to manage today is diverting their executives from pursuing basic business opportunities effectively. Apart from the fact that the society in which business operates is very different today compared with a century earlier, and this just has to be recognized, such a view overlooks the two-way nature of relations between corporations and other institutions. They consist of *inter*dependencies, not simply of dependencies. The reliance which a government places upon a large business corporation for fulfillment of its objectives on, say, regional employment may be quite considerable, just as a financial institution like an insurance company relies upon sustained business performance in order to earn a satisfactory return and to provide continuing security for its policy holders or pension fund clientele.

The recognition that we are dealing with relations in which both corporation and external institution have some degree of interdependence makes relevant the conceptual language of power, influence, and negotiation. Crozier's scheme for analyzing the relative power of different departments within an organization (1964) — to which Bower and Doz refer — could be extended to analyzing the relative power of a business corporation within its environment. If, for example, a corporation operating in a developing country: (1) is providing a service by way of technology, products, employment and so forth which that country's government values highly; (2) cannot readily be replaced by other corporations; and (3) can contribute significantly through its internal trading arrangements to the country's balance of foreign payments when a deficit becomes difficult to finance, then the Crozier-type analysis predicts that the corporation will enjoy high bargaining power with that host country's government. To employ the concepts now in academic use, the corporation enjoys respectively: (1) high *centrality*, (2) low *substitutability*, and (3) controls, via its policies, what is a significant area of financial *uncertainty* for the other party. Insofar as one of the ground rules of entering into negotiation is to appreciate both your own and your partner's strengths and weaknesses, the development of analysis along these lines would be of practical as well as academic value.

Thompson (1967) argued that organizations "subject to norms of rationality" will attempt to manage their interdependencies with parties in the environment. He made the point that the relative power enjoyed by an organization could vary between different external institutions, and so in the management of external relations different approaches may have to be utilized according to the particular power position. Thompson then distinguished between two basic strategies which organizations like corporations can adopt vis-à-vis the environment in order to create conditions favorable to their "strategic vision." Neither strategy is mutually exclusive. The first is to compete on the basis of superior effectiveness. The second is to attempt to secure or improve favorable exchanges with outside

organizations by means of political actions taken with respect to those organizations. Thompson (1967) called this latter a cooperative strategy, and he distinguished three main types: (1) *contracting*, in which an agreement is negotiated for the future; (2) *coopting*, in which new elements are absorbed into the leadership or policy-making structure of an organization — these are normally representatives of influential outside organizations; and (3) *coalescing*, which refers to joint ventures and, at the extreme, to mergers between organizations. Thompson advanced propositions as to the kind of relative power relations between organizations which would promote these alternative arrangements.

There is a growing literature of research into the process of negotiation (see Rubin and Brown, 1975), largely following Walton's and McKersie's seminal work on *A Behavioral Theory of Labor Negotiations* (1965). This literature, while tending to concentrate on formal negotiation, is currently being applied in training on labor relations and thought could well be given to developing equivalent training for the kind of strategic negotiation in which top management is involved. Researchers such as P. Abell (1975) and Pettigrew (1975) are developing models of decision making within organizations which take account both of relative power positions enjoyed by individuals, groups or departments, and of the moves they may adopt to influence decisions under negotiation and/or to secure support for their activities. These are major contributions which Bower and Doz would have found useful in developing an appreciation of the internal social and political processes involved in strategy formulation. They also have considerable potential for aiding our understanding of external strategic negotiation. Abell's work in particular adopts a bargaining framework, which recognizes that decision making is likely to proceed over several stages. The initial preferences held by a manager, and perhaps embodied in his own initial "strategic vision" are likely to be modified and/or crystallized through an informal process of comparing notes and reaching understandings with other decision makers prior to a formal decision making or negotiating session. A similar conclusion has been reached by Pahl and Winkler

(1974) from their study of the activities of British company directors.

An equivalent in the management of external relations to this informal internal process is lobbying. Fidler (1977) concluded from his study of British top businessmen that while they could not normally hope to dissuade politicians from enacting major pieces of legislation, much could be done to affect the wording of legislation. The executives he interviewed mentioned between them eleven recent Parliamentary Bills on which they as individuals had lobbied, claiming some success on nine of them. There are also other matters which are not the subject of legislation in Britain, such as import tariffs, export licenses, planning permission for plant expansion and subsidiaries, on which businessmen claimed lobbying could also be effective. The methods of lobbying they use vary from the use of personal friendships and private connections to the more direct approach such as a lunch invitation. Assael (1968) has examined the conditions under which American trade associations have become actively involved in lobbying for their members, and this is a further channel for exerting influence in the environment.

Studies of interest groups, such as that of the British medical profession conducted by Eckstein (1960), also spell out some of the tactics of lobbying and exerting informal pressure on government which top businessmen might examine carefully as part of a business policy training. Indeed, the literature of political science has given considerable attention to the ways in which organizations can exercise influence and exert pressure in modern society. Castles et al. (1971) provides a collection of relevant articles.

One of the more difficult practical problems in the management of external relations involves establishing what is a socially acceptable basis upon which negotiation can take place and contracts secured. Unless there is the rare case where either the business corporation or the outside organization can, and wishes, completely to dominate the other party, some means must be found of establishing what is "the norm of reciprocity" (Gouldner, 1960). On what basis of exchange, in other words, can a contract or working arrangement be formed? What is expected of business by the outside parties in one part of the world may not be regarded as legitimate in their home country, as is clearly illustrated by the "scandal" of multinational bribery in some countries. There is, thus, a cultural dimension to the norm of reciprocity which can cause problems of inconsistency in business practice, but which is too important strategically to be ignored. For example, a multinational corporation operating in India was wise enough to offer its network of outlets for the distribution of contraceptives in support of the Indian government's birth control campaign. In return, this corporation received favored treatment from that government. One good turn deserves another is the norm of reciprocity. It is of the utmost importance for the top management of a firm to understand this in order to secure adequate strategic opportunities in a centrally controlled economy, of which there are many in the world today. The lesson also applies, of course, to bargaining with other external parties.

Coopting is the second non-competitive way that Thompson distinguished of managing interdependence with the environment. There are now several studies which show that cooptation of strategically significant external parties can be an effective way of managing the environment. Selznick (1949) in his study of the Tennessee Valley Authority described how that organization was able partly to neutralize the strong opposition it faced to its strategic mission by bringing representatives from those groups onto its governing boards. Pfeffer (1972a) using data on 80 large U.S. non-financial corporations concluded that their use of cooptation was related to their dependence on outside resource providers. For instance, the more that external capital was required, the higher tended to be the percentage of board members representing financial institutions. Corporations which deviated from an empirically estimated equation for the number of outside directors, incorporating size, degree of debt financing, local and national regulation, were found to perform more poorly compared to standards for their industry.

Dooley (1969) examined interlocking directorships among the 250 largest U.S. corporations in 1935 and 1965 and concluded that most have been interlocked with other large corporations for many decades. Nearly one in every eight interlocks involved companies which are competitors, even though this is illegal under the Clayton Act. The most prevalent type of interlocking directorship connects corporations which have their head offices within the same commercial center, such as New York or Chicago. Dooley concluded that this degree of interlock points to a constraint upon autonomy in corporate strategy formulation — "Within its own walls it faces the constraining influence of the financier, the local interest, and the competitor" (Dooley, 1969: 323) — and this reminds us that "outsider" directors can be imposed on, as well as coopted by, a corporation. Nevertheless, it does overlook the positive role that interlocking can serve in strategy formulation as a source of information and support from the environment.

Pfeffer (1972b) also points out that cooptation may carry certain disadvantages as a strategy for managing external relations. As Selznick (1949) found with the TVA, absorption of representatives of powerful outside groups into the organization's boards may divert it from its original objectives and set constraints on its strategy formulation. In addition, recruits suited to cooptation by dint of their power and resources may possibly not be available. Other means of managing external relations may therefore be required. Apart from securing long-term contracts or informal understandings via negotiation, this leaves the third strategy identified by Thompson, namely coalescing.

Pfeffer (1972a) examined one form of coalescing — the merger. He identified three different purposes for different types of mergers: (1) reducing "symbiotic interdependence" through vertical integration, (2) reducing "commensalistic (competitive) interdependence" via horizontal merger, or (3) reducing dependence on one market and/or seizing new opportunities for profitable expansion via diversification mergers. Pfeffer then analyzed Federal Trade Commission data on mergers between 1948 and 1969 and concluded that the higher the interdependence in inputs and outputs between firms (and also between industries) the more likely were mergers to take place. Mergers between

competitors were an "inverted-U" function of the number of competitors in an industry — there were proportionately more mergers in industries around the 40 percent concentration ratio level than industries with higher or lower concentration ratios. Finally, mergers aimed at diversification appeared to be used particularly frequently by firms located in industries with a heavy reliance on government business, suggesting that diversification merger is a way of reducing commercial dependence on the government.

Joint programs and joint ventures are another coalescing strategy for managing the environment. These may be distinguished from mergers in that they do not involve a combination of *all* the assets of two or more corporations. Broden's research (1976) into Swedish prefabricated housing manufacturers showed how entering into joint programs with construction firms provided a basis for reducing uncertainty and securing more rapid growth. Pfeffer and Nowak (1976) review other studies into joint ventures and conclude that these tend to be used to organize groups of organizations and also tend to occur among either competitors or organizations which are in a buyer-seller relationship. Their research also indicated that factors such as purchase and sales interdependence, combined with knowledge of industry concentration and certain other variables, may go some way towards predicting a propensity to engage in joint ventures.

Earlier in this commentary, it was pointed out that in the maintenance of joint programs specialist "link" roles will probably have to be created. This serves to draw attention to another area of enquiry which is only just beginning to be explored, namely the importance which the personality of executives or staff engaged in managing external relations may have for their effectiveness. This factor could be of critical importance for the success of informal negotiations, while, at a more specialized staff level, the tolerance for ambiguity of those in organizational boundary roles may directly affect their ability to evaluate and convey complexities and uncertainties to strategic decision makers (McCaskey, 1976). If further research establishes that people of a certain personality type are better able to cope with managing external relations, this would have obvious practical implications for personnel selection.

CONCLUDING QUESTIONS AND REMARKS

This commentary has pointed to a social and political aspect of the strategy formulation process which is not adequately covered in Bower and Doz's paper. It has argued that the management of social and political external relations is of strategic significance for the business corporation, and deserves more attention. Relevant concepts and research were then briefly reviewed in order to indicate that some understanding of managing external relations can already be gleaned from disciplines such as organizational behavior and political science.

Many questions remain unanswered and little researched. What, for example, should govern the choice between alternative cooperative methods of managing the environment, given that each one involves a trade-off between gains in resources and/or reduction of threat and uncertainty, on the one hand, and some loss in autonomy, on the other hand? In what circumstances would it benefit a firm to lobby through a trade association rather than independently? What is an appropriate style for managing external socio-political relations and how does this vary according to the country and the type of external institution in question? Can a business corporation go beyond negotiation with relevant government agencies and also attempt to influence their staffing and policies, employing a kind of informal cooptation? What kind of criteria should be applied in evaluating the degree of success a corporation has in managing external relations? Indeed, do we accept that in a so-called "pluralist" society, it could be undesirable for a corporation to be too successful in managing external parties simply to create conditions for the strategy *its* top management wishes to pursue?

The problem also remains of how research into these issues could be conducted. Such research needs to be sufficiently intensive to afford insight into decisions and processes of consider-

able complexity, and yet also needs to offer carefully drawn comparisons in order to provide an opportunity for reaching conclusions on the effectiveness of alternative approaches to managing external relations. It is likely that only senior managers intimately concerned with an organizations' strategic management processes can provide the necessary degree of insight for two reasons. First, and more obvious, the outside researcher is unlikely to obtain full access to such significant and sensitive matters. Second, the top manager's own construction of reality and those of the external parties with whom he is negotiating will be critical to the understanding of what takes place between them. For this is a level of management where the impersonal conformity of rules has little part to play in the decision making process, while personal initiative and interpersonal process has a great deal of influence.

The problem remains of how to make comparisons between cases where much of the relevant data are personal qualitative accounts of how judgment, ideology and partial information were welded into strategic action in the context of negotiating with others. Clearly, a partnership between researcher and strategist is required. The researcher has the freedom to range between different cases and the training to categorize and apply rudimentary measurement in so doing. Such categorization is, however, largely meaningless unless the researcher really understands the substance of what is at issue and this is where he needs help from those involved. On the other hand, without categorization, comparison becomes impossible and without comparison an assessment of the efficacy of alternatives cannot be made. Since every corporation is unique and since we cannot treat corporations as objects of experiment, any comparisons between them will be subject to limitation. This is simply to say that in the strategic area we shall always be in difficulty when attempting to assess what knowledge is valid, both theoretically and prescriptively (since a valid theory is the basis for valid prescription). Despite these problems, however, much more investigation should be made into the kind of questions raised earlier in this section, and we have as yet barely made a start on that endeavor.

Section 3 References

Abell, Derek. "Competitive Market Strategies: Some Generalizations and Hypotheses." Cambridge, Mass.: Marketing Science Institute, Report No. 75-107. April 1975.

Abell, P. *Organizations as Bargaining and Influence Systems.* London: Heinemann, 1975.

Abernathy, William J. and Phillip L. Townsend. "Technology, Productivity and Process Change." *Technological Forecasting and Social Change,* Vol. 7, No. 4, 1975.

Abernathy, William J. and Kenneth Wayne. "Limits of the Learning Curve." *Harvard Business Review,* September–October 1974.

Abt, Clark, et al. "A Scenario Generating Methodology," in Bright, James R. and Milton Schoeman (editors). *A Guide to Practical Technological Forecasting.* Englewood Cliffs, N.J.: Prentice-Hall, 1973.

Ackerman, Robert W. "Influence of Integration and Diversity on the Investment Process." *Administrative Science Quarterly,* September 1970.

Ackoff, Russell. *A Concept of Corporate Planning.* New York: Wiley, 1970.

Ackoff, Russell. *Redesigning the Future.* New York: Wiley, 1974.

Aguilar, Francis J. *Scanning the Business Environment.* New York: Macmillan, 1967.

Aharoni, Y. *The Foreign Investment Decision Process.* Boston, Mass.: Division of Research, Graduate School of Business Administration, Harvard University, 1966.

Aiken, M. and J. Hage. "Organizational Interdependence and Intra-Organizational Structure." *American Sociological Review,* Vol. 39, pp. 912-930, 1968.

Allan, Gerald B. and John S. Hammond, III. "Note on the Use of Experience Curves in Competitive Decision Making." Boston: ICCH, #4-175-175, 1975.

Allen, Michael G. "Strategic Problems Facing Today's Corporate Planner." Presentation to the Academy of Management. Kansas City, Mo., August 1976.

Allen, T. J., et al. "Regulation and Innovation in Five Industries in Europe and Japan." *Research Policy* (forthcoming).

Allison, Graham T. "Policy Process and Politics." Doctoral diss., Harvard University, 1968.

Allison, Graham T. *Essence of Decision: Explaining the Cuban Missile Crisis.* Boston: Little, Brown, 1971.

Ament, Robert G. "Comparison of Delphi Forecasting Studies in 1964 and 1969." *Futures,* March 1970.

Anderson, Carl R. and Frank T. Paine. "PIMS: A Re-examination." Presentation to Academy of Management. Orlando, Florida, August 1977.

Andrews, Kenneth. *The Concept of Corporate Strategy.* Homewood, Ill.: Dow-Jones-Irwin, 1971.

Anshen, Mel and William D. Guth. "Strategies for Research in Policy Formulation." *Journal of Business,* October 1973.

Ansoff, H. Igor. *Corporate Strategy: An Analytic Approach to Business Policy for Growth and Expansion.* New York: McGraw-Hill, 1965.

Ansoff, H. Igor and Richard C. Brandenburg. "A Program of Research in Business Planning." *Management Science,* February 1967.

Ansoff, H. Igor, Roger P. DeClerck and Robert L. Hayes. *From Strategic Planning to Strategic Management.* New York: Wiley, 1976.

Ansoff, H. Igor and James C. Leontiades. "Strategic Portfolio Management." *Journal of General Management,* Autumn 1976.

Ansoff, H. Igor and John M. Stewart. "Strategies for a Technology-Based Business." *Harvard Business Review,* November–December 1967.

Ansoff, H. Igor, J. Avener, Richard G. Brandenburg, F. E. Portner, and Raymond Radosevich. *Acquisition Behavior of U. S. Manufacturing Firms.* Nashville, Tennessee: Vanderbilt University Press, 1971.

Ashby, W. R. *Design for a Brain* (2d revised edition). London: Chapman and Hall, Ltd., 1960.

Assael, H. "The Political Role of Trade Associations in Distributive Conflict Resolution." *Journal of Marketing,* April 1968.

Ayres, Ralph U. *Technological Forecasting and Long-Range Planning.* New York: McGraw-Hill, 1969.

Barnard, Chester I. *The Functions of the Executive.* Cambridge, Mass.: Harvard University Press, 1938.

Baumol, William J. "Entrepreneurship in Economic Theory." *American Economic Review,* May 1968.

Bell, Daniel, et al. "Toward the Year 2000: Work in Progress." *Daedalus,* Summer 1967.

Benson, J. K. "The Interorganizational Network as a Political Economy." *Administrative Science Quarterly,* June 1975.

Berg, Norman A. "The Allocation of Strategic Funds in a Large, Diversified Industrial Company." Doctoral diss., Harvard University, 1964.

Berg, Norman A. "Strategic Planning in Conglomerate Companies." *Harvard Business Review,* May–June 1965.

Berg, Norman A. "What's Different About Conglomerate Management?" *Harvard Business Review,* November–December 1969.

Biggadike, Ralph. "Entry, Strategy and Performance." Doctoral diss., Harvard University, 1976.

Birch, David L. *The Economic Future of City and Suburb.* New York: Committee on Economic Development, 1970.

Blackman, A. W. "The Rate of Innovation in the Commercial Aircraft Jet Engine Market." *Technological Forecasting and Social Change,* Vol. 2, 1971.

Blackman, A. W., et al. "An Innovation Index Based on Factor Analysis." *Technological Forecasting and Social Change,* Vol. 4, No. 3, 1973.

The Boston Consulting Group. *Perspectives on Experience.* Boston: The Boston Consulting Group, Inc., 1968.

Bower, Joseph L. "Strategy as a Problem Solving Theory of Business Planning." Boston, Mass.: Intercollegiate Case Clearing House Report No. BP894, 1967.

Bower, Joseph L. "Descriptive Decision Theory from the 'Administrative' Viewpoint," in Bauer, Raymond A. and Kenneth J. Gergen. *The Study of Policy Formation.* New York: The Free Press, 1968.

Bower, Joseph L. *Managing the Resource Allocation Process: A Study of Corporate Planning and Investment.* Boston: Division of Research, Graduate School of Business Administration, Harvard University, 1970.

Bower, Joseph L. and C. K. Prahalad. "Power in the Multinationals." Monograph to be published in 1978.

Braybrooke, David and Charles E. Lindblom. *A Strategy of Decision.* New York: The Free Press, 1963.

Bright, James R. "Evaluating Signals of Technological Change." *Harvard Business Review,* January–February 1970.

Broden, P. *Turbulence and Organizational Change.* University of Linköping Studies in Science and Technology, Sweden, No. 7, 1976.

Brown, James W. "Perceived Environmental Uncertainty and the Two-Step Flow Process of Scientific and Technical Communication in Research and Development Laboratories." Doctoral diss., Indiana University, 1976.

Buckley, Walter. *Sociology and Modern System Theory.* Englewood Cliffs, N.J.: Prentice-Hall 1967.

Burns, Tom and G. M. Stalker. *The Management of Innovation.* London: Tavistock Publications, 1961.

Business Week. "Corporate Planning: Piercing Fog in the Executive Suite." April 28, 1975.

Buzzell, Robert D., Bradley T. Gale and Ralph G. M. Sultan. "Market Share — A Key to Profitability." *Harvard Business Review,* January–February 1975.

Cadbury, G. A. H. "Company Environment and Social Responsibility," in Bull, George A. (editor), *The Director's Handbook.* New York: McGraw-Hill, 1977.

Cannon, J. Thomas. *Business Strategy and Policy.* New York: Harcourt, Brace and World, 1968.

Carter, E. Eugene and K. J. Cohen. "Portfolio Aspects of Strategic Planning." *Journal of Business Policy,* Summer 1972.

Castles, F. G., D. J. Murray and D. C. Potter (editors). *Decisions, Organizations and Society.* Harmondsworth: Penguin, 1971.

Chamberlain, N. W. *A General Theory of Economic Process.* New York: Harper, 1955.

Chambers, John C., S. K. Mullick and D. D. Smith. "How to Choose the Right Forecasting Technique." *Harvard Business Review,* July–August 1971.

Chandler, Alfred D. *Strategy and Structure: Chapters in the History of the Industrial Enterprise.* Cambridge, Mass.: M.I.T. Press, 1962.

Channon, Derek F. "Strategic Planning Portfolio Models: Practical Progress and Problems in Practice." Manchester Business School, draft, 1976.

Channon, Derek F. "Strategy Formulation as an Analytical Process." *International Studies of Management and Organization,* Vol. 7, Summer 1977.

Channon, Derek F. "Use and Abuse of Analytical Techniques for Strategy Making." TIMS Conference, Athens, 1977.

Channon, Derek F. and R. M. Jalland. *Multinational Strategic Planning.* New York: Macmillan, 1978.

Charpie, Robert A. "Technological Innovation and Economic Growth," in *Applied Science and Technological Progress.* Report to the Committee on Science and Astronautics, U.S. House of Representatives, by the National Academy of Science. Washington, D.C.: U.S. Government Printing Office, June 1967.

Chevalier, Michel. "The Strategy Spectre Behind Your Market Share." *European Business,* Summer, 1972.

Child, John. *The Business Enterprise in Modern Industrial Society.* London: Collier-Macmillan, 1969.

Christensen, C. Roland, Kenneth R. Andrews and Joseph L. Bower. *Business Policy: Text and Cases.* Homewood, Ill.: Richard D. Irwin, 1973.

Christensen, H. Kurt. "Product, Market and Company Influences Upon the Profitability of Business Unit Research and Development Expenditures." Doctoral diss., Columbia University, 1977.

Churchman, C. W. *The Design of Inquiry Systems.* New York: Basic Books, 1971.

Coates, Joseph F. "Some Methods and Techniques for Comprehensive Impact Assessment." *Technological Forecasting and Social Change,* Vol. 6, No. 4, 1974.

Coates, Joseph F. "The Role of Formal Models in Technological Assessment." *Technological Forecasting and Social Change,* Vol. 9, Nos. 1–2, 1976.

Cohen, Kalman J., and Richard M. Cyert. "Strategy: Formulation, Implementation, and Monitoring." *Journal of Business,* July 1973.

Collings, R. L. "Scanning the Environment for Strategic Information." Doctoral diss., Harvard University, 1968.

The Conference Board. "Planning Under Uncertainty: Multiple Scenario and Contingency Planning." 1978.

Connolly, Terrance. "The Effects of Uncertainty on Communication in a Diffuse Decision Process, with an Application to Budgeting Decisions in NASA." Doctoral diss., Northwestern University, 1972.

Cooper, Arnold C. and Dan E. Schendel. "Strategic Responses to Technological Threats." *Business Horizons,* February 1976.

Coyle, R. G. "Systems Dynamics: An Approach to Policy Formulation." *Journal of Business Policy,* Spring 1973.

Crozier, M. *The Bureaucratic Phenomenon.* London: Tavistock Publications, 1964.

Cunningham, M. T. "The Application of Product Life Cycles to Corporate Strategy: Some Research Findings." *British Journal of Marketing,* Spring 1969.

Cyert, Richard M. and James G. March. *A Behavioral Theory of the Firm.* Englewood Cliffs, N.J.: Prentice-Hall, 1963.

Dalkey, Norman D. and Daniel L. Rourke. *Experimental Assessment of Delphi Procedures with Group Value Judgments.* Santa Monica, Calif.: The RAND Corp., R-612-ARPA, February 1971.

Daniells, Lorna M. *Business Forecasting for the 1970's: A Selected Annotated Bibliography.* Boston: Graduate School of Business Administration, Harvard University, Baker Library, 1970.

Day, George S. and Allan D. Shocker. "Identifying Competitive Product Market Boundaries: Strategic and Analytical Issues." Report No. 76-112. Cambridge, Mass.: Marketing Science Institute, 1976.

Delbecq, André L., A. H. Van de Ven and D. H. Gustafson. *Group Techniques for Program Planning: A Guide to Nominal Group and Delphi Processes.* Glenview, Ill.: Scott, Foresman, 1975.

Denning, B. W. "The Integration of Business Studies at the Conceptual Level." *Journal of Management Studies,* February 1968.

Dhalla, Nariman K. and Sonia Yuspeh. "Forget the Product Life Cycle Concept!" *Harvard Business Review,* January–February 1976.

Dooley, P. C. "The Interlocking Directorate." *American Economic Review,* June 1969.

Dory, John P. and Robert J. Lord. "Does TF Really Work?" *Harvard Business Review,* November–December 1970.

Douglass, Merrill E. "Organizational and Environment Interaction Testing a Comparative Methodology." *Academy of Management Proceedings,* 1973.

Doz, Yves. "National Policies and Multinational Management." Doctoral diss., Harvard University, 1976.

Duncan, Robert B. "Characteristics of Organizational Environments and Perceived Environmental Uncertainty." *Administrative Science Quarterly,* September 1972.

Dunckel, Earl B., W. K. Reed and I. H. Wilson. *The Business Environment of the Seventies: A Trend Analysis for Business Planning.* New York: McGraw-Hill, 1970.

Dutta, Biplab K. "Competitive Analysis to Support Strategic Planning: A Metagame — Theoretic Interactive Modeling Approach." Doctoral diss., University of Pittsburgh, 1977.

Eckstein, H. *Pressure Group Politics: The Case of the British Medical Association.* London: Allen and Unwin, 1960.

Edwards, Ward, et al. "Probabilistic Information Processing Systems: Design and Evaluation." *IEEE Transactions on Systems Science and Cybernetics.* September 1968.

Emery, F. E. and E. L. Trist. "The Causal Texture of Organizational Environments." *Human Relations,* February 1965.

Encel, Solomon, Pauline Marstrand and William Page. *The Art of Anticipation.* London: Martin Robertson, 1975, as reviewed by Harman, Willis and Peter Schwartz in "Towards a Doctrine for Futures Research." *Futures,* June 1976.

Evered, Roger D. "A Typology of Explicative Models." *Technological Forecasting and Social Change,* Vol. 9, No. 3, 1976.

Ewing, David W. "Corporate Planning at the Crossroads." *Harvard Business Review*, July–August 1967.

Fahey, Liam and William R. King. "Environmental Scanning for Corporate Planning." *Business Horizons*, August 1977.

Farmer, Richard N. "Looking Backward at Looking Forward." *Business Horizons*, February 1973.

Farris, George F. "Colleague Roles and Innovation in Scientific Teams," Sloan School of Management Working Paper No. 552-71. Cambridge, Mass.: Massachusetts Institute of Technology, July 1971.

Fidler, J. *Report on a Study of Top Businessmen in Britain*. Birmingham: University of Aston Management Centre, July 1977.

"Flexible Pricing: Industry's New Strategy to Hold Market Share Changes the Rules for Economic Decision-Making." *Business Week*, December 12, 1977.

Forrester, Jay W. *Industrial Dynamics*. Cambridge, Mass.: M.I.T. Press, 1961.

Forrester, Jay W. "Business Structure, Economic Cycles and National Policy." *Futures*, June 1976.

Fruhan, William E., Jr. *The Fight for Competitive Advantages*. Boston: Division of Research, Graduate School of Business Administration, Harvard University, 1972.

Fusfeld, Alan R. and Richard N. Foster. "The Delphi Technique: Survey and Comment." *Business Horizons*, June 1971.

Galbraith, Jay R. "Achieving Integration Through Information Systems." *Academy of Management Proceedings*, 1968.

Galbraith, Jay R. "Organization Design: An Information Processing View." Sloan School of Management Working Paper No. 425-69. Cambridge, Mass.: Massachusetts Institute of Technology, October 1969.

Galbraith, Jay R. "Environmental and Technological Determinants of Organization Design: A Case Study," in Lorsch, Paul R, and Jay W. Lawrence (editors). *Studies in Organization Design*. Homewood, Ill.: Richard D. Irwin, 1970.

George, K. H. "Social and Political Projections Towards 2001: Delphi Study of Youth's Future." Master's diss., Massachusetts Institute of Technology, 1971.

Gershefski, George W. "Building a Corporate Financial Model." *Harvard Business Review*, July–August 1969.

Gerstenfeld, Arthur. "Technological Forecasting." *Journal of Business*, January 1971.

Gilfillan, S. Colum. "The Prediction of Inventions," in U.S. National Resources Committee. *Technological Trends and National Policy*. Washington, D.C.: U.S. Government Printing Office, 1937.

Gilmour, S. D. "The Divestment Decision Process." Doctoral diss., Harvard University, 1973.

Gordon, T. J., et al. *A Forecast of the Interaction of Business and Society in the Next Five Years*. Report R-21. Middleton, Conn.: Institute for the Future, 1971.

Gordon, William J. J. *Synetics: The Development of Creative Capacity*. New York: Collier Books, 1968.

Gouldner, A. W. "The Norm of Reciprocity." *American Sociological Review*, April 1960.

"The Grand Scale of Federal Intervention." *Business Week*, April 4, 1977.

Grant, John H. "Management Implications of Systems-Oriented Strategies within Selected Industrial Firms: A Developmental Model." Doctoral diss., Harvard University, 1972.

Greenberger, Martin, et al. *Models in the Policy Process*. New York: Russell Sage Foundation, 1976.

Grinyer, Peter H. "Some Dangerous Axioms of Corporate Planning." *Journal of Business Policy*, Autumn 1972.

Guth, William D. "The Growth and Profitability of the Firm: A Managerial Explanation." *Journal of Business Policy*, Spring 1972.

Gutmann, Peter M. "Strategies for Growth." *California Management Review*, Summer 1964.

Hage, J. and R. Dewar. "Elite Values versus Organizational Structure in Predicting Innovation." *Administrative Science Quarterly*, September 1973.

Hall, William K. "Strategic Planning Models: Are Top Managers Really Finding Them Useful?" *Journal of Business Policy*, Winter 1973a.

Hall, William K. "Strategic Planning, Product Innovation and the Theory of the Firm." *Journal of Business Policy*, Spring 1973b.

Hamermesh, R. G. "The Corporate Response to Divisional Profit Crises." Doctoral diss., Harvard University, 1976.

Hammond, John S. III. "Do's and Don'ts of Computer Models in Planning." *Harvard Business Review*, March–April 1974.

Hammond, Kenneth R., et al. "Social Judgement Theory," in Kaplan, Martin F. and Steven Schwartz (editors), *Human Judgement and Decision Processes*. New York: Academic Press, 1975.

Hanna, Richard G. C. "The Concept of Corporate Strategy in Multi-Industry Companies." Doctoral diss., Harvard University, 1968.

Hatten, Kenneth J. "Strategic Models in the Brewing Industry." Doctoral diss., Purdue University, 1974.

Hedley, Barry. "A Fundamental Approach to Strategy Development." *Long Range Planning*, December 1976.

Henderson, Bruce D. "The Experience Curve. . . ." Boston Consulting Group, 1974.

Herold, David M. "Long-Range Planning and Organizational Performance: A Cross-Validation Study." *Academy of Management Journal*, March 1972.

Hofer, Charles W. "Toward a Contingency Theory of Business Strategy." *Academy of Management Journal*, December 1975.

Hofer, Charles W. "Research on Strategic Planning: A Survey of Past Studies and Suggestions for Future Efforts." *Journal of Economics and Business*, Spring–Summer, 1976.

Howard, N. *Paradoxes of Rationality: Theory of Metagames and Political Behavior*. Cambridge, Mass.: M.I.T. Press, 1971.

Institute of Life Insurance. *Trend Analysis Program Reports*. New York: The Institute of Life Insurance (quarterly — various dates).

Jantsch, Emil. "Forecasting and Systems Approach: A Frame of Reference." *Management Science*, Vol. 19, 1973.

Jauch, Lawrence R., Richard N. Osborn and William F. Glueck. "Success in Large Business Organizations: The Environment Strategy Connection." *Academy of Management Proceedings*, 1977.

Jopling, David G., Stephen Gage and Milton Shoeman. "Forecasting Public Resistance to Technology: The Example of Nuclear Power Reactor Siting," in Bright, J. R. and M. E. Shoeman (editors), *A Guide to Practical Technological Forecasting*. Englewood Cliffs, N.J.: Prentice-Hall, 1973.

Jurkovich, Ray. "A Core Typology of Organizational Environments." *Administrative Science Quarterly*, September 1974.

Kahn, Herman and A. J. Wiener. *The Year 2000*. New York: Macmillan, 1967.

Karger, D. W. and F. A. Malik, "Long-Range Planning and Organizational Performance," *Long-Range Planning*, December 1975.

Katz, Robert L. *Cases and Concepts in Corporate Strategy*. Englewood Cliffs, N.J.: Prentice-Hall, Inc., 1970.

Keegen, Warren, J. "Scanning the International Business Environment: A Study of the Information Acquisition Process." Doctoral diss., Harvard University, 1967.

Keegan, Warren J. "Multinational Scanning: A Study of Information Sources Utilized by Headquarters Executives in Multinational Companies." *Administrative Science Quarterly*, September 1974.

Kefalas, Asterios and Peter P. Schoderbek. "Scanning the Business Environment: Some Empirical Results." *Journal of the American Institute for Decision Sciences*, January 1973.

Kempner, T., K. Macmillan and K. Hawkins. *Business and Society*. Harmondsworth: Penguin, 1976.

King, William R. and David Cleland. "Information for More Effective Strategic Planning." *Long Range Planning*, February 1977a.

King, William R. and David Cleland. *Strategic Planning and Policy*. New York: Petrocelli/Charter, 1977b.

Kirchhoff, Bruce A. "Empirical Analysis of Strategic Factors Contributing to Return on Investment." *Academy of Management Proceedings*, 1975.

Kitching, John. "Why Do Mergers Miscarry? *Harvard Business Review*, November–December 1967.

Klein, Harold E. and Robert E. Linneman. "Adoption of Multiple Scenario Analysis in Corporate Long Range Planning Processes: An Empirical Study." Working paper, Temple University, 1978.

Klein, Harold E. "Incorporating Environmental Examination into the Corporate Strategic Planning Process." Doctoral diss., Columbia University, 1973.

Kotler, Philip. "Competitive Strategies for New Product Marketing Over the Life Cycle." *Management Science*, December 1965.

Kudla, Ronald J. "The Effects of Strategic Planning on Common Stock Returns." Doctoral dissertation draft, University of Pittsburgh, 1977.

Lawrence, Paul R. and Jay W. Lorsch. *Organization and Environment: Managing Differentiation and Integration*. Boston: Graduate School of Business Administration, Harvard University, 1967.

Learned, Edmund P., C Roland Christensen, Kenneth R. Andrews and William D. Guth. *Business Policy: Text and Cases*. Homewood, Ill.: Richard D. Irwin, 1965.

Lebell, Don and O. J. Krasner. "Selecting Environmental Forecasting Techniques from Business Planning Requirements." *Academy of Management Review*, 1977.

Lenz, Ralph and H. W. Lanford. "The Substitution Phenomenon." *Business Horizons*, February 1972.

Levitt, Theodore. "Exploit the Product Life Cycle." *Harvard Business Review*, November–December 1965.

Lindblom, Charles E. "The Science of 'Muddling Through.' " *Public Administration Review*, Spring 1959.

Linneman, Robert E. and John D. Kennell. "Shirt-sleeve Approach to Long Range Planning." *Harvard Business Review*, March–April 1977.

Linneman, Robert and Harold E. Klein. "The Use of Multiple Scenarios by U.S. Industrial Corporations." *Long Range Planning*, forthcoming, 1978.

Lintner, John. "Security Prices, Risk and Maximal Gains from Diversification." *Journal of Finance*, December 1965.

Litschert, Robert J. "Some Characteristics of Long-Range Planning in Industry." *Academy of Management Journal*, September 1968.

Litschert, Robert J. "The Structure of Long-Range Planning Groups." *Academy of Management Journal*, March 1971.

Litwak, E. and L. F. Hylton. "Interorganizational Analysis: A Hypothesis on Coordinating Agencies." *Administrative Science Quarterly*, March 1961.

Long Range Planning. Prepared by the Congressional Research Service for the Committee on Science and Technology of the U.S. House of Representatives. Washington, D.C.: U.S. Government Printing Office, May 1976.

Lorange, Peter. "Strategic Control: A Framework for Effective Response to Environmental Change." Working paper, Sloan School of Management, Cambridge, Mass.: Massachusetts Institute of Technology, 1977.

Lorange, Peter and Richard F. Vancil (editors). *Strategic Planning Systems*. Englewood Cliffs, N.J.: Prentice-Hall, 1977.

Luck, D. J. and A. E. Prell. *Market Strategy*. New York: Appleton, 1968.

Lupton, T., et al. "Integrated Organizational Strategy." *Journal of Management Studies*, February 1969.

Macintosh, N. B., H. Tsurmi and Y. Tsurmi. "Econometrics for Strategic Planning." *Journal of Business Policy*, Spring 1973.

MacMillan, Ian C. "An Analysis of Certain Power and Influence Relations between the Firm and Its Environment." Master's diss., UNISA, Pretoria, 1972.

MacMillan, Ian C. "Business Strategies for Political Action." *Journal of General Management*, Vol. 1, No. 1, 1974.

MacNulty, Christine A. R. "Scenario Development for Corporate Planning." *Futures*, April 1977.

Mandelker, Gershon. "Risk and Return: The Case of Merging Firms." *Journal of Financial Economics*, December 1974.

Mansfield, Edwin. "Technical Change and the Rate of Imitation." *Econometrica*, October 1961.

Marchal, J. "The Construction of a New Theory of Profit." *American Economics Review*, September, 1951.

Martino, J. *Technological Forecasting for Decision-Making*. New York: Elsevier North-Holland, 1972.

Mason, Richard O. "A Dialectical Approach to Strategic Planning." *Management Science*, April 1969.

Mason, R. H. and M. B. Goudzwaard. "Performance of Conglomerate Firms: Portfolio Approach." *Journal of Finance*, March 1976.

McCaskey, M. B. "Tolerance for Ambiguity and the Perception of Environmental Uncertainty in Organization Design," in Kilman, R. H., L. R. Pondy and D. P. Slevin (editors), *The Management of Organization Design*. New York: Elsevier North-Holland, 1976.

McHale, John and Magda C. McHale. "An Assessment of Futures Studies Worldwide." *Futures*, April 1976.

McKinsey, J. C. C. *Introduction to the Theory of Games*. New York: McGraw-Hill, 1952.

McLean, Mick and Paul Shepard. "The Importance of Model Structure." *Futures*, February 1976.

Mead, Margaret. "Toward a Human Science." *Science*, March 1976.

Meadows, D., et al. *The Dynamics of Global Equilibrium: Collected Papers*. Cambridge, Mass.: Wright-Allen Press, 1973.

Metzner, H. E., J. L. Wall and W. F. Glueck. "Product Life Cycle and Stages of Growth: An Empirical Analysis." *Academy of Management Proceedings*, 1975.

Miles, Ian. *The Poverty of Prediction*. Lexington, Mass.: Lexington Books, 1975, as reviewed by Harman, Willis and Peter Schwartz in "Towards a Doctrine for Futures Research." *Futures*, June 1976.

Miles, Raymond E., Charles C. Snow and Jeffrey Pfeffer. "Organization-Environment: Concepts and Issues." *Industrial Relations*, October 1974.

Miller, Ernest C. *Advanced Techniques for Strategic Planning*. New York: American Management Association, 1971.

Miller, Roger E. *Innovation, Organization and Environment*. Sherbrooke, Canada: Institut de Recherche et de Perfectionnement en Administration, 1971.

Mintzberg, Henry. *The Nature of Managerial Work*. New York: Harper and Row, 1973.

Mintzberg, Henry. "Policy as a Field of Management Theory." *Academy of Management Review*, January 1977.

Mintzberg, Henry, D. Raisinghani and A. Theoret. "The Structure of 'Unstructured' Decision Processes." *Administrative Science Quarterly*, June 1976.

Mitroff, Ian I. "A Communication Model of Dialectical Inquiring Systems — A Strategy for Strategic Planning." *Management Science*, June 1971.

Mitroff, Ian I., Vincent Barabba and Ralph Kilmann. "The Application of Behavioral and Philosophical Techniques to Strategic Planning: A Case of a Large Federal Agency." *Management Science*, Vol. 24, 1977.

Mitroff, Ian I. and Murray Turoff. "The Whys Behind the Hows." *IEEE Spectrum*, March 1973.

Mitroff, Ian I. and Murray Turoff. "Philosophical and Methodological Foundations of Delphi," in Linstone, H. A. and M. Turoff (editors), *The Delphi Method.* Reading, Mass.: Addison-Wesley, 1975.

Moose, S. O. and A. J. Zakon. "Frontier Curve Analysis: As a Resource Allocation Guide." *Journal of Business Policy*, Spring 1972.

Morris, DuBois S. *Perspectives for the '70's and '80's: Tomorrow's Problems Facing Today's Management.* New York: National Industrial Conference Board, 1970.

Nanus, Burt. "Annual Report 1976." Los Angeles: University of Southern California, Center for Futures Research, 1976.

Naylor, Thomas H. and Horst Schauland. "A Survey of Users of Corporate Planning Models." *Management Science*, May 1976.

Negandhi, A. and B. S. Prasad. *The Frightening Angels: A Study of Multinationals in Developing Nations.* Kent, Ohio: Kent State University Press, 1975.

Neustadt, R. E. *Presidential Power.* New York: Signet Books, 1960.

Noland, Richard L. and K. Eric Knutsen. "The Computerization of the ABC Widget Company." *Datamation*, April 1974.

North, Harper Q. and Donald L. Pyke. " 'Probes' of the Technological Future." *Harvard Business Review*, May–June 1969.

Nowill, P. "The Impact of Company Characteristics on Business Level Profitability." Cambridge, Mass.: Marketing Science Institute, July 1974.

Osborn, R. N. and J. G. Hunt. "Environment and Organizational Effectiveness." *Administrative Science Quarterly*, June 1974.

Padbury, Peter and Diana Wilkins. *The Future: A Bibliography of Issues and Forecasting Techniques.* Monticello, Ill.: Council of Planning Librarians, 1972.

Pahl, R. E. and J. T. Winkler. "The Economic Elite: Theory and Practice," in Stanworth, P. and A. Giddens (editors), *Elites and Power in British Society.* Cambridge: The University Press, 1974.

Palmer, Michael and Gregory Schmid. "Planning with Scenarios." *Futures*, Vol. 8, pp. 472–484, 1976.

Patton, Arch. "Stretch Your Product's Earning Years: Top Management's Stake in the Product Life Cycle." *Management Review*, June 1959.

Patton, G. Richard. "A Simultaneous Equation Model of Corporate Strategy: The Case of the U.S. Brewing Industry." Doctoral diss., Purdue University, 1976.

Pestel, Edward and M. D. Mesarovic. *Mankind at the Turning Point: The Second Report to the Club of Rome.* New York: Dutton, 1974.

Pettigrew, A. M. "Strategic Aspects of the Management of Specialist Activity." *Personnel Review*, Vol. 4, pp. 5–13, 1975.

Pfeffer, Jeffrey. "Size and Composition of Corporate Boards of Directors: The Organization and Its Environment." *Administrative Science Quarterly*, June 1972a.

Pfeffer, Jeffrey. "Merger as a Response to Organizational Interdependence." *Administrative Science Quarterly*, September 1972b.

Pfeffer, Jeffrey and P. Nowak. "Joint Ventures and Interorganizational Interdependence." *Administrative Science Quarterly*, September 1976.

Polli, Rolando and Victor Cook. "Validity of the Product Life Cycle." *Journal of Business*, October 1969.

Prahalad, C. K. "The Strategic Process in a Multinational Corporation." Doctoral diss., Harvard University, 1975.

Rao, Ram C. and David Rutenburg. "Strategic Timing of the First Plant: Analysis of Sophisticated Rivalry." Working paper, Pittsburgh, Pa.: Carnegie-Mellon University, 1977.

Regan, M. D. "Management of Exploration in the Metals Mining Industry." Master's diss., Sloan School of Management, Massachusetts Institute of Technology, June 1971.

Rhenman, Eric. *Organization Theory for Long-Range Planning.* New York: Wiley, 1973.

Rink, David R. "A Theoretical Extension of the Product Life Cycle Concept." *Pittsburgh Business Review*, December 1977.

Roberts, Edward B. "Exploratory and Normative Technological Forecasting: A Critical Appraisal." *Technological Forecasting and Social Change*, Fall 1969.

Robinson, David A. (editor). *The Business Environment in 1975–1985.* Croton-on-Hudson, N.Y.: The Hudson Institute, 1974.

Rodriguez, Jaime I. "The Design and Evaluation of a Strategic Issue Competitive Information System." Doctoral diss., University of Pittsburgh, 1977.

Rosenstein, A. J. "Quantitative — Yes Quantitative — Application for the Focus Group." American Marketing Association. *Marketing News*, May 21, 1976.

Rubin, J. Z. and B.R. Brown. *The Social Psychology of Bargaining and Negotiation.* New York: Academic Press, 1975.

Rue, Leslie W. and Robert M. Fulmer. *The Practice and Profitability of Long Range Planning.* Oxford, Ohio: Planning Executives Institute, 1973.

Rumelt, Richard P. *Strategy, Structure and Economic Performance.* Boston: Division of Research, Graduate School of Business Administration, Harvard University, 1974.

Rumelt, Richard P. "Diversity and Profitability." Working Paper No. MGL-51, University of California at Los Angeles, 1977.

Rutenberg, David P. "What Strategic Planning Expects from Management Science." Working Paper No. 89–75–76. Carnegie-Mellon University, 1976.

Sackman, Harold. *Delphi Critique: Expert Opinion Forecasting and Group Process.* Lexington, Mass.: Lexington Books, 1975.

Salter, Malcolm S. "Stages of Corporate Development." *Journal of Business Policy*, Vol. 1, No. 1, 1970.

Schelling, Thomas C. *The Strategy of Conflict.* New York: Oxford University Press, 1960.

Schendel, Dan E. "Designing of Strategic Planning Systems." Institute for Research in the Behavioral, Economic and Management Sciences, Working Paper 616, Purdue University, 1977.

Schendel, Dan E. and G. Richard Patton. "Corporate Stagnation and Turnaround." *Journal of Economics and Business*, Spring–Summer 1976.

Schendel, Dan E., et. al. "Can Corporate Strategy Be Modelled?" Institute for Research in the Behavioral, Economic and Management Sciences, Working Paper 517, Purdue University, June 1975.

Scherer, F. M. *Industrial Pricing.* Chicago: Rand McNally, 1970a.

Scherer, F. M. *Industrial Market Structure and Economic Performance.* Chicago: Rand McNally, 1970b.

Schoeffler, Sidney. *PIMS Newsletters*, Nos. 1 and 2. Cambridge, Mass.: Strategic Planning Institute, 1977.

Schoeffler, Sidney, Robert D. Buzzell and Donald F. Heany. "Impact of Strategic Planning on Profit Performance." *Harvard Business Review*, March–April, 1974.

Schramm, C. J. "Thompson's Assessment of Organizations: Universities and the AAUP Salary Grades." *Administrative Science Quarterly*, March 1975.

Schultz, Randall L. and Dennis P. Slevin (editors). *Implementing Operations Research/Management Science.* New York: Elsevier North-Holland, 1975.

Schumpeter, J. A. *Capitalism, Socialism and Democracy.* New York: Harper, 1942.

Schwartz, J. J. "The Decision to Innovate." Doctoral diss., Harvard University, 1973.

Scott, Bruce R. "An Open System Model of the Firm." Doctoral diss., Harvard University, 1962.

Scott, Bruce R. "Stages of Corporate Development." Harvard Business School, Boston, Mass.: Intercollegiate Case Clearing House, ICCH #9-371-294, 1971.

Scott, Brian W. "Some Aspects of Long-Range Planning in American Corporations with Special Attention to Strategy Planning." Doctoral diss., Harvard University, 1963.

Seiler, Robert E. *Improving the Effectiveness of Research and Development.* New York: McGraw-Hill, 1965.

Selznick, P. *TVA and the Grass Roots.* Berkeley: University of California Press, 1949.

Selznick, P. *Leadership in Administration.* New York: Harper and Row, 1957.

Shocker, Allan D. (editor). *Analytical Approaches to Product and Marketing Planning.* Cambridge, Mass.: Marketing Science Institute, 1978.

Shubik, Martin. "On Gaming and Game Theory" (Part 2). *Management Science*, January 1972.

Shubik, Martin. *Games for Society, Business and War: Towards a Theory of Gaming.* New York: Elsevier North-Holland, 1975.

Simmonds, W. H. C. "Toward an Analytical Classification of Industry." *Technological Forecasting and Social Change*, Vol. 4, No. 4, 1973.

Simmons, W. W. "A Strategic Planning Program for the Next Decade." *Advanced Management Journal*, Winter 1976.

Simon, H. A. *Administrative Behavior* (1st edition). New York: The Free Press, 1945.

Smith, Adam. *The Wealth of Nations.* Edinburgh: Nelson, 1776. (See also London: Dent, 1957–58.)

Smith, J. "The Management of Social Responsibility in Multinational Companies and Its Effect on Corporate Planning." M.B.A. diss., Manchester Business School, 1977.

Spender, J-C. "Programmes of Research into Business Strategy." Paper presented at the City University, London, April 26, 1976.

"SPI Guide to Portfolio Analysis." Cambridge, Mass.: Strategic Planning Institute, 1977.

Starbuck, William H. "Organizations and Their Environments," in Dunnette, M. D. (editor),

Handbook of Industrial and Organizational Psychology. Chicago: Rand McNally, 1976.

Staw, B. M. and J. Swajkowski. "The Scarcity/Munificence Component of Organizational Environments and the Commission of Illegal Acts." *Administrative Science Quarterly,* September 1975.

Steinbruner, J. D. *The Cybernetic Theory of Decision.* Princeton, N.J.: Princeton University Press, 1974.

Steiner, George A. *Managerial Long-Range Planning.* New York: McGraw-Hill, 1963.

Steiner, George A. *Multinational Corporate Planning.* New York: Macmillan, 1966.

Steiner, George A. *Top Management Planning.* New York: Macmillan, 1969.

Terleckyj, Nestor E. *Improvements in the Quality of Life: Estimates of Possibilities in the United States, 1974–1983.* Washington, D.C.: Planning Association, 1975.

Terreberry, Shirley. "The Evolution of Organizational Environments." *Administrative Science Quarterly,* March 1968.

Thompson, James D. *Organizations in Action.* New York: McGraw-Hill, 1967.

Thune, Stanley S. and Robert J. House. "Where Long Range Planning Pays Off." *Business Horizons,* August 1970.

Thurston, Philip H. "Make TF Serve Corporate Planning." *Harvard Business Review,* September–October 1971.

Trevelyan, E. W. "The Strategic Process in Large Complex Organizations: A Pilot Study of New Business Development." Doctoral diss., Harvard University, 1974.

Turk, H. "Comparative Urban Structure from an Interorganizational Perspective." *Administrative Science Quarterly,* March 1973.

Turoff, M. "The Design of a Policy Delphi." *Technical Forecasting and Social Change,* Vol. 2, No. 2, 1970.

"Use of Delphi Growing." *Business Week,* March 14, 1970.

Utterback, James M. "The Process of Technological Innovation: A Study of the Origination and Development of Ideas for New Scientific Instruments." *IEEE Transactions on Engineering Management,* November 1971.

Utterback, James M. and William J. Abernathy. "A Dynamic Model of Product and Process Innovation." *Omega,* Vol. 3, No. 6, 1975.

Utterback, James M. and James W. Brown. "Monitoring for Technological Opportunities." *Business Horizons,* October 1972.

Utterback, James M. and Elmer H. Burack. "Identification of Technological Threats and Opportunities by Firms." *Technological Forecasting and Social Change,* Vol. 8, No. 1, 1975.

Vancil, Richard F. "Strategy Formulation in Complex Organizations." *Sloan Management Review,* Winter 1976.

Van de Ven, A. H. "On the Nature, Formation and Maintenance of Relations Among Organizations." *Academy of Management Review,* Vol. 1, No. 4, 1976.

Vernon, R. *Sovereignty at Bay: The Multinational Spread of U.S. Enterprises.* Harmondsworth: Penguin, 1973.

Von Neumann, T. and O. Morgenstern. *Theory of Games and Economic Behavior* (2d edition). Princeton, N.J.: Princeton University Press, 1947.

Walton, R. E. and R. B. McKersie. *A Behavioral Theory of Labor Negotiations.* New York: McGraw-Hill, 1965.

Warren, R. L. "The Interorganizational Field as a Focus for Investigation." *Administrative Science Quarterly,* December 1967.

Wasson, Chester R. *Dynamic Competitive Strategy and Product Life Cycles.* St. Charles, Ill.: Challenge Books, 1974.

Watt, Kenneth E., et al. *A Model of Society.* Davis, Calif.: Environmental Systems Group, Institute of Ecology, University of California, April 1969.

Wheelwright, Steven C. and Spyros Makridakis. *Forecasting Methods for Management.* New York: Wiley, 1977.

Wheelwright, Steven D. and Darral Clarke. "Corporate Forecasting: Promise and Reality." *Harvard Business Review,* November–December 1976.

Wilson, I. H. "Reforming the Strategic Planning Process." *Long Range Planning,* October 1974.

Wise, George. "The Accuracy of Technological Forecasts, 1890–1940." *Futures,* October 1976.

Wise, T. A. "The Rocky Road to the Marketplace." *Fortune,* October, 1966.

Zald, M. N. "Political Economy: A Framework for Comparative Analysis," in Zald, Mayer N. (editor), *Power in Organizations.* Nashville, Tenn.: Vanderbilt University, 1970.

Zaleznik, A. and M. F. R. Kets de Vries. *Power and the Corporate Mind.* Boston: Houghton Mifflin, 1975.

Zentner, R. D. "Scenarios in Forecasting." *C & E News,* October 6, 1975.

Zysman, S. J. "Top Management and Decentralized Firms: A Comparative Study." Doctoral diss., Harvard University, 1973.

4

STRATEGY EVALUATION

Evaluation of Strategy: Theory and Models

RICHARD P. RUMELT
University of California at Los Angeles

Commentary

BRUCE A. KIRCHHOFF
University of Nebraska at Omaha

Strategy evaluation is not commonly elevated to separate status alongside the formulation and implementation tasks in most currently existing models of the strategic management area. Yet strategy evaluation is a fundamental challenge and one deserving far more attention than it has received because of the important role strategy plays in influencing overall organizational performance.

Strategy not only relates an organization to its environment, but also is a mechanism for integrating the various functional areas of single product firms, and the various businesses in multi-industry firms. It also provides guidelines for major resource allocation decisions. In doing these basic things, strategy is a major determinant of the organization's long-run performance as indicated by the Boston Consulting Group (1968), Rumelt (1974), Hatten (1974), Patton (1976), and the Strategic Planning Institute through its PIMS program. Because of strategy's important impact on overall economic performance, it is essential that existing and proposed strategies be evaluated in terms of their economic impact. Such evaluations must be accurate because it is both difficult and time-consuming to reverse the impact of strategy once implemented. Moreover, it is essential that a strategic control system be developed to insure that the strategy implemented is the one selected for implementation.

To be of value in the strategic management process, strategy evaluation must answer two basic questions. First, will the organization's *existing* strategy lead to the achievement of its goals and objectives (intended results), subject to the environmental conditions it is expected to encounter? If not, then it will be necessary to change the existing strategy. Second, will any *proposed strategy* alternate lead to the achievement of these goals and objectives subject to the expected environmental conditions? Unless the proposed strategy alternate does, it is not worthy of implementation. However, if no strategy can be identified that will lead to achievement of the desired objectives, then it will be necessary to alter the organization's desired objectives. In such instances, the results of an effective strategy evaluation should be helpful in selecting the new goals and objectives, as well as in choosing the strategy to achieve them.

TYPES OF STRATEGY EVALUATION APPROACHES

There are five approaches that can be used to evaluate an existing or proposed strategy. They involve the assessment of: (1) the internal consistency of the organization's goal structure; [1] (2) the quality of the process(es) and underlying analysis used to formulate the strategy; (3) the content of the strategy; (4) whether the organization can implement or execute the strategy effectively and efficiently; and (5) early performance result indicators. Exhibit 4.1 indicates where each of these evaluation checks would be performed in the strategic management process. It also indicates the degree of overlap that exists among the various tasks included in the strategic management process.

GOAL CONSISTENCY. Although we have argued elsewhere (Hofer and Schendel, 1978) that there should be a separation of goals and objectives from strategy, others have defined strategy to include goals and objectives (e.g., Andrews, 1971). Whether goals and objectives are separate or included in the definition of strategy one cannot assess the effectiveness of a particular strategy without knowing what it is supposed to accomplish. The internal consistency of the goals should be assured before a reasonable strategy can be formulated and evaluated, whether this is done as separate goal and strategy formulation processes, or whether these processes are combined. Thus, the first step of effective strategy evaluation should be to determine whether the organization's goal structure is internally consistent.

STRATEGY FORMULATION PROCESS DESIGN. Both theoretically and practically, it is clear that some processes produce results that are consistently superior. Hence, an effective, although indirect, way to assess the adequacy of a proposed strategy is to evaluate the quality (comprehensiveness, consistency, accuracy, reliability, sensitivity, etc., of the analytical and informational analyses, as well as the organizational and political components)

---

[1] Technically, the assessment of the internal consistency of goals and objectives should be part of an organization's goal formulation process. Such checks are often not done in practice until it becomes clear that no strategy will accomplish the organization's objectives. We have included this inconsistency check in the evaluation process to avoid a later finding of an inconsistent goal structure or incongruence beween goals and environmental expectations.

Exhibit 4.1 An Overview of the Strategic Management Process

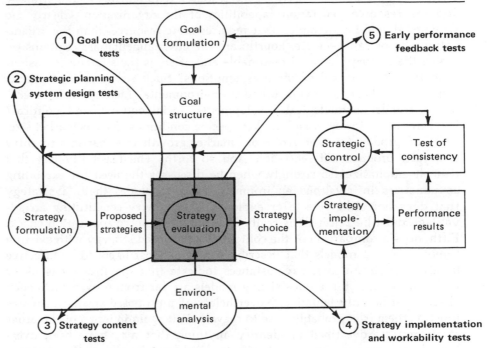

of the process used to formulate it. Thus, if the overall process and its components are of high quality then the probability that the strategy they produce will be effective will be greater than if they are of low quality. This conclusion is further supported by the research reviewed by Lorange in the next set of papers (see Section 5). Additional research is needed to find more effective means of conducting quality assessments of both the informational/analytical and organizational/political aspects of strategy formulation processes as a means of evaluating the quality of a proposed strategy. This approach to strategy evaluation is not covered by Rumelt, and only tangentially by Kirchhoff. Nevertheless, it represents a significant tool in strategy evaluation, especially where there is little knowledge or experience upon which to base an evaluation of the substantive content of a proposed strategy.

STRATEGY CONTENT. It is the content of strategy that has the greatest impact on performance results. Hence, substantive content should be evaluated directly if this is at all possible. There are at least six different means of assessing strategy content. First, both existing and proposed strategies should be checked for completeness and to insure internal consistency in terms of their various components (scope, resource and skill deployment, competitive advantage, and synergy). Second, the consistency of the strategy with the objectives it is intended to achieve should be tested to insure that the firm will be able to achieve the results intended. Third, a check should be made between the resource requirements of the strategy and the resource generation capabilities of the organization. Clearly, no strategy should be attempted that requires more resources than the organization has or can generate. Fourth, are the environmental assumptions on which the strategy is based reasonable and, if so, is the strategy consistent with the most critical of these assumptions? Such environmental checks range from those involving broader environmental factors, such as economic trends, technological developments, social/cultural, and political/legal trends, to industry and market specific conditions, such as market size, stage of product/market evolution, market growth rate, barriers to entry and exit, product differentiation, and so forth. The feasibility test that Rumelt emphasizes so strongly when he discusses the need for exploiting asymmetries in rivalrous environments and concludes that "a strategy that does not either create or exploit an asymmetry constituting an advantage must be rejected" is really a corporate resource application check. Fifth, does a comparison of the content of a proposed strategy with existing hypotheses and models that describe strategies most likely to be effective in given environmental circumstances indicate that the strategy is likely to be successful? Since our existing models are far from proven facts such checks can be only tentative. Nevertheless, if a proposed strategy violates most of them it is probably wise to reevaluate it again in terms of the other strategy tests described to identify anything that may have been overlooked. In any case, this test by itself should not invalidate the strategy. Finally, any proposed strategy's content must be evaluated in terms of its acceptability to the personal values, goals and especially the risk preferences of the principal stakeholders (Mintzberg's internal and external influencers) of the organization.

STRATEGY IMPLEMENTATION. A necessary *ex ante* evaluation test is to assess whether the strategy can be implemented by the organization. At least these issues must be investigated: (1) Do the necessary resources exist (or can they be acquired) and can they be deployed as required by the strategy? (2) Can the organizational structure and the various organizational systems and processes do the work necessary to make the proposed strategy work? (3) Do the organization's members have the will and interest to implement the strategy? (4) How will the organization's political and social processes alter the strategy and will such alterations make the strategy infeasible? Such evaluation checks have an organizational and behavioral foundation, and as Rumelt points out, he has omitted them from his paper. Several of them are covered in Kirchhoff's paper, however.

EARLY PERFORMANCE INDICATORS. While the prior evaluation approaches all are of value in choosing a strategic alternative to be used, there is still one more approach that can and should be used to evaluate any strategy once selected. That approach is to monitor performance indicators that are directly linked to the strategy and provide early indications of its longer run effectiveness. For example, do measures of market share, return on sales, response of competitors, and so forth, suggest that the strategy is having its intended impact? Such early assessments are important both to effective strategy implementation and to the reformulation of ineffective strategy because the ultimate test of any strategy is in the marketplace.

OBSERVATIONS ON RUMELT'S AND KIRCHHOFF'S PAPERS

This general framework of strategy evaluation approaches can be used to assess the Rumelt and Kirchhoff papers. Rumelt begins his paper with a discussion of the different definitions of the strategy concept which exist in the policy literature today. Next, he notes that all these definitions have two common characteristics: (1) they involve hierarchies of policies, i.e., they distinguish between more important and less important policies, and (2) they view strategies as a paradigm for helping to structure ill-structured situations. He then defines strategy for his purposes as "a description of what an organization is trying to accomplish and to what ends it is channeling its critical resources and problem-solving energies." (Note that Kirchhoff believes this definition needs clarification.)

Rumelt goes on to point out that, "it is helpful to cast the evaluation problem in terms of the negative logic of hypothesis testing, i.e., on what grounds may a proposed strategy be refuted or rejected." Armed with this view of the evaluation problem and the two common strategy characteristics noted above, Rumelt proceeds to demonstrate that all strategies, regardless of the type of organization or environment involved, must simultaneously meet four "context free" tests. These are: (1) a goal consistency test, (2) a "frame" test, (3) a competence test, and (4) a workability test.

The goal consistency test is like the one categorized above. The frame test is one that insures the strategy is identifying relevant strategic issues facing the organization. The competence test is one that checks whether the strategy in fact is breaking the ill-structured strategic problem into a series of problems that are treatable and solvable by the organization. Finally, the workability test checks whether the resources available to the organization are sufficient to implement the strategy and produce the outcomes desired.

In the remainder of his paper, Rumelt describes six different types of contextually based strategy evaluation models, proceeding from those that have the widest applicability to those with the narrowest. The six are: (1) the asymmetry test, (2) classical evaluation models, (3) life cycle models, (4) cross-sectional models, (5) strategic group models, and (6) experience curve models. After this review, Rumelt concludes that "strategy evaluation is still pretty much of an art." It is hard to disagree with this assessment, although a start has been made to better structure the process and with future research the art content should decrease.

Rumelt suggests six areas in which future research is needed if advancements are to be made in strategy evaluation. These are: (1) the development of better models and theories that can capture the multidimensional nature of how firms actually compete; (2) the inclusion of manufacturing as a vital element of strategy; (3) the development of more complex measures of organizational success that go beyond profitability to consider specific strategies and environments; (4) the development of ways to supplement statistical tests of theories intended to explain specific strategic situations; (5) the development of better understanding of the determinants of industry structure along the lines of the strategic group concepts, which recognize the influence of strategy, and away from single measures of structure, such as concentration; and (6) the need to create and legitimize methodologies for testing the validity of frame models and statements. He also describes specific research opportunities based on life cycle models, the PIMS data base, and the BCG experience curve model. He closes by noting a major implication of such research, namely, the potential for influencing public policy in areas such as anti-trust, industry regulation, and so on, which are now based on the axiomatic theory of welfare economics, which "assumes away" phenomena "central to strategic theory." Furthermore, such phenomena in many cases are antithetical to the economic theory that underlies so much public policy.

In his commentary on Rumelt's paper, Kirchhoff critiques three aspects of Rumelt's discussion and then suggests several additions to it based on a somewhat broader view of strategy evaluation and its place in the strategic management process. Kirchhoff's principal critiques are that Rumelt has not defined the term strategy as carefully as he should have, that his discussion of rivalry is at times inconsistent with microeconomic theory, and that he varies his definition of "frame" model to include literature that would not otherwise fit in this category. Kirchhoff's major extensions of Rumelt's paper are: (1) a discussion of the need to evaluate the strategy formulation process using behavioral tools, (2) the need to include organization's aspiration levels (that is, what the organization hoped for, not just the results it was able to achieve) when trying to evaluate the effectiveness of strategy content, and (3) the need to develop better criteria for evaluating implementation capacity.

Rumelt's distinction between context-free and contextual models in strategy evaluation is an important contribution. He also identifies four types of context free models that apply to strategies at all organization levels (e.g., to corporate, business, and functional area strategies) and to all types of organizations, resources, and environments. These tests, which are a useful extension of the literature, rest on his definition of strategy and what he calls two basic properties of all strategies, that they contain hierarchies of policies and that they break up unstructured situations into a series of structured problems capable of solution by the organization.

In his discussion of contextual evaluation models, Rumelt shows the need to establish competitive advantage in imperfectly competitive markets, and based on this conclusion he suggests that an important test of strategy is whether it in fact can (or does) establish such an advantage. However, in his discussion of contextual strategy evaluation models, Rumelt does not clearly indicate the levels of strategy to which each model applies. Most of the contextual strategy evaluation models Rumelt reviews apply primarily, if not exclusively, to business level strategy.

An interesting question can be raised as to whether there are any contextual models useful in evaluating corporate level strategy. Similarly, functional area strategies demand better contextual models than are currently available. Direct evaluation of functional area strategies in terms of corporate level objectives, for example, profitability, would appear to be inappropriate since it is difficult if not impossible to evaluate the profit contribution made by only a part of the business.

More emphasis should also be given to organizational (versus analytical), political, and other process approaches to strategy evaluation, as Kirchhoff notes. His call for the need to use behavioral tools to evaluate the strategy formulation process and for better criteria for assessing implementation capacity are important contributions. In addition, more attention should be focused on early performance indicator approaches to strategy evaluation than is suggested by Rumelt or Kirchhoff.

ADDITIONAL AREAS FOR RESEARCH ON STRATEGY EVALUATION

There are several other aspects of strategy evaluation that should provide fertile ground for research in the near future. Among the more important of these are the need for:

(1) Better criteria and techniques for evaluating the content of political strategies;

(2) Better criteria for assessing the readiness and ability of the structural, systems, people, and political character of the organization to implement proposed strategies;

(3) Better systems of early performance indicators for evaluating and controlling strategy;

(4) Recognition of the different evaluation problems at the corporate, business, and functional area levels of strategy. Especially needed are evaluation methods for corporate level portfolio strategies; and,

(5) Better ways to evaluate strategy in not-for-profit organizations that have multiple, conflicting goals (and which are also often protected from rivalrous competition).

Evaluation of Strategy: Theory and Models

RICHARD P. RUMELT
University of California at Los Angeles

The formulation of organizational strategy, when it occurs, is problem solving of the most unstructured sort. What little is known about how ill-structured problems are, or should be, dealt with suggests a three-part cycling process among: (1) problem structuring activities, (2) the generation of tentative solutions, and (3) the testing or evaluation of proposed solutions. The creative phases of this process draw heavily on perceptual skills and imagination. Here, pattern recognition and the ability to perceive new meanings amidst complexity play key roles. By contrast, it is the evaluation phase that presents the greatest opportunity to employ rational analysis. The situation is directly analogous to the scientific process wherein hypothesis generation remains a high art; the full power of the scientific method comes into play only after a clear hypothesis has been formulated.

If "evaluation" is the phase of strategy-making that is most amenable to analytic thought, what is the current state of the art? To treat this question, consider the following idealized problem: suppose one is given a reasonably comprehensive description of an organization, its environment and a proposed strategy. What are the legitimate grounds for evaluating the strategy and to what theories, knowledge, or models can one turn for help in making such an evaluation? The purpose of this article is to examine these questions in the light of recent research and conceptual contributions.

The idealized problem posed is somewhat artificial in that descriptions of strategy, organization, and environment are rarely "comprehensive" and strategy evaluation is more often an organizational process than an analytical task. But our interpretation of "state of the art" is that it implies the "best" that can be done rather than what some do, what might be done, or what is most frequently done. Accordingly, the primary concern will be with the limits of rational evaluation — with identifying the cutting edge between what can be said with reasonable surety about general classes of situations and those aspects of evaluation that remain heavily dependent upon intuition, insight, and sharply situational knowledge.

Strategy is a strongly contextual concept. At the core it deals with the adjustment of specific policies to particular situations. In looking at strategy evaluation, therefore, it will be helpful to associate methods of analysis with their appropriate contexts. We will begin with a discussion of the strategy concept itself, establish the functions it is supposed to perform, and identify those evaluation criteria that are context free — that are always valid. Central to this discussion will be the distinction between a solution to *a* problem and solving the *right* problem. We introduce the idea of "frame" as a way of speaking more precisely about this issue and indicate the special characteristics of "frame theories" that are useful in strategy evaluation.

The broadest context in general use is that of "rivalry." In discussing the context of rivalry we will show that many of the traditional tests for evaluating strategy are logical consequences of the nature of the strategy concept and the assumption of rivalry.

Armed with these observations and tools, a variety of models and theories will be discussed. In each case, the relevant context will be identified, the frame content examined, and the specific "tactical" content of the approach noted. After summarizing our analysis we will point out what seem to be the most fruitful directions for further research.

THE STRATEGY CONCEPT

To evaluate an entity is to determine its utility, truth, or efficacy. This, in turn, requires an appreciation of the function the entity is supposed to perform. Therefore, it will be helpful to examine the special characteristics of the concept of strategy and the role it is supposed to play in the guidance of organizations. Only then can the legitimate grounds for its appraisal be established.

The term "strategy" has a range of related meanings and authors have generally felt quite free to use it quite idiosyncratically. For game theorists, strategies are concrete actions or rules for choosing actions in a conflict situation; for some strategy is "high-level" or "long-term" planning, while others see it as referring only to broad gauge issues of "mission." Still others use it to denote any decision that is "important." The concept of strategy that will be explored here, and that has come to play such an important role in the study of organizational guidance, contains elements of all of the above notions. Its special focus, however, is on the relationship between a whole organization and its external environment.

POLICY HIERARCHIES. An observable aspect of organizations is that they develop hierarchies of policy (rules for defining contexts and making choices). While one frequently speaks of policy-makers as selecting courses of action, the choices are almost always policies or frameworks for guiding action. Even such a seemingly concrete decision as to "increase plant capacity by twenty-five percent within the next nine months" can also be seen as the precursor to a complex cascade of problem-solving activity. Because policy structures are hierarchical, one can speak of "top-level" policy or organizational "strategy" without meaning the combined totality of *every* policy and rule in the organization.

If each level of an organization supplies structure to the task environment of lower levels, what is the framework for guiding the selection of the top-most level of policy? Unidimensional objectives that call for the maximization of profits, happiness, or the public welfare are quite useless for guiding action. Unless they are expanded into specific rules or policies for their achievement, such objectives can only function as rejection criteria. Thus the postulate of some unidimensional objective does not solve the problem of choosing top-level policy and the

assumption of some set of actionable goals as "given" assumes the problem away. Somehow, the organization must maintain and make occasional changes in a set of "local" goals, or policies, that are specific enough to serve as criteria for the selection of other policies. We reserve the term "strategy" for this set of primary goals and policies.

The strategist is thus concerned with at least two levels of objectives. A substantial part of the art of strategy-making lies in discriminating among those objectives which act like values, being fixed and context free, and those which are really tools of administration, changing as strategy changes. In general, fixed objectives serve to constrain the selection of strategy, while operating objectives serve to express a strategy.

While the separation of fixed from operating objectives is a critical part of strategy formulation, it is of little concern in strategy evaluation. In appraising a strategy, the question is whether or not various objectives are consistent with one another, with the chosen context, and with policy. It does not matter where the objectives come from. Therefore, for our purposes, it will be most convenient to simply include all goals and objectives in our definition of strategy.

It is a frequent observation that one person's strategy is another's tactics — that what is strategic depends upon where you sit. One can easily find references to national, political, and industry strategies, to corporate, product, and manufacturing strategies, and even to strategies for conducting an individual interview. Common to all these problem situations is a generic type of poorly structured dilemma: a set of higher-level objectives, frequently flowing from the resolution of a higher-level strategic problem, must be translated into local objectives and the translation depends upon both the objectives, the means at hand, and the detailed content of the situation. Without denying that strategic problems occur on many levels, our primary concern here is with organizational strategy — the problem facing fairly autonomous organizations of selecting domains of activity and ways of coping with those domains.

As a descriptive tool, strategy is the analog of the biologist's method of "explaining" the structure and behavior of organisms by pointing out the functionality of each attribute in a total system (or strategy) designed to cope with or inhabit a particular niche. The normative use of strategy has no counterpart in biology (as yet!), but might be thought of as the problem of designing a living creature (or species) to exist within some environment. The hierarchical nature of policy has its analog in the fact that living systems are not homogeneous but consist of linked subsystems; the "designer," or strategist, can specify the need for "binocular vision" or "integrated production facilities" secure in the knowledge that the problems of creating such entities are solvable.

It is again the hierarchical nature of policy that provides the justification for calling some issues "important" or "critical." Rhenman (1973) notes that most of the problems organizations face are dealt with by standard procedures — they are problems that may be unpleasant, but which the system is designed to cope with. Critical or strategic problems, by contrast, lie outside the limits of the organization's repertoire of coping behavior and may require a redesign of the system. In our biological analogy, strategic issues are ones that lead to extinction unless mutation (or its behavioral equivalent) occurs. Thus, the idea of *critical problems* is not a capricious simplifying assumption, but has firmly grounded analogs in such concepts as "system stability ranges" and "design tolerances."

PROBLEM STRUCTURING. The kinds of situations that call for strategic thinking are termed ill-structured. They are characterized by difficulty, ambiguity, and the lack of established methods for moving towards clarification. According to Simon (1958):

Ill structured problems are difficult because the essential variables are not numerical at all, but symbolic or verbal. . . . the goal is vague and nonquantitative. . . . Finally, there are many practical problems — it would be accurate to say "most practical problems" — for which computational algorithims simply are not available. Facing facts, we are forced to admit that the majority of decisions that executives face every day — and certainly a majority of the very most important decisions

— lie much closer to the ill-structured than to the well structured end of the spectrum.

To this description it is necessary to add two important sources of difficulty. First, ill-structured problems pose very real challenges in simply defining what the problem is. Even the term "ill-structured problem" tends to suggest some type of obstacle to be overcome. In reality, strategists often face situations in which there are many conflicting signs of health and disease, opportunity and risk. Arriving at a formulation of the nature of the situation may well be the principal and most crucial task. Second, the assumption of vague and nonquantitative goals is too strong to be general. In many cases, strategy-making is concerned with the creation of reasonable purposes — with moving from a general awareness of discontent to having identifiable desires.

When confronted by an ill-structured situation an individual or organization may either: (1) classify it and apply standard procedures (the bureaucratic response); or (2) seek some way of structuring the problem that is "meaningful," i.e., that suggests how current knowledge and experience can be brought to bear. The latter, more creative, response requires what Vickers (1965) calls an "appreciation" of the situation and a reduction in ambiguity through the perception of pattern. Little is known about how insight actually operates, but Schon (1963) suggests that metaphor and analogy are the substance of creative thought. New concepts arise, he contends, by the stretching and adapting of old metaphors to meet new situations. The traditional open ended question, "What business are we in?" can be seen as an invitation to metaphor generation. When Timex revolutionized the watch industry with its inexpensive disposable watches, distributed through drug stores, it changed the prevailing metaphor from "a watch is an item of jewelry" to "a watch is a convenience item like a mechanical pencil." Similarly, when diversification away from a traditional area of business induces the senior management group to stop viewing that area as one in which new markets are "conquered," old ones "defended," distributors "strengthened," and advertising "campaigns" launched, and to see it instead as a "mature field" from which funds are "harvested" for reinvestment in more "fertile fields," a change in metaphor has taken place. The managers are, of course, neither generals nor absentee farmers, but both metaphors, though hardly "models," may provide helpful ways of organizing perceptions.

Whether or not metaphor plays a role, the primary task when facing an ill-structured problem is to reduce ambiguity by structuring the problem. Thus, for our purposes, strategy-making is a response that does not necessarily "solve" the problem, but which redefines it in terms of more familiar subproblems. When, for example, a military commander decides on a strategy of using feints to split the opposing forces into two segments, he is leaving a great many issues unresolved. He is, however, drastically reducing the ambiguity inherent in the original problem and providing a framework for further activity. Unlike rational-analytic problem solving, the function of strategy is not to "solve" a problem, but to so structure a situation that the emergent problems are solvable.

A strategy, then, is a description of what an organization is trying to accomplish and to what ends it is channeling its critical resources and problem-solving energies. As such, it may be regarded as a set of goals and policies, as a way of structuring an ill-structured situation, or as an allocation of resources. None of these views contradicts the others and all are helpful in grasping different aspects of strategy and strategy-making.

STRATEGY EVALUATION CRITERIA

Suppose that an analyst is presented with a reasonably comprehensive description of an organization, its environment, and a proposed strategy. What criteria can and should be used in evaluating the strategy?

There may be many features of the proposed strategy that are attractive, insightful, and potentially effective. It takes, however, only one major flaw to invalidate the strategy. Thus, it is helpful to cast the evaluation problem in terms of the negative logic of hypothesis testing: on

what grounds may a proposed strategy be "refuted" or rejected?

If the type of organization or environment is not specified, there are four discernible context-free tests, each following directly from the definition and purpose of strategy, that a proposed strategy must pass: (1) the goal consistency test, (2) the frame test, (3) the competence test, and (4) the workability test.

THE GOAL CONSISTENCY TEST. In mathematics, conflicting objectives imply a null set of feasible solutions. Similarly, a strategy that contains goals, objectives, and policies that are mutually inconsistent must be rejected. The objective of "growth," for example, is not consistent with that of "maintaining a small informal management team."

Strategies authored by a single individual rarely suffer from such gross inconsistencies, but those that evolve from political processes often do. However, in appraising such strategies, one must realize that publicly announced goals are frequently part of the tactics for implementing an implicit strategy. President Carter's energy program, for example, contains inconsistent goals and policies: "energy conservation, promoting new energy sources, equity of sacrifice, and special taxes and penalties." Yet these statements actually represent political tactics within a larger strategy of relying heavily on legislative, rather than market, mechanisms to reduce U.S. dependence on Arab oil and soften the economic shocks forecasted to occur when oil production begins to decline.

THE FRAME TEST. A principal function of strategy is to structure a situation — to separate the important from the unimportant and to define the critical subproblems to be dealt with. An aspect of evaluation must be an appraisal of how well these tasks have been accomplished. Before one can decide whether or not a given strategy will "work," some indication that the right issues are being worked on is needed.

The distinction between problem solving and defining the relevant problems is important in all decision situations, but especially so in strategy-making. It is analogous to Drucker's (1967) distinction between efficiency and effectiveness and the organizational roles of generalists and specialists. In common parlance, the ability to discriminate the important from the unimportant is usually termed "wisdom." For the sake of discussion we shall call schemes for making this kind of distinction "frame theories" to distinguish them from theories whose purpose is to specify interrelationships among known entities.

To carry out the frame test, an evaluator must have or construct a frame theory that identifies the critical issues within the chosen domain. If the strategy's basic policies and objectives do not address these issues, it must be rejected.

General frame theories, applicable to all situations, do not exist and it is doubtful if such a thing is even possible. There are, however, theories and models of varying power that serve to distinguish the important from the unimportant within specific contexts. For example, as a product/market arena evolves from the early growth to the maturity phase of its life-cycle, currently employed models predict that: (1) market share positions become entrenched; (2) cost-based competition becomes ascendant; and (3) the new stability will permit efficiency gains through vertical integration. Such statements are part of *frame models* because they are directed towards revealing the critical *issues* rather than solutions to them. Similarly, assertions that "size is vital in the automobile industry, location in retailing, and image in the liquor business," are pure frame theories (though perhaps untested) in that they indicate what one should have as an objective rather than how to accomplish it.

Many of the complaints concerning the vagueness, incompleteness, and nonoperational nature of such models stem from a basic misunderstanding of their purpose. Frame models need not, and often should not, address the question of exactly how a particular objective or requirement should be achieved. Thus, a frame theory of coal mining might note the pivotal importance of labor productivity while a frame model of oil refining would surely ignore that issue and highlight instead the need for assured sources of supply. In each case, there are various ways in which a strategist might deal with the pivotal issue. One oil refiner might move to integrate back into tanker operations, while

another, serving a relatively isolated region, might simply depend on its ability to afford a higher purchase price. Richer and more complex contexts support a greater variety of strategies, but must be framed more abstractly.

Most frame models in current use take the form of rules of thumb: focus your efforts, specialization is vital for the smaller enterprise, segment your market, etc. Some of these are of dubious generality and may apply, if at all, only to special contexts, but others represent the distillation of rather sophisticated theory. In a section that follows we shall discuss an important subset of frame models, masquerading as rules of thumb, that arise under the special context of rivalry.

THE COMPETENCE TEST. Since a key purpose of a strategy is to structure a situation in a way that creates solvable subproblems, strategies that do not result in solvable subproblems must be rejected. Such strategies simply substitute one ill-structured dilemma for another.

A strategy of competing in the electric typewriter market, for example, by creating a radically cheap yet durable machine defines a subproblem (inventing the machine) that is probably no more amenable to attack than the original strategic problem. The "invention" of such a device is quite unlikely unless some special resources or conditions exist. If the firm in question had a demonstrated competence at similar cost-saving innovations or held a relevant patent, the strategy might be acceptable. Thus, the idea that the subproblems defined by a strategy should be better structured than the original problem has an operational interpretation in the context of organizations — the subproblems should be ones that can be dealt with by existing and demonstrated organizational skills, resources, and competences. While it is not strictly necessary for the strategist, or strategy evaluator, to know "how" such subproblems will be solved, an appreciation for the solvability of various kinds of subproblems is required.

What is particularly interesting about this observation is that the standard rules of thumb, "build on your strengths" and "first understand your strengths and weaknesses" can be deduced from the basic proposition that strategy is problem structuring and organizational policies are hierarchical. They *do not* depend on assumptions about the nature of competition or the stressfulness of the environment and, consequently, apply equally to business and not-for-profit organizations. They are simply a convenient way of expressing the idea that the most direct measure of whether a subproblem is solvable, and therefore simpler than the original strategic problem, is to compare it to problems the organization has had to cope with in the past.

THE WORKABILITY TEST. If a strategy has a consistent goal set, passes the frame test, in that it focuses on the critical issues, and passes the competence test, in that it avoids unreasonable demands on subsequent policy-making, there still remains the question: "Will it work?" Will the proposed policies and actions work together to produce the results sought?

The issue of workability is what most formal planning documents and procedures address, and there are an enormous variety of tools, theories, and methods for making this evaluation. Most can be placed in one of two rough groups: (1) those that are concerned with the availability and deployment of resources, and (2) those that attempt to predict the outcomes associated with particular actions. The first group contains methods for financial, plant capacity, personnel, logistics, and materials flow planning. Encompassing a great deal of what is taught in formal management education, these methods range in sophistication from simple tables of cash flow to complex computer simulations and linear programming models. Their general intent is to permit proposed actions to be tested for consistency with one another and the available resources.

The second group includes procedures and models for estimating demand, price, future technology, competitive reaction, market share, etc. The best developed methods in this group are those for predicting demand. Macroeconomic models, input-output models, industry models, trend analysis, and other techniques can significantly reduce the uncertainty associated with estimates of future demand. Less well developed are models for predicting which firms, following which strategies, will satisfy this demand. Thus, while reasonably accurate forecasts of the future demand for computer peripherals are available, the rigorous prediction of the market share attainable by a specific set of price, line breadth, technical quality, and support policies is largely beyond the current state of the art. Most practical planning systems rely heavily on judgment, intuition, and debate as means of establishing these estimates. Because, except for the roughest of checks, the workability test usually requires inputs from a variety of specialized viewpoints and disciplines, it is largely carried out by a multilevel process in most organizations. (See, for example, Berg, 1965; Bower, 1970.)

This article is not an appropriate forum for surveying all, or even the most important, of the detailed methods for associating actions with results. Firmly rooted within specific functional disciplines, requiring specialized training for their use, they need to be restructured and adapted to each new problem. There are, however, a growing class of models, or theories that attempt to associate policy with results at high levels of abstraction. These shall be termed "tactical" models to stress the idea that their concern is with the manipulation of policy-type variables *within* a frame, rather than the choice of frame or the explosion of policy into detailed subcomponents. A model giving the direction and approximate magnitude of the associations among profitability, promotional effort, and dealer exclusivity (within, say, Porter's [1976] "nonconvenience" frame) would be classified *tactical*. A method for estimating segment-specific price elasticities of television sets would be classified below the tactical level of abstraction.

In general, most of the current strategy oriented research has both frame and tactical content. The builder of frame models will usually at least offer conjectures about the range of appropriate tactics within a context and the builder of tactical models is, at least implicitly, identifying the chosen parameters as critical within the given frame. Thus, as we turn to an examination of specific theories and models useful in strategy evaluation, no strenuous attempt will be made to discuss frame and tactical models in separate sections. Instead, we shall follow a general path from those approaches that are appropriate in the widest contexts to those that are more narrowly focused. The models and theories covered include: (1) the assumption of rivalry in nonperfect markets, (2) classical evaluation approaches, (3) life cycle models, (4) empirically based frame and tactical models, (5) strategic group models, and (6) experience curve models.

RIVALRY AND ASYMMETRY: THE MOST GENERAL CONTEXT

The widest context that provides usable theory for strategy-making and evaluation is that provided by the simple assumption of rivalry. Strategy, as a concept, has its roots in the consideration of pure rivalry, so this should not be surprising.

Pure rivalry, as arises in games, military combat, and other interactions in which the stakes are well defined and cooperation unlikely, is a powerful simplifying assumption. Under conditions of pure rivalry, the solution, or outcome, is indeterminate under symmetry. No one can predict which of two identical opposing armies or corporations will prevail. A determinate solution only becomes possible when certain asymmetries exist, such asymmetries being termed "advantages." The winning strategy (as opposed to tactics) is always the same — play only those games in which you have an advantage. Somewhat less mechanistically, one wins games by exploiting asymmetries that make a difference. Thus, in pure rivalry, a frame model is one that tells the strategist which asymmetries constitute advantages.

One interesting consequence of pure rivalry is that the outcomes of balanced confrontations under conditions of full information will necessarily be determined by details not included in current theories of strategy. If all contenders have equal access to the available strategic knowledge, which need not be very good, the only confrontations of interest are those in which, according to the current state of strategic theory, the outcome is indeterminate. Faced with such a situation, the determined strategist will try to discover new sorts of advantages hitherto unrealized. The approach to such discovery would have to be through the study of situational asymmetry rather than the examination of theory. Once the outcome has been determined, the potential store of knowledge will have been increased — a new type of asymmetry will have been tested as to whether or not it constitutes an advantage. Therefore, in a world of pure rivalry, strategists either know in advance the outcome of a confrontation or they are pure situational thinkers. Researchers, in this imaginary world, would have to gain knowledge by the arduous and undignified method of studying a myriad of individual cases, looking for clues as to which asymmetries were critical in each.

Traditional microeconomic theory is based on the assumption of pure rivalry and frames the strategic issues quite simply: the only asymmetry that can constitute an advantage is cost. The theory goes on, of course, to make further assumptions which, in the end, guarantee equilibrium — a condition of complete symmetry. From our perspective, microeconomics is a wide context frame model with this content: (1) Cost asymmetries are critical advantages for business firms. (2) If costs are equal, the nature of advantage is beyond the scope of the theory. Of course, if an economy were in *real* equilibrium, not all variables would be symmetrical, but no advantage would be attainable. In a world in which people learn, in which new insights can occur, and in which every situation contains a universe of complex potential asymmetries, it is doubtful if equilibrium is a conceivable state of affairs for anything but physical systems.

The kind of rivalry characteristic of today's economy is far from "pure rivalry." Perhaps the most important difference is its ecological nature. Not all firms are pitted against one another, protected niches exist, "mutations," in the form of innovations, constantly open up new possibilities and obsolete old sources of advantage. More important still, asymmetries that are not advantages in one arena may be critical advantages in another — we live in a world of multiple contexts. If two firms have identical costs, microeconomic theory predicts a standoff. Suppose, however, that one firm possesses a particularly rich source of raw materials and the other a special manufacturing process. Each potential advantage reduces cost by the same amount so no cost asymmetry is produced. A strategist, however, might notice that the special process of the first firm gives it an advantage abroad, where it has not yet been introduced. The second firm cannot exploit the cost advantage of its raw material supply at such distances and cannot follow. It may, however, choose to investigate the use of its material advantage in other products. One firm becomes a multinational, and the other diversified. Strategy, in other words, still depends on asymmetry, but under "impure" rivalry advantages other than cost exist, information is far from perfect, and the recognition of asymmetry is as vital as its exploitation.

Rivalrous environments reward the exploitation of asymmetry and the exploitation of asymmetry, in turn, leads to the formation of niches and specialization as a means of adapting to niches. The rivalrous environment, therefore, simplifies the analytical job by usually restricting attention to the immediate niche in question and its close neighbors. Furthermore, in a particular niche, rivalry tends to be on certain key factors. Accumulated histories have given the competing organizations (or organisms) roughly equivalent endowments in the basic functions necessary for survival; factors that formed the center of strategic battles in the past (e.g., coping with labor unions, use of EDP technology) come into balance for the survivors and competition extends to new grounds.

The implications of assuming rivalry for strategy-making and the appropriate focus of strategy analysis are rarely made explicit. We have dwelt on them because statements that are frequently passed off as simply heuristics, or rules of thumb, are often deductions from a model of rivalrous competition. The model lacks the rigor so attractive to those trained in economics or the physical sciences, but is more accurate in its essentials than any available rigorous model. Biologists studying niches, ecologies, and species adaptation realize the enormous variety of solutions to competitive problems that evolving organisms can produce, and employ the same kind of situational functional analysis as

do students of organizational strategy in their search for understanding. The assumption of rivalry, in sum, can be seen as a frame model that (1) invites a focus on the comparison of roughly similar entities rather than elaborate models of an entire system, (2) implies that strategic factors are discoverable through the inspection asymmetries rather than common factors, (3) implies that stable solutions to strategic problems take the form of niches and niche maintenance behavior, and (4) implies that the fundamental threats to stability will arise from changes in the climate and innovation (mutation).

The assumption of rivalry, therefore, allows the use of a powerful rejection rule in evaluating strategy: *a strategy that does not either create or exploit an asymmetry constituting an advantage must be rejected.* Which asymmetries produce advantages is determined either from an appropriate frame model or situational analysis. The rule is *powerful* in the same way that the conservation of energy law permits one to reject proposed perpetual motion machines without studying their inner logics.

CLASSICAL EVALUATION APPROACHES

The strategy concept as described here developed out of the contributions of a number of scholars. While Reilley (1955) and Kline (1955) were among the earliest authors to apply the term "strategy" to the idea of a comprehensive business plan, the first well articulated descriptions of strategy as a mechanism for adapting an organization to its environment were those of Selznik (1957), Chandler (1962), Tilles (1963), Learned *et al.* (1965), and Ansoff (1965). While Chandler saw strategy as mediating between environment and organizational structure, and Selznik saw "mission" as the essence of organizational leadership, neither author dwelt on either the formulation or evaluation of strategy. We take, therefore, Tilles's approach to evaluation, which is a distillation of the Harvard Business School concept of strategy later published by Learned *et al.*, and Ansoff's normative prescriptions for strategy formulation and evaluation, as the "classical" approaches.

Identifying strategy as a "set of goals and major policies," Tilles suggested that strategy be evaluated on six criteria: (1) internal consistency, (2) consistency with the environment, (3) appropriateness in the light of available resources, (4) satisfactory degree of risk, (5) appropriate time horizon, and (6) adequacy of results achieved. Tilles's terminology, of course, does not match our own, but his discussion makes it clear that his first criterion corresponds to our test for goal consistency and the resource oriented part of our workability test. By "consistency with the environment" Tilles means a requirement that the strategy address and deal with the critical success factors and problems within the chosen domain — this corresponds to our frame test. The third criterion, Tilles makes clear, is a test of whether certain resources are employed to "advantage" by the strategy. Specifically mentioned are money, competence, and physical facilities. The fourth and fifth criteria are suggested elements or characteristics of the goal set and the sixth refers to *a posteriori* appraisal.

The Tilles aproach can be seen as a simple frame model of general business rivalry — it posits the need for some type of workability test and suggests that advantage be sought in the three broad areas of money, competence, and physical facilities. Admittedly general, the model stands in striking contrast to many prior approaches to the guidance of corporations that emphasized such factors as forecasting, superior product quality, and low costs or that suggested that success would be attained by those who possessed "vision," "aggressiveness," or "sound management practice." While the frame model employed by Tilles is quite broad, his article recounts a number of anecdotes which serve to suggest a number of specific issues that may be critical in certain situations. Similarly, the Learned *et al.* text on the evaluation of strategy relies on a series of cases to make explicit the issues that the authors believe to be critical in selected situations.

Ansoff presents a normative approach to strategy formulation that emphasizes the issue of diversification. Paralleling Tilles and the Harvard group in his approach to intra-industry strategy, Ansoff suggests that diversification

strategy be framed by consideration of: (1) the available funds, (2) the available level of general management skills, (3) the demand/capacity relationship in the area being considered, (4) the barriers to entry, and (5) the potential synergy. The synergy idea is the heart of the matter and, in its raw form, is simply a measure of increased efficiency through combination of activities. Ansoff, however, requires that synergy be compared to the profile of strengths and weaknesses of the firms operating in the area being considered for entry. Thus, it actually becomes a measure of the degree to which a corporate resource is capable of being an advantage in the new area. The synergy argument, therefore, amounts to the proposition that the firm should possess resources that can be used to advantage in the proposed new venture. Where Ansoff differs from Tilles and the Harvard group's approaches is over the issue of whether such advantage is *required* — while Ansoff values its presence highly, he does not reject the idea of diversification if synergy is absent.

In summary, these two "classical" approaches to strategy evaluation provide some very wide context frame models, but no explicit tactical theories for the evaluation process. They do provide the first comprehensive descriptions of the strategy concept, emphasize the importance of deploying resources in ways that produce relative advantage, and suggest a number of areas in which advantage will normally be found. In short, the classical approach is roughly equivalent to our basic frame of rivalry. Drawing its power from its generality, it remains the approach to which one must turn when context-specific theories or models are not available.

LIFE CYCLE MODELS

The product/market life cycle concept provides a powerful frame theory that has yet to be fully developed. Originally employed as a tool for marketing specialists, the (product) life cycle concept has been gradually elaborated to include such factors as industry structure and raw material sourcing patterns. Hofer (1975) succinctly summarizes most of the comprehensive life cycle models, including those of Levitt

(1965), Fox (1973), and Wasson (1974), and also gives his own synthesis.

Most product/market life cycle models divide the evolution of a product/market area into five contexts: introduction, growth, shakeout, maturity, and decline. Ideally, if formulated as a pure *frame* model, a product/market life cycle model would identify those areas or issues which form the primary basis of rivalry in each context. Such a model would, for example, indicate how rivalry in the maturity phase differs from rivalry in the growth phase, point out the issues that would be considered strategic in each phase, and highlight the areas in each phase in which asymmetry may produce advantage. Most of the product life cycle models that have been put forward, however, are mixtures of descriptions of activities, suggested actions, and frame models. Fox (1973), for example, indicates that during the growth phase rivalry will be among a few firms offering similar products, production should be centralized, and manufacturing efficiency will be the critical focus. The first point is descriptive, providing what is actually a key for identifying the phase, the second is a normative proposition (of questionable generality), and the third a frame-type statement (i.e., that advantages in efficient production will be critical) that may or may not be valid.

In most product/market life cycle models the area of greatest interest is the transition from growth to maturity, with some type of passage through a "shakeout" phase in the process. The basic idea is that the basis of rivalry and the activities of rival firms change as this transition takes place. While much of the information provided by the life cycle theorists describes "normal" or "common" activities that will occur during each phase, there is a consensus frame model, albeit broad, that is useful in strategy formulation and evaluation. Obviously pertaining only to fairly standardized products aimed at a variety of buyers, the consensus frame is approximately as follows:

In the growth phase, demand pull provides margins that may allow relatively inefficient producers to survive. Rivalry focuses on product performance, price, access to distribution channels and the identification of viable market segments and the special product charac-

teristics appropriate to each. Depending on the competences of the rival firms and the nature of the market, strategies will be fashioned to take advantage of asymmetries in cost, product quality, distribution channels, and image in or access to market segments.

Shakeout is signaled by falling margins and a reduction in the rate of demand growth. By this time, market segments have been defined and footholds gained. Those with inferior products, poor distribution, high costs, or indefensible segmentation commitments have either fallen by the wayside or soon will. Rivalry shifts to a new phase — segments are cleared of weaker competitors and strategic advantage is sought in production efficiency, selling efficiency, and distribution intensity *within* segments. While the factors that were important during the growth phase continue to be necessary, rivals with a chance at survival already possess these skills or resources. Efficiency in one's chosen segments, and efficiencies gained by scale economies of linked segments are translated into increased ability to advertise and promote the product.

Once maturity sets in, relative stability reigns. The maturity phase, almost by definition, is one in which the rivals have established defensible territories and the attainment of critical advantage is virtually impossible. Strategy shifts to niche maintenance and the honing of established skills and tactics. Without innovation or a major change in the environment, there is no way of "winning" in a mature market unless rivals commit blunders.

As Hofer (1975) has pointed out, for the product/market life cycle frame to be truly useful in strategy evaluation, more specific contexts must be defined. The variables he suggests as important delimiters of different contexts include product differentiability, purchase frequency, nature of the buyer's needs, rate of technological change, the ratio of distribution costs to value added, price elasticity of demand, marginal plant size, and others. Hofer and other researchers are currently attempting to build a "contingency" theory of strategy by using such variables to predict the emergent winning strategies. Hofer's fundamental frame theory is that the product/market life cycle is the most critical determinant of strategy, followed closely by the nature of buyer needs (economic vs. noneconomic) and the degree of product differentiation. He goes on to specify sets of resources or market characteristics that are most significant in each stage of the life cycle and offers a number of hypotheses concerning the appropriate tactics in quite specific contexts.

The contingency approach is not only a potentially fruitful source of frame and tactical theory, it also permits theory building to be directly tied to case-type data. We do, however, disagree somewhat with the idea that the models can be used to (and be validated by) successfully predict(ing) winning strategies. There is a subtle difference between trying to predict what a firm's strategy should be in a particular context and trying to identify the issues with which it must come to grips. The predictive approach, if successful, amounts to describing the *common* characteristics of all surviving rivals. However, *among* those rivals it is still asymmetry and uniqueness rather than commonality that will govern and structure the nature of current and future rivalry. Our position is that, to be useful in the formulation and evaluation of strategy, a model must not only describe what is necessary for existence in a given context, it must also indicate what the rivalry is about — the areas in which advantage will make a critical difference. How a particular firm uses its unique history and position to attain an advantage is, ultimately, beyond the reach of general theory.

A true frame model that bears a close resemblance to life cycle theories is Abernathy's model (Abernathy and Utterback, 1975; Abernathy and Townsend, 1975) on the ways in which standardization and variety act as conflicting forces to affect relative emphasis on product vs. process innovation. According to this model, the period immediately following the introduction of a complex (composed of many subunits and requiring a wide variety of materials and specialized production steps) innovative product is one in which rival firms jockey for position by testing alternative designs. During this period, constant changes in the design of the product and the wide variety of alternate forms necessary to explore the environment limit the usefulness of highly standardized production or vertical integration. Rivalry is essentially on the basis of product performance, and

product innovation is the strategic issue. Eventually, the model holds, product design and the environment come into balance and a "dominant design" appears — the model T Ford, the DC-3, the vinyl LP stereo disc, etc. The consequent stability in product and reduction in variety now permit backward integration, standardization of manufacturing process, and economies of scale in integrated production to become strategic factors. While during the product innovation phase the fluidity of design did not permit a firm to firmly commit to a particular set of subassemblies or production processes, the era of stability allows production efficiency and process innovation to become critical competitive factors.

The Abernathy model also predicts that the advantages gained by standardization will eventually work against the firm if product innovation activity is renewed. Simply stated, the strategies required for success in the stable phase make the firm more and more vulnerable to the next cycle of product innovation. Of course, the reverse may also be possible — the advantage gained by the integrated producer, particularly if significant *process* innovation is involved, may be sufficient to ensure the economic viability of its version of the dominant design for a very long period of time. Nevertheless, the idea that strategy can be *too* focused, producing barriers to future adaptation in addition to barriers to entry, has direct analogs in biology and provides an intriguing counterpoint to received microeconomic equilibrium models. Some empirical support for these notions comes from the Cooper and Schendel (1976) study of how the dominant producers in seven industries responded to significant technological innovations by "outsiders." Their principal finding was that, over the long run, the traditional firms that tried to participate in the new technology were not successful.

EMPIRICALLY BASED FRAME AND TACTICAL MODELS

Cross sectional analyses of policy-performance relationships in various contexts can provide valuable insights into the underlying parameters that influence variation among firms and the range of attainable states. Such studies can produce both frame and tactical theories but remain limited by the fundamental limitation of cross sectional analysis — the observed associations do not imply causality. Two examples of fairly comprehensive cross sectional studies are the PIMS project (see Schoeffler *et al.*, 1974; Buzzell *et al.*, 1975) and Rumelt's (1974) study of diversification strategy.

The discovery of policy-performance relationships on a business level has historically been hampered by the unavailabiltiy of data on anything but the firm level. The PIMS project is an on-going study that is continually building a data base of business-level statistics. Administered by the Strategic Planning Institute (SPI), the project's member firms pay a fee in order to add their business-level data to the bank and, in return, gain access to the project's proprietary programs and results. SPI ensures confidentiality and supports research based on the accumulating data.

The central theme of the PIMS results is the association between market share and return on investment (ROI). This association turns out to be quite strong and is enhanced when capital intensity is low, when the product is sold to industrial customers, when product differentiation is increased, purchase frequency decreased, and in a variety of other circumstances. The published two-way contingency tables also indicate positive associations between product quality and ROI and a host of other associations. Thought provoking and suggestive, the two-way displays unfortunately leave unanswered the question of whether or not these associations continue to hold as other conditions are changed.

The PIMS data provide what is perhaps the most potent *general* tactical model that is available for strategy evaluation at the business level. By selecting a subsample which occupies the general context of interest, the analyst can explore, on an ad hoc basis, the historical and cross sectional associations between variations in policy and changes in outcomes. No strong theory lies behind the observed associations, and quantitative theories concerning relationships among variables of this type simply do not exist.

In addition to providing immediate tactical tests of strategy workability, the PIMS data can be a rich source of frame theories. While much attention has been paid to the factors that influence profitability, an important empirical finding is that only a *few* factors explain the preponderance of profitability variance, and that these factors *change* as context changes. For example, while capital intensity is strongly associated with profitability among firms with moderate to low market shares, it is much less important in explaining profitability variations among firms with high market shares. It is from collections of such observations and their detailed analysis that future frame theories can be constructed.

Rumelt's (1974) study of 273 large industrial corporations focused on the relationship between profitability and diversification strategy. After defining eight patterns of diversification posture, ranging from single-business to unrelated-portfolio, tests for long-term profitability differentials were performed. It was found that the critical explanatory factor was *not* the absolute degree of diversity, but the way in which businesses had been related to one another. In particular, the highest levels of profitability were associated with firms that were diversified but which related the majority of their activities to some central core skill, competence, or resource. The lowest levels of profitability were displayed by vertically integrated raw material producers and slowly growing conglomerates. Like the PIMS results, Rumelt's findings cannot be interpreted causally — it remains unclear whether the high performing group is profitable because of its strategy or whether the strategy of limited diversity reflects an unwillingness to abandon a highly profitable area. Nevertheless, the study provides this frame content: when diversification is at issue, the degree and type of interrelationships among activities tends to be a more critical decision area than the absolute degree of diversity.

In a more recent study, Rumelt (1977) has found that the high profitability of related-constrained firms is due to their ability to consistently take positions in industries characterized by high levels of return on capital. Furthermore, these "high-profit" industries are themselves largely composed of related-business firms.

The emergent picture is one of a class of high-profit industries existing chiefly as the intersections of related-business firms rather than as separate fields dominated by specialists. It appears that both the industry and firm phenomena are reflections of a more fundamental determinant of profitability: extensible skills together with activity in product/market arenas subject to product differentiation and market segmentation.

In summing up empirical studies on the effectiveness of strategy content, it seems evident that cross-sectional methods can be used to separate the important from the unimportant within a variety of contexts. In addition, with access to sufficient data, strong mutual associations among variables can be used as tactical models. The fact remains, however, that without an underlying theory to explain *why* the observed associations occur, there are distinct limitations on these models' ability to aid one in understanding the detailed forces at work in a particular situation.

STRATEGIC GROUPS MODELS

A branch of strategy research that promises to provide a rich source of both frame and tactical models is concerned with the discovery and understanding of heterogeneous competitive groups within industries. The traditional assumption that has guided economists in the study of industrial organization is homogeneity — that firms within an industry differ only with respect to scale. A dubious assumption at best, this approach has led inexorably to characterizing industries in terms of concentration (relative size being, after all, the only attribute the model allows) or in terms of characteristics possessed collectively by all firms in the industry (e.g., entry barriers). While the roots of an effective challenge to this tradition are many, the significant contributions currently defining the field have been made by Hatten (1974) and Patton (1976) from Purdue, strongly influenced by Schendel, Cooper, and Bass (see Bass, 1969; Hatten and Schendel, 1977; Schendel and Patton, 1976), and Hunt (1972), Newman (1973), and Porter (1976) from Harvard, strongly influ-

enced by Bower and Caves (see Caves and Porter, 1977).

Hatten studied the brewing industry between 1952 and 1971 by building a linear regression model relating observable policy variables (e.g., number of plants, price, number of brands, market share, etc.) to return on equity. Using a clustering algorithm together with a statistical test for homogeneity of regression models, he showed that the industry could actually be broken into subindustries, each with its own distinct policy-performance relationship. The five clusters corresponded to large national brewers, smaller national brewers, strong regional, weak regional, and small regional brewers. Patton used the same data but a different approach — he grouped the firms into three clusters (national, large regional, and small regional) and fitted simultaneous equation regression models to each cluster with the cyclic independent variables being return on equity, market share, and efficiency (price-cost margin).

Perhaps most striking among Patton's findings is that while market share is positively and significantly related to return on equity (ROE) for the industry taken as a whole, the relationship is negative within each cluster. In other words, the national brewers have higher levels of both market share and ROE than do regional brewers, but marginal additions to market share by either group of firms lowers profitability. The regression equations thus reveal the type of niche structure that has long been the mainstay of qualitative strategic analysis.

Taken as a frame model, Patton's results suggest that rivalry among the national brewers has been essentially on efficiency and promotion — exploiting economies of scale and the efficiency of new automated facilities in order to support massive promotional campaigns. The regional firms, by contrast, cannot play this game and, rather than being direct rivals, compete with the national firms by focusing all their efforts on one or two brands in a limited, but heavy beer drinking, region.

The beer industry is one of the most mature industries and one would not expect to find either incompetent firms or hidden winning strategies that have been missed. It is, therefore, somewhat surprising to find the model suggesting that brand proliferation strategies and plant acquisition programs by regional brewers have generally been both unsuccessful and damaging. Of course, the model cannot tell us what would have happened to firms undertaking these programs had they not done so, nor can it reveal whether the relationship is causal or just a reflection of firms in trouble taking such actions as "last ditch" efforts. Still, the general picture presented is that efficiency on a national level is the critical issue for the large brewer, and maintaining some defensible hold on a regional area, and *not* expansion, is the critical issue for the smaller brewer.

Patton's model also provides a tactical model that is useful in strategy formulation and evaluation. The regression equations that have been fitted to the brewing industry are the substance of that model and provide the strategy evaluator with a description of the "strategy possibility," or feasibility, frontier. More simply, the equations provide a check on the consistency of a set of goals and policies.

Intriguing questions remain with regard to the Hatten and Patton studies. How unique is the beer industry? Why have so few beer firms diversified to any extent? Is the observed pattern generalizable or a function of the rather unique characteristics of the beer market (e.g., unusually high resistance to new brands)?

Porter's investigation of bilateral market power provides a new frame model and additional support for the strategic group concept. Focusing on the interaction between manufacturers and retailers, Porter hypothesized that the manufacturer's profits would, other things being equal, decline as retailer bargaining power increased. That power, he reasoned, depends chiefly on the retailer's ability to help differentiate the product. Splitting retailers (and products) into "convenience" (frequently purchased goods sold through self-service outlets) and "nonconvenience" (shopping goods sold through specialty stores and/or dealers) outlets, the latter would be expected to have a greater impact on product differentiation. Manufacturers' primary weapon in countering retailer power is strongly advertised brands since stores can hardly deny shelf space to items that consumers demand. Using these and other arguments, Por-

ter built a model predicting that manufacturer profit rates would vary strongly with advertising intensity in convenience goods, but that advertising intensity would have a much smaller influence on the profitability of makers of nonconvenience goods. The prediction was strongly supported by several tests comparing the form of traditional industry structure models in each of the two contexts.

Porter states quite clearly that his intention was to build and test a frame-type model (1976: 234): "The model identifies what strategic elements are crucial in determining profits and which ones have little effect." His results not only suggest that strong brands are the critical issue in convenience goods, but that *there is little room for strategic variability in convenience goods*. A simple bilateral model explains a great deal of the profitability variance. By contrast, branding and advertising are less critical issues in nonconvenience goods *and* the room for strategic variability is much greater. Thus, while there are only a few viable strategies in the convenience goods arena, nonconvenience goods businesses can seek advantage in many different ways (e.g., branding, service, product quality, geographical specialization, type of outlet, and so on). Porter has not only provided a new model, he has significantly increased our ability to speak clearly about and validate frame-type models.

THE BCG EXPERIENCE EFFECT

The Boston Consulting Group (1968) has taken the well-known learning curve effect, generalized it to apply to whole business units, and built a fairly elaborate structure that is essentially a strongly quantitative tactical model. According to BCG, the cost elements of value added tend to drop by 20 to 30% each time *accumulated* production (in units) doubles. In essence, BCG is arguing that the general observable trend of decreasing costs (adjusted for inflation) is due to a special type of scale-economy that must be earned by experience rather than purchased. The immediate consequences of this proposition are: (1) of firms following roughly parallel expansion paths, the one with the largest market share will have the lowest unit costs; (2) as long as the product does not change radically, and providing that the market leader commits no blunders, trailing firms will never be able to overtake the market leader; (3) accumulated experience, or its proxy, market share, is a valuable resource and rational strategy-making requires that it be treated as an investment; and (4) eventual market dominance is determined early in the struggle for position.

Economics is supposed to be the "dismal" science; the BCG theory is dismal news indeed for many strategists. It suggests that most market positions currently being worked on are hopeless, that taking high profits in a growth industry is the road to disaster, and that the game, in the end, goes to the swiftest and most efficient.

The basic model's frame content is straightforward. The areas in which advantage occur are in having a good product ready to market earlier than one's rivals and in having the financial and organizational strength to sustain more rapid growth (at perhaps a lower margin!) than one's rivals. Like all frame models, this one is silent on the issues of gaining these advantages in the first place. BCG tends to suggest that a properly managed diversified firm has the best mix of resources to provide these advantages. In theory this may be true, but few diversified firms have been able to solve the problems of getting innovative new products to market early and of supporting division-level strategies of foregoing current profit for future return.

The BCG framework is also a powerful tactical model, especially when combined with some model of price elasticity of demand. The analyst can, by setting a few key parameters, estimate the cash flow accruing to the firm under a variety of pricing and growth policies.

The major stumbling block in using the BCG model is that the contexts in which it is valid are not well established. The electronics industry, among others, appears to be a context which supports the model, but it is not clear to what degree it applies in areas characterized by heavy branding and promotion, highly segmented markets, custom engineered products, etc. In addition, anyone who has tried to tie down the concept of "market share" in any but the simplest industries is aware how vague a concept it really is.

Our conjecture is that the BCG model will continue to be elaborated and the contexts within which it is appropriate will become better defined. In addition, it seems probable that the concept of "shared experience" among different products will ultimately prove to be a more fertile ground for strategic models than the raw experience effect theory. For example, current strategic theories almost invariably imply that persistently profitless business areas be dropped. The idea of shared experience, by contrast, suggests that careful attention must be paid to the possibility of continuing to gain experience in a low profit area in order to lower costs in a related, but more profitable, business.

SUMMARY AND SUGGESTED DIRECTIONS FOR FURTHER RESEARCH

Focusing on analytical approaches, we began our examination of strategy evaluation by noting that the primary function of strategy is to provide a consistent set of objectives and policies that restructures an ambiguous reality into a set of organizationally solvable subproblems. We then argued that this purpose implied four tests that must be passed if a strategy is to be judged acceptable. They were:

1. *The Goal Consistency Test* — a proposed strategy must be rejected if it contains mutually inconsistent goals, objectives, and/or policies.

2. *The Frame Test* — the strategy must be rejected if it does not address those issues or problem areas which are crucially important within the chosen context. Assuming rivalry, the strategy must exploit asymmetries which constitute advantages within the chosen domain.

3. *The Competence Test* — the strategy must be rejected if the subproblems it poses do not lie within the realm of those that are solvable by demonstrated resources or organizational skills and competences.

4. *The Workability Test* — the strategy must be rejected if the combined policies are infeasible from a resource point of view or if available knowledge indicates that the desired objectives will not be obtained by the policy set.

These tests are context free and apply to any organization in any environment. Turning to the problem of making these tests operational, we examined, in progressively narrower contexts, the frame and tactical aspects of a number of recent research efforts and contributions to theory building pertaining to the content of effective strategies.

What, then, is the state of the art? Our survey of approaches was illustrative but necessarily incomplete. Omitted was the vast literature on industrial organization, a goodly number of specific tactical models, many insightful, but as yet untested, normative propositions, the whole political process approach to the strategy formulation/evaluating issue, and many other worthwhile contributions. Nevertheless, even if our survey had been comprehensive, the simple answer would have to be that strategy evaluation is still pretty much of an art. Progress is being made, but that progress is itself an art practiced by individuals with widely varying points of view, employing disparate techniques, and aiming toward different goals. Knowledge is accumulating, but there has not, as yet, appeared a paradigm powerful enough to permit its integration. Strategy continues to be studied because of its importance rather than its tractability.

A more complete answer would have to begin by noting that the approaches examined in this article appear to conform to a pernicious variant of Heisenberg's uncertainty principle: apparently, one can gain concreteness only through a narrowing of scope, and breadth of vision is purchased at the price of essential detail. The classical approach permits the consideration of the broadest range of issues, but provides only the flimsiest structure and no calculus for the manipulation of the constructs it suggests. The BCG model, by contrast, attains a crystal clear inner logic by focusing almost entirely on the single issue of unit cost.

FURTHER DIRECTIONS. Accepting the need for work to continue on several levels of abstraction, some of the crucial questions that future research should probably address if a coherent body of knowledge is going to evolve are the following:

1. Much better models and theories are needed of how firms actually compete. How do book publishers and motion picture producers compete? What is the nature of the rivalry among aerospace contractors and among office equipment manufacturers? Microeconomics is essentially a system of logic which, once one understands what contributes to "cost" in a given situation, can always provide an *a posteriori* explanation. What is needed is a simplified model of rivalry that still captures its multidimensional nature.

2. Manufacturing has been woefully neglected as an aspect of strategy. Scherer's (1975) study of the economies of multiplant operation provides more insight into the policy issues surrounding manufacturing than any "policy" text.

3. Studies that use profitability as the dependent variable tread very thin ice. If we believe our concepts concerning adaptation to niches, specialization, segmentation, and rivalry based on asymmetry, comparing profitabilities across niches (or even strategies) tells us very little about "success."

4. Statistical tests of theories need to be supplemented with tests of their efficacy in aiding understanding of specific strategic situations. McDonald's (1975) game theoretic analysis of the Ford-GM confrontation shows what can be done with the simplest tools. If our theories are more sophisticated, cannot we do more?

5. We need an improved understanding of the determinants of industry structure and a better language for describing the structure of industry. The strategic groups concept represents a beginning of the move away from equating structure with concentration, but much more work is required.

6. Methodologies for testing the validity of frame statements and frame models need to be created and legitimized. Porter's (1976) study provides an important example of how this can be done.

Turning to a more specific set of research opportunities, the life cycle models focus on the issue of adaptation to change, and particularly change that is induced by the rivalry itself rather than from external sources, but need to be more sharply focused on the nature of rivalry in each phase. By contrast, the Hatten-Patton type of model reveals the inner structure of rivalry in sharply quantitative terms, but has been applied so far only to an atypically stable situation. What might be fruitful would be a study that applied the Hatten-Patton method to a competitive group in the growth phase and then again in the maturity phase of the life cycle. Several of the key hypotheses of the life cycle theory might be tested by such an approach.

The PIMS data base will obviously provide fertile territory for a number of studies. In addition to supporting further tests of the life cycle theories, it should also provide the means to test a broad range of frame models. Perhaps most intriguing will be research aimed at explaining some of the counter-intuitive results already reported by PIMS. The negative association between R and D intensity and profitability has already been the subject of a prize-winning thesis by Christensen (1977).

The Boston Consulting Group's model will undoubtedly spawn a variety of operations research oriented elaborations, but its real utility in strategy formulation and evaluation will only be realized if the contexts within which it is valid are better established. A practical place to begin examining this issue might be an identification of the factors which influence the degree to which experience is a firm versus industry effect. It may well be that such factors are the real elements of strategy in situations where the experience effect is strong.

A CLOSING NOTE. In addition to its obvious value to practicing managers, the major opportunity that beckons in the study of strategy and strategy evaluation is a significant restructuring of the theory of the firm and the theory of industrial structure. Although this opportunity is, perhaps, more a function of the slowness of professional economists to come to grips with these issues than of great strides on the part of students of corporate strategy, it nonetheless exists. Economic studies of competitive behavior have traditionally been oriented towards a particular set of audiences: other economists, Congress, the Federal regulatory agencies, the Department of Justice, and the courts. The theories developed have generally been designed to help determine whether or not markets are "competitive," to evaluate certain practices as to fairness, and are heavily influenced by the axiomatic theory of welfare economics.

What the economics profession has not been able to deal with are precisely those issues that are central to strategic theory: the rivalry of firms, the inner details of industries, the dynamics of competition based on innovation, product differentiation, segmentation, and the shifting defense and exploitation of changing territories. These phenomena have not been ignored because they are invisible, but because the bulk of traditional economic models assume away such behavior. Good economists talk about these issues, using the symbol system of economics, and are fully aware of their importance. The overwhelming weight of traditional theory, however, tends to relegate such observations to the status of folklore — they are fascinating, but not suitable subjects for rigorous theorizing.

This opportunity is a significant one because it holds out the promise that public policy may ultimately be influenced by a more valid view of the functioning of a modern economy.

Commentary

BRUCE A. KIRCHHOFF
University of Nebraska at Omaha

This comment on Rumelt's paper focuses on three major points: strategy definitions, evaluation criteria and a comment on his literature review of strategy evaluation research. Then, Rumelt's thoughts are placed in the broader context of strategy as a totality: formulation, content and implementation, with some remarks as to where it all points.

STRATEGY DEFINITION

Rumelt begins by defining strategy, selecting observations on the subject from many sources and correctly noting that the strategy concept can be applied to activities at all levels of an organization. But rather than weave an hierarchical explanation upon which to base the rest of his remarks, Rumelt leaves the reader with an interesting array of possible choices, but no clear understanding of what he means by strategy. Rumelt apparently considers strategy to be top level managers' goals and policies that structure an otherwise ambiguous organization-environment interrelationship. Unfortunately, within this definition, Rumelt fails to separate the formulation process of those goals and policies from the "... set of goals and policies ..." that emerge from the process. It is wise, however, to separate process from content for evaluation purposes, for, contrary to Rumelt's opening statement, all aspects of ill-structured problem solving offer outstanding opportunities for rational analysis.

EVALUATION CRITERIA

Rumelt suggests four context-free tests by which goals and policies may be evaluated: (1) goal consistency, (2) frame, (3) competence, and (4) workability. Goal consistency, competence, and workability are concepts familiar to strategy evaluators, but the frame test as Rumelt presents it is unique in the strategy literature. According to Rumelt, frame theories are schemes for discriminating important from unimportant issues within unstructured situations. He acknowledges that "general frame theories applicable to all situations do not exist ..." and likens them to "rules of thumb" by which "critical issues" are identified. This definition implies that frame theories can be used in the strategy formulation process. Thus, frame theories are not solely tools of evaluators, but also of formulators, a

confusion which is endemic in theoretical efforts to separate evaluation from formulation.

Foremost among frame models, Rumelt says, is the model of "rivalry." His discourse on the theory of rivalry makes inaccurate references to micro-economic theory and fails to provide convincing logic that rivalry is more accurate or different from micro-economic theories of competition. More importantly, he correctly states that under conditions of competition, strategies must create or exploit advantages. He is correct in noting that micro-economic theories inadequately express the complexities of strategies. But this is primarily because of their unrealistic assumptions, especially the assumption of maximum profits as the sole goal of business firms.

LITERATURE REVIEW OF EVALUATION RESEARCH

Rumelt provides a thorough and useful, organized review of the available literature on techniques of evaluating organizational goals and policies. He attempts to apply his unique concept of "frame models" as a link to connect the otherwise diverse literature. Frame models, however, do not fit all the literature, so application of the concept requires variation in its meaning. For example, Tilles' six evaluation criteria are not tools for separating the important from the unimportant as is required by Rumelt's definition of a frame model. Tilles' tests of (1) internal consistency, (2) environmental, (3) resource appropriateness, (4) degree of risk, (5) appropriate time horizon, and (6) adequacy of results are applied after the critical issues have been identified. On the other hand, the (product) life cycle theory fits the frame model concept as Rumelt suggests.

In his search for frame models within the literature, Rumelt overlooks a significant empirical research contribution. He cites Patton's (1976) dissertation and notes its importance for "strategic group models." He overlooks Patton's most important contribution however, which is the use of multiple equations to express the true context of multiple goal seeking organizations. Micro-economists have unrealistically assumed away multiple goal strategies, choosing instead to maximize profit. Strategy researchers have, by and large, followed this lead by choosing ROI as the measure of overall firm success. However, Patton breaks with this tradition, using the rigor of statistical analysis to create multiple "goal" equations.

A BROADER CONTEXT

Strategy evaluation is as broad as Rumelt suggests, perhaps broader. Thus, one should examine aspects of managerial behavior along with evaluation of content of goals and policies when evaluating strategy.

By defining strategic management to mean the overall managerial process for establishing strategy (goals and policies) and guiding the organization's actions towards their attainment, the broader context of strategy evaluation becomes more evident. In examining this broader context, evaluation can be divided into three parts: (1) evaluation of the strategy formulation process, (2) evaluation of strategy content, and (3) an evaluation of strategy implementation capability.

Evaluation of the Strategy Formulation Process

Strategy formulation is a behavioral process, involving thought patterns and behaviors of individuals and groups as they perceive and process information in their efforts to structure unstructured situations. As a behavioral process, it requires behavioral evaluation tools. Decision behavior research is a broad field and no comprehensive compendium of empirical findings exists. Projections of future research directions, however, have been offered by activists in this field. Noteworthy among these are Mintzberg (1973) with his unique insights, McClelland (1967) who has identified power, affiliation and achievement motivation among managers, and Van de Ven (1975) who has explored group planning processes.[1]

[1] Editor's note: A very profitable direction for future policy research would be to integrate some of these findings into the models used by practitioners to evaluate the effectiveness of the strategy formulation process.

Strategy Content Evaluation

Current empirical research thrusts in strategy content evaluation are directed towards converting subjective tools into analytical models. The focus of these efforts is relating organization performance to strategy through the underlying assumption that performance is a result of organization actions intended to achieve objectives, subject to certain conditions.

PIMS (Buzzell, et al., 1975) researchers, Hatten (1974), Kirchhoff (1975a), and Patton (1976) use multiple regression with results that suggest the methodology is appropriate. These models, though, suffer one or both of two limitations: (1) their narrow perspective on performance (must use only ROI as a performance measure), and (2) their exclusion of organization aspirations as evaluation criteria. As already emphasized, Patton's multiple equation model is free of the first limitation, but subject to the second.

The problem of incorporating organization aspiration (goals and objectives) in strategy evaluation is complex. If organization aspirations are used to guide actions, then the actual results of these actions should be measured relative to the desired results. This forms a rigorous test of goal content feasibility. Researchers should develop methods of operationalizing this concept. For example, many organizations have formal planning systems, so written records of goals should exist. Based on such records, the ratio of actual ROI divided by goal ROI could be substituted for raw ROI as a performance measure.

Evaluation of Strategy Implementation Capability

Analytic models built upon examinations of performance results assume that organizations can act so as to cause performance results. By implication, the researcher assumes that organization goals and strategy are directly translated into actions. This assumption is drawn from the classical model of bureaucracy, i.e., top management sets goals and organization members pursue them. But organization theory (March and Simon, 1958; Perrow, 1961) and empirical research (Likert, 1967; Stogdill, 1974; Fiedler, 1967) question this assumption. Thus, strategy implementation capability cannot be assumed and must be evaluated along with content and formulation capability.

Evaluation of implementation capability should focus on whether managers at top, middle and lower levels actually connect their day-to-day work to the organization's goals. This is again a behavioral research problem. A review of empirical research on leadership reveals an immense number of laboratory and field research studies bearing on this question, but this research draws data primarily from lower level managers, workers, and other non-managers, and measures performance in terms more tactical than strategic, e.g., job satisfaction, role conflict, absenteeism, etc., and in terms that do not deal with overall organization performance.

A review of the leadership literature gives some clues to useful research on the evaluation of implementation capability, but provides few appropriate instruments for assessing how top level managers pursue goals and generally use strategy to guide operations. For example, Kirchhoff's (1971) survey research work found upper level managers occasionally refused to respond on Likert's (1967) "Profile of Organization Characteristics" instrument and Fiedler's (1967) "Least Preferred Co-worker" instrument. Post test interviews revealed that these top level managers felt intimidated and/or alienated by the concepts and vocabulary of these instruments.

Because of these difficulties, Kirchhoff (1975b) created a measuring instrument using vocabulary and conceptual schemes familiar to upper level managers. His "Managerial Style Questionnaire" (MSQ) has had a high response rate, even in mail surveys. It measures the extent to which managers use objectives and goals in performing their managerial duties. Based upon responses of middle and top level managers in twelve organizations, the MSQ

satisfactorily meets psychometric standards for validity and reliability. Research results so far indicate: (1) that the use of objectives varies from organization to organization; (2) that existence of formal written objectives is positively related to the use of objectives, but does not guarantee their use; and (3) that managers can be trained to use objectives. In addition, the use of objectives by organizations has been found to be positively correlated with overall performance within 31 profit centers of a large U.S. manufacturing corporation (Kirchhoff and Schendel, 1977).

The need for better criteria to evaluate implementation capability poses a challenge to behaviorally-trained researchers to define new, broad behavioral constructs and to operationalize them for field research with top level managers. Strategists need to know more about how goals and strategy translate into actions, and what kinds of managers within different organizations effectively carry out actions intended to reach goals. The use of such new behavioral constructs can help improve our knowledge of these processes.

SUMMARY

The evaluation of implementation capacity brings us full circle back to strategy formulation, for many implementors are also formulators. In reality, the formulation, content and implementation of strategy are inseparable parts of the strategic management process. Conceptually, however, they must be separated to differentiate evaluation methods and direct future research. At this stage of development of strategy evaluation research the real challenge for strategy evaluation researchers is to incorporate economics, sociology, psychology and working manager pragmatism into a comprehensive model for evaluation of strategy and performance. The pursuit is *multi*-disciplinary.

Section 4 References

Abernathy, William J. and Phillip L. Townsend. "Technology, Productivity, and Process Change." *Technological Forecasting and Social Change*, Vol. 7, No. 4, 1975.

Abernathy, William J. and James M. Utterback. "Innovation and the Evolving Structure of the Firm." Harvard Business School Working Paper 75–18, 1975.

Andrews, Kennth. *The Concept of Corporate Strategy*. Homewood, Ill.: Dow-Jones-Irwin, 1971.

Ansoff, H. Igor. *Corporate Strategy: An Analytical Approach to Business Policy for Growth and Expansion*. New York: McGraw-Hill, 1965.

Bass, Frank. "A New Product Growth Model for Consumer Durables." *Management Science*, January 1969.

Berg, Norman A. "Strategic Planning in Conglomerate Companies." *Harvard Business Review*, May–June 1965.

Boston Consulting Group Staff. *Perspectives on Experience*. Boston: The Boston Consulting Group, 1968.

Bower, Joseph L. "Planning within the Firm." *American Economic Review*, May 1970.

Braybrooke, David and Charles E. Lindblom. *A Strategy of Decision*. New York: The Free Press, 1963.

Buzzell, Robert D., Bradley T. Gale and Ralph G. M. Sultan. "Market Share — Key to Profitability." *Harvard Business Review*. January–February 1975.

Caves, R. E. and M. E. Porter. "From Entry Barriers to Mobility Barriers: Conjectural Decisions and Contrived Deterrence to New Competition." *Quarterly Journal of Economics*, May 1977.

Chandler, Alfred D. *Strategy and Structure: Chapters in the History of the American Industrial Enterprise*. Cambridge, Mass.: M.I.T. Press, 1962.

Christensen, H. Kurt. "Product, Market, and Company Influences upon the Profitability of Business Unit Research and Development Expenditures." Doctoral diss., Columbia University, 1977.

Cooper, Arnold C. and Dan Schendel. "Strategic Responses to Technological Threats." *Business Horizons*, February 1976.

Dhalla, Nariman K. and Sonia Yuspeh, "Forget the Product Life Cycle Concept!" *Harvard Business Review*, January–February 1976.

Drucker, Peter F. "The Effective Decision." *Harvard Business Review*, January–February 1967.

Fiedler, Fred E. *A Theory of Leadership Effectiveness*. New York: McGraw-Hill, 1967.

Fox, Harold. "A Framework for Functional Coordination." *Atlanta Economic Review*, November–December 1973.

Gale, Bradley T. "Market Share and Rate of Return." *Review of Economics and Statistics*, November 1972.

Hatten, Kenneth J. "Strategic Models in the Brewing Industry." Doctoral diss., Purdue University, 1974.

Hatten, Kenneth J. and Dan E. Schendel. "Heterogeneity Within an Industry: Firm Conduct in the U. S. Brewing Industry 1952–1971." *Journal of Industrial Economics*, December 1977.

Hofer, Charles W. "Toward a Contingency Theory of Business Strategy." *Academy of Management Journal*, December 1975.

Hofer, Charles W. "Research on Strategic Planning: A Survey of Past Studies and Suggestions for Future Efforts." *Journal of Economics and Business*, Spring–Summer 1976.

Hofer, Charles W. and Dan Schendel. *Strategy Formulation: Analytical Concepts*. St. Paul, Minn.: West Publishing Company, 1978.

Hunt, Michael S. "Competition in the Major Home Appliance Industry, 1960–1970." Doctoral diss., Harvard University, 1972.

Kirchhoff, Bruce A. *A Foundation for the Measurement of Management by Objectives*. Salt Lake City: Bureau of Economic and Business Research, University of Utah, 1971.

Kirchhoff, Bruce A. "Empirical Analysis of Strategic Factors Contributing to Return on Investment." *Academy of Management Proceedings*, August 10, 1975a.

Kirchhoff, Bruce A. "A Diagnostic Tool for Management by Objectives." *Personnel Psychology*, Autumn 1975b.

Kirchhoff, Bruce A. and Dan Schendel. "Linking Strategy and Operations through MBO." Presented at the Academy of Management National Meetings, Orlando, Florida, August 1977.

Kline, C. H. "The Strategy of Product Policy." *Harvard Business Review*, July–August 1955.

Learned, Edmund P., C. Roland Christensen, Kenneth R. Andrews and William D. Guth. *Business Policy: Text and Cases*. Homewood, Ill.: Richard D. Irwin, 1965.

Levitt, Theodore. "Exploit the Product Life Cycle." *Harvard Business Review*, November–December 1965.

Likert, Rensis. *The Human Organization: Its Management and Value*. New York: McGraw-Hill, 1967.

March, James G. and Herbert A. Simon. *Organizations*. New York: Wiley, 1958.

McClelland, David C. *The Achieving Society*. New York: The Free Press, 1967.

McDonald, John. *The Game of Business*. Garden City, N.Y.: Doubleday and Co., 1975.

Mintzberg, Henry. *The Nature of Managerial Work*. New York: Harper and Row, 1973.

Newman, Howard H. "Strategic Groups and the Structure-Performance Relationship." Doctoral diss., Harvard University, 1973.

Patton, G. Richard. "A Simultaneous Equation Model of Corporate Strategy: The Case of the U.S. Brewing Industry." Doctoral diss., Purdue University, 1976.

Perrow, Charles. "The Analysis of Goals in Complex Organizations." *American Sociological Review*, December 1961.

Porter, Michael E. *Interbrand Choice, Strategy, and Bilateral Market Power*. Harvard Economic Studies, Vol. 146. Cambridge, Mass.: Harvard University Press, 1976.

Reilley, E. W. "Planning the Future Strategy of the Business." *Advanced Management*, December 1955.

Rhenman, Eric. *Organization Theory for Long Range Planning*. New York: Wiley, 1973.

Rumelt, Richard P. *Strategy, Structure, and Economic Performance*. Boston: Division of Research, Graduate School of Business Administration, Harvard University, 1974.

Rumelt, Richard P. "Diversity and Profitability." Managerial Studies Center Working Paper MGL-51, Graduate School of Management, University of California at Los Angeles, 1977.

Schendel, Dan E. and G. Richard Patton. "A Simultaneous Equation Model of Corporate Strategy." Institute for Research in the Behavioral, Economic and Management Sciences. Paper No. 582. Purdue University, July 1976.

Scherer, Frederic M. *The Economics of Multi-Plant Operation: An International Comparison Study*. Cambridge, Mass.: Harvard University Press, 1975.

Schoeffler, Sidney, Robert D. Buzzell and Donald F. Heany. "Impact of Strategic Planning on Profit Performance." *Harvard Business Review*, March–April 1974.

Schon, Donald A. *Displacement of Concepts*. London: Tavistock Publications, 1963.

Selznik, Phillip. *Leadership in Administration*. New York: Harper and Row, 1957.

Simon, Herbert A. "Decision Rules for Production and Inventory Controls with Probability Forecasts of Sales." O.N.R. Research Memorandum, Carnegie Institute of Technology, 1958. Quoted in Shull, F. A., A. L. Delbecq and L. L. Cummings. *Organizational Decision Making*. New York: McGraw-Hill, 1970.

Stodgill, Ralph M. *Handbook of Leadership*. New York: The Free Press, 1974.

Tilles, Seymour. "How to Evaluate Corporate Strategy." *Harvard Business Review*, July–August 1963.

Van de Ven, Andrew H. *Group Decision Making and Effectiveness: An Experimental Study*. Kent, Ohio: Administrative Research Institute, Kent State University, 1975.

Vickers, Sir Geoffery. *The Art of Judgment: A Study of Policy Making*. New York: Basic Books, 1965.

Wasson, Chester R. *Dynamic Competitive Strategy and Product Life Cycles*. St. Charles, Ill.: Challenge Books, 1974.

5

STRATEGY IMPLEMENTATION

This section of the text contains two sets of papers. The first by Lorange, Hekhuis, and Henry deals with formal planning systems and their role in strategy formulation and implementation. The second by Galbraith and Nathanson, Wrigley, and Miner, deals with the role of organizational structure, processes, and behavior in the implementation of strategy. The pairing of these two sets of papers may appear unusual, since formal planning systems are generally considered to include the organizational mechanism by which strategies are formulated. A question can be raised, therefore, as to why we have placed this material on formal planning systems and strategy implementation in the same section.

Our reasons are these. First, although it is conceptually useful to separate the formulation and implementation tasks for research and teaching, in practice they must be integrated if organizational purpose is to be achieved. Sometimes this is done informally; sometimes through a partially developed planning system; and sometimes formally through a single, integrated formal planning system that includes the strategic planning system and the operating planning system (e.g., budgeting, scheduling and control systems). However done, linkages between strategy formulation, strategy implementation, and operations are essential, even though this fact is sometimes overlooked by academics. Inclusion of the formal planning systems discussion in this section helps highlight and emphasize this essential linkage.

The second reason for discussing formal planning systems in this section is that, in many instances, such systems are used more for implementation than for formulation. Systems used in this way tend to emphasize the extrapolation of the organization's existing activities into the future through inertial forecasts. While such extrapolation is necessary in strategic planning, indeed, in all forms of planning, systems that are used in this manner do not consider change from the perspective of formulating strategy. Rather, they seek out the organizational, administrative, and operating issues that will have to be resolved to effectively implement strategic decisions made outside the planning system. Perhaps it would be better, following Henry's commentary, to acknowledge that such systems are not really strategic planning systems. Rather than trying to change the use of terminology too violently, it seems more productive to us to note that many formal planning systems are used primarily for implementation tasks.

A final reason for discussing formal planning systems in this section is that the design and operation of such systems must be done in terms of, and be consistent with, the extant structure and processes of the organization; for example, a firm cannot design, install, and operate an advanced, sophisticated formal planning system if the remainder of its structure and processes are not sophisticated enough to supply to the planning system its information and other needs.[1] Hence, even though one of the responsibilities of the formal planning system is to help formulate strategy, the system itself is a part of the total structure of the organization, that is, it achieves its analytical ends through administrative means. Thus, to consider formal planning systems in the same section in which the other elements of structure are discussed is appropriate.

[1] This fact means that structure may well affect strategy, a point noted later by Galbraith and Nathanson, among others. The reasoning here derives from the general systems notion that process may affect output.

FORMAL PLANNING SYSTEMS: A LINK BETWEEN FORMULATION AND IMPLEMENTATION

Although formal planning systems are not depicted explicitly in our systems diagram of the strategy management process (see Exhibit 5.1) it is clear from the above discussion that they provide the organizational context necessary to support the strategy formulation, evaluation, implementation, and control processes. As such, they are clearly one of the most important tools available to organizations today for implementing the strategic management process.

Lorange explores three aspects of formal planning system design and use in his paper. First, he reviews the literature pertaining to the benefits to be derived from the use of formal planning systems in strategy formulation. He concludes that organizations that use formal planning systems perform better. He notes in this regard that, while a cause-and-effect relationship has not yet been established (and perhaps never can be established), there does seem to be a strong correlation between the use of formal planning systems and better economic performance.

Second, he surveys the literature on the acceptance and use of formal planning systems, giving particular attention to a series of studies that describe the pitfalls that organizations may encounter in attempting to introduce and use formal planning systems.

Exhibit 5.1   An Overview of the Strategic Management Process

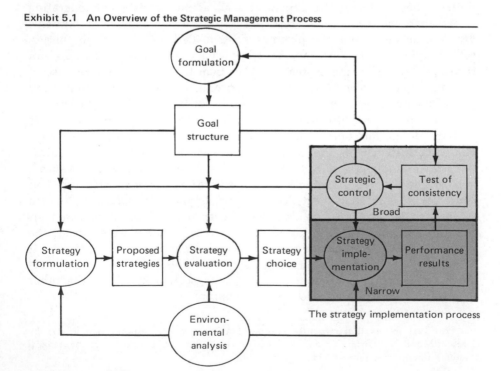

Finally, he examines the literature pertaining to various broad parameters of formal planning system design, such as the kinds of linkage that should exist between an organization's strategic planning system and its operations planning, the technical complexity of the system, and the financial orientation of the system.

A major thesis advanced by Lorange, and one that seems most sensible, is that formal planning system design must be of a contingent nature. There do not appear to be any absolutes available for designing a formal planning system that will be usable by all organizations — in Lorange's paper, tailor-made is a recurrent phrase used to express the need for contingent designs. However, after recognizing that such tailor-making is required, Lorange does not offer the building blocks or components that might be used to construct such a system, nor does he review the literature devoted to such components, or the manner in which they are linked and so on. It should be possible to define such components or building blocks of a formal planning system and still remain consistent with the contingency notion with respect to the overall systems design as Schendel (1977) indicates, and a conclusion with which Henry agrees. Nevertheless, Lorange's conclusion that we have much to learn about the contingent design and implementation of formal planning systems seems irrefutable.

Hekhuis, a corporate planning staff member at General Electric, one of the foremost organizations in the world in terms of the development and use of formal planning systems, endorses the need for planning systems that can do more to: (1) cope with the increasing complexity and range of social and political issues confronting business enterprise today; (2) assist with problems of resource management in light of growing resource scarcities; and (3) assist in the integrating/coordinating activities necessary across business and organizational levels in order to fully accomplish strategic planning tasks and objectives. Hekhuis also notes that: (1) CEO involvement is the most important factor influencing planning system effectiveness; (2) the degree of CEO involvement will depend primarily on the benefits that the system can produce; and (3) the ability to squeeze time for thinking about the future out of crowded executive calendars may be the single most important contribution of a formal planning system insofar as top managers are concerned.

Henry's commentary complements Lorange's paper by focusing on formal planning system philosophies, components, responsibility assignments, and procedures, topics which Lorange did not address in great detail. Henry agrees with Lorange on the need for a much better understanding of formal planning system utilization in order to identify ways to improve their design and effectiveness. In this regard, he suggested a number of topics on planning system utilization that might be addressed by future research.

In any such future research on formal planning systems, however, there seems to be a need, based on the observations of the authors in this section, to recognize the following factors: (1) that contingency-based planning system design and implementation is probably necessary; (2) that the distinction between strategic and operations planning needs to be carefully drawn; (3) that research will need to be somewhat clinical in nature and is, therefore, probably not amenable to large sample studies; and (4) that planning systems are of a proprietary nature and thus not easy to gain access to for detailed study.

STRATEGY IMPLEMENTATION: THE ROLE OF STRUCTURE AND PROCESS

All of the tasks comprising the strategic management process discussed so far go for nought if the strategy they produce is not used by the organization to guide and actuate operations. The strategy implementation task is, therefore, of great importance. It has also received considerable attention in terms of both policy and organizational behavior research. In its essence, strategy implementation is an administrative task. Thus, while it would be possible, although in our opinion undesirable, to conduct all the tasks of the strategy formulation and evaluation tasks analytically and without resort to the organization, or at least most parts of the organization, it would not be possible to implement strategy without doing it through and with the help of the organization. Moreover, strategy formulation and evaluation that do not consider the problems associated with implementation risk being ineffective. From a process viewpoint, this raises a question regarding the degree to which implementation issues should influence strategy content.

Conceptually, the implementation process begins after the selection and evaluation of strategy, as indicated in Exhibit 5.1. Narrowly defined, it would end with a set of organizational actions that relate the organization to its environment and determine its overall performance. Broadly defined, it would include the strategic control process through which the organization would attempt to respond to deviations from the planned strategy or between expected and actual levels of performance.

The implementation task itself is accomplished through a variety of administrative tools. These tools can be grouped into three categories: (1) *structure*, including these tools: physical structure, methods of specialization, methods of departmentalization, methods of coordination, delegation of authority, and informal organization; (2) *processes*, including these tools: resource allocation systems, information systems, measurement and evaluation systems, rewards and sanctions, and personnel selection, development, and promotion systems; and (3) *behavior*, including these tools: interpersonal behavior, leadership style, and use of power. Note that structure is often not defined as broadly as has been done here.

The key questions for effective implementation are: (1) Are there any universal or contingent principles that should be followed in the application of these tools? (2) If so, what are they?

Galbraith's and Nathanson's paper attempts to answer these questions through an extremely comprehensive survey of past research on organizational structure and processes. They begin by reviewing Chandler's thesis: (1) that organizational structure follows growth strategy; (2) that firms evolve through a stepwise development sequence; and (3) that organizations do not change their structures until they are provoked to do so by inefficiencies. Next, they discuss two conceptual extensions of Chandler's thesis: (1) that strategy/structure fit influences performance, and (2) that (1) holds, but only under competition. They then look at two different explanations of the evolution of structural forms: one by Williamson (1975), from the point of view of transaction costs and uncertainty; and the other by Thompson (1967), from an open systems, behavioral viewpoint. Next, they examine a number of streams of research drawn from the policy and organizational theory literature that bears on these hypotheses. These include: (1) studies of the relationship between strategy and structure; (2) studies on resource allocation, evaluation and reward, and people and careers; (3) studies relating strategy, structure, and competition; (4) studies relating structure, competition, and performance; (5) studies relating organizational structure and processes; and (6) studies of organizational growth and development.

Based on this review, they concluded that the strategy/structure/competition performance fit thesis has received substantial support, although other explanations are also possible because no study has examined all of the parameters at once, or their interactions. They also develop an extended organizational growth model that includes several types of transitions not included in prior models. Unlike Chandler, however, Galbraith and Nathanson suggest that organizations need not grow, that is, they may choose to stay in a particular stage; and, when they do change, they may change in several ways. For example, they might just as easily modify their strategy to fit their structure as vice versa. The important thing is not what they do, but that they do it consistently.

Wrigley's commentary adds some necessary perspective and additional insights on the research cited by Galbraith and Nathanson in several ways. First, he notes that all the researchers from Chandler onward have used situational, open systems models to explain their findings. Wrigley's point is not that the use of such models was wrong, but rather than no one questioned their use or the implications that such use might have for the conclusions developed by these studies. Second, he points out that Chandler's research affected entire schools of thought, not just the thinking of individual researchers. However, he also notes that most recent research has intellectual debts beyond those owed to Chandler.

Perhaps Wrigley's most important observation was to note that Chandler's research was different from most of the more recent studies of organizational structure with respect to its assumptions about environmental discontinuities and the historical concept of man. In this regard, Wrigley argues that long-term longitudinal studies of managerial responses to environmental discontinuities are needed to reveal the creative achievements of managers. Thus, he eschews an approach that searches for a deterministic science of man, suggesting instead the need to move to the middle ground of a search for regularities and common patterns among populations of firms.

Finally, Wrigley suggests that the major limitation of research on organizational structure to date has been a lack of interaction among different schools of thought.

Miner, in his commentary, argues that while the strategy/structure hypothesis developed from Chandler's work may be interesting theory, it has yet to be strongly corroborated statistically. He further argues that, in light of all the research done in this area to date, "it is time to take critical stock of the theory in order to avoid, if possible, investing further time and resources in extensive research which might ultimately yield only a small payoff." After critically reviewing several of the major research studies that purportedly support the strategy/structure hypothesis, Miner puts forward an alternate explanation for the existing findings, that is, a structure/people fit hypothesis. Miner suggests that this hypothesis not only explains the major research to date very well but is further corroborated by additional studies he has done (see his Exhibit 6.3). He argues that the structure/people fit hypothesis is more parsimonious than the strategy/structure/competition/performance hypothesis that others are offering, and therefore a better theory so long as it explains the facts.

Miner's views are controversial, to say the least. What are the counter-arguments? First, as was noted by Bower at the conference, most of the studies involved included much rich descriptive data beyond the statistics cited by Miner, most of which support the strategy/structure hypothesis. Second, it may be that the strategy/structure/people fit hypothesis and Miner's structure/people fit hypothesis both have elements of truth to them. It may be that the strategy/structure fit can be a loose one, while the structure/people fit must be a tighter one. In other words, it may be that there are a number of strategies and structures that will fit together well, although to be consistent with Chandler's and some of Rumelt's data, there would be others that would not fit. By contrast, the range of variation between structure/people might be more constrained. For example, most structures may require a particular type of person, and/or most persons may work best in a particular type of structure. The fact that this explanation is consistent with both sets of data does not mean that it is correct. More research on a different data base would be needed to corroborate it. Nor does the fact that this explanation fits the data preclude other explanations.

Two points are clear, however, First, Miner has raised a provocative challenge to the now almost traditional strategy/structure hypothesis. Second, more research is obviously needed to differentiate among the various competing hypotheses.

A review of these papers as a set raises several additional issues and questions beyond those suggested by the papers individually. First, one wonders whether it will be possible to develop large-domain contingency theories in this area. For instance, can we really say anything about how different structural forms, processes, and behavior should be integrated, both at a given point in time and over several stages of organizational evolution, in order to effectively implement strategy? Or, as Brandenburg notes in a later commentary, how can different strategies for different businesses in a multi-business firm be accommodated by mixed structural forms within the same corporate structure? Or, in the same vein, how does the relative importance of structure, process, and behavior change with stage of organization evolution, and with environmental circumstance?

The implementation area also needs to proceed from a sounder concept of the nature and relationship of this task to other tasks in the strategic management process. For instance, much of the research done on implementation tools proceeds either from a very macro level, such as the stages of development model, or from a very micro level, as is characterized by much of the organizational behavior literature. These two types of work need to reinforce one another far better than they do now, for, at root, they are not competing explanations but complementary explanations of different aspects of the implementation process.

Finally, as these papers so convincingly demonstrate, whenever doing research, it is desirable to understand as fully as possible the intellectual roots of the different theories and streams of research in the area.

Formal Planning Systems: Their Role in Strategy Formulation and Implementation

PETER LORANGE
Massachusetts Institute of Technology

INTRODUCTION*

This paper attempts to survey the empirically based research literature on long-range formal planning processes for corporations, and to assess the state-of-the-art of the research-based body of knowledge on formal planning systems. Its scope is thus limited in several ways. First, I will deal solely with the planning processes of profit-making corporations. Thus, although the discussion might have relevance for a broader set of applications, planning in organizations such as those in the public sector will not be discussed. Further, the discussion will be limited to *formalized* planning processes. Formalized systems become particularly useful in instances where the company has grown too diverse, big, or interrelated to handle planning informally. Not surprisingly, therefore, most of the research findings to be discussed will be dealing with larger organizations. And since formal planning concepts have been extensively developed by companies in the industrial sector, the discussion will be confined to planning efforts in large, complex industrial corporations.

It seems increasingly clear that the systems approach to strategy formulation and implementation, as signified by formal planning systems, is only one of many aspects relating to effective strategy formulation and implementation; that is, several other factors might contribute equally or more to a corporation's strategic success. One is the intellectual process of developing a good, substantive strategy, without which no formal planning system or process can suffice. Although the formal planning system is intended to facilitate the development and implementation of the company's strategy, it is clear that the element of managerial vision, strategic understanding, and "feel" is critical.

* The author wishes to acknowledge helpful comments from Richard F. Vancil.

No formal strategic planning system can compensate for managerial insight and the will to manage strategically. As a corollary, it becomes difficult to discuss planning systems in isolation from the substantive strategic decisions that might face the firm.

Organizational structures and processes are two other key areas that affect strategy implementation. Formal planning systems cannot function in a vacuum but need to be reinforced by other formal systems, such as management control, managerial accounting, management information, and management incentives and compensation. Again, however, at the expense of being unrealistically narrow, this paper will not discuss the issue of how the formal planning system can be positioned as one element of an overall strategic system.

In summary, then, the focus of this paper has been kept intentionally narrow in several ways, by only dealing with research on formal planning systems in relatively large, profit-making industrial organizations, by separating the issue of designing a planning system from the decision-making tasks of facing specific substantive strategic choices, and by not focusing on other interrelated systems that also play important roles in the formulation and implementation of strategy.

METHODS FOR CLASSIFYING RESEARCH ON FORMAL PLANNING SYSTEMS: AN OVERVIEW

There are several potentially useful ways of classifying the research literature on formal planning systems for the purpose of a survey like the one undertaken here. A conceptually appealing approach would be to outline a normative/theoretical framework for long-range planning and then to compare the various empirical research findings against this conceptual scheme. This would allow one to assess the extent to which the various aspects of the conceptual framework seem to be validated by the empirical findings, or, alternatively, to specify areas of modifications that seem to be called for in order to improve on the relevance of the conceptual scheme. This logico-experimental approach, although superior from a research methodology point of view, does, however, raise several practical problems if attempting to apply it in the present task.

A primary concern is the newness of long-range planning as a field for research. Consequently, a commonly accepted conceptual scheme has hardly yet emerged; on the contrary, the nature of much of the research at this embryonic stage has been focused on delineating what might be relevant parameters in a conceptual scheme for planning. This paper, therefore, might be characterized as a preliminary step anticipating the evolution of the field to a stage where the state-of-the-art can be sufficiently operationally described to allow for a logico-experimental research thrust.

A second concern is the difficulty of reconciling in the discussion a broad set of empirical studies done during the recent two decades that reflect dramatic progress in our understanding of formal planning systems as a management tool, but that were also often done with vastly differing research purposes in mind. A framework following strict conceptual lines would blur one's sense of direction of progress over time, an important consideration for being able to understand where the field might be going.

Consequently, the discussion will be organized in such a way that the dynamic direction of progress in the field gets highlighted. It will, therefore, be useful to first review the rather broad research literature which attempts to address the rationale for formal planning in general — why do we need a planning approach and what might be its payoffs — and then to review a set of studies which have a somewhat sharper focus in that they address issues of how to establish a long-range planning system, such as what seem to be the most common general pitfalls in implementation.

Next will be a review of the literature on how to design different aspects of a formal planning system to reflect differing corporate situational settings, and to address the question of what seems to work for different types of companies. This topic covers the bulk of the research activities in the field today. The logical next step, then, is to ask what will be likely and useful directions for research to take from here, a question that will be addressed in a sequel section on potential research directions.

The discussion of the empirical knowledge-base on formal planning — retrospective, perspective, and prospective — cannot be properly interpreted, however, without a recognition of what seem to be some of the major problems and challenges in doing research in this area. This paper will thus conclude with a few caveats for doing research on planning systems.

Before embarking on this review, however, one overall generalization should be made about the studies as a whole, as well as one general limitation with respect to the discussion. As will be seen, there seems to be a reasonably strong empirical verification that formal planning systems have reached a high degree of usefulness and are seen to be generally beneficial. Also, the areas of general pitfalls of doing formal planning seem to have been extensively researched. However, when it comes to research that focuses on contingency-related issues for planning systems design, there seems to be much less research undertaken and, not unexpectedly, also a less clear pattern of consensus as to the implications of the research results. Thus, the interpretations and viewpoints of this reviewer become relatively more important during this portion of the discussion. This subjective element will be even more pronounced when it comes to discussing fruitful research directions. Thus, although an attempt has been made to be as objective as possible in the review of the various stages of research in this field, it is inevitable that some element of personal bias will be present. Most important in this respect is probably the reviewer's belief that formal long-range planning systems might contribute more usefully to strategy formulation and implementation when such "systems" are seen primarily as decision-process elements of a larger strategic management process, rather than being isolated as a separable body of knowledge about formal planning systems as such.

THE USE AND BENEFITS OF FORMAL PLANNING SYSTEMS

This section will discuss the empirical research literature that deals with issues relating to the general acceptance and payoffs of formal planning. Based on surveys of the degree to which planning is being used, Ringbakk (1972) asserts that very few corporations had adopted what would presently be called systems for corporate planning prior to 1960. The major waves of adoption came from 1962 to 1965 for U.S. firms, and from 1964 to 1969 for European firms (Ringbakk, 1972). Studies by Ringbakk (1968, 1969) for the U.S.A. and by Hewkin and Kempner (1968) and Taylor and Irving (1971) for the United Kingdom indicate that the degree of use of formalized corporate planning is somewhat less than might have been expected. According to Ringbakk (1969):

Organized corporate long-range planning is neither as well accepted nor as well practiced as suggested by the literature on the subject.

And Taylor and Irving (1971) add:

Corporate planning in major U.K. companies is neither as well developed nor as fully accepted as one might expect.

A number of studies have attempted to establish the potential payoff of using formal planning systems. Thus, Thune and House (1970) undertook a study in which, from an initial sample of 96 corporations, 26 were matched in terms of industry and size into six industry groups. Their study showed that, when measured in terms of earnings, companies with formal planning tended to achieve better performance after this. Herold (1972) attempted to extend the Thune and House study for several more years. Because of mergers and consolidations, he was able to examine only two industries with a sample of five pairs of companies in each. Seen in terms of both sales and profits, the companies with formal planning systems performed better than those who planned informally. Later, Karger (1973) reported on a study comparing high-growth with low-growth U.S. corporations in which "93 percent of high-growth companies rated the 'Setting of Basic Objectives' and the 'Setting of Goals for the Years Ahead' as important factors, whereas low-growth companies rated these items 81 and 88 percent respectively." Although these differences are not large, they nevertheless may suggest that the goal-setting process is more emphasized in effective corporations than in less effective ones. In this regard, Taylor and Irving's (1971) study of 27 large U.K. companies indicated that,

while any assessment of planning benefits must be largely subjective, it is perhaps worth noting that virtually all respondents were enthusiastic about the benefits to be derived.

A concurrent study by Perkins and Sugden (1971) also attempted to evaluate the general overall effectiveness of formal planning systems. This study was part of a large empirical research project on formal planning systems undertaken at the Harvard Business School, which will be discussed more fully later. After stating definitions of the "purpose" of planning and planning's "effectiveness," Perkins and Sugden developed an index of planning effectiveness, which expressed the relationship between purpose and effectiveness in a single quantifiable measure. However, the study failed to come up with significant results.

At about the same time, a team of researchers under the leadership of Ansoff (1971) undertook a study of the potential payoff from planning when making acquisitions. Their study addressed solely the phenomenon of diversification planning undertaken at the corporate level of the organizations involved. Ninety-three corporations which had acquired 299 other firms were studied. Two different types of planning behavior were identified: namely, those firms which took an unplanned opportunistic approach and those which planned systematically. Measures of success included both objective measures such as profits and stock performance, which were taken from the Compustat tapes, and perceived effectiveness measures, such as management's assessment of how well they met their objectives. The main results, which were all significant within reasonable confidence levels, were as follows:

Although subjective evaluation of results by management does not differ greatly between planners and non-planners, objective financial measurements show a substantial difference. ... On virtually all relevant financial criteria, the planners ... significantly outperformed the non-planners.... [Also,] they performed more predictably than non-planners. Thus, planners appear to have narrowed the uncertainty in outcomes of acquisition behavior.

Lorange (1972, 1973b) also undertook a study of what seem to be more effective as opposed to less effective designs of planning systems for major capital expenditures. This study was heavily based on the contingency theory concept. In it, he attempted to correlate the "tailoring" of a system to the setting of the company, and measured systems effectiveness according to an index of perceived effectiveness. With this, he found significant differences at the 95% or better level between the more effective and the less effective subsamples on two of the ten possible systems design elements. Using an index for the rate of financial growth as an alternative effectiveness measure, he found significant differences at the 95% or better level between more and less effective subsamples for only one of the ten design factors. A third alternative effectiveness measure, an index measuring "the degree of confronting as a problem solving style," gave no significant differences between the more effective and the less effective subsamples along any of the ten systems design dimensions.[1]

Given the apparent difficulties of estimating the effects of formal planning based on real-life company data, one might speculate that experimental research design approaches could be an alternative. Surprisingly, the author found only two experimental studies on the effects of the use of formal planning systems. The first was a study by McKinney (1970), which focused on how systematic approaches to strategic planning might aid in developing better corporate strategies. The effects of two alternative formal approaches to strategic planning were tested, namely,

The dominant concept for a formal approach to strategic planning — it focuses on allocating corporate resources to meet opportunities in the environment. The other approach is oriented instead at detailing desirable improvements in the corporate strategy — at the tactical elements that make up corporate strategy.

These procedures were based on Cannon's (1968) strategy concepts. The strategies were operationalized as computer-based check-lists and made available in the form of an experiment to Master's students for solving a policy case. Judges then rated the quality of the strategies developed by the students. An important result emerged: the performance of the students using the formal planning system which laid out a pattern of resource allocation for achieving an overall set of opportunities was much higher than the performance of the students using an increments-driven "tactical" planning system. Thus, a formalized overall approach to strategic planning seems advantageous as a tool for making better strategic decisions.

In the second experimental study, Lee (1976) analyzed the performance of competing "companies" run by teams of senior executives as well as Master's students in the context of a management game situation. He found that teams that formulated more focused corporate goals and objectives tended to outperform teams that took a more informal approach toward goals and objectives-setting. It seems particularly interesting that in a setting with high time-pressures, such as when playing a management game, a more formalized approach toward planning and policy formulation seemed to pay off. A total of 24 teams of four to seven students were part of the study. There was

---

[1] This surrogate measure for systems effectiveness had been suggested by Lawrence and Lorsch; see P. R. Lawrence and J. W. Lorsch, *Organization and Environment*, Division of Research, Harvard Business School, Boston, Mass., 1967.

no difference between the performance of the teams composed of senior executives versus those composed of Master's students when it came to the benefits from formalized planning; in both instances the more formal approach seemed to pay off.

The general pattern of the results from the studies just reviewed seems to indicate that formal long-range planning is indeed an accepted management tool that might provide competitive advantages to those companies that adopt such systems. Thus, at a highly general level there seem to be strong indications that planning might pay off. This conclusion is, however, neither particularly surprising, nor particularly useful. What would be potentially useful to know, but what most of the studies do not shed much light on, is the question of specifically what potential benefits arise from different types of planning approaches. However, given the number of factors that might affect the performance of a corporation, such as the degree of effectiveness of management systems other than the planning system, the quality of the strategic choices actually made by managements as well as a component of "sheer luck," it seems unlikely *a priori* that one should be able to establish empirically strong causal relationships between a firm's adoption of a formal planning system and its performance, at least not unless the company's performance is judged over an extensive period of time. Therefore, it is probably not surprising that no more specific conclusions as to what are the more tangible benefits from the use of formal planning systems seems to emerge from the studies just reviewed.

Two potential shortcomings in the designs of several of these studies might, however, also account for the inability to verify more specifically the ways in which effective formal planning might pay off. First, several of the studies neglected to specify the types of planning they were trying to study, e.g., corporate level portfolio planning, or divisional level business planning, or functional planning.[2]

Thus, except for the studies by Ansoff et al. (1971) and Lorange (1972), formal planning was treated as a broad phenomenon, and little effort was being made to distinguish what sort of formal planning one was dealing with. Thus, a problem still remains in deciding what type of formal planning activities proved advantageous. In future attempts to establish the usefulness of formal planning systems, care should be taken to focus on each particular type of planning separately, for if this is not done, some potential patterns of differential effectiveness might be "averaged" out.

Second, the measures of effectiveness of formal planning systems that have been used have not been as relevant as one might wish; many of these measures were based on some general surrogate variable, when it probably would have been more relevant to measure effectiveness as a function of how well the formal planning system's capabilities were able to meet the specific planning needs at hand for a given company (Lorange, 1977b). Such an approach for studying whether there is a relationship between high performance and high planning system effectiveness, when effectiveness is defined as the degree of "match" between a particular firm's specific planning needs and its specific planning capabilities, would, however, probably require clinically based research design, emphasizing an in-depth assessment of planning needs and capabilities for the given firm. Such an approach would, therefore, involve smaller samples than was the case for the studies discussed in this section.

While the primary focus of the research discussed this far has been on establishing that formal planning systems are a useful management tool, little attention has been given to the specific factors that may have to be considered in the implementation of such formal planning systems in order to achieve the potential benefits they offer.

---

[2] It is outside the scope of this paper to discuss conceptual approaches to the structure of formal planning systems. However, there seems to be a general consensus that it is useful to consider three levels of strategic planning, as indicated above. See, for instance, R. F. Vancil, "Strategy Formulation in Complex Organizations," *Sloan Management Review*, Winter 1976, or P. Lorange and R. F., Vancil, "Strategic Planning in Diversified Companies," *Harvard Business Review*, January–February, 1975.

MAKING FORMAL PLANNING
SYSTEMS WORK

In this section, several studies will be discussed which address the question of how to make formal planning systems work. In this regard, Ringbakk (1971) reported on a survey study of 350 companies, 65 of which participated in an interview survey and 285 responded to a questionnaire which listed a total of 32 planning problem issue questions. These companies were based in both the United States and Europe. The study revealed ten common reasons why formal planning processes typically might malfunction. These were:

1. Corporate planning has not been properly integrated with the rest of the company's management system.
2. There may be a lack of understanding of certain dimensions of planning, such as lack of consideration of alternative strategies or exclusion of alternative courses of action.
3. Management at various levels in the organization may not be participating properly in planning.
4. A staff planning department, not the line, has gotten the brunt of the planning responsibility.
5. There may be a misconception among many managers in that they actually expect the plans to be realized, despite the fact that new events almost inevitably will change the assumptions of the plan.
6. Often, too much may be attempted at once when starting formal planning.
7. There may be a lack of willingness among management to follow the plan in their operating decisions.
8. Extrapolations and projections may be confused with planning.
9. There may be elements of inadequate or unbalanced inputs in planning, such as too little environmental input, or too little participation in projections by top management, engineering or marketing personnel.
10. Small planning details may distract and hamper the development of an overall view of planning.

Some of these reasons, notably 4, 6, and 8, seem to indicate a lack of general competence among management with respect to how to approach the task of implementing formal planning. The other reasons, however, suggest that the formal planning process in this large sample of real-life companies does not seem to resemble what is often called rational or optimal decision-making behavior. Rather, the nature of most of the implementation problems seems to indicate that the long-range planning activities in most companies more closely resemble so-called organizational/political decision-making approaches. (Look at problem 2, for example!) This conclusion is consistent with the view taken by the "behavioral theory" school which views the planning process primarily as one of facilitating changes in organizational direction as a result of a combined set of inputs of limited rationality, rather than as one of making rational choice with respect to one unified directional thrust for the organization (Cyert and March, 1963; Cohen and Cyert, 1973; Allison, 1971). Thus, it seems as if the behavioral "realities" of planning imply a process characterized by limited search, bounded rationality and suboptimization.

Unfortunately, empirical data is available only to verify problems 2, 7, and 9 on Ringbakk's list. Also, since his findings were not cross-tabulated against subgroups of respondents, it is not possible to conclude whether the findings are relevant to *all* types of formal planning or only to a particular type of planning, e.g., to portfolio planning or to business planning. This limitation seems particularly critical because Ringbakk's sample includes mining and raw materials processing corporations as its largest industry group. Such companies would normally be managed in a more centralized way than firms in several of the other industry groups included in the study. Thus, the fact that the findings are not reported by subgroups, especially by subgroups for which one would expect the planning process to differ, significantly limits the usefulness of the results. Also, the variance in the sales volume and number of employees per firm is high, which indicates a heterogeneous sample, another reason why a contingency analysis of the type described above seems appropriate.

At the same time, Taylor and Irving (1971) undertook a survey study of corporate planning practices in 27 large United Kingdom-based corporations. They defined formal planning to be:

1. The formal process of developing objectives for the corporation and its component parts, evolving alternative strategies to achieve these objectives and doing this against a background of a systematic appraisal of internal strengths and external environmental changes.

2. The process of translating strategy into detailed operational plans and seeing that these plans are carried out.

Thus, they limited their study to corporate level portfolio planning and were explicit about the type of planning they were studying. On the other hand, since they solicited responses only from corporate planners and not from line managers, there might be a systematic "optimistic" bias in the data they reported.

One of their findings was that formal planning seems to require a particular type of systematic upper management attitude, and that informally managed organizations will have to change their management style to undertake such formal planning systems. This seems to raise the question of style as an independent variable in planning system design. That is, the failure of efforts to use formal planning systems may result from the fact that the design of the planning system may fail to reflect the managerial style of the organization.

Taylor and Irving also reported twelve major and several minor reasons why formal planning was needed; 36% of these related to "external" factors, 40% related to "internal" needs and 24% were unclassified. The principal external factor reported was the need to develop better responses to environmental changes, while the major internal need was to coordinate overall internal activities better following decentralization. These results correspond to the hypotheses of a number of normative studies on planning, namely, that a formal planning system should fulfill two major types of tasks, namely, adaptation to environmental opportunities and/or threats and integration of the

internal pattern of functional activities so as to reap benefits from strengths and/or ameliorate effects from weaknesses (Lorange, forthcoming; Hax and Majluf, 1977a, 1977b; Malm, 1975).

Taylor and Irving's data were not detailed enough to corroborate or refute some of the more detailed hypotheses, however. For instance, Gordon and Miller (1976) postulated that the formal planning system's capacity to facilitate adaptation through "opportunistic surveillance" (Thompson, 1967) will probably be relatively more important when the environment is rapidly changing than when it is more stable. Similarly, Kimberly (1976) hypothesized that its capacity to facilitate integration will probably be relatively more important when the company's functional activities are relatively task specialized or when the firm itself is larger or diversified.

As to which factors had provided major stimulus for the implementation of formal planning, Taylor and Irving's study indicated that the occurrence of tangible events such as major personnel turnover, organizational changes, or some sort of a crisis seemed to be very significant. This finding seems to be consistent with similar findings relating to the implementation of other management systems such as management information systems (Keen, 1975). It also seems consistent with the clinical intervention theories for organizational change developed by Schein (1969), Beckhard (1969), and others.

The major internal "political" problems arose, according to Taylor and Irving, when the formal planning system was seen as embracing activities traditionally carried out by other functions. Thus, careful and open information and communication, attempts not to preserve old interests, and the active role of the top management were seen as important factors in removing such political problems. This seems consistent with the clinical findings of Lorange (1978), which indicate that a major barrier to more effective implementation of strategic planning programs is a tendency among the various functional areas not to adequately cooperate in what might be seen as a predominantly cross-functional process. Consequently, an important general management function seems to be to facilitate such cooperation on the implementation of strategic planning programs. Several interesting case studies have also been reported which illustrate the need to create a strategic mode of cooperation among management which might differ from the operating mode (Goggin, 1974; Lorange and Vancil, 1977).

As to the role of the planner, Taylor and Irving (1971) found that ". . . the common theme was that *planning is a line job*. The role of the planner therefore is not to do the planning, but to design, sell and direct the planning effort." Since Taylor and Irving looked at planning at the corporate level only, it seems quite reasonable that they found that the planner should be a system's "catalyst," not a plans "analyst." This is consistent with the normative arguments of others (Ackerman, 1977; Lorange, forthcoming), and is also supported by case study profiles that indicate that this seems to be the appropriate role for the corporate planner.[3] However, at the divisional or functional levels, the role of the planner does not necessarily have to serve an identical function. In fact, these planners are probably doers" much more than catalysts.

As to the chief executive's involvement, Taylor and Irving found that 33% of the chief executives were said not to be personally involved in strategic planning. This seems to be consistent with Ringbakk's (1971) finding that only 10% of the chief executives participated in the original development of plans. Three major reasons were cited for the top executive's lack of involvement: (1) misunderstanding about the nature of the planning process, (2) a short-term operations orientation, and (3) the lack of planning philosophy by the firm.

Taylor and Irving also indicated that line managers had various types of motivations for using formal planning, the most important being that such planning would help them do a better job (30% response frequency), and the second being corporate pride (22% response

frequency). On the other hand, only 3% indicated an interest in the role of formal planning in capital expenditure allocations and its linkage to management control. This seems to indicate that the formal planning systems role in the resource allocation process is unemphasized, that is, that line managers do not see the full value of formal planning as a tool for "narrowing down options." Taken as a whole, according to Taylor and Irving's study the predominant characteristics of the formal planning process seem to resemble the behavioral model, and in this respect their findings seem to agree with Ringbakk's.

Based on Steiner's (1972) earlier work, Steiner and Schollhammer (1975) undertook a study of pitfalls encountered in long-range planning in 460 large multinational corporations, about half of which were headquartered in the U.S., and the others headquartered in Japan, Canada, Great Britain, Italy and Australia. The ten most important pitfalls to be avoided when implementing formal planning, according to their study, were as follows:

1. Top management's assumption that it can delegate the planning function to a planner.

2. Top management becoming so engrossed in current problems that it spends insufficient time on long-range planning, with the result that the process becomes discredited among other managers and staff.

3. The failure to develop company goals suitable as a basis for formulating long-range plans.

4. The failure to create a climate in the company which is congenial and not resistant to planning.

5. Top management's failure to review with departmental and divisional heads the long-range plans which they have developed.

6. The failure of major line personnel to assume the necessary involvement in the planning process.

7. Assuming that corporate comprehensive planning is something separate from the entire general management process.

8. Failing to make sure that top management and major line officers really understand the nature of long-range planning and what it will accomplish for them and the company.

---

[3] See, for example: "The State Street Boston Financial Corporation," in P. Lorange and R. F. Vancil, eds., *Strategic Planning Systems*, and E. G. & G. (A) and (B), Intercollegiate Case Clearing House, ICCH 9–376–187 and 9–376–188, Boston, Mass., 1976.

9. Failing to locate the corporate planner at a high enough level in the managerial hierarchy.

10. The failure to use plans as standards for measuring managerial performance.

It turned out that, in general, there was little difference between companies of different country origins, except for a few relatively minor characteristics. The most important pitfalls were also classified by organizational size. There was also surprisingly little difference in the choice and ranking of variables due to size differentials. In this regard, it is interesting to note that while Steiner and Schollhammer (1975) found that size differentials among large companies had little effect on the design of their formal planning systems, Lorange (1977a) found that similar size differentials among small companies had a rather noticeable effect on the designs of their formal planning systems. Specifically, after examining the planning practices of 95 companies with annual sales in the five to fifty million dollar range, Lorange found that the formality of planning in companies larger than twenty-five million dollars in sales was significantly greater than that of smaller companies along several design dimensions. This finding might underscore the fact that there typically is a relatively large, one-shot investment in setting up a formal planning system, requiring a certain size before formal planning becomes affordable as an overhead item. Above this critical size range, however, the formality of the planning system and the costs of such planning do not seem to grow at as rapid a rate as sales. Hence, there is less variation in formal planning systems design due to differentials in sales above a certain level.

Steiner and Schollhammer (1975) also identified ten pitfalls of relatively low importance, and these revealed even less disparity among the different groups of respondents than was

the case with the important ones.[4] In addition, Steiner and Schollhammer made an assessment of the effects of the various pitfalls they identified on the perceived effectiveness of the long-range planning system. It turned out that the two pitfalls that most reduced the effectiveness of the formal planning system (and which therefore definitely should be avoided) were: (1) top management's lack of awareness of the importance of the planning system, and (2) the failure to state corporate goals in clear and operational terms. In terms of overall satisfaction, there did not seem to be as much dissatisfaction with formal planning systems as one might have expected. However, divisionalized corporations tended to be slightly more satisfied with their planning systems than more centralized corporations. Further, there was a strong positive correlation between the satisfaction with the formal planning system and the degree of formality of the system, and with the extent of written plan documentation, as well as some with the "age" of the planning system; that is, the older the system the greater the satisfaction.

In general, two broad observations may be made with respect to the findings of Steiner and Schollhammer (1975). First, the general nature of the ten most important pitfalls to the effective implementation of formal planning which they found seems to verify some of the earlier findings of Ringbakk (1969, 1971, 1972) and Taylor and Irving (1971); namely, that effective long-range planning should be viewed as a strategic decision-making process, involving the line managers of the organization, and reflecting the fact that a relatively large number of managers will be involved in it; thus the process more closely resembles behavioral/political models of organizational decision-making than rational/analytical ones. Such corroboration is especially significant because of the extreme care that was given to research

---

[4] While Steiner and Schollhammer called these the ten least important pitfalls, they were least important only in the sense that they received the lowest rankings of the fifty pitfalls contained in their questionnaire. Since some of these had been regarded as potentially important when they sent out their questionnaire, this low ranking was a

significant finding. On the other hand, there were several other pitfalls that were written in by respondents that had lower rankings, and some that were dropped during the construction of the questionnaire because of the low scores they received on preliminary tests.

design and pilot testing in the study by Steiner and Schollhammer.

Second, Steiner and Schollhammer, unlike the earlier researchers, Ringbakk and Taylor and Irving, report on the contingency results of their study. In this regard, it is a significant finding that many of the demographic factors they controlled for, such as nationality of headquarters location and size, do not seem to be as important as one might have expected in calling for different planning systems designs. It is also particularly interesting that Steiner and Schollhammer attempted to measure user satisfaction with the formal planning system, and found that the users' perceptions do seem to differ. This might call for using a measure of perceived effectiveness of formal planning systems as a criterion for assessing its success, rather than using criteria based on the organization's performance per se. This issue shall be pursued further in the next section.

It is also interesting that Steiner and Schollhammer find degree of diversity/decentralization of the organization and the maturity of the formal planning system to be two important situational factors influencing success, a finding which verifies several hypotheses advanced by Lorange and Vancil (1976).

Thus far some relatively broad evidence has been presented indicating that formal planning systems are a useful and valuable management tool. In addition a set of common factors has been identified that seems to be important for the effective implementation of formal planning systems. The next question, then, is to address the issue of how one should approach the more specific aspects of the design of such formal planning systems, with particular attention given to the problems of how to "fit" such systems to the settings of different corporations.

THE DESIGN OF FORMAL PLANNING SYSTEMS: SOME CONTINGENCY VIEWS

There have been a number of what might be called special-purpose studies that focus on different aspects of the design of formal planning systems which, when taken together, might take us one step further toward understanding the elements of a more full-fledged contingency-based theory of formal planning systems design.

Several early attempts at such contingency-based special-purpose studies stemmed from the so-called Harvard Business School Data Bank Project (Aguilar, Howell, and Vancil, 1970; Vancil, 1971; Vancil, 1972). During the years 1970 and 1971, under the direction of Vancil, an extensive set of data was collected from 60 and 90 large corporations, respectively, encompassing detailed measures of the several situational characteristics of the businesses, a large number of planning systems design parameters and practices, and several criteria for measuring the effectiveness of their planning. Since it is possible that the situational factors (i.e., the set of independent variables) may partly or entirely relate to several systems design characteristics (i.e., sets of dependent variables), there is potentially great economy in building a data bank as a research tool, e.g., the background information — the independent variables — may be collected once and remain constantly accessible in the data bank while the dependent variables may then be collected separately by means of a number of short questionnaires, each addressing the particular research question.

One of the Harvard Data Bank studies, undertaken by Lorange (1972, 1973b), addressed some of the design problems which arise when trying to develop formal planning systems to handle major investment decisions in large industrial companies. Specifically, Lorange attempted to evaluate the supposition that, in order to be effective, a formal system for capacity expansion planning would have to be designed in such a way that the specific situational setting of the firm be reflected in the design. Focusing attention on behavioral situational variables in particular, he proposed that ten controllable systems design factors, or dependent variables, be considered as elements of such a planning system, and seven situational human behavior factors, or independent variables, be used to reflect the setting of a firm. In order to explore the relationship between dependent and independent variables in effective systems, he developed an index of perceived effectiveness. Out of a total of 87 respondents, 30 turned out to be highly effective, 40 were moderately effective, and 17 were less effective. By means of multiple regression, Lorange then estimated the multivariate relationships between the seven independent variables and each of the dependent variables, both with the effective and the less effective samples as bases.

Only four of his predictions were highly significant. These were that in the more effective firms: (1) the degree of linkage of the project to plans and budget tended to be tighter; (2) the incorporation of the shape of the cash-flow pattern tended to be more explicit; (3) the degree of generality of the analytical approach tended to be less; and (4) the commitment to improvement of the planning method tended to be higher. Running factor analyses on the dependent and independent sets of variables, four situational "independent" factors and four "dependent" factors were identified. It turned out that one design factor, the degree of detail in the system, depended strongly and positively on management's conflict resolution behavior. Two other design factors, the technical complexity in the system and the commitment to system's improvement, depended negatively on three factors: management's conflict resolution behavior, management's R&D orientation, and management's concern for operations. The final design factor, the financial orientation of the system, depended positively on both management's conflict resolution behavior and the planner's competence.

In general, the multivariate analysis based on the factor analysis reached similar conclusions to those arrived at in the multiple regression analysis. Although not revealing an overly conclusive general pattern of statistically significant results, the study is significant in that it provided an early empirical verification of the merits of contingency-based formal planning systems design approach through the identification of four instances in which effective performance depended on varying the design of the system to fit the characteristics of the companies involved.

Another study that tested the validity of the contingency approach to formal planning systems design was undertaken by Vancil (1971b), who addressed the question of how to develop schemes for effective business level planning, which he carefully distinguished from corporate level portfolio planning. He started by running several simple correlations between a number of industry characteristics and business characteristics, as well as correlations *within* the two sets of characteristics. Perhaps the most significant result he found at this stage was that a large number of paired relationships seemed to exist, and that any one industry or business characteristic might be related to several others. Vancil also undertook a number of different analyses of independent variables relating to a given design feature. First, he ran simple correlations with the dependent variable. Then, he selected significant correlations for multiple regression analysis, while progressively reducing the number of independent variables in order to finish with the "best" ones. Unfortunately, the approach did not reveal many meaningful results.

Vancil concluded that the lack of large numbers of significant multivariate relationships might perhaps be expected for a project attempting to describe systematic patterns of differences in planning practices at the business planning level. That is, one might expect that a pattern of causal relationships might be particularly difficult to detect at the business level where extensive differences among various businesses can be expected to be the rule, thereby making it quite difficult to develop robust contingency-based rules in business level planning systems design practices.

The difficulty of developing a contingency-based business level planning systems approach was corroborated by Lorange (1977a), who compared the nature of the formality of the planning systems of well-performing and less well-performing companies which were predominantly in high-growth businesses versus predominantly in more mature businesses. In general, he found relatively few significant differences in systems design, except for a far greater formal emphasis on the preparation of funds flow forecasts for the more effective firms in high-growth business areas, and a greater formal emphasis on efficiency-related planning issues among the more effective firms in predominantly mature business.

It is particularly worthwhile noticing that thus far researchers have been unable to come up with a relatively robust contingency-based approach to business level planning systems design, given what seems to be an emerging consensus on what seem to be the relevant dimensions in the substantive strategic choices in business level strategizing, both conceptually (Boston Consulting Group, 1971; Arthur D. Little, 1974), as well as empirically (Strategic Planning Institute, 1977). Stated differently, far less is known about how to design formal planning systems as an implementation tool at the business level than is known about the characteristics of effective strategies at that level.

In addition to the research reported above, a number of other studies were undertaken on the Harvard Data Bank to explore other aspects of formal planning systems design. In general, these were rather explanatory in nature and will be dealt with only cursorily here. First, there seemed to be a difference between a corporate planner's and a divisional planner's involvement in the process (Lorange, 1973a). Second, for effective planning the "track record" of the planner was often important (Greiner, 1970), and line executives had to be centrally involved (Ewing, 1970). The goal-setting process was also found to be an important part of planning (Aguilar, 1970; Murrah and Tuxbury, 1971). In addition, it was found that the planning system tended to become more tightly linked to the management control system as time evolved in terms of similarity of the plan's and budget's content, the timing of the planning-budgeting sequence, as well as the degree of contact between the planner's and controller's offices (Shank, 1970; Camillus, 1973).

More recently, Lorello (1976) has done a survey study of the linkage practices of 92 companies in an attempt to verify the findings of Shank (1970). He generally comes up with corroborating results. It was also found that the formal planning system and the planner might play a useful role in identifying areas of acquisition (Tennican, 1970; Cash and Revie,

1971). These findings on acquisition planning were strongly corroborated by Ansoff et al. (1971).

A recent study by Anand (1977) explored further the relationship between capital budgeting, resource allocation, and strategic planning. His study revealed that senior managers typically consider a large number of dimensions when making up their decisions with regard to resource allocation alternatives. Specifically, based on in-depth data collected in 13 firms, he found that the number of dimensions considered increased with the degree of uncertainty of the firm's environment, and also that as the amount of planning done prior to the investment evaluation increases, the dimensions used by managers for this evaluation shift from a combination of externally oriented as well as internally oriented ones to predominantly internally oriented factors. His data did not indicate large differences due to different degrees of diversity of the firms, however.

Overall, there seem to be relatively few potential generalizations that emerge from these contingency-based studies, and even these few are tentative in nature. In the next few pages, an attempt will be made to summarize these conclusions and then to discuss why a more unidirectional pattern or direction for contingency-based formal planning systems design does not seem to emerge.

In total, only three generalizations with regard to contingency-based formal planning systems design seem possible. First, it seems as if a contingency-based approach toward the design of formal planning systems is necessary in order to achieve more effective systems. Thus, one probably should not expect to arrive at a general theory of planning systems design.

Second, several situational factors seemed to emerge as potentially important for assessing the needs of a particular corporate setting when it comes to the design of a formal planning system. For instance, demographic factors such as the size of the company and maturity of the planning system seem important. Also, factors relating to the strategic posture of the firm seem relevant, including the diversity of its portfolio of businesses and the nature of the product/market setting of its various businesses. Finally, management style factors, such as management's perceptions about the needs for planning, seem important.

Third, several systems design factors seem important in terms of choosing how to tailor-make them into a formal planning system for a particular situation. Such factors include: (1) the top-down versus bottom-up orientation of the system, especially with regard to the division of labor between the corporate and the divisional levels in initiating, formulating, reviewing and executing plans; (2) the relative emphasis on longer-term objectives-setting versus near term action programs; (3) the selection of various devices for linking together elements of the planning process, such as timing, plan content and organizational linkages; and (4) the role of the corporate planner as well as other staff and line executives in the planning process.

Admittedly, however, nothing more than a few rudiments of a contingency-based approach of formal planning systems design seems yet to have emerged. Largely, this is what one would expect; it is a formidable research task to explore relatively exhaustive sets of situational and design variables in various types of settings. Even more monumental is the task of increasing our understanding about the specific nature of the interrelationship among these variables. Thus, our present findings should be considered as a mere start-up.

Several research methodological issues may also have contributed to the relatively low degree of conclusiveness that has emerged from the contingency-based thrust of studies in this area of data. One is a lack of precision in hypothesis formulation in many of the studies (some of the studies did not state hypotheses at all). Another is the lack of precision in data gathering in many of the studies. Still another might be the typically high degree of variability of the underlying data. Thus, several of the research designs were inadequate to study such a large and apparently complex set of problems as contingency-based design of formal planning systems. For instance, although the Harvard Data Bank contained a large number of "cases" with data on various corporations' formal planning practices, the causal relationships among variables may well be so unique for each case that it may be unrealistic to expect general relationships to emerge through such cross-sectional studies. This may be so even if the sample size had been substantially increased. Finally, in some of the studies discussed there was a tendency to "over-kill" the data by "forcing" it to be analyzed by means of powerful multivariate techniques, often violating the data-requirements assumptions of these statistical techniques. Simple gross classification systems, frequency distributions, and cross-tabulations might often have yielded more meaningful research insights than were generated through the use of techniques such as correlation, multiple regression and factor analysis.

SOME POTENTIAL DIRECTIONS FOR RESEARCH ON FORMAL PLANNING SYSTEMS

As indicated at the outset of the present discussion, one of the key purposes of this paper is to establish a reasonably clear sense of direction with regard to the evolutionary direction that research on formal planning systems has been taking and from this to suggest potential future research directions. Thus, a brief recap of the major conclusions of the empirical studies reviewed so far is in order. There are three such overall conclusions. First, there seems to be substantial empirical evidence that long-range and strategic planning has received widespread use in practice, and that such planning seems to pay off for the corporations that use it and is therefore a useful management tool. There is also a strong body of empirical knowledge relating to the general pitfalls that might detract from the effectiveness of such overall planning processes. Second, there is some empirical evidence, although less clear than that cited above, that indicates that the nature of the planning process is multifaceted, not monolithic, that there seem to be several types of planning at work, and that a design approach which is contingency-based seems to be necessary. Third, there are a few instances of piecemeal and sporadic evidence about the relationship among the variables that are part of such a contingency-based theory of formal planning systems design, although in these instances the evidence is not strong.

It seems clear from the above that the thrust of future research efforts should be toward a better understanding of the situational design and implementation of formal planning systems. It is in the area of specific, contingency-based research that new efforts are particularly needed, rather than within areas of more "global" planning issues. More specifically, the challenge seems to be to better understand how formal planning systems can be used more effectively for different organizations' strategy formulation and implementation efforts. In this regard, there will probably be a need for better insights with respect to contingency-related planning systems design issues. In fact, until we more fully understand how to better tailor-make formal planning systems to particular situational settings, the use of such systems to help corporations formulate and implement strategy will probably not be nearly as effective as it might be. In sum, the issue of how to improve a formal planning system's usefulness and role in a firm's strategic decision-making processes is indeed a major challenge and seems to represent the most significant research problem ahead.

To address this issue well calls for a continued emphasis on contingency-based research, so that one can continue the progress of better being able to understand how to tailor-make the design of a formal planning system so that it is as responsive as possible to each given corporate setting. However, a significant shift in the nature of this research is also to be called for. What is needed is to shift the emphasis more toward the explicit recognition of an organization's strategic setting itself as the key situational factor. That is, the particular strategic setting that a company is in will probably dictate the particular needs that this firm has with respect to formal planning systems design in a better way than any other situational factors.

To further pursue the issue of strategic setting as a prime determinant of planning needs and systems design, consider the following example. The organization involved is a division

of a company that typically carries out business activities in several products and markets, commonly denoted "Strategic Business Units" (SBU's). For each such SBU there will probably be different needs for planning depending on where the SBU is positioned strategically in terms of the relative attractiveness (say, market growth position) of its business as well as in terms of its positioning of relative competitive strength (say, relative market share).

In such a situation, what specifically are the differences in planning needs between SBU's that are enjoying fundamentally different strategic positions? How can the formal planning system be designed to meet these needs? These are key questions about how to achieve a strategy-determined situational design for the formal planning system. Analogous questions could be raised for the firm's division level planning needs — how can the planning system meet the strategic planning needs of divisions with different SBU structures and different patterns of interdependence ("consolidation attractiveness") between the SBU's — as well as at the corporate portfolio level — how can the planning system be tailor-made to meet the strategic needs stemming from different portfolio strategy directions? Unfortunately, we do not have many empirically tested answers with regard to questions like these. It should be a high-priority challenge for future research to attack such issues.

This leads to a second and related research area. If we understand how to better tailor-make a planning system's capabilities to an organization's strategy-driven planning needs, then how should modifications in the design of the organization's planning system be undertaken so as to meet modified needs for planning due to a change in the organization's strategy? This question calls for an expanded role for formal planning systems in that we want to become able to manage the evolution of the system so that it will support and reinforce decisions regarding shifts in strategy. Thus far, however, little research has been done on the issue of managing the evolution of formal planning systems. Some research questions that, in all likelihood, would have to be addressed in order to develop an operational approach for designing a strategy-driven planning system's evolution might include: What design factors seem particularly effective in enhancing a desired change in a planning system's capabilities? What features should be relatively more as well as relatively less emphasized? How might such an actively managed evolutionary approach, which would imply moderating frequent changes in the planning system, be integrated with the operating line organization? What would be the relationships between the planning system and other formal systems that have a bearing on the firm's strategies? Will an overall strategic management system emerge, and, if so, what would this imply for the organization's formal planning system? In such systems, what would be the role of the corporate planner given that he or she would be more directly involved in being a change agent for the corporation's strategic shifts? And so on.

In terms of potential future research directions, then, we anticipate a shift in emphasis toward better understanding formal planning's role as a tool in strategy formulation and implementation, the issue becoming how to achieve an appropriate match between strategic needs and capabilities. We also expect the emphasis on contingency-based designs to continue, but with a shift in focus from demographic-type contingencies to strategic position contingencies. In addition, the contingency approach is taking on a second, dynamic dimension in the form of an active management of the evolution of formal planning systems design in order to be able to meet emerging strategic needs.

An emerging issue at this point is the question of what might be useful research approaches for tackling the research problems just outlined. The following will address this issue as well as discussing some general caveats about doing research in the planning system area.

SOME CAVEATS FOR DOING RESEARCH ON PLANNING SYSTEMS

Having gone through a considerable body of literature for the purpose of this survey, we are left with the uncomfortable feeling that it is difficult to fit the bits and pieces together. There seems to be considerable lack of consensus in the literature when it comes to such central questions as what are the critical elements of the nature of planning systems, what constitute relevant empirical areas of research, and so on. Also, the common vocabulary is surprisingly small and too often lacks adequate definitions. Research designs frequently are less precise than desirable, particularly when they fail to state assumptions which might limit the universality of the research findings. The reasons for this fragmentation and lack of synthesis may derive from the general nature of the research problem itself. We are studying a very complex administrative phenomenon, consisting of a number of different planning types (e.g., systems for corporate planning, business planning, and functional planning), and a number of sequentially related analytical styles (e.g., objectives-setting, multiyear programming, and budgeting), each of these factors interrelated. Added complexity arises from the vast differences in situational settings between corporations and, therefore, the requirement to tailor strategies and planning systems to each company. Finally, given the rapid changes now so typical for corporations' situational settings and environments, the task of upgrading the planning system in response to such dynamic change seems formidable. Thus, it seems prudent not to have too high a hope of arriving at a more general theory of formal planning systems concepts. However, even though it may be unrealistic to expect a more orderly pattern of research output in this field, it may also be that some of the research in the area has started out from unnecessarily narrow or inaccurate premises, thereby making it less reconcilable with other studies than otherwise might have been the case.

The nature of our research problems is also influenced by the fact that we are dealing with a relatively recent addition to management's tools. This is evidenced in several ways. For instance, the data for longitudinal field studies may simply not exist, while the data available for cross-sectional surveys may not accurately represent the phenomenon under study. Also, most of the progress in the "art" of designing long-range planning systems has been spearheaded by business organizations themselves. Understandably, there may be reluctance on their part to give out data about these often sensitive systems developments. Measurement problems and complications due to lack of a well-established common language are present — as they typically are for most emerging fields.

Consequently, choice of research methodologies for the research problems we have identified above is not easy. Our feeling is that researchers in the area to an increasing degree will have to work with a small number of companies over considerable periods of time in order to make further progress. In addition, a necessary requirement for getting access to companies and developing working relationships will probably be that the researchers be prepared to "give something back" to the companies in the form of advice and insights. Stated differently, more traditional, predominantly one-way information-gathering research approaches are not likely to be adequate in securing the cooperation necessary to get relevant information at this stage. Thus, the future research challenges in the area seem to be calling for highly interactive studies by researchers with considerable knowledge of planning systems and with the willingness and patience to engage in longitudinal projects of considerable duration.

SUMMARY AND CONCLUSIONS

This paper has surveyed the empirical research literature concerning formal planning systems, and attempted to outline some fruitful directions for future research in the area. Our major conclusions, which also provide a picture of the evolution of research and thinking on formal planning systems, were as follows:

1. Formal planning systems as a management technique seem to be well accepted at this point and their payoffs seem to be adequately recognized.

2. The process of implementing formal planning systems seems to have become relatively well understood, with a relatively standard set of issues emerging in terms of pitfalls to be avoided.

3. Attempts to design formal planning systems on a contingency basis are still in their infancy, and are relatively heavily oriented toward acknowledging demographic-type factors as characterizing the situational setting, with little or no emphasis on how the strategic setting should influence the design of such systems.

4. Future research will focus on bringing formal planning systems designs more in line with the particular strategic settings of the company involved so that such systems can contribute more effectively toward strategy formulation and implementation.

In summary, then, formal planning systems have evolved a long way, and are today important and integral tools in many companies' strategic decision-making. Moreover, we expect that they will play an increasingly important role in the corporate strategizing process in the future.

Commentary

Dale J. Hekhuis
General Electric Company

Rather than critique Lorange's paper, this commentary will highlight and extend his remarks based on my experience at General Electric as a planning practitioner. First, some of the forces supporting further development of formal planning systems are described. Then a brief overview of General Electric's strategic planning system is presented, and finally, using this system as a background, several areas where research might be done are suggested.

TREND TOWARD FORMAL PLANNING SYSTEMS

Formal planning systems will be increasingly adopted for the development and implementation of strategic plans in large, diversified companies.

The impetus for this will come from the following:

1. *The need to cope with the increased complexity and range of public issues impacting on the corporation — political, social, legal, international, etc.* This need is requiring increased activity by large, diversified firms in anticipating, defining and analyzing issues for the purpose of assessing corporate impact and formulating policies, initiatives, and responses. It will also probably increase the significance and vitality of environmental analysis activity in the planning process by providing a sharper work focus. Simultaneously, top executive involvement in the management of strategic issues will increase because of the significance of such issues for the very vitality and survival of the corporation.

2. *The increasing importance of resource management in the light of growing resource scarcities.* Coping with sharp increases in costs of materials and energy and, in some cases, simply preserving access to commodity or money markets are according increased emphasis to resource strategy formulation and implementation. Thus, the development of functional plans — human resources plans, financial resources plans, technology resources plans, and materials procurement plans—and the role and significance of functional managers in strategic planning are being accorded higher priority.

3. *A substantial increase in integrative/coordinating type activity in the strategic planning process.* This type of activity will increase as a consequence of responses to external developments — insuring a touch-all-bases corporate response to complex, multi-faceted issues — and as a consequence of an internal need to achieve more effective international or technological integration across SBUs or divisions. And, as the number of SBUs or divisions expands, or as the extent of diversification increases, coordination type activity will probably increase more than proportionately.

The foregoing developments will place increased demands on corporate management for *time and attention.* A formal planning system is one of the few effective means for squeezing time out of a crowded corporate calendar. In fact, this ability to program an executive's time may be the single most important contribution of formal planning systems. My guess is that the very processes of issue definition and response and of resource strategy formulation will reinforce an already developing trend toward what Lorange has called "a strategic administrative system." This system will increasingly link up a variety of management systems with the planning system, including measurement/control, management information and manpower/compensation systems.

OVERVIEW OF A FORMAL PLANNING SYSTEM

Exhibit 5.2 shows a simplified schematic of the corporate strategic planning cycle employed at General Electric. The following is a brief chronological summary of the major steps in the cycle:

1. *January:* A corporate-level review of the environment identifies issues of corporate-level concern across the company, such as the impact of double-digit inflation or of an energy crisis. SBUs receive corporate-level guidelines indicating the company's major priorities and goals.

2. *February–June:* Each Strategic Business Unit (SBU) updates its five-year strategic plan. A major focus is on enhancing its long range competitive position. In addition, it determines its response to corporate guidelines.

3. *July–September:* The Corporate Management Committee, comprised of the Chairman, Vice Chairmen and top staff officers review the SBU plans. They judge plan quality, assess risks, and decide on resource allocation priorities. Corporate management concentrates on objectives and resource requirements, minimizing its involvement in specific SBU strategies to achieve objectives.

4. *October–December:* Each SBU develops detailed operating programs and budgets for the coming year.

Exhibit 5.2   General Electric's Corporate Strategic Planning Cycle

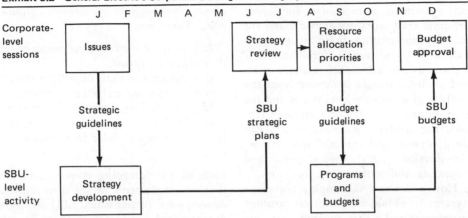

5. *December:* SBU budgets receive final approval at corporate level; they provide the basis for measuring operations in the coming year.

SOME SUGGESTED AREAS FOR RESEARCH

I would like to suggest the following areas of research which could be directed toward making formal planning a better strategic management tool:

1. How Can Formal Planning Systems More Effectively Serve and Involve the CEO?

The Chief Executive Officer has been the single most important factor in the corporate decision to employ or not to employ a formal planning system. Hence, research which can shed light on ways and means for improving the effectiveness of formal systems for CEO or corporate usage should have a significant payoff. Most CEOs are a skeptical lot when it comes to judging the payoff from planning systems, so research will have to come up with some convincing findings to achieve an impact. The following are some areas which might pay off:

(a.) How can the planning system help the CEO to cope with continuing high levels of environmental uncertainty by formulating corporate-wide strategies that demonstrably cope with this uncertainty? An example is the formulation of a corporate-wide energy strategy in the face of extreme levels of uncertainty.

In this case, the first step was to formulate a series of alternative energy situations or strategic scenarios, that spanned a broad range of energy events. These included the following:

— A base-case scenario based on continuation of past trends.
— An oil-dislocation scenario.
— A nuclear-dislocation scenario.
— A low or zero energy-growth scenario.

The second step was an analysis made to identify those strategy elements common to all of the scenarios and those that lacked commonality. It was surprising to see the number of areas or strategy elements that were found to be common to all scenarios, which made it possible to pursue major strategic thrusts based on their likely occurrence over a wide range of scenarios. For example, three strategy elements common to all scenarios included the development and utilization of the U.S. coal reserve, the development of energy-saving products and services and the development of energy systems based on renewable energy resources. Those elements not common to all scenarios indicated a need for hedge strategies that included defensive measures and contingency plans.

(b.) How can the CEO use the formal planning system as a mechanism for laying out corporate staff work assignments and for subsequently integrating these assignments into a document known as a Corporate Plan? Given the crush of additional strategic analysis and position papers stemming from the proliferation of corporate-level issues and the increased emphasis on resource strategy formulation, the strategic planning system can provide a context and administrative framework for developing a staff work agenda and for integrating and coordinating this work.

(c.) How can the CEO employ the planning system to obtain insights into earnings and investment risks that confront the corporation? Having gained these insights, how can the system help him to manage or contain these risks?

(d.) How can the flexibility and response time of planning systems be improved so as to be responsive to "what-if" queries of the CEO?

(e.) The aggregation of five-year earnings forecasts for the total number of SBUs in a firm typically has a strong upward bias and is therefore overly optimistic. Moreover, it is my experience that unexpected earnings surges very rarely outweigh unexpected earnings collapses. Given this situation how can "discounted" forecasts be developed that are credible to the CEO?

(f.) How can the CEO effectively use the planning system as a means for reporting to the Board of Directors?

(g.) How can the planning system help the CEO to adapt company policies and operations to the political realities of international markets, recognizing that disparate economic and social systems will require varying investment approaches for market participation?

2. What Is the Distinct Role and Value-added Contribution of Corporate-level Planning Activity vs. Individual SBU Planning Activity?

Answers to this question can help shed light on the "worth" of corporate-level planning activity. My experience with a large, diversified corporation suggests five distinct, corporate-level roles. These are:

(a.) Shaping the corporate business scope and diversification thrust,

(b.) Setting corporate objectives and priorities,

(c.) Developing a risk containment system,

(d.) Establishing resource allocation priorities,

(e.) Designing supporting management systems which are circular in response characteristics.

Each of the foregoing corporate planning activities complements rather than duplicates the development of individual SBU strategies on a decentralized basis. All of these activities can provide the appropriate internal environment for decentralized business planning without usurping the creative strategy formulation job. In summary, this approach adds up to strategy leadership without dictatorship.

3. What Can U.S. Planners and Researchers Learn from the Japanese in the Design and Application of Formal Planning Systems and Procedures?

Some possibilities are the following:

(a.) The Japanese Trading Companies, originally formed to arrange for raw material imports, subsequently have gone far beyond this function. In effect, they have become the *integrative force* behind major Japanese industrial groups, with an ability to cut across the companies of a group to put together consortia and bring all relevant capabilities to bear.

This integrative capability in a resource-scarce environment is very important for assuring that an organization's resources, wherever located, can be directed to opportunities and problems, wherever located.

The question can be asked: Are there any insights to be gained from the integrative mechanisms used by Japanese trading companies that might improve the plan integration capabilities of U.S. planning systems?

(b.) The Japanese, through their trading companies, also appear to have developed a highly sophisticated international commercial intelligence gathering and processing tool. Again, are there any insights to be gained relative to the design and use of corporate competitor and commercial intelligence systems?

CONCLUSIONS

It seems likely that more and more large, diversified corporations will install and develop formal planning. Additional research on how to make planning systems more useful for the practitioner is needed. Such research must recognize the dramatically changing environment and the problems of managing within more complex environments. Three questions worth study are: (1) How can formal planning systems more effectively serve and involve the CEO?, (2) What is the distinctive and value-added contribution of corporate-level planning activity vs. individual SBU planning activity?, and (3) What can U.S. planners and researchers learn from the Japanese in the design and application of formal planning systems and procedures?

Commentary

HAROLD W. HENRY
University of Tennessee

INTRODUCTION

Lorange has reviewed both prescriptive and empirical studies on formal planning systems and has proposed many areas for additional research. This paper will define the functions of a formal planning system, challenge some of Lorange's views, and outline a topical framework for future research on formal planning systems.

FUNCTIONS OF A FORMAL PLANNING SYSTEM

Planning is the primary function of management in any formal organization, for decisions on goals, resource needs, resource allocation, and action plans should precede specific actions. *Execution* of plans is the second basic management function and *control* to insure that desired results are obtained is the third. Thus, the management cycle of planning, execution, and control is repeated continually by managers at all levels in every successful organization.

In the past two decades, "formal planning systems" have evolved in major U.S. and for-

eign corporations and in other institutions. The degree of formality varies, but empirical studies by Henry (1967, 1976) and others have shown that "formal" systems for planning have these characteristics:

1. planning activities are assigned to specific individuals,
2. planning activities are scheduled during each year,
3. analytical methods and premises are standardized,
4. resulting plans are reduced to writing.

The purpose of such "formal" systems is to provide a continuing, systematic, and effective means of deciding on future courses of action which are most likely to achieve enterprise objectives. Informal planning systems are more haphazard and reactive in nature and have proven to be generally less effective. Formal planning systems are often fully integrated with the managerial subsystems for execution and control in large firms today, so the same managers have the major responsibility for all three functions in each unit of an organization. In other cases, the planning function is assigned to a separate group which does not execute or control.

By definition, the planning process ends when a plan of action is developed and approved. Thus, a formal planning system is not expected to execute plans or to control performance. However, when such a system is viewed as an integral part of the management system, all aspects of management are integrated. This broader system is often called a "strategic management" system. This approach to management, in which formal, strategic, (long-range) planning is the central and most critical element in the system, has been adopted by many organizations during the past few years. In spite of some disappointing results, formal planning remains a vital function in many firms today. Henry (1976) found that several very large U.S. firms had redesigned their planning systems in the early 1970's in an effort to improve performance in a very competitive and rapidly changing environment.

It is the function of the most fully developed strategic planning systems today to:

1. determine organizational purpose and management philosophy,
2. identify internal strengths and weaknesses,
3. monitor changes in the external environment,
4. forecast future conditions and establish planning premises,
5. determine threats and opportunities,
6. formulate specific goals,
7. identify and evaluate alternative policies and strategies,
8. select the best strategic plan,
9. prepare functional action plans,
10. prepare financial plans.

One of the most vital planning elements, based on empirical studies by Henry and others, is the process of formulating strategies. Alternative strategies are identified in progressive firms today after monitoring their external environment to identify threats and opportunities and after appraising the internal environment to determine company strengths and weaknesses. The process of internal appraisal is very important to system design as well. Lorange does not em-

phasize the necessity of including these components in planning system design. These elements cannot be overlooked because the heart of a strategic planning system is strategy identification, evaluation, and selection, and further understanding of how these processes are performed is a very important topic for future research.

For many years, formal long-range planning efforts focused primarily on operational planning, or on planning how to continue the firm's current activities. Only in the past decade has the emphasis shifted to strategic planning, or planning how best to use limited resources in pursuit of company goals in a competitive environment. Many more options are evaluated by firms with a strategic management outlook. While Lorange does not distinguish between operational and strategic planning, such distinctions are necessary in formal planning system design.

The "contingency approach" which Lorange advocates for designing planning system research projects is very global and impractical. The general notion that planning system effectiveness is a function of several variables in a particular firm is valid and has been supported by various empirical studies. For example, Henry (1967) identified four important variables in company approaches to long-range planning, as follows:

1. the philosophy and leadership of top executives,
2. the orientation of the company to change,
3. the organization for long-range planning, and
4. the activity focus of forward planning.

Thus, future research studies on formal planning systems need to focus on specific variables which may be important in several firms or on specific cause and effect relationships which exist in different firms.

FRAMEWORK FOR RESEARCH ON FORMAL PLANNING SYSTEMS

Research on formal planning systems can be logically classified under three categories, as follows:

1. planning system design,
2. planning system utilization, and
3. planning system performance.

Specific topics appropriate for future research are outlined under each of these categories below:

PLANNING SYSTEM DESIGN

Even though many descriptive studies of planning system design have been done in the past, as summarized by Hofer (1976), additional empirical studies of this type will be fruitful in the future. Henry (1976) found that designs change over time as the business changes, as performance declines, or as external conditions change. Thus, longitudinal studies to identify the types of changes, reasons for the changes, and results of the changes will be beneficial. Also, as more medium-sized and small firms and other institutions adopt formal planning, research on design features should prove valuable to determine if some characteristics of the planning system design are related to size, location, and type of industry or activities. Finally, when more advanced research on planning system utilization and performance is undertaken, the initial part of such studies should include a clear definition of the planning system design in the organization being studied.

Some of the key design variables to be determined include:

1. primary planning responsibility assignment — line or staff units,
2. planning unit size, scope of activities, and criteria for including smaller units in each basic planning unit,
3. degree of decentralization of the planning function or the types of decisions permitted in various organizational units,
4. staff involvement in the planning process — types of staff units, number of levels (corporate, divisional, plant), and the specific assigned planning functions,
5. line manager involvement in the planning process, and

6. schedule of planning activities and its rationale.

PLANNING SYSTEM UTILIZATION

Specific topics to study in planning systems as they are actually utilized include:

1. roles performed by various line and staff "actors" in the system — as initiators, analysts, information gatherers, information disseminators, forecasters, evaluators, screeners, or approvers,
2. extent and nature of individual *vs.* group effort,
3. degree of actual standardization of procedures, terminology, premises, techniques, forms, and plan formats among organizational units,
4. specific procedures for evaluating internal strengths and weakness, including variables evaluated, methods of measurement, time period covered, standards used as bases for evaluation, and weighting procedures for combining evaluations of separate variables.
5. specific procedures for monitoring and evaluating changes or trends in the external environment,
6. specific procedures for formulating strategies at corporate level, divisional (or planning unit) level, and in functional or operating units, including sources of ideas on alternative strategies, evaluation procedures, and the use of outside profilers.
7. procedures for developing specific operational plans,
8. techniques used to evaluate competing investment proposals,
9. extent of integration of various types of planning activities — goal setting, strategy formulation, operational planning, capital budgeting, facilities planning, expense budgeting, programming, human resource planning, and organizational planning,
10. methods of developing managers, especially with respect to changing their attitudes and practices when introducing a new strategic planning system,
11. criteria for selecting and assigning managers to implement a particular strategic plan,
12. extent to which the *implementation* of strategic and operational plans is considered

and planned for in the regular planning cycle, and

13. methods for evaluating and improving the system internally, including the persons involved, the frequency, the criteria, methods for changing the system, and the use of outside consultants.

PLANNING SYSTEM PERFORMANCE

Regardless of the degree of sophistication in planning system design and utilization, the ultimate test of the system's effectiveness and justification for its existence is the impact it has on organizational performance. To measure planning system effectiveness in all types of organizations, correlation studies are needed which relate a composite quantitative index of system design and utilization to various specific measures of organizational performance. The most difficult aspect of such research is the development of a scale or methodology for rating a particular planning system. One approach would be to design a point rating system, using several key design or utilization factors and several possible degrees of achievement for each factor. Another approach which was applied to bank planning systems by Wood (1977) is the Guttman scaling technique.

Once an overall numerical index of planning system performance or effectiveness is determined for several firms in a given industry, a correlation can be made between this index and each of several measures of organizational performance. For example, in business firms, performance measures could include return on equity, return on assets, earnings per share growth rate, sales growth rate, and assets growth rate.

SUMMARY AND CONCLUSIONS

Some limitations of Lorange's paper have been discussed, but the primary focus of this paper has been to define the functions of a formal planning system and to outline some specific topics for future research on formal planning systems. These topics were classified under: (1) planning system design, (2) planning system utilization, and (3) planning system performance.

The potential is great for much fruitful research in the future on formal planning systems. Such systems are relatively new and require many years to reach maximum effectiveness. Formal planning systems are being adopted by a growing number of business firms and have spread from industrial firms to banks, government agencies, and other institutions. Studies cited by Lorange have shown significant improvements in organizational performance as a result of using systematic strategic planning. Thus, empirical studies in all of the above organization types can lead to a much better understanding of the management process. In addition, present and future managers can benefit from the results of such studies, and this is a primary goal of research in any applied science.

The methodology for research on formal planning could include field studies, mail questionnaires, analysis of company publications and public documents, and statistical analysis of data collected in central data banks. However, personal interviews with key managers and planning specialists, using formats which are not highly structured, are considered by the author to be one of the most productive methods to gain insight into the actual use and worth of planning systems.

The Role of Organizational Structure and Process in Strategy Implementation

JAY R. GALBRAITH
The Wharton School

DANIEL A. NATHANSON
The Wharton School

The recent scholarly interest in strategy and structure connections was impelled by the publication of Chandler's research in *Strategy and Structure* (Chandler, 1962). On the basis of a historical study of seventy of America's largest firms, he formulated several hypotheses that stimulated much of the subsequent work. First, he proposed the principle that organization structure follows the growth strategy of the firm. Second, he proposed a stagewise developmental sequence for the strategies and structures of American enterprises. Third, he theorized that organizations do not change their structures until they are provoked by inefficiency to do so. In part, this is because the formulator of strategies is rarely the creator of organizations.

Chandler's work is best known for the first hypothesis that is suggested in the title of his book. "The thesis deduced from these several propositions is then that structure follows strategy and that the most complex type of structure is the result of the concatenation of several basic strategies" (Chandler, 1962: 14). Thus, the structure of an organization follows from its growth strategy. Specifically, as organizations change their growth strategy in order to employ resources more profitably in the face of changing technology, income, and population, the new strategy poses new administrative problems. These administrative problems are solved only by refashioning the organization structure to fit the new strategy. A corollary to this thesis is that if a structural adjustment does not take place, the strategy will not be completely effec-

tive, and economic inefficiency will result. Chandler proposed a sequence consisting of new strategy creation, emergence of new administrative problems, decline in economic performance, invention of a new appropriate structure, and subsequent recovery to profitable levels.

In his historical study, the above sequence was seen to be repeated often as American firms grew and changed their growth strategies. Initially most firms were units such as plants, sales offices, or warehouses in a single industry, a single location, and a single function of either manufacturing, sales, or wholesaling. Initial growth was simply *volume expansion*, but it created a need for an administrative office. Next, a *geographic expansion* strategy created multiple field units in the same function and industry but in different locations. Administrative problems arose concerning degrees of centralization and standardization. Exhibit 5.3 shows the strategies and the resulting structures that evolved.

The next stage in the historical development consisted of the strategies that involved *vertical integration*. That is, successful business firms stayed in the same industry but acquired or created other functions. Manufacturing plants created their own warehouses and wholesaling operations and their own sales force. New administrative problems arose in the effort to balance the sequential movement of goods through the interdependent functions. This led to the development of forecasts, schedules, and capacity balancing techniques that were managed through the functional organization.

The last strategy analyzed by Chandler was the one of *product diversification*. Firms moved into new industries in order to employ existing resources as primary markets declined. The new

Exhibit 5.3 Strategies and Structure

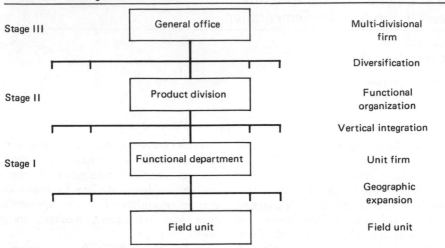

problems in this case centered on the appraisal and evaluation of product divisions and alternative investment proposals. Time had to be allowed for the strategic management of this capital allocation process. The multi-divisional structure shown in Exhibit 5.3 was the new form of organization that evolved. This form, which created a division of labor based on time horizon, was superior to the functional organization as a means of managing capital allocation in the face of diversity. The divisions were responsible for short-run operating decisions; the central office was responsible for strategic, long-run decisions. The office was to be staffed with general managers who were not responsible for short-run operating results and were thereby given the time and psychological commitment necessary for long-term planning in the interest of the corporation as a whole. There were enough general managers, usually group executives, to tie strategic direction to internal control of divisional performance. However, there was not the excessive management which often led to local interference. In this way the divisional form was superior to the functional organization and the holding company.

Chandler traces the development of this new form throughout American enterprise. However, not all of the firms adopted the multi-divisional form. The copper and aluminum companies, for example, did not. These were the companies that did not diversify product lines, however; they grew in one industry and supplied the same customers. Thus, structure follows strategy. Those firms that remained and grew within a single industry retained the centralized functional organization; those that diversified adopted the multi-divisional structure. This strategy-structure linkage has been the part of Chandler's work that has been examined and reformulated most in subsequent studies.

The relationship between organization structure and process and the product/market strategy of the firm is the primary focus of this paper. In subsequent sections we will review the conceptual and empirical extensions of Chandler's hypothesis. Several studies have examined the relation between strategy and structure. When the relation was found to be weak, the degree of competition was offered as a moderating variable. A few studies have examined the relation between strategy, structure, and competition. More recent research has focused on strategy, structure, and economic performance. Thus, subsequent research has led to an examination of our interrelated factors — strategy, structure, competition and economic performance. These factors are shown schematically in Exhibit 5.4. Different researchers have focused on various combinations of these four factors, but no one has examined all of them in one comprehensive study. In the next sections we will review these studies starting with the strategy and structure research, then we will add competition and performance before we attempt a critique and summary. The stages of development and new forms of organization structure make up the final sections.

STRATEGY AND STRUCTURE CONCEPTUAL EXTENSIONS

The idea that strategy and structure are closely linked was picked up quickly by a number of different disciplines. In business schools, the business policy, organization behavior, and management groups all incorporated it into their literature. Most empirical work has come from these sources. In addition, economists and sociologists with an interest in organization theory have adopted it to confirm some of their ideas, making some conceptual elaborations and extensions of the concepts.

MARKETS AND HIERARCHIES: AN ECONOMIC PERSPECTIVE

The most extensive study of structure that has been made by an economist is that of Oliver Williamson (1970, 1975). Williamson is a leading theorist in the new field of institutional economics, which has developed methods of analyzing microeconomic phenomena in a detailed yet rigorous manner. The primary focus of such research is on the cost of transactions. This focus leads Williamson and others to examine different institutional arrangements for conducting economic activity. In the past, economists have been primarily preoccupied with prices and markets as the only institutions through which efficient economic transactions could take place. The institutionalists, however, see markets and firms as alternative institutions through which to conduct economic transactions.

Williamson makes an argument that is obvious to business policy and organization theorists but not necessarily to economists: internal organization makes an economic difference. Specifically, he suggests that when there are exchange circumstances characterized by uncertainty, and by idiosyncratic knowledge, small numbers, and opportunistic behavior, then market prices and market substitutes such as con-

Exhibit 5.4 The Extended Chandler Model

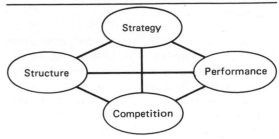

tracting are inefficient or unfair. Instead, it is more efficient to use an administrative process which takes an adaptive approach to uncertainty by making a sequence of decisions and transmitting the newly acquired information between the interested parties. He suggests that internal organization and administrative processes as we know them are the result of the forementioned market failures. That is, under circumstances of uncertainty, of differentially distributed information, of opportunism, and of small numbers of participants, the invisible hand fails to do its job of clearing markets in an economically efficient manner. An inventor of an institutional form to replace the defective market can reap the benefits of increased economic efficiency. Such is the case with vertically integrated work flows managed through functional organizations instead of bilateral monopoly bargaining. Such is also the case with diversified businesses managed through the multi-divisional structure, rather than by a capital market allocating funds to functional organizations.

Williamson's view of the multi-divisional firm as a miniature capital market is an interesting one. He sees the multi-divisional form as a response to the inability of both functional organizations and capital markets to regulate decision-making discretion in organizations following both a substantial separation of management and ownership and an increase in a firm's size and complexity. Williamson argues that for large firms operating in diverse businesses, the multi-divisional structure is a more effective means of allocating capital in order to maximize profit than either the functional organization, the holding company, or businesses operating as independent units regulated only by product and capital markets.

Domain and Structure: A Sociological Perspective

A second conceptual framework comes from James D. Thompson, a sociologist, whose distinctive approach is nonetheless very similar to Williamson's, because it also studies uncertainty, diversity, and bounded rationality (Thompson, 1967, Chapters 3 to 6). Thompson's interpretation provides the most complete statement of how organizations both shape and are shaped by their environments, because his propositions relate to choices of strategy as well as to those of structure.

Thompson begins his analysis of organization-environment interaction with the proposition that organizations stake out domains; that is, they make claims that they will offer certain products or services to certain customers or clients. In the terminology of business policy, this is simply the firm's product/market strategy. The term *domain* is used in organizational sociology to denote a generalization to all types of organizations. The significance of the choice of domain or product/market strategy is that, together with the choice of technology, it determines the points at which the organization is dependent upon the cooperation of others for the resources, referrals, and other types of support required for its survival.

Domains are not unilaterally determined, however. Given scarcity of resources and competitors for domains, environmental support must be earned and sustained. A domain becomes operational only when the organization's rights to the domain are recognized by those whose support is needed. Once the expectations of the environmental groups on which the organization is dependent have been met, a consensus concerning domain exists. The concept of domain consensus is similar to the business policy concept of product/market distinctive competence. The difference appears to be that distinctive competence is defined from the point of view of the focal organization, and domain consensus is defined from the point of view of environmental groups. Thus far, there has been little cross-fertilization between the groups using these separate but similar terms.

The next step in Thompson's scheme is to recognize that domain consensus must be in the context of changing technology, population, and competition. Given change and dependency on others, Thompson expects organizations to manage these dependency relations by trading on the dependencies of other organizations in the environment. This view causes him to focus on power-dependence relations among organizations.

Thompson's descriptive propositions concerning environmental management differ from the normative strategy literature at this point, but they are nonetheless very relevant to it. Thompson's view is also very close to Williamson's. In managing power-dependence relations, organizations promote distinctive competence when faced with large numbers of suppliers and users. This is the competitive response, and theories of prices and markets apply. However, when suppliers and users become concentrated (Williamson's small numbers condition), the organization seeks to gain power relative to those sources upon which it depends by exploiting its own dependency. He develops a number of propositions about how organizations defend their domains and analyzes the conditions under which they will reduce the uncertainty surrounding their dependency by means of contracting and by either co-opting dependent elements or coalescing with them through joint ventures. Each of these cooperative moves reduces uncertainty about the continued support from sources on which the organization is dependent and thus guarantees viability.

The defense of domains can become costly, however. If an organization has strong technological dependencies and is operating under unstable conditions, continued support from the environment becomes a serious problem. It requires finding and holding a position that is recognized by all environmental groups as more worthwhile than other alternatives. One would expect, therefore, that organizations would minimize the need for this environmental maneuvering by incorporating critical dependencies within the boundaries of the organization.

Thompson poses a number of hypotheses that predict the direction in which an organization will grow on the basis of its critical dependence upon an environmental component. He uses much of Chandler's work as data to support the growth strategy propositions, employing the concept of interdependence to distinguish between different kinds of dependencies. Organizations are predicted to grow by incorporating within their boundaries those elements that, if left outside, would pose critical contingencies for viability and be costly to manage by contracting.

Both Thompson and Williamson have generated conceptual contributions from which further theoretical and empirical work can continue. The compatibility of their concepts, Chandler's concepts, and the concepts used in business policy and organization design is striking. This is both encouraging and disheartening, however, because although a number of people are independently moving toward a consensus on strategy and structure, little of business policy thinking and language enters the other models, and vice versa.

STRATEGY AND ORGANIZATION STRUCTURE

The empirical studies that will be described in this section fall into several categories. First, there are a number of studies, all done at Harvard, that directly test the Chandler hypothesis. Next, there are some other studies that relate centralization to strategy. Third, there are the studies from organization theorists interested in structural variations. The next two sections focus on coordination processes that lead to matrix organizations and the many other processes such as planning, reward and evaluation, and management development. Finally, the concept of congruence between strategy, structure, and processes is described.

The Harvard Studies

The Harvard Studies, some of which are summarized by Scott, contributed several refinements and extensions of the Chandler thesis. First, they refined the theory of diversification strategy by distinguishing between different types of diversification (Wrigley, 1970). Second,

they demonstrated that not all multi-divisional structures are alike by identifying different structural forms. Third, they carried the analysis to European countries (Channon, 1971, 1973; Pooley-Dias, 1972; Pavan, 1972; Thanheiser, 1972). Finally, international strategies for American (Stopford and Wells, 1972) and for European firms (Franko, 1974, 1976) were considered.

The first study refined the concept of diversification and compared the strategies with regard to structural form (Wrigley, 1970). Taking a sample from the *Fortune* 500, Wrigley distinguished four different strategies that were being followed. Some firms stayed in a *single product business*. Another group diversified, but still had a single *dominant business* that accounted for 70 to 95 percent of sales. Still another group diversified into related businesses and had more than 30 percent of their sales outside their main business. Finally, the last group diversified into completely *unrelated businesses* and had more than 30 percent of their sales outside the main business. From data reported by Scott (1973), it is clear that the more diversified the strategy, the more likely one is to find the multi-divisional structure. Single product or business firms are always organized functionally. Wrigley observed a hybrid form of structure also in use in the dominant business category. This group managed the dominant business through a functional structure and the diverse products through a divisionalized structure. This amounts to a partial move toward the multi-divisional structure. Those companies that diversified into related and unrelated businesses overwhelmingly chose multi-divisional structures. These results support the thesis that structure follows strategy in general, and that diversification leads to multi-divisional forms in particular.

The same type of analysis was replicated for firms in the U.K. (Channon, 1971), France (Pooley-Dias, 1972), Germany (Thanheiser, 1972), and Italy (Pavan, 1972). For all countries there is an increase in the amount of diversification between 1950 and 1970. Similarly, there is an increase in the use of the multi-divisional structure at the expense of functional and holding company alternatives.

The most comprehensive example of this research is the study by Rumelt (1974). He further elaborated the types of strategies of diversification. Through the use of subjective judgments and some quantitative measures, he created nine different strategies to characterize a sample of U.S. firms from the *Fortune* 500. The single business category remained as defined above, but the other three categories were elaborated.

The dominant product business (70 percent < dominant business sales < 95 percent) was divided into four subcategories. The first subcategory was vertically integrated firms. These firms were classed as having sales outside the dominant business, but the products sold were by-products taken out of the sequential flow between stages of production. This strategy was different from those strategies involving independent businesses. The second, third, and fourth categories also apply as subclasses of the related business category. They characterize the degree of relatedness of the businesses into which the firm diversified. Some stayed "close to home" by adopting only products that utilized a common technology or market channel. These firms were classed as dominant-constrained. That is, their diversification was constrained by the desire to exploit a particular advantage. The next type was a firm that diversified in a manner that maintained links between businesses but was not constrained by one unifying link. That is, some products shared a common technology. Some of the technology sharers also shared a common distribution channel with another group of businesses. Viewed as a whole, the businesses appear unrelated, but there are links of varying types between all of them. This category was called dominant-linked. The last category was simply dominant-unrelated; it characterized firms diversifying into business totally unrelated to the dominant and other businesses.

The related category, as suggested above, was divided into related-constrained and related-linked. The unrelated category was also subdivided into two types. The purpose was to create a separate category for the acquisitive conglomerate. So the unrelateds were classed on the basis of their aggressiveness in acquiring other firms. This classification led to categories for the unrelated-passive and the acquisitive

conglomerate and made nine categories in all.

These strategies were then related to the type of structure. Rumelt classed structures as being functional, functional with subsidiaries, multi-divisional (both product and geographic divisions), and holding companies, the last being a divisional structure characterized by highly autonomous divisions with a miniscule formal organization above them. Strategies and structures employed by the sample were examined from 1949 to 1969.

Several results emerged from the analysis. First, American firms increased the degree to which they diversified product lines over the twenty year period. Second, the use of the functional organization declined and the use of the multi-divisional structure increased. Third, when strategy and structure were matched, the Chandler thesis was supported. The single and dominant business strategies were conducted through functional organizations. The greater the diversity, the more likely one was to find the multi-divisional form. Over time, an increasing percentage of firms falls into step; by 1969, functional and holding company models give way to the multi-divisional structure. Relations between strategy and structure eventually come into line.

A second group of studies came from the Harvard International Project (Fouraker and Stopford, 1968; Stopford, 1968; Stopford and Wells, 1972; Franko, 1974, 1976). This group has followed the changes in structure that have accompanied strategies of international expansion for U.S. and European firms.

Stopford studied a sample of U.S. firms taken again from the *Fortune* 500. To qualifiy, a firm had to have six manufacturing subsidiaries in foreign countries in 1963 in which it had at least 25 percent ownership. These were firms that expanded internationally during the 1950s, largely exploiting technological innovations to overcome lower labor costs elsewhere. These firms were classified using the Stage I, II (functional), and III (multi-divisional) categories. As the degree of domestic product diversification increased, measured as a percentage of sales outside the primary industry, structure moved increasingly to a Stage III type. There were no functional organizations with more than 6 percent of their revenues coming from outside their primary industry. In addition, the results show that it was the divisionalized companies that adopted an international strategy.

Stopford traces these firms as they expanded internationally during the 1960s. In so doing, he finds that American firms adopted common structures when following common strategies. The first major structural change adopted by the firms was the establishment of an international division that was added to the existing product divisionalized structure. Thus, the initial structural response was to create an international division that differentiated all international activity from domestic business.

The international division, was a transitory form, however, and gave way to another, more global form. Which global form a company moved to depended on the firm's international growth strategy. Those firms that took their entire diversified domestic product line abroad would eventually adopt worldwide product divisions. Those firms that expanded internationally with only their dominant business adopted geographic divisions that divided the world into areas. Each of these strategies set up forces that led to the abandonment of the international division. Why did the international division get disbanded?

Stopford's explanation is the Chandler thesis. One cannot manage high diversity within a single structure, be it functional or, in this case, geographic. That is, the international division was usually organized geographically, and the European and Latin American departments had to manage the entire diversified product line. New product introductions usually led to problems and a reorganization to worldwide product divisions. Product diversity is best managed through product divisionalized firms.

The next question is, Why did the international division disappear for firms that did not diversify abroad, but grew in a dominant business? One reason might be that geographic diversity presents the same problems as product diversity and overloads the executive, who is trying to manage multiple countries and regions. However, Stopford's data do not show that geographic diversity leads to the abandonment of the international division and the adoption of the area divisions. In part, this result is expected because the international division itself was already organized on a geographic basis. Thus, it was already prepared to manage this source of diversity.

The explanation offered by Stopford is a political one based on two observations. First, area divisionalized firms had the highest percentage of total revenue coming from foreign sources. (It is important that it is percentage of total sales and not the absolute amount.) A second, and more detailed, observation was that the area division was adopted at a time when the international division grew to a size equal to the largest U.S. domestic division. It was therefore hypothesized that a coalition of the domestic divisions caused the breakup of the international division, which was beginning to get the lion's share of the capital and research and development budget, and of the managerial talent and other resources. The explanation is post hoc and has not been directly tested. However, it fits with numerous case study interpretations.

The results of Stopford's work are shown graphically in Exhibit 5.5. The Stage II firms and Stage III firms with an international division are all located inside the boundary running between 10 percent diversification and 50 percent foreign sales. With an increase in sales or diversification, the firm crosses the boundary, abandons the international division, and adopts a global Stage III form. Which form is adopted depends on the growth strategy pursued by the firm. Sales growth in a dominant product line leads to area divisions. Diversification in foreign as well as domestic markets leads to worldwide product divisions. Again, structure follows strategy, this time in the international context.

Stopford raises an interesting question that is not answered by his data. What happens as area divisionalized firms diversify, or worldwide product firms increase foreign sales? Some mixed forms were observed where the firm had area divisions, but one large and unique product had been organized as a worldwide product division. One of Stopford's firms had been organized as a matrix or grid form by simultaneously assuming a geographic and a product form. This type will be treated later in more detail. For the moment the question of, What

Exhibit 5.5 Foreign Sales, Product Diversity, and Organization Structure

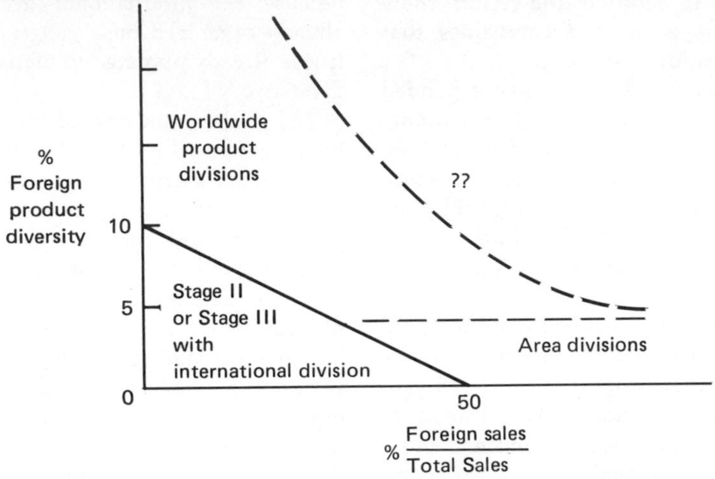

lies on the other side of the next boundary? is the state-of-the-art question. We will return to it later.

OTHER STUDIES

Several other studies are relevant to the strategy-structure relation. Those studies use a different methodology than those quoted above and also look at different structural dimensions. Up to now, only the divisional structure was discussed. In subsequent sections we will add other dimensions of organization structure such as the degree of centralization, resource allocation processes, reward systems and so on.

The first study is a case study reported by Galbraith (1971). He analyzed the changes in the structure of the Commercial Airplane Division of the Boeing Company following changes in their strategy and market. The Division added new programs such as the 737 and 747 to the existing 707 and 727 programs. The market for commercial jet aircraft also became more competitive. The result was a change from a centralized, functional organization to a decentralized, divisional structure in which each program was a division. Again, diversity appears to be best managed through a divisional structure.

The question of centralization is more directly addressed in the work of Berg (1965) and Lorsch

and Allen (1973). Berg addressed the question of structural differences in explaining why the conglomerates of the 1960s were effective. He noted that there were two types of divisional structures, the conglomerate and the diversified majors. The diversified majors, which were the multi-divisional type of form described by Chandler, usually had several hundred people in the corporate office. They coordinated divisional activity through corporate policies and direct participation of corporate offices. In contrast, the conglomerate, similar to the holding company, would have ten to twenty general managers with specialists only in the tax, legal, and financial areas. The conglomerate, then, placed nearly all functions within the division and eliminated the need for coordination. Corporate divisional interests were coordinated through the reward system.

The greater decentralization in the conglomerate case was justified because they managed greater diversity. Berg describes them as diversifying into unrelated businesses, to use Rumelt's categories. The diversified majors were less diverse and followed a strategy of diversifying into related businesses. The relatedness of these divisions required some coordination in the corporate interest, thereby necessitating more corporate management. Thus, greater diversity of a quantitative and qualitative nature requires greater divisional autonomy and smaller corporate offices.

The second study that addresses the centralization issue is based on an empirical study of six divisionalized firms (Lorsch and Allen, 1973). The firms varied in the degree of diversity, the degree of uncertainty, and the amount of interdivisional trading. Indeed, two firms had sufficient interdivisional transfers to be called vertically integrated.

Three of the conglomerates fit the pattern suggested by Berg. They had small corporate offices and performed few divisional functions. The one conglomerate that operated as a vertically integrated firm was also the poorest performer. The vertically integrated units, in contrast, were larger, performed more corporate functions, and served in some operating as well as policy roles in these functions.

Lorsch and Allen also measured the amount of integrating effort expended at corporate offices on corporate-divisional relations and interdivisional relations. The lower performing vertically integrated firm was shown to spend too little effort in integrating the interdependent divisions. On the other hand, the lower performing conglomerates were characterized by too much integrative effort. Some effort is surely attributable to lower performance per se, but the conclusion is that strategies characterized by diversity and uncertainty require greater decentralization and self-containment of divisions. When autonomy is not given, lower performance results. Strategies leading to interdivisional interdependence, such as vertical integration, require more corporate integrative effort. When too little is given, lower performance results. The extent of decentralization follows from the strategy.

CONTINGENCY THEORIES OF ORGANIZATION

The field of organization theory should have a great deal to contribute to questions of strategy and structure linkages. However, the amount of relevant work falls short of one's expectations. Only recently have theorists studied environmental linkages through a so-called open systems perspective. Even then they have not directly addressed either strategy or strategy-structure relations per se. However, some of the work is relevant and is briefly reviewed here.

The portion of organization theory that is relevant to considerations of strategy and structure is the work usually summarized as contingency theory. The theory states that there is no best way of organizing, but that all ways of organizing are not equally effective. That is, the choice of organization form makes a difference in terms of economic performance. The choice depends, however, on the situation. Therefore, contingency theorists have concentrated on situational attributes that make a difference.

The initial impetus came from British sociologists. Joan Woodward (1965) proposed that manufacturing technology was a primary determinant of organization form. Subsequent research has substantiated some of her original findings and modified others (Pugh *et al.*, 1969; Child and Mansfield, 1972; Blau *et al.*, 1976).

Two other British sociologists suggested that it was the rate of change of the environment that determined organization form (Burns and Stalker, 1961). They suggested that in industries characterized by high rates of change of markets and technology, successful firms adopted what they called an "organic form." An organic organization was decentralized with ambiguous roles and a great deal of lateral communication. In industries with stable markets and product lines, the firms adopted a "mechanistic" organization. This form was characterized by centralization and well-defined roles, with communication following the chain of command. This form was hypothesized to be successful for the stable markets. Thus, the type of organization (structure) is contingent upon the rate of change in the environment (strategy). Those firms in high technology industries and in markets characterized by rapid change following strategies of new product introduction, such as the semiconductor industry, should adopt decentralized organic forms.

The results of these studies, when combined with emerging contingency theories of leadership (Fiedler, 1967), small group processes (Leavitt, 1962), preindustrial societies (Udy, 1959), and Chandler, gave impetus to the belief that a new discovery was in the making. A great deal of research then followed from these original studies. Some work was conceptual (Perrow, 1967; Thompson, 1967); some research was empirical (R. Hall, 1962; Hage and Aiken, 1969); and other studies concentrated upon measuring uncertainty (Duncan, 1972; Van de Ven and Delbecq, 1974). The rationale for contingency theory, however, was established by the publication of *Organization and Environment* by Lawrence and Lorsch in 1967.

The Lawrence and Lorsch study examined ten firms in three different industries. There are several portions to their research, but one piece is directly relevant here. Using measures of perceived hierarchical influence, they showed that high performing firms in an uncertain environment had greater decentralization than low performers, and that in the predictable industry, the high performer was the more centralized. The high performers in both industries had achieved a fit with their environment. The addition of the performance measures gave contingency theory the necessary credibility. Textbooks have now picked up the results of the study, and contingency theory is the dominant school of thought in organization behavior.

In summary, organization theorists have adopted their own contingency theory of structure. Instead of focusing upon strategy, they have considered various dimensions of the task to be performed. Usually, task uncertainty is the dimension that is to vary with organization structure. This point of view is consistent with the Chandler hypothesis, since uncertainty and diversity tend to vary together. These studies give still more weight to the strategy-structure thesis.

Coordination Processes

Organizations have created a number of information sharing decision making processes to integrate or coordinate activities, particularly those activities that cut across divisional and departmental boundaries. These processes vary from simple spontaneous meetings to complicated matrix forms. Our task here is to identify these processes, to order them in a way that will allow them to be related to strategy, particularly product/market strategies, and to iden-

tify the conditions under which the different processes should be chosen for implementing strategy.

Organization theorists had occasionally performed studies that examined interdepartmental contact and communication. However, the results were not very operational because it was not clear what were the mechanisms that produced the contact. The Lawrence and Lorsch work made a significant step toward providing a language for talking about these lateral processes. They postulated two dimensions that were important for organizational effectiveness. First, organizations had to differentiate their functions so that each functional department could deal with its different subenvironment. Second, it had to integrate the differentiated functions around the interdependencies brought on by the key competitive requirements of the industry. For those firms where new product introduction was the key competitive issue, the integration problem was one of coordinating marketing and research and development. Where on-time delivery was the key competitive issue, the integration problem was one of coordinating marketing and production. The Lawrence and Lorsch thesis was that the most effective firms would be those that had differentiated their functions to the extent needed to adapt to functional subenvironments and had simultaneously found mechanisms to integrate the differentiated functions in order to deal with the competitive issue of the overall corporate environment.

In summary, there are a number of specific mechanisms that are used to achieve interdepartmental coordination. These mechanisms vary from hierarchical referral to the addition of integrating departments such as product management departments. An enlarged list of mechanisms is shown below:

— Hierarchy
— Rules
— Goal Setting (Planning)
— Direct Contact
— Interdepartmental Liaison Roles
— Temporary Task Forces
— Permanent Teams
— Integrating Roles
— Integrating Departments

Organizations select from the list those mechanisms that will permit them to implement their strategy. The selection is not random, however; choice makes a difference.

The list of coordination mechanisms is an ordered list. Each step down the list represents the commitment to a more complicated and more expensive mechanism of coordination. The increasing expenditure of resources for coordination results, first, because integrating departments are more expensive than temporary task forces using line managers. But expenditures increase also, because mechanisms at the bottom of the list are added to, not substituted for, those higher on the list. They are not direct substitutes. Therefore, an organization should select from the list starting at the top and going down only as far as is necessary in order to implement its strategy. Lawrence and Lorsch's (1967) successful container firm stopped at direct contact, while their successful food processor stopped with integrators (product managers), and the plastics firm adopted all of them in order to be successful. The more new product activity, the higher the level of technology and uncertainty and the more the hierarchy needs to be buttressed with cross-departmental coordination mechanisms. Therefore, those organizations pursuing strategies characterized by interdepartmental activity, high uncertainty, and high diversity will select mechanisms farther down on the list than those organizations pursuing strategies characterized by low uncertainty and diversity.

The hypothesis that strategies characterized by uncertainty and diversity lead to cross-departmental processes (teams) and integrating roles is supported and elaborated by the work of Corey and Star (1971). They studied various types and responsibilities of integrating roles (program structures, in their terminology) in functional business structures. First, they described the same type of integrating role that characterized the Lawrence and Lorsch plastics firms. Next they found that some organizations adopted market based integrating departments. Finally, they presented some organizations like IBM and Du Pont, who have experienced both market and product diversity. The response of these organizations has been to organize simultaneously by markets, products, and functions. Thus, diversity is handled within functional organizations by developing integrating roles around the sources of diversity.

The second point made by Corey and Star was that the greater the diversity and the greater the amount of new product introduction, the greater the likelihood of integrating roles and departments and the greater was their influence. Thus, integrating roles represents one of the principal means with which to implement diversification strategies *without reorganizing* into a product divisionalized structure.

In summary, organizations create integrating mechanisms in order to cope with general management problems of interdepartmental coordination caused by product and market diversity. The mechanisms, such as product task forces, are information and decision processes that are general manager substitutes, but are less than full-time equivalents that result from product divisionalized structures. These mechanisms vary in their cost and their ability to cope with uncertainty and diversity. The more diversity in the business strategy, the greater the number of mechanisms adopted. For diverse and uncertain strategies, separate roles are created around the sources of diversity. These roles, such as product management roles, represent the move to simultaneous structures, which are structures in which the organization is simultaneously product and functional, or any other combination.

SIMULTANEOUS OR MATRIX STRUCTURES

The adoption of coordination mechanisms with which functional organizations can manage diversity suggests that there are a number of transition phases between the functional and multi-divisional structures. Indeed, each step down the list of coordination mechanisms represents a step toward more product oriented decision making. Thus, the change from functional to product structures need not be a major discrete alteration, but can be an evolutionary movement. There is a continuous range of distribution of influence between product and functional orientations. This description is shown in

Exhibit 5.6. One moves along the distribution of influence by adding additional coordination mechanisms and adding power to integrating roles. The point at which product and function are of equal power is called the matrix organization. At that point, there are simultaneously two line organizations of equal power. The organization is simultaneously functional and product. Equal power is obtained through multiple authority relations. The chart for such a company is shown in Exhibit 5.7. It shows a matrix organization for a geographically organized bank that is pursuing a strategy of segmenting markets and creating new financial services for those markets. The resulting market diversity forces the bank into a simultaneous structure built around markets and geography. At some point, the two structures must intersect. In Exhibit 5.7 the market organization and geographic organization intersect at the country level. The individual who manages multi-national corporate banking has two bosses — the country manager and the market manager. The

task of that individual is to integrate the two perspectives for that business in that country.

One could also move to the right-hand side of the diagram in Exhibit 5.6, where product divisions are dominant and the functional managers play integrating roles. Thus, organizers are not faced with a choice of function versus product (or market or geography) divisions, but with a choice of whether to give priority to product or function. Organizations nowadays are simultaneous structures (simply a generalization of line-staff models), with product and functional managers reporting to the general manager. Multi-national firms add a third geographic dimension. Which dimension is more influential and has higher priority depends upon several factors, including the strategy and the business environment.

Several factors favor emphasizing the product side. As already mentioned, diversity and new product introductions are best managed through product oriented structures. One would move to the right of the diagram as a result. Also,

Exhibit 5.6   The Range of Alternatives

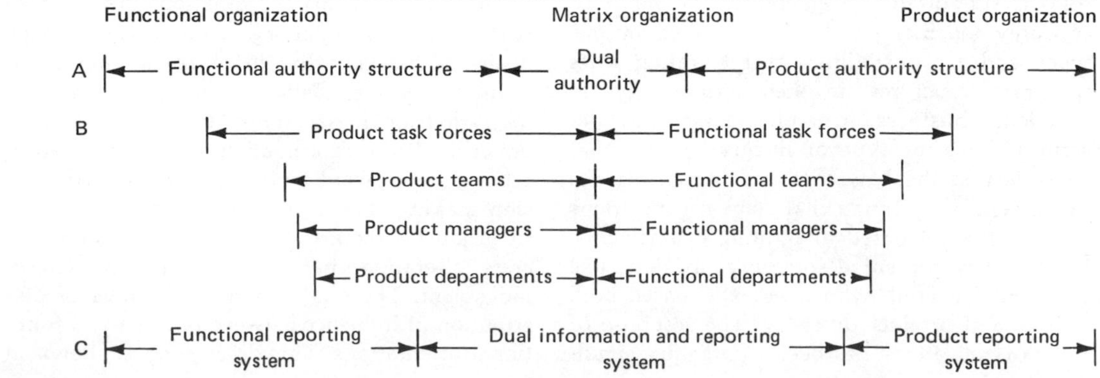

Exhibit 5.7   Worldwide Matrix for a Banking Firm

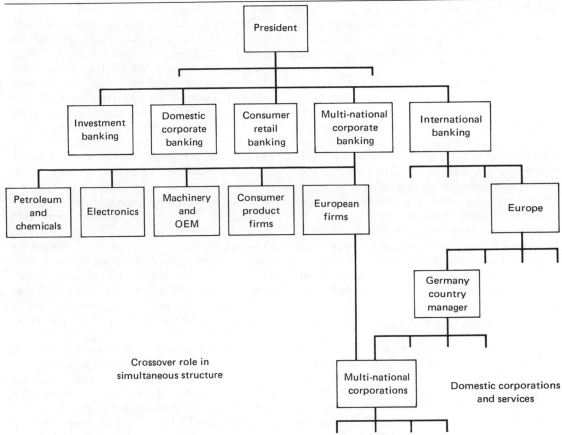

increasing interdependence among functional departments and increased need for responsiveness to the market favor a product or project orientation. However, these generalizations must be qualified by considerations of size. Self-contained product divisions may be too small to have their own sales force or to achieve size economies in production. Therefore, the larger the organization, the more likely the establishment of product or project divisions. The smaller the organization, the more likely the establishment of product or project integrating departments. The longer the life cycle of the product or project, the more likely that a self-contained division will be created.

A couple of factors favor the functional organization. Economies of scale in the functions mitigate against breaking them up and distrib-

uting the pieces among the product divisions. The need for special expertise and career paths for specialists are facilitated by the functional form. Therefore, firms pursuing state-of-the-art technology should have strong technical functions. The uncertainty connected with high technology also argues for a coordination capability across functions. It is usually the high technology firms that adopt some form of the matrix, which simultaneously gives them high technology and high coordination.

OTHER SYSTEMS AND PROCESSES

The phenomena that constitute organizations are not only structural in nature. There are other phenomena such as resource allocation processes, performance evaluation and reward systems, integrating mechanisms, and many others, all of which constitute the form of the organization. This section reviews the relevant research analyzing the relationship of strategy to these processes.

The importance of these other phenomena was noted by Chandler. In discussing the General Motors case, he spent a great deal of time discussing the invention of accounting practices, such as standard volume and other performance measurement and reporting systems, the implementation and linkage of interdivisional committees, the creation of new roles, such as the group executive, and the difference in personality between managers who invented the strategy and those who invented the structure. In this section, we will examine resource allocation processes, then performance evaluation and reward systems, and finally the human issues of career and management development.

RESOURCE ALLOCATION PROCESSES

Organizations undertake a myriad of activities in allocating their resources. These activities are usually labeled as budgeting, and planning and control processes. Although a great deal of scholarly attention has been devoted to methods of allocating resources rationally from an economic viewpoint, much less attention has been given to examining the decisions as organizational and political processes. There are a few exceptions, however, and these studies provide a good base for further exploration. Most of the studies are of a general descriptive nature, but some compare process differences based upon differences in strategy or structure.

Some of the studies use Cyert and March's *Behavioral Theory of the Firm* as their point of departure (1963). The behavioral theory was intended to introduce a better description of how decisions actually were made rather than how they should be made. Their work prompted others to view resource allocation not as single choices, but as organizational processes (Aharoni, 1966). Another study that illustrates how the processes in an organization actually differ from the rational economic model is one done by Carter (1971). He showed how strategy affected decisions and confirmed the lack of analysis in decision making.

The last general descriptive study to be mentioned here is the specific examination of the resource allocation process in a large diversified company by Bower (1970). He distinguished three sequential steps that took place at three different levels of the organization. First, was the *definition* phase at the division level, where a need for investment was recognized and a proposal created to reduce a discrepancy. Next, the proposal was given *impetus* when a division manager bought it and agreed to back it and commit himself to it. Finally, there was the *approval* by corporate management in the allocating of scarce funds. Bower's work is a thorough description of this process for four investments. He too was interested in describing the actual process and in distinguishing it from more quantitative, but naive versions of investment decisions. No attempt was made by Bower or the other researchers mentioned above to distinguish variations in the process and to relate them to variations in strategy.

Subsequent work has introduced variations in process that accompany variations in structure and strategy. Ackerman (1970) used the Bower model to compare paper manufacturing divisions in two integrated paper companies and in two diversified multi-divisional firms. Holding industry constant, he assigned variations in process to variations in structure. The result was greater centralization of the definition and impetus stages in the vertically integrated company.

The work of Berg (1969) provides another comparative study. His approach was to contrast the conglomerate with the more standard multi-divisional form. The conglomerates usually pursue even more diverse strategies than the multi-divisionals. Their resource allocation processes are even more decentralized than those described by Ackerman. However, they did use a few sophisticated financial planning and control information systems. From Berg's study, one gets the impression that the modern conglomerate finds companies that need better management, acquires them, and turns them around. The turnaround is accomplished by a corporate group skilled in general management that acts like a consulting firm with ownership clout. Many of the reasons for the success of these organizations and their processes are attributable to their growth by acquisition rather than by internal development; they seek businesses with no relationship to existing businesses, instead of exploiting a distinctive functional competence.

Pitts (1977) has outlined some of the differences between firms that pursue internal diversification strategies and those that diversify by acquisition. The internal diversifier is characterized by larger corporate staffs, more interdivisional transfers, a more subjective performance appraisal, and, in short, more interdivisional sharing of resources. The internal diversifier, then, actively exploits opportunities for resource sharing; the acquisitive diversifier deliberately foregoes such opportunities. The main strength of the internal diversifier is that it brings to a new business its ability to draw upon the combined resources of its numerous dimensions, especially in the technological area. On the other hand, the key capability of the acquisitive diversifier rests in its ability to attract and retain acquired managers who themselves possess expertise in newly entered fields. They are then given high division autonomy, financial backing, general management coaching, and performance targets. Pitts points out that, because of the fundamental differences between the two strategies, any attempt to define a compromise position somewhere between the two might very well prove disastrous.

In summary, progress has been made in developing an understanding of processes by which organizations allocate strategic resources. Some progress has also been made in creating a language for discussing and comparing these different processes. A few studies have found variations in process to be related to different strategies. One study suggests that these variations lead to more effective economic performance. One of the reasons that resources are effectively allocated is that evaluation and reward systems are tied to planned resource usage.

EVALUATION AND REWARD SYSTEMS

One of the most important components of an organization form is the system by which performance is measured, evaluated, and rewarded. The study of rewards and punishments from a motivational view has been a major research area for organization behavior specialists. Most of this work has been directed at testing various models of motivation, at questions of whether extrinsic or intrinsic rewards are more motivating, and at examining various policies to make work more satisfying. Much of this research also concentrates on lower and middle level personnel. The best recent paper summarizing research on reward systems, and compensation in particular, is that of Lawler (1971, 1977). Lawler suggests that the research confirms the conventional wisdom that when pay is tied to performance, it motivates higher performance. But despite its obviousness, this is not a unanimous view (Meyer, 1975).

Lawler's work has also led to a typology of the different kinds of pay plans and their likely motivational consequences. First, money rewards can be given as salary increases or bonuses. The reward can be given on the basis of individual, group, or organization-wide performance. Second, performance can be measured by productivity or profit, by cost effectiveness or cost reduction, or by superior's rating. Lawler rates these pay plans according to their ability to tie pay to performance, to produce dysfunctional side effects (such as encouraging short-run performance at long-run expense), to encourage cooperative behavior between people, and to promote employee acceptance. The last point raised by Lawler is the concept of system congruence. That is, there is no single best reward system. The best depends on the organization's task and strategy, and on the fit of the reward system with the organization's structure, processes, and other systems.

The linkage between compensation policy and strategy has been considered and elaborated by Salter (1973). When considering incentive or bonus compensation for group and division executives, several choices are available. First, there is a choice of financial instruments such as cash, stock, deferred cash, and several others. Second, there is the choice of performance measure and the amount of discretion in allocating the rewards. Finally, the amount of bonus is considered. In choosing a plan, Salter suggests that management analyze the strategy in order to examine the time horizon of the decision maker (short- vs. long-run), the amount of risk taking to encourage, the degree of cooperation with other managers that is required, and the likely differences between corporate and division goals. His recommendations, which are generally consistent with those of Lawler, give management some basis for designing reward policies.

In summary, the Lawler and the Salter schemes require that the reward system designer start with the strategy of the organization in order to determine the behavior that is necessary for implementation of that strategy. They identify some behavior types for us, such as degree of cooperation between units and need for goal congruence between successive layers. The reward system chosen will be a trade-off between the various incentives for particular behaviors. A typical trade-off is between division profit incentives and total corporate profit. The total figure will encourage cooperation and congruence between division and corporate goals, but will reduce the degree to which an individual's performance is linked to his or her bonus. A balanced incentive scheme should be formulated according to the strategy, the interdependence between units, and the individualism of the managers in question.

A few of the research studies mentioned earlier also have compared reward system variation with strategy and structure variation. Berg credits the conglomerate with motivating managers rather than coordinating them (1969). The interdependence and need for cooperation between divisions is eliminated, and managers are rewarded generously on the basis of financial performance, usually with equity compensation. Thus, they are encouraged to take risks, to take a short- and long-term view, and to balance division versus corporate goals. Cooperation is voluntary and encouraged only if it pays off for the division.

Lorsch and Allen (1973) also compared the performance evaluation systems of their sample of diversified and integrated companies. Their results are consistent with the results of Ackerman and Berg. The diversified companies rewarded division managers against explicit *a priori* goals. Rewards were tied directly to the accomplishment of end results. The pool of funds from which rewards were given resulted directly from division profits against the budget. In contrast, division performance evaluation for integrated firms was more informal and was less explicitly related to profit. There was no formula for determining bonus awards, and management exercised more discretion in awarding year end incentive compensation.

PEOPLE AND CAREERS

Chandler's original research focused on differences in personality between the strategy formulator and the structure innovator. Nowhere was the contrast greater than between Billy Durant and Alfred P. Sloan at General Motors. The pattern repeated itself at Du Pont and other organizations, which suggested something systematic. Several approaches to considering variations among people are relevant to this issue. First, there is some recent research that attempts to match people with variations in structure and task. Second, there is a great deal of attention now being given to careers and to management development. Finally, practitioners and consulting firms are promoting schemes based on matching individual variations with structure-strategy variations.

A number of studies have attempted to relate variations in personality to variations in task and structure (Morse and Young, 1973; McCaskey, 1976; Kilman and Mitroff, 1976). There is some evidence that there are systematic relations between types of people, types of structure, and the degree of task uncertainty.

Most of the research has not explored the consequences of a lack of fit. Presumably, people are most satisfied and performance is higher when congruence among all the factors is achieved. One study has examined this feature, however (Lorsch and Morse, 1974). The sample consists of ten matched organizations. Four manufacturing firms, two high performers and two low performers, are compared with six research and development laboratories, three high performers and three low performers. The research and development labs performed uncertain tasks, while the manufacturing plants' task was more predictable. As predicted, low tolerance for ambiguity was found among the people in the manufacturing plants and high tolerance at the research and development labs. The high performing plants had mechanistic structures, the low performing plants had less mechanistic structures. The high performing research and development labs had organic structures, and the low performers had more formal mechanistic ones. Thus, when there was a fit between structure, task, and people, there was higher performance and also greater motivation and satisfaction. Low performance and motivation occur when the structure is out of line with the task and people. Unfortunately, the sample did not contain a situation where personality was out of line with the task. Therefore, alternative explanations as to causation cannot be rejected. But, Lorsch and Morse's evidence supports the congruence or fit hypothesis.

The second approach that is relevant for this review is the focus on careers, management development, and career development. A great deal of current research is focused on these topics (Campbell, Dunette, Lawler, and Weick, 1970; Hall, 1976; Van Maanen and Schein, 1977). However, very little of this research addresses how variations in strategies and structures are matched with variations in management development. So far, however, the emphasis of empirical work has been upon the individual; macroperspectives simply have not been taken in empirical studies. A start in this direction, though, is a study comparing the uses of managerial transfer in European multi-national firms (Edstrom and Galbraith, 1977). The authors hypothesize that large numbers of transfers of many nationalities lead to a decentralized subsidiary structure. The work of Pitts (1977) is also relevant here. He finds that firms that grow internally and presumably pursue "related diversification" strategies make use of interdivisional careers to a greater extent than do external growth firms pursuing unrelated diversification strategies. The need for technology transfer of the "related" competence is satisfied by interdivisional transfers. Similarly, most organizations that operate a mature matrix organization have career paths that encourage multidivisional and multi-functional experiences. This

form of organization, which arises to handle diversity while sharing resources, requires generalists who know all the diverse markets, products, countries, and functions. These renaissance people are grown and developed internally by diverse sets of managerial experiences arranged through the career path.

The third approach to the people dimension is taken by consulting firms selling strategy making packages to multi-divisional firms. The idea is to match the product division manager with particular stages on the product life cycle, or with whether the product is a "star" or "cow." These ideas are very much like Chandler's concepts. However appealing these ideas are, they have yet to be tested. The types of people are also quite vague, being characterized as entrepreneur, sophisticated manager, opportunistic milker, and so on. However, the approach continues to be adopted by companies and by consulting firms.

In summary, there is some evidence that there is something to be gained through systematically matching structure, strategy, and people. At best, such matching gives both human satisfaction and effective organizational performance. Also, there is a great deal that needs to be done in examining which management development and career process best fits different product/market strategies and different structures.

THE CONCEPT OF CONGRUENCE

Our review, thus far, has examined relationships between various dimensions of organization structure and process and the firm's product/market strategy. With a few exceptions, the relationships examined were between a particular organization dimension, such as the departmental structure or the reward system, and strategy. However, each organizational dimension must be consistent not only with the strategy, but also with the others. All the dimensions, such as structure, reward systems, and resource allocation processes, must constitute an internally consistent organizational form. Organizations are packages or mosaics in which all pieces must fit together. This concept of fit, or congruence, was raised earlier in connection with personality types. It will be raised again here, because it is the key concept of current organization design theory and practice.

The concept of fit or congruence among all the dimensions of the organization has emerged from several sources. Scott began talking of his stages as consisting "of a cluster of managerial characteristics" (Scott, 1971: 6). In addition, he suggested that a cluster was not just an organizational form, but a "way of managing," even a "way of life." He then identified the characteristics and specified them for each stage. These are shown in Exhibit 5.8.

The same scheme has been elaborated by consulting firms in their own strategy and structure packages. They distinguish between products or businesses in a multi-divisional firm by the stage of the product life cycle. Then they assume that the "way of managing" will vary with the stages. They go on to prescribe managerial characteristics that are appropriate for the various stages. The main point is that business divisions need to adopt an internally consistent set of practices in order to implement the product strategy effectively.

Another source of development of the congruence or fit concept is organization theory. Leavitt (1962, 1965) was one of the first to discuss the degree to which task, structure, people, and processes form an integrated whole. He suggests that organizational change strategies should take all dimensions into account. One cannot successfully change structure without making compensating and reinforcing changes in information and budgeting systems, career systems, management development practices, and compensation policies. In organizations, everything is connected to everything else.

The major developer and empirical investigator of the fit concept has been Jay Lorsch (Lawrence and Lorsch, 1967; Lorsch and Allen, 1973; Lorsch and Morse, 1974). Much of his work has already been discussed in the sections devoted to the individual dimensions. He is the primary investigator to examine structure, task, people and administrative practices, the congruence between these dimensions, and the degree to which congruence is related to organizational performance. The results of his research support the hypothesis that a fit between the dimensions leads to high organizational performance. Those organizations that were not high performers were experiencing a situation in which either structure or process did not fit with the degree of task uncertainty.

Some further conceptual development has recently appeared (Galbraith, 1977). Galbraith has built upon both the Lorsch scheme and the Lorsch research. He has attempted to identify the major design variables to be considered when matching organization form to strategy. Specifically a congruence between people, rewards, information and decision processes, and structure is needed to effectively implement a given strategy.

There is a great deal of research yet to be done in testing the concept of congruence, because it comprises many interacting variables. Although the concept of fit is a useful one, it lacks the precise definition needed to test it and to recognize whether an organization has it or not. There is also a trade-off between short-run fit and long-run fit. That is, the short-run congruence between all the organization design variables may be so good that they cannot be disentangled and rearranged into a new configuration in order to meet an environmental challenge or to implement a new strategy. For example, the Swiss watch makers achieved an excellent fit between strategy and structure for the making of mechanical watches. However, the institutionalization of the mechanical technology has prevented these firms from adapting to the new electronic technology. Thus the corporate designer must choose a time period over which to optimize the fit.

STRATEGY, STRUCTURE, AND COMPETITION

In the previous section we examined the relation between strategy and structure. The work in that area generally confirmed the Chandler thesis, expanded the concept of organization to include processes in addition to static structural dimensions, and introduced the concept of congruence. In this section the moderating effect of competition on the strategy-structure relation is discussed.

The Harvard research on strategy and structure in Europe, which was summarized by Scott (1973), initially raised the competitive issue.

Exhibit 5.8 Three Stages of Organizational Development

Company characteristics \ Stage	I	II	III
1. Product line	1. Single product or single line	1. Single product line	1. Multiple product lines
2. Distribution	2. One channel or set of channels	2. One set of channels	2. Multiple channels
3. Organization structure	3. Little or no formal structure—"one man show"	3. Specialization based on function	3. Specialization based on product/market relationships
4. Product-service transactions	4. N/A	4. Integrated pattern of transactions → Market	4. Not integrated (A B C → Markets)
5. R&D	5. Not institutionalized-oriented by owner-manager	5. Increasingly institutionalized search for product or process improvements	5. Institutionalized search for *new* products as well as for improvements
6. Performance measurement	6. By personal contact and subjective criteria	6. Increasingly impersonal using technical and/or cost criteria	6. Increasingly impersonal using *market* criteria (return on investment and market share)
7. Rewards	7. Unsystematic and often paternalistic	7. Increasingly systematic with emphasis on stability and service	7. Increasingly systematic with variability related to performance
8. Control system	8. Personal control of both strategic and operating decisions	8. Personal control of strategic decisions, with increasing delegation of operating decisions based on control by decision rules (policies)	8. Delegation of product/market decisions within existing businesses, with indirect control based on analysis of "results."
9. Strategic choices	9. Needs of owner vs. needs of firm	9. —Degree of integration —Market share objective —Breadth of product line	9. —Entry and exit from industries —Allocation of resources by industry —Rate of growth

It was noticed that in Europe the strategy of product diversification spread more rapidly than the multi-divisional structure. One could find firms with diversified product lines but with functional and holding company structures. The explanation offered was that in many European countries the markets were less competitive and there was, therefore, less need for efficient allocation of resources through structures that matched strategies.

The competitive hypothesis was put to a direct test by Franko (1974, 1976). He took a sample of European firms from the *Fortune* 200 for the largest non-American firms. His initial findings did not support the Chandler thesis. The vast majority of European multi-nationals in 1961 were organized around an international holding company/domestic functional model, which Franko labeled the mother-daughter form. However, things began to change in the late 1960s. The mother-daughter form began disappearing. By 1971, the numbers of mother-daughter forms had dropped from sixty-one out of seventy in 1961 to twenty-five out of seventy. More revealing was the observation that between 1968 and 1972, forty-four firms changed their structures to the multi-divisional structure. Why? Franko suggests that it is the breakdown of the negotiated environment in Europe.

The strength of Franko's case rests on the fact that the environment did not change equally in all countries or in all industries. The largest number of and earliest changes to multi-divisional forms occurred in the U.K., the country with the least government planning, the most antitrust enforcement, and the greatest penetration by non-European countries. French companies show the least penetration by outside firms. Similarly, in the pharmaceutical and chemical industries, where the largest number of antitrust suits existed and where the only fines occurred, all fourteen companies have adopted the multi-divisional structure. The greater the penetration by outside competitors and the greater the amount of antitrust activity, the more likely one will find a move toward the multi-divisional structure. In industries where the same negotiated environment exists, the functional and holding company models are still used.

Thus, country and industry comparisons support the case that diversity combined with competition leads to the multi-divisional form. Neither alone is sufficient to provoke a change to the new structure. It appears that structure follows strategy only when structure makes a difference. When diversifying under monopoly conditions, however, strategy can be implemented independent of structure. The status quo structure offers the solution with the least resistance. It is only when competition causes performance deterioration that structural adjustment is needed to restore profits to acceptable levels.

Organization theorists have also done some work on the competitiveness issue. There are no studies that directly examine the strategy and structure relation, but there are several that have examined the degree of competition in an industry and its effect on structure.

Some discussion of the sample populations is needed before the results are interpreted. All the following studies examined small manufacturing operations. They did not sample from the *Fortune* 500. Most of the organizations were of a size equal to a division in a multi-divisional firm. Some care should be taken, therefore, in generalizing to multi-divisional firms. Also, there was no examination of the departmental structure. The primary interest was in decentralization and in formalization of procedures.

There are two studies which report results from Indian (Negandhi and Reimann, 1972, 1976) and from Mexican and Italian firms (Simonetti and Boseman, 1975). Both studies found that the more competitive the industry the more decentralized the organization. The more effective the organization, the stronger the relation.

A study by Khandwalla adds more support to the previous findings (1973). Using a sample of ninety-eight U.S. manufacturing firms, he measured industry competition, the amount of delegation of decision making, and the extent of the use of sophisticated management controls such as cost and variance analyses. He found that decentralization is coupled with the use of formal control systems and is most extensive under competitive conditions.

The last study that will be reported here related competition, dimensions of structure and process, and various types of strategy and technology (Pfeffer and Leblebici, 1973). They took their measures from a sample of thirty-eight small manufacturing firms. They found that the greater the competition, the greater the degree of specification of procedures (formalization) and the more frequent the reporting of results. These findings support the previous studies. The relation between decentralization and competition was again positive, but this time it was small and not statistically significant. In part, this result is attributable to the lack of control for economic effectiveness and to a different measure for decentralization (the amount of money a department head can spend without higher authorization).

The second part of the study examined relations between strategic variables such as number of product changes, structure, and process variables. There is a mixture of results. Under competitive conditions, organizations reduce spans of control and add levels to the hierarchy; under noncompetitive conditions, organizations stay flat and increase spans of control and number of departments. Also, the greater the number of changes to products, the greater the formalization and written reporting of performance. The results for decentralization are mixed, with some positive results for competitive and some for noncompetitive conditions. In part, this could arise from a confounding with size as well as the previously mentioned economic performance. The larger the organization, the greater the amount of money a manager can spend without higher approval.

These results can be interpreted as being consistent with previous results. Greater competition brings on a need for greater coordination and control. The increase is obtained through the use of formalized systems and procedures for measuring and reporting performance and a greater delegation of decision making discretion within those systems and procedures. As a matter of fact, some current theorists argue that narrowing spans of control occur under uncertain conditions and are associated with decentralization (Perrow, 1977). Under this interpretation, all the previous studies lead to the same results. Competitiveness affects organizational structure and process. The effects are decentral-

ization and formalization. The more a firm is decentralized and formalized in a competitive environment, the stronger the relation with economic performance. The need for coordination and control is thus created in the competitive environment. There is simply less need for coordination in noncompetitive conditions, and it is less important in order to obtain economic performance. These results support the view emerging from the studies of strategy and structure.

STRUCTURE, COMPETITION, AND PERFORMANCE

Two of the studies reported in the section above tested the relation between structure, competition, and performance (Negandhi and Reiman, 1972, 1976; Simonetti and Boseman, 1975). Initially, the hypothesis was that decentralized firms would be most effective in competitive markets and centralized firms more effective in less competitive markets. Instead, one finds little relation between structure (decentralization) and performance under less competitive conditions. Actually the authors find a positive relation between the lack of competition and economic effectiveness. This result is consistent with the findings of economists (Bain, 1958). However, there is a relation under competitive conditions. The more decentralized the organization, the greater the economic and behavioral effectiveness. Again structure only matters in competitive circumstances. There were measures or controls for strategy.

STRATEGY, STRUCTURE, AND PERFORMANCE

There are a number of studies that examined pairwise relations between strategy, structure, and performance. Some have examined all three. But an analysis of variance that separates the individual and interaction effects is still lacking.

The empirical evidence presented above certainly supports the hypothesis that strategy and structure are related. With due regard for competition, diversification leads to the multi-divisional structure. However, it has not yet been demonstrated that structure contributes to economic performance or that firms that have matched strategy and structure perform better than those that have not.

Rumelt examined the financial performance of the firms in his sample in order to test strategy-structure-performance relations. First, economic performance and type of strategy were compared. The finding was that the type of diversification, not the amount, was related to economic performance. Both constrained strategies, dominant and related, were the top performers in almost all categories, such as return on equity, stability, and various categories of growth. Thus, a strategy of controlled diversity is associated with high stable economic performance, because it neither commits the organization to a single business nor stretches it across industries. Instead, controlled diversity reflects the reason for the entry into related businesses: that all may draw upon a common strength or a distinctive competence. However, controlled diversity may not necessarily be the cause of economic performance; it may also result from it. The low performing related-constrained types may leave to try related-linked businesses, leaving the high performing related-constrained firms. Cause and effect statements cannot be made yet.

The multi-divisional structure per se was the high performer in all growth areas and in risk-adjusted growth in earnings per share. It had average return on equity and capital. This finding is interesting, because often growth is assumed to be purchased at the expense of reduced profitability. Instead, growth and profitability were positively related, and the multi-divisional firms were able to increase profits faster than functional organizations, while maintaining the same return on capital. The reason is assumed to be the planning, control, and reward systems used in multi-divisional structures.

Again, it is not only the divisional structure, but also the matching of processes and systems to strategy, as well as to the achievement of short-run profit in the divisions and long-term growth overall, that is important.

The tests of the fit of strategy-structure-performance were not conclusive. Two tests were attempted. First, it was hypothesized that in science-based industries divisionalized structures would be superior to nondivisionalized struc-tures. Actually, the reverse was found to be true, but was not statistically significant. In part, the test was invalid because of the rare occurrence of nondivisionalized firms.

Rumelt's second test controlled for strategy. Within the related strategies (constrained and linked), it was hypothesized that the multi-divisional would outperform the functional organization. Partial support for this proposition was found. Return on equity, return on capital, and price earnings ratios were higher, but they were not statistically significant. Growth in earnings per share which was higher for functional organizations was also not statistically significant. The only significant difference was that multi-divisionals produced higher sales growth. So, four out of five hypotheses were in the predicted direction, and one was significant. This is supportive, but not overwhelming evidence.

In summary, the Rumelt study caps the Harvard research that shows the diversification of large firms in the Western world and the continuing adoption of the multi-divisional form to manage that diversity. The program supports the thesis that structure follows strategy but raises as many questions as it answers. The failure to show that high performance comes from a match of strategy and structure suggests that either controls on life cycles are needed, or that economic performance is independent of strategy-structure congruence. Large samples, longitudinal data, and sophisticated, time phased econometric techniques are needed.

Channon (1973), in a study of British service industry firms such as banks, insurance companies, and hotels, using the categories of single business, dominant business, diversification into related businesses, and diversification into unrelated businesses, found that the single and related business categories were superior on a number of measures of growth and returns, with the related businesses being marginally superior overall. This suggests that diversification is pursued only after the single business begins to decline. If prospects are good, no diversification occurs. When diversification does occur, however, greater success is achieved by going into related businesses, as opposed to unrelatedness.

The structure results were somewhat similar

to those found by Rumelt. The multi-divisional firms had high growth results for sales, assets, and earnings per share while maintaining above average returns. The functional organizations had slightly higher returns, and holding companies were the poorest performers. Unfortunately, there was no test for the fit between strategy and structure.

Another study tested the effects of using a profit center structure, presumably a multi-divisional, versus not using one, presumably a functional organization (Poensgen, 1974). Using financial data taken from Compustat tapes and structure categories from a questionnaire (Mauriel and Anthony, 1966), correlation with controls for factors such as size and industry were computed for 364 American firms. The result shows that profit center structures are more profitable with structure explaining about 10 percent of the variance in return on equity. This is one of the few measures of importance and indicates that structure can have an effect of up to 10 percent. Cause and affect analyses yielded no results. Before and after data did not show an increase in profitability after going to the profit center structure. Finally, Rumelt's results of low association between returns and growth for profit centers were reproduced. Presumably with one group working on returns (divisions) and one group working on growth (corporate), the association between the two is less. Growth, in a multi-divisional structure, does not depend on profit from current operations to the degree that it does in a functional organization.

The last study to be reported here examined the economic performance of eighty-two British firms (Cable and Steer, 1977). The primary independent variable was optimal organization form. Optimal forms are multi-divisional forms, with separation of division and corporate interests based on time horizon, and functional organizations in a single business. Nonoptimal are holding companies, multi-divisionals with corporate offices too involved in division activities, and diversified functional forms. Controlling for size, industry, ownership, and growth, the authors found that organization form is a significant predictor of return on equity and assets. Organization can account for between 7 percent and 9 percent difference in returns. Overall, the au-

thors explain about 50 percent of the variance. Unfortunately, the criteria for determining the optimal organization are not explicit. However, the inclusion of several regressions with questionable cases omitted or reclassified produces little change in overall results. Some care should be taken in interpreting the authors' conclusion that organization makes a difference. Involvement by corporate superiors may be a response to, not a cause of, poor performance. The nonoptimal classification distorts the effect of organization. The results, like those of other correlation studies, should be interpreted with respect to causation.

CONTINGENCY THEORY: FIT AND PERFORMANCE

Several of the studies discussed above measured performance outcomes and tested contingency theory hypotheses. In this section, we want to review that literature in its entirety. Recall the contingency hypothesis that the structure of the organization must fit the environment in which the firm is operating. If it does not, the firm should be less effective.

The hypothesis originated with the findings of Woodward and Lawrence and Lorsch. In both cases, the less effective firms deviated from the hypothesized fit with technology and environment. A number of subsequent studies have confirmed that relation, although two have not.

Lorsch and his colleagues have twice replicated his original results. As reported earlier in this paper, a study of corporate-divisional relations demonstrated that low performers deviated from the optimal fit, and high performers did not (Lorsch and Allen, 1973). In another study to be described later, Lorsch and Morse found that high performers on routine tasks had mechanistic organizations, and high performers on nonroutine tasks had organic structures (Lorsch and Morse, 1974). The low performers had mechanistic structures for nonroutine tasks and organic structures for routine ones.

Khandwalla (1974) attempted to replicate the Woodward (1965) results. Using a scale that measured the degree to which a firm used mass production or continuous process techniques, he predicted that mass and continuous production would be associated with the acquisition of prior and subsequent operations in the work flow, delegation of authority, and coordination through sophisticated control systems. In general, the hypotheses held, but it was the high performers that conformed more to the hypothesis than the low performers. Again, the high performers achieved a better fit.

Child has examined structure and performance in six industries in Britain (1974, 1975). He was interested in the effects of size and dynamic environments on the degree to which firms acquired formal control and staff specialists, and the degree to which they delegated authority. Increases in each are referred to as the degree of bureaucratization. The high performing firms acquired bureaucracy at a faster rate when they grew than did the poor performers. With size should come bureaucracy. Although the high performers in dynamic environments acquired bureaucracy at a slower rate than the high performers in stable industries, they did so faster than low performers in both environments. In a dynamic environment, a balance must be struck between bureaucracy for size and responsiveness for change. Again, the notion is one of fit.

The studies in the previous section should also be cited here. Negandhi and Reimann (1973) and Simonetti and Boseman (1975) both found that in competitive environments, decentralization led to high performance. Presumably, operations need to be decentralized in more dynamic competitive situations in order to fit with the environment. Here again one must exercise the usual caution about cause and effect when interpreting performance-decentralization relations.

These studies all support the fit hypothesis. However, several problems are present. First is the notion of causation. It is not clear whether low performance causes centralization, or vice versa. Decentralization is always one of the structural variables used. Second, the importance of structure is not clear. There appears to be a relation between structure and performance, but it may be weak or strong. The earlier Poensgen and Cable and Steer studies give us some idea of this relationship, but there is no analysis of variance among the contingency studies.

Finally, there are two studies that do not report results that support the fit hypothesis. In both cases, there was no support for a direct test that organic or decentralized organizations perform better than centralized organizations in uncertain environments (Mohr, 1971; Pennings, 1975). Both studies have experimental holes of their own, primarily because their samples were taken from a single context. Therefore, they examined a restricted range of variation. However, the studies do give cause for skepticism and for avoiding hasty adoption of simple contingency relations.

A more recent view is that congruence among organizational structure, processes, and systems is the important factor, not fit with the environment. Two studies are consistent with this hypothesis.

Using the same data base mentioned before, Khandwalla (1973) proposed that internal consistency of structural design was related to performance. He found that it was the more effective firms that adopted uncertainty reducers, internally differentiated their structures, formalized procedures, and decentralized decisions all in proportion to one another. There was far less congruence between these practices in less effective firms. These findings led him to suggest that it was the whole package or gestalt that was more important than any single factor alone.

Some preliminary results of a study by Child also reinforce this hypothesis. He is studying five international airlines, their structures and their performance. In examining the two most profitable airlines, he finds that they have contrasting administrative practices and structures even though they face similar problems, have similar route structures, and equivalent sizes. But the one feature they have in common is congruence among their processes and structure. One is not divisionalized, has short time horizons, is centralized, and uses high and continuous involvement of the top management team which meets often. It operates a personal control process and has open communications among a management cadre which has long tenure. Conflicts are expressed and decisions are made and acted upon rapidly. The other airline has a multi-divisional, regional form with decentralized profit centers. It operates with impersonal controls and sophisticated planning processes. It has a large number of administrative staff personnel who operate the impersonal control system. These observations lead Child to suggest that it is the consistency among these practices, structure and people that makes them effective.

The poor performers also had multi-divisional structures for decentralization, but placed restrictions on the amount of discretion that could be exercised. Although they had the structure and incurred the administrative cost of large staff overhead, they received none of the benefits of decentralization. Child's explanation of the effect of inconsistency among structural variable upon performance is based on the impact of such inconsistency on managerial behavior. Such inconsistent practices give mixed signals that frustrate managers and weaken their motivation.

Thus, there are three researchers who have offered data to support the structural consistency or congruence hypothesis. These studies should be followed by others using different methodologies, however, because the above research is methodology bound. That is, each of the studies is a small sample, cross-sectional, comparative study. This methodology could lead to rejection of the fit hypothesis and has not. But it has several flaws. The concept of fit involves consistency among multiple organizational dimensions, performance, and strategy. Consequently, a small sample size does not permit a fully orthogonal experimental design. Thus, there are still multiple interpretations that cannot be rejected either. Some of these interpretations concern causation. For example, does noninvolvement of corporate offices create the autonomy that divisions use to respond to the uniqueness of their market, thereby performing at a high level? Or, does high divisional performance create confidence in the minds of corporate management, who then give high performing divisions autonomy, while concentrating on the low performing divisions? Here the cross-sectional nature of the research does not permit a rejection of the alternative explanations. Some large sample and longitudinal empirical studies

are needed to complement and build upon the Lorsch, Khandwalla, and Child research.

GROWTH AND DEVELOPMENT MODELS

Every area of inquiry has its own stages of growth model. One can find proposed stages of growth in individual cognitive development and socioemotional development, in group development, and in the economic development of countries. Organization and management theory is no exception. Several reviews of this literature already exist and will not be repeated here (Starbuck, 1965, 1971; Child and Keiser, forthcoming). Instead, we will select only those models that are relevant to choices of strategy and structure. These models are referred to as metamorphosis models, as opposed to continuous, smooth development models.

A number of metamorphosis growth models have been offered. They vary in the number of stages that constitute the developmental sequence, in the number of organizational strategy and structure dimensions that are included, and in the particular determinant that drives the metamorphosis, for example, age, size, or complexity. The latter distinction accounts for the greatest variance in the models. For example, James (1973) has proposed a growth model based on time phases or age of the organization, whereas Pugh and his colleagues (1969) propose that size is the primary driving force generating changes in organization form. The problem with all of these models is not that they are wrong, but that they are only partially correct. Clearly young organizations are different from old ones. They have fewer institutionalized practices and are more entrepreneurial, creative, informal, and fragile. Similarly, a fifty person organization is very different from one that has fifty thousand, and there are major transitions along the way to the latter size. In reality, age, size, and complexity are confounded, and it is virtually impossible to disentangle their separate effects. All contribute to development. Which model one uses will vary to some extent with the questions that one is asking. Because we are interested in choices of strategy and structure, the complexity models are most relevant for our purposes.

In the next sections, we will review the most

relevant complexity models that have followed from Chandler's work, giving particular attention to the empirical studies that have also followed. We want to focus upon the following questions: What constitutes a stage in these developmental sequences? How many are there? Is the sequence unalterable? And how do you know one stage from another?

Chandler's work has been summarized and extended by Scott (1971), whose model was presented earlier in the chapter on contingency relations. The essence of the Chandler and Scott sequences is the successive addition of new sources of diversity which result in more complexity. Starting with the simple firm which is single product, single function, and single region, there are successive adoptions of multiple regions, then multiple functions, and finally multiple products as the firm becomes a Stage I, Stage II, and finally Stage III organization. The change from stage to stage constitutes a metamorphosis.

SALTER'S MODEL

The Scott model has been analyzed and extended by Salter (1970). He suggested that the Scott model misses two forms of organization and thereby also misses the possible alternative paths that can be taken through developmental sequences. For example, the multi-divisional forms that were adopted by General Motors and Du Pont were achieved through different transitions. General Motors was a holding company, while Du Pont was a Stage II functional organization. The holding company form is not in the model. In addition, Salter proposes that the geographic multidivisional form should be a separate stage. Thus, he splits Scott's Stage III form into a Stage 3, the geographic form, and a Stage 4, the product form. However, he does not include the holding company as a separate form or stage.

The Salter work raises the question of what constitutes a stage. A multidivisional structure around geographic areas is different from a multidivisional structure around product lines. But is it different enough to constitute a separate stage? How different must it be? How does one tell? Our view is that the geographic

profit center is not a separate stage. Although the transition from geographic to product divisionalized form or vice versa would require a major change in the power structure of an organization, it would not constitute a major change in the "way of life" in the organization. It is still a profit center or investment center of one dimension (i.e., product or region). The managerial style is still one of delegation of operations to the divisions, and rewards are based on bottom line results. There is nowhere near the magnitude of change that occurs in the change from a functional form to a profit center form. It is our contention that characteristics of structure, process, reward, and people are quite similar for all multidivisional forms regardless of what the one dimension is. That is, the multidivisional structure can be based upon products, regions, markets, industries and so on, and the "way of life" will be similar. That way of life will change only when other dimensions or sources of diversity are added, or when the geographic expansion is international rather than domestic.

STOPFORD'S MODEL

Another extension of the Scott model has been proposed by Stopford to account for the international expansion of American firms (Stopford, 1968; Stopford and Wells, 1972). Recall from our review of his work that he identified a two stage model involving international markets. First, the firms formed an international division and attached it to their domestic product divisions. Then the division was disbanded, and either worldwide product divisions or area divisions were adopted. Product divisions resulted from high foreign product diversification, and area divisions were adopted for low product diversity. However, Stopford did not suggest that these structural forms constituted a new stage. Instead he called them Stage III with an international division and Stage III other, meaning that the form could be product, area, or even some mixture of the two. The question naturally arises whether these two types are, in fact, stages IV and V, that is a type of organization genuinely different from Stage III domestic firms. Our view is that the international division is not a new stage. The addition of a new geographic division, even an international division, has about the same impact as the addition of new business or product division. The move to a global structure of either worldwide product divisions or area divisions poses a problem, however. On the one hand, the global structures are still uni-dimensional profit centers. On the other hand, the global structures are significant departures from the pure domestic multi-divisional structure. In addition, there is no single global form. An organization can be a global-divisional structure as already mentioned, a global holding company, or a global functional organization.

Our view is that the transition to a global form constitutes a metamorphosis. There are changes in the financial control system designed to handle such factors as national variations, profits by product and region, and transfer pricing. Different and multiple standards of evaluation appear; and compensation practices are changed; new committees and staffs evolve. Most important, an international mentality gets created to various degrees. All together, we feel these changes constitute a different "way of life" and therefore a different form.

The global form is not, however, a single distinct form like a functional or holding company form. There is no single global form. In its different manifestations, it resembles the multi-divisional forms which are all profit centers, but in which the profit center could be based on products, markets, or regions. Global structures can also assume any of those three multi-divisional forms, or they can take global, functional or a holding company form. In fact, Franko's descriptions of European mother-daughter forms are descriptions of global holding companies. Thus, we conceive of four different types of organization, each of which constitutes a distinct way of life — the simple, the functional, the holding company (or conglomerate), and the multi-divisional form. Each of these, but probably only the latter three, can exist in a domestic or in a global form. We prefer to talk about these eight possible organizations as forms rather than stages. All the forms are possible. Whether there are stages is in part an empirical question. Two studies have addressed themselves to this question.

STOPFORD AND FRANKO STUDIES

Two major empirical studies by Stopford and Wells (1972) and Franko (1974, 1976) have dealt with the stage of growth of American multi-nationals and European multi-nationals, respectively. These studies have both been discussed earlier in this paper. It is important at this point, however, to focus on their findings concerning the sequence of the stages. Exhibit 5.9 illustrates, comparatively, the sequence of both American and European multi-nationals (Franko, 1976).

The American multi-national's first phase in international growth is characterized by an initial period of autonomy for the foreign subsidiary. The second phase is a period of organizational consolidation when an international division is developed. The international division is typically considered an independent enterprise and is not subject to the same strategic planning that guides domestic activities. In the third phase, strategic planning is carried out on a consistent and worldwide basis, and the structure of the foreign activities is altered to provide closer links with the rest of the structure. As indicated by the chart, most American firms went through one of two major sequences of structural change. Either they moved from a functional Stage II structure to a divisional Stage III structure for their domestic businesses before adding an international division, or they added an international division to a domestic Stage III structure. The Exhibit also indicates that forty-nine of fifty-seven firms that replaced their international divisions did so after they had developed Stage III structures for their domestic activities. The few firms that moved directly from a Stage II structure with an international division to a global system are exceptions to the trend, and all of them adopted area divisions. According to Stopford and Wells (1972: 28):

Only twenty-four firms, or *14 percent of the 170 firms*, have moved directly from the phase of autonomous subsidiaries to a global structure without ever using an international

Exhibit 5.9 International Organizational Evolution of Multi-national Enterprise

Continental Multi-national Enterprise

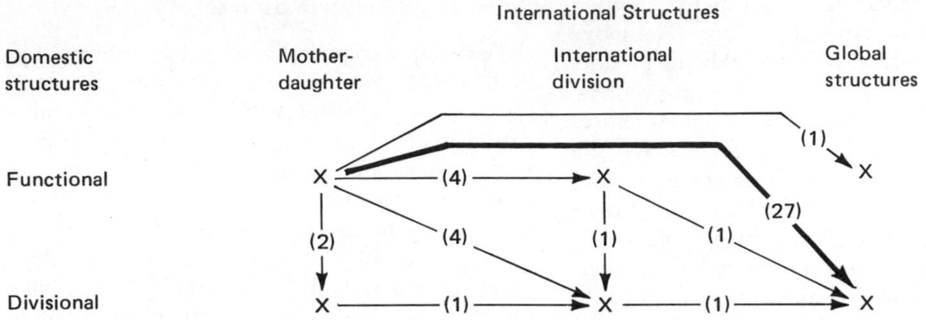

International Structures

American Multi-national Enterprise

International structures

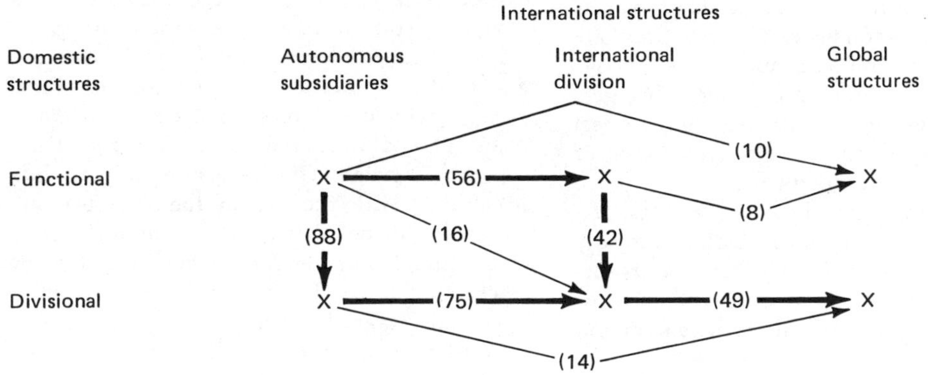

division. In almost every instance, these firms have expanded abroad primarily by acquisitions or mergers with other firms that had international interests.

Only six cases of firms reversing the directions of change shown in Exhibit 5.9 were observed. These reversals are associated with failures in the decentralized systems and with decisions to recentralize authority and to establish tighter controls.

Unlike American multi-nationals, the continental enterprises that adopted supranational organization structures typically did so after achieving a relatively large spread of multinational operations. Moreover, when the continental multi-nationals changed their organization structures, they also did so in a sequence very different from that followed by their American counterparts.

One sees that most continental firms simply skipped the international division phase passed through by nearly 90 percent of the 170 American multi-nationals surveyed by the Comparative Multi-national Enterprise Project. One also observes that in all but three cases, continental moves to the global forms of worldwide product divisions, area divisions, or mixed and matrix structures accompanied rather than followed divisionalization moves at home. In contrast, more than three-quarters of the American enterprises classified as multi-national saw fit to change their domestic organization structure from functional to divisional prior to adopting one of the so-called global structures.

In the competitive environment of their home market, American firms adapted their structures to their product diversification strategies. In practice, this meant that diversified American firms forsook functional for divisional organization structures well before they had had much of a chance to involve themselves in foreign operations.

Further examination of the data reveals some consistency between the European and American experiences. Those firms that did establish international divisions were French and German firms which came from large countries with large domestic markets. Also, if Europe is considered a single market, then many firms manage the rest of the world through an international division. Both these observations lend support to the international division stage, provided that there is a large domestic market.

In summary, these studies support the stagewise thesis of growth from a domestic functional organization to global multi-divisional structures. They also repeat Salter's assertion of alternate paths to worldwide structures. As organizations come from different sized countries, face domestic markets varying in competitiveness, and grow by acquisition rather than internally, they choose different but predictable paths to a similar final stage. However, the more detailed the specification of the stage, the less predictable the sequential movement. As long as we conceive of only three stages, with global forms considered to be a Stage III type, the stages of growth model holds. As soon as we consider other types of global structure or con-

sider substages such as the international division phase, more alternate paths appear, more outcomes are possible, and more detailed specifications of strategy, such as Rumelt's nine categories, are required to match strategy with structure and process.

A REVISED MODEL

In this section, we would like to offer our model of growth and development which summarizes the thinking of others and builds on the empirical evidence. The model is based upon several assumptions and empirical findings. First it is assumed that, starting with the simple form, any source of diversity could be added to move to a new form. There is no set sequence through which firms must move in lock steps. An organization could add functions, products, and geography and wind up with a global multi-divisional form along the way. Or it could add functions, geography, and products and still wind up with a global multi-divisional form, bypassing instead through functional and global functional forms as intermediate transitions. As a result of this assumption, alternate paths through the developmental sequence are possible. The comparison of American and European multi-nationals is a case in point.

Although there are possible alternative paths, a dominant sequence emerges empirically. Both Franko and Stopford report dominant sequences when multiple sequences are possible. This result is attributable in part to the effects of the environment. When faced with similar environments, firms choose to do similar things. The particular scenario that emerged consisted of specific patterns of population growth, economic growth, technological change, political changes, and world wars. Particular strategies resulting in particular structures proved to be profitable at various times. However, if a different scenario could have emerged, then a different dominant sequence would be observed. The point is that there is no set sequence; in all cases, however, development was dominated by the particular pattern of organization growth. Even though a pattern dominates, there are other routes taken by a minority of the firms.

Another feature of all developmental models is that an organization can stop anywhere along the way. Not every American organization is going to become a global, multi-divisional form. Also, a firm can reverse direction and retrace its steps. Some firms are busy selling off their international subsidiaries and could very well move back to a domestic multidivisional form.

Finally, the resulting structure of any sequence of development is, as Chandler suggested, a concatenation of all previous steps. If one examined global structure based on areas, one would find that, within an area, substructure is based on products. Within the product substructure, the organization could be market based by breaking out government and commercial sectors. Within a market sector, the substructure is probably functional. Thus each level of the hierarchy is a mechanism for coping with a source of diversity.

The resulting stages model is shown in Exhibit 5.10. The starting point is the simple structure with one function and product line. The first major structure change results from a growth in volume. The increased size brings about a division of labor and the simple functional organization to coordinate the divided work. From this structure several paths are possible. Some firms with crucial supply or distribution problems will pursue strategies of vertical integration. These firms will continue to elaborate their functional organization until they become large, centralized firms. The mining companies are good examples. Other organizations will diversify product lines through internal growth and acquisition. The internal developer tending to pursue a related diversification strategy will adopt the multi-divisional structure. The third path an organization can follow is to diversify through acquisition and pursue an unrelated diversification strategy. These firms would adopt a holding company or conglomerate form. In each case, the structure fits the strategy.

Although the next stages increase rapidly in number of possibilities, empirically there is a dominant movement. The majority of large enterprises have moved to the multi-divisional form either from a holding company type like General Motors, or from a functional form as did Du Pont. In the former case, the move is an attempt to consolidate acquisitions, exploit a source of relatedness, and switch to internal growth. The latter case is the classic example of a functional organization unable to manage diversity.

Two other possible paths are not observed in the particular sample of firms that make up the empirical study. The multi-divisional could change to the centralized functional form or to the holding company model. A firm could introduce standardization across related product lines and attempt to exploit economies of scale by moving to the functional organization. General Motors may be an example. In its automobile business, General Motors moved toward a functional organization by placing all manufacturing in a GM Assembly Division. Alternatively, the multi-divisional firm could pursue external growth and diversify into less related businesses. A transition to a holding company could occur if the new acquisitions are not integrated into the existing structure. The original core business will probably become an autonomous group managed from a small headquarters office that has been removed from its original location. There probably are examples of organizations not on the *Fortune* 500 that have followed these paths.

The next different stage of development for those organizations that choose to pursue strategies of international expansion is the global form. Most organizations will adopt either the area or product global form as indicated in the Stopford research. Global holding companies and global functional forms are possible too, although less likely.

In summary, firms do follow developmental sequences characterized by a metamorphosis between the stages. There is also a dominant path that has been followed by large American enterprises. However, alternative paths are possible. The multi-divisional form need not be Stage III. It can be Stage II for some firms who adopt a holding company form for Stage III. Thus, the model proposed here allows alternative paths, permitting organizations to stop at any form and even to reverse direction. The primary point of the discussion is to separate what has been observed in a biased sample from what is possible.

Exhibit 5.10 A Summary of Stages Model

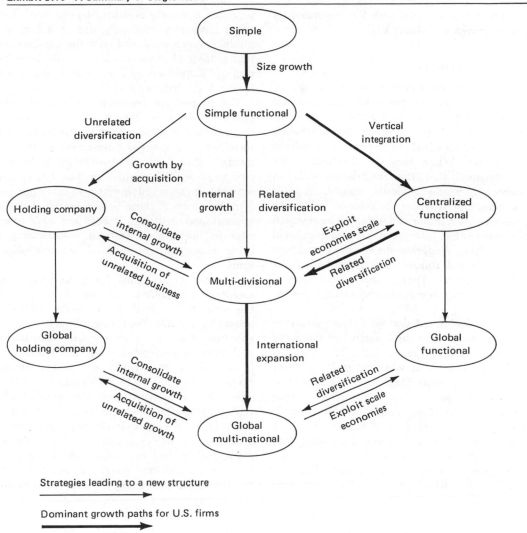

A second feature of the model is that it does identify some sequences of development. Not all paths are possible. An organization cannot move to a global form without passing through a domestic form as well. A simple organization cannot become a global multi-divisional without passing through at least one transitional form. That is, an organization must learn to manage one and two sources of diversity before handling a third. In this sense we can speak of stages, but we cannot equate any of the types of structure, after the simple structure, with a particular stage. Therefore, it is preferable to refer to types of organization form rather than to stages. Our model illustrating the organizational characteristics associated with five organization types is shown in Exhibit 5.11.

OVERVIEW OF RESEARCH

Many studies have been reviewed throughout this paper. In general, the thesis that structure follows strategy receives substantial support. Large American and European manufacturing and service enterprises are diversifying products and markets. When they do, they adopt the multi-divisional structure. The relation is shown in numerous studies. Clearly, something is at work here, but whether the relation is the one suggested by Chandler is not clear. The research has created other interpretations and additional variables that moderate the strategy-structure relation. We will follow the Scott and Chandler stages model here. There is no loss of general applicability as a result of substituting type for stage.

Chandler suggested that the Stage I structure was invented to solve the problems of the Stage I strategy (volume expansion). The Stage II structure was invented when Stage I structures could not manage the Stage II strategies, and so on. Thus, effective performance is achieved only when Stage N strategy is matched with Stage N structure. When management adopts an $N + 1$ strategy, there is a decline in performance that provokes the shift to the $N + 1$ structure, which then increases performance. This sequence depicts the events at Du Pont that were described by Chandler. The observed lags in changes to multi-divisional forms following diversification also fit the interpretation. Thus, a mismatch in strategy and structure causes a decline in performance that is restored when a match is finally achieved.

The direct tests of this hypothesis have not been conclusive and are subject to alternative explanations. Rumelt ran into difficulty, because he could not always find mismatches in sufficient numbers to permit statistical tests. This fact could be taken as data that natural selection is at work forcing mismatches into matches. But the fact may be attributed to other factors, such as imitation of other organizations. In addition, the mismatches, although few in number,

are sometimes the high performers. This observation is usually explained by the firm's having a temporary monopoly due to a hot, new product. When combined with the European research these observations lead to the introduction of competition as a moderating variable in the strategy-structure relation.

The proposition becomes: Only under competitive conditions does a mismatch between strategy and structure lead to ineffective performance. If a firm has power over its environment so that it can control prices because of monopoly position, tariffs, or close ties to government, it can maintain effective economic performance even if there is a mismatch between strategy and structure. It does not have to engage in the difficult task of restructuring to bring about efficient internal resource allocations.

A couple of scenarios for firms under noncompetitive conditions are possible to augment the scenario put forth by Chandler and illustrated by the Du Pont case. One is that the adoption of an $N + 1$ strategy does not lead to a decline in performance at all. Thus, there is no motive for structural change. Second, there may be a decline in performance that is restored not by restructuring, but by influencing relevant actors in the environment. Thus, the relation is not always a simple sequential process of change of strategy, decline in performance, restructuring, and restoration of performance. The relation becomes instead a complicated interplay between strategy, structure, performance, and competitiveness of markets.

The second scenario raises another possible sequence of events. Under competitive conditions, an $N + 1$ strategy and a Stage N structure will lead to a decline in performance. The interesting question is, What is the response of the organization to the information about performance? Presumably, performance can be restored either through restructuring or by influencing relevant actors in the environment. A third alternative is to return to the Stage N strategy and abandon the unfamiliar Stage $N + 1$. Conceivably, this third alternative may also restore performance.

The three possible scenarios, which could follow from a performance decline due to a mis-

Exhibit 5.11 Model Illustrating Five Organizational Types

Type / Characteristic	(S) Simple	(F) Functional	(H) Holding	(M) Multi-divisional	(G) Global—(M)
Strategy	Single product	Single product and vertical integration	Growth by acquisition unrelated diversity	Related diversity of product lines—internal growth, some acquisition	Multiple products in multiple countries
Interunit and market relations					
Organization structure	Simple functional	Central functional	Decentralized profit centers around product divisions, small headquarters	Decentralized product or area division profit centers	Decentralized profit centers around world-wide product or area divisions
Research and development	Not institutionalized random search	Increasingly institutionalized around product and process improvements	Institutionalized search for new products and improvements—decentralized to divisions	Institutionalized search for new products and improvements—centralized guidance	Institutionalized search for new products which is centralized and decentralized in centers of expertise
Performance measurement	By personal contact subjective	Increasingly impersonal based on cost, productivity but still subjective	Impersonal based on return on investment and profitability	Impersonal, based on return on investment profitability with some subjective contribution to whole	Impersonal with multiple goals like ROI, profit tailored to product and country
Rewards	Unsystematic, paternalistic based on loyalty	Increasingly related to performance around productivity and volume	Formula based bonus on ROI or profitability, Equity rewards	Bonus based on profit performance but more subjective than holding—cash rewards	Bonus based on multiple planned goals. More discretion. Cash rewards.
Careers	Single function specialist	Functional specialists with some generalist interfunctional moves	Cross-function but intra-divisional	Cross-functional interdivisional and corporate-divisional moves	Interdivisional. Intersubsidiary. Subsidiary/corporate moves.
Leader style and control	Personal control of strategic and operating decisions by top management	Top control of strategic decisions. Some delegation of operations through plans, procedures	Almost complete delegation of operations and strategy within existing businesses. Indirect control through results and selection of management and capital funding	Delegation of operations with indirect control through results. Some decentralization of strategy within existing businesses.	Delegation of operations with indirect control through results according to plan. Some delegation of strategy within countries and existing businesses. Some political delegation.
Strategic choices	Need of owner vs. needs of firm	Degree of integration. Market share. Breadth of product line	Degree of diversity. Types of businesses. Acquisition targets. Entry and exit from businesses	Allocation of resources by business. Exit and entry from businesses. Rate of growth.	Allocation of resources across businesses and countries. Exit and entry into businesses and countries. Degree of ownership and type of country. Involvement.

match, introduce another relevant variable — the power distribution among the top managers. Undoubtedly, proponents for all three alternatives can be found inside the firm. The functional vice-presidents will favor a return to the dominant business, whereas the younger managers with cross-functional experience and MBAs will favor reorganization to the multidivisional form. Both positions are self-serving. In the absence of a clear-cut solution, the chosen alternative is the result of political processes. The greater the ambiguity, the greater the influence of politics in determining the outcome and the greater the influence of the current distribution of power. Thus, structure will influence strategy. It is also for this reason that a change in the chief executive is often needed to bring about the change in strategy and structure. The current organization has institutionalized the previous strategy, and role occupants stand to lose status and power by adopting a new strategy and, therefore, a new structure.

Thus, the complete explanation of the relation between strategy and structure must consider a number of other factors. Exhibit 5.12 introduces these factors and illustrates some likely

Exhibit 5.12   Schematic of Possible Strategy, Structure, and Performance Relations

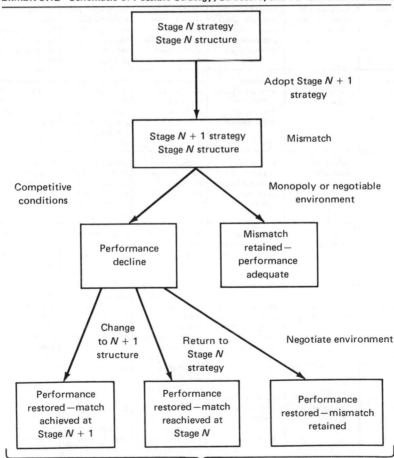

Result of political processes among top managers

scenarios that can follow each condition. An adequate understanding requires knowledge of market conditions, performance, and the relative power of the dominant managers. An historical perspective of the individual firm is required in order to untangle the interplay of these various factors.

The schematic shown in Exhibit 5.12 and the discussion in the paragraph above raise the issue of influence of structure upon strategy formulation. In the developmental sequence of: Strategy I → Structure I → Strategy II → Structure II → Strategy III → Structure III, Chandler focused upon the relation between Stage N Structure and Stage $N + 1$ Strategy. Strategy can follow structure, also! Perhaps structure or organization can explain why some Stage II organizations adopted Stage III strategies, and some did not. If Stage II strategy is matched with Stage II structure, why change? Chandler suggests that changes are a response to the need to employ resources more profitably because of shifts and growth in population, changes in technology, and so on. But if you are already profitable, why do something unfamiliar? Some recent work by Miles and Snow (1978) begins to look at that question. They focus on the values and attitudes of the dominant management group. The management groups are then classified into types such as prospectors, adapters, defenders, and so on. The prospectors are managers who see environments as turbulent and act accordingly, thereby causing in part the turbulence that they see. Adapters are not the seekers of opportunity that prospectors are but will, as their name implies, change as they are forced to do so. They do not initiate, however. The defenders are those who stick to their dominant business and defend it. They see stability and arrange their environment so that it remains stable. How an organization reacts depends upon which of these groups holds the levers of power and what are the objective industry conditions. Successful organizations can be found among all groups. The important point here is that there must be consistency between strategy and all elements of the structure. It is not really important whether structure causes strategy, or vice versa, but whether they are

eventually brought into line. There are many causal sequences in which change of strategy may precede change of structure. Or, performance may decline, precipitating first a strategy change and then a structure change. Or, structure may be changed first, in order to bring in new managers who will formulate the new strategy. There is no simple one-to-one relation.

SUMMARY

The point of this elaboration is to move us beyond a simple one-to-one relation such as structure follows strategy. Clearly, there are times when it does, but there are also times when it does not. Our purpose here was to identify a few factors that elaborate the relation without unduly complicating it, so that we can understand the choices available. Each factor (strategy, structure, and competition) has been shown to have its own independent effect upon performance. We wanted to identify when their combined effects were more important than each factor alone. The interaction of performance data and the power distribution among managers are the processes by which the alignment between the factors takes place.

Our position is, "It doesn't matter what you do, just so long as you do it well." That is, there are multiple solutions to any situation. What is important is to choose one of those solutions and pursue it. The firm should match its structure to its strategy, match all the components of the organization with one another, and match the strategy with the environment. The challenge is to understand, to learn how to manage, and to learn how to talk about the power dynamics that take place in the determination of the chosen strategy and structure. When stakes are high, when capable people win and lose and some people are hurt, these are crucial choices. The choices require greater understanding from theoretical, practical and ethical perspectives.

Commentary

LEONARD WRIGLEY
University of Western Ontario

INTRODUCTION

Every progressive society is confronted with the question how better to accommodate individual drives for self-achievement with the advantages of cooperative effort (specialization, profitable transaction between people, social élan, etc.). The problem, fundamentally, arises from scarcity of resources and the difficulty men have in trusting their fellow men. The question immediately is how to develop those institutions that best provide the necessary accommodations.

No society starts with a blank sheet of paper. Hence, "to develop institutions" means just that: how to attend to the existing arrangements to better balance the claims of the individual with the needs for social action. For Western societies, this has meant how to develop the structures either of the market, or of the corporation, or both.

Part of the answer has been to provide for scholarly research on such structures. Today, each Western society contains schools of economics, where the structure of markets is studied, and schools of business administration, where the structure of the corporation is studied. Thus, those responsible for developing the market or the corporation are not, or are no longer, without scholarly advice.

This paper will discuss Galbraith and Nathanson's survey of empirical research in the area of organizational structure. Galbraith and Nathanson also surveyed research on other aspects of strategy implementation, including the design of organization processes and organization evolution. These will not be discussed in this commentary in order to permit fuller discussion of the structural research they reported. In total, Galbraith and Nathanson examined some 40 recent studies on structure. They noted that almost all these studies had been stimulated by or derived from Chandler's now classic work *Strategy and Structure: Chapters in the History of the American Industrial Enter-*

prise (1962). To Galbraith and Nathanson three aspects in Chandler seemed particularly influential, namely:

1. The proposition that structure follows strategy;
2. The stages of corporate growth and development model;
3. Chandler's documentation of the proposition and model using data from "*Fortune* 500 enterprises."

However, Galbraith and Nathanson were concerned not only with the similarities, but also the differences between the various later research studies on organizational structure and that of Chandler. Consequently, Galbraith and Nathanson's survey could also be entitled "Similarities and Differences in Recent Studies of Corporate Organizational Structure."

The purpose of this paper is twofold. First, to arrive at a judgment on the state of the art in organizational studies in Business Policy. Second, to consider what new developments may be expected in research in this area over the next decade. Although this was also Galbraith's and Nathanson's objective, this paper reaches slightly different conclusions by focusing more intensively than Galbraith and Nathanson did on the following four related themes: (1) the similarity of thinking of all recent research on organizational structure, Chandler included; (2) the influence of Chandler's work on more recent research on organizational structure; (3) the differences in the viewpoints of recent research on organizational structure, Chandler included, and (4) the differences between Chandler's view and those of all other recent researchers on organizational structure.

SIMILARITIES IN THINKING ABOUT ORGANIZATIONAL STRUCTURE

There are important similarities between all the recent researchers on strategy and structure in the way they thought about organizations. All, even those who were case oriented, arranged their data in some kind of a pattern. This is not to say they were dogmatic, along the lines, say of Fayol or Taylor or Urwick, about the dominant role of principles in organization — principles which are both fixed and pervasive — according to which corporate management should or does develop organizations by a set of rigid rules. The notion of principles of this kind has been rejected in all the recent studies; but the contrary notion of bare facts — facts which are nothing but facts, hard, inescapable, untainted by arrangements in man-made patterns — has also been rejected. Rather, all the researchers have arranged, classified, and contrasted their data, have seen patterns of lesser or greater complexity in their arrangements, and have regarded their efforts not as a peculiar kind of thinking, but as thinking itself.

All these researchers recognized the "situational" validity of their ideas about structure. If and when they accused their colleagues of bias or distortion, or of too weak a sense of evidence, they did so not on some notion of an absolute standard of truth, valid at all times, everywhere, for all organizations, in a timeless and universal sense, but because their colleague's ideas deviated too far, or contrasted too harshly with their own ideas or with their own canons of verification and interpretation. Each researcher accepted that he was in bondage to some Idol of history, or Tribe, or even of a Cave, but seemed not greatly tolerant of other Idols, or of those who were in bondage to these other Idols.

All the researchers used an open system model of the corporation (I exclude Boulding here) which means the profession as a whole has transferred emphasis from study of internal organizational interactions to interactions between an organization and its environment. However, the new kind of studies, for example, Lawrence and Lorsch's (1967) study of the relationship between environmental uncertainty and organizational structure, are not necessarily less or more detailed or accurate than earlier studies, such as Woodward's (1965) investigation of the relationships between types of tech-

nology and characteristics of organizational structure. The more recent studies have been written merely from a different perspective, a different concern with what goes with what, reflecting a shift of interest in the question asked and, consequently, in the models used.

In sum, all the new concepts and methodologies spring from no single or permanent source. Some researchers have made a successful attempt to adapt a technique developed originally in another branch of human enquiry, such as biology or physics, while others have developed their own concepts and techniques. All have been influenced in lesser or greater measure by Chandler, but none have been dominated by him. Given the common use of open systems models, a similarity of the various writers turns out to be the diversity of their source of ideas.

Yet it is also true that in their thinking about organizations, none of the researchers have been wholly capricious. None have merely borrowed techniques developed in other fields. All are part of a tradition — comparative studies that consider differences as well as similarities in social actions (which can be traced, historically, to Montesquieu's *The Spirit of the Laws*, written in the early eighteenth century) — and use the tradition to derive patterns relevant to new problems and to new methodologies.

THE INFLUENCE OF CHANDLER

A correlation is not a structural relationship, however. Certain similarities between Chandler and later researchers must be attributed either to a common heritage (already considered) or a common environment. In the late 1950's, the time Chandler wrote, the notion of economic growth through conscious effort and planning had already seized the popular imagination. This was the era of determinism or historical inevitability or at least of regularity in patterns of human progress; and this was the age when bigger meant better. What Chandler provided the literature was a way of expressing ideas which many were groping toward; and this he did with style.

But Chandler did more than just express the

organizational concerns of his time. He wove together a multiplicity of factors shaping the modern corporation during the middle years of the twentieth century. His influence was not just a proposition ("structure follows strategy"), nor a model ("stages of corporate growth and development"), nor a methodology (case studies in a framework provided by 70 large enterprises), but all three, which at once provided policy research with both respectability and an example.

The breadth and depth of Chandler's influence can be seen by reference to Exhibit 5.13, which traces the influence relationships between

30 studies, 25 of which are discussed in more depth by Galbraith and Nathanson.

Clearly, the relationships between researchers depicted in Exhibit 5.13 are simplified, but if the pattern is not an aid to specialist enquiry, neither can it be dismissed entirely. What the Exhibit illustrates most effectively is that Chandler's ideas affected entire schools of thought and not just the thinking of individual writers, i.e., Chandler's influence was both direct, and — through interpretation of others — indirect. Thus, his work, *Strategy and Structure: Chapters in the History of the American Industrial Enterprise,* can truly be said to con-

Exhibit 5.13   Relationships of Chandler to Other Writers of Organizational Studies in Recent Times

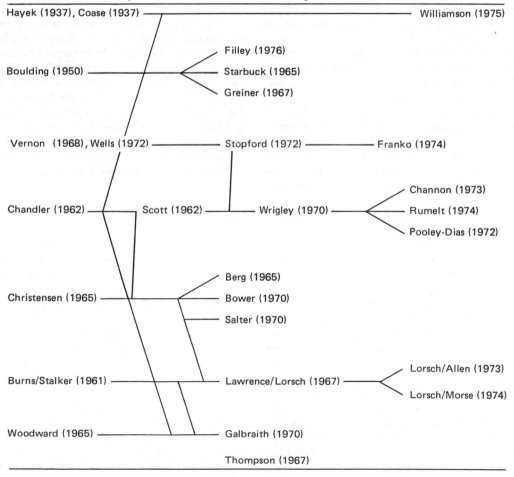

stitute a watershed between an old world, where firms were seen merely to respond to their environment, and a new world, where firms were seen to act upon and in measure shape their environment.

DIFFERENCES AMONG RESEARCHERS

If the similarities among researchers are important, the differences are no less profound. Immediately, these differences can be traced to background, interests, and schools:

1. Williamson, an economist, is concerned with comparing the market and the corporation as alternative systems for enabling transactions among people under conditions of uncertainty, with his roots in Coase, Hayek (and Thirlby?) of the London School of Economics.

2. Starbuck, Filley, and Greiner are building models of growth, and may be seen as rooted in Boulding, with his (biological) life cycle model of the firm.

3. Scott, Wrigley, Stopford, and Rumelt are most central with Chandler, yet here distinctions are also necessary. Scott's *An Open Systems Model of the Firm* (1962), which was to impact on Wrigley, owes much to Christensen (and to Homans and Rostow), but nothing to Chandler, although Scott's later work on stages of growth was strongly influenced by Chandler. Wrigley combined transaction cost theory from the London School of Economics with Scott's open system model to develop the notion of "core skill" from which he generated various categories of multi-divisional firms' strategies and structures. Stopford next added the methodology for documenting mathematically the general propositions of Business Policy, while Rumelt brought in management science and consulting skills to take Chandler, perhaps, to its ultimate destination.

4. Bower, Berg and Salter, by contrast, were concerned with the effects the subtle interplay of human ambitions, vision, and skills had on the way resources were allocated within the organizational framework of multi-divisional enterprise, and to this extent, they are the strongest force behind the notion that it is strategy which follows structure. Although indirect, Christensen certainly had great influence here.

5. Lawrence and Lorsch and also Galbraith and Nathanson owe much of their frameworks to Burns and Stalker, and are in a research stream going back to Woodward with her interest in different technological states, and the impact of this on the organization.

6. Thompson, a sociologist, is opposite to Williamson in theoretical base (soft vs. hard concepts), though sharing a common interest in environment and organization interactions and in experiments using original conceptual apparatus.

Fundamentally, the differences between and among these writers can be traced to a distinction which seems to divide all schools of management thought, and, it may be, scholars in general. This is the distinction between those who believe in the ability of a single unified (meta) theory to explain how an organization, and, perhaps man in general, works, and, those who are concerned with solving real world management problems and who will use whatever model or theory or system that will aid them in their endeavors. Chandler, Scott, Wrigley and Rumelt are examples of the problem solving theorists and researchers in the organizational structure area while, at the other extreme, Williamson and Thompson are the system builders, the conceptualizers par excellence for the implementation area.

Of course, this distinction, if pursued, becomes simplistic, and, ultimately, absurd, but those who miss it entirely, e.g., those who think only of the distinction between case oriented and discipline oriented writers or schools, miss out on an important division within the field.

SOME UNIQUENESSES OF CHANDLER

This final section will explore some unique aspects of Chandler's work that have not yet, with minor exceptions, been reflected in the work of those who followed him. Allow me to start with an analogy. It makes a point.

Leo Tolstoy, in one of those sermons which are more often in his writing than is usually supposed, opened the novel *Anna Karenina* with the words: "Happy families are all alike; each unhappy family is unhappy in its own particular way." Like all his sermons, this one is exactly what Tolstoy believed, and exactly the opposite of what he saw and described in his writings. Happy families, like happy — that is to say important — scholars, tend to have an individuality of their own which cannot be emulated.

As already mentioned, later researchers have followed Chandler with respect to his proposition, his model and his methods of documentation. Yet, while these later researchers cannot follow all aspects of Chandler's work, there are two particular aspects of his approach which seem important, appear transportable, but have not yet been taken by other studies. These are his concern for the impact of environmental discontinuities on organizational states, and his historical concept of man.

Both these aspects seem central to Chandler's theme, and are interrelated. He takes environmental discontinuities, such as an economic slump, and dwells carefully on the role of the general manager attempting to overcome organizational resistance to the changes in strategy and structure needed to meet these discontinuities. His descriptions of these moments are rich in the multiplicity of detail and awareness of feelings, and present to the reader the challenge of an unusual and sustained experience. Without such descriptions, *Strategy and Structure* would be dull and lifeless — the description of proposition and model take their meaning and significance from the context.

The difference here between Chandler and other writers, with perhaps the exception of Bower and Galbraith, is significant. Comparisons between two different environmental states (e.g., certain and uncertain) and two different organizational structures (e.g., authoritative and participative) are of a different kind than Chandler's complex and rich descriptions, especially with respect to the roles of general management. Thus, it is necessary to insist that there are important distinctions to be made between a study of organizational change and a

study of two different organizations, i.e., between longitudinal and cross sectional studies. Quite simply, only longitudinal studies, i.e., studies of organizational change in response to an environmental discontinuity can portray the general manager in significant creative achievement.

Curiously, a number of case studies written about the time Chandler was completing his work, in the early 1960's, also picked the theme of the role of general managers changing their organization in response to environmental discontinuity. The Midway Foods, Grangesberg, and International Manufacturing Company cases provide the obvious examples. (Christensen and Scott were the principal case writers for these cases.) Since then, this theme seems to have disappeared, both from research and case writing, although at the University of Western Ontario, both Thain and Little have picked it up again, Thain with respect to firms in Canada, and Little with respect to a firm in Sweden. Yet, in thinking of increased government or worker impact on the environment, the theme seems of continued relevance. Perhaps the reason for the disappearance has been the retirement to limbo of the historical concept of man, at least as a manager.

CONCLUSION

This paper has attempted to present the similarities and differences of recent organizational studies — using Chandler as a landmark — to enable an assessment of the "state of the art" and to consider what to expect and hope for in the future.

If the Galbraith-Nathanson list is representative, and it appears to be, then the area is in good shape, both in terms of recent progress, and in comparison with other areas. True, much of the research is not as centrally concerned with the role, or of the practical problems of general managers as some would wish, but this may reflect the difficulty of research and model building with multiple variables, in ill structured situations, rather than lack of concern for the general management viewpoint. If a definite fault had to be identified, a real candidate is the lack of interaction between schools of thought. Perhaps, Chandler's influence was too strong for easy interaction; but, it seems to me more conceptual progress would have been made had more attention been paid to what other writers from other schools had achieved. Instead, we have been a successful, but a jealous breed of scholar; a little intolerant of Idols other than our own. Such is my assessment.

We can expect in the future that the general similarity will continue in our thinking about organization–comparative studies, over time or between institutions — for we all draw on the same traditions, and it has served us well. But the basis of comparison might change from inter-firms to market/corporation comparisons. My reasoning here is twofold. First, the era of market inefficiency/corporate efficiency seems ending, and the big question may be identification of the truly distinctive competence of organizational relationships vis-à-vis market relationships, as now attempted theoretically by Williamson, and empirically by Crookell/Killing/Wrigley. Second, both Williamson's *Markets and Hierarchies* (1975) and Wrigley's *Transactions in Technology* (1975) have enabled both the fast track doctoral thesis and new conceptual development, a combination which traditionally has proven compellingly attractive. I would expect also a retreat from the notion of "a science of man" with its deterministic connotations and a move to the middle ground of a search for regularities and common patterns among populations of firms (hopefully not all large firms), in regard to organizational change. Such are my expectations.

I would hope for more problem related, longitudinal research particularly on patterns of organizational/general management response to environmental discontinuities — especially those promoted by political and social forces — for here there exists both a lacuna in the literature and a high probability of the existence of major management problems. It would be good if there was more concern with the real problems of today rather than the hypothetical problems confronting "tomorrow" — confronting our children, or our children's children (children, I might add, who are not yet born, and who might never be born). The essence of Business Policy/General Management/Strategic Management is concern for corporate survival and growth over the short (five year) term, and there, one would hope, is where we have to be concerned — for if not us, who?

Commentary

John B. Miner
Georgia State University

The major theme integrating the various components of the Galbraith and Nathanson paper is the theory of strategy-structure-people fit. This theory, which also has been considered by the senior author elsewhere (Galbraith, 1977), is as yet somewhat loosely defined, a not surprising state of affairs in view of its tremendous scope — ranging from business policy to personality theory.

The basic assumption of the theory is that there are certain fits or congruencies between types of strategies, organizational forms, and the personality characteristics of organization members which are necessary if an organization is to cope with its environment in an effective manner. Accordingly, it is a normative theory. Although the theory in its present form does not indicate in detail the exact nature of the fits needed to achieve organizational effectiveness under various environmental conditions, Galbraith and Nathanson, drawing on a very comprehensive literature review, have performed an extremely valuable service by delineating at least some of the relationships that should be built into such a theory. Thus, a framework has been developed and we are well down the road "toward a theory," if not actually at the point of true "scientific theory." Furthermore, the names and works of some of the major contributors to both the policy/strategy field and the organization theory field have been marshalled in support of this approach.

Against this background it appears appropriate to take critical stock of the theory in order to avoid, if possible, investing further time and resources in extensive research which ultimately might yield only a very small payoff. Based on the current evidence does strategy-structure-people fit theory appear to offer a viable framework for understanding strategy implementation and organizational functioning? The following discussion cannot hope to deal with this question in its totality. However, consideration will be given to some of the key research findings that bear on the validity of the theory, and to their interpretation.

Ideally, of course, the relevant research would deal with the full range of the theory. Not surprisingly, however, the tendency has been to consider limited components and linkages. Thus, a particular strategy has been studied in relation to a particular organization structure, or alternatively, a specific structure has been related to the characteristics of those who operate within it.

THE LORSCH AND MORSE RESEARCH

The major study designed to deal with the full range of the theory, although not explicitly with strategies, is that conducted by Lorsch and Morse (1974). This study was concerned with environmental uncertainty levels, organizational structure and process, and personality characteristics of organization members as related to unit effectiveness in five companies. In two of these companies, manufacturing plants were studied (certain environments) and, in the other three, research laboratories were studied (uncertain environments). The *personality variables* considered did not differentiate within types of

organizations, but they did differentiate types of organizations (and by implication levels of uncertainty faced). The findings were as follows:

Research (uncertain)		Manufacturing (certain)
High	Integrative complexity	Low
High	Tolerance for ambiguity	Low
High	Independence of authority	Low
High	Individualism	Low

Furthermore, a number of *structure and process variables* were found to differentiate high and low performing units within organization types. The *more effective* units were found to be characterized as shown on page 291.

Quite evidently there are real differences between the two contexts. These are attributed by Lorsch and Morse to the degree of fit between levels of uncertainty of environments (and by implication to strategies for dealing with certainty-uncertainty), organizational structures, and people characteristics. Where the fit is good, one gets high performance; otherwise one does not.

However, there is an alternative, and more parsimonious explanation. The research profession per se attracts people who are characterized by integrative complexity, tolerance for ambiguity, independence of authority, and individualism, whereas manufacturing does not. There is considerable prior evidence to support this conclusion (Pelz and Andrews, 1966; Barron, 1969). The effective research units, furthermore, appear to have relied strongly on professional norms to induce and control individual efforts toward goal achievement. The less effective research units appear to have confounded the already existing professional system of norms by adding in a sizable amount of hierarchic pressures as well. That this should create role conflict and lower performance levels is entirely consistent with the research findings of Szilagyi, Sims, and Keller (1976).

The effective manufacturing plants, on the other hand, clearly placed strong reliance on

Research (uncertain)	Manufacturing (certain)
High concern for scientific goals	High concern for efficiency and productivity goals
Low formality of structure	High formality of structure
High influence at the professional level	High influence at the top of the hierarchy
Highly participative supervision	Highly directive supervision
Low levels of coordination	High levels of coordination
High use of confrontation to resolve conflict	High use of confrontation to resolve conflict
High sense of competence	High sense of competence
Long time orientation	
High reliance on professional standards	

hierarchic authority to induce goal contributions. The data Lorsch and Morse present appear to indicate that the low performing manufacturing plants are often characterized by a basically laissez-faire approach, where strong inducements of any kind are lacking. Extrapolation from research on leadership would indicate that just such performance problems should occur in a laissez-faire context (Stogdill, 1974). In addition, there is some basis in the data for concluding that, on occasion, low performance in the manufacturing context was associated with a confounding of a hierarchic authority system with an inducement system which made strong use of group norms and pressures (participative decision making of a kind) to induce contributions. Again, the potential for role conflict was sizable, and the likelihood that this contributed to the performance deficiencies considerable.

Accordingly, the results of the study can be explained in terms of such variables as inducement systems, role conflict, laissez-faire, and personality constructs without recourse to an added level of environmental variables and the strategies to deal with them. This is not to say that this has been shown to be the correct interpretation, only that it is more parsimonious and thus probably theoretically desirable to do so.

THE STRATEGY-STRUCTURE RESEARCH

The pioneering work of Chandler (1962) is often cited in support of strategy-structure-people fit theory or at least in support of the linkage of the first two types of variables. Chandler's conclusions ultimately emerge as both descriptive theory, indicating an essential causal link running from strategy to structure, and normative theory as well. The work is an admirable example of creative, inductive theory building, but the data cited by Chandler cannot be used to test the theory, since the theory grew out of them. To draw on Chandler's own findings for validation of his theory is to engage in self-fulfilling prophecy post hoc.

Yet as Galbraith and Nathanson indicate, subsequent research offers only very limited support of Chandler's hypothesis. Descriptively, certain product and market strategies do appear to go with certain structural forms, but the nature of the causal relationships is uncertain; any of three possibilities may be operative:

Strategy ⟶ Structure

Structure ⟶ Strategy

A third variable (x) ⟶ Strategy and structure

A likely source of x over the period of much of the strategy-structure research is the influence of the large international management consulting firms, which have been espousing and introducing both product diversification strategies and product-line divisionalization structures throughout the industrialized world for many years.

Furthermore, there is little support for the normative form of the theory, that strategy-structure fit causes success and that nonfit is likely to result in failure. As Galbraith and Nathanson note, the major study conducted to test this proposition (Rumelt, 1974) yields equivocal results against profitability criteria. Again the theory cannot be totally rejected on empirical grounds, but neither can it be accepted, at least as of the present time.

THE LAWRENCE-LORSCH-ALLEN RESEARCH

Another major line of evidence adduced in favor of the strategy-structure component of the theory is the research conducted by Lawrence and Lorsch (1967) and Lorsch and Allen (1973). The basic hypothesis of these studies is that those strategies required to cope with uncertainty in the environment create a need for differentiation of structure and integration, if profitability is to be attained.

Although the authors generally interpret their data as supporting this hypothesis, their statistical data are not entirely consistent with such a conclusion. Thus, in the Lawrence and Lorsch study, among six plastics firms operating in uncertain environments, the relationships of performance levels to the rankings of the firms on differentiation of structure and integration were as follows:

Performance	Differentiation	Integration
High	1	1
High	4	2
Medium	5	3
Medium	2.5	4
Low	2.5	5
Low	6	6

It is apparent that integration levels are strongly related to performance, but differentiation is much more weakly related, if at all. Furthermore, other data indicate that the relationship between integration and performance noted above holds irrespective of the degree of uncertainty characterizing industry environment, i.e., integration is associated with profitability whether or not a company develops strategies to cope with environmental uncertainty.

Lorsch and Allen report a highly significant correlation between integration scores and division performance for sixteen divisions in four conglomerates; the value is .62. However, their differentiation scores show no significant relationship to performance. Similarly, a comparison of the same departments in two paper companies indicated higher integration as characteristic of the more profitable firm, but no differences in differentiation. Subsequent analyses indicated that the conglomerates faced much greater environmental uncertainty than the paper companies. Yet the pattern of success being associated with integration, but not differentiation, is characteristic of both contexts.

Taken as a whole the Lawrence-Lorsch-Allen research provides little support for the concept of environmental-structural fit and thus, by implication, little support for strategy-structure fit. What it does show is a very marked association between extent of integration and profitable performance, irrespective of environmental conditions.

AN EXPLANATION OF STRUCTURAL ADVANTAGES

If the fit with strategy is not used to explain the widespread effectiveness of the divisionalized structure for large firms, and in particular divisionalization which emphasizes related businesses having a common theme (Scott, 1973; Hofer, 1976), how can such structural effectiveness be explained?

The major problem for the holding company or federated form, often a conglomerate whose growth has occurred through the acquisition of unrelated businesses, appears to be that of laissez-faire leadership. It is very difficult to maintain the kind of appropriate controls that are needed for success in this kind of structure (Khandwalla, 1973; Negandhi, 1975). Yet if controls are not maintained, the performance effects of laissez-faire management can be anticipated.

The functional structure, on the other hand, tends to foster highly cohesive groups at the top levels of the organization. In some cases, these groups form around existing professional norms and, in other cases, they generate their own value systems. In either case, pronounced clique formation tends to occur. As the organization grows to substantial size and these cliques are represented at the highest levels, the cliques grow in size and take on sufficient power so that their internal norms and values (professional and/or group) become major competitors with the hierarchic system of authority and sanctions. The result is not only role conflict for many key individuals in the organization, but overt intergroup conflict at the top which saps the organization of energy needed for goal accomplishment.

The strength of the divisionalized structure, with sufficiently closely related businesses that corporate management can truly understand them all, is that the hierarchic inducements to goal directed behavior can be maintained without basic threats to their effectiveness. Laissez-faire conditions are less likely because corporate management can retain adequate information to know what and how to control without overload. Conflict from professional and functional group norms is less likely because these individuals are pushed down in the system to less powerful positions and because they are separated from each other, thus reducing opportunities for clique formation.

These interpretations are not proven by existing data, but they do explain the findings at the purely organizational level through resort to concepts such as a lack of adequate inducements to channel energy to organizational goals, or conflicting inducements. They do not require adding the less parsimonious and more cumbersome strategy fit hypothesis to the formulations. They also suggest that the divisionalized structure should prove effective in implementing a variety of strategies given sufficient organizational size. Thus, a single product, high market share strategy, although perhaps not as desirable in itself as a strategy, would be expected to be *best implemented* through the use of multiple geographical or customer-type divisions.

STRUCTURE-PEOPLE FIT

In contrast to the rather shaky status of the strategy-structure part of the theory, the structure-people aspect seems to have considerable empirical support. The Galbraith and Nathanson paper reviews much of the data, but there are two other lines of evidence that should be considered.

Organizational structures have been classified in numerous ways, but a particularly fruitful approach appears to be to classify them in terms of the method used to induce or channel motivational effort toward organizational goals (Miner, 1975, 1978). Four different types of inducement systems have been identified as important for organizational performance and, in each instance, key individuals or groups of individuals can be designated whose personalities must fit the structure if the organization is to be effective.

The first and most widely used inducement approach is hierarchic. If relies upon legitimized authority and the manipulation of sanctions to achieve its ends. The formal bureaucracy is the predominant manifestation, as used, for instance, in the successful manufacturing plants described by Lorsch and Morse (1974). The key people are the managers since they must orchestrate the authority and sanctions that make the organization function.

A second source of inducement is the profession and the norms and values which are instilled in and guide its members. Professional norms serve to channel organizational energy most effectively in the professional organization structure or, as in the case of the more effective research laboratories described by Lorsch and Morse (1974), a truly professional unit of a hierarchic organization. The key people for the professional norm based structure are the full-fledged professionals and, in particular, those senior professionals whose behavior most closely matches the values of the professional system.

Exhibit 5.14 Significant Relationships between Motivation to Manage and its Components and Success Criteria within the Management of Hierarchic Systems and in Other Contexts

Studies Related to Hierarchic Management

N	Criterion	Design	Total MSCS score	Positive attitude toward authority	Desire to compete (games)	Desire to compete (situations)	Assertive motivation	Desire to exercise power	Desire to stand out	Desire to perform routine administrative functions
R and D managers—oil company										
100	Grade level	Concurrent	<.01	—	—	<.01	—	—	—	—
81	Performance rating	Concurrent	<.05	<.01	—	<.05	—	<.01	—	—
81	Potential rating	Concurrent	<.01	<.05	<.05	<.01	—	<.05	<.01	—
R and D managers—oil company										
49	Grade level change	Predictive	<.05	<.01	<.05	—	—	—	<.01	—
Marketing managers—oil company										
81	Grade level change	Predictive	<.01	<.01	—	<.01	—	<.01	—	—
R and D and marketing managers—oil company										
61	Performance rating	Predictive	<.01	<.01	<.05	<.01	<.01	<.01	—	—
Managers—department store—Miner (1965)										
70	Grade level	Concurrent	<.01	not reported	—	<.05	—	<.05	—	<.05
70	Performance rating	Concurrent	—	not reported	—	—	—	—	—	—
70	Potential rating	Concurrent	<.05	—	—	—	—	<.05	—	<.05
Scientists and engineers—government R and D laboratory										
117	Peer rating—Supervisory Potential	Concurrent	<.01	not reported	—	—	—	—	—	—
Scientists, engineers, and managers—government R and D laboratory										
95	Promotion into management	Predictive	<.05	—	<.05	<.05	—	<.05	—	—
Undergraduate students in a simulated bureaucratic organization—Western Michigan University										
415	Promotion into management	Concurrent	<.01	—	<.05	<.05	—	—	<.05	<.01
Personnel and industrial relations managers										
101	Composite success measure	Concurrent	<.01	<.01	—	—	—	—	—	—
101	Compensation	Concurrent	<.05	<.01	—	—	—	—	—	—
101	Position level	Concurrent	<.01	<.05	<.05	<.01	<.05	—	—	—
Personnel and industrial relations managers										
142	Position level	Concurrent	<.05	<.01	<.05	—	—	<.05	—	—
Graduate students in business—University of Oregon										
106	Choice of a managerial career	Concurrent	<.01	<.01	<.05	<.01	<.01	<.01	<.05	<.01
Undergraduate students in business—University of Oregon										
108	Choice of a managerial career	Concurrent	<.05	—	—	<.01	—	—	—	—
Managers—various companies										
395	Position level	Concurrent	<.01	<.01	—	<.01	<.01	—	—	<.05
School administrators—large city										
82	Grade level	Concurrent	—	—	—	—	—	—	—	—
82	Compensation	Concurrent	<.05	—	—	—	—	—	—	—
82	Performance rating	Concurrent	<.01	<.05	<.05	<.01	<.01	—	<.05	—
82	Potential rating	Concurrent	<.01	—	—	<.01	<.05	—	<.05	—
Graduate students in business—Georgia State										
47	Promotion into management	Concurrent	<.05	not reported	—	—	—	—	—	—
Female managers—department store										
44	Grade level	Concurrent	<.05	—	—	—	—	<.05	<.05	—
Undergraduate students—RPI										
40	Selection as fraternity president	Concurrent	<.05	—	—	—	—	<.05	—	<.05
Undergraduate students—Georgia State										
190	Selection for student office	Concurrent	<.01	—	—	<.05	—	<.01	—	<.05

Exhibit 5.14 Significant Relationships between Motivation to Manage and Its Components and Success Criteria within the Management of Hierarchic Systems and in Other Contexts (Continued)

Studies Not Related to Hierarchic Management

N	Criterion	Design	Total MSCS score	Positive attitude toward authority	Desire to compete (games)	Desire to compete (situations)	Assertive motivation	Desire to exercise power	Desire to stand out	Desire to perform routine administrative functions
R and D researchers—oil company										
19	Grade level change	Predictive	(<.05)		Not reported					
Undergraduate students—University of Oregon										
190	Grade point average	Concurrent	—		Not reported	Not reported				
Scientists and engineers—government R and D laboratory										
117	Promotion rate	Concurrent	(<.05)		Not reported	Not reported				
Management consultants—6 U.S. offices										
51	Performance rating	Predictive	—	—	—	—	—	<.05	—	—
51	Potential rating	Predictive	—	—	—	—	—	<.05	—	—
51	Compensation	Predictive	—	—	—	—	—	<.01	—	—
51	Per diem charge for services	Predictive	—	—	—	—	—	<.01	—	—
Management consultants — 6 foreign offices										
30	Performance rating	Predictive	None significant							
30	Potential rating	Predictive	None significant							
30	Compensation	Predictive	None significant							
30	Per diem charge for services	Predictive	None significant							
Management consultants—single U.S. office										
24	Performance rating	Concurrent	None significant							
24	Potential rating	Concurrent	None significant							
24	Compensation	Concurrent	None significant							
Undergraduate students in small, unstructured groups—University of South Florida										
72	Peer rating— Management potential	Concurrent	None significant							
Business school faculty members										
49	Academic rank	Concurrent	None significant							
49	Promotion into administration	Concurrent	None significant							
School administrators—medium city										
57	Grade level	Concurrent	None significant							
57	Compensation	Concurrent	None significant							
57	Performance rating	Concurrent		<.05		—	<.01	—	—	—
57	Potential rating	Concurrent		<.05		—	<.01	—	—	—
School administrators—small city										
44	Grade level	Concurrent	None significant							
44	Compensation	Concurrent	None significant							
44	Performance rating	Concurrent		<.05		<.05		—		—
44	Potential rating	Concurrent		—		<.05		—		—
School administrators—consolidated district										
36	Grade level	Concurrent	None significant							
36	Compensation	Concurrent	None significant							
36	Performance rating	Concurrent	None significant							
36	Potential rating	Concurrent	None significant							
Dealer salesmen—oil company										
65	Sales figures	Concurrent	None significant							

( ) Negative relationship

A third source of induced effort is pressure within face-to-face groups which have achieved some degree of cohesiveness. Here leadership positions exist only to carry out the will of the majority and leadership is of an emergent nature. Voluntary and legislative structures are of this kind; people act as they do because strong conformity pressures are exerted on them. The key individuals are group members in good standing, especially those with the social skills to monopolize communication and influence processes.

A fourth type of inducement approach involves pressures built into the job itself; the pulls and pushes inherent in the very nature of certain tasks. For organization theory, the most significant example of this form is the small entrepreneurial firm. Here the ever present pull of profits and the push of potential bankruptcy exert an influence on all members to some degree, but the key person is the entrepreneur, or in some cases the entrepreneurial group.

There is considerable evidence which suggests that to function effectively, the organization spawned by the pushes and pulls of entrepreneurial inducements requires a sizable dose of achievement motivation, especially in the entrepreneur himself. Components of this achievement motivation include a desire for personal responsibility and credit, moderate risk taking, feedback on results, opportunity for innovation, and a future-oriented time perspective. The literature supporting the fit between the entrepreneurial structure and achievement motivated people has been reviewed by McClelland and Winter (1969) and more recently by Steiner and Miner (1977).

A second program of research provides strong support for a fit between the hierarchic structure and motivation to manage in the key managerial component (Miner, 1965, 1977). Motivation to manage includes a favorable attitude upward (to authority), a desire to compete with peers, a desire to exercise power (over subordinates), assertiveness, a desire to stand out and assume a distinctive position, and a sense of responsibility for routine administrative activities. Data on relationships with success criteria obtained within the key managerial components of hierarchic organizations and in other contexts are

given in Exhibit 5.14. It is clear that the fit of managerial motivation is unique to hierarchic management.

CONCLUSIONS

On the evidence, the theory of strategy-structure fit does not appear to offer a very powerful tool for understanding at the present time. The role of environmental factors, in particular the concept of environmental uncertainly, is itself very uncertain insofar as organization structures and processes are concerned (Downey, Hellriegel, and Slocum, 1975; Miles, Snow, and Pfeffer, 1974). This is not to say that environmental circumstances are not an important factor in strategy formulation per se. However it would appear that the same strategy can be implemented equally effectively through different structures depending on organizational size and the most appropriate inducement system, among other considerations. Furthermore, an existing structure can be mobilized behind a wide range of strategies provided that appropriate role prescriptions to guide implementation behaviors are specified in some manner.

On the other hand, the theory of structure-people fit does appear to have considerable validity and value. There is sufficient evidence regarding these fits for hierarchic and entrepreneurial task inducement systems and their key people to provide encouragement for research to fill out the specifics of the theory further. In particular, knowledge is needed regarding the operation of professional norm and group pressure inducement systems and the people who are able to implement them most effectively. In addition, we need a much greater understanding of what happens at the interfaces of inducement systems, as for example, in the matrix structure and in very large organizations staffed primarily with professionals but with a hierarchic overlay. What kinds of people fit best in these inducement system boundary roles? One would anticipate that it would be those relatively rare individuals who possess the motivational patterns required by *both* of the interfacing systems, but research to date is mute on this subject.

Section 5 References

Ackerman, Robert W. "Influence of Integration and Diversity on the Investment Process." *Administrative Science Quarterly*, September 1970.

Ackerman, Robert W. "Role of the Corporate Planning Executive," in Lorange, Peter and Richard F. Vancil (editors), *Strategic Planning Systems*. Englewood Cliffs, N.J.: Prentice-Hall, 1977.

Aguilar, Francis J., Robert A. Howell and Richard F. Vancil. *Formal Planning Systems — 1970*. Boston: Graduate School of Business Administration, Harvard University, 1970.

Aguilar, Francis J. "Setting Corporate Objectives," in Vancil, R. F. (editor), *Formal Planning Systems — 1971*. Boston: Graduate School of Business Administration, Harvard University, 1971, pp. 13–21.

Aharoni, Yair. *The Foreign Investment Decision Process*. Boston: Division of Research, Graduate School of Business Administration, Harvard University, 1966.

Allen, Stephen A. "Fourth Generation Organizations: Problems, Emerging Solutions and Human Implications." Unpublished paper presented at IEEE Systems, Man and Cybernetics Conference, Boston, Mass., November 1973.

Allen, Stephen A. "A Taxonomy of Organizational Choices in Divisionalized Companies." Working paper, IMEDE, Lausanne, Switzerland, October 1976.

Allison, Graham T. *Essence of Decision: Explaining the Cuban Missile Crisis*. Boston: Little, Brown, 1971.

Anand, S. "Resource Allocation at the Corporate Level of the Firm: A Methodological and Empirical Investigation of the Dimensions Used by Managers for Evaluating Investments." Doctoral diss., Sloan School of Management, Cambridge, Mass., 1977.

Ansoff, H. Igor, J. Avner, R. G. Brandenburg, F. E. Portner and R. Radosevich. "Does Planning Pay? The Effect of Planning on Success of Acquisitions in American Firms." *Long Range Planning*, December 1971.

Arthur D. Little, Inc. *A System for Managing Diversity*. Cambridge, Mass., 1974.

Bain, Joe. *Industrial Organization*. New York: Wiley, 1958.

Barron, Frank. *Creative Person and Creative Process*. New York: Holt, Rinehart and Winston, 1969.

Beckhard, Richard D. *Organization Development: Strategies and Models*. Reading, Mass.: Addison-Wesley, 1969.

Berg, Norman A. "Strategic Planning in Conglomerate Companies." *Harvard Business Review*, May–June 1965.

Berg, Norman A. "What's Different About Conglomerate Management?" *Harvard Business Review*, November–December 1969.

Blake, Robert R. and Jane Mouton. *The Managerial Grid*. New York: Gulf Publishing, 1964.

Blau, Peter, Cecilia M. Falbe, William McKinley and Phelps Tracy. "Technology and Organization in Manufacturing." *Administrative Science Quarterly*, March 1976.

Boston Consulting Group. *Growth and Financial Strategies*. Boston: Boston Consulting Group, 1971.

Boulding, Kenneth, E. *A Reconstruction of Economics*. New York: Wiley, 1950.

Bower, Joseph. *The Resource Allocation Process*. Boston: Division of Research, Graduate School of Business Administration, Harvard University, 1970.

Burns, Tom and G. M. Stalker. *The Management of Innovation*. London: Tavistock Publications, 1961.

Business Week. "GE's New Strategy for Faster Growth," July 8, 1972.

Cable, John and Peter Steer. "On the Industrial Organization and Profitability of Large U. K. Companies." Unpublished working paper, Liverpool Polytechnic, February 1977.

Camillus, John C. "Formal Planning: Creativity vs. Control." Doctoral diss., Harvard University, 1973.

Campbell, John P., Marvin D. Dunnette, Edward E. Lawler and Karl E. Weick. *Managerial Behavior, Performance, and Effectiveness*. New York: McGraw-Hill, 1970.

Cannon, J. Thomas. *Business Strategy and Policy*. New York: Harcourt, Brace and World, 1968.

Carter, E. Eugene. "The Behavioral Theory of the Firm and Top Level Corporation Decisions." *Administrative Science Quarterly*, December 1971.

Cash, W. H. and J. M. Revie. "The Long-Range Planner and Acquisition Planning," in Vancil, R. F. (editor), *Formal Planning Systems — 1971*. Boston: Graduate School of Business Administration, Harvard University, 1971, pp. 206–234.

Chandler, Alfred D. *Strategy and Structure: Chapters in the History of the American Industrial Enterprise*. Cambridge, Mass.: M.I.T. Press, 1962.

Channon, Derek F., "The Strategy and Structure of British Enterprise." Doctoral diss., Harvard University, 1971.

Channon, Derek F. *The Strategy and Structure of British Enterprise.* Boston: Graduate School of Business Administration, Harvard University, 1973.

Channon, Derek F. "Strategy, Structure and Performance in the British Service Industries." Unpublished manuscript, 1977.

Child, John. "Organizational Structure, Environment and Performance — The Role of Strategic Choice." *Sociology,* January 1972.

Child, John. "Managerial and Organizational Factors Associated with Company Performance — Part I." *Journal of Management Studies,* October 1974.

Child, John. "Managerial and Organizational Factors Associated with Company Performance — Part II, A Contingency Analysis." *Journal of Management Studies,* February 1975.

Child, John. *Organization: A Guide for Managers and Administrators.* New York: Harper and Row, 1977.

Child, John and Alfred Keiser. "The Development of Organizations Over Time," in Nystrom, P. and W. Starbuck, *The Handbook of Organization Design,* Vol. 1, forthcoming.

Child, John and Roger Mansfield. "Technology, Size and Organization Structure." *Sociology,* Vol. 6, pp. 369–393, 1972.

Christensen, Roland C. Internal Memorandum. Graduate School of Business Administration, Harvard University, 1965.

Coase, R. H. "The Nature of the Firm." *Economica N. S.,* Vol. 4:386–405, 1937. Reprinted in Stigler, G. J. and K. E. Boulding, editors. *Readings in Price Theory.* Homewood, Ill.: Richard D. Irwin, 1952.

Cohen, Kalman J. and Richard M. Cyert. "Strategy: Formulation, Implementation, and Monitoring." *Journal of Business,* July 1973.

Corey, E. Raymond and Steven H. Star. *Organization Strategy: A Marketing Approach.* Boston: Graduate School of Business Administration, Harvard University, 1971.

Cyert, Richard M. and James G. March. *A Behavioral Theory of the Firm.* Englewood Cliffs, N.J.: Prentice-Hall, 1963.

Downey, H. Kirk, Don Hellriegel and John W. Slocum. "Environmental Uncertainty: The Construct and Its Application." *Administrative Science Quarterly,* December 1975.

Duncan, Robert. "Characteristics of Organizational Environments and Perceived Environmental Uncertainty." *Administrative Science Quarterly,* September 1972.

Edstrom, Anders and Jay Galbraith. "Transfer of Managers as a Coordination and Control Strategy in Multi-National Organizations." *Administrative Science Quarterly,* June 1977.

Ewing, David W. "Involvement of Line Executives in Planning," in Aguilar, F. J., et al. *Formal Planning Systems — 1970.* Boston: Graduate School of Business Administration, Harvard University, 1970, pp. 65–68.

Fiedler, Fred E. *A Theory of Leadership Effectiveness.* New York: McGraw-Hill, 1967.

Filley, Alan C., Robert House and Steven Kerr. *Managerial Process and Organizational Behavior.* Glenview, Ill.: Scott, Foresman, 1976.

Fouraker, Lawrence E. and J. M. Stopford. "Organizational Structure and Multinational Strategy." *Administrative Science Quarterly,* June 1968.

Franko, Lawrence. "The Move Toward a Multi-Divisional Structure in European Organizations." *Administrative Science Quarterly,* December 1974.

Franko, Lawrence. *The European Multinationals.* Stamford, Conn.: Greylock Publishers, 1976.

Galbraith, Jay R. "Environmental and Technological Determinants of Organization Design," in Lawrence, Paul and Jay W. Lorsch (editors), *Studies in Organization Design.* Homewood. Ill.: Richard D. Irwin, 1970.

Galbraith, Jay R. "Matrix Organization Designs." *Business Horizons,* February, 1971.

Galbraith, Jay R. *Designing Complex Organizations.* Reading, Mass.: Addison-Wesley, 1973.

Galbraith, Jay R. *Organization Design.* Reading, Mass.: Addison-Wesley, 1977.

Goggin, William. "How the Multi-Dimensional Structure Works at Dow-Corning." *Harvard Business Review,* January–February 1974.

Gordon, I. E. and D. Miller. "A Contingency Framework for the Design of Accounting Information Systems." *Accounting, Organizations and Society,* 1976.

Greiner, Larry E. "Patterns of Organizational Change." *Harvard Business Review,* May–June 1967.

Greiner, Larry E. "Integrating Formal Planning Into Organizations," in Aguilar, F. J., et al. *Formal Planning Systems — 1970.* Boston: Graduate School of Business Administration, Harvard University, 1970, pp. 85–109.

Hage, J. and M. Aiken. "Routine Technology, Social Structure and Organizational Goals." *Administrative Science Quarterly,* September 1969.

Hall, Douglas T. *Careers in Organizations.* Santa Monica, Calif.: Goodyear Publishing, 1976.

Hall, Richard. "Intraorganizational Structure Variation." *Administrative Science Quarterly,* December 1962.

Hax, Arnold C. and Nicholas S. Majluf. "Towards the Formalization of Strategic Planning — A Conceptual Approach." Technical Report No. 2, Sloan School of Management, Cambridge, Mass., 1977a.

Hax, Arnold C. and Nicholas S Majluf. "A Methodological Approach for the Developing of Strategic Planning in Diversified Corporations." Technical Report No. 3, Sloan School of Management, Cambridge, Mass., 1977b.

Hayek, F. A. von. "Economics and Knowledge." *Economics*, February 1937.

Henry, Harold W. *Long Range Planning Practices in 45 Industrial Companies.* Englewood Cliffs, N.J.: Prentice-Hall, 1967.

Henry, Harold W. "An Empirical Study of Strategic Planning Processes in Major U.S. Corporations." Unpublished paper presented at the Academy of Management Meeting, Kansas City, Mo., August 1976.

Henry, Harold W. "Formal Planning in Major U. S. Corporations." *Long Range Planning*, October 1977.

Herold, David M. "Long Range Planning and Organizational Performance: A Cross Valuation Study." *Academy of Management Journal*, March 1972.

Hewkin, J. W. M. and T. Kempner. "Is Corporate Planning Necessary?" *BIM Information Summary*, December 1968.

Hickson, D., Derek Pugh and Diana Pheysey. "Operations Technology and Organizational Structure." *Administrative Science Quarterly*, September 1969.

Hofer, Charles W. "Research on Strategic Planning: A Survey of Past Studies and Suggestions for Future Efforts." *Journal of Economics and Business*, Spring–Summer 1976.

Hofer, Charles W. and Dan E. Schendel. *Strategy Formulation: Analytical Concepts.* St. Paul: West Publishing, 1978.

James, Barrie G. "The Theory of the Corporate Life Cycle." *Long Range Planning*, June 1973.

Karger, D. W. "Integrated Formal Long Range Planning and How to Do It." *Long Range Planning*, December 1973.

Keen, Peter G. W. (editor). *The Implementation of Computer-Based Decision Aids.* Cambridge, Mass.: Center for Information Systems Research, Sloan School of Management, 1975.

Khandwalla, Pradip N. "Effect of Competition on the Structure of Top Management Control." *Academy of Management Journal*, June 1973.

Khandwalla, Pradip N. "Mass Output Orientation of Operations Technology and Organization Structure." *Administrative Science Quarterly*, March 1974.

Kilman, Ralph and Ian Mitroff. "On Organization Stories: An Approach to the Design and Analysis of Organizations Through Myths and Stories," in Kilman, Pondy and Slevin (editors), *The Management of Organization Design*, Vol. 1. Amsterdam: Elsevier North-Holland, 1976.

Kimberly, J. R. "Organization Size and the Structuralist Perspective: A Review, Critique and Proposal." *Administrative Science Quarterly*, December 1976.

Klein, H. E. "Incorporating Environmental Examination into the Strategic Planning Process." Doctoral diss., Columbia University, 1973.

Lawler, Edward E. *Pay and Organizational Effectiveness: A Psychological View.* New York: McGraw-Hill, 1971.

Lawler, E. E. "Reward Systems," in Hackman, J. R. and J. L. Suttle (editors), *Improving Life at Work.* Santa Monica, Calif.: Goodyear Publishing, 1977.

Lawrence, Paul R. and Stanley Davis. *Matrix Organization*, Reading, Mass.: Addison-Wesley, 1977.

Lawrence, Paul R. and Jay W. Lorsch. *Organization and Environment: Managing Differentiation and Integration.* Boston: Graduate School of Business, Harvard University, 1967.

Leavitt, Harold J. "Unhuman Organizations." *Harvard Business Review*, July–August 1962.

Leavitt, Harold J. "Applied Organizational Change in Industry," in March, James (editor), *The Handbook of Organizations.* Chicago: Rand McNally, 1965.

Lee, Dennis. "Strategic Decision Making in a Management Game: An Experimental Study of Objectives Setting and Consistency in Complex Decision-Making." Cambridge, Mass.: Sloan School of Management Working Paper No. WP 887-76, 1976.

Lorange, Peter. "Tailoring the Capital Budgeting System to the Behavioral Style of Management." Doctoral diss., Harvard University, 1972.

Lorange, Peter. "The Planner's Dual Role — A Survey of U.S. Companies." *Long-Range Planning*, March 1973a, pp. 13–16.

Lorange, Peter. *Behavioral Factors in Capital Budgeting.* Bergen, Norway: Norwegian University Press, 1973b.

Lorange, Peter. "Administrative Practices in Smaller Companies." Paper presented at TIMS/ORSA Conference on Strategic Planning, New Orleans, 1977b.

Lorange, Peter. "An Analytical Scheme for the Assessment of a Diversified Company's Corporate

Planning System: Needs; Capabilities; Effectiveness." Cambridge, Mass.: Sloan School of Management Working Paper No. 964-77, 1977a.

Lorange, Peter. "Implementation of Strategic Planning Systems," in Hax, A. C. (editor), *Studies in Operations Management*. New York: Elsevier North-Holland, 1978.

Lorange, Peter. *Corporate Planning: An Executive Approach*. Englewood Cliffs, N.J.: Prentice-Hall, forthcoming.

Lorange, Peter and Richard F. Vancil. "Strategic Planning in Diversified Companies." *Harvard Business Review*, January–February 1975.

Lorange, Peter and Richard F. Vancil. "How to Design a Strategic Planning System." *Harvard Business Review*. September–October 1976.

Lorange, Peter and Richard F. Vancil. *Strategic Planning Systems*. Englewood Cliffs, N.J.: Prentice-Hall, 1977.

Lorello, Benjamin. "Plan-Budget Linkage." Master of Science diss., Cambridge, Mass.: Sloan School of Management, 1976.

Lorsch, Jay W. and Stephen A. Allen, III. *Managing Diversity and Interdependence: An Organizational Study of Multidivisional Firms*. Boston: Graduate School of Business Administration, Harvard University, 1973.

Lorsch, Jay W. and John J. Morse. *Organizations and Their Members: A Contingency Approach*. New York: Harper and Row, 1974.

MacMillan, Ian C. *Strategy Formulation: Political Concepts*. St. Paul: West Publishing, 1978.

McCaskey, Michael. "Tolerance for Ambiguity and the Perception of Environmental Uncertainty in Organization Design," in Kilman, R., L. R. Pondy, and D. P. Slevin (editors), *The Management of Organization Design*, Vol. 2. Amsterdam: North-Holland, 1976.

McClelland, David C. and David G. Winter. *Motivating Economic Achievement*. New York: The Free Press, 1969.

McKinney, G. W., III. "An Experimental Study of the Effects of Systematic Approaches to Strategic Planning." Doctoral diss., Stanford University, 1970.

Malm, Allan T. *Strategic Planning Systems*. Lund, Sweden: Student Litteratur, 1975.

Mauriel, John and Robert Anthony. "Misevaluation of Investment Center Performance." *Harvard Business Review*, March–April 1966.

Meyer, H. "The Pay-for-Performance Dilemma." *Organization Dynamics*, Winter 1975.

Miles, Raymond E., Charles C. Snow and Jeffrey Pfeffer. "Organization-Environment: Concepts and Issues." *Industrial Relations*, October 1974.

Miles, Raymond E. and Charles Snow. *Environmental Strategy and Organization Structure*. New York: McGraw-Hill, 1978.

Miner, John B. *Studies in Management Education*. Atlanta, Ga.: Organizational Measurement Systems Press, 1965.

Miner, John B. "The Uncertain Future of the Leadership Concept: An Overview," in Hunt, J. G. and L. L. Larson (editors), *Leadership Frontiers*. Kent, Ohio: Kent State University Press, 1975.

Miner, John B. *Motivation to Manage*. Atlanta, Ga.: Organizational Measurement Systems Press, 1977.

Miner, John B. *The Management Process: Theory, Research and Practice*. New York: Macmillan, 1978.

Mohr, L. B. "Organization Technology and Organization Structure." *Administrative Science Quarterly*, December 1971.

Morse, John and Darroch Young. "Personality Development and Task Choices: A Systems View." *Human Relations*, Vol. 26, No. 3, 1973.

Murrah, T. F. and W. F. Tuxbury, "Plan Review Process: Negotiated Goal Setting," in Vancil, R. F. (editor), *Formal Planning Systems — 1971*. Boston: Harvard Business School, Harvard University, 1971, pp. 34–56.

Negandhi, Anant R. *Organization in an Open System*. New York: Dunellen, 1975.

Negandhi, Anant R. and Bernard C. Reimann. "A Contingency Theory of Organization Reexamined in the Context of a Developing Country." *Academy of Management Journal*, June 1972.

Neghandhi, Anant and Bernard C. Reimann. "Organization Structure and Effectiveness: A Canonical Analysis," in Kilman, R., L. R. Pondy, and D. P. Slevin (editors), *The Management of Organization Design*, Vol. 2. Amsterdam: North-Holland, 1976.

Pavan, Robert. "Strategy and Structure in Italian Enterprise." Doctoral diss., Harvard University, 1972.

Pelz, Donald C. and Frank M. Andrews. *Scientists in Organizations*. New York: Wiley, 1966.

Pennings, Johannes. "The Relevance of the Structural-Contingency Model for Organizational Effectiveness." *Administrative Science Quarterly*, September 1975.

Perkins, A. E. and B. K. Sugden. "Purposes and Effectiveness of Formal Planning Systems," in Vancil, R. F. (editor), *Formal Planning Systems — 1971*. Boston: Graduate School of Business Administration, Harvard University, 1971.

Perrow, Charles. "A Framework for the Comparative Analysis of Organization." *American Sociological Review*, April 1967.

Perrow, Charles. "The Bureaucratic Paradox: The Efficient Organization Centralizes in Order to Decentralize." *Organization Dynamics*, Spring, 1977.

Pfeffer, Jeffrey and Huseyin Leblebici. "The Effect of Competition on Some Dimensions of Organizational Structure." *Social Forces*, December 1973.

Pitts, Robert A. "Incentive Compensation and Organization Design." *Personnel Journal*, May 1974.

Pitts, Robert A. "Strategies and Structures for Diversification." *Academy of Management Journal*, June 1977.

Poensgen, Otto. "Organizational Structure, Context and Performance." European Institute for Advanced Studies in Management, Working Paper No. 74-49, November 1974.

Pooley-Dias, Gareth. "Strategy and Structure of French Enterprise." Doctoral diss., Harvard University, 1972.

Pugh, Derek, D. J. Hickson, and C. R. Hinings. "An Empirical Taxonomy of Structures of Work Organizations." *Administrative Science Quarterly*, March 1969.

Ringbakk, Kjell-Arne. "Organized Corporate Planning Systems — An Empirical Study of Planning Practices and Experiences in American Big Business." Doctoral diss., University of Wisconsin, 1968.

Ringbakk, Kjell-Arne. *Organized Planning in Major U.S. Companies — A Survey*. Menlo Park, Calif.: Stanford Research Institute, 1969.

Ringbakk, Kjell-Arne. "Why Planning Fails." *European Business*, Spring 1971.

Ringbakk, Kjell-Arne. "The Corporate Planning Life Cycle — An International Point of View." *Long Range Planning*, September 1972.

Rumelt, Richard P. *Strategy, Structure, and Economic Performance*. Boston: Graduate School of Business Administration, Harvard University, 1974.

Salter, Malcolm. "Stages of Corporate Development." *Journal of Business Policy*, Vol. 1, No. 1, 1970.

Salter, Malcolm. "Tailor Incentive Compensation to Strategy." *Harvard Business Review*, March–April 1973.

Schein, Edgar A. *Process Consultation: Its Role in Organization Development*. Reading, Mass.: Addison-Wesley, 1969.

Schein, Edgar A. "Increasing Organizational Effectiveness Through Better Human Resource Planning and Development." *Sloan Management Review*, Fall 1977.

Schendel, Dan. "Designing Strategic Planning Systems." Institute for Economic, Management and Administrative Science. Paper No. 616, Purdue University, 1977.

Scott, Bruce R. "An Open Systems Model of the Firm." Doctoral diss., Harvard University, 1962.

Scott, Bruce R. "Stages of Corporate Development." Harvard University, Intercollegiate Case Clearing House Report No. 9-371-294 BP 998, Boston, Mass., 1971.

Scott, Bruce R. "The Industrial State: Old Myths and New Realities." Boston, Mass.: Intercollegiate Clearing House #9-371-294.

Shank, John K. "Linkage Between Planning and Budgeting Systems," in Aguilar, F. J., et al. *Formal Planning Systems — 1970*. Boston: Graduate School of Business Administration, Harvard University, 1970.

Simonetti, Jack and F. Glenn Boseman. "The Impact of Market Competition on Organization Structure and Effectiveness: A Cross Cultural Study." *Academy of Management Journal*, September 1975.

Smith, William and R. Charmoy. "Coordinate Line Management." Working paper, Searle International, Chicago, Ill., February 1975.

Starbuck, William. "Organizational Growth and Development," in March, J. G. (editor), *Handbook of Organization*. Chicago: Rand McNally, 1965.

Starbuck, William. *Organizational Growth and Development*. London: Penguin, 1971.

Steiner, George A. *Pitfalls in Comprehensive Long Range Planning*. Oxford, Ohio: Planning Executives Institute, 1972.

Steiner, George A. and John B. Miner. *Management Policy and Strategy*. New York: Macmillan, 1977.

Steiner, George A. and Hans Schollhammer. "Pitfalls in Multi-National Long Range Planning." *Long Range Planning*, April 1975.

Stevenson, H. H. "Defining Corporate Strengths and Weaknesses." *Sloan Management Review*, Spring 1976.

Stogdill, Ralph M. *Handbook of Leadership*. New York: The Free Press, 1974.

Stopford, John. "Growth and Organizational Change in the Multinational Field." Doctoral diss., Harvard University, 1968.

Stopford, John and Louis Wells. *Managing the Multinational Enterprise*. London: Longmans, 1972.

The Strategic Planning Institute. *Nine Basic Findings on Business*. Cambridge, Mass., 1977.

Szilagyi, Andrew D., Henry P. Sims and Robert T. Keller. "Role Dynamics, Locus of Control, and

Employee Attitudes and Behavior." *Academy of Management Journal*, Vol. 19, pp. 259–276, 1976.

Taylor, Bernard and P. Irving. "Organized Planning in Major U.K. Companies." *Long Range Planning*, June 1971.

Tennican, Michael L. "Diversification by Acquisition," in Aguilar, F. J., et al. *Formal Planning Systems — 1970*. Boston: Graduate School of Business Administration, Harvard University, 1970.

Thanheiser, Heinz. "Strategy and Structure of German Firms." Doctoral diss., Harvard University, 1972.

Thompson, James D. *Organizations in Action*. New York: McGraw-Hill, 1967.

Thune, Stanley S. and Robert J. House. "Where Long Range Planning Pays Off." *Business Horizons*, August 1970.

Udy, Stanley. *Organization of Work*. New Haven, Conn.: Human Resources Area Files Press, 1959.

Vancil, Richard F. (editor). *Formal Planning Systems — 1971*. Boston: Graduate School of Business Administration, Harvard University, 1971a.

Vancil, Richard F. (ed.). *Formal Planning Systems — 1972*. Boston: Graduate School of Business Administration, Harvard University, 1972.

Vancil, Richard F. "Strategy Formulation in Complex Organizations." *Sloan Management Review*, Winter 1976.

Van Maanen, John and Edgar Schein. "Career Development," in Hackman, R. J. and J. L. Suttle (editors), *Improving Life at Work*. Santa Monica, Calif.: Goodyear Publishing, 1977.

Van de Ven, Andrew H. and Andre L. Delbecq. "A Task Contingent Model of Work-Unit Structure." *Administrative Science Quarterly*, June 1974.

Vernon, Raymond. *Manager in the International Economy*. Englewood Cliffs, N.J.: Prentice-Hall, 1968.

Wells, Louis in Stopford, John and Louis Wells. *Managing the Multi-National Enterprise*. London: Longmans, 1972.

Williamson, Oliver. *Corporate Control and Business Behavior*. Englewood Cliffs, N.J.: Prentice-Hall, 1970.

Williamson, Oliver. *Markets and Hierarchies*. New York: The Free Press, 1975.

Wood, Dexter Robley, Jr. "An Analysis of the Strategic and Operational Planning Systems in Large United States Banks." Doctoral diss., University of Tennessee at Knoxville, 1977.

Woodward, Joan. *Industrial Organization: Theory and Practice*. London: Oxford University Press, 1965.

Wrigley, Leonard. "Divisional Autonomy and Diversification." Doctoral diss., Graduate School of Business Administration, Harvard University, 1970.

Wrigley, Leonard. "Transactions in Technology." Internal memorandum, University of Western Ontario, 1974 (appearing in Killing, Peter, "Manufacturing Under Licensing," Doctoral diss., University of Western Ontario, 1975).

6

STRATEGIC MANAGEMENT AND ORGANIZATION TYPES

Strategic Management: New Ventures and Small Business

ARNOLD C. COOPER
Purdue University

Commentary

JEFFREY C. SUSBAUER
Cleveland State University

KARL H. VESPER
University of Washington

Strategic Management: The Multi-Business Corporation

NORMAN BERG
Harvard University

ROBERT A. PITTS
Pennsylvania State University

Commentary

RICHARD G. BRANDENBURG
The Carborundum Company

Strategic Management: Not-for-Profit Organizations

MAX S. WORTMAN, JR.
Virginia Polytechnic Institute and State University

To this point, we have been examining the strategic management paradigm in terms of its various components. In this set of papers, it is examined in terms of three organization archetypes: (1) newly founded firms, small and ongoing; (2) multi-industry businesses; and (3) not-for-profit organizations. Our interest will be in exploring the commonalities and differences in the strategic management process in terms of each type of organization. Of particular interest will be those aspects of the strategic management process that are unique to each particular type.

Cooper authors the topic paper on new ventures and small on-going businesses, the latter a very prevalent form of business organization and one that spawns almost all larger business organizations. His paper is discussed by Susbauer and Vesper. Berg and Pitts examine some of the unique aspects of the strategic management processes in large, multi-industry businesses, probably the most successful of all forms of business organizations in the world today. Brandenburg comments on their paper from the perspective of the practitioner. Finally, Wortman explores the strategic management issues associated with not-for-profit, nonbusiness organizations, which he classifies under three general types: (1) public; (2) third sector; and (3) institutional, excluding profit-making organizations.

Before commenting on the papers individually, we shall first examine the commonalities and differences among these organization archetypes with respect to six different aspects of the strategic management paradigm: (1) purpose and mission, (2) general management roles, (3) environmental analysis, (4) strategy content, (5) strategy implementation, and (6) organizational evolution.

GENERAL OBSERVATIONS

PURPOSE AND MISSION

Insofar as business and nonbusiness organizations are concerned, an immediate and important distinction to note is the differences in their mission, that is, in the purposes for which they are formed. It is from purpose that the goal structure that motivates action is derived, and it is the goal structure, in turn, that is the end point that strategy attempts to reach. As Mintzberg, Richards, and Murray have shown earlier, goal structures are complex, and if the motivation they provide is to be fully understood, it is necessary to understand how goals are formulated, the nature of their content, and the impact of that content on the organization. Thus, for business organizations, one must appreciate the powerful constraint that economic goals play in conditioning strategy formulation and implementation if one is to understand the strategic management process in such organizations. On the other hand, economic constraints, while important to a greater degree than any short-term examination is likely to show, have much less immediacy for the not-for-profit organization and thus have much less impact on its strategic management process.[1]

In the new venture, and in most small, ongoing firms as well, the goal formulation process lies almost entirely in the hands of the entrepreneur-founder and the discipline of the market. Moreover, in most such firms, mere survival takes primacy over other goals as the firm tries to be repaid for the benefits it provides to its markets and society. The role of purpose and resulting goal structures is to be very plainly seen in such small businesses, as Susbauer notes so well. Moreover, there is much that can be learned about goal trade-offs and the role of goals in the study of strategic and operating management practices of small firms.

The contrasts between goals and goal formulation processes of new ventures and small, ongoing firms, and those of the multi-industry, multi-cultural firm are dramatic. First, goal formulation in the multi-industry firm is much more complex, as there are many more individuals in both external and internal coalitions who play a part in the process. The goal structure is also far more complex not only because of the need to reflect the interests of the external and internal coalitions, but also because it is necessary to develop subunit goals for each level of the organization. In addition, survival is rarely an issue in the well-established firm, a fact which permits organizational slack and discretion on the part of stake-holders regarding which goals receive priority. Such complexities clearly would not be possible in any firm struggling for economic survival.

The primary goals of not-for-profit organizations are noneconomic in nature. Nevertheless, economic goals are of more long-run importance than is usually recognized because unless the organization provides net benefits over its costs it will not survive. Still, even over the long-run, the primary goals of not-for-profit organizations remain noneconomic in nature. While such principal goals are usually clearly understood, their social (and political) character makes it difficult to develop a set of indices for measuring them which can be used to determine whether they have been achieved. Lacking such clear-cut indices, it is also difficult to develop a hierarchical goal structure to guide the day-to-day activities of such organizations' various components. The primacy of a set of difficult-to-measure, socially oriented goals also permits greater social and political inputs to the goal formulation process than is possible where there exists one dominant, easy to measure, externally oriented economic goal.

Even though there are substantial surface differences in the purposes, missions, and resulting goal structures of the three organizational archetypes examined here, the uses of such goal structures in the management

---

[1] It is perhaps this characteristic that has led many behavioralists, who have used not-for-profit organizations as their principal objects of study, to play down the importance of rationality and the "discipline" that the need for profits places on the discretion and freedom of business organizations to choose other goals, and to play up the degree to which social and political processes operate within them.

of the organization are really much the same. Goals serve as criteria for strategic problem identification, evaluation, and choice. Further, they provide the basis upon which the evaluation and control of: (1) overall organizational performance, (2) the activities of various organizational components, and (3) the task behavior of individuals can be based.

THE ROLE OF GENERAL MANAGEMENT

A second area in which new ventures, multi-industry businesses, and not-for-profit organizations differ in their strategic management processes is in the nature of the role of general management. In all organizations the general manager responsibilities differ from those of functional managers. The general manager has final responsibility for the overall health and welfare of the organization, while the functional manager is responsible primarily for a set of specific administrative and technical tasks.

Management responsibilities can be distinguished on other than a parts/whole basis, however. The principal distinction made by the strategic management paradigm is between the day-to-day management of existing processes, products, markets, and technologies (called operations management) and the management of strategy, that is, the management changes in the relationships between the organization and its environment (called strategic management). The primary differences in the general management role in the three organizational archetypes are the extent and the ways the general manager is involved in operations and strategic management.

In the new venture and small business type, the entrepreneur clearly performs both operating and strategic management functions. However, because of time pressures and limited resources, he is usually so heavily involved with operating management tasks that he spends little time with strategic management tasks.

In the not-for-profit organization type, the general manager is also often primarily involved in operations management, but for far different reasons. Because of the organizational arrangements of most such organizations and the encouragement of public administration literature, the goal formulation process in most such organizations is performed primarily by the legislative or other members of the external coalition. Thus, the general manager sees himself as an implementer rather than as a formulator of strategy/policy, although he may try to influence strategy through explicit political actions.

In the multi-industry firm, by contrast, the strategic and operating management tasks have been separated, with different levels of general and functional managers involved with each. Thus, some general managers are responsible for the operational management of existing products and markets, others for the strategic management task at a business level, and still others for the strategic management task at the corporate level.

Two interesting questions arise with respect to these patterns of general management work. The first is: How can improvements be made with respect to the general management functions in each archetype? The second is: Will a separation of the process of achieving social and political legitimacy (Ansoff's environmental strategy) eventually be separated from the corporate strategy formulation task in multi-industry firms, necessitating still another level in the general management superstructure?

ENVIRONMENTAL ANALYSIS

The third way new ventures, multi-industry businesses, and not-for-profit organizations differ with respect to the strategic management paradigm is in the nature of their environments and environmental analysis processes. All organizations need to perform some type of environmental analysis. These analytical processes may differ, however, with respect to: (1) the type of environments examined; and (2) the size, scope, and relative importance of the organization's proximate and nonproximate environments.[2]

In new ventures and small businesses, the proximate environment is limited in scope, but far more important than the nonproximate environment. In the multi-industry business, the proximate environment is still the more important of the two, but it is a more complex environment because there is a greater scope to it, and more opportunities for interaction between the greater numbers of environmental factors. In the not-for-profit organization, the relationship between proximate and nonproximate environments varies substantially, with some appearing like new ventures and others like multi-industry firms. The distinguishing characteristic here, however, is that both the organization's nonproximate and proximate environments involve social/political interactions to a far greater degree than in either type of business organization.

STRATEGY CONTENT

New ventures, multi-industry businesses, and not-for-profit organizations also differ in the nature of their strategy content. In each, strategy consists of four components as noted earlier, that is: (1) scope, (2) resource deployments and distinctive competences, (3) competitive advantage, and (4) synergy.

In the new venture and/or small business, however, the key to effective strategy is the creation of a unique match of scope and skills and resources at the individual product/market segment level, that is, the key is to provide a unique product or service to a small, specialized group of cus-

---

[2] An organization's proximate environment includes all those external factors that have a direct and immediate impact on its strategy and operations. Its nonproximate environment includes all those external factors that affect the organization indirectly, that is, either through their effect on factors in its proximate environments or through other nonproximate variables.

tomers. In the multi-industry firm, product/market segment strategy is often formulated three or more layers deep in the organization. Moreover, since such strategies usually pertain to an entire market or industry rather than to one small protected portion (niche) of it, it is more appropriate to call such strategies business strategies. At the corporate level, however, the primary strategy focus is on the formulation of portfolio strategies for the firm as a whole, rather than to examine any product/market segment in particular. Thus, at the corporate level, scope is usually a more important component than distinctive competences. By contrast, many not-for-profit organizations have no internally consistent strategy at all. They may have goals and perhaps even a goal structure, and they usually have policies to be adhered to. Seldom do they develop explicit strategies to tie the two together, however. Moreover, in the not-for-profit organizations that do attempt such links, resources deployments and distinctive competences are usually far more important than scope, since the latter is often specified for the organization.

STRATEGY IMPLEMENTATION

In general, strategies are implemented through the application of three broad sets of tools: (1) structure, (2) systems and process, and (3) behavior. Although all of these are useful, new ventures, multi-industry businesses, and not-for-profit organizations differ in the importance of these tools to the strategy implementation task, as well as in the ways these tools are used.

In the case of the new venture and small business, organizational structure, systems, and procedures are usually informal or nonexistent as noted by the various stage-of-growth theories. Consequently, implementation is normally accomplished through specific individual task assignments, and the leadership style of the entrepreneur. In the multi-industry business, by contrast, a variety of formal structural configurations typically exist side by side. Systems and procedures are also well developed and are tied closely to the formal structure. All three sets of factors are important to implementation and usually have to be "fitted" together to achieve maximum effectiveness. In some ways, implementation is most problematic in the not-for-profit organization. Here, the structure may often be specified by law and the use of reward and sanction systems strongly circumscribed. Thus, charismatic leadership, interpersonal style, or the acquisition and use of power are often needed to carry the day.

ORGANIZATIONAL EVOLUTION

The evolution of the firm from a single manager, new venture to a moderate-sized functional area organization, on to the product/market division, multi-industry organization, leads to the question as to why such evolution occurs in the first place. Chandler's answer to this question was that it permitted certain strategies to be used, strategies which permitted size to be managed both efficiently and effectively. But our broader view of strategy as an integrating concept makes evolution a much more complicated phenomenon than just one of size. Thus, entrepreneurship is also necessary in the large organization, where it is much more diffuse in nature than in small firms.

However, except for the growth that each type of not-for-profit organization enjoys, there does not appear to be an evolutionary model to be studied across organization types in the not-for-profit sector of our economy. Nevertheless, increases in size do add complexity to strategic management processes of such organizations, but the rather poor development of practice and research in this area does not permit even tentative conclusions to be drawn.

STRATEGIC MANAGEMENT: NEW VENTURES AND SMALL BUSINESS

Cooper's leadoff paper and the commentary of Susbauer and Vesper are occupied with four themes that are worth attention: (1) the classification of small business types and the use of such a taxonomy for study of the strategic problems unique to each; (2) the role of the entrepreneur in such organizations (this may be the simplest, cleanest, and easiest environment in which to see the basic strategic management tasks); (3) the fact that new ventures and small businesses provide a ready laboratory for study of strategic management variables without the confounding of a large number of other variables as would be characteristic of larger, more complex firms; and (4) the need for better data bases on such firms if they are to be used in such research.

A viewpoint shared by Cooper, Susbauer, and Vesper is that the most ubiquitous small business, the "mom-and-pop" store, does not warrant much further attention. Rather, they argue that the newly founded, growing, high-potential small business is where research attention should be focused, not only for better understanding of strategic management issues in general, but also because of the eventual importance of such firms to our economy.

However, while the small, emerging business does offer a useful "laboratory" for some studies in strategic management without the confounding of complex, extraneous, and nonstrategic variables, it also poses some problems to the researcher, among the more important of which is the lack of objective financial data for assessing organizational performance. Nevertheless, small firms are widespread and easily available to researchers, regardless of location, which makes the problem of getting sufficient sample sizes for such research far less difficult.

Besides the specific suggestions for possible research direction contained in these papers, a further major point emerges from them. That is the way that different conceptualizations of a phenomenon or different ways of classifying and partitioning a territory can give rise to further possible research ideas. Thus, Susbauer's paper shows in some depth the types of research questions that can be produced through a modification of Cooper's system for classifying small businesses. Vesper's paper then shows how the construction of entirely different classification schemes and conceptual constructs can produce an entire range of additional insights and questions. The reader is thus challenged to consider how each of the other topic papers in this text could be conceptualized differently and to think about the different types of research ideas and questions that such new conceptualizations would produce.

Some additional questions that might be raised with respect to new ventures and small businesses are the following:

1. The major reasons given for new-venture failure are:

    (a) Lack of well-rounded experience on the part of the entrepreneurs, especially in the areas of sales and production;

    (b) Inadequate capitalization of the venture; and,

    (c) Lack of an adequate financial control system.

Do these factors apply equally to all types of new ventures? To all types of entrepreneurs? If not, then what factors do lead to failures for each type of new venture? For each type of entrepreneur?

2. Do all types of new ventures follow similar evolutionary patterns? If not, how do these patterns vary by type of venture?

3. Are particular types of entrepreneurs associated with particular types of ventures? If so, what are these associations?

STRATEGIC MANAGEMENT: THE MULTIBUSINESS FIRM

Berg and Pitts begin their paper with a taxonomy of strategic management tasks that they limit to strategy formulation (and evaluation, since they include the evaluation step) and strategy implementation. For the purpose of summarizing research on multibusiness firms, they separate their consideration of strategy formulation into two subtopics, that is, the "content" of strategy and the "processes" used to formulate strategy. They divide strategy implementation into two parts as well, with strategy diversification-divisionalization issues separated from the administrative problems associated with the headquarters'/divisional linkage issues in such firms. Next, Berg and Pitts note that there are really just two evolutionary patterns that lead to the creation of the multi-industry firm, that is, internal development versus external acquisition. Their research also indicates that firms which evolve through internal development are managed differently from firms that evolve via acquisition. Berg and Pitts then survey the research in each of the four categories noted above and speculate as to the most promising directions for future research in each area.

With respect to strategy content, they note that most of the research done to date has attempted to develop classification systems for describing such strategies. Most of these frameworks utilize one or more of the following variables to construct categories: (1) the degree of diversification of the firm (e.g., single product line, dominant product line, diversified); (2) the extent to which the firm's different businesses are tied to some common core skill (e.g., related, unrelated); and (3) the pattern by which such firms have diversified (e.g., internal diversification, acquisition). They then indicate the need to develop even better ways for describing and classifying corporate-level strategy and, in particular, the need to better understand how corporate-level strategies relate the multi-industry firm to the totality of the environment in which it operates.

With respect to strategy formulation processes, Berg and Pitts believe that most of the research done to date has focused on the social and political aspects of the process. This research has corroborated the impact of such factors on the process and the role of business-level managers and suggests that corporate-level management may be better able to influence the strategic decision process by "its manipulation of structure than by making substantive inputs to the strategic decisions themselves." Berg and Pitts then suggest the need for further research that examines the strategy formulation process in different types of multi-industry firms, as well as for different types of strategic choices. With respect to diversification and divisionalization, Berg and Pitts briefly recount the "stages of development" model and suggest that "further efforts to establish levels and trends of diversification and subsequent divisionalization may yield only marginal payoffs" and that more useful research efforts in strategy implementation might focus on headquarters/divisional relationships.

With respect to such relationships, they note that a few studies have been done regarding the differences in which "internal and acquisitive diversifiers" have carved out activities such as R&D, marketing, and so on, at the corporate level, as well as differences in the ways they transfer and compensate divisional managers. However, more research is needed, they argue, on topics such as how such firms differ in the way they handle interdivisional relationships, such as transfer pricing.

Berg and Pitts conclude their paper by suggesting that future research on multi-industry firms will be most effective if: (1) it appreciates the complexity of the corporate-level general management tasks in such firms; (2) draws on a mixture of clinical field observations and broader-based survey methodologies; (3) is problem oriented rather than tool oriented; and (4) will focus on the general manager in organizations rather than looking at the general manager, the organization, or the environment separately.

Brandenburg complements the Berg and Pitts discussion by suggesting additional areas for research on multi-industry firms based on his experience in the Carborundum Company. In terms of strategy formulation and content in the multibusiness firm, he indicates a need for research on such topics as: (1) a better understanding of the range of applicability of the various analytical tools and concepts used in the strategy formulation process; (2) the classification and study of the performance characteristics of different business portfolios; (3) improved techniques for analyzing the actions and intentions of competitors; and (4) a better understanding of strategies for capital-intensive industries and resource-constrained environments.

In terms of planning processes, Brandenburg suggests these research needs: (1) the development of ways to improve "bottom-up" strategic planning which can incorporate specific technical knowledge of individual businesses and their management personnel; (2) better measures of general and functional managers' performance at the business level with respect to the quality of their strategies and operating decisions; (3) how to make cost-effective use of staff in planning and auditing or controlling plans of businesses; (4) how to more effectively iterate between corporate- and business-level strategies; (5) better understanding of how to link strategic and operating plans and control processes; (6) the development of techniques to audit planning processes to improve such processes over time; and (7) better understanding of how top management's efforts should be allocated between strategic and operating management.

In terms of strategy implementation and organization structure, Brandenburg suggests that a problem exists within a multibusiness firm in managing different businesses or divisions that themselves are in different stages of evolution. Such mixed-mode organization structures create problems for corporate managers. He also shows a concern for where new business development activities should be assigned in multi-industry companies. Here, the problem of entrepreneurship and organizational renewal crops up, as it has in all of the papers in this section. Clearly, entrepreneurship, whether in starting new companies or new businesses within existing firms, is a problem worth much further research than it has received to date.

In reviewing the Berg and Pitts and Brandenburg papers, the reader should note that Berg and Pitts have focused their attention solely on those aspects of strategy formulation and strategy implementation in which the multi-industry firms differ from those of less diversified firms, while Brandenburg has commented on all aspects of strategy formulation and implementation. Thus, Brandenburg's remarks help put Berg's and Pitts's observations into a broader context. At the same time, some of Brandenburg's observations more appropriately reflect on earlier papers in this book, e.g., those of Grant and King, and Lorange.

Comprehensive as both of these papers are, it is interesting to note that they fail to discuss several aspects of strategic management in multi-industry firms. Specifically, neither Berg and Pitts nor Brandenburg comment on the goal structures or goal formulation processes of such firms; they are silent on the concept of strategic control; and their discussion of environmental analysis is quite limited.

It is also interesting to note that research cited by Berg and Pitts deals primarily with the internal organizational, social, and political aspects of the strategic management processes in multi-industry firms. Since they argue that the intellectual task of comprehending the totality of strategy is different in kind at the corporate level of multi-industry firms than at the business level of such firms, or at the corporate level of simpler firms, the research done to date would seem to imply that such complexity can be handled only by organizational means, not by the development of new intellectual concepts. Brandenburg's comments, which deal with both the organizational and the analytical aspects of such work, seem to refute this contention. The contrast in these points would seem to indicate that academic research has been unbalanced in its focus on the strategy problems and practice of multi-industry firms.

As a set, these two papers suggest several interesting questions regarding the application of the strategic management paradigm to multi-industry firms. A few of these are: (1) Why have multibusiness firms evolved? (2) What do we know about the content of corporate-level strategies in such firms? (3) How should strategic and operating management tasks be divided within the general management hierarchy?

The first question raises a number of important managerial and public policy issues. For example, does antitrust policy pursue social good when it attempts to break up large, multi-industry corporations, or do such corporations possess synergies other than scale economies in areas such as manufacturing, marketing, and distribution? In terms of managerial practice, does the conglomerate form raise any cost-of-capital and risk issues? As noted in Section 5, Williamson argues that multi-industry firms are better able to allocate capital among related businesses than are capital markets, because they have more relevant information with which to do so than do capital markets. On the other hand, behavioral scientists argue that such agglomeration is owed primarily to the search for stronger power bases by the top management of such firms. Perhaps both explanations, and still others, are necessary to understand fully why multi-industry firms have evolved and what their implications for society are.

The second question highlights the fact that while we have learned a great deal about strategy content, there is much more still to be learned, especially at the corporate level. For instance, we need to know more about the problems of building and balancing portfolios of businesses in multi-industry firms, a central issue in corporate strategy determination.

The strategic management paradigm describes six types of tasks that management must perform to effectively relate the organization to its environment. Yet the third question reveals our meager knowledge of strategic management processes. The paradigm does not specify how the six tasks should be accomplished organizationally, nor how the accomplishment of such tasks should be related to the operating management work of the organization. It is clear, however, that multi-industry firms have given more thought to these issues than any other organizations in our society.

Such study is reflected in the structures and systems they have developed, and, especially, in the nature of the general management hierarchies they have created and in the ways they have designed their formal planning systems. It would seem appropriate to reexamine past studies of the nature of managerial work to see if they accurately reflect general management practice in multi-industry firms.

STRATEGIC MANAGEMENT: NOT-FOR-PROFIT ORGANIZATIONS

Wortman's paper is built around a typology of three major types of not-for-profit organizations: (1) public organizations (composed of executive agencies and departments, urban organizations, and environmental organizations); (2) third-sector (quasi-public/private) organizations; and (3) institutional (charitable, educational, religious, trade union, etc.) organizations. He examines these organizational types in terms of: (1) the literature available on each type; and (2) the research needs that seem to exist, as well as the research techniques that appear most applicable for each type. In performing this review, Wortman uses a conception of the strategic management paradigm that is somewhat different from that used in the remainder of this text.

Several conclusions seem apparent from Wortman's survey. First, not-for-profit organizations are, unfortunately, managed much more in a short-term operations sense than in a strategic sense. Second, very little research has been done on any aspect of the strategic management process in such organizations. Thus, while it appears that goal formulation in such organizations is very politically oriented and unconcerned with economic issues, at least in the short run, there is little systematic evidence to support this conclusion or its converse. In attempting such research, it would be interesting to try to apply Mintzberg's power configuration typologies to the various types of not-for-profit organizations, not only to empirically test the typologies, but also to learn more about the goal formulation processes of such organizations.

There is also a lack of research on the other components of the strategic management process for such organizations, including environmental analysis, strategy formulation, strategy content, strategy implementation, and strategic control. In fact, there is some evidence that some of these organizations have no strategies at all. Rather, they seem motivated more by short-term budget cycles and personal goals than by any interest in reexamining their purpose or mission in light of altered environmental circumstances. Similarly, management control is not based on objectives or intended outcomes but on inputs; the focus is on costs and expenditures, not on investments and returns. Research on the evaluation of the structural design of such organizations in response to changes in the strategic issues facing them is also lacking, despite the many studies done by organizational behavioralists in these types of organizations.

In sum, there is, as Wortman points out, a strong need for many research studies done at much higher levels in these organizations. Especially fruitful would be comparative studies of business and nonbusiness organizations on all aspects of the strategic management process. In contemplating such studies, we would challenge the reader to consider the additional perspectives and insights that would be produced by using a classification system different from that constructed by Wortman for the examination of such organizations, a technique that Vesper used in his consideration of new ventures and small businesses.

SUMMARY

This section has been concerned with exploring the variations in the concept of strategy and the strategic management process associated with three different organizational archetypes: (1) new ventures and small businesses, (2) multi-industry business firms, and (3) not-for-profit organizations. Since these are three of the most important archetype organizations in our society, this focus is not inappropriate. However, the reader should further contemplate the types of variations that would be produced in the strategic management process by a study of other organizational archetypes, such as high-technology firms.

Strategic Management: New Ventures and Small Business

Arnold C. Cooper
Purdue University

New and small firms provide a distinctive environment for the formulation and implementation of strategy. This paper reviews the literature relating both to the processes by which strategy is developed in such firms and the nature of the resulting strategies. Because new ventures within established firms have many of the characteristics of new and small businesses, strategic management within this context will also be considered.

Most businesses in this country are small. Approximately 95% of all U.S. businesses have fewer than 20 employees (*1967 Enterprise Statistics, Part 1*: 164). About 86% of all businesses are organized as proprietorships or partnerships; of the remaining 14% of businesses organized as corporations, 57.7% have less than $100,000 in assets (*Statistical Abstract of the United States*, 1976: 507 and 515). A substantial number of these companies are new. The process of creating new and small firms continues; in a typical 40 hour week, about 158 new corporations are created per hour and almost as many are discontinued (*Statistical Abstract of the United States*, 1976: 507).

The diversity among these small firms is enormous, so that statements which are descriptive of some groups of small firms do not apply to others. They differ in types of founders, in management sophistication, in stage of development, and in performance. Vesper has suggested that small firms might be classified as "mom and pop" companies, stable high-payoff companies, and growth-oriented companies (Hosmer, *et al.*, 1977). Liles (1974) has developed similar categories. Although these classifications are impressionistic and have not been the subject of explicit research, they help to distinguish among different types of smaller firms.

By far the majority of small businesses would be classified as mom and pop firms, particularly in retailing and service industries. Many

have no hired employees and rely only on the proprietor or members of the family. Their founders often lack formal managerial training, but may have technical skills, such as being able to sell real estate, cut hair, or do automobile repairs. Capital barriers to entry are usually low, management methods intuitive, and profits moderate or low. Start-ups and discontinuances are frequent and the founders often move from blue-collar or clerical jobs to entrepreneurship and back again. Some such places of business need revolving doors, not for the few customers, but for the entrepreneurs who come and go.

Some small retail and service firms and a higher percentage of small manufacturing firms might be classified as stable, high-payoff companies. Their founders often have more formal education and higher expectations than the mom and pop founders. Often they enjoy strong competitive positions deriving from specialized know-how, patents, or a virtual monopoly in a particular local market. Management methods, although informal by large company standards, may be very effective. Without the pressures of growth, the founder may be able to engage in civic activities or achieving a lower golf handicap, while maintaining a high standard of living.

Growth-oriented small firms offer the possibility of high payoff through selling out, through floating public issues of stock, or through controlling a large enterprise. They are started more often by groups, with the founders usually having had managerial experience. Their strategies usually position them in growing markets or involve innovative methods or products which give them clear competitive advantages. However, their growth may impose heavy demands on the founders, in personal commitments and the need to take risks. Capital requirements may bring outside investors and loss of control. Management methods may change to such a degree that the original founders must be replaced.

These classifications are fluid and it is certainly possible for a firm to move from one category to another. However, in general, these types of firms start with different resources, follow different growth paths, and involve different environments for the formulation and implementation of strategy.

The context within which strategy is managed also varies by the stage of development of the small firm. The literature on stages of development involves many ways of classifying the phases through which a growing firm passes. In this paper, we shall focus upon three stages:

1. *The start-up stage,* including the strategic decisions to found a firm and to position it within a particular industry with a particular competitive strategy;

2. *The early-growth stage,* when the initial product/market strategy is being tested and when the president maintains direct contact with all major activities (many firms stabilize at this stage);

3. *The later-growth stage,* often characterized by multiple sites for retail and service businesses and by some diversification for manufacturing firms; organizationally the firm usually has one or more levels of middle-management and some delegation of decision-making.

All of the types of firms just considered pass through the start-up stage and, if they are successful, move on to an early-growth stage. However, only the growth-oriented firms are likely to be found in the later-growth stage.

As a firm grows, at what point is it no longer small? Any answer to this question is somewhat arbitrary, but the focus here, even for firms in the later-growth stage, will be upon organizations with less than 500 employees.

TYPES OF LITERATURE

The literature on strategic management in new and small firms might be considered according to the following typology (based in part upon a paper by Douds and Rubenstein, 1975).

1. *Discursive writings* — based upon wisdom, observation, and general experience, usually prescriptive in character;

2. *Case studies* — based upon intensive study of selected cases; data can be from secondary sources or field studies;

3. *Field surveys* — data gathered from many respondents through survey techniques;

4. *Field research* — includes comparative case studies, longitudinal studies, field experiments.

The dominant type of literature on new and small firms is discursive, wisdom-based, and prescriptive. The wisdom may be sound and reflect broad experience, but the reader must trust the author as there is no explicit presentation of the results of a specific study or experiment. Often, this literature is not focused on strategy; most is concerned with operating problems, although some observations are clearly applicable to strategic management. Unfortunately, much of this prescriptive literature is mechanistic, intended to present broad approaches to an unsophisticated audience, and not sensitive to the special problems of new and small firms.

There is, however, a growing number of research studies relating to some aspects of new and small firms. Much of this explicit research has been on entrepreneurship, with the focus on the founding of new firms. (Entrepreneurship is used here in the narrow sense of only being concerned with the starting of new companies, rather than including the management of risky, innovative ventures within established organizations.) Included have been large sample studies of the characteristics of entrepreneurs, some longitudinal studies of founding characteristics associated with survival and success, and several studies of those factors which seem to be related to how companies are started at particular times and places.

The research on strategic management in existing small firms has been based largely on case studies and to a lesser degree on field surveys. Much of this research has been inductive in character with the generalizations and hypotheses at the end of the studies rather than at the beginning.

We shall now consider the literature on strategic management and opportunities for research relating to each of the three stages of development within which small firms might exist — the start-up stage, the early-growth stage, and the later-growth stage. The special problems of new ventures within established organizations will be considered separately.

STRATEGIC MANAGEMENT IN THE START-UP STAGE

The decision to found a new firm is, in every sense, a strategic decision by the entrepreneur. It involves non-routine decisions to commit major resources to create a particular new business at a particular time and place. The new business then has a strategy (which may or may not have been carefully considered); it provides selected goods or services to particular markets and it emphasizes (whether wisely or not) particular policies to provide a way of competing.

The decision to found a new firm seems to be influenced by three broad factors (Cooper, 1971). They are: (1) the entrepreneur, including the many aspects of his background which affect his motivations, his perceptions, and his skills and knowledge; (2) the organization for which the entrepreneur had previously been working, whose characteristics influence the location and the nature of new firms, as well as the likelihood of spin-offs; and (3) various environmental factors external to the individual and his organization, which make the climate more or less favorable to the starting of a new firm.

Of these three broad factors, the characteristics of the entrepreneur have been most extensively researched. Psychological research suggests that founders have a high need for achievement and a belief that they can control their own fate (McClelland, 1961; Shapiro, undated). One group of manufacturing entrepreneurs was characterized as having had poor relations with their fathers, their teachers, and their employers. They seemed to be driven to entrepreneurship by their need to avoid being in a subordinate relationship to others (Collins and Moore, 1970). A number of studies have shown that entrepreneurs often come from families where the father or a close relative was in business for himself (Roberts and Wainer, 1971; Shapero, 1975). A number of studies have also demonstrated that some sub-groups of a society have higher rates of entrepreneurship than others; young members of such sub-groups (such as the Chinese in South-East Asia or the Indians in East Africa) are surrounded by "role-models" of entrepreneurship. They may also choose this career path because other career paths are closed to them in the larger society (Hagen, 1971). The thrust of these various research studies is that some people, by virtue of their family background and early childhood influences, are much more likely to start businesses. However, entrepreneurial inclinations, like musical talent, may or may not be capitalized upon. A number of other factors, discussed below, interact to create a climate more or less favorable to starting a new business.

The typical entrepreneur with technical or managerial training starts his business when he is in his thirties (Cooper, 1973; Liles, 1974). It is then that he has the track record, experience, and savings to make founding feasible, while still having the energy level and willingness to take risks which are necessary. Thus, the conditions which exist when potential technical entrepreneurs are in their thirties, including the organizations they then work for and the environmental climate then extant, determine whether they will be likely to found new businesses. However, evidence on the founders of mom and pop firms suggest a wider range of ages at the time of founding (Mayer and Goldstein, 1961).

A second major factor influencing whether a potential entrepreneur will start a new business is the nature of the organization for which he works. This organization, which might be termed an incubator, seems to play a particularly important role in the founding of high-technology firms. It locates the potential founder in a particular geographic area which may or may not have a favorable entrepreneurial climate. (A number of studies have shown that most entrepreneurs start their businesses where they are already living and working; it is the rare founder who moves at the time he is starting a new business. (Susbauer, 1972; Cooper, 1973).

The incubator organization also provides the entrepreneur with the experience which leads to particular managerial skills and industry knowledge. Since industries vary widely in the extent to which they offer opportunities for new ventures, this means that the strategy of the incubator organization determines to a great extent whether its employees will ever be in a position to spin off and start their own businesses. Thus, an established organization in a mature industry with little growth and heavy capital requirements is unlikely to have many spin-offs. Its employees, no matter how motivated, are not acquiring the technical and market knowledge which can easily be translated into the strategic decision to start a new business.

The policies of potential incubator organizations also appear to determine, to a marked degree, the motivations of the entrepreneur. In response to brief questionnaire surveys, founders tend to report the socially acceptable reasons as to why they became entrepreneurs; these include such factors as the desire for independence and financial gain. However, depth interviews often disclose that the founder was "pushed" from the parent organization by frustration (Cooper, 1973; Shapero, 1975). Studies of spin-off rates from established organizations show that internal factors influence spin-off rates, with internal problems being associated with high rates of spin-off and placid times being associated with low rates (Cooper, 1973). Thus, the extent to which the strategic and operating decisions of the established firm satisfy or frustrate its employees influences whether spin-offs occur.

A complex of factors external to the individual and to the parent organization also appears to influence entrepreneurship. Much of the research in this area is only suggestive, but it seems that climates can change over time and that past entrepreneurship makes future entrepreneurship more likely. A number of researchers report that the credibility of the act of starting a company appears to depend, in part, upon whether the founder knows of others who have taken this step (Shapero, 1975). Venture capital availability and particularly the existence of well-developed communication channels vary across geographic regions and help to determine the feasibility of entrepreneurship. The presence of experienced entrepreneurs also influences future entrepreneurship; they serve as sources of advice and venture capital and they sometimes do what they know best — start additional new businesses (Lamont, 1972; Cooper, 1973). Their companies become excellent incubators for other spin-offs and also offer consulting opportunities for fledgling founders who are seeking income while trying to get started. It seems clear that past entrepreneurship influences the climate for future entrepreneurship. What is not so clear and what deserves additional research is how an area begins to become entrepreneurially active or how an area which has been active becomes less so.

The three broad factors just discussed influence the entrepreneurial decision as summarized in Exhibit 6.1.

There are many opportunities for further research relating to the start-up stage of new firms, several of which are discussed below:

1. To what extent are there differences across geographic regions or across different segments of the population in what might be termed an "entrepreneurial environment"? This would reflect differences in knowledge about entrepreneurship and perceptions of the risks and rewards associated with starting new firms. Is it possible to measure an "entrepreneurial environment"? Is it possible to change such an environment and to measure the changes?

2. Communication networks presumably bring entrepreneurs and sources of venture capital together. What are the processes by which entrepreneurs make contact with non-institutional sources of venture capital? Are there regional differences in communication networks? Is it possible to create or modify communication networks to facilitate the process by which particular kinds of entrepreneurs make contact with particular kinds of venture capital sources?

3. How do regions change to become more or less entrepreneurial over time? In particular, in an area with very little entrepreneurship, how do the first businesses get established? How do entrepreneurially-active areas become less ac-

Exhibit 6.1 Influences upon the Entrepreneurial Decision

ANTECEDENT INFLUENCES
UPON ENTREPRENEUR

1. Genetic factors

2. Family influences

3. Educational choices

4. Previous career experiences

INCUBATOR ORGANIZATION

1. Geographic location

2. Nature of skills and knowledge acquired

3. Contact with possible fellow founders

4. Motivation to stay with or to
   leave organization

5. Experience in a "small business" setting

ENVIRONMENTAL FACTORS

1. Economic conditions

2. Accessibility and availability
   of venture capital

3. Examples of entrepreneurial action

4. Opportunities for interim consulting

5. Availability of personnel and supporting
   services; accessibility of customers.

> Entrepreneur's decision

tive? What is the role of the life cycles of the dominant industries in such regions in influencing entrepreneurship?

4. The role of the incubator organization has been investigated primarily in relation to the founding of high-technology firms. Research might focus upon whether it helps to explain how other kinds of new firms are started at particular times and places.

THE COMPETITIVE STRATEGY OF THE NEW FIRM

The decision to start a new firm is clearly a strategic decision. However, also of interest here is the cluster of decisions which determine the nature of the new business, including the products or services to be offered, the markets to be served, and the policies to be emphasized. What has been learned about the influences upon these decisions in the new firm and about the relationship between particular strategies and performance?

Since the new business draws primarily upon the knowledge and skills of the entrepreneur, one might expect that the product/market choice would be closely tied to the experience gained in the incubator organization. For the most part this is true, although it varies by industry. New companies are closely related to the nature of the business of the parent firms for about 80% to 85% of high-technology firms; for non-technical manufacturing and service firms, the corresponding percentages are 50% to 55% (Mayer and Goldstein, 1961; Hoad and Rosko, 1964; Cooper, 1973). For new franchises, the percentage is probably very low, since the franchisor supplies the expertise rather than the founder.

There has not been much explicit research on how the founder decides what policies to emphasize in trying to establish a competitively viable business. We can draw some inferences from general descriptions of the process and from case studies. For larger, more professionally-based ventures, and particularly for those seeking venture capital, there typically is a new business plan. Such a plan describes the way in which the proposed firm is to compete and presumably reflects considerable thought. For that much larger group of new ventures which starts without the discipline of seeking outside capital, the process of deciding upon a basis of competition seems to be informal and intuitive. It may be based upon an excellent, first-hand "feel" for the market. However, many new service businesses of the mom and pop type seem to be started opportunistically, with the availability of particular facilities or sites being important determinants (Mayer and Goldstein, 1961).

There has been little explicit research on the relationships between characteristics of founders, the strategies of their firms, and subsequent performance. There has been some research on high-technology firms, though, which suggests that successful new firms are more likely than unsuccessful new firms to be started by multiple founders, have more initial capital, transfer more technology from the parent organization, are more likely to have a marketing function, show greater concern for personnel matters, and are more likely to have spun-off from large organizations than from small ones (Roberts, 1972; Cooper and Bruno, 1977). With regard to strategy, those new high-technology firms whose strategies were related to the parent firms, in markets served and technology utilized, were more likely to be successful. In addition, a longitudinal study of 95 new manufacturing firms indicated that those judged to be successful were more likely to have been started by two or more founders and more likely to have founders with both relevant experience and post high school education (Hoad and Rosko, 1964).

Research opportunities, focusing upon the strategy of the new firm, might include the following:

1. The process by which entrepreneurs choose strategies for new firms might be examined. These processes are probably related to characteristics of the entrepreneurs. Subsequent performance might also be related to the processes followed by the founders.

2. Much more needs to be learned about the relationship between new firm performance and the chosen strategy. Important dimensions might include the product/market choice, the basis of competition or the business strategy, and the relationship to the industry life cycle.

STRATEGIC MANAGEMENT IN THE EARLY GROWTH STAGE

As a new firm becomes established, the founder typically continues to be in direct contact with all activities and decisions. Many businesses of modest potential stabilize at this point, often with no hired employees. Other firms continue to grow, adding employees and sometimes additional management. When this occurs the founder or founders may delegate operating decisions, but not strategic decisions. As indicated in the stages of growth literature, management methods continue to be informal, with few policies and with control exercised primarily through direct contact (Westfall, 1969; Uyterhoeven *et al.*, 1973; Hosmer *et al.*, 1977).

As the new business gets started, it immediately begins to receive "feedback" from the market. Sometimes, the assumptions underlying the new firm's strategy prove to be faulty, with the result that the firm often runs out of cash before reaching the break-even point. There has been no explicit research on the nature or frequency of change in the strategies of new firms; however, cases and anecdotal evidence suggest that some founders do change their strategies shortly after startup. Thus, an electronics component manufacturer switches to sub-contract work, or an ice-cream parlor becomes a steakhouse. At this point, the entrepreneur has the opportunity to "change on a dime;" there is no organization to convince and there is little commitment to the status quo. However, much will depend upon how the entrepreneur perceives the environment, whether he perceives it as it really is or as he would like to see it (Schrage, 1965). Founders are sometimes stubborn people with a dream who are not really amenable to dispassionate analysis of their plans.

As the new firm becomes established, the extent to which management confronts strategic decisions varies with the kind of firm and the characteristics of its industry. For the mom and pop business in a stable environment, the focus is usually upon operating decisions. Whether the strategy is reexamined and whether opportunities are then pursued appears to depend on the characteristics of management. In experiments conducted in India, owner-managers who had received achievement-motivation training frequently investigated or undertook changes in strategy (McClelland, 1965). There has been very little research on the frequency or nature of strategic change in such firms. There would seem to be research opportunities in examining the stability or flexibility of their strategies and relating these to environmental turbulence and characteristics of the entrepreneurs.

For those businesses which grow to become what we have classified as stable, high-payoff firms or growth-oriented firms, there are decisions associated with evolving successful strategies. However, we lack systematic research to indicate whether these firms have high-potential strategies from the time of founding or whether these strategies evolve from the feedback of the market place. One study of 270 manufacturing firms indicated that companies which achieved annual sales of $100,000 or more in sales did so in their first ten years; old small companies usually didn't grow (McGuire, 1963). The firms in this sample also showed great stability in their strategies, with only one in twelve making substantial product changes in a nine year period.

There is substantial "wisdom-based" literature analyzing the characteristics of small firms and suggesting the most suitable strategies. Small firms, particularly those in the early stages of evolution, have limited financial and human resources. They have almost no reputation and little in the way of economies of scale or benefits from experience curves. There is a concentration of risk in one or a few products, markets, and people; there is usually no cushion to absorb the results of bad luck or bad decisions. The capabilities of the new firm are often uneven, reflecting the unbalanced experience of the entrepreneur (Buchele, 1967).

Against these disadvantages, the new firm has no ties to the past; it can innovate, without worrying about the effect on existing sales. This, coupled with the talents and drive of the founding group, is undoubtedly one reason why new and small firms have been such remarkably fertile sources of technical innovation, accounting for major new innovations all out of proportion to their R&D expenditures (Charpie, et al., 1967). (Of course, most small firms are not particularly innovative; it is the growth-oriented small firms which are most likely to have this characteristic.) New firms also have the ability to move quickly; the chain of command is short and decision methods are informal and, if not carefully documented, at least timely. Management often has a first-hand "feel" for the realities of customers and operations, based not upon the abstractions of reports, but upon day-to-day contact. Small firms also can avoid the departmentalization and coordination problems which characterize large, complex organizations. There may be a lack of staff specialists and formalized analysis, but there is the opportunity to focus the attention of the organization upon opportunities. The small organization, with its shared sense of the need to survive, can create a cost consciousness and dedication which are difficult to achieve in large, profitable firms where each individual knows that his contributions are only a small part of the whole. Of course, in all instances there are potential advantages which may or may not be realized, depending upon the competence and commitment of management.

The advice of most writers seems to be that

the small firm should choose a "niche" and avoid direct competition with larger companies. Some would modify this advice to say that direct competition is possible, but that the small firm should concentrate where it has a competitive advantage, or where the large firm is complacent or doing a poor job (Bursk, undated; Kline, 1955; Hosmer, 1957; Gross, 1967b; Katz, 1970). Thus, large firms tend to concentrate on mass markets, so small firms should concentrate on specialized markets. Large firms tend to be slow to react, so small firms should concentrate on opportunities arising from rapid market change. Large firms tend to be organized to produce in large production runs and to offer standardized service. Small firms can concentrate on short production runs, quick delivery, and extra service. Large firms must be concerned about whether raw material supplies, work forces, and manufacturing and personnel policies are suitable for large volume operations. Small companies can use scarce materials, locate in areas with small labor forces, and utilize unique approaches, unconcerned about the implications if these were applied throughout a large corporation. Large firms must be concerned about government regulatory attitudes and their visibility to communities and unions. Small firms have a low profile and can move more quickly and be less concerned about the reactions of such groups. The evidence supporting these recommendations is anecdotal and is based upon general observation. Much of it appears to be sound, but there is no systematic research examining the strategies of large numbers of firms and their performance over time.

The process of strategic planning in small firms has received attention in several articles (LeBreton, 1963; Steiner, 1967; Gilmore, 1971; Wheelwright, 1971). The small firm environment makes heavy demands upon management for day-to-day operations and there are usually no staff specialists to provide support. Explicit efforts to set aside blocks of time for planning and to shield management from day-to-day pressures may be necessary (Golde, 1964). Structured approaches to the process of planning have been recommended by several authors. Unlike large organizations, the emphasis is not upon deciding how to allocate resources among businesses or upon formal planning as a communication mechanism. The primary focus is upon mechanisms for identifying problems and for "stepping-back" to look at the implications of current strategy. Recognizing the flexibility of small firms, particular emphasis should be placed on short-term planning (Cohn and Lindberg, 1972, 1974).

The early growth stage of new firms offers a number of opportunities for further research:

1. The relationships between performance and strategy might be studied for a number of types of firms. One particularly interesting group includes those stable, high-payoff companies which enjoy unusually high rates of return. Many of the most profitable firms in American industry are in this category (Hosmer, et al., 1977). Identification of their strategies and careful examination of their reasons for success could be a fruitful study.

2. The frequency and nature of strategic change in new firms might be examined. Change in strategy would probably be related to environmental change or stability and to the characteristics of the entrepreneurs. It might also be related to the degree of success of the initial strategy.

STRATEGIC MANAGEMENT IN THE LATER GROWTH STAGE

Many small businesses stabilize and maintain an internal environment in which the president is in direct contact with the key activities, possibly with a small management team, each member of which is responsible for a key function. However, growth-oriented small businesses may continue to grow, adding additional levels of management.

The internal environment for management then begins to change, as the sheer volume of activities compels the founder to turn some duties over to others (Buchele, 1967; Westfall, 1969). Typically, the role of the founder changes, with "doing" activities largely delegated and with the job becoming more managerial in character (Hosmer, et al., 1977). Many operating decisions may be delegated, although the president continues to be deeply involved in strategic decisions. One of the distinguishing characteristics of the very small firm, the president's direct contact with employees, products, and customers, begins to change. More formal ways must be developed to keep management informed and to control operations. Policies must be developed and increased formality occurs (Scott, 1971; Uyterhoeven, *et al.*, 1973). Top management must try to develop new skills in managing through others and in developing an organization. Some entrepreneurs are not suited for this kind of managerial task and their shortcomings may prevent the firm from growing successfully or may lead to the entrepreneur's departure (Mancuso, 1973; Snyder, 1974).

These changes in the internal environment both aid and hamper effective strategic management. The growth in the organization may give the president more time for planning. The growing firm may have more resources to pursue particular activities and to withstand competitors' challenges. However, growth may cause management to "lose touch"; control of operations may suffer and management's feel for markets, competitors, and organizational capabilities may diminish. Implementation of strategy, which is typically one area where a small firm has a real advantage, becomes more of a problem as the organization grows. Case and anecdotal data, as well as a number of authors, document these kinds of changes. However, there has been little investigation of whether these problems develop gradually or whether there are continuous changes.

Many growth-oriented small firms seem to be positioned in newly-developing industries. As such, management faces the challenges of adapting strategy to the changing demands of an evolving industry. The strategic implications of industry life cycles become particularly important for these firms (Hofer, 1975). It is widely believed that new industries are characterized by a high rate of new company formation and a high rate of entry by established firms, both small and large. Later, there is often a "shake-out" as the stronger competitors enlarge their market shares. The extent to which small firms survive as an industry matures appears to vary

widely. In those industries in which a shake-out process occurs, some small firms survive and even prosper. Research focusing upon the strategies of surviving and non-surviving small firms in industries undergoing great change would seem promising.

We might speculate that the increasing emphasis upon experience curve theory and the importance of market share may mean that small firms will have fewer opportunities in the early stages of industry development than in the past (*Perspectives on Experience*, 1968). As has occurred in the semi-conductor industry, larger firms may increasingly price on the basis of future costs, thereby pre-empting opportunities and making the costs of "staying in the game" too high for smaller firms. On the other hand, emphasis on having a dominant market position may lead more large firms to withdraw from industries where their market shares are low, thereby creating opportunities for smaller firms.

Growth-oriented small firms sometimes owe their success to innovative strategies. A number of authors have commented on how the small firm environment is conducive to innovation, with its informal decision processes in which relatively few executives must be convinced, its lack of commitment to the status quo, its low sales requirements to be successful, and its low costs of development (Cooper, 1966; Charpie, *et al.*, 1967). The increasing emphasis upon short-term performance measurement in large firms may cause decreased emphasis on innovation, particularly of radically different products and processes. This environmental change may create added opportunities for the innovation minded small firm. However, the small firm may sometimes pioneer and then be faced with severe competition. What is surprising is that there has been very little research on the most appropriate strategies for small firms which have been successful in innovation, but then face severe competition in a growing market.

The growth-oriented small firm has the potential for substantial economic impact and also offers the opportunity for interesting research. In addition to topics already discussed, the following might be investigated:

1. Systematic examination of the strategies of small firms experiencing high growth would be useful. One interesting aspect to examine would be the extent to which these high growth firms compete directly with large companies; much of the literature implies that, in seeking a niche, small firms should avoid direct competition with large companies.

2. The founders of growth-oriented firms face the challenge of changing and of developing new skills as their organizations grow. Research focusing upon the changing roles of founders in growing organizations would be interesting.

3. The planning of the organizational structure and the determination of the appropriate degree of formality and structure is a continuing problem in the growing small firm. Research might examine the changes necessary, the signals which indicate a need for organizational change, the determinants of the timing of those changes, and the problems to be overcome.

STRATEGIC MANAGEMENT IN INTRACORPORATE VENTURES

A number of writers have suggested that large firms seem to be better at developing existing businesses than at growing new ones (Peterson, 1967; Hill and Hlavacek, 1972; Hanan, 1976). The large firm can bring great resources to bear upon new opportunities and can absorb failures. However, performance measurement systems often penalize those divisions and executives who assume risks. New ventures can disrupt existing manufacturing and marketing activities. New ventures often require different kinds of people and facilities and an orientation toward working closely with customers, short production runs, and continually changing technology (Fast, 1977).

An increasing number of corporations have developed new venture departments to facilitate intracorporate entrepreneurship. Several surveys have examined the extent of this practice, the different forms of new venture activities, and the problems encountered in implementation. Two surveys, both published in 1973, indicated that the number of new venture departments was increasing (Susbauer, 1973; Vesper and Holmdahl, 1973). As might be expected, large firms have adopted formal intracorporate entrepreneurship programs to a greater degree than smaller firms (Susbauer, 1973). However, more recent research suggests that many new venture departments are short-lived (Fast, 1977).

New venture department organizations may range from *ad hoc* task forces with no formal training, to departments with established budgets, to separate legal entities. Typically, these intracorporate entrepreneurial groups study proposed ventures and sometimes proceed to start new businesses — developing, producing, and marketing new products. They usually can call upon the resources of the larger organization, although this sometimes presents problems because of lack of authority over other departments. The performance measurement system may be modified to place less emphasis on short-run profits. If the product is promising or becomes firmly established, it may be transferred to an existing department or become the basis for a new department.

Practices vary in the extent to which new ventures are separate, the timing of when products are transferred to the regular organization, and how venture managers are rewarded. An extreme form of venture management might be termed "sponsored spin-offs" in which, with the parent firm's blessing, a separate new enterprise is created, possibly with the parent company holding some of the equity (Cooper and Riggs, 1975). There have been no published studies of the long-term success of operating companies acting as venture capitalists.

Some of the issues associated with organizing venture management departments include determining how managers are to be rewarded and how their careers are affected if they return to the main organization. Other issues relate to the extent to which they can call upon resources from the main organization and the degree of delegation — the extent to which they can act as if they were managing their own firms.

Research by Fast (1977) indicated that new venture departments usually evolve, becoming operating divisions, staff departments, or new venture departments which differ in size, objectives, and corporate impact from their earlier versions. Sometimes the departments are disbanded. The two major influences upon the evolution of a new venture department appear to be the changing nature of the firm's venture strategy and its political support within the organization.

To date, the literature on venture management activities has been primarily of two types: surveys of existing practices or case-based studies in which the approaches of particular firms are described. There has been little research in which specific practices have been compared across companies of different types, with emphasis upon trying to determine the most effective venture management approaches for different kinds of environments.

OPPORTUNITIES FOR FUTURE RESEARCH

The literature on strategic management in small business and new ventures has been primarily discursive, wisdom-based, and prescriptive in character. Some of this literature has been based upon shrewd observation and testing within the environments of particular firms. However, systematic, formal, empirical research, of the sort that has helped move other fields forward, has been notable by its absence. Most of the formal research which has been done has related to the start-up stage, and especially to the strategic decision to start a new venture.

Empirical research on new and small firms must overcome certain inherent problems. There is little published data about individual smaller firms. It is true that for firms whose stock is traded over-the-counter there are annual reports and other financial data; however, most small firms are not publicly held and, even for those companies which are, the amount of published data is quite limited compared to that available on larger firms. One result is that research on new and small firms usually must be field research, involving direct contact with the firm or the entrepreneur. In pursuing field research in large organizations, written records and procedures can be helpful in understanding both historic decisions and the processes by which decisions have been made and implemented. By contrast, the researcher within the smaller com-

pany usually can find very little documentation on past decisions or procedures. Both must be determined through interviews and observation. Much of the process of planning occurs inside the minds of one or two people.

Performance data for smaller companies are difficult to interpret. In closely-held companies, reported profits may be minimized through large executive salaries and perquisites and through payments to relatives. New companies, particularly those which are growth-oriented, may invest heavily in product and market development, resulting in losses or low profits even when the firms are well-managed. Furthermore, the corporate goals may be intertwined with the personal values of the owner-managers to a marked degree; the satisfactions and life-styles of the founders may be difficult to measure in any systematic way.

However, research on smaller firms also has advantages. There are many small businesses, so that it may be possible to build up substantial samples. Although small company managers are busy and sometimes secretive, many are willing to cooperate. In addition, all the researchers must do is convince the president; there are no delays while the question of whether to cooperate is passed up the line. Smaller companies also are simpler and easier to comprehend. Since they are usually not diversified, performance may be related more directly to particular product/market strategies.

As previously noted, the literature on new ventures and small businesses is characterized by some survey and case research and a great deal of discursive writing. A particular need exists for field research in which hypotheses or research questions are formulated and data are gathered to test these hypotheses. All of the topic areas considered could benefit from, and in fact now cry out for, this kind of empirical research.

A number of specific research opportunities have been discussed in the preceding sections. To summarize one of the major themes, studies are needed which would relate the strategies and the performance of small firms in particular industries. More specifically, research could focus upon the strategies and the performance of small firms which have different resource positions and which compete in industries in different life cycle stages. Longitudinal studies, looking at the performance associated with different strategies over time, seem desirable; one alternative would be to examine an industry undergoing great change and to analyze successful and unsuccessful small firm strategies under those conditions. Studies which would compare and contrast the processes by which strategic decisions are made and implemented in large and in small organizations would be useful. Since growing small firms experience such great internal change, research could focus upon the changing processes of management, including the changing role of the president. In regard to the strategic decisions associated with starting new firms, experimental research, examining the effect of action programs to change the environment, are promising; some programs of this sort are already being supported by the National Science Foundation (Colton and Udell, 1976).

As to types of businesses, the mom and pop firms are the most numerous; they are of particular interest to the Small Business Administration because most of its clients are of this type. However, the economic impact of each individual firm is limited, many are very poorly managed, and the percentage of owner-managers willing to cooperate with university researchers is probably lower than for other categories.

Growth-oriented firms, particularly high-technology firms, have been the subject of previous research. Their economic potential makes them of obvious interest and their managers, often university trained, are likely to be cooperative. However, the number of such firms is relatively small and in some parts of the country researchers do not have ready access to many such companies.

Stable, high-payoff companies may be a fruitful area of study. Some of these companies are extremely profitable, although most of the profits may be paid out in salaries and perquisites. The most successful firms in this category are probably achieving the highest returns in American industry.

Strategic management in new and smaller firms appears to operate with both constraints and opportunities different from those in large organizations. As a field of research, the potential is great and the benefits, in terms of improved economic performance, can be substantial.

Commentary

JEFFREY C. SUSBAUER
Cleveland State University

Cooper's paper has delineated the range of prior research on small business and internal new venturing as it relates to policy research. This paper focuses attention on two topics discussed by Cooper from a different perspective, and suggests the need for more formal and utilitarian data bases if policy research in this area is to advance beyond discursive wisdom.

It has been well-documented elsewhere (*Statistical Abstract*, 1976) that in our free enterprise system, it is extremely easy to initiate a new venture, and it is almost as easy to fail. The majority of small firms do not reach maturity, and of those which survive, there are relatively few that achieve high success as defined by "normal" criteria of ROI, profitability, market share, and so on (Susbauer, 1969; Hoffman and Shapero, 1971; Cooper and Bruno, 1977).

Despite the failure rates, there are many reasons why small firms and new ventures are appropriate subjects for policy research. Among these are:

1. A pervasive fascination with the Great American Dream. Given this fascination, it is

appropriate to investigate what makes successful and surviving enterprises.

2. A growing popularity of courses dealing with small businesses, including the business policy course. The student appeal of such course content suggests a need to address the policy and strategy issues of such firms with the rigor and insights traditionally used for the study of the larger firm.

3. From a pragmatic viewpoint, to provide some answers to questions of improving small firm performance and the success rate of internal new ventures. If policy research can improve the survival and success rates, then society, government and the enterprises themselves benefit.

4. The small firm can represent a microcosmic image of the larger enterprise without much of the distortion that the more complex organization's size, human interactions, structure and history creates. Thus, observation and translation of the significant variables in organization and policy processes can sometimes be seen and evaluated more clearly in small firms than in larger enterprise.

THE NEED FOR A DATA BASE

If a valid purpose of policy research is to effect change in the performance of firms and enable growth to potential, then policy research on smaller enterprises should concentrate on those classes of firms which can be most easily identified, manipulated and evaluated. There is a crucial data base problem associated with developing streams of policy research in small firms because the data currently available is not well organized and does not reflect the different orientations of enterpreneurs and their firms.

There appears to be a need for a national data bank developed for small firms that is organized in appropriate ways to take the key variables into account. Research in other countries has already addressed this problem with some success by an orientation to data gathering on the basis of industry (Bolton Report, 1971; Meredith, 1975; Smyth, 1975; Watkins, 1975). Robert Morris Associates and various trade associations regularly gather operating

performance data on small firms in the U.S. However, these data have not been systematically culled for insights into operating and strategy performance for different classes of small firms. It would appear that a comprehensive effort would be the logical starting point for any large-scale effort to create such a data base.

A SMALL FIRM TYPOLOGY

Both Cooper's paper and Hosmer, Cooper, and Vesper (1977), have created typologies of small firms which are discussed by Cooper and Vesper in this set of papers and need not be repeated here. A different, but parallel typology continuum is discussed below that should be considered in developing appropriate data bases from which to elicit policy research.

The following typology is based on differing definitions of "success" for small enterprises. If Dun & Bradstreet is correct, success for the fledgling firm in very high-failure industries may well be equated with "survival." For other small enterprises, success might be defined in terms of the total compensation the entrepreneur is able to extract from the enterprise. In still others, success might be defined as a situation where the firm is leveraged to the maximum to enable high growth.

Without claiming exhaustion of the possibilities on the "success" continuum, there appear to be four types of small enterprise with sufficiently different characteristics that warrant discussion:

1. The survival firm
2. The attractive growth potential firm
3. The underachieving firm
4. The high success growth firm

Each type is described briefly below, with some discussion about the applicability of policy research to firms fitting these criteria.

THE SURVIVAL FIRM

The first class of firm to be considered is often referred to in popular jargon as the "mom and pop" store. The vast majority of all American business firms can be so categorized. Independent franchises — a dying breed in America — also fit this category. The firm fitting this stereotype is usually undercapitalized, undermanaged, and has extremely limited potential. It may fill a market niche, but it is unlikely to be even regional in scope. This kind of enterprise has the highest failure rate, and *succeeds by surviving*.

Government assistance programs, such as those devised by the U.S. Small Business Administration, are directed at attacking the problems of the "mom and pop" firm. In the decade of the 1960's, a descriptive research program was conducted to gather data about these firms (e.g., Mayer and Goldstein, 1961; Delano et al., 1966). The recommendations of these studies have largely been implemented where practicable. However, the research that was conducted has not seemed to affect the survival rate of such firms to any marked degree.

Policy research could be directed at the "mom and pop" store, but it is unlikely that significant impact will result because the entrepreneur will not usually comprehend or generally accept and implement strategic changes, even if he or she has the financial and/or managerial capability to do so. Given the problems associated with improving the performance of these firms, and in the absence of social, political and economic barriers to market entry, time and effort might be better spent encouraging Congress to pass a "Mom and Pop" Welfare Bill than to perform policy research on these firms. For these reasons, policy research on small firms is better directed elsewhere.

The Attractive Growth Potential Firm

The second type of small firm also defines success in terms of survival, at least initially. However, the survival criterion is simply an intermediate step on the way to more substantial financial performance. High technology firms frequently fall into this category. Regionally-based retailers, multi-location service firms and some manufacturing and wholesaling firms also may be placed in this slot.

The attractive growth potential firm is similar to the multiple-founder spin-off described by Cooper and Bruno (1977). These firms usually target a specialized market, are growth-oriented, have professional management and management assistance, and are backed by proper capitalization.

The policy research problems here lie in identifying attractive growth potential firms and in studying their characteristics. Within a given industry, such firms will usually be in the minority. By definition, the attractive growth potential firm has survived, but has not yet achieved "normal" success as measured by criteria such as ROI, market share, profitability, and so on. Consequently, there will be a real reluctance on the part of the entrepreneur to have the characteristics of the firm and its strategic secrets researched. Given problems of identification, access and secrecy, it is doubtful that policy research efforts will produce transferable data or findings that will be authorized for release.

The Underachieving Firm

In terms of research potential, the underachieving firm may be far more fruitful than the survival or attractive growth potential firm. In underachieving firms, anecdotal evidence suggests that a market niche has generally been established, and that the entrepreneur has reached a stage where he/she is able to derive a substantial standard of living from the fruits of the enterprise. The "true" potential of the firm is not being realized however.

Underachievement appears to be of two basic types. The first is a *conscious* underachievement; the second is *unintentional* sub-optimization of company potential.

CONSCIOUS UNDERACHIEVEMENT. Consciously underachieving entrepreneurs and their firms can be found in areas where there appear to be excellent and expanding markets, current technology, and good growth potential. The conscious part of the underachievement generally is rooted in the basic character of the entrepreneur. Such entrepreneurs may recognize their limited capability to grow the firm, may desire to keep the enterprise privately held, or have a value system that recognizes leisure as being as important as the hard work of growth.

When academic researchers observe firms like this, their perception is usually one of wasted potential. However, instead of viewing these firms as underutilizing their potential, policy researchers might consider the non-traditional criteria that may govern the behavior of such entrepreneurs and their firms. *Fortune, Duns,* and similar periodicals feature articles describing the views of large firm executive officers and relating how their philosophies and ambitions affect the performance and shape of their companies. Why not analogous research into the insights that might be furnished by consciously underachieving entrepreneurs?

The underachievement philosophy has negative ramifications for the satisfaction of subordinate and market needs, but as our society moves towards increasing leisure time, the study of consciously underachieving entrepreneurs and their firms may be a fruitful area of research. There may be problems of identifying firms in which to conduct such research, but secrecy and access should not present major obstacles. Truthfulness in relating strategy and the accuracy of perceptions of the entrepreneur may be an issue in such research, but that is beyond the scope of the present discussion.

UNINTENTIONALLY UNDERACHIEVING FIRMS. Some small companies do not achieve their potential, not because of the personal aspirations of the entrepreneur, but because the potential is unintentionally thwarted by actions (or inactions) on the part of the entrepreneur. The anecdotal evidence suggests that unintentional underachievement may be linked to a mismatch of technology, market, finance, and/or management capabilities.

Where unintentional underachievement is the case, it would appear that fruitful policy research could be performed with a pragmatic eye to multiplying findings so that effective policy/strategy options can be developed as guidelines for entrepreneurs creating and managing firms. Identifying unintentional underachievers may be somewhat difficult, particularly in the absence of the appropriate data base, but access to and sharing of information should not be difficult once identification has been accomplished.

THE HIGH SUCCESS GROWTH FIRM

Growth enterprises that have survived and are achieving their potential constitute the fourth stereotypical firm in the continuum. Such firms may still be managed by their founding entrepreneur, and may maintain a high degree of continuing entrepreneurial activity in the firm, as business planning techniques begin to rationalize behavior in the firm, and strategic issues become of direct concern as old products cycle to maturity, new products are created to fill new niches, and the firm expands.

The usual success criteria are appropriate for measuring the performance of this type of firm. The successful growth firm most closely resembles the *Fortune*-listed company, and thus has the most promise for policy/strategy research. Unlike the promising high growth firms, normal restrictions, secrecy and access are no longer significant issues to the successful growth firm: Hence, high success growth firms frequently can be identified, but are still not easily accessed, in the earlier stages of their growth.

There are some advantages of researching policy and strategy issues in high success growth firms. These firms are still on a high growth track, and still operate semi-entrepreneurially without many of the bureaucratic trappings of more mature enterprises. Consequently, some of the confounding variables that organization structure, largeness itself, and professional management by committee bring to the very large firm, do not dominate to as great an extent when the researcher studies the high success growth enterprise. The growth strategy may be clearer and more "pure" in such a firm. For those interested in successful decision processes, the track record exists, but is not obscured by as much shared decision responsibility as in the larger firm.

While the high success growth firm mirrors its larger cousin in many respects, the chief advantage of studying its character and strategy lies in its relative simplicity. The danger, of course, lies in the appearance of truth versus the actuality of what "is." This is a continual danger, given the anecdotal nature of most policy research on even larger small enterprises. This danger is minimized somewhat by the application of more normal success criteria appropriate to high success growth companies.

INTERNAL NEW VENTURES

Once growth is achieved, a major question confronting management is the maintenance of growth. There may be clues from policy research on small firms that can assist this strategic process in large firms.[1]

There are many strategic options for growth. Among them are development of new products, penetration of new markets with old products, acquisitions, licensing, joint venturing, and other options which are essentially combinations of two or more of the above (Baker and Susbauer, 1977a). Internal options for growth may include the creation of entirely new ventures within the existing corporation.

Some growth options require an entrepreneurial thrust to achieve effective results. Unfortunately, as organizations grow larger, it becomes more difficult to attract and retain entrepreneurial individuals in the corporation (Susbauer, 1973; Baker and Susbauer, 1977a). Moreover, the entrepreneur finds it more difficult to maintain his/her entrepreneurial integrity in the face of the dominant corporate policy which demands conformity. Entrepreneurs within the large corporation also face substantial problems in acquiring (pirating?) resources to test their new venture ideas (Anagnostopoulos, 1975).

Large corporations can provide a significant amount of creature comforts that can individually and collectively threaten an entrepreneur. When an independent entrepreneur fails, the data show that a large percentage simply begin acquiring resources to start over (Shapero et al.,

1969; Susbauer, 1969). When an entrepreneur within a large firm creates a failure, this usually jeopardizes his/her status, role, and bargaining power to either begin again or re-blend into corporate structure. Failure of an internal new venture can substantially damage corporate performance and limit options for the entire firm.

On the positive side, the independent entrepreneur can generally obtain a direct correlation between success and material achievement for himself. The internal entrepreneur bucks existing corporate policy which generally limits the individual up-side potential rewards for venture success (Baker and Susbauer, 1977a).

Internal new venturing is also thwarted by the size of the parent firm. This has at least two dimensions. The relatively small, but larger, established firm has a difficult financial and philosophical time with the internal entrepreneur who has a market/product concept that might translate into a new venture which would equal or exceed the parent enterprise. By contrast, the very large firm has a difficult time perceiving the worth of a potential internal new venture which does not have an apparent market of $50–$100 million within five years of start up. This latter orientation is also currently shared by professional venture capital firms, to the woe of many would-be entrepreneurs with good ideas for smaller sized market niches (Hoffman and Shapero, 1971; Griggs, 1972; Baker and Susbauer, 1977b).

SUMMARY AND CONCLUSIONS

New venturing, whether independently or internally, is a high risk/high reward strategy. Policy research needs to be directed at isolating and identifying appropriate strategies which can reduce the risk for both the entrepreneur and the firm while retaining the potential rewards.

To achieve these ends, and to achieve substantial advancement of an organized body of knowledge about policy and strategy in entrepreneurial endeavors, the problems of inadequate and inappropriate data bases must be overcome. The data available do not generally recognize different entrepreneurial orientations,

---

[1] The question of growth itself is an issue among researchers. E. F. Schumacher (1973) postulates appropriate technology in a movement back to smallness. The Club of Rome (Meadows, et al., 1972) advocates "limits to growth" on the grounds that bigness is too resource consuming. Yet, the fact remains that without growth, peoples' aspirations, needs and ambitions cannot be achieved.

and ignore the stage of development of the firm.

There is little reason to research policy questions in most small firms. The degree to which small firms and new ventures grow and develop to their potential appears to directly reflect the aspirations, education, experience and training of the entrepreneur and his/her team, and the extent to which the entrepreneur can make the transition from entrepreneur to manager. In the case of internal new ventures, the critical variables also appear to include corporate understanding of entrepreneurship and venture nurturing.

Small venture success will remain elusively defined as long as researchers continue to apply traditional success criteria associated with large firms to various stage small enterprises. The formal recognition by policy researchers of the differences and similarities between small and large companies would appear to be essential to the development of the policy discipline and the firms themselves.

Commentary

KARL H. VESPER
University of Washington

INTRODUCTION

Extensions will be suggested here to complement the Cooper and Susbauer schemes for viewing research on entrepreneurship and small business to reveal gaps and opportunities for research in addition to those they have suggested. The Cooper and Susbauer papers have reviewed quite thoroughly the research to date in entrepreneurship and small business, pointing out what is known and where opportunities for additional study lie. Rather than attempting to embellish their summary by adding mention of a few more studies, this paper will seek to explore limitations of the conceptual frameworks they used for examining the entrepreneurship area in particular. Then other frameworks will be offered which both complement the Cooper and Susbauer schemes and, at the same time, reveal other directions for future research.

LIMITATIONS OF THE COOPER AND SUSBAUER SCHEMES

The framework erected by Cooper to display the existing literature on entrepreneurship and small business does so quite well, and therein lies its weakness. Because the literature, as Cooper points out, is very limited in relation to the field to be covered, its display does not demand as comprehensive a framework as the field deserves. His paper offers three main schemes for classifying research. First, three different types of companies: "Mom 'n Pop," Stable High Payoff and Growth Oriented. To this might be added another category he discusses: the new venture inside a larger organization, also referred to as internal entrepreneurship, or in Susbauer's paper intracorporate entrepreneurship. Second, Cooper suggests classification into three stages of company development: Startup, Early Growth, and Later Growth. Third, he suggests classification by four types of literature: Discursive, Case Studies, Field Surveys, and Field Research. He points out limitations and opportunities for further research, particularly for each of the three stages of company development, for intracorporate ventures, and to a lesser extent for each of the three different types of companies. Susbauer's discussion illustrates how finer gradation of company types than Cooper's first scheme can reveal more areas for study when he notes that not all companies with growth potential are growth oriented. There are those that may have growth potential but don't know it, and those that know they have it but do not choose to be growth oriented anyway. These can be important distinctions to note in pursuing research aimed ultimately at serving managers because they may reveal linkages between personal entrepreneurial desires and company strategic outcomes.

By comparing Cooper's first two schemes, company types and company development stages, some other gaps can be seen. The three developmental stages, startup, early growth and later growth, may seem to imply that startup is generally followed by growth. But in fact it is not. As Cooper notes, most companies are proprietorships or partnerships. Most of these fall into the Mom 'n Pop category, a lesser number into the stable high payoff category, and very few of them are destined for growth. Hence another developmental stage is implied which involves maturity without growth. Susbauer's expansion of Cooper's framework covers this category to some extent, by noting companies that barely survive and other companies that could grow, but have not. Susbauer leaves out companies that do more than survive, maybe even are fairly high payoff, and that want to grow, even try to grow, but find they can't. This seems a very worthwhile direction for study, first because, by definition, it represents an area where managers find themselves frustrated. Second, the number of client firms in this category is likely very large, considering the number of firms that remain small and the pervasiveness of the "growth ethic" throughout American business (and according to Parkinson non-business as well). Third, methodical research on why some types of firms stay small, even though they may prefer not to, is virtually nonexistent.

Another developmental stage which could be added to those given by both Cooper and Susbauer is that of longer range disposition of the firm. The company may be dissolved, may be taken over and carried on in its small form by new management, may grow into a large company, or may be merged with one or more other firms to take on quite a different organizational form. Each of these four general types of outcomes could represent a substantial field for investigation. There have been some studies of failures (Etcheson, 1962), but not on what variables a manager can control during dissolution and to what effect, nor on how the economic gap left by the dissolved company is refilled by the economic system and the attendant strategic opportunities that may go with it. The second general outcome type, continuance as a small firm through management succession, has been little studied. One investigation (Christenson, 1953) looked at this question and there have been some of the sorts of magazine articles Cooper categorizes as "discursive," but little else. Acquisition by individuals is a major personal strategy used by entrepreneurs for business entry, but except for individual case studies, little has been written either to pull together what the experience of those entrepreneurs teaches or to explore how else it could be done. The view from inside the firm concerning management succession in small companies would seem a likely subject for organizational behavior researchers, but their efforts to date seem confined only to large organizations. It would also seem that within those large organizations they might find opportunities to study the third type of general outcome, the effects of merger on the small firm, but that too has been left for future study. Only the fourth outcome type, growth into a large company, has been much treated in the literature, and even there, as can be seen in Cooper's discussion, the treatment has been light.

SOME OTHER CLASSIFICATION SYSTEMS

By devising and applying other classification schemes two effects are produced. The first is to demonstrate that entrepreneurship and small business are not, as the paucity of academic attention to date might imply, narrow and limited fields for study but are rather enormous. The second is to reveal and help define further gaps in the existing literature where worthwhile research opportunities lie. Two schemes will be suggested here for further unfolding the field of independent entrepreneurship.

One derives from the Schreier and Komives bibliography (1973) in which it is shown that there have been at least some scholastic publications within each of the following categories:

1. *Tycoon History* — The studies summarized by Cooper all focus on current or recent entrepreneurial activities. However, many of the most dramatic entrepreneurial adventures, like those of Ford, Carnegie and Rockefeller, occurred much further back and constitute a field of history, or business, depending upon personal viewpoint, as interesting and possibly instructive as any other.

2. *Psychology of Entrepreneurs* — How entrepreneurs perform on mental texts measuring achievement motivation, inner versus outer locus of control, risk propensity, and the like are classified by Cooper in connection with the startup phase. Approaching from the direction of psychology may extend the apparent research frontier.

3. *Sociology of Entrepreneurs* — This sub-field concerns how the psychology of entrepreneurs may be influenced by characteristics of the groups to which they belong: minorities, females, immigrants, etc. The resultant social mores and values, in turn, may enhance or repress entrepreneurial tendencies. Cooper alludes to part of this sub-field in mentioning impact of role models on startups. But references in the Schreier-Komives bibliography and books, such as that of Kilby (1971), suggest that there is much more to this aspect than a brief mention can suggest.

4. *Economics of Entrepreneurship* — Cooper refers to environmental factors of influencing startup, with particular reference to recent empirical studies of regional high technology entrepreneurship, and suggests some interesting lines for further research. It is also a ripe field for theoretical speculation as well as empirical investigation from several points of view, including those of entrepreneurs, politicians, investors, and rulemaking bureaucrats as well as academics. How entrepreneurial activity responds to governmental changes in the rules — OSHA, the SEC, the IRS, the Federal Reserve, the EPA, etc. — may be an increasingly important question on which no research has yet been produced.

5. *Startup Methodology* — This subject concerns specific tools of use to entrepreneurs in creating new ventures, planning techniques, checklists, strategic options, deal packages, flow diagrams, career planning tactics, and so forth. Cooper alludes to part of this category in discussing competitive strategies of new firms, and the paucity of research he associates with it is characteristic of the broader category as well. To date, publications treating this subject have mainly been of a discursive or exhortatory nature. One likely direction of research suggested by this fact would be to explore the extent to which entrepreneurs follow the advice which the literature offers. Another would be to see whether those who do follow that advice fare better than those who don't.

6. *Venture Finance* — Although not brought out by Cooper, this subject area, which concerns how money for startups is obtained, has received more than its share of the publication compared to other subjects in the Schreier-Komives bibliography. However, as with the other subjects, most of this publication has been of a discursive rather than a methodical research nature. It is a natural field for academic study because within it numbers abound; numbers which can readily be compared and contrasted with other established data bases. It would be interesting, for instance, to compare the rates of return enjoyed by self-employed entrepreneurs with those in other categories of employment involving less risk. This might hold implications for future economic contributions to be expected from entrepreneurial startups compared to those of the past.

Each of these sub-fields has implications for strategic management in new ventures. The strategic management of new ventures itself is a subject which may conveniently be divided into two categories: (1) strategies employed by the entrepreneur personally to reach a position for starting a venture, and (2) strategies of the actual venture itself. Cooper discusses the second of these two categories in his section on the competitive strategy of the new firm, pointing out that little research on it has been done. However, he does not discuss the first category explicitly, although it is to some extent implied in his mention of the entrepreneur as one of three factors influencing the decision to start a company. If the three stage model for viewing startups — which Cooper presents as startup, early growth and later growth, and to which might also be added "final disposition" — were expanded to include pre-startup considerations, then it might encompass personal strategies of the entrepreneur. From anecdotal accounts of entrepreneurs, it appears that two general types of pre-startup personal strategies exist. One type is the deliberate planning and striving that some people do when they know in advance they want to start companies and then work at it until they succeed, or fail. The other is the happenstance or implicit strategy by which people enter into entrepreneurship through unforeseen events and without a long history of startup ambition. The vast majority follow the latter approach, but what the implicit or explicit strategies are within each approach has not been methodically studied, nor have the relative degrees of effectiveness of different personal strategic approaches.

It is a weakness in many studies of entrepreneurs that they talk about "the" entrepreneur, as if there were really only one type. Perhaps it is a failing brought to entrepreneurship by the academic fashions of statistics to seek out central tendencies, the mean, the norm rather than the range or spectrum of possibilities. If, as conventional wisdom has it, entrepreneurs tend often to be mavericks and to defy typicality, then there may be more to learn by seeking to identify the spectrum that exists rather than searching for its center. To begin with, it can be noted that at least nine different types of entrepreneurs can be identified according to kinds of economic functions they perform. These are:

1. *Solo Self-Employed Entrepreneurs* — The independent theatrical agent, plumber or physician.
2. *Workforce Builders* — Those who start and build up independent machine shops, commuter airlines, engineering service firms, or other small firms that serve large firms.
3. *Product Innovators* — Tektronix, Hewlett-Packard and many similar (and dissimilar companies) were founded by entrepreneurs with new products.
4. *Unutilized Resource Exploiters* — Mining prospectors, war surplus dealers, and real estate developers would all fit within such a category and, at the same time, illustrate its potential diversity.
5. *Economy of Scale Exploiters* — Discount store builders of the "50's" and mail order operators illustrate this type.
6. *Pattern Multipliers* — Formulas of the McDonald Brothers and of Colonel Sanders were exploited by franchise entrepreneurs. In an earlier age, chain builders multiplied patterns in other ways.
7. *Takeover Artists* — If the company continues beyond its founder it is because it has either been absorbed by a larger company or has been taken over by another entrepreneur of another type.
8. *Capital Aggregators* — Specialists in marshalling front money can start businesses like banks and insurance companies that cannot be started without resource aggregations.
9. *Speculators* — Although they often do not start or build businesses, those who trade in ownership paper of various types sometimes do build fortunes, and thereby become known as a type of entrepreneur.

One value of having such an array of different types of entrepreneurs can be to display for would-be entrepreneurs what some of their career options may be in this field. But for each of these types there are undoubtedly many alternative strategies for pursuing each particular career, and such strategies have as yet not even been listed, let alone methodically evaluated regarding effectiveness. Observation suggests that opportunities for some of these types are heavily time dependent. War surplus tends to be more available following wars, and new product opportunities tend to follow technological breakthroughs. There was much entrepreneuring in the discount store business at one time in history, chain store business at another time, mutual fund creation at another, semiconductor electronics another, and so forth. But neither the cycles, nor the time dependence of these venture opportunities periods have been examined in the literature.

Even the very fundamental issue of how entrepreneurs discover the opportunities they exploit remains unstudied. Some exhortatory works (Morrison, 1973) discuss how their authors think entrepreneurs *should* discover opportunities, while others such as Swayne and Tucker (1973) simply presume the idea has been discovered and go on from there. But no research has been published evaluating the efficacy of either approach.

The multitude of other directions in which research could proceed is quickly suggested when cross comparisons are made between the various classification schemes. Exhibit 6.2 lists the four sets of categories treated thus far in the discussion. Theoretically, the number of possible combinations of topics is the product of the numbers of items on all the lists multiplied together ($5 \times 5 \times 6 \times 9 = 1,350$). This number should be reduced by elimination of redundancies. For instance, Mom 'n Pop ventures tend to include solo self-employed entrepreneurs, though the overlap is not necessarily complete. But even after such elimination, the number remains very large. Moreover, it can be further extended by considering other classification criteria. Historical periods, mentioned above

as being associated with certain venture types, could be one. Classification by industry could be another. It may be a weakness of the present literature, for instance, to group "high technology" startups together when, in fact, what high technology means is "mostly electronic but including a smattering of other technologies as well." Further industrial stratification of the data might reveal important differences, such as perhaps the educational requirements for participation.

Where the most important intersections of these classifications are is an open issue, which itself could be the basis for a substantial academic exploration. From patterns in the existing literature, it can be seen that some categories have been much more studied than others (Vesper, 1977). But none have received anything approaching the magnitude of attention given other academic areas such as accounting, operations research, or human relations.

Especially deserving of more research attention in the future may be the area of internal or intracorporate entrepreneurship. The U.S. economy has been for many years on a trajectory of aggregation in which a major portion of its industry, particularly in manufacuring, is managed by large companies and also in which progressively more of its resources are man-

Exhibit 6.2 Four Classification Schemes

Venture types	Venture stages	Academic sub-fields	Entrepreneur types
1 Mom 'n Pop	1 Pre-startup	1 Tycoon history	1 Solo self-employed
2 High payoff Small, stable	2 Startup	2 Psychology of entrepreneurship	2 Workforce builders
3 Conscious under-achieving	3 Profitability	3 Sociology of entrepreneurship	3 Product innovators
4 Unintentional underachieving	4 Later growth	4 Economics of entrepreneurship	4 Unutilized resource exploiters
5 High growth	5 Disposition	5 Startup methodology	5 Economy of scale exploiters
6 Intracorporate		6 Venture finance	6 Pattern multipliers
			7 Takeover artists
			8 Capital aggregators
			9 Speculators

aged by the federal government. In short, it is a trajectory in the direction of socialism in which small industrial units (i.e., ventures) emerge only at the sufferance, and under the power of large scale organization.

It is unlikely that private entrepreneurship will ever be entirely extinguished by such a trend. Even in the Soviet Union where entrepreneurship is against the policy in all cases, against the law in some cases, and even carries the death penalty in others (here called speculation, there called "profiteering") entrepreneurs still abound, as witnessed by both the black market and occasional executions. But it is possible that progressively more entrepreneurs may find themselves playing more the game of internal, rather than independent entrepreneurs. Consequently, a better understanding of internal entrepreneurship as developed through industrial experimentation tracked by methodical researchers may be of use to an increasing number of would-be entrepreneurs. At the same time, from a social point of view, it would be desirable for the country to be able to reap as fully as possible the benefits of innovative initiative which entrepreneurs have traditionally provided. Hence, the trend toward industrial aggregation and socialism makes it desirable that economic planners, whether in the bureaucracies of large corporations or that of the federal government have a better understanding of internal entrepreneurship and how it can be made to work.

PROBLEMS AND POTENTIALS IN RESEARCHING ENTREPRENEURSHIP

Attempting to perform research on entrepreneurship within larger organizations poses one set of difficulties and advantages to the researcher, while attempting to study entrepreneurship in smaller firms presents quite a different set. Some advantages in studying larger companies are that data on them are readily available in libraries, that they have large staffs who can afford time to respond to questionnaires and the like; and that they often provide generous support for such research, since the cost of doing so is usually negligible in relation to their total net income, even though the consequences of the research may not be. They also offer the attraction of lucrative consulting fees to those academics they believe may be helpful to them. Their main disadvantage is that their headquarters (and hence their strategy formulating nerve centers) are clustered in a very few cities, so that to reach them is inconvenient from most schools, whose policy researchers are therefore confined to secondhand data from libraries or else mail and telephone surveys.

Small companies offer complementary advantages and disadvantages for research. As Cooper notes, their large number allows statistically more elegant sampling, their smallness makes for easier access to their presidents for top level management studies. Being less complex, they allow easier comprehension of each enterprise in totality, and, by virtue of narrower specialization they offer more sharply defined strategies for studying strategic cause and effect. In addition, it can be noted that virtually all metropolitan schools have hundreds of small firms of many industrial types nearby, and hence convenient for study.

A major handicap for small business as an area of research is that they usually cannot afford to financially support such research because of their limited earnings, nor can they offer the several hundred dollars per day consulting rates that make large company studies so alluring to academics. But compensating factors are emerging. The number of schools offering small business courses has multiplied several fold since the Small Business Administration introduced its *Small Business Institute* program in 1972 and rapidly expanded it to nearly 400 schools. Through the "hands on" interaction between students and top managers of small firms in this program, a torrent of real world experience and data have begun pouring into business schools. Faculty are beginning to draw upon this experience and data for academic research papers, and new journals are beginning to emerge. The number of schools offering entrepreneurship courses has, for reasons somewhat different than the SBI program, also been growing rapidly (Vesper, 1976). In addition, programs have been established at Carnegie-Mellon, MIT, and Oregon to experiment with different ways of starting or helping start new companies. These experiments are being studied by other researchers to see which approaches seem most effective. Such campus experimentation may add a fifth type of literature to the other four (Discursive, Case, Field Survey, and Field Research) suggested by Cooper.

SUMMARY AND CONCLUSIONS

Entrepreneurship and small business are academic research areas which may at first encounter seem narrow, but upon closer examination are clearly enormous. As Cooper and Susbauer have pointed out, the literature at present is largely exhortatory, anecdotal, and opinionated. Methodical research to date has been limited in quantity. By considering different schemes for analyzing these fields, it is further apparent that the research to date has left some areas entirely untouched, while many others have barely been considered. Hence, the potential for future development of the field is great. Moreover, it is important! Entrepreneurship has been not only the original source of nearly all U.S. industry, but it continues to account for a major share of the country's innovations. Small business serves not only as the source of companies that grow into large businesses, but also as a major employment and economic productivity sector in its own right. If the country continues to move more in the direction of aggregation of power in larger organizations and the federal government, the concept of intraorganizational entrepreneurship in particular may become increasingly more important, but independent small business as a promising field for academic research seems bound to continue strongly as well.

Strategic Management: The Multi-Business Corporation

Norman Berg
Harvard University

Robert A. Pitts
Pennsylvania State University

INTRODUCTION

This paper deals with past and suggested future research directed at bettering our understanding of how the dual general management tasks of strategy formulation and implementation are being executed at various levels in multi-business firms. A number of management problems as well as four separate but related research streams are identified, two bearing on the former of these tasks, two on the latter. The contribution of each is assessed, and avenues for potentially fruitful further research explored. In concluding, the interrelationships among the four streams and possible patterns of continued research along them are briefly discussed.

The most important form of industrial organization in this country in terms of sales and assets is the diversified company. Although precise measures of diversity from the viewpoint of the managerial problems created do not exist, it has been clearly established by Wrigley (1970) and Rumelt (1974), for example, that the amount of diversity in American industry has increased dramatically since World War II and is currently high. Their estimates place the proportion of the *Fortune* 500 largest industrials that are diversified and multi-divisional at around 80%–85%. Since the *Fortune* 500 are commonly regarded to account for roughly two-thirds of the output, investment, employment, and three-quarters of the profits of U.S. industry, the prevalence and importance of diversified companies is clear.

Chandler (1962), in his landmark study of diversification by American industrial corporations in the early part of this century, established a clear relationship between increasing managerial complexity, brought on by strategies of product diversification, and the divisional form of organization, brought on by the attempts to deal with this increasing complexity. The focus of this paper will be on the research opportunities stemming from those aspects of the general manager's job which are significantly different, in degree or kind, in the diversified, divisionalized industrial company than in the single-business company. The term "general manager" will be used to refer to the person with substantial, although seldom complete, responsibility for either a single business unit or an aggregation of such units. In the typical large diversified company there will therefore be several levels of general management and consequently many general managers, with specific organizational titles differing among companies.

The job of the general manager of a single business division in the diversified company is most like that of his counterpart in the single-business independent company. As one proceeds up through the levels to a group vice president (commonly responsible for a number of divisions) and on to the president or chief executive officer of the entire organization, new tasks and complexities arise.

PROBLEM AREAS AND RESEARCH STREAMS

This paper will suggest a few broad problem areas in which there appear to be interesting, important, and hopefully "do-able" research projects with regard to the management of diversified companies. Attention will be focused on the management problems which tend to be unique to companies either diversified or considering becoming so, and not to problems which are common and important to the general management task in any enterprise. Consequently, issues of environmental protection, minority employment, product safety, government and public attitudes toward business, the role of boards of directors, or international business are not treated since they have relatively little to do with the fact that a company is diversified.[1] Such issues are more directly related to the size and location of a company and its facilities, the nature of its products, and its own past policies than to its level of diversification. By contrast, the following categories of problems seem of particular relevance to the general management task in diversifying and diversified companies.

The Corporation Product-Market Portfolio

Of primary importance are questions of whether, when, and how to either diversify or divest. These are basic strategic questions for corporate management as they determine the products and markets in which the corporation will invest resources. Diversification can be by internal development or by acquisition, and divestiture can be accomplished by a gradual "phasing out" of a business no longer considered desirable, by a sale of the division as an ongoing business, or by liquidation. The strategic choice at the corporate level is primarily one of a selection of products and markets in which to engage, and not the question of product/market strategy for each individual business, although it is apparent that the product/market choices at the corporate level cannot be made in isolation from product/market strategies at the division level. We will turn first to the broad area of diversification decisions, about which much has been written, before addressing the divestiture problem.

Some large, dominant product companies have perhaps waited too long to diversify, and now have their physical and managerial assets committed to the production of commodity products in industries of periodic and perhaps chronic overcapacity and often high capital investment needs, with consequent depressed earnings and

stock multiples (Rumelt, 1974; Levitt, 1975). A variety of conditions (Jacoby, 1969) which contributed to the acquisition and merger atmosphere of the late 1960s, on the other hand, enticed some companies to diversify perhaps too fast, as their subsequent difficulties with individual acquisitions and overall spotty performance has indicated (Lynch, 1971; Malkiel, 1975).

The decisions to diversify, or to continue with diversifying acquisitions or internal development, involve far more than an analysis of target industries or companies. It is clear that some industries are consistently more profitable over a long period of time than others, but the issue for any single company is the potential of a virtually unlimited choice of diversification alternatives for *that* company, compared to continuing with its own businesses or investing in forward or backward vertical integration. Andrews (1965)[2] articulates a broad approach to the problems of strategic analysis of the single industry which contains most of the elements still commonly found in that vast literature, and Ansoff (1965) at about the same time outlined an approach to the analysis of diversifying activities which also has many of the features still common to the literature in that field.

Diversification can be either by internal development or by acquisition, and each has its particular hazards and advantages. For example, Fast (1977) recently studied the internal diversification efforts of a number of large companies, and demonstrated well the unhappy experiences of many "New Venture Divisions" formed for the purpose of developing significance new lines of business for the parent company. Pitts (1977b) recently looked at the relative contributions of diversification via internal development and diversification via acquisition in 17 large, successful diversified firms. Diversification via either approach has implications for the tech-

---

[1] With the exception of the important public policy issues related to the growth and existence of large, diversified enterprises, which will not be addressed in this paper.

[2] Andrews' concepts were first presented in the text portion of *Business Policy: Text and Cases.* Homewood, Ill.: Richard D. Irwin, 1965, by Learned, Christensen, Andrews, and Guth, and later published separately in Andrews, *The Concept of Corporate Strategy.* Homewood, Ill.: Dow Jones–Irwin, 1971.

nical competence required, the types of diversification sought, and the administrative skills and structure needed.

Diversification by internal development involves questions of the management of innovation and the development of new enterprises; diversification via acquisitions involves basic strategic assessments as well as the technical fields of the tax, legal, and financial aspects of mergers and acquisitions. Neither body of specialized literature or knowledge is likely to be of much direct help to the general manager trying to decide which, if either, strategic course his company should follow, since both approaches can be successful.

Corporate level product/market choices involve questions of exit as well as entry (Porter, 1976). One of the most frequently given justifications for the advantages of diversification is that a constant "upgrading" of the product portfolio can occur via judicious acquisitions or internal expansion and equally astute divestiture of less promising activities. Recommended criteria range from the relatively simple concepts of forecasts of safety and growth in sales and earnings and timing of cash flows to the more intangible measures of strategic fit or the more analytically sophisticated criteria underlying efficient financial portfolio selection. The logics underlying attempts at such continual portfolio upgrading are impressive, but both the intellectual and administrative difficulties of achieving these objectives are substantial. There is abundant evidence that the portfolio management efforts of professional money managers as a group have contributed little if anything to the performance of their portfolios in comparison with broad market averages, and money managers do not even have to deal with the administrative side of the problem that complicates the life of the general manager.

Are companies in fact successful at portfolio selection and upgrading, and how does one know? The authors would surely not want to defend the proposition that the ability of group and corporate management to select companies and lines of business for inclusion in their product portfolio is no better than the record of portfolio managers in "beating the market." That expensive mistakes are made by highly competent and experienced managements is evident, however. Witness, for example, the recent divestitures of the computer operations by General Electric and RCA, and of a number of large units by both Singer and Westinghouse. Somewhere in the area of strategic analysis or administrative implementation there are still some unsolved problems worthy of investigation.

Strategy Formulation Research Streams on Multi-industry Firms

The general management tasks and problems described in the previous sections are generally included under the broad heading of strategy formulation by those who study the process. It is far easier for us as observers and researchers to separate the logics of strategic planning than it is for the manager to manage the process in isolation of his many other tasks. The literature on strategic planning is extensive, and an excellent summary is contained in a recent work by Hofer (1976).* A more recent book by Vancil and Lorange (1977) deals specifically with strategic planning in the diversified firm. The problem of strategic planning in the diversified company is significantly different than that of the single-business company because of the diversity of business — each requiring its *own* strategic plan and funding — and the multiple levels of management involved in the process.

There are two major research streams bearing on strategy formulation in multi-business firms. One deals with the *process* of strategy formulation, the other with the *content* of strategy in this kind of firm.

Stream 1: Research on the Nature of Strategy Formulation Processes in Multi-industry Firms

A number of researchers have attempted to describe the process by which strategic decisions are made in multi-business firms. Among the

* Editor's note: As noted in Section 5, a distinction needs to be made between strategic planning as a process dealing with strategy formulation and/or strategy implementation, and the strategic management process which incorporates but is not limited to strategic planning.

earliest and most detailed works in this category are those by Berg (1965), Aharoni (1966), Ackerman (1968), and Bower (1970). Each examines in depth the influences upon strategic decisions within large, diversified firms.

A number of interesting conclusions emerge from these studies. Two of the most important to our discussion here are perhaps the following:

1. A strategic decision in a large multi-business firm is frequently the net result of a series of choices made over time by numerous decision-makers located at various organizational levels, often with goals that differ from level to level; and

2. Top corporate management can influence the strategic decision process more readily through its manipulation of structure (organization design, information and reward systems, etc.) than by making substantive inputs to strategic decisions themselves.

The research supporting these conclusions suffers some methodological limitations, of course. First, it is based on a relatively small sample of firms which may not reflect very well the population of multi-business firms in general. For example, all of the firms examined in the studies cited above were large well-established enterprises whose growth and diversification had resulted primarily from internal developments generated by vigorous R&D programs.

Second, the studies in this stream are limited with respect to the kinds of strategic decisions they examine. For example, Aharoni limited himself to foreign investment decisions, Bower to capital investment decisions, Ackerman to research and development expenditures, and Berg to "strategic funds" expenditures (i.e., funds expended to improve future rather that current period profitability).

These limitations offer interesting opportunities for further research. They suggest, for example, a clear need to track the strategic decision process within different kinds of multi-business firms from those studied so far. A particularly intriguing candidate for future study would be one of the newer multi-business firms whose diversification has resulted from acquisi-

tions rather than from technology-based internal developments. There is also a need to investigate strategic choices other than foreign investment, capital investment, research and development, and "strategic funds" expenditures, and to compare the results with the findings noted above.

It is likely that research along either of these lines may reveal different patterns of decision-making influence than those described above. For example, one would expect that an investigation of the strategic decision process in an acquisitive conglomerate might reveal that corporate management had less substantive input into product/market strategic decisions at the division level than in the firms studied so far, but perhaps more with respect to some other categories of strategic decisions such as acquisitions and divestitures.

Stream 2: Research on the Content of Strategic Decisions in Multi-industry Firms

In the section above, attention was focused on the process by which strategy is formulated in multi-business firms. This section will consider the content of strategy itself in this kind of firm.

It is reasonable to assume that strategy at the level of individual divisions of multi-business firms may be quite similar to that of independent firms operating in single business areas. But what about strategy at the corporate level? How can the notion of strategy be usefully applied there? What different kinds of strategy are multi-business firms in fact pursuing? In what terms, for example, can one usefully develop and state the *corporate* strategy of a company such as General Electric or Litton? It is surely not just a collection of divisional strategies, but at the same time it needs to be something more operational than "do whatever we are good at" or "seek out good opportunities." Hanna (1968) investigated this question in three large companies that had grown by acquisition, but more needs to be done. In the diversified company, the development of a truly corporate strategy as well as the determination of the useful roles and contributions of various levels of management to the development of strategic plans for the divisions is significantly different, and substantially more challenging, than comparable processes in the single-business company.

While research directed at these questions has been very limited to date, there have nevertheless been some initial efforts to deal with them. For the most part, these have taken the form of attempts to classify multi-business firms into broad strategic categories.

One of the earliest of these was Berg's (1973) identification of two quite different kinds of multi-business firms — "diversified majors" and "conglomerates." He defined the former as firms which "had become diversified" largely by the means described by Chandler: "(1) as part of a long-term trend starting in the 1920s, (2) with a characteristic pattern of (a) initial expansion and accumulation of resources in a single business, (b) rationalization in the use of resources, (c) expansion into new (often related) markets and product lines to help assure the continuing full use of resources, and (d) development of new administrative structures to deal with the new management problems."

Conglomerates, by contrast, were characterized as multi-business enterprises which had: "(1) achieved most of their growth and diversification within the last 5–15 years, (2) followed a characteristic pattern of expansion (a) largely by a series of acquisitions, rather than internally generated diversification, (b) often into widely unrelated areas, and (c) often by means of aggressive financial policies rather than with excess resources" (Berg, 1973).

Pitts subsequently simplified Berg's classification somewhat by ignoring all but a single attribute of multi-business firms — namely, their mode of diversification (Pitts, 1976a). Using this narrower perspective, Pitts attempted to capture the essence of Berg's "diversified majors" and "conglomerates" by designating them simply "internal" and "acquisitive" diversifiers. Pitts (1977b) in a later investigation identified two additional, less common multi-business strategies. One of these he characterized as "simultaneous pursuit of a *mixture* of internal and acquisitive diversification;" the other as acquisi-

tion of "companies whose products are closely related technologically."

One of the most comprehensive efforts to classify multi-business firms according to strategy, structure, and performance is that of Rumelt (1974), which built on the work of Wrigley (1970). Several major and sub-categories emerge from his effort. The most important major categories are those of "related" and "unrelated" diversification. The former includes two subcategories ("constrained" and "linked" diversification); the latter, two more ("passive" and "acquisitive conglomerate" diversification).

While very useful as an initial step toward clarifying the nature of corporate-level strategy in multi-business firms, Stream 2 research suffers from two serious limitations. First, few of the studies included in this stream have been comprehensive in their selection of firms for study. For example, the sample studied by Berg (1973) and several of those investigated by Pitts (1974, 1976b) were selected not on any random basis, but because they were thought to represent extremes along a continuum between internal and acquisitive diversification. Even though the sample sizes involved at least ten companies, care must be taken in generalizing the findings drawn from these samples to other types of companies. Rumelt's work (1974), based on a sample of about 100 firms selected from the *Fortune* 500, is a major exception, as are some of Pitts' later investigations (1976a, 1977a).

A perhaps more serious limitation of Stream 2 research is its failure to probe beyond what might be considered somewhat superficial aspects of strategy. Consider, for example, the designations "internal" and "acquisitive" diversification (Pitts, 1976b). While these terms do perhaps signify two quite different strategic orientations, they do not very satisfactorily clarify the nature of these strategies. Particularly disconcerting is their failure to pinpoint clearly the environmental opportunities toward which each is directed and to identify the organizational competences underlying each. Hanna (1968), Lynch (1971), and Pitts (1976b) probed these questions to some extent, but more needs to be done. Our expectation is that further efforts along these and related lines will eventually reveal that the corporate-level strategy of many multi-business firms is more highly articulated and plays a more important role in the performance of many companies than Stream 1 findings to date would suggest.

IMPLEMENTING STRATEGY

The discussion above has dealt with the problems of the multi-business top manager in his capacity as formulator of strategy. This section will consider him in his role as architect of organizational structure and processes designed to support and implement strategy.

The roles and functions of the various levels of general management in the diversified company, and the relationships among these levels, are the essence of the ongoing general management task in diversified companies. The pressures which led to the establishment of the product division form of organization were well described by Chandler (1962). Many of the managerial changes which accompany the change from functional, single-business to multi-business management are described in "Stages of Corporate Development" by Scott (1971), and others. That the approach to organization differs considerably among different types of diversified companies in practice has been demonstrated by Berg (1973), Pitts (1976a), and Allen (1976).

The broad issue underlying all of these studies is one that is a continuing issue for managers: given the multiple levels of general management created in response to the demands of managing diversity, how shall the management tasks be split up? In a given situation, what should be the content of the division manager's job, the group vice president's job, and the president's job, and what should be the relationships among them? What line of staff functions should be performed at the division level, and what at the group or corporate levels? What are the relative advantages of various approaches for various types of companies and specific industries? What are the key factors that affect the answers for the specific company?

Such questions get to the heart of everyday, ongoing administration. Included are the ongoing tasks of evaluating and helping to improve the present performance, as well as assessing the future promise, of both businesses and managers that the corporate-level executive cannot know in as much detail as he would like. Many analytical aids to the strategic analysis of the product portfolio are available — The Boston Consulting Group product portfolio matrix, the McKinsey evaluation of Strategic Business Units (SBU's) as developed in conjunction with General Electric, the PIMS Project on determinants of business profitability, also originally developed at General Electric, and so on. All of these provide convincing logical reasons and approaches for milking the "Cows" to support the "Stars" or "Question Marks" while selling the "Dogs." Progress in the use of these techniques will come not so much from improving the logic of the analysis, in our opinion, as from increasing understanding of the administrative difficulties of making decisions and taking action (see Bower and Doz, Section 3), and in obtaining and structuring the data so that it can be applied to the specific situation.

The broad questions that must be addressed with regard to designing the roles of the various levels of general management in the diversified company can be stated as: (1) what can the division do for the parent and for other units in the company — e.g., provide earnings, business expertise, technological cooperation, and so on; and (2) what can the parent do for the division — e.g., provide access to capital markets, specialized staff assistance, better controls, etc. The big question to be answered is why the division will perform better because it is part of a diversified company than as an independent unit, and why the parent will perform better because it includes the division. An example of a research effort to address these questions is that of Grant (1972) who examined efforts by several multi-business firms to produce and market systems involving the products of numerous divisions. If the reasons for expecting the whole to be greater than the sum of the parts are not better understood and articulated, management will have little by which to guide their approach to administration. The concept of synergy is a fascinating one, but it must be expressed in operational terms in order to be useful in a specific situation.

RESEARCH STREAM: STRATEGY IMPLEMENTATION

There are two major research streams bearing upon interunit relationships in multi-business firms. One deals with the important phenomenon of divisionalization, the other with the relationship between headquarters and the divisions.

STREAM 3: RESEARCH ON DIVERSIFICATION AND DIVISIONALIZATION IN MULTI-INDUSTRY FIRMS

As noted above, a number of studies have shown that as firms diversify they tend to divisionalize — i.e., to create separate organizational units called "divisions," which are assigned individual responsibility for different businesses. Among the earliest and best known of these is that of Chandler (1962). Several subsequent investigations patterned on Chandler's work have confirmed his findings across large, randomly-selected samples of multi-business firms both in the U.S. and Europe. Specifically, these issues were investigated in the U.S. (Wrigley, 1970), Britain (Channon, 1971), Italy (Pavan, 1972), France (Pooley-Dias, 1972), and Germany (Thanheiser, 1972) in a series of doctoral theses supervised by Scott at the Harvard Graduate School of Business Administration.

In light of the extensive Stream 3 research already completed, further efforts to establish the level and trends of diversification and subsequent divisionalization may yield only marginal payoffs. More useful at this point, perhaps, would be efforts: (1) to identify differences in the way the corporate-level manages their divisions, and (2) to establish how these differences may relate to differences in corporate environments, resources, strategy, and performance.

STREAM 4: RESEARCH ON HEADQUARTERS-DIVISIONAL RELATIONSHIPS IN MULTI-INDUSTRY FIRMS

One of the earliest field studies dealing with headquarters-divisional relationships was that of Mace (1962). His examination of problems associated with managing acquisitions revealed a clear pattern of increasing corporate involve-ment in the affairs of the acquisitions, often as a result of crisis rather than design. Berg (1973) later investigated headquarters-divisional relationships in a selected sample of internal and acquisitive diversifiers. He found substantial differences between the two kinds of firms in the activities carried out respectively at the corporate level in areas such as R&D, marketing, manufacturing, purchasing, and traffic. Heau (1976) studied the relationship in divisionalized firms between corporate influence on divisional long-range planning and the extent of the firm's diversification, and found that influence to be more substantive as the diversity decreased.

Two subsequent studies by Pitts (1974, 1977a) have uncovered other structural differences between these two species of multi-business firms. In one, internal diversifiers were found to be transferring managers much more frequently across division lines than acquisitive diversifiers. In the other, the manner of measuring divisional performance for incentive compensation purposes was found to be substantially different in these two kinds of firms.

While the studies in this stream provide some interesting initial insights into the relationship between structure and strategy in multi-business firms, they leave many important questions still unanswered. For example, they provide little data indicating whether structural differences along dimensions other than those already studied (with respect to transfer pricing, for example) may exist between firms pursuing internal vs. acquisitive diversification. Nor do they shed light on how multi-business firms which are diversifying by a combination of internal developments and acquisitions may be structuring themselves.

The need to find answers to these questions presents opportunities for further research. One interesting illustration of research along these lines is that of Corey and Star (1971). They traced in considerable detail the relationship between organization structure and strategy in more than a dozen large multi-business firms pursuing a variety of different strategies. While their case study findings are difficult to generalize, their approach, if applied over time to a larger number of multi-business firms, might eventually contribute significantly to our understanding of the constraints which structure and strategy pose for each other in this kind of enterprise.

RELATING THE STREAMS

So far the four streams discussed above have been treated as relatively independent fields of activity. In reality, they are closely related, each acting both to simulate and be stimulated by the others. Consider the following two examples — one drawn from the past, one from what we perceive as a possible future course of research on the strategic management of multi-business firms.

A Past Example

As one scans the historical development of the four streams, it seems clear that Stream 3, Diversification/Divisionalization, has played an extremely important role to date. It is the oldest of the four chronologically, it includes some of the most comprehensive studies, and in a sense it "spawned" the other three. Only after Chandler (1962) and other Stream 3 researchers had established that firms tend to divisionalize as they diversify, and that these patterns were widespread, were researchers led to ask the questions such as the following which generated the other three streams:

1. What role do managers at various levels in this new kind of organization play in the strategic decision process (Stream 1)? What role should they play?
2. What intellectual input, if any, does corporate management, which can comprehend only superficially the competitive specifics of its various businesses, make to this process (Stream 2)? What input should it make?
3. How autonomous in fact are the divisions within the new divisionalized organization (Stream 4)? How autonomous should they be?

A Possible Future Research Direction

In this concluding section, some speculations are offered about the course of future research on the strategic management of multi-industry firms, both in terms of how such research might relate to the four major research streams discussed above, as well as the broad characteristics which seem desirable for such research.

Regarding the former issue, the following evolution seems plausible:

1. Future research on the content of strategy at the corporate level (Stream 2) uncovers a number of heretofore undiscovered, or at present only partially comprehended, multi-business strategies. In describing such strategies, this research is able to clarify both the nature of the opportunities toward which they are directed and the sources of competitive competence which underly them.
2. These insights feed back on research in the process of strategy formulation (Stream 1) in the following way. As researchers begin to recognize the variety and sophistication in the corporate strategies of many multi-business firms, they are likely to become increasingly uncomfortable with currently accepted Stream 1 theory which portrays corporate management of multi-business firms as providing only minimal substantive input to the strategy formulation process at the business level. In reaction, they hopefully undertake additional Stream 1 research, perhaps along the lines outlined above.
3. These same Stream 2 developments feed back on research on Headquarters-Divisional Relationships (Stream 4) in the following way. As the competences underlying different multi-business strategies become better understood, Stream 4 researchers are prompted to investigate the nature of the structural and process characteristics underlying such competences.

The possible paths of such research are obviously numerous, and many scenarios in addition to the above could be constructed. For example, a considerable body of research dealing with the application of financial theory — primarily portfolio models — to conglomerate diversification exists, as do some empirical studies on the performance of conglomerate companies or their securities. Much of this has been done by financial economists and reported in finance and economics journals, and as yet seems to have had little impact on managerial decisions in diversified firms. As another example, several streams of research around the theme of "decentralization" could be identified, with emphasis on either the organizational behavior or the planning and control aspects.

Regardless of the specific questions investigated, the following are some general characteristics that are likely to be present in the most useful research on these topics:

First, it will be based on an appreciation of the *complexity* of the task facing corporate and divisional general managers of such companies. The management task is different in part because there are new tasks and more strategic options available, but it is also different — especially at the group and corporate levels — because there are simply more of the familiar problems with which to deal. There is always the temptation to believe that if one could specify the approach for solving problems individually — as for instance, the problems of any one division, operating in largely a single industry — one will have improved the ability of the organization to solve large numbers of these same types of problems as well. That this is not necessarily true is the very reason for the creation of multiple levels of management and the product division form of management. The president of a single-business company can play a certain role because he can immerse himself in an industry and understand that industry, as well as his own organization and people, exceptionally well. The president, or even a group vice president, of a General Electric or a Westinghouse manifestly cannot do the same. Prescriptions which do not take into account the increased intellectual and administrative complexities that arise from dealing with a large number of seemingly familiar problems are not likely to be of much help to the president concerned about managing forty divisions or even the group vice president responsible for five divisions.

Second, the research will incorporate or draw upon a mixture of clinical field observation and broader-based survey methodologies. The major limitation of clinical research is the difficulty of generalizing to other situations because of the limited sample size, an unavoidable consequence of the time consuming nature of such research. By contrast, the major limitation of large-scale survey research, either field or library based, is the difficulty of addressing it to important administrative situations. It is not necessary or often possible for every researcher to do both, but we feel the most significant research on the management of multi-industry firms will come from efforts which draw upon and can be related to both types of work. The sequence of effort is not crucial; each type of research can be a source of inputs (hypotheses or corroboration) for the other.

In this regard, one of the principal difficulties in relating clinical research to broader-based survey methods is in devising useful classification schemes and measurement procedures which will enable one to relate the findings of one approach to those derived via the other approach. It is apparent that not all significant data can readily be quantified, nor can all the contingencies relevant to various situations be readily determined or expressed in comparable terms.

Third, the most useful research on managing multi-business companies will originate with an interest in an understanding of a problem of general management rather than an extension of a specific analytical technique or a particular research methodology. It will be a problem in search of a solution, not a solution in search of a problem. The risk of the former approach is that the solutions or insights offered may not be rigorous or elegant either in their development or proof; the risks of the latter are that the solutions may be rigorous and elegant, but largely irrelevant to the practice of business administration because of the number of limiting assumptions made. At this time, the former risks seem preferable.

Fourth, such research will not focus solely on the general manager, or the organization, or the environment, but will reflect an understanding of the tasks facing general managers functioning in real multi-industry organizations, coping with a complex and changing environment. If we are to make progress in relating theory and practice, a quotation from Roethlisberger (1968: x) in the study of administration is just as relevant for policy researchers as for the audience for which his remarks were originally intended:

> ... Although by abstraction man could be studied apart from organizations and organizations apart from man, this person I called the administrator could not be studied even

abstractly this way. He was *par excellence* man-in-organization, and the relation between what he thought he was doing or should be doing and what he in fact was doing was critical. Only by keeping the focus on man-in-organization could the gap between theory and practice be bridged.

Commentary

RICHARD G. BRANDENBURG
The Carborundum Company

Understanding what general managers of multi-industry businesses do and how they do it, what Berg and Pitts call appreciating the "complexity of the task," is a useful perspective for considering possible directions for research on strategy and strategic planning in such firms. In this regard, the initiatives and involvement of different general managers at different organizational levels and locations in multi-industry firms can have a major impact on the number and quality of the strategic opportunities the firm identifies for achieving its operating income and return on investment (ROI) objectives. However, Berg and Pitts do not, in my opinion, emphasize such initiatives and involvement that are necessary from different managers at different organizational levels if the firm is to diversify or divest effectively, make its planning systems work, or establish appropriate corporate-divisional relationships.

My viewpoints result from my close involvement for the past year with formal strategic planning in a "multi-industry business" — The Carborundum Company. Based on what I have observed, I will suggest some needs and opportunities for further research besides those identified by Berg and Pitts. These opportunities correspond to real challenges our senior executives are facing in their commitment to continuously improve strategic planning as a key management discipline for guiding the purposes and performance of The Carborundum Company.

These opportunities and needs are not unique to our Company. The following outline highlights areas where I believe that applied research could improve the strategic management capabilities of executives in most multi-industry businesses.

INFORMATION REQUIREMENTS

ASSESSMENT OF TOOLS FOR STRATEGIC PLANNING

Strategic planning methods have proliferated to the point where a useful service to managers would be rendered by sorting the techniques out. Techniques need to be classified in terms of where they fit best among the conceptual stages of the strategic planning process. Uses and limits of different tools need to be compared. A mapping is needed which pulls together, interprets and evaluates the best of the state of the art for both the "substance" and "process" of strategy planning and implementation. For instance, evaluation criteria for assessing the quality of strategy and its applicability, such as those suggested by Ansoff and Hayes (1972), should be developed and tested.

The overall result should help general managers of multi-industry business do three things:

1. Avoid reinventing the wheel, by learning more efficiently from the cumulative experience

of others about what works, what doesn't and why.

2. Know where and when to call for outside consulting help, and how to make cost-effective use of such consultants.

3. Tailor processes of strategic planning to particular needs of the different business segments which make up a multi-industry firm as a whole.

Business Performance Taxonomies

There is still much work to do on taxonomies of business performance designed to assist general managers in isolating the small number of factors most important to the operating income and ROI of different businesses compared to the large number of factors on which businesses could be planned, measured and controlled. For multi-industry businesses, there are two requirements:

1. Evaluating the performance characteristics of different business portfolios to help answer "what if" questions about possible acquisitions and divestments.

2. Pinpointing key leverage points in established business units to guide selection, rewards and incentives, and priority setting for business unit managers.

Competitor Analysis

A third knowledge gap which needs to be closed is competitor analysis. Profiles of strengths and weaknesses of competitors must be translated into their consequences for strategies of the business. In multi-industry businesses, however, keys to competitive analysis are processes for collecting, updating, and facilitating timely transfer of information among different monitoring and decision points in the organization.

WHICH STRATEGIES ARE MOST IMPORTANT?

Multi-industry businesses need multiple strategies. Emphasizing only diversification or divestment decisions could result in a misalloca-

tion of research efforts in business policy and planning. More attention should be given to improving the strategies of ongoing, established businesses. Here are three examples of ways this might be done:

Generating Strategy Alternates

Arthur D. Little has developed a matrix of "generic" business strategies, linked to where a business is in its overall life cycle: embryonic, growth, mature or aging. Generic business strategies it includes are market penetration, maintenance of present competitive position, product line rationalization, technological efficiency, etc. Such approaches help managers of established businesses to generate possible strategy alternates and to think explicitly about which ones to rule out and why. Any construct which enhances the efficient examination of strategy alternates under the time and information processing pressures of most formal strategic planning systems used by multi-industry businesses is worth exploring.

Strategies for Capital-intensive Businesses

Boston Consulting Group has developed some concepts for strategy formation and evaluation in the very difficult competitive environment of capital-intensive businesses. Making preemptive capital investment strategies work poses complex timing and risk factor challenges for general managers. Evaluation of such strategies usually requires consideration of detailed manufacturing-logistics economics specific to the business, the impact of lead times for manufacturing capacity additions on competitor costs, EPA and OSHA regulations, and the magnitude of cost reductions that can be achieved through investments in scale. As Bruce Henderson, President of the Boston Consulting Group, puts it, the purpose of such preemptive strategies is to "persuade your competitors not to invest in added capacity at the same time you do." General managers in mature capital-intensive businesses must know the strategic importance of factors internal to their business and their competitors' businesses. In particular, they must understand productivity of assets, both those that are fixed and those which vary with sales. Such managers could use some applied research help in deciding when and how to formulate and execute major capital investment strategies.

Resource Strategies

Strategies for procurement of major materials and energy forms are becoming more essential to the viability of more businesses. Such strategies must encompass conservation, anticipation of price increase discontinuities, and contingency plans to protect assets and/or maintain customer service in the face of curtailments or shutoffs. Other resource needs include the identification of the businesses and selection of which operating locations are most vulnerable to shifts in supply availabilities, the rational allocation of scarce energy resources among different units within a multi-industry business, and the interactions between energy-materials, cost changes, and product pricing strategies. Resource strategies also should assess energy impacts on the sales levels of key customers and suppliers, and make energy conservation and alternate fuel flexibility explicit factors in plans for facilities and equipment investments. Related work is needed on systems for tracking energy and materials usage against business plans and objectives.

THE PROCESS OF PLANNING

There is no argument with Berg's and Pitts' conclusion that development of a truly corporate strategy for a multi-industry business is different from and more challenging than for a single business. Here are a few ideas on what needs to be done about it.

"Bottom-up" Strategy Plans

More research should be directed to improving the "bottom-up" phases of strategic planning processes. It is necessary to determine the levels and locations at which the main opportunities for operating income and ROI improvement will be defined and where the main action

programs to capitalize on such opportunities will be put together and put to work. Some key questions include:

1. How to measure general and functional managers at division levels with respect to the quality of their strategies vs. their tactics?
2. How to design planning systems which make cost-effective use of functional staff in preparing plans vs. auditing or critiquing plans once prepared?
3. How to iterate back and forth between corporate objectives and division strategies within time and resource constraints, recognizing that strategic planning should be triggered by the significance of opportunities open to particular business segments, while operating planning, budgeting and programming are triggered by fiscal-calendar year time frames?

Links between Strategic and Operating Plans

Senior executives influence strategic planning decisions made by different components and levels within multi-industry businesses by managing the couplings between strategic planning, operating planning, and organizational control processes.

Research on how to make different modes of coupling more responsive to the requirements of different business segments at different points in time would be valuable. A key difference should be clarified here. Certainly, it is necessary to make sure that operating plans, programs and budgets are on track, approved, and committed to strategic plans, as Hobbs and Heany (1977) suggest. However, of equal importance to corporate level executives is design for couplings which lead to formation of better quality strategic plans to begin with by appropriately balancing "realism" and "reach," as discussed by Shank, Niblock, and Sandells (1973).

Evolution of Planning Systems

Research to determine when and how to change the design of the strategic planning process is badly needed. For example, when should responsibility for the content of strategic plans shift from business division units to world-wide product units? How should the planning process of several different business units be combined and interconnected to achieve better planning, implementation, and control for the multi-industry business as a whole?

Another issue here is how to "audit" the strategic planning process so that lessons learned from experience can be used to make improvements in future planning cycles. It should also be noted that changes in planning procedures can reach a point of diminishing returns, because operating managers eventually are unable to gain enough experience with any one procedure to do a good job. Furthermore, there is a dangerous tendency for the number of changes in strategic planning system procedures to increase until the capacity of each corporate functional staff to tinker with its piece of the procedural machinery is exhausted. What is needed is a rational way of eliminating two things for every new thing added to the planning instructions. Thus, methods for making strategic planning systems evolve toward more selectivity in highlighting the smallest number of key strategies which have the largest impact on the performance of each business segment would be important steps in the right direction.

Allocating Management Efforts

How should management efforts be allocated among strategic planning, operations planning and performance measurement and control in order to best contribute to operating income and ROI? For multi-industry businesses there obviously is more than one right answer. The answers depend on the capabilities, values and styles of key managers; on distinctions in the competitive and customer-market environments of different business units; and on variations in the strategic factors which characterize the operations of different businesses. Research which helps to make effort allocations congruent with the values senior management place on strategic inventiveness vs. operations consistency and comparability would be of practical value.

Dynamics of Organizations

The highest priority strategic challenge facing general managers of most multi-industry businesses is in determining the types of organizations they should use to integrate and balance three simultaneous performance modes:

1. Maximizing operating income/ROI from operations of existing businesses.
2. Developing new businesses with favorable future operating income/ROI potentials.
3. Building and using the systems required to support present business operations and new business developments.

There often are multiple organizational forms within multi-industry businesses. The Carborundum Company is a good example. Five Group Vice Presidents report to our Chief Operating Officer. Two of the groups are geographical region oriented: Europe, Africa and the Middle East; and Latin America and the Pacific. The other three are product-customer need oriented: Abrasives Systems, Resistant Materials, and Environmental Systems.

The Europe, Africa and Middle East group has just gone through a phased reorganization, from legal entity to an entity manager/product manager matrix, to directors of major businesses with responsibilities for providing a family of products to meet a family of customer-market needs throughout the region. The Latin America and Pacific Group is organized by geographical entity. Our Abrasives Systems Group has a technology center and marketing division which serve all of the manufacturing divisions. In Resistant Materials and Environmental Systems, product development and marketing responsibilities are lodged with each operating division. Moreover, in the past two years, several established business divisions have been split into two or more separate new business divisions.

The point is that different organizational forms exist side by side, as needed to meet different business objectives and priorities at different points in time. Decisions as to which organization forms are initiated, modified, or dropped and when business functions should be reassigned where, result from conscious and continuing strategic leadership applied by our Chief Executive Officer.

Investment and operating expenses for management itself are a major cost of running multi-industry business. Executives must plan what kinds of managers and management organizations are consistent with what they want their businesses to become in the future and how they will develop the capabilities required to get them there. There is more gold to be mined by researchers in the ways in which structures should follow strategies, and how combinations of structures can best support formation and execution of combinations of strategies.

Several other kinds of organizational considerations are important in multi-business firms. They include:

1. Gauging the capacities of management to simultaneously direct and control various changes in various businesses. A key limiting factor to strategy can be corporate management overload, just as much as operating management overload.

2. Comparative analysis of different modes of corporate functional staff working relationships with operations, and the corresponding differences in the results accomplished are worth undertaking.

3. Methods for efficient transfer of product-process technology and know-how among various business units need to be developed.

4. Assignments of authority and responsibility for new business development initiatives

among various managerial units which make up a multi-industry business should be made.

The challenge posed by each of the above considerations is to determine what organization design criteria should apply, given the objectives to be accomplished, the nature of the businesses and their environments, and the styles and values of key executives.

CONCLUSION

My outline of some of the needs for improving strategic management capabilities of management in different levels and functions throughout multi-industry businesses leads to a basic question about characteristics of useful research. Many multi-industry businesses are very sophisticated and experienced in formal strategic planning. Carborundum is a case in point. Therefore, the most useful research in areas I have suggested should involve a strong clinical orientation, tailor methodologies to the real situation, and give practical assistance to managers in understanding and improving their strategies. Academic researchers must be more discriminating in focusing on their own comparative advantages. In this regard, they must determine what kinds of research they can do best as compared to the work of outside professional consultants and line and staff planners within multi-industry businesses.

Strategic Management: Not-for-Profit Organizations

MAX S. WORTMAN, JR.
Virginia Polytechnic Institute and State University

One of the most fruitful areas for research in strategic management today is that of not-for-profit organizations. It truly is virginal territory for the strategic management researcher. When one thinks of organizations that are poorly managed over the long term, have few or no long-range goal structures (or ones that are ill-defined), and have different constraining characteristics than profit-making organizations (Newman and Wallender, 1978), one probably thinks of organizations such as not-for-profit hospitals, colleges and universities, welfare agencies, urban housing authorities, and churches. Few of these can be acknowledged as being creditably managed in either the short or long term.

Although many not-for-profit organizations have goals, these goals frequently are short range and poorly defined. Some not-for-profit organizations, such as those in the performing arts, have not only ill-defined goals in both the short and long range, but different goals in these periods. Some officials in public organizations are interested primarily in being re-elected and may not be concerned with the attainment of long-range goals of the government. Some public executives are interested primarily in retaining their jobs, not in the established goals (short or long term) of their agency. As a result of these differing perceptions of what the long-term goals of an organization ought to be, how they should be analyzed, how they should be formulated, and how they should be evaluated, not-for-profit organizations probably can be helped more through rigorous, empirical studies in strategic management than can profit-making organizations. Through such studies, not-for-profit organizations would become more concerned with their long-range goals and appropriate courses of action to achieve them and would be more responsive to their various constituencies.

This paper examines strategic management for not-for-profit organizations by: (1) delineating a format for analyzing each type of not-for-profit organization; (2) evaluating the current strategic management research in each of those types of organization; (3) discussing further research needs, and (4) suggesting approaches that may be taken toward further research in strategic management of not-for-profit organizations.

STRUCTURE OF STRATEGIC MANAGEMENT IN NOT-FOR-PROFIT ORGANIZATIONS

Although some would argue that the management of not-for-profit organizations is significantly different than the management of profit organizations because of differing organizational characteristics, there are few or no major studies indicating that this is the case. There is one study indicating that some organizational characteristics are different in not-for-profit organizations than in profit organizations. Newman and Wallender (1978) note that these constraining characteristics seem to account for unusual managerial problems, but that such characteristics also appear to a greater or lesser extent in profit-oriented organizations. These characteristics include:

1. *Service is intangible* and hard to measure. This difficulty is often compounded by the existence of *multiple* service objectives.

2. *Customer (client) influence may be weak.* Often the enterprise has a local monopoly, and payments by customers may be a secondary source of funds.

3. Strong *employee* commitment to *professions* or to a cause may undermine their allegiance to the organization.

4. *Resource contributors may intrude* into

internal management — notably fund contributors and government.

5. *Restraints on the use of rewards and punishments* result from parts 1, 3, and 4 above.

6. *Charismatic leaders* and/or the "mystique" of the enterprise may be an important means of resolving conflict in objectives and overcoming restraints (Newman and Wallender, 1978).

Therefore, this study assumed that some characteristics of not-for-profit organizations and profit organizations differ, but that there is too little known about these differences in characteristics to be able to establish a systematic classification framework based upon them.

Therefore, a strategic management framework was taken for the structure of this study. Based upon a survey of the literature in public administration, urban administration, environmental administration, and institutional administration,

a typology of organizations related to these fields was developed. A similar typology has been developed by Newman and Wallender (1978). Each type of not-for-profit organization will be discussed using their typology, which is shown in Exhibit 6.3.

Based upon this classification system, more than 150 different periodicals were examined to identify the research studies on strategic management in each of the five broad types of not-for-profit organizations. The literature dealing with such organizations is quite voluminous. Unfortunately little of it deals with strategic management, or any of the components of strategic management.

Each research study of a not-for-profit organization that was identified was analyzed to determine if the research involved a single segment of the strategic management process (namely, whether it involved analysis, formulation, implementation, interpretation, or evalua-

---

Exhibit 6.3   A Typology of Different Types of Not-for-Profit Organizations

I.   Public organizations

    A. Executive agencies and departments
        (other than urban and environmental)
        Federal, state, and local governments
        Military

    B. Urban organizations

        Fire
        Police and law enforcement
        Public housing authorities
        Social services and welfare
        Transportation
        Human resources (manpower)

    C. Environmental organizations

        Conservation
        Water resources
        Air resources
        Energy resources

II.   Third sector organizations

    Public-private agencies
    (COMSAT, AMTRAK, etc.)
    Not-for-profit consultants
    Research institutes
    Consumer cooperatives

III.   Institutional organizations

    Education
    Hospitals and health care
    Trade unions
    Political parties
    Churches
    Libraries
    Performing arts
    Voluntary associations
    Organized charities

tion)[1] *or* whether more than one segment of strategic management was involved. In the former case, each study was classified in terms of the segment it involved. In the latter, a study was classified as comprehensive.

Furthermore, each study was classified by the research method involved. The following classification system was followed: *documentary*, which included both archival, historical, and secondary source data; *case study; survey; models and simulation; quantitative*, which includes mathematical models; *statistical*, which includes hypothesis generation and hypothesis testing; and *experimental*. The research techniques used in each study were also varying from interviews to questionnaires to group meetings.

Obviously other typologies and classifications could have been used in the evaluation of this body of literature on not-for-profit organizations. Indeed, as the years pass, other schemata will be undoubtedly suggested and used. The following sections will evaluate the literature in the not-for-profit field.

PUBLIC ORGANIZATIONS

In general, the literature on public organizations (excluding urban and environmental) with respect to strategic management seems to be highly descriptive. In other words, writers throughout the field are urging professionals to adopt their particular point of view, their new technique, or their new method (Hovey, 1968; Rabinovitz, 1969; Ranney, 1969; *Public Administration Review*, 1969; Schwarz, 1977). Unfortunately they seldom document their reasoning with empirical data of any type. Furthermore, the little empirical research on strategic management that does exist is primarily descriptive (see Exhibit 6.4).

---

[1] This system of classifying the strategic management process was derived from Hodgetts and Wortman's (1975) definition of administrative policy science. (Editor's note: the reader should note that Wortman's description of the strategic management process differs from that used throughout the remainder of this text.)

In federal organizations, the emphasis seems to be upon analyzing the role of federal executives approximately every ten years (Stanley, 1964; Corson and Shale, 1966). Usually some type of questionnaire or interview method has been used to obtain the data. Seldom are statistical analyses employed. Experimental methods are non-existent. Recently evaluation in the federal government has become fashionable and a few survey studies have been made (Katz, 1975; Wholey, et al., 1975). The terms "long-range planning" and "strategic management" seem never to have been heard in the federal bureaucracy. Analysis of administrative processes in top level management of the federal government in a rigorous, demanding series of studies has not yet occurred.

Similarly, there has been little strategic management research at the state level in government. Almost all of the literature that does exist is descriptive. The analysis of specific structures for the establishment of policy has been one area of study (Brief, Delbecq, et al., 1976).

At the local level of government, the emphasis seems to have been on examining the role of city managers (Almy, 1977; Lyden and Miller, 1976, 1977). Lyden and Miller (1976, 1977) have completed one of the only longitudinal studies on not-for-profit organizations. Little or no research on strategic management has been attempted at the local government level including county and metropolitan governments (Rugman, 1973).

Although the use of strategic management concepts by the military is well established in the literature, actual in-depth empirical evaluation of such applications is not wide-spread (Lang, 1965). One of the most recent successful attempts at analysis of governmental and military operations was the study by Allison (1971) of the Cuban missile crisis.

FURTHER RESEARCH NEEDS. In sum, the examination of strategic management in public organizations has barely been initiated even after many years of continuing political control by one party at city, county, state, and federal levels in the United States. The role of the executive in these governments badly needs to be examined in rigorous well-designed research

Exhibit 6.4 Strategic Management for Public Organizations: Examples of Current Research

Types of research	Studies done by	Content of the study	Characteristics of research		
			Types of organizations studied	Nature of studies	Research techniques used
A. Federal government					
Comprehensive	David and Pollock (1957)	Characteristics of federal executives.	Federal agencies	Survey	Interviews
	Stanley (1964)	Career patterns of federal executives.	225 Federal executives, GS 15–GS 18	Survey	Interviews Questionnaires Statistical analyses Group meetings
	Corson and Shale (1966)	Characteristics of top level federal executives.	424 Federal executives	Survey	Questionnaire
	Kaufman (1976)	Analysis of life cycle of government agencies.	175 Federal agencies— 1923 394 Federal agencies— 1973	Documentary/ Longitudinal	Federal register and federal documents
Evaluation	Katz (1975)	Evaluated government operations and relationship to client population.	1,431 Adults—Institute of Survey Research national survey	Survey	Interviews
	Wholey (1975)	Analyzed impact of federal programs.	15 Federal programs	Survey/Documentary	Interviews Examination of documents and studies
B. State government					
Comprehensive	Brief, Delbecq, et al. (1976)	Analysis of innovation proneness, adoption potential, and problem severity in elite groups.	7 Staff agencies 15 Service agencies 11 Boards, committees, commissions	Survey/Statistical	Questionnaires Statistics/correlation
C. Local government					
Comprehensive	Cousins (1976)	Influence of voluntary organizations upon local government.	3 Boroughs in London and 1,500 voluntary associations	Case study	Observation Interviews
	Kraemer, et al. (1976)	Evaluation of impact of information systems upon local government operations.	U.S. cities over 50,000 population	Model	Statistical/correlation

Exhibit 6.4 Strategic Management for Public Organizations (Continued)

Types of research	Studies done by	Content of the study	Characteristics of research		
			Types of organizations studied	Nature of studies	Research techniques used
	Buchanan (1974)	Comparison of business and government managers on commitment to objectives of organization.	279 managers in 3 industrial organizations and five government agencies	Survey	Questionnaire Instruments Statistical/Multiple regression
	Lyden and Miller (1976)	Characteristics of city managers.	83 City managers in 1966 and 82 in 1974 in Washington, Oregon, Idaho	Survey/Longitudinal	Questionnaire—Structured
	Lyden and Miller (1977)	Analysis of policy orientation of city managers.	83 City managers in 1966 and 82 in 1974 in Washington, Oregon, Idaho	Survey/Longitudinal	Questionnaire—Structured Forced choice options
	Almy (1977)	Analysis of city manager influences upon public expenditures.	645 City managers	Survey	Multi-purpose mail survey
Formulation	Rugman (1973)	Corporate planning in local government.	Kent County Council, England	Case study/Model	Observation Interviews
	Wolensky and Groves (1977)	Impact of planners and city officials upon local planning.	26 Planning commission chairmen, 29 mayors, 23 professional planners in 29 cities	Survey	Qualitative Interview Semi-structured Field research techniques
D. Military *Comprehensive*	Levine (1972)	Analyzes redundancy in military policy.	3 Cases—World War II, NATO, and Vietnam	Case study/Documentary	Documents
	Lang (1965)	Analysis of all types of military organization.	Military organizations	Documentary	Documents
	Allison (1971)	Analysis of Cuban missile crisis.	Executive branch of federal government	Case study/Documentary/Model	Documents

studies rather than in the descriptive fashion of the past. Commissions, boards, committees, and similar organizations which have major impacts upon executives in their decision making should be examined in terms of their roles, their interactions with the executives, their impacts upon decision making, and the ways in which they utilize strategic management concepts, if at all. Analysis of tri-partite bodies consisting of bureaucrats, client members (those to be served), and the public and their impact upon the strategic management of large governmental agencies serving client populations should be attempted. Such groups frequently have or seem to have a major input into strategic decisions affecting those client populations.

Not only should well-designed studies be attempted of governmental strategic management, but conceptual papers that outline hypothesis and propositional inventories are badly needed for the theoretical development of the field. Although policy scientists (using their base in political science) have clearly done some outstanding work in the conceptual area (primarily large-scale theoretical overviews of policy at multi-national, national, and regional levels of government), they have not delineated clearly what practical issues should be attacked in strategic management. Such hypotheses and propositions would establish priorities for systematic research in the strategic management of public organizations.

FURTHER RESEARCH APPROACHES. Although most of the work on public organizations has been descriptive, further well-designed exploratory studies on practically any aspect of strategic management would be useful. For example, studies which determine the nature of the strategic management process in governmental operations at any level of government would assist researchers in their comparison of strategic management processes in profit versus not-for-profit organizations. Such studies would be able to ascertain whether the segments of strategic management processes are similar or whether they are different (and if they are different, in what ways). Furthermore, analysis of the impact of long-range goals established by the federal government upon the long-range goals of state and local governments on a cross-sectional basis or longitudinal basis would be useful.

Even additional descriptive studies, including case studies and surveys, would be helpful in establishing the parameters of strategic management practice in public organizations. For example, the amorphous goals and goal structures could be meaningfully examined in such descriptive studies. Moreover, there are few well-designed documentary studies on strategic management in public organizations. Therefore, documentary studies based on archival sources could be useful in longitudinal studies of strategic management. In this regard many universities have large archives which are seldom used by policy researchers.

URBAN ORGANIZATIONS

Although there is some overlap between urban organizations and public and environmental organizations, there is a clearly defined area of urban problems which has become increasingly important to everyone as our society has become more and more urbanized. Briefly, research studies on urban organizations tend to be highly descriptive or to utilize mathematical models of very narrow issues (Exhibit 6.5). First, these descriptive documentary or case study analyses of urban organizations have not been gathered together in any systematic fashion for a total overview of the parameters of strategic management practices in urban organizations. Thus, the most rudimentary analyses of the segments of such strategic management practices in urban organizations have not been attempted. Second, the mathematical models employed frequently have not been based upon any empirical data nor have they been field-tested rigorously after they have been developed. Therefore, the net addition to the understanding of strategic management in urban organizations has not been as substantive as it could have been if these models had been tested empirically.

The analysis of strategic management in large fire departments in urban settings is nonexistent. One significant study identified was that of the New York City Fire Department by

Blum (1972). Not only was a mathematical model developed, but it was based upon some observation and a departmental data base. But fire-fighting literature is bereft of any attempt at studying the strategic management issues involved in fire-fighting. For example, long-term operations normally might be construed to be the question of when a given fire truck ought to be purchased.

Due to the emphasis upon law enforcement during the past decade, significant efforts have been made to improve the long-term management of police operations and the criminal justice system. But most of these efforts have been oriented toward short-term gains and improvements in law enforcement. Few efforts have been directed at the strategic management of the total law enforcement system including its components such as the in-field police officer, prosecution of cases, prisons, and assistance for ex-offenders. One model describing a total criminal justice system has been developed by Blumstein and Larson (1972). By developing such a model, they have taken a first step toward considering how the strategic management of such a total criminal justice system including its long-range goals and operations could be improved. Presently the individual parts of the system seem to be tinkered with at different periods. The total criminal justice system never seems to be analyzed in a systematic fashion. In one study, an analysis of the goals, policies, and operations of police officials and professionals was a first step toward research on strategic management in law enforcement (Hudzik and Greene, 1977).

An analysis of the literature on public housing authorities indicates there has been no research on strategic management. Clearly, in light of the scandals related to the financing (both short and long term) of such large-scale structures, of the poor construction of many public housing units (e.g., St. Louis), and of the continued poor administration of such authorities, research should have been centered on the strategic management of such housing authorities at a much earlier date.

In similar fashion, social services and welfare organizations seem to have grown indiscriminately with little or no thought given to some logical, coherent way of managing such huge

organizations efficiently and effectively in the long term. In these organizations, little or no consideration has been given to strategic management. With the implicit long-term structure of these agencies, research into their strategic management seems to be crucial. But few academics or practitioners have been willing to tackle such organizations, probably because of inadequate data bases and a reluctance by executives in these organizations to become involved in such research.

Although recent studies have been case oriented or documentary in transportation organizations (Carlson, 1976; Gakenheimer and Wheaton, 1976), there are some seminal studies in the evaluation of some aspects of strategic management in these organizations (Kobayashi, Aoki, and Tani, 1975). Unfortunately, research on transportation organizations has been dominated by those who are not empirically oriented.

In human resources or manpower organizations which deal with large-scale employment and training of the unemployed and disadvantaged, there has been little or no concern about the strategic management of such organizations. Indeed, there has been little or no concern about even the short-term management of such programs. But these programs are long-term programs and should be considered from a strategic management viewpoint. For example, manpower programs initiated under the Manpower Development and Training Act of 1962 are still around in one form or another under the Comprehensive Employment and Training Act of 1973.

FURTHER RESEARCH NEEDS. Since most of the writing on urban organizations in strategic management has been descriptive, practically any well-designed exploratory study would be fruitful. This would be true in all types of urban organizations.

Fire-fighting organizations apparently have not been studied to any appreciable extent. The strategic management of fire operations could have significant efficiency and effectiveness impacts upon city government in the long run. Studies of goal structures in fire-fighting operations, urban or rural, would be extremely useful. Analysis of the decision-making processes

Exhibit 6.5 Strategic Management for Urban Organizations: Examples of Current Research

Types of research	Studies done by	Content of the study	Characteristics of research		
			Types of organizations studied	Nature of studies	Research techniques used
A. Total urban systems					
Comprehensive	Rogers (1971)	Analysis of top management of three cities.	New York, Philadelphia, Cleveland	Case study	Observation Interviews
	Rosenbloom and Russell (1971)	Analysis of urban management in four cities.	Dayton, Ohio; New York City; New Jersey; Columbia, Maryland	Case study	Observation Interviews Operations analysis
	Morse (1972)	Analysis of urban organizations.	Many different urban organizations	Models/Mathematical	Quantitative
	Sweet (1972)	Analyzes models of urban structure.	Many different urban organizations	Models/Mathematical	Quantitative
	Scheff (1976)	Analyzes social planning.	Social organizations	Descriptive	Observation
	Goldberg (1977)	Simulates models of cities.	Vancouver, Canada Bay Area	Models/Mathematical	Simulation
Evaluation	Albert and Kamrass (1974)	Examines social experiments and evaluation.	Many different urban organizations	Case study/Models	Quantitative Observation
B. Fire					
Comprehensive	Blum (1972)	Examines New York City Fire Department.	New York City Fire Department	Case study/Model	Observation Quantitative

Exhibit 6.5 Strategic Management for Urban Organizations (Continued)

Types of research	Studies done by	Content of the study	Characteristics of research		
			Types of organizations studied	Nature of studies	Research techniques used
C. Police					
Comprehensive	Blumstein and Larson (1972)	Analysis of total criminal justice system.	Total criminal justice system	Model	Quantitative
	Hudzik and Greene (1977)	Study of goals, policies, activities.	7 Command officers in Midwestern sheriff's office	Case study	Interviews Open-end
Analysis	Levine (1975)	Effectiveness of police departments.	U.S. cities over 500,000	Documentary	Documents
	Skogan (1976)	Strategy on different types of crime.	386 U.S. cities more than 50,000 in 1970	Documentary	Statistics/correlation
D. Housing					
E. Social services and Welfare					
F. Transportation					
Comprehensive	Gakenheimer and Wheaton (1976)	Examines priorities in transportation research.		Documentary	Documentary
Analysis	Carlson (1976)	Examines failing system.	Santa Clara County Transit District	Case study	Observation
Evaluation	Kobayashi, Aoki, and Tani (1975)	Develops planning transportation system.	150 Office workers 1 Tokadai New Town	Case study/Survey	Questionnaires
G. Human resources					

of fire-fighting executives would lead to the further exploration of improving operations on a long-term basis.

In police and criminal enforcement organizations, practically any kind of well-designed study of any aspect of strategic management would be helpful. The roles of police commissions, citizen advisory committees, civilian review boards, court officials, penal officials and executives, and similar official positions throughout criminal enforcement could be analyzed. Advisory groups which are related to police operations should be evaluated in terms of their impact upon long-run operations of police departments and justice departments. Furthermore, the interaction of decisions by such executives and actual operations could be examined fruitfully. Theoretical, conceptual, and review studies which outlined the parameters of the problems faced by police executives could be extremely useful in establishing the broad general outlines for research on strategic management. Total systems conceptual models of the criminal enforcement system would be particularly useful in establishing the boundaries of the area.

In housing, social services, and welfare organizations, any work on the strategic management process would be useful. Presently the information on strategic management in these types of organization is non-existent. As noted earlier, the immensity of the problems, lack of adequate data, and ill-defined or implicit goals have frightened many researchers away from interesting policy-oriented studies in large-scale operations. In housing authorities, researchers may wish to look at long-term financing strategies of providing adequate housing for urban populations. In all of these types of organizations, there should be an examination of why implicit (or ill-defined explicit) long-range goal structures in these organizations seem to fail more than they succeed. Are their goal structures indeed different than those in other types of public organizations, not-for-profit organizations, or profit-oriented enterprises? Studies should be made of the ways in which inputs are gathered from interested parties and pressure groups in the establishment of goals in these organizations. Moreover, significantly dif-

ferent types of goal structures and processes for establishing these goal structures may have to be developed for this type of organization as contrasted with other public and private organizations. Lastly, an analysis of the environments within which these organizations operate would be useful in the determination of whether or not there is a disproportionate impact of external factors upon the goal-setting process as compared to other organizations.

Similarly, practically any type of systematic study on strategic management in transportation and human resources or manpower organizations would be helpful. Strategic management studies and pragmatic models of large-scale transportation systems on a national, state, or local basis would assist governments to clarify extremely unwieldly systems of transportation for the future. An examination of the impact of long-term planning upon manpower and human resource programs would undoubtedly provide leadership in a field where there has been little interest in strategic management. Moreover, the roles of executives in the goal-setting process in these organizations clearly needs to be analyzed. Contrasting studies of executives in day-to-day operations of these organizations with those in profit-oriented organizations could be useful to both types of organization.

FURTHER RESEARCH APPROACHES. Through this section on urban organizations, the stress has been on the fact that any systematic, well-considered research probably would be useful to the development of the field. Similarly, any research technique could be used in the development of these research areas, ranging from the simple exploratory case study to the statistically designed study. Presently, the study of strategic management in urban organizations badly needs some descriptive, exploratory studies upon which to base more extensive analyses. Analyzing strategic management in these types of organizations truly is a case where the researcher would not know what variables to study without initiating some exploratory, descriptive studies. Even surveys may not be useful since we do not know what variables to study. Therefore, surveys, quantitative analyses, statistical studies, and experimental designs probably would not yield significant understanding of the strategic management process in urban organizations. Techniques such as structured and unstructured questionnaires, interviews, and observation probably would be the most useful in such analyses.

ENVIRONMENTAL ORGANIZATIONS

Environmental organizations are, in general, one of the newest groups of not-for-profit organizations. They include conservation organizations (including groups like the Sierra Club and National Audubon Society) which attempt to maintain and improve the environment in which society exists; water resources organizations which include not only large urban water plants and waste disposal operations, but also multistate corporations which attempt to provide water resources in each of the states; air resources organizations which are primarily interested in maintaining the quality of the air we breath through the operations of pollution control commissions, advisory committees, and lobbying groups; and not-for-profit energy organizations which are interested in procuring additional energy sources and conserving those which exist. Because of the newness of the area almost all the materials are documentary (Exhibit 6.6) (Hutchinson, 1972; Edmunds and Letey, 1973; Preiser, 1973).

The management of conservation, water resources, and air resources is discussed in the literature. But this does not mean management in the usual sense, nor does it mean strategic management. Normally conservation management means the actual management of a forest, the actual management of a conservation area in terms of trees, picnic areas, and hiking trails, or the actual management of a farm pond. Management of water resources means the operations of a water treatment plant or a waste water disposal plant. The management of air resources means to fit "scrubbers" on utility chimneys or to hold down the amount of air pollution in a large urban center. None of these is directly related to strategic management. Similarly, energy management may mean a whole host of different things from energy manage-

ment in your home to the management of energy in large-scale industrial operations to the management of an oil refinery. Most of these are not directly related to strategic management (Eppen, 1975; O'Toole, 1976).

Therefore, research into strategic management in these areas would be exceptionally fruitful. Not only have these organizations not been studied, they probably would be glad to have strategic management researchers study their critical problems because many of the problems faced in conservation, water resources, air resources, and energy resources are truly problems involving long-range implications.

FUTURE RESEARCH NEEDS. Clearly a well-defined study of goals and goal structures in any of these types of organizations would be extremely useful. Moreover, an analysis of the roles of executives, their goals and aspirations, their impact upon operations, and their understanding of operations and of their field would be most helpful. Studies of the structure of such organizations could lead to their useful expansion in other areas, including public, urban and third sector organizations. Studies of the interrelationships between conservation, water resources, and air resources and the ways in which they are managed could be useful to a long-term strategy of integrating all of them in the same type of organization.

FURTHER RESEARCH APPROACHES. With little or no research into strategic management in these areas, almost any type of rigorously defined, well-designed research study would be welcome. Conceptual and theoretical studies are badly needed to define the parameters of strategic management in a given resource area. Documentary studies could be utilized as back-up material for such conceptual attempts. Case studies could be quite useful in the initial exploration of these types of organization. Surveys, based upon one or more case studies, also would be useful in the initial exploration of the field. At this time, quantitative, statistical, and experimental studies probably would not be very useful due to the lack of understanding of what it is we are trying to measure in strategic management in these types of organizations.

Exhibit 6.6 Strategic Management for Environmental Organizations: Examples of Current Research

Types of research	Studies done by	Characteristics of research			
		Content of the study	Types of organizations studied	Nature of studies	Research techniques used
A. Conservation					
Comprehensive	Hutchinson (1972)	Examined organizations involved in pollution.	Primarily those related to pollution	Documentary	Documentary
	Edmunds and Letey (1973)	Analysis of environmental organizations.	All types of environmental organizations	Documentary	Documentary
	Preiser (1973)	Studied environmental organizations.	All types of environmental organizations	Documentary	Models Statistics Simulation Questionnaires
B. Water resources					
C. Air resources					
D. Energy					
Comprehensive	Eppen (1975)	Analyzed energy related problems.	All types of energy related problems	Documentary	Documentary
	O'Toole et al. (1976)	Analyzed energy related problems.	54 Experts from academia, business, and government	Documentary/ Statistical	Delphi techniques

THIRD SECTOR ORGANIZATIONS

According to most definitions, third sector organizations are those not-for-profit organizations that have a private-public legal base and that attempt to do things that private corporations and the government either have not done, have not done well, or are not doing often enough (Levitt, 1973). Although third sector organizations have been around for a long time, their specific labelling as third sector organizations did not occur until the 1970's and little research was done on them prior to this time. Consequently, almost all of the research that has been done is documentary (Levitt, 1973; Cassell, 1975; Etzioni, 1975; McGill and Wooten, 1975; Parker and Gilbert, 1977). Most writers are attempting to establish a conceptual framework for such public-private organizations and to estimate the strategic impact of these organizations upon the society as a whole (Exhibit 6.7). With the development of more and more third sector organizations such as AMTRAK, COMSAT, etc., the strategic management of such organizations becomes critical.

FUTURE RESEARCH NEEDS. There is a tremendous need for strategic management research on such third sector organizations. As Etzioni (1975) and Levitt (1973) have pointed out, more and more of the economy is likely to become third sector-oriented. Therefore, it is critical that we have a clear understanding of what happens to the goals and goal structures of such organizations, that we comprehend the roles of executives in such organizations, and that we know the relationship of the executive to the operations of such organizations and to their advisory boards, committees, boards of directors, and commissions.

Continuing research on the conceptualization and theory pertaining to such organizations must continue. What is an appropriate mix of public-private involvement in such public-private organizations? Would the goals and goal structures be similar or dissimilar to those of other organizations? Based upon such concepts, theoretical hypotheses and propositions should be established which can be tested empirically. Hopefully, such testable concepts would also include methods of testing such hypotheses and propositions.

FURTHER RESEARCH APPROACHES. The present exclusive documentary approach to third sector organization research is inadequate. First, case studies of the strategic management practices of a third sector organization would be most useful. Through such exploratory studies, appropriate variables could be identified and future research planned with more sophisticated methods. Later, surveys of executives, directors, members of commissions, and members of committees to determine their roles and their impact upon the organization would be helpful. Without a number of in-depth exploratory studies to establish the parameters of future research, it will be extremely difficult to model, to statistically analyze, or to experimentally design studies in third sector organizations.

INSTITUTIONAL ORGANIZATIONS

Institutional organizations are those organizations which consist of generally well-established and highly-organized groups, societies, and foundations that are supported by the society as a whole. These include educational institutions, hospitals and health care institutions, trade unions, political parties, churches, libraries, performing arts organizations, voluntary associations, and organized charities (see Exhibit 6.8). With the exceptions of higher education and health care, these organizations have had little or no research on management, much less strategic management. Clearly, there is a need to study strategic management in each of these not-for-profit organizations because they have an impact upon the society as a whole.

Higher educational organizations are highly visible today because of the public concern about the increasing costs of sending children to college. Many higher educational organizations are poorly managed, both short and long range. Therefore, an increasing amount of attention should be paid to the strategic management of higher education institutions (Hosmer, 1972). To date, the research in higher educational institutions has been primarily documen-

Exhibit 6.7 Strategic Management for Third Sector Organizations: Examples of Current Research

Types of research	Studies done by	Content of the study	Characteristics of research		
			Types of organizations studied	Nature of studies	Research techniques used
Comprehensive	Levitt (1973)	Studies private-public organizations.	Private-public organizations (NAB, NOW, etc.)	Documentary	Documentary
	Etzioni (1975)	Studies private-public organizations.	Private-public organizations (COMSAT, etc.)	Documentary	Documentary
	McGill and Wooton (1975)	Studies private-public organizations.	Private-public organizations (AMTRAK, etc.)	Documentary	Documentary
	Cassell (1975)	Studies private-public organizations.	Private-public organizations (NASA, etc.)	Documentary	Documentary
	Parker and Gilbert (1977)	Analyzes ConRail and AMTRAK operations.	ConRail and AMTRAK	Documentary	Documentary
Implementation	Yavitz and Schnee (1977)	Examines NASA operations	NASA	Case study	Observation

Exhibit 6.8 Strategic Management for Institutional Organizations: Examples of Current Research

Types of research	Studies done by	Content of the study	Characteristics of research		
			Types of organizations studied	Nature of studies	Research techniques used
A. Higher education *Comprehensive*	Rourke and Brook (1966)	Management in higher education.	290 State colleges and universities	Survey	Questionnaires Interviews
	American Educational Research Association (1967)	Educational organization and administration.	None	Documentary	Literature Review
	Casasco (1970)	Corporate planning model for universities.	None	Documentary/Model	Documentary
	Mazze (1971)	University planning model.	None	Documentary/Model	Documentary
	Oliver (1972)	University planning.	None	Models/Mathematical	Quantitative
	Heron and Friesen (1973)	Analyzes community colleges in U.S.	Community colleges in the U.S.	Documentary	Documentary
	Churchman (1974)	Organization of future universities.	None	Documentary/Model	Documentary
	McKay and Cutting (1974)	Long-range planning model in higher education.	None	Documentary/Model	Documentary
	McConnell (1975)	Examined coordinating structures in higher education.	50 States' coordinating structures in higher education	Documentary	Documentary
	Miller and Rice (1967)	Examined non-profit institutes.	Non-profit research institutes	Documentary	Documentary
	Ikenberry and Friedman (1972)	Analyzed executives in research centers and institutes.	125 Research center and institute directors	Survey	Questionnaires Interviews Telephone Observation
	Orlans (1972)	Examined non-profit institutes.	Non-profit research institutes	Documentary	Documentary
	Peterson (1975)	Analyzed effectiveness of new and old college and university presidents.	26 College and university presidents, 12 new and 14 experienced	Survey	Interviews Critical incident technique
	Stringer (1977)	Analyzed "assistant to" in higher education.	1 Large public university; 17 superiors, 18 "assistant to's"	Survey/Case study	Interviews Questionnaire Structured
Analysis	Conrad (1974)	Studied operative goals in university.	None, university goals	Documentary	Documentary
	Lewis and Dahl (1976)	Analyzed operations of deans and chairpersons.	1 Major American university; 8 chairpersons and directors; 4 deans	Case study/Statistical	Extensor unit (Time measure) Regression
Implementation	Maciariello and Enteman (1974)	Long-range planning in a college.	Union College	Case study	Model
	Escher (1976)	College planning model.	1 Catholic liberal arts school	Case study	Observation
Interpretation	Newby (1976)	Long-range planning in a college.	1 Free Methodist liberal arts college	Case study	Observation
	Mood, et al. (1972)	Management efficiency in higher education.	Private college and universities in California	Models/Mathematical Survey	Quantitative

Exhibit 6.8 Strategic Management for Institutional Organizations (Continued)

Types of research	Studies done by	Content of the study	Characteristics of research		
			Types of organizations studied	Nature of studies	Research techniques used
Evaluation	Fenker (1975)	Evaluation of university administrators.	Evaluation of faculty and administrators at Texas Christian University	Case study	Instruments
B. Hospitals and health care					
Comprehensive	Georgopoulos (1967)	Characteristics of American general hospital.	41 General hospitals—2,400 respondents	Survey	Questionnaire/Semi-structured/ Interviews Statistics/Correlation
	McNamara and Todd (1970)	Characteristics of group practice in the United States.	6,371 Medical group practices with 3 or more physicians	Survey	Questionnaire
	Freidson and Mann (1971)	Dimensions of large-scale group medical practice.	125 Medical group practices with 10 or more physicians	Case study/Survey/ Statistical	Questionnaire Factor analysis
	Georgopoulos (1972)	Entire hospital field.	Hospitals	Documentary	Literature review
	Hickey (1972)	Functions of hospital boards of directors.	527 Directors from 105 short-term general hospitals of 100 beds or larger in Arkansas, Louisiana, New Mexico, Oklahoma, and Texas	Survey	Questionnaire
	Pfeffer (1973)	Hospital boards of directors.	57 Hospitals in a Midwestern state	Survey/Statistical	Ranking instrument Questionnaire Statistics/Correlation
	Georgopoulos (1975)	Entire hospital field.	Hospitals	Documentary	Literature review
	Lum (1975)	Profiles of health maintenance organization directors.	67 Health maintenance organizations	Survey	Questionnaire/Likert scale
Analysis	Baldwin (1972)	Impact of organizational differentiation and integration on hospital performance.	14 Florida hospitals (210 to 500 beds), 209 managerial and affiliated physicians	Survey	Questionnaire Interviews Statistical records
	McClain and Rao (1974)	Evaluation of health system alternatives.	25 Health care executives	Model/Statistical	Statistics/Correlation Cluster analysis
Formulation	Thompson (1974)	Financial planning in an HMO.	1 San Francisco health maintenance organization	Case study/Model	Statistical Simulation
	Webber and Dula (1974)	Long-range planning committees.	Long-range planning committees in hospitals	Documentary	Observation
	Cleverley (1975)	I-O analysis and hospital budgeting.	1 Northern California short-term hospital with 210 beds	Case study	Statistical model
	Waters (1976)	State comprehensive health planning.	42 State comprehensive health planning agencies	Survey/Case study	Questionnaire Observation
	Glueck and Mankin (1977)	Strategic planning in hospitals.	15 Missouri general hospitals	Survey	Field interviews Questionnaire
	Schmidt and Madoff (1977)	Organization of public health laboratories.	11,903 Clinical laboratories	Survey/Documentary	Survey questionnaire

Exhibit 6.8 Strategic Management for Institutional Organizations (Continued)

Types of research	Studies done by	Content of the study	Characteristics of research		
			Types of organizations studied	Nature of studies	Research techniques used
Implementation	Veney, et al. (1971)	Implementation of health programs in hospitals.	480 Short-term general non-federal hospitals	Statistical	Questionnaires, Multiple factor design
	Anderson (1976)	Hospital utilization model.	Short-term general hospitals in New Mexico, 1970 census data	Model/Statistical	Simultaneous equations
	Meyers, Dorwart, and Kline (1977)	Using citizen boards in health planning.	37 Mental health planning citizen boards (21 persons on a board)	Documentary/Statistical	Statistical/Factor analysis
Evaluation	Palmiere (1972)	Health facilities planning councils.	46 Facilities' planning councils	Survey	Questionnaire
	Grimes and Moseley (1976)	Index of hospital performance.	32 Texas hospitals—40 experts in the field	Statistical	Delphi technique
C. Trade unions					
D. Political parties					
E. Churches					
Comprehensive	Hussey (1974)	Corporate planning in a church.	A small Methodist church	Case study	Observation
Interpretation	Webb (1974)	Organizational effectiveness in the church.	15 Presbyterian churches; 304 church members	Survey/Statistical	Interviews, Questionnaire, Cluster analysis, Regression
F. Libraries					
Comprehensive	Morse (1972)	Library models.	None	Model/Mathematical	Quantitative
	McGrath (1973)	Long-range planning in university library.	Cornell University Library	Survey	Questionnaires, Interviews, Observation
	Kennington (1977)	Long-range planning in public libraries.	23 Library directors and experts in library science	Survey	Delphi technique
G. Arts organizations					
Comprehensive	Adizes (1972)	Boards of directors in performing arts.	156 Artistic directors, managers, members of artistic organizations, and active and inactive members of performing arts companies; 33 performing arts companies	Survey	Interviews, Observation
	Zelermyer (1976)	Management of art gallery.	None	Documentary	Documentary, Observation
H. Voluntary associations					
Comprehensive	Pennock and Chapman (1969)	Operations of voluntary organizations.	Various types of voluntary organizations	Documentary/Models	Documentary, Models/Non-mathematical
I. Organized charities					

tary (American Educational Research Association, 1967; Miller and Rice, 1967; Casasco, 1970; Mazze, 1971; Orlans, 1972; McKay and Cutting, 1974; Churchman, 1974) and survey data (Rourke and Brooks, 1966; Ikenberry and Friedman, 1972; Peterson, 1975; Stringer, 1977) (Exhibit 6.8). In most of the research on comprehensive strategic management in higher education, there is the propensity to develop models based upon documentary evidence or upon experience. Few of these models are developed from empirical data. Those studies that have utilized data usually have employed interviews, questionnaires, and observation. Most of the research in the comprehensive strategic management area has centered on structural components of higher education in terms of the institution itself (Rourke and Brooks, 1966; Heron and Friesen, 1973), coordinating structures (McConnell, 1975) and non-profit research institutes (Miller and Rice, 1967; Hutchinson, 1972; Orlans, 1972). Normally when executives are studied in higher educational institutions, the president of the college or university is analyzed (Peterson, 1975). Other executives in the top corporate structure of higher educational institutions seldom are studied (Stringer, 1977).

In analyzing problems in higher educational institutions, studies have utilized documentary and case study approaches (Exhibit 6.8). Some studies have analyzed university goals and goal structures (Conrad, 1974), while others have measured the ways in which time is spent by university administrators (Lewis and Dahl, 1976). In examining the implementation of policy, most studies of higher educational institutions have been experiential case studies, which have used observation and experiential techniques to obtain data (Maciariello and Enteman, 1974; Escher, 1976; Newby, 1976). In research which has attempted to interpret policy, some studies have used models, while others have used surveys (Mood, 1972). Lastly, the evaluation of policies in recent years has been attempted by the faculty in examining and evaluating how top administrators in a university or college have carried out established policies set by the trustees or the faculty (Fenker, 1975).

With more and more of our economic dollars moving into the health care field, the issue of strategic management of health care has become more and more critical. Clearly, this importance is reflected in the growing numbers of solid empirical research articles in the literature and in the establishment of new research journals in hospital administration. Although many of the studies in the hospital and health care field are surveys or case studies, there are increasing numbers of literature review articles which should lead to further development of the health care field (Georgopoulos, 1972, 1975) (Exhibit 6.8).

Operations of hospitals (Georgopoulos and Matejko, 1967), group medical practices (McNamara and Todd, 1970; Friedson and Mann, 1971), health maintenance organizations (Thompson, 1974; Lum, 1975), hospital boards of directors (Hickey, 1972; Pfeffer, 1973) and health care councils, advisory committees, and boards have demonstrated the increasing concern of the health care field about the strategic management of health care operations and the rising costs of health care itself. The study of executives in health care operations has not been as extensive as it should have been (Baldwin, 1972; McClain and Rao, 1974).

In terms of the segments of the strategic management process, more studies seem to have been done in this type of not-for-profit organization than any other. Studies have been done in analysis (Baldwin, 1972; McClain and Rao, 1974), formulation (Thompson, 1974; Webber and Dula, 1974; Cleverley, 1975; Waters, 1976; Glueck and Mankin, 1977; Schmidt and Madoff, 1977), implementation (Veney, 1971; Anderson, 1976; Meyers, Dorwart, and Kline, 1977), and evaluation (Palmiere, 1972; Grimes and Moseley, 1976). In terms of research methodology, they vary widely from documentary studies to statistical studies (Exhibit 6.8). Most of the studies are survey-oriented and tend to be descriptive in nature. Observation, interviews, and questionnaires are widely used to gather the data. But the major thrust of the health care administration field seems clearly to be toward a tightening of research design and the testing of hypotheses. In the future, we should see both statistical and experimentally designed studies in the health care administration field.

Strategic management research for trade

unions is non-existent. The word "management" is an anathema to a trade union leader. The literature certainly backs this contention. Little or no research has ever been done on "strategic management" in trade unions. But the trade union movement today probably needs as much analysis of its goals and goal structure as any other type of not-for-profit organization because of its seeming lack of forward progress by both the union membership and the American public.

In political parties, the orientation is toward winning elections. Almost all of their strategic management focus currently appears to be short term. Little or no overt strategic planning or strategic management seems to be attempted by a political party. The leaders of the party are primarily interested in retaining their posts long enough to carry out the objectives of the party, as well as their own objectives. Therefore, there is no literature on strategic management in political parties.

In recent years, there has been a swing toward some management studies of the operations of the church. The classic model of a hierarchical structure was the Catholic church. Today there are a few studies of strategic management in the church (Hussey, 1974; Webb, 1974). These generally are case studies or surveys. Many are oriented toward the examination of goals and goal structures to determine what the church is doing right or doing wrong according to its constituency. Observation, interviews, questionnaires, and statistical analyses have been used in such studies (Exhibit 6.8).

In general, libraries have been poorly managed. A professional librarian does not automatically make a good manager (similar to professionals in any field). With the increasing costs of books and periodicals, libraries have began to look at how they are managed. Strategic management may become of critical importance to libraries. Recent strategic management studies in libraries have ranged from models (Morse, 1972), to case studies (McGrath, 1973), to surveys (Kennington, 1977). These studies generally are concerned with long-range planning.

Arts organizations have generally been unconcerned with their managements. If the orga-nization did not meet its budget, it went to the community and asked for more money. Today, with increasing financial constraints upon all parts of society, more and more arts organizations are becoming concerned about management and, more specifically, strategic management. In the context of arts organizations, strategic management means almost the same as it does in other profit and not-for-profit organizations. Goals and goal structures are crucially important to these organizations. For example, they must have as one long-range goal the survival of the organization. With the increasing costs of operation, arts organizations are beginning to look toward better management as a means of survival in the short term and, hopefully, will begin to look at better strategic management practice for both the long and short term. In this vein, one author has written a book on gallery management (Zelermyer, 1976). Adizes (1972) has studied executives in 33 performing arts companies. In his study, interviews and observations were used as the primary means of obtaining data.

Voluntary associations are beginning to consider how they manage themselves. As time passes, they probably will be more interested in strategic management (Pennock and Chapman, 1969). Presently there is no literature on strategic management in voluntary associations. Similarly, there is no research or literature on organized charities.

FUTURE RESEARCH NEEDS. Throughout this section on institutional organizations, it is clear that all of these organizations are having an increasingly difficult time from a financial standpoint. Therefore, they should be looking toward strategic management as a way out of these financial difficulties. Higher educational organizations already have the strongest research base. Yet much of the research is insufficiently backed by rigorous empirical studies, with few of the strategic management models validated empirically.

In higher educational institutions, top level executives need to be studied in depth as to their roles, goals, and their impact upon the organization. Governing boards and their impact upon institutions of higher education need to be analyzed. Goals and goal structures within the university, within the board, within faculty governance units, and within the executive structure should be examined. Structural operations of such institutions need to be revaluated for maximum efficiency and effectiveness.

Although the health care organization area is moving along in the analysis of its strategic management needs, its emphasis has been upon total operations of hospitals, health maintenance organizations, group medical practices, etc. Analysis of the executives in such organizations has not been as thorough or as rigorous as it ought to be if we truly want to understand the roles of executives in health care management operations. Certainly theoretical and conceptual papers in the area of health care administration are badly needed. Of course, such papers should be well documented rather than attempting to transfer the "executive image" from modern business to the modern health care facility. Perhaps such executives really are different from their counterparts in industry, and perhaps they are more aware of the political realities of their various constituencies they serve. Furthermore, research in the health care field has advanced sufficiently so that surveys and statistical studies could be employed to create and test hypotheses about goals and goal structures, the roles of executives, and the integration or lack of integration of the segments of the strategic management process in health care operations. The field is not yet ready for experimentally designed studies.

Many trade unions are in trouble today because of the lack of strategic management. Successful trade unions should be analyzed to determine the reasons for their long-term success and to see how they performed their strategic management tasks in the past. Furthermore, their current goals and goal structures (whether explicit or implicit) should be studied to learn how they might utilize strategic management today.

Political parties at the national level should be examined to determine if there are any reasons that they should be engaged in strategic management. Their goal structures and goals should be analyzed to determine if they truly are non-strategic management-oriented and whether they should remain that way.

Churches, libraries, arts organizations, voluntary associations, and organized charities are generally so poorly managed that an examination of the strategic management concept for these organizations should start at the beginning with simple conceptual and theoretical papers with hypotheses and propositional inventories which probably would be prescriptive rather than descriptive. Exploratory case studies could also be initiated to determine the goals and goal structures of each of the different types of organizations. Surveys could conceivably be used. Statistical and experimental design studies are not in the picture at this time.

FURTHER RESEARCH APPROACHES. With the exception of higher educational institutions and health care organizations, the institutional organizations identified in this section really are in the exploratory stage of research on strategic management. Conceptual and theoretical papers on how they could use strategic management concepts would be helpful to each of the different types of organizations. Hypotheses and propositions of a prescriptive nature would be useful in such organizations. Case studies and surveys as exploratory devices could be used to determine the limits of strategic management in each type of organization. Except for higher educational institutions and health care organizations, these institutions will not be using statistical or experimental design research in the foreseeable future.

CONCLUSIONS

Not-for-profit organizations are just in the initial stage of using the strategic management concept. Many of them could indeed use it today. But many are ill-prepared to do so, because of inadequate managements, ill-defined data bases, poorly defined goals, and poor or no comprehension of the concept. The research needs on strategic management are enormous in not-for-profit organizations. Indeed, rigorous empirical research is needed on all such organizations.

Throughout this study, there is a major recurring theme — that of the need for simple exploratory studies of goals and goal structures for all types of not-for-profit organizations. Although some would argue that goals and goal structures in not-for-profit organizations are significantly different than those in profit-oriented organizations, there is little or no evidence that they are similar or dissimilar. Therefore, studies of the strategic management process in not-for-profit organizations must begin at the very earliest stages of that process — namely goals and goal structures. When these exploratory studies have been completed and

the variables identified, other studies with more sophisticated research methods and techniques can be undertaken on the process itself. Additional exploratory studies analyzing the relationship between different environmental conditions and these goal structures, and the roles of executives in achieving those goals would also be needed.

The researcher looking for fruitful areas in which to do strategic management research would be well advised to consider the possible study of not-for-profit organizations.

Section 6 References

Abbanat, Robert. "Strategy of Size." Doctoral diss., Harvard University, 1967.

Ackerman, Robert W. "Organization and Investment Process: A Comparative Study." Doctoral diss., Harvard University, 1968.

Adizes, Ichak. "Boards of Directors in the Performing Arts: A Managerial Analysis." *California Management Review*, Winter 1972.

Aharoni, Yair. *The Foreign Investment Decision Process*. Boston: Division of Research, Graduate School of Business Administration, Harvard University, 1966.

Albert, James G. and Murray Kamrass (editors). *Social Experiments and Social Program Evaluation*. Cambridge, Mass.: Ballinger Publishing, 1974.

Alderson Associates. "The Strategy of Business Growth," in Gross, A. and W. Gross. *Business Policy: Readings and Commentaries*. New York: The Ronald Press, 1967.

Allen Stephen A. "A Taxonomy of Organizational Choices in Divisionalized Companies." Working paper, IMEDE, Lausanne, Switzerland, October 1976.

Allison, Graham T. *Essence of Decision: Explaining the Cuban Missile Crisis*. Boston: Little, Brown, 1971.

Alm, Kent G., et al. "Managing Faculty Reductions." *Journal of Higher Education*, March–April 1977.

Almy, Timothy A. "City Managers, Public Avoidance, and Revenue Sharing." *Public Administration Review*, January 1977.

Altshuler, Alan A. *City Planning Process: A Political Analysis*. Ithaca, N.Y.: Cornell University Press, 1965a.

Altshuler, Alan A. "The Goals of Comprehensive Planning." *Journal of the American Institute of Planners*, August 1965b.

Amara, Roy C. "Toward a Framework for National Goals and Policy Research." *Policy Sciences*, March 1972.

American Educational Research Association. "Educational Organization, Administration, and Finance." *Review of Educational Research*, 1967.

American Institute of Planners. "Improving State and Metropolitan Planning." *Proceedings of Two Technical Seminars*—Washington, D.C., January 6–7, 1969.

Anagnostopoulos, C. E. "Management of New Ventures in a Mature Organization." *Proceedings of Project ISEED*. Milwaukee, Wis.: Project ISEED, Ltd., 1975.

Anderson, James G. "A Social Systems Model of Hospital Utilization." *Health Services Research*, Fall 1976.

Andrews, Kenneth R. *The Concept of Corporate Strategy*. Homewood, Ill.: Dow Jones–Irwin, 1971.

Angell, Robert C. and Ronald Freedman. "The Use of Documents, Records, Census Materials, and Indices," in Festinger, Leon and Daniel Katz (editors), *Research Methods in the Behavioral Sciences*. New York: Holt, Rinehart and Winston, 1953.

Ansoff, H. Igor. *Corporate Strategy: An Analytic Approach to Business Policy for Growth and Expansion*. New York: McGraw-Hill, 1965.

Ansoff, H. Igor. "The State of Practice in Planning Systems." *Sloan Management Review*, Winter 1977.

Ansoff, H. Igor and Robert L. Hayes. "Role of Models in Corporate Decision-Making," in Ross,

M. (editor). *Operational Research*. Amsterdam: North Holland, 1972.

Baker, Robert J. and Jeffrey C. Susbauer. "The Venture Formation/Development Process — A Framework for Evaluation of Venture Assistance Experiments." *Proceedings of Project ISEED*. Milwaukee, Wis.: Project ISEED, Ltd., 1975.

Baker, Robert J. and Jeffrey C. Susbauer. "New Venture Development and Corporate Growth Strategy and Tactics." Unpublished working paper, 1977a.

Baker, Robert J. and Jeffrey C. Susbauer. "Venture Capital and Other Frivolous Acts of Man." Unpublished working paper, 1977b.

Baldwin, L. Eugene. "An Empirical Study: The Effect of Organizational Differentiation and Integration on Hospital Performance." *Hospital Administration*, Fall 1972.

Barzun, Jacques. *The American University*. New York: Harper and Row, 1968.

Berg, Norman. "Strategic Planning in Conglomerate Companies." *Harvard Business Review*, May–June 1965.

Berg, Norman. "Corporate Role in Diversified Companies," in Taylor, B. and K. MacMillan (editors). *Business Policy: Teaching and Research*. New York: Wiley, 1973.

Beyle, Thad L. and George T. Lathrop. *Planning and Politics*. New York: Odyssey Press, 1970.

Biggadike, Ralph. "Entry, Strategy and Performance." Doctoral diss., Harvard University, 1976.

Black, James A. and Dean J. Champion. *Methods and Issues in Social Research*. New York: Wiley, 1976.

Blum, Edward H. "The New York City Fire Project," in Drake, A. W., R. L. Keeney and P. Morse (editors). *Analysis of Public Systems*. Cambridge, Mass.: M.I.T. Press, 1972.

Blumstein, Alfred and Richard C. Larson. "Analysis of a Total Criminal Justice System," in Drake, A. W., R. L. Keeney and P. Morse (editors). *Analysis of Public Systems*. Cambridge, Mass.: M.I.T. Press, 1972.

Bolton Report. *Small Firms: Report of the Committee of Inquiry on Small Firms*. HMSO Report Cmnd. 4811. London, England, November 1971.

The Boston Consulting Group. *Perspectives on Experience*. Boston: Boston Consulting Group, 1968.

Boswell, Jonathan. *The Rise and Decline of Small Firms*. London: Allen and Unwin, 1972.

Bower, Joseph L. *Managing the Resource Allocation Process: A Study of Corporate Planning and Investment*. Boston: Graduate School of Business Administration, Harvard University, 1970.

Brewer, Garry D. "The Policy Sciences Emerge: To Nurture and Structure a Discipline." *Policy Sciences*, September 1974.

Brief, Arthur P., Andre Delbecq, et al. "Elite Structure and Attitudes." *Administration and Society*, August 1976.

Brooks, Philip C. *Research in Archives: The Use of Unpublished Primary Sources*. Chicago: University of Chicago Press, 1969.

Buchanan, Bruce, II. "Government Managers, Business Executives, and Organizational Commitment." *Public Administration Review*, August 1974.

Buchele, Robert. *Business Policy in Growing Firms*. San Francisco: Chandler Publishing, 1967.

Buchele, Robert. "Coping with the Key Crises in Growing Firms." *Proceedings of Project ISEED*. Milwaukee, Wis.: Project ISEED, Ltd., 1975.

Bursk, Edward. "Pointers on Meeting Competition." Small Business Administration, Management Aids for Small Manufacturers, No. 134.

Campbell, Donald T. and Julian C. Stanley. *Experimental and Quasi-Experimental Designs for Research*. Chicago: Rand McNally, 1963.

Carlson, Robert C. "Anatomy of a Systems Failure: Dial-a-Ride in Santa Clara County, California." *Transportation*, March 1976.

Casasco, Juan A. "Corporate Planning Models for University Management." *Report No. 4*. Washington, D.C.: ERIC Clearinghouse on Higher Education, 1970.

Cassell, Frank H. "The Politics of Public-Private Management," in Wortman, Max S. and Fred Luthans (editors). *Emerging Concepts in Management* (2d edition). New York: Macmillan, 1975.

Chandler, Alfred D. *Strategy and Structure: Chapters in the History of the American Industrial Enterprise*. Cambridge, Mass.: M.I.T. Press, 1962.

Channon, Derek F. "The Strategy and Structure of British Enterprise." Doctoral diss., Harvard University, 1971.

Channon, Derek F. *The Strategy and Structure of British Enterprise*. Boston: Graduate School of Business Administration, Harvard University, 1973.

Charpie, Robert, et al. *Technological Innovation: Its Environment and Management*. Washington, D.C.: U.S. Government Printing Office, 1967.

Christenson, C. Roland. *Management Succession in Small and Growing Enterprises*. Boston: Graduate School of Business Administration, Harvard University, 1953.

Churchman, C. West. "On the Organization of Exoteric Universities," in Leavitt, Harold, Lawrence Pinfield and Eugene Webb (editors). *Organizations of the Future.* New York: Praeger, 1974.

Clayton, Ross, Patrick Conklin and Raymond Shapek (editors). "Policy Management Assistance —A Developing Dialogue." *Public Administration Review, Special Issue,* December 1975.

Cleverley, William O. "Input-Output Analysis and the Hospital Budgeting Process." *Health Services Research,* Spring 1975.

Cochran, William G. and Gertrude M. Cox. *Experimental Designs* (2d edition). New York: Wiley, 1957.

Cohn, Theodore and Roy A. Lindberg. *How Management Is Different in Small Companies.* New York: American Management Association, 1972.

Cohn, Theodore and Roy A. Lindberg. *Survival and Growth: Management Strategies for the Small Firm.* New York: AMACOM, 1974.

Collins, Orvis and David Moore. *The Organization Makers.* New York: Appleton-Century-Crofts, 1970.

Colton, Robert and Gerald Udell. "The National Science Foundation's Innovation Centers — An Experiment in Training Potential Entrepreneurs and Innovators." *Journal of Small Business Management,* April 1976.

Conrad, Clifton. "University Goals: An Operative Approach." *Journal of Higher Education,* October 1974.

Cooper, Arnold. "Small Companies Can Pioneer New Products." *Harvard Business Review,* September–October 1966.

Cooper, Arnold. *The Founding of Technologically-Based Firms.* Milwaukee, Wis.: The Center for Venture Management, 1971.

Cooper, Arnold. "Technical Entrepreneurship: What Do We Know?" *R&D Management,* February 1973.

Cooper, Arnold and Albert Bruno. "Success Among High-Technology Firms." *Business Horizons,* April 1977.

Cooper, Arnold and Arthur Riggs, Jr. "Non-Traditional Approaches to Technology Utilization." *Journal of the Society of Research Administrators,* Winter 1975.

Corey, E. Raymond and Steven H. Star. *Organization Strategy: A Marketing Approach.* Boston: Graduate School of Business Administration, Harvard University, 1971.

Corson, John J. and Paul R. Shale. *Men Near the Top: Filling Key Posts in the Federal Service.* Baltimore, Md.: Johns Hopkins and the Committee for Economic Development, 1966.

Cousins, P. F. "Voluntary Organizations and Local Government in Three South London Boroughs." *Public Administration* (London), Spring 1976.

David, Paul T. and Ross Pollock. *Executives for Government.* Washington, D.C.: The Brookings Institution, 1957.

Delano, Miles, D. W. Johnson and R. T. Woodworth. "Entrepreneurial Report." Graduate School of Business, University of Washington, March 1966.

Douds, Charles and Albert Rubenstein. "Methodology for Behavioral Aspects of Innovation," in Kelly, P., M. Kranzberg, et al. *Technological Innovation: A Critical Review of Current Knowledge, Vol. II.* Washington, D.C.: U.S. Government Printing Office, 1975.

Drake, A. W., R. L. Keeney and P. M. Morse (editors). *Analysis of Public Systems.* Cambridge, Mass.: M.I.T. Press, 1972.

Dror, Yehezkel. "Prolegomena to Policy Sciences." *Policy Sciences,* Spring 1970.

Dror, Yehezkel. *Design for Policy Sciences.* New York: Elsevier North-Holland, 1971.

Dror, Yehezkel. "Policy Sciences: Some Global Perspectives." *Policy Sciences,* March 1974.

Eddison, Tony. *Local Government: Management and Corporate Planning.* London: L. Hill, 1973.

Edmunds, Stahrl and John Letey. *Environmental Administration.* New York: McGraw-Hill, 1973.

Eppen, Gary (editor). *Energy: The Policy Issues.* Chicago: University of Chicago Press, 1975.

Escher, Firmin, Sr. "College of Saint Benedict: A Planning Model That Works." *New Directions for Higher Education,* No. 15, Autumn 1976.

Etcheson, Warren W. *A Study of Business Terminations.* Seattle, Wash.: University of Washington Business School, 1962.

Etzioni, Amitai. "The Third Sector and Domestic Missions," in Wortman, Max and Fred Luthans (editors). *Emerging Concepts in Management* (2d edition). New York: Macmillan, 1975.

Fast, Norman. "The Evolution of Corporate New Venture Divisions." Doctoral diss., Harvard University, 1977.

Fenker, Richard M. "The Evaluation of University Faculty and Administrators." *Journal of Higher Education,* November–December 1975.

Fowler, Frank P. and E. W. Sandberg. *The Relationship of Management Decision Making to Small Business Growth.* Fort Collins, Colo.: Colorado State University, 1964.

Freidson, Eliot and John H. Mann. "Organizational Dimensions of Large Scale Group Medical Practice." *American Journal of Public Health,* April 1971.

Friend, John K. and W. N. Jessop. *Local Government and Strategic Choice.* Beverly Hills, Calif.: Sage Publications, 1969.

Gakenheimer, Ralph and William C. Wheaton. "Priorities in Urban Transport Research." *Transportation,* March 1976.

Georgopoulos, Basil S. (editor). *Organization Research on Health Institutions.* Ann Arbor, Mich.: Institute for Social Research, University of Michigan, 1972.

Georgopoulos, Basil S. *Hospital Organization Research: Review and Source Book.* Philadelphia: Saunders, 1975.

Georgopoulos, Basil S. and Aleksander Matejko. "The American General Hospital as a Complex Social System." *Health Services Research,* Spring 1967.

Gilmore, Frank F. "Strategic Planning's Threat to Small Business." *California Management Review,* Vol. 9, Winter 1966.

Gilmore, Frank F. "Formulating Strategy in Smaller Companies." *Harvard Business Review,* May–June 1971.

Glueck, William F. and Douglas C. Mankin. "Strategic Planning." *Hospital and Health Services Administration,* Spring 1977.

Goldberg, Michael A. "Simulating Cities: Process, Product, and Prognosis." *Journal of the American Institute of Planners,* April 1977.

Golde, Roger. "Practical Planning for Small Business." *Harvard Business Review,* September–October 1964.

Grant, John. "Management Implications of Systems Oriented Strategies within Selected Industrial Firms: A Developmental Model." Doctoral diss., Harvard University, 1972.

Griggs, Jack. "The Commercial Banker and Industrial Entrepreneurship: The Lending Officer's Propensity to Make Loans to New and Different Companies." Doctoral diss., The University of Texas at Austin, 1972.

Grimes, Richard M. and S. Kelley Moseley. "An Approach to an Index of Hospital Performance." *Health Services Research,* Fall 1976.

Gross, Alfred. "Coping with Radical Competition," in Gross, A. and W. Gross. *Business Policy: Readings and Commentaries.* New York: The Ronald Press, 1967a.

Gross, Alfred. "Meeting the Competition of Giants." *Harvard Business Review,* May–June 1967b.

Hagen, Everett. "The Transition in Columbia," in Kilby, P. (editor). *Entrepreneurship and Economic Development.* New York: The Free Press, 1971.

Hall, Owen P., Jr. "A Policy Model Appraisal Paradigm." *Policy Sciences,* June 1975.

Hanan, Mark. "Venturing Corporations — Think Small to Stay Strong." *Harvard Business Review,* May–June 1976.

Hanna, Richard. "The Concept of Corporate Strategy in Multi-Industry Companies." Doctoral diss., Harvard University, 1968.

Hardy, James M. *Corporate Planning for Nonprofit Organizations.* New York: Association Press, 1972.

Hass, Raymond M., et al. *Long-Range Planning for Small Business.* Bloomington, Ind.: Indiana University, Bureau of Business Research, 1964.

Heau, Dominique G. "Long Range Planning in Divisionalized Firms: A Study of Corporate Divisional Relationships." Doctoral diss., Harvard University, 1976.

Heron, R. P. and Friesen, D. "Growth and Development of College Administrative Structures." *Research in Higher Education,* 1973.

Hickey, W. J. "The Functions of the Hospital Board of Directors." *Hospital Administration,* Summer 1972.

Hill, Richard and James Hlavacek. "The Venture Team: A New Concept in Marketing Organization." *Journal of Marketing,* July 1972.

Hoad, William and Peter Rosko. *Management Factors Contributing to the Success or Failure of New Small Manufacturers.* Ann Arbor, Mich.: University of Michigan, 1964.

Hobbs, John M. and Donald F. Heany. "Coupling Strategy to Operating Plans." *Harvard Business Review,* May–June 1977.

Hodgetts, Richard M. and Max Wortman, Jr. *Administrative Policy: Text and Cases in the Policy Sciences.* New York: Wiley, 1975.

Hofer, Charles W. "Toward a Contingency Theory of Business Strategy." *Academy of Management Journal,* December 1975.

Hofer, Charles W. "Research on Strategic Planning: A Survey of Past Studies and Suggestions for Future Efforts." *Journal of Economics and Business,* Spring–Summer 1976.

Hoffman, Cary A. and Albert Shapero. *Providing the Industrial Ecology Required for the Survival and Growth of Small Technical Companies.* Austin, Tex.: MDRI Press, 1971.

Hosmer, L. T. "Academic Strategy: The Formulation and Implementation of Purpose at Three New Graduate Schools of Administration." Doctoral diss., Harvard University, 1972.

Hosmer, L. T., Arnold Cooper and Karl Vesper. *The Entrepreneurial Function.* Englewood Cliffs, N.J.: Prentice-Hall, 1977.

Hosmer, W. Arnold. "Small Manufacturing Enterprises." *Harvard Business Review*, November–December 1957.

Hovey, Harold A. *The Planning-Programming-Budgeting Approaches to Government Decision-Making.* New York: Praeger, 1968.

Hudzik, John K. and Jack R. Greene. "Organizational Identity and Goal Consensus in a Sheriff's Department: An Exploratory Inquiry." *Journal of Police Science and Administration*, March 1977.

Hussey, David. "Corporate Planning for a Church." *Long Range Planning*, April 1974.

Hutchinson, Colin. "People and Pollution: The Challenge to Planning," in Taylor, Bernard and Kevin Hawkins (editors), *Handbook of Strategic Planning.* London: Longmans, 1972.

Ikenberry, Stanley O. and Renee C. Friedman. *Beyond Academic Departments.* San Francisco: Jossey-Bass, 1972.

Irwin, Patrick. "Towards Better Strategic Management." *Long Range Planning*, December 1974.

Jacoby, Neil. "The Conglomerate Corporation." *The Center* [for the Study of Democratic Institutions] *Magazine*, July 1969.

Katz, Daniel, et al. *Bureaucratic Encounters: A Pilot Study in the Evaluation of Government Services.* Ann Arbor, Mich.: Survey Research Center, University of Michigan, 1975.

Katz, Robert. *Management of the Total Enterprise.* Englewood Cliffs, N.J.: Prentice-Hall, 1970.

Kaufman, Herbert. *Are Government Organizations Immortal?* Washington, D.C.: The Brookings Institution, 1976.

Kennington, Don. "Long Range Planning for Public Libraries — A Delphi Study." *Long Range Planning*, April 1977.

Kilby, Peter. *Entrepreneurship and Economic Development.* New York: The Free Press, 1971.

Kline, Charles. "Strategy of Product Policy." *Harvard Business Review*, July–August 1955.

Kobayashi, Kenzo, Yoichi Aoki and Akira Tani. "A Method for Evaluating Urban Transportation Planning in Terms of User Benefit." *Transportation Research*, February 1975.

Komives, John. "Characteristics of Entrepreneurs." *Business Quarterly*, Summer 1972.

Kraemer, Kenneth L., et al. "A Future Cities Survey: Research Design for Policy Analysis." *Socio-Economic Planning Sciences*, Vol. 10, pp. 199–211, 1976.

Lahti, Robert E. *Innovative College Management.* San Francisco: Jossey-Bass, 1973.

Lamont, Lawrence. "What Entrepreneurs Learn from Experience." *Journal of Small Business Management*, July 1972.

Lang, Kurt. "Military Organizations," in March, James G. (editor), *Handbook of Organizations.* Chicago: Rand McNally, 1965.

Lasswell, Harold D. "The Emerging Conception of the Policy Sciences." *Policy Sciences*, Spring 1970.

Lasswell, Harold D. *A Pre-view of the Policy Sciences.* New York: Elsevier North-Holland, 1971.

Lazarsfeld, Paul F. "The Policy Science Movement (An Outsider's View)." *Policy Sciences*, September 1975.

Learned, Edmund P., C. Roland Christensen, Kenneth R. Andrews and William D. Guth. *Business Policy: Text and Cases.* Homewood, Ill.: Richard D. Irwin, 1965.

LeBreton, Preston, *A Guide for Proper Management Planning for Small Business.* Baton Rouge, La.: Division of Research, College of Business Administration, Louisiana State University, 1963.

Levine, Robert. *Public Planning: Failure and Redirection.* New York: Basic Books, 1972.

Levine, Robert. "The Ineffectiveness of Adding Policy to Prevent Crime." *Public Policy*, Fall 1975.

Levitt, Theodore. *The Third Sector.* New York: AMACPM, 1973.

Levitt, Theodore. "Dinosaurs Among the Bears and Bulls." *Harvard Business Review*, January–February 1975.

Lewin, Arie Y. and Melvin F. Shakun. *Policy Sciences: Methodologies and Cases.* New York: Pergamon, 1976.

Lewis, Darrell R. and Tor Dahl. "Time Management in High Education Administration: A Case Study." *Higher Education*, February 1976.

Lightwood, Martha B. *Public and Business Planning in the United States: A Bibliography.* Detroit: Gale Research Co., 1972.

Liles, Patrick. *New Business Ventures and the Entrepreneur.* Homewood, Ill.: Richard D. Irwin, 1974.

Lum, Doman. "The Health Maintenance Delivery System: A National Study of HMO Project Directors on HMO Issues." *American Journal of Public Health*, November 1975.

Lyden, Fremont J. and Ernest G. Miller (editors). *Planning-Programming-Budgeting: A Systems Approach to Management.* Chicago: Markham, 1967.

Lyden, Fremont J. and Ernest G. Miller. "Why City Managers Leave the Profession: A Longitudinal Study in the Pacific Northwest." *Public Administration Review*, March–April 1976.

Lyden, Fremont J. and Ernest G. Miller. "Policy Perspectives of the Northwest City Manager,

1966–1974." *Administration and Society*, February 1977.

Lynch, Harry H. *Financial Performance of Conglomerates.* Boston: Division of Research, Graduate School of Business Administration, Harvard University, 1971.

McCarthy, William G. "Historiography and Historical Research," in Jones, Ralph H. (editor). *Methods and Techniques of Educational Research.* Danville, Ill.: Interstate Printers, 1973.

McClain, John O. and Vithala Rao. "Trade-Offs and Conflicts in Evaluation of Health System Alternatives: Methodology for Analysis." *Health Service Research*, Spring 1974.

McClelland, David. *The Achieving Society.* Princeton, N.J.: D. Van Nostrand, 1961.

McClelland, David. "Achievement Motivation Can Be Developed." *Harvard Business Review*, November–December 1965.

McConnell, T. R. "Coordinating Higher Education." *Higher Education Review*, Autumn 1975.

Mace, Myles L. and George C. Montgomery, Jr. *Management Problems of Corporate Acquisitions.* Boston: Division of Research, Graduate School of Business Administration, Harvard University, 1962.

McGill, Michael E. and Leland Wooten. "Management in the Third Sector." *Public Administration Review*, September–October 1975.

McGrath, William E. *Development of a Long-Range Strategic Plan for a University Library: The Cornell Experience: Chronicle and Evaluation of the First Year's Effort.* Ithaca, N.Y.: University Libraries, Cornell University, 1973.

McGuire, Joseph W. *Factors in the Growth of Manufacturing Firms.* Seattle, Wash.: Bureau of Business Research, University of Washington, 1963.

Maciariello, J. A. and Willard Enteman. "A System for Management Control in Private Colleges." *Journal of Higher Education*, July 1974.

McKay, Charles W. and Guy D. Cutting. "A Model for Long Range Planning in Higher Education." *Long Range Planning*, October 1974.

McNamara, Mary E. and Clifford Todd. "A Survey of Group Practice in the United States, 1969." *American Journal of Public Health*, July 1970.

McNeil, Keith A., Francis J. Kelly and Judy T. McNeil. *Testing Research Hypotheses Using Multiple Linear Regression.* Carbondale, Ill.: Southern Illinois University, 1975.

Malkiel, Burton G. *A Random Walk Down Wall Street.* New York: W. W. Norton, 1975.

Mancuso, Joseph. *Fun and Guts: The Entrepreneur's Philosophy.* Reading, Mass.: Addison-Wesley, 1973.

Marney, Milton. "Interdisciplinary Synthesis." *Policy Sciences*, September 1972.

Mason, R. S. "Production Diversification and the Small Firm." *Journal of Business Policy*, Spring 1973.

Mayer, Kurt and Sidney Goldstein. *The First Two Years: Problems of Small Firm Growth and Survival.* Washington, D.C.: U.S. Government Printing Office, 1961.

Mayer, Robert R. *Social Planning and Social Change.* Englewood Cliffs, N.J.: Prentice-Hall, 1972.

Mayhew, Lewis B. *The Carnegie Commission on Higher Education.* San Francisco: Jossey-Bass, 1973.

Mazze, Edward M. "University Planning: An Organization Model." *Long Range Planning*, December 1971.

Meadows, Donella H., Dennis L. Meadows, Jorgen Randers and William W. Behrens, III. *The Limits to Growth* (first report of the Club of Rome). New York: Universe Publishers, 1972.

Mehsenberg, Michael. *Environmental Planning: A Guide to Information Sources.* Detroit: Gale Research Co., 1976.

Meredith, G. G. "Sustaining Ventures after Formation." *Proceedings of Project ISEED.* Milwaukee, Wis.: Project ISEED, Ltd., 1975.

Meyers, William, Robert Dorwart and David Kline. "Social Ecology and Citizen Boards: A Problem for Planners." *Journal of the American Institute of Planners*, April 1977.

Miller, E. J. and A. K. Rice. *Systems of Organization.* London: Tavistock Publications, 1967.

Mills, Edwin S. *An Aggregate Model of Resource Allocation in a Metropolitan Area.* Baltimore, Md.: Johns Hopkins University Press, 1965.

Mood, Alexander M., et al. *Papers on Efficiency in the Management of Higher Education.* Berkeley, Calif.: Carnegie Commission on Higher Education, 1972.

Morrison, Robert S. *Handbook for Manufacturing Entrepreneurs.* Cleveland: Western Reserve Press, 1973.

Morse, Philip M. "Library Models," in Drake, A. W., R. L. Keeney and P. M. Morse (editors). *Analysis of Public Systems.* Cambridge, Mass.: M.I.T. Press, 1972.

Morse, Richard. "Variety and Selectivity in Entrepreneurial Development Programs." *Proceedings of Project ISEED.* Milwaukee, Wis.: Project ISEED, Ltd., 1975.

Murthy, K. R. Srinavasa. *Corporate Strategy and*

Top Executive Compensation. Cambridge, Mass.: Harvard University Press, 1977.

National Research Council, Committee on Social and Behavioral Urban Research. "A Strategic Approach to Urban Research and Development." Publication No. 1728. Washington, D.C., 1969.

National Research Council, Committee on Urban Technology. "Long-Range Planning for Urban Research and Development." Publication No. 1729. Washington, D.C., 1969.

Neimann, Max. "Analogues and Policy Analysis: An Alternative Strategy." *American Politics Quarterly*, January 1977.

Newby, John M. "Spring Arbor College: Implementing Comprehensive Long-Range Planning." *New Directions for Higher Education*, Autumn 1976.

Newman, William H. and Harvey W. Wallender, III. "Managing Not-for-Profit Enterprises." *Academy of Management Review*, January 1978.

1967 Enterprise Statistics, Part 1. Washington, D.C.: U.S. Government Printing Office, 1972.

Novick, David (editor). *Program Budgeting: Program Analysis and the Federal Budget*. New York: Holt, Rinehart and Winston, 1969.

Oliver, Robert M. "Operations Research in University Planning," in Drake, A. W., R. L. Keeney and P. M. Morse (editors). *Analysis of Public Systems*. Cambridge, Mass.: M.I.T. Press, 1972.

Orlans, H. *The Non-Profit Research Institute: Its Origins, Operation, Problems, and Prospects*. New York: McGraw-Hill for the Carnegie Commission on Higher Education, 1972.

O'Toole, James and the University of Southern California Center for Futures Research. *Energy and Social Change*. Cambridge, Mass.: M.I.T. Press, 1976.

Owen, A. Knorr (editor). *Long Range Planning in Higher Education*. Boulder, Colo.: Western Interstate Commission for Higher Education, 1965.

Palmiere, Darwin. "Lessons Learned from the Experience of Health Facilities Planning Councils." *American Journal of Public Health*, September 1972.

Parker, Francis H. and Gilbert, Gorman. "Rail Planning: Crisis and Opportunity." *Journal of the American Institute of Planners*, January 1977.

Pavan, Robert. "Strategy and Structure in Italian Enterprise." Doctoral diss., Harvard University, 1972.

Pennock, J. Roland and John W. Chapman (editors). *Voluntary Associations*. New York: Atherton, 1969.

Perkins, J. A. (editor). *The University as an Organization*. New York: McGraw-Hill for the Carnegie Commission on Higher Education, 1973.

Peterson, Russell W. "New Venture Management in a Large Company." *Harvard Business Review*, May–June 1967.

Peterson, W. D. "Critical Incidents for New and Experienced College and University Presidents." *Research in Higher Education*, Vol. 3, 1975.

Pfeffer, Jeffrey. "Size, Composition, and Function of Hospital Boards of Directors: A Study of Organization-Environment Linkage." *Administrative Science Quarterly*, September 1973.

Pitts, Robert A. "Incentive Compensation and Organization Design." *Personnel Journal*, May 1974.

Pitts, Robert A. "Strategies and Structures for Diversification." *Eastern Academy of Management Proceedings*. Washington, D.C., May 1976a.

Pitts, Robert A. "Distinctive Competence for Diversification." *Academy of Management Proceedings*. Kansas City, August 1976b.

Pitts, Robert A. "Unshackle Your 'Comers.'" *Harvard Business Review*, May-June 1977a.

Pitts, Robert A. "Organizing R&D Activity in Large Diversified Firms: Correlating Centralized vs. Decentralized Approaches." *Eastern Academy of Management Proceedings*. Hartford, Conn., May 1977b.

Pooley-Dias, Gareth. "Strategy and Structure of French Enterprise." Doctoral diss., Harvard University, 1972.

Porter, Michael E. "Please Note Location of Nearest Exit: Exit Barriers and Strategic and Organizational Planning." *California Management Review*, Winter 1976.

"The Practical Uses of Planning Theory: A Symposium." *Journal of the American Institute of Planners*, September 1969.

Preiser, Wolfgang (editor). *Environmental Design Research: Volume 2, Symposia and Workshops*. Stoursburg, Pa.: Dowden, Hutchinson, and Ross, Inc., 1973.

Prybil, Lawrence D. and David B. Starkweather. "Current Perspectives on Hospital Governance." *Hospital and Health Administration*, Fall 1976.

Putt, William and Kenneth Germeshausen. "Business Strategy and Development," in Putt, W. (editor). *How to Start Your Own Business*. Cambridge, Mass.: M.I.T. Press, 1974.

Rabinovitz, Francis F. *City Politics and Planning*. New York: Atherton, 1969.

Radnor, Michael. "Management Sciences and Policy Sciences." *Policy Sciences*, December 1971.

Ranney, David C. *Planning and Politics in the Metropolis*. Columbus, Ohio: Merrill, 1969.

Reynolds, James F. "Policy Science: A Conceptual and Methodological Analysis." *Policy Sciences*, March 1975.

Rigby, Paul. *Conceptual Foundations of Business Research.* New York: Wiley, 1965.

Roberts, Edward. "Influences Upon Performance of New Technical Enterprises," in Cooper, A. and J. Komives (editors), *Technical Entrepreneurship: A Symposium.* Milwaukee, Wis.: The Center for Venture Management, 1972.

Roberts, Edward and Alan Frohman. "Internal Entrepreneurship: Strategy for Growth." *Business Quarterly,* Spring 1972.

Roberts, Edward and H. Wainer. "Some Characteristics of New Technical Enterprises." *I.E.E.E. Transactions on Engineering Management,* Vol. EM-18, No. 3, 1971.

Roethlisberger, F. J. *Man-in-Organization.* Cambridge, Mass.: Harvard University Press, Belknap Press, 1968.

Rogers, David. *The Management of Big Cities.* Beverly Hills, Calif.: Sage Publications, 1971.

Rosenbloom, Richard S. and John R. Russell. *New Tools for Urban Management.* Boston: Graduate School of Business Administration, Harvard University, 1971.

Rourke, Francis E. and Glenn E. Brooks. *The Managerial Revolution in Higher Education.* Baltimore, Md.: Johns Hopkins University Press, 1966.

Rugman, A. "Corporate Planning in Local Government." *Long Range Planning,* September 1973.

Rumelt, Richard P. *Strategy, Structure and Economic Performance.* Boston: Graduate School of Business Administration, Harvard University, 1974.

Sackman, Harold and Ronald L. Citrenbaum (ed.). *On-Line Planning: Towards Creative Problem Solving.* Englewood Cliffs, N.J.: Prentice-Hall, 1972.

Scheff, Janet. "The Social Planning Process: Conceptualizations and Methods." *Planning Series S-2, Graduate Program Planning.* San Juan, Puerto Rico: University of Puerto Rico, 1976.

Schmidt, Robert M. and Morton A. Madoff. "The State and Territorial Public Health Laboratory: Program Activities, Organization and Prospects for the Future." *American Journal of Public Health,* May 1977.

Schrage, Harry. "The R&D Entrepreneur: Profile of Success." *Harvard Business Review,* November–December 1965.

Schreier, James W. and John L. Komives. *The Entrepreneur and New Enterprise Formation.* Milwaukee, Wis.: The Center for Venture Management, 1973.

Schumacher, E. F. *Small Is Beautiful — Economics as if People Mattered.* New York: Harper and Row, 1973.

Schwarz, B. "Long Range Planning in the Public Sector." *Futures,* April 1977.

Scott. Bruce R. "Stages of Corporate Development — Part I." Intercollegiate Case Clearing House Report No. 9-371-294, Boston, Mass., 1971.

Shank, J. E., E. G. Niblock and W. T. Sandells. "Balance Creativity and Practicality in Formal Planning." *Harvard Business Review,* January–February 1973.

Shapero, Albert. *An Action Program for Entrepreneurship.* Austin, Tex.: MDRI Press, 1969.

Shapero, Albert. "Entrepreneurship and Economic Development," in *Entrepreneurship and Enterprise Development: A Worldwide Perspective. Proceedings of Project ISEED.* Milwaukee, Wis.: Project ISEED, Ltd., 1975.

Shapero, Albert. "The Role of Entrepreneurship in Economic Development at the Less-Than-National Level." Report prepared for the Office of Economic Research, Economic Development Administration.

Shapero, Albert, Cary A. Hoffman, Kirk Draheim and Richard P. Howell. *The Role of the Financial Community in the Formation, Growth and Effectiveness of Technical Companies.* Austin, Tex.: MDRI Press, 1969.

Simon, Julian L. *Basic Research Methods in Social Science.* New York: Random House, 1969.

Skogan, Wesley G. "Efficiency and Effectiveness in Big-City Police Departments." *Public Administration Review,* May–June 1976.

Smith, Thomas B. "The Policy Implementation Process." *Policy Sciences,* June 1973.

Smyth, Gerry A. "Management Development for Owner-Managers." *Proceedings of Project ISEED.* Milwaukee, Wis.: Project ISEED, Ltd., 1975.

Snyder, Arthur. "Entrepreneurs — God Bless Them," in Putt, William (editor). *How to Start Your Own Business.* Cambridge, Mass.: M.I.T. Press, 1974.

Stanley, David T. *The Higher Civil Service.* Washington, D.C.: The Brookings Institution, 1964.

Starbuck, William H. "Organizational Growth and Development," in March, J. G. (editor), *The Handbook of Organizations.* Chicago: Rand McNally, 1965.

Statistical Abstract of the United States, 1976. Washington, D.C.: U.S. Government Printing Office, 1976.

Steiner, George A. "Approaches to Long Range Planning for Small Business." *California Management Review,* Fall 1967.

Steinmetz, Lawrence L. "Critical Stages of Small Business Growth." *Business Horizons,* February 1969.

Stringer, Jeremy. "The Role of the 'Assistant To' in Higher Education." *Journal of Higher Education*, March–April 1977.

Susbauer, Jeffrey. "The Technical Company Formation Process: A Particular Aspect of Entrepreneurship." Doctoral dissertation, The University of Texas at Austin, 1969.

Susbauer, Jeffrey C. "U.S. Industrial Intracorporate Entrepreneurship Practices." *R&D Management*, June 1973.

Swann, Ken. "Entrepreneurship in Large Companies." *Journal of General Management*, Summer 1975.

Swayne, Charles, and William Tucker. *The Effective Entrepreneur*. Morristown, N.J.: General Learning Press, 1973.

Sweet, David C. (editor). *Models of Urban Structure*. Lexington, Mass.: D. C. Heath, 1972.

"Symposium: Planning-Programming-Budgeting Systems Reexamined: Development, Analysis, and Criticism." *Public Administration Review*, March–April 1969.

Taylor, John L. and Richard N. Maddison. "A Land Use Gaming Simulation: The Design of a Model for the Study of Urban Phenomena." *Urban Affairs Quarterly*, June 1968.

Thanheiser, Heinz. "Strategy and Structure of German Firms." Doctoral diss., Harvard University, 1972.

Thompson, David A. "Financial Planning for an HMO." *Health Service Research*, Spring 1974.

Tilles, Seymour and Arthur Contas. *Planning in the Family Firm*. Boston: The Management Consulting Group (undated).

U.S. Congress, Joint Economic Committee. "The Analysis and Evaluation of Public Expenditures: The PPB System, Compendium of Papers." Washington, D.C.: U.S. Government Printing Office, 1969.

Uyterhoeven, Hugo, Robert Ackerman and John Rosenblum. *Strategy and Organization*. Homewood, Ill.: Richard D. Irwin, 1973.

Vancil, Richard F. and Peter Lorange. *Strategic Planning Systems*. Englewood Cliffs, N.J.: Prentice-Hall, 1977.

Veney, James E., et al. "Implementation of Health Programs in Hospitals." *Health Services Research*, Winter 1971.

Vesper, Karl H. *Entrepreneurship Education, A Bicentennial Compendium*. Milwaukee, Wis.: The Center for Venture Management, 1976.

Vesper, Karl H. "Sub-Fields of Entrepreneurship Research." *Academy of Management Proceedings*, Orlando, Florida, 1977.

Vesper, Karl H. and Thomas Holmdahl. "How Venture Management Fares in Innovative Companies." *Research Management*, May 1973.

Vickers, Geoffrey. "Commonly Ignored Elements in Policymaking." *Policy Sciences*, July 1972.

Vickers, Geoffrey. "Values, Norms, and Politics." *Policy Sciences*, March 1973.

Waters, William J. "State Level Comprehensive Health Planning: A Retrospect." *American Journal of Public Health*, February 1976.

Watkins, David S. "Regional Variations in the Industrial Ecology for New, Growth-Oriented Businesses in the U.K." *Proceedings of Project ISEED*. Milwaukee, Wis.: Project ISEED, Ltd., 1975.

Webb, Ronald J. "Organizational Effectiveness and the Voluntary Organization." *Academy of Management Journal*, December 1974.

Webber, James B. and Martha A. Dula. "Effective Planning Committees for Hospitals." *Harvard Business Review*, May–June 1974.

Weiner, Aaron, *The Role of Water in Development: An Analysis of Principles of Comprehensive Planning*. New York: McGraw-Hill, 1971.

Weisberg, Herbert and Bruce D. Bowen. *An Introduction to Survey Research and Data Analysis*. San Francisco: Freeman, 1977.

Westfall, Steven. "Stimulating Corporation Entrepreneurship in U.S. Industry." *Academy of Management Journal*, June 1969.

Wheelright, Steven C. "Strategic Planning in the Small Business." *Business Horizons*, August 1971.

Whittick, Arnold (editor). *Encyclopedia of Urban Planning*. New York: McGraw-Hill, 1974.

Wholey, Joseph S., et al. *Federal Evaluation Policy: Analyzing the Effects of Public Programs*. Washington, D.C.: The Urban Institute, 1975.

Williams, Walter. *Social Policy Research and Analysis*. New York: Elsevier North-Holland, 1971.

Wolensky, Robert P. and David L. Groves. "Planning the Smaller City: Major Problems and a Possible Solution." *Socio-Economic Planning Sciences*, 11, 1977.

Woodward, Herbert N. "Management Strategies for Small Companies." *Harvard Business Review*, January–February 1976.

Wrigley, Leonard. "Divisional Autonomy and Diversification." Doctoral diss., Harvard University, 1970.

Yavitz, Boris and Merome E. Schnee. "Managing the Impacts of Large Scale Public Programs." *Long Range Planning*, February 1977.

Zelermyer, Rebecca. *Gallery Management*. Syracuse, N.Y.: Syracuse University Press, 1976.

7

THEORY BUILDING AND THEORY TESTING IN STRATEGIC MANAGEMENT

Commentary

J-C. Spender
City University Business School (London)

Contingency Theories of Strategy and Strategic Management

George A. Steiner
University of California at Los Angeles

Commentary

Frank T. Paine
University of Maryland

Qualitative Research Methods in Strategic Management

Robert B. Duncan
Northwestern University

Quantitative Research Methods in Strategic Management

Kenneth J. Hatten
Harvard University

Commentary

William Naumes
Clark University

To this point, our focus has been on the content of the research findings and on possible areas for future research in strategic management, not on the methods by which these findings have been made. Yet, it is impossible for any field to advance without developing and using research methods suited to the problems and issues characteristic of that field. Strategic management is a young field. Like many new fields, it does not yet have a strong research tradition, and it is still searching for its first organizing paradigm. We believe that paradigm is the one developed here, but whether it is or not, there is no doubt that research in the field is at a relatively early stage of development, with more promise ahead of it than results behind it.

Research means many things to different people. In business policy, it has typically meant "case research" based on a small number of in-depth field or clinical studies. While a number of concepts and hypotheses have been derived from case studies, most of these concepts and hypotheses, as well as the studies from which they were developed, are of a descriptive, historical character and address a small portion of the field. It would not be stretching the truth to label them "surveys of past practice," although a few suggest new concepts and ideas of a more global sort.

As the papers in this book attest, the field now has a sufficient variety of concepts and hypotheses of both a descriptive and a normative character to form the basis of a scholarly discipline. At the same time, most of these concepts and hypotheses have never been subjected to adequate empirical testing to determine their domain of applicability or, in some cases, whether they are even valid for any set of organizations. Moreover, most of the studies that have been done and which continue to be done reflect an inadequate appreciation of the scientific method — some because they continue to draw maps of the territory when hypothesis testing is what is needed, some because they try to test hypotheses when the basic phenomenon in question is still inadequately understood. In part, this is due to the complexity of the field. In part, it stems from the lack of an accepted research paradigm in the field. In part, it is a reflection of inadequacies in the research training of some researchers in the field. And in part, it reflects the lack of established research centers and research journals which makes it difficult for scholars in the field to communicate with one another.

The new threshold that strategic management research is now on suggests that more rigor in research methodology is required, not only to test existing concepts and hypotheses, but to go on to build better theory than now exists. For purposes of the conference we chose to focus on qualitative versus quantitative research methods and asked Duncan and Hatten to prepare papers to cover these methods. The discussion at the conference indicated that our conception was inadequate, however, and that, in fact, what was needed was an appreciation of the totality of the research process in light of the state of research progress in the field. Fortunately, several authors showed greater wisdom than we did and responded to our challenge to complement the views of others in such a way that we have been able to put together such a broad view for this text. To provide this perspective, we shall first present a conceptual overview of the theory-building/theory-testing process and then describe how the various papers illuminate different aspects of this process.

THEORY BUILDING AND THEORY TESTING: A CONCEPTUAL OVERVIEW

THE NATURE OF THEORY

According to *Webster's New Collegiate Dictionary* (1974), a theory is "a plausible or scientifically acceptable general principle or body of principles offered to explain phenomena." Parsons (1961) defines theory as, "a logically integrated set of propositions about the relations of variables, that is, abstract conceptual entities, in which many statements of fact can be systematically related to each other and their meanings for the solution of empirical problems interpreted," that is, it is a simplified, abstract map of reality. Parsons goes on to state:

> Besides the all important empirical relevance, the principal criteria of good theory are conceptual clarity and precision, and logical integration in the sense not only of the logical compatibility of the various propositions included in a theoretical scheme, but of their mutual support, so that inference from one part of the scheme to other parts becomes possible.

To these criteria the concept of parsimony should be added. A good theory must be rich enough to capture all the important variables and interactions in the territory. But, since the power of a theory is inversely proportional to the number of variables and relationships it contains, good theory should contain the minimum possible number of variables and relationships that are needed to adequately explain the phenomenon in question.[1]

Theories can be of many types. For our purposes, the principal distinction to be made is between descriptive and prescriptive theory. A descriptive theory is one that accurately describes "what is" and does this for all elements in its domain. Thus, a theory that describes strategy formulation as a political process could be regarded as good descriptive theory only if: (1) it were shown empirically that all or almost all organizations do formulate strategy this way (observation of a sufficient proportion of rational, comprehensive processes would throw the theory out) — in this

---

[1] Newton's and Einstein's laws of motion provide a good example of this dilemma. Newton's laws are not sufficiently rich to adequately explain the movement of bodies at speeds close to that of light. Here Einstein's laws are used. In day-to-day affairs, however, Newton's laws are still used, as the extra richness of Einstein's laws is not needed to explain motion within the required range of accuracy.

case it would be a universal descriptive theory, or (2) if it were shown that all or almost all organizations of a particular type formulate strategy this way — in this case, it would be a limited domain theory.[2] Descriptive theories may or may not contain variables that are controllable by management.

By contrast, prescriptive theories are theories that describe "what can be" and do this accurately for all elements in their domain. They do not need to describe the totality of "what is," since they make no claim to describe what will happen if their "prescriptions" are not followed. They must accurately predict outcomes if the "prescription" is followed, however. By definition, prescriptive theories must contain variables controllable by management; otherwise, there would be no way for management to intervene and "apply the prescription."

The Nature of the Theory-Building/Theory-Testing Process

Theory building and theory testing are diametrically opposed processes in terms of purpose. Theory building is a creative process that seeks to put forward new concepts, ideas, and hypotheses to explain phenomena. Theory testing, by contrast, seeks to refute null hypotheses (although in the hope that the refutation will support real hypotheses).[3]

Theories typically evolve through a sequence of five steps. These are: (1) exploration, (2) concept development, (3) hypothesis generation, (4) hypothesis testing for internal validity, and (5) hypothesis testing for external validity (see Exhibit 7.1). The process can be entered at any step, and may recycle at any time. However, except for recycling, progress is always from left to right, as shown in Exhibit 7.1.

In the exploration step, the purpose is to explore the territory, that is, to identify the phenomena of interest and describe its key characteristics. All disciplines emerged from this stage. To become a discipline, however, they must progress past it. In evolving disciplines, the proportion of research in this stage will decrease as the discipline matures, and in mature disciplines the proportion of exploratory research will be fairly small, although it may still be significant at the fringes of the discipline, or when a discovery of major impact to the whole field occurs.

The second stage is concept development. In it, the purpose is to draw maps of the territory, that is, to identify the key variables that may be used to describe the phenomena of interest. These could include not only

---

[2] If a sufficient number of limited domain theories can be combined so that they cover the entire territory, then this combined theory can be called a universal "contingency" theory, or contingency theory for short.

[3] This discussion refers to the testing of "real" hypotheses, not "null" hypotheses. The latter are logical inferences of the "real" hypotheses established to be rejected. Rejection of "null" hypotheses thus offers some measure of support to the "real" hypotheses. Such support is not always as strong as most assume, however, as Spender notes later in his commentary.

the object of interest but the factors (variables) that appear to influence it. At some point, the concept development stage merges into and becomes the hypothesis generation stage. Here the purpose is to improve the maps of the territory, primarily by specifying the relationships (hypotheses) that exist among the variables identified in the concept development stage. Some new variables are found and old ones are defined more precisely as cycling occurs between the concept development and hypothesis generation stages.

Once a reasonably consistent set of hypotheses has been developed concerning a particular phenomenon, the next step is to test the validity of these hypotheses. This is usually done in one of two ways, although the approaches are sometimes combined. Initially, the concepts and hypotheses are tested for their internal validity, that is, to see whether they really do accurately describe the phenomenon in question, and in the domain in which it has been observed in the past. Such testing will usually lead to the modification or acceptance of the hypotheses, although in some instances such hypotheses have been rejected at this stage.

Assuming that a hypothesis or set of hypotheses survive the internal validity check, they should then be tested for external validity, that is, to determine the extent of the domain to which they apply. Here rejection is more likely. When it happens, it is sometimes possible to modify the hypotheses (and theory on which they are based) so that they are corroborated for the larger domain.[4] Another possibility when rejection occurs, however, is that the hypotheses (and theory) cover a limited domain. That is, the hypotheses (and the theory on which they are based) are valid for their original domain, but not for the more extended one. If external validity tests fail, one should usually repeat internal validity tests unless it seems clear that inadequate concept development is the root cause of the difficulty, in which case, a return to earlier stages of theory building is necessary.

This continuous process of cycling and recycling is the way both theories and disciplines develop using scientific method. The patterns of such cycling usually vary with the maturity of the theory or field, however. Two points should be made with respect to such cycling in a developing field such as strategic management. First, it is possible to try to advance too rapidly, that is, to jump to hypothesis generation and testing before the phenomenon is adequately understood or described. This is a reason why Mintzberg's (1977) call for more descriptive research makes sense. We would join his call, but add a qualification. Also, make the research *normative*. As long as one is observing practice, examine the best practice when possible so that it is known to be worth emulating.

The second point regarding cycling is that at some point the field must move forward toward hypothesis testing. Descriptive theory is fine. But at

---

[4] It is never possible to "prove" a hypothesis is true. All that is possible is to show that, insofar as it has been tested, it is not false. Since falsification is always possible with new evidence, "truth" can never be established.

Exhibit 7.1 Theory Building and Theory Testing: A Conceptual Overview

Characteristics of the research process → Types of research	Theory building			Theory testing	
	Exploration	Concept development	Hypothesis generation	Hypothesis testing internal validity	Hypothesis testing external validity
Purpose	Explore territory	Draw maps of territory	Improve maps of territory	Test maps of the territory	
Nature of research question	What's there? and What are the key issues?	What are the key variables?	What are the relationships among variables?	Are the theories really valid?	Where do the theories apply?
Nature of research design	In-depth unfocused longitudinal case study	Few focused comparative longitudinal case studies	Several focused comparative longitudinal case studies	Large-scale sample of original population	Large-scale sample of multiple population
Data-gathering methods	Observation Unstructured interviews Documents	Observation Structured interviews Documents	Observation Structured interviews Documents Small-scale questionnaire	Structured interviews Documents Open- and closed-ended questionnaires Lab experiments Field experiments	Structured interviews Documents Open- and closed-ended questionnaires Lab experiments Field experiments
Data analysis methods	Insight Categorization	Factor analysis Semantic differentials Multidimensional scaling		Sign test χ^2 Kendal's Tau Correlation analysis of variance Pearson's Product Moment Correlation	
				Multiple regression	Simultaneous regression
Nature of results	Identification and description of phenomenon	Refined description of phenomenon	Development of hypotheses about phenomenon	Corroboration or refutation of hypotheses for similar organizations	Corroboration or refutation of hypotheses for different organizations

Normative / Descriptive

some point such theories must be tested to see whether they apply beyond the small set of cases studied. A descriptive theory that applies to only one case example is not a theory: it is a random aberration. In fact, a descriptive theory that appears to apply to a small sample (less than, say, ten in number) may still be an aberration. Consequently, additional testing is needed to determine whether the theory is an aberration, a limited domain theory, or a universal theory.

The Nature of Research and the Research Process

Ideally, theories evolve through the sequence of five steps identified above. The actual process of theory building and theory testing can occur in a number of ways, however. New theories and concepts can be discovered by chance (serendipity), by intuitive insight, or by inductive or deductive reasoning from a known set of facts. Similarly, theories and concepts can be refuted by accidental observation; by a massive, but random comparison with known facts; or by a systematic, scientific process of examining every element and relationship in the domain of the theory.

A discipline cannot afford to rely on accident or haphazard investigation. Consequently, paradigms have been developed to guide the theory-building/theory-testing research effort in a thorough, systematic (scientific) manner. In general, one can distinguish between two types of research: (1) descriptive research, and (2) normative research, each differing with the other as to their purpose and research design. (The word "descriptive" can be and is applied both to theories and to research; the term "prescriptive" applies only to theories, and the term "normative" applies only to research.) Descriptive research aims only at describing "what is," that is, at developing a model of the phenomena that are observed or identified. By contrast, the purpose of normative research is to help develop prescriptive theory. It attempts to describe what "can be" insofar as any given "can be" is possible in the real world.

This difference manifests itself in the sample selection process. In descriptive research, any organization in which the phenomenon of interest occurs is as good as any other. As long as the research is done well, and while the resulting theory may have a limited domain and may not be prescriptive in that it does not contain variables management can control, still descriptive theory is produced. In normative research, however, it is not enough to select any organization in which the phenomenon occurs. Organizations (sample) with a range of performance outcomes should be selected in sufficient numbers as to be able to represent the population (domain) to which the resulting theory is to be applied.

In spite of these differences, both types of research follow the same general paradigm. It contains these steps: (1) the selection of a topic to be researched; (2) the development of the research questions(s); (3) the selection of a research design; (4) the selection of the method(s) that will be used to generate and gather data; (5) the selection of the method(s) that will be used to analyze the data; (6) the analysis of the data; and (7) the interpretation of the results. Usually, these steps are followed in the sequence given, although steps 1 and 2 and steps 3, 4, and 5 are often considered simultaneously.

The selection of a topic for research involves two to three substeps. First, a field of interest must be chosen; in our case, strategic management. Then, a particular subfield or broad topical area has to be selected; for example, if one used the strategic management paradigm presented in this text, one might choose to study goal formulation processes, strategy content, new ventures, and so on. Finally, some particular topic within the subfield must be focused upon; for example, strategic failure, business strategies or turnaround strategies. The breadth of the final topic will depend on the nature of the project on which the researcher is working, but it should usually be defined as narrowly as possible. Choice of a topic for research will reflect the researcher's interests and training. The topic chosen will be further constrained by paradigms already used and by research already done in the field.

Once a specific topic has been chosen, it is useful to frame the researcher's specific interest in the topic in the form of a set of research questions. These should be stated as precisely as possible and in operational terms. In the case of hypothesis-testing research, the questions would normally be stated in the form: Are hypotheses $H_1, \ldots, H_n$ true? (More precisely, this means, Can $H_1, \ldots, H_n$ stated in null form be rejected? If so, support for the real hypotheses is gained.)

The next task in the research process is the determination of the research design and data-gathering methods that will be used. Selecting a research design involves three interrelated subchoices: (1) sample size, (2) sample (site) selection, and (3) time period of observation. The choice that will be made on each of these factors will be determined by the purpose of the research and the nature of the research question(s) asked. The choice of sample-size and data-gathering methods will usually reflect the state of the evolution of theory on the topic in question. For example, in exploratory research little is known about the territory, and so it is almost impossible to frame detailed questions about variables and relationships of importance beforehand, thus ruling out questionnaires, except of the broadest kind, structured interviews, lab experiments, or other non-time-consuming data collection methods. Instead, it is usually necessary to use observation and unstructured interviews, coupled perhaps with secondary data from documentary sources. Since causal relationships are also not known at this stage, the research usually has to be longitudinal so that causal patterns, especially ones with time lags, can reveal themselves. These two choices, when combined with the typical time and resource constraints, usually mean that the sample size must be very small (sometimes $n = 1$), that site selection is important, and that such selection be done in a nonrandom manner, with a preference for either leading or average organizations. In short, the research design usually involves an in-depth, unfocused, longitudinal field (case) study of one or two organizations that are leaders with respect to the topic in question.

Hypothesis-testing studies, by contrast, usually involve medium- to large-scale samples of either the original or extended populations, using questionnaires, structured interviews, or data bases such as COMPUSTAT tapes to generate data. Usually, the sampling procedures will be random from the population or random from classes within the population. The time period covered will vary with the need to support causality inferences and the time lags hypothesized between cause and effect.

In general, research designs and data-gathering methods will vary with the type of research involved, as indicated in Exhibit 7.1. A further point needs to be made regarding sample (site) selection though. It is that sample (site) selection is usually carefully thought out through the hypothesis generation phase, becoming random only in the hypothesis-testing state. This reflects the different purposes of the research and, in fact, could almost be used as an indicator of the dividing line between the two types.

Data analysis methods depend, quite obviously, on the types of data collected (and vice versa). Typically, they vary with the type of research done, as indicated in Exhibit 7.1. As Hatten notes, most policy research studies have not taken advantage of the wide variety of statistical tools available for analyzing data.

The Need for Research Paradigms

The commentary above has described the general relationships that exist between various characteristics of the research process and the stage of evolution of theory in a field. There are exceptions to these statements as there always are.

One of the unique burdens of the strategic management field, however, is that all of the time and resource constraints normally associated with research are magnified by the complexity of the phenomena being studied. As a consequence, policy researchers face a special challenge of trying to develop new research paradigms that will help overcome some of these difficulties. The use of preexisting secondary documentary "case" data is one step in this direction. The PIMS data base is another. Still other options exist and need to be developed.

OBSERVATIONS ON THE PAPERS

Spender's commentary discusses the theory-building/theory-testing process in more depth and from a more theoretical perspective than is done in the remarks above. Of nearly equal importance are his observations on the ways vocabularies and underlying conceptual constructs structure the way situations are perceived. In this regard, he examines the basic differences between functional theories, exchange theories, and conflict theories as paradigms for viewing a situation.[5] Analyzing a strategic decision-making process from all three points of view might lead to some interesting insights, as Allison's (1971) study of the Cuban missile crisis indicates. Spender also suggests that we may be able to enrich our vocabularies by working more closely with practicing managers.

Steiner's paper examines the nature of contingency theories in strategy and strategic management. He suggests that they represent a useful middle ground between the "universal-truths" type of theories and the assumption that "each situation is unique," which admits no theory at all, and that "inherent in the contingency theory idea is more rigor and a deeper appreciation of the interrelations in situations" than is reflected in the universal principles approach to theory building.

Steiner then surveys various contingency theories of strategy content, of strategy formulation processes, of organization design, of implementation processes, and of leadership style. He classifies these in four categories according to the school of thought from which they were derived: (1) theories based on the case tradition; (2) theories derived from organization theory work; (3) theories derived from empirical research and tradition; and (4) theories developed through conceptualization. Based on this review, he then makes several suggestions for future research in the area and concludes that "business policy is a discipline of its own and is reaching for some maturity."

Additional research ideas could probably be generated by classifying these contingency theories in still different ways; for example, by the level of the organization to which they apply. The major limitation of Steiner's paper, however, is its failure to distinguish between two types of contingency theories. The first type assumes that all combinations of contingency variables are possible, which is the case with most contingency theories derived from the organization behavior/organization theory tradition. The second type assumes that a number of possible combinations of the contingency variables are null spaces (forbidden regions), which is the case with some, but not all, of the theories derived from the case tradition. The fundamental differences between these two types of contingency theories is the richness of the theory they permit for a given degree of parsimony.

In this regard, those which assume forbidden combinations of variables are richer because they permit a more precise specification of variables for a given degree of parsimony, as Exhibit 7.2 indicates. Given the joint need for richness in order to adequately describe the complexity of strategic management issues, and for parsimony to produce theoretical power and

---

[5] Spender fails to note, however, that each of these three types of theories can be regarded as interaction theories which differ only with respect to the degree of commonality (overlap) that exists in the participants' goal structures, as is reflected in the following associations: functional theories/great commonality; exchange theories/some commonality; conflict theories/little commonality.

Exhibit 7.2 Different Types of Contingency Theories

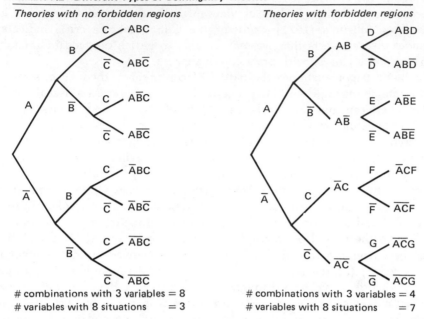

Theories with no forbidden regions

combinations with 3 variables = 8
variables with 8 situations   = 3

Theories with forbidden regions

combinations with 3 variables = 4
variables with 8 situations   = 7

permit more effective empirical investigation, contingency theories of the second type, those with forbidden regions, hold greater promise for theory development in the strategic management area than those which admit all possible combinations of variables.

In his commentary, Paine decides against trying to extend Steiner's survey because of "its completeness." Instead, he suggests one way in which the various contingency theories of strategy content, strategy formulation process, organization design, organization context, leadership style, and so on, drawn from the organization theory tradition might be combined into a single contingency theory of strategic management. Space does not permit Paine to reveal all the assumptions he has made, or all the reasons he has combined the various individual theories as he has done, or why he has rejected other possible methods of integration. Nevertheless, he does provide a good illustration of how more global theories can be built from a sequence of limited domain theories. An additional observation worth making is that when building such "global" theories, they should be constructed to the extent possible using limited domain theories that are well corroborated empirically.

Duncan's paper examines some of the philosophical differences between qualitative and quantitative research. He then points out the need for additional qualitative research in the policy field based on an examination of some of the research questions it faces, after which he discusses the pros and cons of various qualitative data-gathering methods that may be used in policy research, giving examples of how each might be used. Duncan may have overstated the case for qualitative research methods through his selection of Mintzberg's paradigm of the field. If one compares Mintzberg's paradigm (Exhibit 7.11, see page 426) with Exhibit 2 (see page 15) in the Introduction, one immediately notes that Mintzberg has no outputs in his paradigm, only processes. Since quantitative research methods are more amenable to content research than process research, Mintzberg's representation immediately and implicitly overemphasizes the importance of qualitative research to the field. Since many would argue that a study of process is more important than a study of content, it may still be that qualitative research methods are more important to the development of the field. Maybe so, but probably not to the degree Duncan implies.

Hatten's paper makes the case for the use of quantitative research methods in the field. First, he surveys the quantitative research that has been done recently and concludes: (1) that little such research has been done, but (2) that the problem is not caused by a lack of tools available for doing such research. He then examines in some detail the quantitative research that has been done and suggests ways that this research might be built upon in the future. His comments on the strategic group concept are worth particular attention. Next, Hatten notes that most quantitative research in the field to date has focused on content rather than on process questions, but observes that this need not be the case in the future. His following discussion on the ways that quantitative tools such as factor analysis, mulidimensional scaling, and perceptual mapping might be used to study strategic management process is, perhaps, the most provocative in this section of the text.

Like Duncan, Hatten has probably overstated the case for quantitative methods. One of the primary reasons that such techniques have not been used more often is not a total lack of familiarity with the techniques, or the lack of internal data, but that most in-depth field studies (which usually involve primarily nominal and ordinal data) do not involve sample sizes sufficiently large to permit the meaningful use of such techniques, a point supported by Naumes.

In his commentary on Duncan's and Hatten's papers, Naumes points out that the development of various limited domain theories in the policy field should permit more effective future research, since it will no longer be necessary to base future studies on wholistic maps of the territory, and thereby try to cover more territory in less depth. He also points out that future studies should reflect the behavioral side of policy making processes. Naumes then discusses several types of quantitative techniques that may be used for policy research that were not covered by Hatten, including simulation, path analysis, and Q-sorts. One of his more important points is his contention that simulation is a useful tool for research and deserves attention. In this regard, it is interesting to speculate on whether strategic management researchers will be able to build simulation models rich enough to simulate various strategic management issues in the future that would be analogous to the various behavior theory simulations built in other disciplines in the early 1960s. Finally, Naumes echoes Duncan's suggestion that most policy research should use a combination of qualitative and quantitative methods.

SOME CONCLUDING OBSERVATIONS

In summing up our introduction to this section, we would like to reemphasize four points regarding research in strategic management that have been made earlier in this text. First, more empirical research is needed in the field. We do not want for theories, but we do want for theories that have been adequately tested against empirical data. Second, future research should, wherever possible, be normative in character. Purely descriptive research is also needed and welcome. However, a knowledge of best practice and how it compares with average and poor practice is desirable if the field is to advance. Third, we should, to the extent possible, make greater efforts to build on the work of others. Clearly, there will always be a need to explore some totally new territory or to repeat the work of others when the latter has been called into question. To merely duplicate such work without extending it in some way is a waste of resources. Likewise, random studies on widely diverse sets of new topics are not likely to extend the field as much as a series of works integrated and built on one another. Finally, future research should be more rigorous, in a scientific sense, than it has been in the past. We do not mean that an immediate jump to hypothesis testing and falsification is needed. In fact, many studies have tried such an approach without first truly understanding the phenomena in question. At the same time, too many have failed to move forward when such movement was possible. What is needed is not more research of a particular type (i.e., conceptual development, hypothesis generation, or hypothesis testing), but rather, much more research that develops and tests new paradigms for studying the field and which properly uses both quantitative and qualitative techniques to the fullest extent possible to study the phenomena in question.

Commentary

J-C. SPENDER
City University Business School (London)

INTRODUCTION

The title of this section of the text already reveals significant assumptions, and our purposes are served if we clarify these. First, theory is contrasted with the responsibilities of strategic management, which implies a belief that theory is helpful. This is not self-evident and our theorizing is at times widely criticized. It behooves us to be humble about our failings, especially the tendency to pursue theoretical rigor at the expense of practical relevance, a dilemma which we share with economists and others (Gordon, 1976). Some researchers respond with total immersion into practicality, but there is another way, to pursue more empirically significant theory. Although some would argue we have theory enough, we lack good theory so long as management is unimpressed. In general, policy researchers are looking for theories that apply to management's practical concerns rather than those of the pure theorist.

Second, we could follow Galtung's (1967) useful text and just distinguish data collection from data analysis. At first sight more practical, this approach panders to an outdated belief in raw data, marked only by the certainty of commonsense. That all data is theoretically fashioned, whether by observation theories or others, is now a major issue in research design which is particularly relevant to the policy area. The section title, therefore, does not contrast theory with data since if this were the focus, we could easily call the section, "Building and Testing Ways of Collecting, Analyzing and Interpreting Data."

THEORIES THAT APPLY TO STRATEGIC MANAGEMENT

The first difficulty in theorizing about strategic management is in defining the field precisely. A variety of different vocabularies from areas such as economics, finance, marketing, organizational theory, and political science have been used to describe the field, and as yet, there is no agreement on which is most useful. More importantly, some words and concepts are defined differently in the different vocabularies. For example, the word strategy has no universally accepted meaning. Some writers see it as a logical plan to transform received objectives into desired results, while others define strategy to include choices on both objectives and means.

The choice of language is important to theory-building and testing, however. Theorizing depends on making assumptions which reduce the infinite variety of reality. This can be done in many ways through the use of different constructs and vocabularies. Resulting theory is limited to the extent of these assumptions' practicality. For instance, theories that depend on perfect competition are useless to managers facing imperfect markets. The crux of theory-building then is to choose concepts and vocabulary that are rich enough to accurately describe the key interactions in the real world, but which are parsimonious enough that powerful conclusions can be developed from the theories.

THE SCIENTIFIC METHOD

The twin orthodoxies of modern scientific method, the hypothetical-deductive approach (Hempel, 1966) and falsificationism (Popper, 1959), both ignore theory building on the grounds that it is inductive and, consequently, unscientific. Schon (1963: 3) writes: "either they make the process mysterious, and therefore intrinsically unexplainable; or they regard novelty as illusory and, therefore, requiring no explanation." This contrast can be put in its historical context, for the balance between the two activities is being gradually restored. The orthodoxies are under considerable pressure, especially from science historians who argue that progressive science has little to do with such methodological prescriptions (Braithwaite, 1953; Hanson, 1965; Lakatos, 1970; Feyerabend, 1975). Indeed, at the time of Boyle and Newton, scientists abominated hypotheses and focused exclusively on empirical data. They regarded induction as the method of science (Laudan, 1969).

The anti-inductive paradigm still dominating the practice of science only arose when it was realized that there could be no fool-proof logic of discovery. Science's focus then shifted naturally from relevance to rigor after the early natural scientists had mapped the physical universe in a burst of theory-building that still underpins contemporary science. But this universe seems significantly different from the social and economic universes with which managements struggle. Here the changes are rapid and yesterday's relevant theory might well be irrelevant, though still true, today.

In contrast with the methods of physical sciences, there are many discussions of theory-building in social science (e.g., Kaplan, 1964; Zetterberg, 1965; Merton, 1967; Stinchcombe, 1968; Blalock, 1969; Dubin, 1969; Wallace, 1971; Gibbs, 1972; Skidmore, 1975; Olson, 1976). In particular Harvey (1969) offers a comprehensive methodological text. The same general principles are offered throughout.

THE STRUCTURE OF THEORY

Because strategy-making is a type of theory building, a theory of strategy-making is a theory of theory-building. This makes for a certain intellectual complexity which is best addressed by dealing with theory in general before passing on to theory in the strategic area. Theory begins with some assumptions that particular variables are of interest and usefully regarded as attributes of the object or event under investigation. The theory asserts a relationship between the variables. Thus, theories have logical domains, areas in which they are considered applicable, which are determined in terms of these variables. In particular, it is often simpler to argue that some event is outside a theory's domain than to argue that some other event is within it. For instance, it may be easier to argue that strategy-making is outside the domain of microeconomic theory than to delineate those managerial decisions that are within it.

More generally, theory Z might assert a relation between two variables P and Q. (see Exhibit 7.3 for a depiction of the property space.) If the variables appear irrelevant to an event E_1, it might be that it lies outside Z's domain. Yet if P and Q appear relevant to another event E_2,

it does not follow that E_2 is actually adequately covered by the theory. One might discover that some further variable R is actually responsible for E_2. Hence one needs to consider the variables and their connection to the events that are of interest most carefully, noting that asserting the significance of P and Q denies the significance of every other variable through an implicit "ceteris paribus" clause. Similarly, the theory is empty if, at the same time as asserting one kind of relationship between P and Q, it does not also deny all other types of relationships. However, different relationships cannot be distinguished one from another unless both P and Q are scaled, i.e., unless P and Q are variables.

There are a number of options in the ways variables can be scaled. Stevens (1966) showed they range from simple labelling to the application of ratio scales. He divided this range into four regions: nominal, ordinal, interval and ratio. Each region was differentiated by the mathematical structure to which the scores conform. As can be seen in Exhibit 7.4, these structural properties accumulate, ordinal having all the properties attributed to nominal, plus others; interval all those attached to ordinal, plus others, and so forth. Binary nominal scaling is the simplest, and actually dichotomizes the variable, separating "has a particular attribute" from "has not." Thus a firm might be characterized as having a vertically-integrated structure or not. Similarly, a second variable might be membership of a particular industry, such as steel-making. The simplest possible theory asserts a relation between two such dichotomies; P and not-P, Q and not-Q, or, in the example, between steel-making industry membership and vertically integrated organizational structure. The theoretical relationship can be presented as a property-space whose logical properties en-

Exhibit 7.3 Property Space

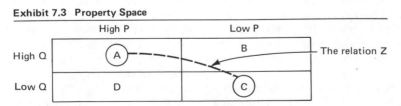

Exhibit 7.4 Scale Systems and Corresponding Properties

Scale system	Defining relation	Possible transformations	Appropriate statistics		
			Central tendency	Dispersion	Tests
Nominal	Equivalence	$x' = f(x)$ where $f(x)$ means any one-to-one substitution	Mode	% in the mode	Chi-square Contingency coefficient Goodman-Kruskal's Lambda phi-coefficient *(Non-parametric)*
Ordinal	Equivalence Greater than	$x' = f(x)$ where $f(x)$ means any increasing monotonic transformation	Median	Percentiles	Spearman's rho Kendall's tau Kolmogorov-Smirnov Goodman-Kruskal's Gamma phi-coefficient *(Non-parametric)*
Interval	Equivalence Greater than Known ratio of any two intervals	Any linear transformation: $x' = ax + b$ $(a > 0)$	Mean	Standard deviation	t-test F-test (analysis of variance) Pearson's r Point biserial (one variable dichotomous) etc. *(Parametric and non-parametric)*
Ratio	Equivalence Greater than Known ratio of any two intervals Known ratio of any two scale values	$x' = cx$ $(c > 0)$	Geometric mean	Coefficient of variation	

capsulate the points made thus far (Barton, 1955); see Exhibit 7.4.

The property-space shows the domain of the theory, asserting a logical space in which every instance can be scored in both P and Q scales. It defines as irrelevant scores against other variables and instances which cannot be scored against both P and Q. It shows what the theory Z asserts, the relation AC, and what it denies, the relations AB, BC, CD, DA and DB. The type of scale can be changed without affecting the logic of the property-space. Scales can also be mixed with, say, P as ordinal and Q as interval.

The theory answers the question, "Why are instances observed and their scores located logically in the property-space in the way they are?" This answer is an "explanation." Kaplan (1964) argued there are two kinds of explanation, hence two kinds of theory, "deductive," which is logical, and "pattern" which is inductive. A deductive theory follows by deduction from some other established theory. If P is pressure and Q temperature, we can deduce a deductive theory (Z') from the general gas law "pressure times volume divided by temperature is constant" by including volume in the ceteris paribus clause and holding it constant. Then Z' is "pressure P over temperature Q is constant." A pattern explanation (Z'') follows whenever an instance can be fitted into an established pattern of instances within the property-space. The two explanations differ because the first is logically true, while the second is dependent on a pattern of experience, an empirical generalization induced from past instances. A great deal of thought has been given to the nature of the differences between these two types of explanation without, as yet, any entirely satisfactory conclusion. However, the second type of theory development, i.e., induction from empirical observation, obviously involves qualities in P and Q which are unnecessary in the first type.

A deductive explanation (Z') does not require that either P or Q be empirically significant; a pattern explanation (Z''), on the other hand, requires that P and Q be observable and measurable, operationally and empirically significant. Operationalizing the P and Q scales transforms the property-space from a logical domain into an operational domain. This is of much greater interest in the development of practical theory. But it also gives any score a double meaning; it is both a member of the set of scores that the property-space encompasses, which can be imagined within the property-space, and a member of the quite different set which the measurement system encompasses. The operational significance of a data point cannot be grasped without also understanding the measurement system which produces it and the way data manipulation is limited by this system's structure. Merton (1967) noted that operational clarification is generally a substantial part of the research task. The operational significance of the variables must be clear enough for data to be manipulated legitimately, and for permissible conclusions to be drawn. The relationship between the logical and operational types of domain is the same as that between the deductive and pattern explanations; thus, in the pursuit of relevant theory we should seek pattern explanation within an operationally defined property-space.

THEORY-TESTING

This property-space can be used in two ways, to test pattern theories or to build them. There are no connections between the scales employed in setting up the property-space and the uses made of it. Nominal scaling can be as usefully employed in the test of a theory as ratio scaling can be employed in the building of another. Hence, as Galtung (1967) observes, covariance is the main analytic tool in all types of social science investigation, equally applicable to both testing and building. As shown in Exhibit 7.5, to test a pattern theory, the property-space must encompass both confirming instances that the theory allows (I_1), and falsifying instances that it denies (I_2).

So long as all the instances within the Z'' domain are confirming ones (I_1's), and there are no falsifying ones (I_2's), the evidence confirms the tenability or the usefulness of Z'' as an explanation of these instances. But if I_2's are found as well as I_1's then their significance must be established. There are many rules for guiding the researcher's conclusions under such circumstances, and these are discussed in Hatten's paper. The point of departure is the need to discriminate between I_2's which are random variations of I_1's, and those which suggest that Z'' is not the appropriate pattern with which to explain the property-space. The conclusions apply to the whole population of possible instances in the domain. But practical property-spaces are arranged to apply to instances which have yet to arise, to extend into the future, to include potential instances in the domain. This, together with a need to generate conclusions from the least data possible, necessitates making inferences about the total population from samples of instances.

The interpretation of the scores depends on the degree to which they depart from what was expected, given that Z'' is tenable. In applying statistics, the logic is reversed and the scores are analyzed to assess the confidence with which the null hypothesis can be rejected. The null hypothesis asserts there is no relation between P and Q, and that the scores are distributed randomly within the property-space, i.e., that the theory Z'' is false. By rejecting the null hypothesis an assertion is made that theory Z'' holds, or is true. Grant (1962) shows the results of this approach are not always what they seem. Likewise, Bakan (1966) notes possible abuses when large numbers of observations have been gathered. Since few natural arising populations are effectively random, the null hypothesis is often false. Hence, quite spurious results can sometimes be obtained, which appear to confirm any Z'' whatsoever, just by making the sample large enough.

THEORY-BUILDING

The theory-building procedure is quite different from that of theory-testing. The most important difference is that there is no hypothesis or theoretical relation being asserted. Theory-building starts merely with the assumption that certain variables are of interest, that there might be the possibility of conjunction between

Exhibit 7.5 Confirming and Falsifying Instances

	High P	Low P
High Q	I_1	I_2
Low Q	I_2	I_1

two measurement systems S and T. There are no assertions about the factual significance of the implicit property-space, which may not contain any events at all. Any event showing a conjunction between S and T is already a tangible result and, by definition, surprises us. It runs counter to the expectation that there ought not be relationships between two arbitrarily chosen variables S and T. In practice, the researcher is usually interested in events of some kind, but is struggling to find some property-space within which to locate them. He explores the usefulness of S and T as variables within which to map these events. Without a prior theory though, he does not expect the events that do occur to fall into any pattern. He can only expect them to be distributed randomly. Moreover, his property-space is not adequately bounded, for he has no way of imagining the domain's total population. In the theory-building mode, therefore, sampling and significance levels are empty ideas. Such conclusions as can be drawn arise directly from the observations and not, as in the theory-testing mode, from the interaction of assertion and observation. Observations can be aggregated to suggest some inductive assertion, but no assertions can be made about instances in the future or about the unobserved remainder of any imagined population.

The essence of induction is surprise at things being similar when there is no reason to think of them as other than diverse. Surprise develops into a pattern as the researcher notes a succession of similarities. As before, though, matters get complicated as soon as the observations vary; the researcher must assess whether the scatter indicates one or several inductive conclusions, or none at all. He arrives at a conclusion only when he feels able to assert that the property-space is patterned, that S and T seem to be related. As depicted in Exhibit 7.6, the pattern (Y'') is the empirical generalization that describes what he has observed in the domain.

Perceiving such similarities, and the patterns they suggest, is no more commonsensical than perceiving the significance of theory-testing data. There have been many recent developments in the quantitative methods by which similarities in a body of data can be drawn out, such as factor analysis and canonical correlation analysis, and Hatten deals with these. It is important to appreciate that the criteria by which observations are judged similar must be imported into these analyses. Thus, while significance levels are imported into the analyses of differences, the conventions are widely accepted. However, similar conventions have yet to be established in the analyses of similarities through techniques such as numerical taxonomy or cluster analysis (Sokal and Sneath, 1963; Cole, 1969; Aaker, 1971; Shepard et al., 1972). Hence the criteria used, as well as the methods themselves, are likely to be criticized by those socialized into the conventions of difference analysis.

Taxonomic analyses attempt to evaluate only the applicability of descriptions to conjunctions observed, and these vary in discriminatory power. At one level, every event is surprising, so that every event shares that as a common description. At the opposite extreme, every event is in some ways unique, so the analyst can vary the extent of the events' grouping or cluster membership to suit his own purposes. To discriminate among his observations, the analyst uses a measure of the distance between them which reflects both variables scored. Each distance score is then sorted to cluster the observations into groups of high similarity, the separation between clusters reflecting major differences. There are many kinds of measures and each demands its own analysis. Choosing among them is a matter of experience rather than theory, as discussed in Everitt (1974), though the final criterion must be fitness to the analyst's purpose and may call for some trial and error on his part.

COMBINING THEORY-BUILDING AND THEORY-TESTING

The theory-tester asserts the future tenability of relations which have passed repeatable tests that conform to canons of scientific rigor. The theory-builder, on the other hand, merely creates a new statement and suggests it has factual significance under specific conditions. Without knowing the extent of the domain implied, it cannot be extended into the future to become a practical guide to action. Hence, although theory-building and testing are quite different procedures which stand in dialectical opposition to each other, they are the interactive parts of progressive science. The output from each procedure is an input to the other. Theory-testing is the methodical criticism of the synthesizing

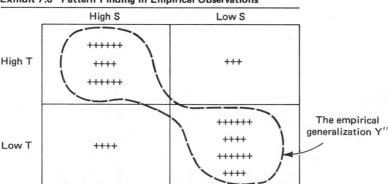

Exhibit 7.6 Pattern Finding in Empirical Observations

	High S	Low S
High T	++++++ ++++ ++++++	+++
Low T	++++	++++++ ++++ ++++++ ++++

The empirical generalization Y''

suggestions generated by the theory-builder. Likewise theory-building begins by accepting the measurement systems involved as operationally tested sub-theories. The relationship is recursive, as Wallace suggests (1971). But it is also progressive, more like a spiral than a circle. A tested and accepted theory Z″ is operationalized into a measurement system S. Two such systems are mapped into a domain and their conjunctions y″ observed to induce the empirical generalization Y″. This is then carefully tested until it is accepted, and so forth, as illustrated in Exhibit 7.7.

Although two variables are sufficient to illustrate the principles involved, practical research may involve many more. The mathematical techniques for handling a multiplicity of variables are known collectively as multivariate analysis. Both difference and similarity handling techniques are included, although they stand in contrast to each other. Similarity analysis techniques, such as graph analysis and numerical taxonomy, are suitable for showing up unexpected similarities in a body of data. Difference-based techniques, such as factor analysis, are appropriate for showing the dimensions in which the differences in a body of data can be maximized (Aaker 1971). The two kinds of technique are complementary in the analysis of complex operational domains (Green and Wind, 1975).

The methods outlined above are general and apply to theory-building and testing in any field of empirical study employing pattern explanations. As Merton (1967: 157) points out, the combination of techniques enables empirical research to fashion a theory's development in four ways; "it initiates, it reformulates, it deflects and it clarifies." By ensuring the relative independence of the measurement systems mapped into the operationally defined domains, continued relevance is ensured and the logical closure of the deductive approach can be avoided. When the variables defining the property-space are both derived from a single theory, empirical evidence is unnecessary for an examination of how the conjunctions are distributed. By sticking to pattern theory the researcher remains open to evidence which can surprise and confound him and lead to rebuilding. But, by the same token, the researcher relies upon operational conventions rather than pure theory to define the domains worked on.

THEORY-BUILDING AND THEORY-TESTING IN THE STRATEGIC MANAGEMENT AREA

Because of these conventions, particular measurement systems and their manipulation become characteristic of particular disciplines and programs of research. The problem of relevance is dealt with through these conventions. An area of empirical enquiry, therefore, is distinguished through the theories operationalized into the measurement systems shown relevant to its particular domain. The choice of variables mapped into a domain is a convention which, in turn,

Exhibit 7.7 Theory-Building/Theory-Testing Process

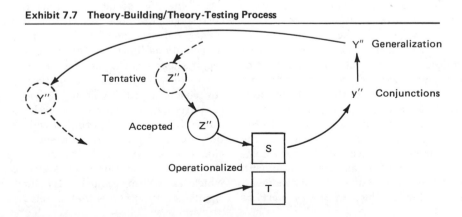

limits the variables that appear in the generalizations made about it. The strategic management area traditionally relies on variables derived either from marketing, financial, and microeconomic-based measurement systems, or from organization theory or political science based measurement systems. Hence, many corporate strategy theories revolve around conjunctions between strategies described in marketing or financial terms, for example, as market posture or resource allocation patterns, and organizational structures described in organization theory terms, illustrated, for instance, in the manipulations and conclusions of Meyer and Glauber (1964), Rumelt (1974), Schoeffler et al. (1974), and Berry (1975). But the traditional variables can also be used as vocabularies, from which theory can be built. The works of Goronzy (1969) and Hatten (1975) show the exploration of the conjunctions observable when the strategy area's variables are scored for populations of firms.

BROADENING THE RANGE OF IDEAS

Organization and political theorists have long been working with other vocabularies which are important additions to those traditional to the policy researcher. These extended vocabularies are evident in the papers by Bower, Mintzberg, Berg and Pitts elsewhere in this book. Because the power of multivariate analysis enables several measurement systems to be embraced at the same time, it is possible to search for wider patterns of conjunction within a single piece of research. The most significant expansion of these vocabularies arose from the work of Lawrence and Lorsch (1967b). Their study led to an awareness of the firm's environment and attempts to describe it. Operationalized measures of technology were applied, enlarging Burns and Stalker's (1961) earlier analysis of environmental variability and uncertainty.

But this is only one kind of extension to the vocabulary the researcher can apply to the firm's environment. To theorize about the relationship between the firm and its environment, the strategist must describe the environment. As soon as he does this, he shares, perhaps

inadvertently, part of the sociologist's task. Sociologists are trying to describe society and explain why it is as it is, and have given considerable thought to possible descriptions of the environment. Wallace (1969) summarizes these and his typology of sociological theories can be seen as a typology of vocabularies that might be usefully mapped into the strategic management area. He distinguishes between treating society as something which imposes itself on all these interactions and treating society as itself arising out of such interactions. It is obvious that much current contingency theory falls into the first part of this typology. It takes society to be *sui generis*, beyond our influence and to be adapted to. Wallace dubs this position "ecologism," and it is vividly illustrated in the "adaption" versus "adoption" argument in microeconomics (e.g., Alchian, 1950; Penrose, 1952). Child (1972) has pointed out such passive acceptance of the environment overlooks management's option to move to a less hostile environment. Hence it overlooks by assumption a whole dimension of the strategist's options for coping with apparent difficulties in the firm's environment. Child's criticism can be generalized to show the necessity of treating the firm's environment as the active product of others' strategic decisions. Dealing with this extension demands the different vocabularies of the second half of Wallace's typology.

If one believes that managers are struggling with a socially constructed environment rather than one which is *sui generis*, then one finds oneself in the mainstream of contemporary sociology. There are three principal ways of describing the social environment and these correspond to three different rationalities for managerial decision. First, one can conceive of all activity as functional, in the sense that auto-repair shops sustain the mobility which is necessary to society's functioning. Second, one can conceive of all activity as an inter-active pattern of purposive and conscious exchange. Adam Smith, for instance, argued that while specialization increased productive efficiency, it made exchange necessary. Third, one can conceive of all activity as a pattern of contained conflict in which each firm competes for limited spoils against every other within a relatively stable economic structure. Clearly, all of these ideas are present in managerial thinking, but that does not make them equivalents. They give rise to quite different theories about society and, therefore, different descriptions of the environment. If the strategic theorist wishes to build good theory, he must be careful with the vocabulary he maps into his area of concern, and this means clarifying the differences between these three views, as well as the interrelated terms within each. For example, strategies designed to beat competitors in an open market place must not be confused with ones which involve cooperation between firms to influence or close markets for their mutual benefit. Likewise, neither of these must be confused with a search for undiscovered business opportunities in a socially predetermined market.

APPEALING TO MANAGERS FOR IDEAS

Each of these views, however, relies upon the prior assumptions about the nature of the environment embedded in the three types of sociological theories that form Wallace's typology. They are functionalism, exchange theory and conflict theory. They can be translated into the strategic management area; thus, the first asserts that the environment is made up of already existing business opportunities, the second asserts that such opportunities are a manifestation of co-operation between firms, while the third asserts that all markets are wholly and perfectly competitive. These are severe abstractions and also of quite different natures, and there is little evidence to suggest that managers apply such sociological schema to their work.

Thus, rather than rely upon the sociologist for his relevance-ensuring conventions, the strategic theorists could turn to the managers themselves and see how they describe and theorize about their firms' environments. This is a profound shift in method, for it adds a further preliminary step to the scientific methodology sketched out in the earlier part of the introduction. There, theory-building is described as the synthesizing of the established measurement systems which convention suggests can be usefully mapped into the area of interest. There is no discussion of where these systems come from, or of how they come to be accepted. Financial and organizational structural descriptions are accepted as relevant, although there is no research to prove that managers either apply these or significantly restrict themselves to such vocabularies. The strategic management researcher may be able to elicit a broader, more relevant set of variables if he abandons his theoretical preconceptions and attempts to get into the manager's particular situation himself. At this point, the strategic theorist and the strategic manager become as one.

These methods, which require the researcher to participate in the situation as an actor rather than as an observer, are based upon an entirely different conception of enquiry. They derive from phenomenology rather than positivism and focus on the subjective aspects of experiencing a situation, rather than the objective aspects of observing it. Although there has been much use of participant-observational methods in organization behavior and theory research, as Duncan's paper illustrates, they have yet to be applied extensively within the policy field. Although attractive, they harbor a number of additional difficulties which have yet to be solved in the fields, for example, psychology, in which they are currently applied. The researcher's first step is to use the experience of participating to identify the classification systems being applied by the managers, and to institutionalize himself into their way of thinking. This requires that he accept whatever objectives they perceive as the sole objective of their decision-making, and reject the essentially normative, results oriented nature of most policy research. The researcher's second step, since he cannot readily evaluate his findings against such prior performance objectives, is to communicate his findings to others who share his interest in the managers' way of thinking. The methodological difficulties of doing this are substantial and are discussed in texts such as McCall and Simmons (1969), Filstead (1970), Diesing (1972), Filmer et al. (1972), and Bogdan and Taylor (1975).

The essential problem with phenomenological methods is that of translating from one culture to another while also denying that all possible cultures are merely instances of the universal laws of human behavior implied in the three sociological models above. In this sense it is not clear how research which reveals the managers' idiosyncratic perceptions of their environment can lead to the kind of understanding and improved performance which policy research is normally directed toward. The difficulties are not trifling, for this focus on the individual and the idiosyncratic runs counter to the objective basis of scientific theory-testing while, at the same time, relevant theory can only be built with variables whose objectivity is accepted. Thus, Nagel (1963) concludes that these methods are not continuous with empirical science, implying that their usefulness in the strategic management area is limited until their own relationship with scientific method is more clearly established (Meltzer et al., 1975).

CONCLUSION

The strategic management theorist has a variety of sources for the variables he maps into the area, those traditional to policy research, those drawn from sociology, psychology, political theory and, possibly, those from the managers themselves. He can improve the generality of his theories by relying on universalistic assumptions about the nature of the firm, its managers or its environment, but only at the expense of practical relevance. By paying attention to the unique, the historical and the individual, he can generate theory that is highly relevant, but of less use in other or future circumstances. The strategic manager faces precisely the same methodological issues, for his effectiveness is reflected in the power of the theories he builds. Not only do they need to grasp the salient facts of the environment, but they must also be projectable to the future, to remain acceptable under new circumstances. Even though few managers have the time to test their theories directly, they have much to gain by understanding the procedures for building and testing the theories they need for the execution of their responsibilities. Certainly, the strategic management scholar must adopt and further methodologies for building and testing theories.

Contingency Theories of Strategy and Strategic Management

GEORGE A. STEINER
University of California at Los Angeles

INTRODUCTION

The purpose of this paper is to review the development of some main concepts and research streams concerned with contingency theories in the strategic management area. Following this evaluation I shall speculate about future research opportunities and methodologies in the area. My intent is to present a broad picture of the state-of-the-art of contingency theories concerning strategy and strategic management. It is not my intent to provide an encyclopedia of all the research findings in the field. Space does not permit such an assessment. Anyway, that has been done in other studies for the entire field (Paine and Naumes, 1974; Steiner and Miner, 1977), and for parts of the field (Hofer, 1975).

THE MEANING OF CONTINGENCY THEORY IN THE STRATEGIC MANAGEMENT AREA

During the past decade organization theorists directed their attention to developing a contingency approach to organization. Succintly, this approach sees "a middle ground between: (1) the view that there are universal principles of organization and management, and (2) the view that each organization is unique and that each situation must be analyzed separately" (Kast and Rozenzweig, 1973: ix). The contingency theory approach is concerned with a midrange body of theory which stands between "universal truths" and "each situation is unique." The contingency approach seeks to determine a relationship in which observable behavioral response in and to organizations is dependent upon specified environmental conditions. The major research thrust has concerned the relationship between environment and organization structure, but the research scope has broad-

ened considerably beyond that in recent years.

The general current concept of contingency theory is typified by the work of Lawrence and Lorsch on *Organization and Environment* (1967b) in which they showed conclusively that although there is no one best way to organize different companies in different industries and situations, environmental forces require different types of organizational structures at different stages in their growth. This work, and subsequent contingency theories, established situational guidelines for managers, which preceding theorists proposing universal principles were unable to provide.

The idea of a contingency theory of strategic management has its roots in the work of theorists extending back many years. For instance, Selznick (1949) showed that different organizations and interest groups in the environment of TVA affected the decisions that managers made. In his study *TVA and the Grass Roots*, he showed how both formal and informal systems of TVA adjusted to the outside environment. He also described the strategy by means of which adjustment was made. This basic concept was followed years later by well-known research of organizational theorists, other than Lawrence and Lorsch noted above (Burns and Stalker, 1961; Chandler, 1962; Woodward, 1965; Thompson, 1967; and Perrow, 1970).

Other scholars also have adopted the contingency approach to research without using that phraseology. It has been evident for a long time that strategies appropriate for one firm under one set of conditions may be quite different for another firm under different or even the same conditions. It was this view, among other things, that fostered the use of the case approach in teaching business policy, a practice extending back many years. Mary Parker Follett in 1925 had the idea of contingency theory in her so-called law of the situation (in Metcalf and Urwick, 1940: 58). Peter Drucker in his *The Practice of Management* (1954), to cite another example, took a contingency approach to management practice and organizational structure although he did not use that word. As Moberg and Koch point out (1975), older universalistic models assumed a form which came close to contingency theory (see also Child, 1974).

What is new with contingency theory is that it takes a new approach in seeking to describe for given situations, structures and actions that best meet the needs of the organization. This is a new unifying approach to organizational design which is now being applied to different areas of management theory, including strategic management. The contingency approach is richer than the universal principles approach to theory-building. Inherent in it is more rigor, a deeper appreciation of interrelationships in situations, and an effort to identify causal relationships.

Since we are dealing with contingency theories concerning strategic management, the latter concept needs definition. The word strategy moved into management literature from its military usage. Strategy was defined as an action taken by a manager to offset actual or potential actions of competitors (Chandler, 1962; Cannon, 1968; Ansoff, 1969; Cooper and Schendel, 1971; Newman and Logan, 1971; Christensen, Andrews, and Bower, 1973). Initially the principal focus was on the concept of strategy and the processes by which it was formulated and implemented. While there is no consensus in the field, many scholars today have broadened these concepts and view "Strategic Management" as including the process by which organizational missions, purposes, objectives, strategies, policies and action programs are formulated, evaluated, implemented, and controlled so that desired organizational ends are achieved. It should also be noted here, that there are as yet no integrated theories of the strategic management process. There are, however, numerous contingency theories that cover different parts of the territory, such as contingency theories of strategy content, of the strategy formulation and implementation processes, of organizational decision, leadership style, and so on. My terrain is, therefore, very broad. In this light, what follows is illustrative only of the subject, it does not exhaust it.

MAJOR THRUSTS IN THE DEVELOPMENT OF CONTINGENCY THEORY FOR STRATEGIES

Four main thrusts can be identified in the recent development of contingency theories in the strategic management area. They are theories based on the case tradition, those derived from organization theory, those derived from empirical research and experience, and conceptualization theories. This division is rather loose and arbitrary and I do not think it is satisfactory, but it is the best I can think of at this time and it does help in classifying different thrusts for discussion. The groupings are not mutually exclusive. Many of the works cited below may be included in more than one of these categories, so the reader may choose to classify some studies differently than I have.

CONTINGENCY THEORIES BASED ON THE CASE TRADITION

What I have in mind in this classification is contingency hypotheses derived from case analysis. This includes not only evaluation of written cases, but field studies of organizations. Research in this area has been growing rapidly and has produced a wide variety of findings which clearly enrich our knowledge about appropriate strategies under different conditions.

Theories derived from written cases of actual situations tend to be rather complex because they embrace a wide range of variables. A typical example is the recent work of Hofer (1975). He begins with the proposition that, "The most fundamental variable in determining an appropriate business strategy is the stage of the product life cycle" (1975: 798). He then proceeds to develop strategies appropriate for different stages of the product life cycle. The variables considered are:

1. *Market and consumer behavior variables* — buyer needs, purchase frequency, buyer concentration, market segmentation, market size,

elasticity of demand, buyer loyalty, seasonality, cyclicality.

2. *Industry structure variables* — uniqueness of the product, rate of technological change in product design, type of product, number of equal products, barriers to entry, degree of product differentiation, transportation and distribution costs, price/cost structure, degree of technological change in process design, experience curves, degree of integration, economics of scale, and marginal plant size.

3. *Competitor variables* — degree of specialization within the industry, degree of capacity utilization, degree of seller concentration, and aggressiveness of competition.

4. *Supplier variables* — degree of supplier concentration, and major changes in availability of raw materials.

5. *Broader environmental variables* — interest rates, money supply, GNP trend, antitrust regulations, growth of population, age distribution of population, regional shifts of population, and life style changes.

6. *Organizational characteristics and resources* — quality of products, market share, marketing intensity, value added, degree of customer concentration, discretionary cash flow, gross capital investment, length of the production cycle, plant and equipment newness, and relative wage rate.

Descriptive propositions are then developed for each stage of the product life cycle, such as the following for the maturity stage: the major determinants of business strategy are the nature of buyer needs, the degree of product differentiation, the rate of technological change in process design, the degree of market segmentation, the ratio of distribution costs to manufacturing, value added, and the frequency with which the product is purchased.

Normative contingency hypotheses are then formulated using these determinants. For the maturity stage, for example: *When*

1. the degree of product differentiation is low,

2. the nature of buyer needs is primarily economic,

3. the rate of technological change in process design is high,

4. the ratio of distribution costs to manufacturing value added is high,

5. the purchase frequency is high,

6. the buyer concentration is high, and

7. the degree of capacity utilization is low,

then businesses should:

1. allocate most of their R&D funds to improvements in process design rather than to new product development,

2. allocate most of their plant and equipment expenditures to new equipment purchases,

3. seek to integrate forward or backward in order to increase the value they add to the product,

4. attempt to improve their production scheduling and inventory control procedures in order to increase their capacity utilization,

5. attempt to segment the market, and

6. attempt to reduce their raw material unit costs by standardizing their product design and using interchangeable components throughout their product line in order to qualify for volume discounts.

In this paper Hofer presents other sets of strategies for different combinations of states of the contingency variables. The results are complex, but do retain much of the richness of the case origins.

A different type of study in a different strategy area is that of Ackerman's (1975) intensive field investigation, extending over several years, of how two large companies institutionalized social programs in their decision making processes. The result is a model to help corporations identify, formulate and implement programs which are socially responsive.

A more ambitious field study project was conducted by Clifford (1973) among 700 publicly owned so-called threshold companies. Threshold companies are those that have grown very rapidly and stand at the point where they become giant corporations if they grow further. Depending upon the industry, the annual sales volume of these companies ranges from $20 million to $200 million. Clifford sets forth in detail the strategies used by these threshold companies in adapting to environmental forces as they grew. His content coverage is wide and includes organization structure, role of chief executive officers, product line strategies and financial strategies. He makes the point that even though each company is unique "there are common threads that run through the fabric of successful — and unsuccessful — growing threshold companies that can provide useful insights to management, and it is these common threads that we seek to draw out in this report" (Clifford, 1973: 5).

In contrast to Clifford's rapid growth companies is the research of Schendel and Patton (1976a) concerning stagnation and turnaround strategies. After examining net income data for 1800 firms, they selected 36 pairs and concluded that declining companies needed some severe jolt to spring them into action, but when they did stir themselves there were identifiable strategies which were appropriate to turning the situation around. Research in this general area is comparatively new. Others have made contributions through case analysis to our knowledge about strategies to prevent failure (Altman, 1971; Ross and Kami, 1973; Wilcox, 1976; Argenti, 1976).

There are many other areas for which contingency theories have been developed through case research. To illustrate, Kitching (1967) examined 181 mergers and acquisitions by 22 companies and found preferred strategies for successful acquisitions. Gutmann (1964) in an earlier study reached conclusions concerning preferred strategies for growth after examining 53 high-growth manufacturing firms. In a more recent study, Miller (1975) examined about 50 written cases and concluded, among other things, "Successful firms used more controls, scanning, delegation, and technocratization, had more resources, and lacked bureaucratic constraints. Their strategy making was more adaptive, innovative, integrated, multiplex, and analytical" (Miller, 1975: 65).

In addition, Hofer (1973) studied business case histories appearing in *Fortune* during the years 1960 to 1972. He examined five categories of strategic challenge in the firms' environment, and ten categories of strategic responses, and concluded that "different types of strategic challenges do indeed elicit different types of strategic responses." For example, the principal responses to increased total demand differs from the responses to saturated or decreased total demand. These differ from responses to technology, and so on.

Most of the above research focuses on strategy content and strategy formulation processes. Other case research has emphasized strategy implementation. The range of research in this area is wide and includes contingency theories of organizational design, budgeting systems design, and managerial style, as well as other aspects of implementation.

Corey and Star (1971: 53, 54) surveyed over 500 companies and found that "the type of program structure (product, market, or both) which a business has is a function of the type(s) of diversity with which it is faced." They also found that "businesses with program organizations seem to have been considerably more successful in developing and introducing new products than businesses without program organizations." Bower (1970) spent two years of field research in a large corporation studying its capital resource allocation process. He found the resource allocation process to be dependent upon a number of forces such as different levels in the organization, the technical and political processes at each level, and the nature of the planning system. Most of the contingency theory concerning implementation of strategy has been developed as a part of research in organization theory.

CONTINGENCY THEORIES DERIVED FROM ORGANIZATION THEORY

The work of organization theorists in recent years has focused on the interrelationships between environment and organizational structures. These efforts have been very helpful in understanding the interplay between the environment and organization design, but have not had quite the operational value to managers as many of the preceding types of research.

Contingency theories derived from organization theory were summarized in Steiner and Miner (1977: 51–52) and are given here in part and with additions, as follows.

The first major analysis of the interrelationships among environment, strategy, and structure was that of Chandler (1962). In a masterful analysis of 50 companies, explained in more detail in Galbraith's and Nathanson's paper, he concluded that strategy was directly related to the application of an enterprise's resources to market demand and that in turn brought major changes in organizational structures.

A step forward in facilitating cross-cultural comparative management studies was made with the work of Richman (1964) and Farmer and Richman (1965). They hypothesized that the practices as well as the effectiveness of managers were a function of external environmental variables. They reasoned that interfirm differences could be explained by variables in the environment and to advance the analysis they, and others (e.g., Schollhammer, 1969) developed classifications of environmental variables affecting the management of business firms. Despite these early typologies, research in the area "has not progressed beyond providing arbitrary classifications for separating environmental factors into certain groups: economic, social, cultural, etc. In other words, various environmental factors have not been operationalized, nor have testable hypotheses emerged from this approach" (Negandhi, 1975: 336).

Lawrence and Lorsch (1967a, 1967b) demonstrated convincingly that environment affects the subsystems of a company differently. If an organization is to be effective, each of its subsystems must react appropriately to its environment, and they all must be properly integrated as they discharge their roles in different ways as determined by the environment.

A large number of additional theories and research have been built upon the seminal works of Chandler (1962) and Lawrence and Lorsch (1967a, 1967b). Among other things, these studies have clarified the impacts of stable versus changing environments on different facets of organizations. For example, early theorists observed that organizations reacted to stable environments with centralized organization, highly specialized task orientation, close supervision of workers, a chain of command that is clear and followed, and inflexibility of procedures (Weber, 1946). On the other hand, more recent research shows that the appropriate response to rapidly changing environments is

decentralization, flatter organization structures (for example, wider span of control), dominance of organizational goal orientation, participation in decision making, and interpersonal managerial styles (Terreberry, 1968; Newman, 1971; Scott, 1973; Emery and Trist, 1965, 1973; Rhenman, 1973).

As researchers have probed deeper, they concluded that the way in which organizations reacted to environment was much more complex than earlier researchers thought. Furthermore, they concluded that there was no one "right" way to respond to changing environments. Rather, organizational design must be tailored to each situation (Emery and Trist, 1965; Lawrence and Lorsch, 1967a, 1967b; Pugh, Hickson, Hinings, and Turner, 1969; Negandhi, 1970; Child, 1972; Rhenman, 1973; Perrow, 1973; Lorsch and Allen, 1973; Emery and Trist, 1973; Miles et al., 1974; Lorsch and Morse, 1974; Negandhi, 1975; Nagashima, 1976; to mention but a few).

In reviewing contingency research based on organization theory, Perrow (1973: 11) concluded that: "As the growth of the field has forced ever more variables into our consciousness, flat claims of predictive power are beginning to decrease and research has become bewilderingly complex." So, as efforts are made to provide greater prescriptive values regarding structure and implementation for operating managers, the complexity of these theories begins to approach the conclusions of research growing out of case analysis.

A substantial body of research, erected on the findings of Chandler, has elaborated in considerable detail relationships between organizational performance and structure. Rumelt (1974), following Wrigley (1970), divided 200 of the largest firms in the United States into twelve classes and drew such conclusions as the following about financial performance:

1. Product-division firms showed average growth rates in earnings per share substantially higher than did the nondivisionalized firms.
2. No science-based company moved into the maturity and decline phase of its life cycle without diversifying and adopting a multidivisional structure.

3. Related business firms will, on the average, have higher profitability, higher rates of growth, and higher price-earnings ratios than other categories of firms.

Perhaps Rumelt's most significant finding is that "the [twelve] categories did separate firms into groups that displayed significant and consistent differences in financial performance." Channon (1973) examined the 100 largest firms in Great Britain and found trends in organization structure, between 1950 and 1970, very similar to the Rumelt results. Scott (1973) compared trends in structure in four European countries (United Kingdom, France, Germany, and Italy) and found comparable organizational structure trends.

Another thrust of organization theory in this general area concerns perceptions of environmental and strategic change. Anderson and Paine (1975) developed a theory of strategy content based on two environmental contingency variables. The first is the perceived uncertainty of the environment (certain or uncertain) and the second is the perceived need for strategic change (high or low). In each case, the relevant perceiver is the strategy decision-maker. Different strategies are proposed for each of the four quadrants. For example, under conditions of perceived environmental certainty and low need for change, strategies should stress defending the domain, expansion in "sure bet" areas only, integration to protect supplies and markets, efficient technological processes and maintenance of market share.

In a somewhat different analysis, Cook (1975) took as contingency variables perceived environmental press (hostile or benign) and organizational responsiveness orientation (stable or dynamic). He derived four hypotheses:

H_1 Stable organizations facing benign press tend to enact intensification (approach/conventional) strategies.

H_2 Dynamic organizations facing benign press tend to enact proactive (approach/creative) strategies.

H_3 Stable organizations facing hostile press tend to enact reactive (avoidance/conventional) strategies.

H_4 Dynamic organizations facing hostile press tend to enact mediative (avoidance/creative) strategies.

Cook undertook empirical tests of his hypotheses using 14 supermarket chains as a data base. The results provide support for his hypotheses. To be determined is the impact on performance of the indicated contingency conditions.

Newman's (1971) work in this area covers a much wider territory. In his study of management design and environment, he developed a matrix with one dimension the need for change (infrequent/frequent) and the other the nature of change (unprecedented/precedented). He then identified industries that fell into each of the quadrants and identified four major responses by management, namely: stable, regulated flexibility, temporary–ad hoc, and adaptive. For the first two and the last, he then postulated different management structures under the following headings: organizing, planning, leading, and controlling. The result, of course, is a contingency theory relating different management processes with different environmental changes and different managerial responses.

In another study focusing primarily on structural relationships, Lorsch and Allen (1973) examined 22 corporate headquarter units and divisional top management groups in six multinational firms to determine factors affecting their interrelationships. They concluded that the relationships were extremely complex and that there was no one best way to organize to assure smooth interrelationships. Using contingency theories of organization, however, they found among other things that lower performing conglomerates had far more complex organizational devices to achieve effective corporate-divisional coordination (or integration) and that they tended to achieve less effective corporate-divisional relationships. They also tended to have less effective interrelationships with their particular industry environments. The major integrating devices for effective interrelationships they found were: an annual budgeting system; an approved system for major capital and expense items; formal goal-setting system (performance evaluation and incentive compensation system); group vice presidents; direct managerial contact; a monthly budget review; and five-year planning systems.

It should be noted that much research has been directed at developing contingency theories of participation and motivation. Some positive conclusions have resulted from this research, but much of it also has been inconclusive. For instance, Searfoss and Monczka (1973: 543) found among other things that "a positive relationship exists between perceived participation in the budget process and the position in the organizational hierarchy." Mitchell (1973) found that in one setting increased participation may raise motivation, whereas in another setting the impact of motivation may be negative.

CONTINGENCY THEORIES DERIVED FROM EMPIRICAL EXPERIENCE

One thrust of research in this classification is the identification of environmental factors which will have the most significant impact on the success of the firm and the strategies to react appropriately to those factors. Some of the research noted above can qualify here, but I also want to focus at this point on features other than organization structure.

One significant thrust concerns the relationship between market share and profitability. An impressive study, which is continuing and is being used by a large number of companies, is PIMS (Profit Impact of Market Strategy) project. This project was first begun at General Electric when a top manager asked the director of market research to find out what information was available concerning the relationship of market share and operating economies. The result was a study initiated by Schoeffler and McKitterick of the performance of nearly 40 of General Electric's operating divisions. The scope of PIMS, now directed by the Strategic Planning Institute, has expanded well beyond the market share/profitability relationship.

PIMS has identified 37 factors that have a powerful and usually predictable influence on profitability, such as long-run industry growth rate, short-run market growth rate, market share, product quality, corporate size, and so on.

The results are given in a set of tables (usually three-by-three matrices). From this research, there has been developed a long list of conclusions, such as the following:

1. Vertically integrated businesses have an advantage, in the long run, in mature industries.
2. High levels of research and development spending pay off most in slow-growing markets.
3. Profitability from new products is greatest in stable markets.
4. The higher the market share the greater is the profitability.
5. Market position is most important when customers buy infrequently (Schoeffler, Buzzell, and Heany, 1974; Schoeffler, 1975).

The Boston Consulting Group has developed a large body of data concerning experience curves and has advanced the concept that all costs decrease with accumulated volume. These curves encompass all costs including capital, administrative, research and marketing. The experience curve is used as a basis for developing strategies about many subjects such as pricing, market entry, competitive stance, and product growth rates, to mention a few. Specific managerial guidelines are developed from these data, such as,

> There is clearly a direct relationship between market share and accumulated experience for a given product. The cost differentials among competitors — which is the critical factor in the ability to survive — should be a direct function of their respective accumulated experience (assuming competence and equal available costs for labor, materials and capital). Over time, then, the competitor with the greatest *sustained* market share should have the greatest accumulated experience and hence the lowest relative costs. Market share over time can therefore be very important to competitive strategy, and when translated into cost differentials, its value can be calculated quite precisely in quantitative terms (Boston Consulting Group, 1968: 30).

Chevalier (1972) and Fruhan (1972b) have reached conclusions in this area that elaborate on the PIMS and BCG research.

Another type of contingency research based upon empirical observation concerns strategic planning. Only two aspects of this research will be mentioned here. The first is a series of theories whose focus is improving strategic planning (Steiner, 1969; Mockler, 1971; Hussey, 1974; Rothschild, 1976; Lorange and Vancil, 1977; Steiner, 1977). Surprising agreement exists among these and other planning researchers about preferred designs for strategic planning systems. The most recent thrust in this area is the broadening of theories of strategy and strategy formulation processes into a contingency theory of strategic management (Ansoff, et al., 1976).

The second are contingency theories concerning different aspects of strategic planning systems. To illustrate, a number of researchers have concluded that formal strategic planning pays off in better sales, profits, and other financial terms. The first research in this area was done by Thune and House (1970). There have been many studies after this, the most recent of which is a study of 90 companies by Karger and Malik (1975). Steiner (1972) and Steiner and Schollhammer (1975) (based on surveys of experience among hundreds of companies in six industrialized countries) set forth pitfalls which should be avoided in strategic planning if effective results are to be achieved. Egerton and Brown (1972) interviewed executives and drafted contingency theories about the role of the chief executive in planning. To mention but one more, Lorange (1975) studied divisional planning systems and developed commonly used processes in those systems which were most effective.

Contingency theories have also been developed in other areas based on empirical observation. An early influential study into leadership was made by Fiedler (1967). He found that leadership effectiveness or success was dependent upon the appropriate matching of the individual leaders' style of interacting and the influence that the group situation provided. Effective leadership is as dependent on the situation as the group situation is on the leader.

There have been many other contingency studies based upon experience but this section will be concluded with mention of only a few, such as research and development strategies (Ansoff and Stewart, 1967); diversification strategies (Mace and Montgomery, 1962); product line strategies (Day, 1975); and financial strategies (Weston and Brigham, 1971).

CONTINGENCY THEORIES BASED ON CONCEPTUALIZATION

There are two types of theories I wish to mention in this classification. First, are the comprehensive conceptualizations such as that of Ansoff's *Corporate Strategy* (1965). This well-known book, whose focus was more on process than content, was a milestone in the development of an integrated theory of corporate strategy formulation.

Second, are listings of hypotheses or propositions. Glueck (1972), for example, set forth 71 hypotheses covering major strategies for a corporation. Many of his hypotheses are expressed in a universal way but a number are of a contingency nature.

Contingency variables proposed are: the degree of dependency of the firm; the extent to which the company is entrepreneurial; complexity of product line, technology, and environment; industry; the presence of long linked, mediating, or intensive technology; market share; stage of the product life cycle; growth rate of the market; volatility of the market; and company size.

Some of these hypotheses refer to a specific theoretical domain rather than subsuming the full variable range as in true contingency theory. Some derive from organization theory and some from case experience. The variable terminology, lack of logical relationships among the hypotheses, and on occasion the total failure to maintain internal consistency almost automatically invalidate such a list as a theory. The list is merely what the author originally presented it as — an attempt to get things started (Steiner and Miner, 1977: 779).

A number of proposition lists have been developed for the product life cycle. Luck and Prell (1968), for example, developed an exhaustive list of proposed strategies for different phases of the product life cycle. A little later Ansoff (1969) presented a list of descriptive propositions for strategic change in the product life cycle. A later listing, not nearly as extensive as that of Luck and Prell, was prepared by Wasson 1974). All these lists are based on contingency variables and thus advance contingency theories for strategy content in product life cycles.

There is another type of finding growing out of conceptualization that should be mentioned. This is illustrated by Drucker's (1974: 77, 79) discussion of company missions. Here is an area of very little published research and one of the major strategy decisions of an organization. He points out that the right mission for an enterprise is generally not obvious and that what is right "never emerges as a logical conclusion from postulates or from 'facts.' " It is, however, contingent on a number of variables, the most important of which are products, markets and top executive values.

SOME CHARACTERISTICS OF THE STATE-OF-THE-ART CONTINGENCY THEORIES OF STRATEGIC MANAGEMENT

Although the research cited above is merely illustrative of a vast literature, it does, I hope, capture the essence of scholarly activity in the development of contingency theories of strategic management. Together with other research, it provides a base for identifying some of the major characteristics of the current contingency theories of strategy content, strategy processes, organizational design, leadership, etc.

RESEARCH VOLUME IS IMPRESSIVE AND GROWING

In contrast to a decade ago, the volume of contingency theory development to date has been most impressive. The mere fact that Steiner and Miner (1977) recently accumulated well over 300 pages of research findings about strategy, a large part of which are from contingency research, and then only touched the surface of the results, underscores this point. It also explains why only a few of the many works and research topics could be included in this paper.

CONTINGENCY RESEARCH COVERS A WIDE RANGE OF SUBJECT MATTER AND IS EXPANDING

In the organization theory field, the first contingency theories concentrated on the relationship between environment and organizational design. Subsequent research in this area not only delved more deeply into details of that relationship, as for instance Rumelt's work, but moved into other directions as noted above. The research based on traditional cases has been rather diffuse from the very beginning, but has expanded its subject matter considerably.

Research has concentrated more on broad organizational design and environmental variables than on other aspects of strategic management, such as capital allocation, managerial styles, objectives and goals, product expansion, and research and development. Most research has concentrated on the organization as a whole rather than on major subparts. More research has related to corporate headquarters than major divisions with particular attention to different control relationships with headquarters and in different environmental settings. More research has been done about contingency theories for business strategies than for strategies at other levels or for other types of organizations. Finally, more research has concerned strategic processes than strategy content.

CONTINGENCY RESEARCH METHODOLOGIES HAVE COVERED A WIDE RANGE

Most of the research has been based upon written or field case surveys. This methodology is logical and necessary in a young discipline. Much of our research has also been based upon conceptualization. A good bit of the research has been quantified and verified by repeated testing, such as PIMS. In addition, some scholars are developing contingency theory from quantitative model building such as that of Hatten, Schendel, and Cooper (1978).

COMPREHENSIVE CONTINGENCY THEORIES OF STRATEGIC MANAGEMENT REMAIN TO BE PERFECTED

Despite the massive research strides that have been made in recent years, we have comparatively few aggregative contingency models and, where they do exist, they are at a rather high level of abstraction. As such, they serve more to illuminate and educate the scholarly observer of organizational strategy than to provide solid guidance to operational managers. Thus, what we have today is, with a few major exceptions, a limited domain theory which focuses on several important theoretical areas while ignoring broad interconnections with other models and systems. This is a point well argued by Moberg and Koch (1975).

Nonetheless, some of this theory and research does provide valuable guides for operating managers. Thus, it sorts out for managers classifications of contingencies from which it is easier to identify strategies which are preferable within a given area and situation. Some of the theories are rather precise in their prescription of preferred strategies, such as the PIMS findings.

Because of the absence of comprehensive contingency theories, and the great complexity of the variables affecting strategy identification, evaluation and implementation, few of the research findings have the power of law. Those that do are at a high level of abstraction and prescribe for broad cases, such as the virtue of divisionalization in a multiproduct organization.

I do believe, however, that in the next few years we shall have more and more guides, based upon research, which strategists in organizations can accept with confidence. As I noted, we do have many today. For a wide range of situations, however, the absence of research, or conflicts in research findings, or a limited focus on one small domain, leaves the operating manager with little or no sure guidance.

Nevertheless, the totality of research effort to date leaves no doubt in my mind that there is a distinct field of scholarly inquiry concerned with strategy and strategic management and that it is moving towards conceptual maturity. As Steiner and Miner (1977: 781–782) have noted, "The key point is that it [the policy/ strategy area] is no longer drawing primarily on other disciplines and functional fields to create an unstable amalgam of theories, hypotheses, and data with little apparent relationship to one another. It is now a discipline that is generating its own indigenous knowledge and with which certain individuals find their primary professional identity." Contingency theory

has had a major part to play in this development.

RESEARCH OPPORTUNITIES AND METHODOLOGIES

FUTURE RESEARCH OPPORTUNITIES

If what has been said so far is anywhere near to picturing realistically the present state-of-the-art of contingency theories in the strategic management area, it is apparent that great opportunities for research exist. The following are a few areas where more research can and should be pursued which conceivably can have an important impact on the development of a comprehensive contingency theory of strategic management:

1. Very little research has been done on the factors determining which missions, purposes, and philosophies are preferred in which environmental (internal as well as external) conditions. This is an extremely difficult area to research because there are so many different variables that can influence conclusions. Nevertheless, decisions made at this level are of the highest importance in strategic decision making throughout an organization.

2. Very little research has been done on factors influencing the design of formal strategic planning systems. There is no such thing as an ideal strategic planning system. Each organization is unique and each system, therefore, differs from all others. But empirical observations show there are common characteristics among planning systems which are influenced by different environmental forces such as managerial style, size of organization, turbulence of environment, intensity of competition, capital/labor intensity of product, and so on. We have not identified very clearly major types of strategic planning systems nor the factors which most influence their design and effectiveness. A valuable start in this direction is that of Lindsay and Rue (1976), who surveyed 198 companies and related the impact of environmental complexity to the use of computers, the setting of goals, the sophistication of the planning design, plan-

ning review intervals, and people participation.

3. Not enough research has been done on preferred strategies concerning social programs pursued by an organization in light of variable environmental forces.

4. Not enough research has been done on preferred strategies to acquire environmental knowledge that is most needed in making decisions in different situations. No company can examine thoroughly all environmental conditions which may influence strategic decisions. How does a company determine precisely what environmental forces to examine in making strategic decisions of particular types? How does a company determine how much effort to devote to what data gathering?

5. Some years ago a study was made about strategic factors most significant in the success of firms in different industries (Steiner, 1969). These factors were found to be common to companies in the same industry, but very different among different industries. Further research in this direction seems warranted.

6. Much has been done, as noted above, regarding strategies for different stages of the product life cycle. This research could be pursued further in different directions. For instance, deeper penetration into specific types of products might well produce useful guidelines to managers. Deeper research would be useful into environmental variables having the most important impact on strategies at each stage in the product life cycle.

7. With the growing interest in more participation in organizations, more research is needed concerning results of participation under different conditions. For instance, what are the preferred relationships among degrees and types of participation (e.g., intimate, need to know, group, etc.), types of decision making (e.g., capital allocations, long-range planning, budgeting), and environmental variables (e.g., large organizations, small organizations, etc.)?

8. Most of the research on contingency theories of strategy content, structure, etc., has been focused on business enterprises. Many of the results are applicable to other organizations, but not-for-profit organizations also have characteristics which differ significantly from business organizations. With the growth in importance of the not-for-profit area much more needs to be done in developing contingency theories of strategic management in the area.

9. Most of the research for business organizations has been focused on corporate headquarters. Great opportunities exist for research in the understanding of preferred relationships between headquarters and divisions and within divisions.

10. We need much replication of past research to see whether different scholars reach the same conclusions. Much of the past research has met high scholarly standards. Nevertheless, most of what has been done needs to be verified with larger samples and/or extended to include more variables. Until this is done questions about the conclusiveness of results are bound to arise.

11. Deeper research is needed in important areas where significant research has already been done. I have in mind, for instance, the excellent work of Fiedler (1967) on leadership, which needs further follow-up. Utecht and Heier (1976) tested Fiedler's contingency model (described above) through structured questionnaires given to 495 military officers and they concluded that Fiedler's "contingency model would be no better than pure chance as a predictor of successful military leadership." This does not mean, of course, that Fiedler's contingency model is not useful. It indeed is. What is needed, of course, is more and deeper research among more variables and situations.

12. Finally, but not least, we need much more study of the manager as a variable. This person's perceptions, biases, irrationalities, and style of management, to note a few variables, have highly significant bearings on strategic choices. A little work has been done in this area, but we have not yet begun to appreciate these variables in decision making let alone understand their influence in different situations and types of strategic decision making.

Research Methodologies

As noted above, a variety of research methodologies has been used in developing and testing contingency theories in the strategic management area. All, of course, should be continued. Among them all, however, I believe most emphasis should be placed on creative and intensive field research. I agree with Mintzberg (1977: 94) when he writes:

> Students of research methodology in the social sciences generally agree that at early stages in the study of a phenomenon, there is a need to use less rigorous, more exploratory approaches, that can encompass more variables. Only by remaining open to the rich complexity of reality can effective theory building be initiated in a new field. This applies especially to phenomena that involve the close interrelationships of many variables, most of which are difficult to measure.

While we have an abundance of hypotheses and theories in certain areas there is a dearth in other areas. We need more inductive research to build new theories. We need more research to link findings in limited domains research with other limited domains research. This will require creativity and imagination of a high order, for we are dealing with messy phenomena and with variables difficult to measure. Field research provides a superb laboratory to find and understand better the rich complexity of forces influencing strategic choices in operational settings.

As research increases, there are certain pitfalls that must be avoided, as Steiner and Miner (1977: 780–781) note:

> One is that hypotheses should not be tested using the same case data that were used to generate them in the first place. Another is that when hypotheses are derived from analyses of a set of cases by factor analysis or some similar technique, the hypotheses cannot be assumed to be true because they derive from data; they must be tested on another independent data set. Another is that causation cannot be attributed to a particular independent variable unless other correlated variables are controlled either statistically or experimentally. And yet another is extrapolating from limited data to widespread applications. Pitfalls of this kind have marred research in the past; they are in fact inevitable in an emerging field. But to obtain valid answers to important research questions, they need to be kept to a minimum.

CONCLUDING COMMENT

Research on contingency theories of strategy and strategic management has advanced significantly during the past handful of years. It has reached the point where policy/strategy is a discipline of its own and is reaching towards some maturity. It is, however, far from becoming a discipline where underlying comprehensive theories tie together major parts of the phenomenon involved. If one accepts the broad concepts of contingency theory and strategic management used in this paper, there are major gaps in our theories. This provides great opportunities for scholars. A wide variety of research methodologies are applicable and needed in exploiting these opportunities. Among them all, however, field research is still a favored method to achieve significant prescriptive theories. Creative conceptualizations are also, of course, major approaches to advancing the theoretical strength in the field.

We should not expect too much too soon, however, by way of comprehensive conclusive theories because much of the strategy area is extremely complex. Even relatively small variances among major variables can result in significant changes, either in strategic choice or outcome. Faced with identical environmental conditions, two managers may make very different strategic choices and each may achieve equally successful outcomes. Despite these problems, which create challenging opportunities for scholars, I anticipate important results from research in the near future.

However, we shall not see soon, in my judgment, a well-rounded comprehensive theory of strategic management. The best we can hope for is more penetrating limited domain contingency theories and more work on integrating such limited domain theories. If that is well done, however, it can illuminate significantly our scholarly knowledge of how organizations operate. It can also produce important prescriptive guidelines for managers in formulating and implementing strategy.

Commentary

FRANK T. PAINE
University of Maryland

INTRODUCTION

Steiner has done a reasonably comprehensive job in discussing the major thrusts in the development of contingency theories of the strategy formulation process, of strategy content and of organizational structure and processes. He also discusses some characteristics of the state-of-the-art of contingency theories in strategic management and the research opportunities and methodologies associated with such theories. Steiner recognizes the lack of integration among contingency theory building in the strategic management area, but does not attempt to pursue such integration.

Because of the comprehensiveness of Steiner's review, this paper will not further evaluate existing limited domain contingency theories, but rather will attempt to pull together some of the broad interconnections in existing limited domain contingency theories to show how a more comprehensive contingency theory of strategic management might be developed. Specifically, this commentary will focus on developing an integrated contingency theory of strategic management applicable to both the corporate and business levels of large firms, based primarily on existing contingency theories of strategy process, strategy content, organization design, etc., derived from the organization theory tradition. No attempt will be made to draw upon or integrate into this model the various contingency theories derived from the case tradition or conceptualization. Nor will it be possible to cite all of the empirical research upon which this model is based or to elaborate on all the concepts introduced.

PREVIOUS ORGANIZATION THEORY, CONTINGENCY THEORIES, AND WHAT'S NEEDED TO TIE THEM TOGETHER

Organization theorists have tended to focus on limited domains within the strategic management-strategy process (e.g., Newman, 1971; Anderson and Paine, 1975), strategy content (e.g., Cook, 1975; Anderson and Paine, 1975), performance outcomes and structure (e.g., Farmer and Richman, 1965; Lawrence and Lorsch, 1967a; Scott, 1973; Emery and Trist, 1973; Channon, 1973; and Rumelt, 1974). To develop an integrated contingency theory of strategic management, the following steps are needed:

1. combine the limited domain theories into an overall contingency framework
2. develop hypotheses about the relationships among the concepts in those theories
3. check for the validity of the relationships, i.e., are they logical? Are they operational? Do they have generality? Are they parsimonious? Is there empirical evidence to support them?

The final form of the integrated contingency theory of strategic management developed here will provide sequential guides for managers to sort out classifications of contingencies from which it will be easier to identify strategies and capabilities which are preferable within a given area and situation. However, this attempt is only a beginning step toward the final form.

THE OVERALL CONTINGENCY FRAMEWORK

The framework to be used in this model includes five main parts: (1) A Contingency Profile of Environmental Uncertainty, (2) A Matrix of Appropriate Contingency Strategies and Capability Profiles, (3) A Contingency Profile of the Firm's (or Business's) Current Position, (4) An Assessment of the Need for Strategic Change, and (5) A Program for Implementing Strategic Change. These parts fit together as shown in the flow diagram in Exhibit 7.8. Each part has sub-parts which will be explained later.

Exhibit 7.8 Overall Contingency Framework

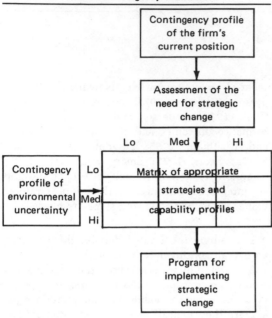

The framework may be used at either the corporate level or at the business level within an organization depending on the nature of the firm's environment. If the firm operates businesses in relatively independent environments, each with its own distinctive threats, trends, and opportunities, then use of the framework for each business segment is analytically meaningful (Ansoff and Leontiades, 1976). To identify such business segments, consideration is given to differences in geography, customers/ clients, technology, product lines and maturity of markets. If significant variations are present in one or more of these variables, sub-divisions should be considered.

PROFILING THE FIRM'S ENVIRONMENTAL UNCERTAINTY

Uncertainty appears to make a difference in type of organization's strategy and structure (e.g., Lawrence and Lorsch, 1967a; Cook, 1975; Galbraith, 1977). Furthermore, uncertainty in the firm's environmental segment(s) can be profiled for a number of attributes, such as lack of

knowledge of threats and opportunities, price competition, promotion and distribution competition, technological change, technological diversity, societal pressures, customer pressures, length of public life cycle, stages in the life cycle, socio-cultural change, and unpredictable shifts in government policies to name a few (Ansoff, et al., 1976; Khandwalla, 1977).

The profile in Exhibit 7.9 highlights the degree (amount) of the uncertainty, as well as the relative importance of the uncertainty, for each attribute. Careful analysis and judgment of the situation relative to other organizations or environmental segments is necessary to develop the profile.

The attributes in the profile can be combined into a composite measure of environmental uncertainty because increases in uncertainty in any of these attributes increases the amount of information that must be processed by the organization (Galbraith, 1977). Therefore, variations in broad strategy and capability profile are hypothesized to be variations in the ability of the organization to process information about events that could not be anticipated in advance. For example, adjusting a strategy toward more integration improves the organization's capability to process information relating to uncertainties among its suppliers and/or distributors.

APPROPRIATE CONTINGENCY STRATEGIES AND CAPABILITIES

Starting with the observation that an organization's broad strategy should reflect the degree of environmental uncertainty it faces, it is postulated that its broad strategy will differ based on the extent of gap between its present position and its goals. Using these two factors — environmental uncertainty and gap size, a matrix of appropriate contingency strategies and capability profiles may be developed (Exhibit 7.10). Hypotheses for only four of the cells are indicated. Some support for these hypotheses exists (Khandwalla, 1976; Paine and Anderson, 1977). For example, if a business faces conditions of environmental certainty and low gap size, its broad strategy and capability profile should stress defending the domain, efficiency

Exhibit 7.9   Profile Levels of Uncertainty in Each Segment

	Low			Medium		High	
State of knowledge about T/O							
Intensity	1	2	3	4	5	6	7
Importance	1	2	3	4	5	6	7
Price competition							
Intensity	1	2	3	4	5	6	7
Importance	1	2	3	4	5	6	7
Promotion and distribution competition							
Intensity	1	2	3	4	5	6	7
Importance	1	2	3	4	5	6	7
Technological changes	Slow			Medium		Fast	
Intensity	1	2	3	4	5	6	7
Importance	1	2	3	4	5	6	7
Technological diversity	Low			Medium		High	
Intensity	1	2	3	4	5	6	7
Importance	1	2	3	4	5	6	7
Societal pressures							
Intensity	1	2	3	4	5	6	7
Importance	1	2	3	4	5	6	7
Customer pressures							
Intensity	1	2	3	4	5	6	7
Importance	1	2	3	4	5	6	7
Product life cycle	Long			Medium		Short	
Intensity	1	2	3	4	5	6	7
Importance	1	2	3	4	5	6	7
Stage of product life cycle	Maturity	Early growth		Late growth		Emergence decline	Shift in stage
Intensity	1	2	3	4	5	6	7
Importance	1	2	3	4	5	6	7

with known technology, maintenance of share, and little risk taking and innovation. By contrast, in businesses where uncertainty and the gap size are high, major reallocations at the organizational level should take place with new products, new markets, new technologies or, if the gap size is too high, divestiture or harvest strategies. A broad turnaround strategy (Schendel and Patton, 1976a) or a threshold strategy for rapid growth also may be needed (Clifford, 1973). However, if the gap size is smaller another broad strategy may be appropriate. Since related business firms have, on the average, higher financial performance than other categories of firms, perhaps diversification into related areas should be stressed (Channon, 1973; Rumelt, 1974).

In addition, the organization's detailed strategy should be formulated by processes and structures consistent with the above factors (e.g., Ansoff and Stewart, 1967; Lorange and Vancil, 1977; Steiner, 1977). In the previous example of low uncertainty-low gap size, an adaptive planning process for strategy making

Exhibit 7.10 An Integrated Contingency Theory Model Gap Between Present Position and Goals

		Low	Medium	High

Environmental uncertainty	**Low**	*Strategy process*
		
		  Adaptive planning
		  Integration of on-going activities
		
		Strategy content
		
		  Defend the domain, efficiency with
		    known technology
		  Maintenance of market share
		  Environmental management stresses
		    independence
		
		Overall capability profile
		
		  Closed/Stable/Mechanistic
		  Reject change
				Strategy process
				
				  Long range planning
				  Integration of on-going activities
				
				Strategy content
				
				  Integration, improve distinctive
				    competence
				  Search for market share
				  Environmental management stresses
				    independence
				
				Overall capability profile
				
				  Closed/Stable/Mechanistic
				  Attitude of accept change as necessary

	Medium			

	High	*Strategy process*
		
		  Adaptive entrepreneur
		  Environmental awareness
		
		Strategy content
		
		  Expansion to related markets & products
		  Know technology, maintain flexibility
		  Environmental management stresses
		    cooperative relationships
		
		Overall capability profile
		
		  Open/Adaptive/Organic
		  Product division, matrix
		  Seek familiar change
				Strategy process
				
				  Entrepreneurial or stress
				  Environmental awareness
				
				Strategy content
				
				  Divestiture, harvest or expansion of
				    markets, new technology, new
				    marketing concepts
				  Environmental management stresses
				    cooperative relationships
				
				Overall capability profile
				
				  Personal control, venture management
				  Risk taking
				  Create change

should be followed with little proactive scanning of the environment. Emphasis in the process should be on linking or integrating on-going activities. By contrast, where uncertainty and the gap size are high, an entrepreneurial approach to planning should be followed resorting to more personal control, innovation and risk taking. The strategy process should focus heavily on environmental awareness.

ASSESSING THE FIRM'S CURRENT POSITION

The firm's current position has three parts which need assessment: (1) its broad Strategy, (2) its Overall Capability Profile, and (3) its Top Management Coalition. These assessments should be independently verified.

BROAD STRATEGY

The broad strategy includes the existing organizational missions, purposes, and objectives; policies to achieve them; and methods needed to assure that the broad strategy is implemented to achieve organizational ends.

OVERALL CAPABILITY PROFILE

The firm's capability profile relative to competition or potential competition makes a difference in the type of broad strategy it should follow. More overall experience than competition, for example, may provide a cost and technological advantage which will permit advantageous pricing strategies (Boston Consulting Group, 1968). The overall capability profile subsumes such variables as cost and technological position, financial situation, knowledge, skill, power, attitudes, processes, roles, programs, and structure. Configuring these capability profiles to maintain more flexibility and autonomy is more necessary when there is high uncertainty in the environmental segment(s) (e.g., Burns and Stalker, 1961; Ansoff, 1976). Configuring the structure into product divisions consistent with a diversification strategy shows, on the average, favorable performance results (e.g., Scott, 1973; Rumelt, 1974).

TOP MANAGEMENT COALITION

The perceptions, values and relative power of this coalition (the inner circle) affect the adjustments of strategies and capabilities to the environmental segment(s) (e.g., Bower, 1970; Child, 1972; Guth, 1972; Khandwalla, 1977; Mintzberg, 1977).

THE NEED FOR STRATEGIC CHANGE

The magnitude of the gap between the firm's current position (in terms of economic performance) and its desired position should be measured. When this is done, the firm could plot where it should be and where it is to determine the need for change in its environmental segment(s), strategy process, strategy content, and capability profile.

IMPLEMENTING STRATEGIC CHANGE

The components in this section of the model include: (1) Environmental Management, (2) Internal Change Strategies, and (3) Portfolio and Business Strategies.

ENVIRONMENTAL MANAGEMENT

First, the appropriate broad strategy should be adopted. The choice of broad strategy will determine the environment, and in particular, the stakeholders (consumers, suppliers competition, regulators) who will be affected by the change. The firm should attempt to manage or modify this environment in order to reduce uncertainty about critical events.

In choosing strategies by which to manage the environment, the organization balances its needs for autonomy and flexibility against the exchange of commitments to reduce uncertainty and get cooperation and coordination. Where there is lower uncertainty, the firm should rely more heavily on strategies which stress independence, that is, competition, public relations, and voluntary response. Other strategies which may be more costly in terms of autonomy reduction, such as contracting (negotiating an agreement), coopting, coalescing, are more necessary when uncertainty is high (e.g., Galbraith, 1977).

INTERNAL CHANGE STRATEGIES

In addition to modifying the environment, the organization can attempt to change its own strategy process and capability profile. There are numerous change strategies available. However, these various change strategies may be placed in three categories: rational-empirical, power-coercive, and normative-reeducation (Chin and Benne, 1976). The selection of a change strategy by the top management coalition is contingent on assumptions about the nature of stakeholders affected.

A rational-empirical change strategy assumes the stakeholders will follow rational self-interest and will thus change if it can be demonstrated that they will benefit by the change. This change strategy involves various methods of educating stakeholders about new and "better" alternatives. A power-coercive change strategy is based on the assumption that the relevant stakeholders are basically motivated by political and economic interests. In dealing with stakeholders who are to be influenced, the organization would try to find out where their vested interests lie and to uncover power and financial motives for change. Normative-reeducative change strategies are more complex and time consuming. They see stakeholders as having varied mixtures of cognitive, affective and social motives. Stakeholders' ideas, feelings about and commitments to certain practices, as well as to the effect of group pressures and norms, are to be considered. Again, however, the relative power of the organization vis-à-vis its stakeholders is important in selecting a change strategy.

PORTFOLIO AND BUSINESS STRATEGIES

The previous description and classification suggests broad categories of actions that might be taken for improving performance outcomes. More specific analysis of contingencies will be necessary to provide detailed guidance.

Before proceeding, however, it is important to distinguish between two distinct areas of strategy: (1) business unit strategy, and (2) portfolio strategy. The basic differences? Business units are concerned with issues such as the marketing mix, cost position, competitive position, and new product/market segments. By contrast, the corporation as a whole is (or should be) concerned with the process of resource reallocation among different business units to improve the corporate portfolio. A business has little value to its stockholders unless it yields cash today or growth and compounded cash later. Since it takes cash to grow, cash is all important. Each business can be categorized according to its cash needs as: (1) fund, (2) maintain, or (3) harvest. The categorization of any business may be based on analysis of market strength, market growth, net cash flow and invested capital (Boston Consulting Group, 1968; Ansoff and Leontiades, 1976). For example, a business with low uncertainty-low gap size-low cash needs would be categorized as

"maintain." A key question, then, is what does the unit have to do to dominate and maintain a defensible (and for profit seeking organizations, a profitable) position? A defensible position permits accumulation of experience with associated relative cost advantages. The experience curve and various contingencies such as stage of product life cycle, length of product life cycle, degree of product differentiation, and rate of technological change, should be used for developing strategies about many subjects such as pricing, promotion, market entry, and research and development to name a few (e.g., Chevalier, 1972; Fruhan, 1972b; Glueck, 1972; Schoeffler, et al., 1974; Hofer, 1975).

Congruency or consistency checks can be made between various strategies and environmental profiles. Investment criteria and feedbacks can be developed appropriate to each strategy by business and cash flow by business. The overall corporate needs can be identified for a different balance in the portfolio for more growth, for more cash and/or for changes in financial arrangements.

Such portfolio balance may provide the organization faced with high environmental uncertainty some degree of protection from risk. However, besides making sure that the organization is not overly dependent on any one business, consideration also needs to be given to possible overdependence on any one external resource area or any one group of stakeholders, otherwise sudden discontinuity might cripple the organization. Environmental management (previously discussed) is needed. Internally, top management may deal with environmental uncertainty by configuring the capability profile of the organization for quick and efficient transferability. A tradeoff may be made with some loss of cost advantage from specialization and experience.

SUMMARY AND CONCLUSION

This paper has tried to develop an integrated contingency theory of strategic management based on various limited domain contingency theories of strategy process, strategy content, and organizational design, etc., coming primarily from the organization theory tradition. It has not tried to bring together all contingency theories from the case or conceptualization tradition. Nor has it included all of the empirical research on these topics. Hopefully it is a useful start, but it is also clear that much more work still needs to be done.

Qualitative Research Methods in Strategic Management

ROBERT B. DUNCAN
Northwestern University

INTRODUCTION

The objective of this paper is to provide an overview of qualitative research methods that can be applied to policy research questions.[1] The paper will cover three areas. First, it will differentiate qualitative and quantitative research methods. Second, it will identify some current policy research questions that require qualitative research methods. Third, it will discuss the different types of qualitative methods and how they can be used in studying policy research questions.

QUALITATIVE VS. QUANTITATIVE RESEARCH METHODS

The focus of this paper is qualitative research methods and thus it becomes important to differentiate these from quantitative research methods. However, in making this distinction it should be clear that the functions of each method are complementary rather than contradictory. Qualitative methods take a phenomenologist reference. The qualitative approach thus is concerned with understanding human behavior from the actor's frame of reference (Weber, 1968). The methods of qualitative research yield descriptive data which enable the researcher to see the situation as the actors see it (Bogdan and Taylor, 1975). The qualitative approach then asks the following questions: (1) What's going on here? (2) What are the forms of the phenomenon? (3) What are the variations in this phenomenon? (Lofland, 1971).

Quantitative analysis takes a different approach, a positivist one. Positivism was developed by Comte (1816) and Durkheim (1938) and focuses on the facts or causes of social phenomena with little regard for the subjective states of individuals. This methodology uses questionnaires, inventories, and demographic analysis which produce "numbers" which can be statistically analyzed to reject relationships between operationally defined variables. The quantitative approach then focuses on the following questions: (1) What are the causes of a social phenomenon, the forms it assumes and the variations it displays? and (2) What are the consequences of the phenomenon, the forms it assumes, the variations it displays? (Lofland, 1971).

One can take issue with quantitative methods' ability alone to truly deal with the issue of causation. Quantitative methods by themselves may ignore much of the process phenomena associated with a particular research question so that a real understanding of what's happened may not exist. For example, an organization may have changed its structure to a more decentralized mode in order to implement its new strategy for diversification. The researchers may have collected performance data to measure what impact this structural change has had on organizational performance. The quantitative data may indicate that in fact this structural change did not work to improve performance. Without qualitative data that focuses on the processes of "what happened," the researchers may never be able to understand why the structural change was not effective in increasing the firm's performance. It may have not been successful because the managers who were required to work in this new structure did not have the skills and abilities to implement this change. The quantitative data by itself may not have information on this breakdown in the implementation process.

It is important here to emphasize that we are

---

[1] This discussion is not meant to be a comprehensive analysis of qualitative research methods. For this the reader should see Lofland (1976), Bogdan and Taylor (1975), Mehan and Wood (1975), and Filstead (1970).

not proposing that one research strategy is more appropriate than the other, or that choosing a quantitative or qualitative approach is an either/or choice. Each form of data is useful for *both* theory verification or testing and the generation of new theory. In fact, in some studies the best strategy may be to use both approaches. The researcher may be interested in both *discovering* the nature and characteristics of the phenomena associated with the research question and, at the same time, *ascertaining causes* and relationships between other phenomena associated with the research question.

CURRENT POLICY RESEARCH QUESTIONS

Whether one pursues a qualitative or quantitative research approach must depend on the kind of research problem one is studying. If one understands what the phenomena are and understands their characteristics, then one is in a better position to start focusing on causes and relationships among the various components of the phenomena and thus start using quantitative techniques. On the other hand, if it is unclear just what the phenomena are, then qualitative research techniques are more relevant. The researcher cannot be concerned with issues of causation when there is little or no understanding regarding the phenomenon in question.

Currently, the policy field is at an early stage of development in that many of the research problems of interest still have not been adequately defined in terms of their components and characteristics. For example, there is much discussion about organizational adaptation, yet very little is known about this phenomenon and its characteristics. It is necessary to first discover what the components of adaptation are before the question of what causes it is pursued.

The current state of development of policy theory and research is due mainly to the complexity of the problems that policy researchers are interested in. It is not that policy researchers are less capable of doing research than, say, their colleagues in organization theory. Rather,

it is that the phenomena they are interested in are very complex. Because of the complexity of the phenomena it focuses on, policy as a field is still in a state of theory development as its primary concern.

Exhibit 7.11 provides a classification of topics in policy. These topics are broken down into two broad areas: inputs to the policy process and the policy making process itself. Managerial roles, organizational design, and organizational processes are the elements that contribute to environmental analysis, strategic decision making, strategy formulation and implementation of strategies in the policy making process.

Exhibit 7.12 presents a list of policy research questions that fall under each of the seven categories in Exhibit 7.11. These questions are not meant to be exhaustive, but rather attempt to representatively illustrate some of the key research questions in policy that can facilitate theory development. These categories of questions will now be briefly discussed.

MANAGERIAL WORK

This set of issues focuses on just what managers do. What are the key activities that managers perform and how do these activities relate to the strategic decision making process and strategy formulation? Here the interest is in just what different roles managers play. What is the process by which managers affect strategic decision making and policy formulation? Also of concern is how managers change the different roles they perform over time. For example, the manager is a decision maker as well as a decision implementer. How does that manager's behavior in terms of interpersonal style, affective orientation, etc., toward others change as he/she performs these two different roles? Initiating and making a decision require reflection, assimilating diverse data, selecting among alternatives — all of which are primarily cognitive, intellectual skills. Implementing the decision requires additional skills. Important implementation skills are related to understanding people, getting their cooperation, etc. Just how do managers make this transition and what are the processes involved?

From the above issues regarding managerial

Exhibit 7.11 Topics of Management Policy

work, one can see that much of our concern is on identifying the phenomenon. Thus, qualitative methodological approaches are required.

ORGANIZATION DESIGN

Here the concern is with how the organization is designed structurally to accomplish its objectives. How does the structure of the organization affect the way decision makers communicate? How does organization structure affect the information flow in the organization? Given that different organizational structures are appropriate for different decision environments, how do organizational decision makers *change* the structure – what are the processes involved? For example, as the organization's environment moves from being relatively stable and simple to more complex and dynamic, just how do organizational decision makers go about changing their structure to be more flexible and less bureaucratic in order to deal with this changed environment?

Another critical design process about which relatively little is known is the process of co-ordination among units that are highly interdependent. For example, the logic of the decentralized organization structure is that it allows the organization to segment its environment and organize around markets or product areas. This organization design strategy then reduces the information requirements any one organizational unit will require. It will have its own resources and will only have to deal with its particular environment rather than the overall environment of the firm. This strategy works well until some interdependence develops between two decentralized units. Now the units will have to coordinate their activities. What are the components of this coordination process? How does one manage coordination? Once again the attempt is to *identify* the phenomenon involved.

A particularly important issue regarding organization design is how does structure affect the strategic decision making process and policy

Exhibit 7.12   A Sampling of Current Policy Research Questions

Managerial roles

1. What are the key tasks of managerial work?
2. How do these key tasks vary from manager to manager and across different organizations?
3. What roles do different managers emphasize?
4. How do managerial roles change over time given the key problems facing the organization?

Organization design

1. How does structure affect *process* of communication, decision making, goal setting, etc.?
2. Given that different structures are appropriate for different decision environments—how do decision makers *change* the structure over time to deal with different situations?
3. How does one design-structure the organization to respond most effectively to a changing environment?
4. How are coordination processes set up in very decentralized organizations to deal with interdependence that may exist between divisions?
5. What impact does organization structure have on the formulation of strategy?
6. Does strategy lead to structure or does structure determine strategy?
7. How do influences from the environment of the organization affect organization structure?

Organizational processes

1. How do power relationships within the organization affect the decision making process?
2. What is the political behavior of individual managers as they attempt to get organization to act in line with their interest?
3. How is the organization's dominant coalition set up and how does it change over time and what are factors leading to membership in the dominant coalition?
4. How does the organization's ideology (values—beliefs) get shaped and shift as powerful and influential interest groups take control of the organization?
5. How do external coalitions (those influences outside the organization) and internal coalitions (those influences inside the organization) attempt to influence decision making?
6. What kinds of power configurations develop within and between internal and external coalitions?
7. What factors facilitate information exchange across divisional boundaries in organization?
8. What factors facilitate more effective headquarters field relations?

Environmental analysis

1. What are the major constraints in the environment as they affect strategic decision making?
2. What are changing demands the organization's environment is making on the organization?
3. What information does the organization need from the environment to anticipate changes and where does this information come from?
4. How can the organization anticipate environmental changes so that it will be in a better position to influence the direction of these changes?

Making strategic decisions

1. What are the key stages of strategic decision process?
2. What is the process by which strategic decisions are identified by managers and the strategic decision situation then diagnosed?
3. How might the nature of strategic decisions in terms of stimuli evoking them, their solutions, and processes used to arrive at them affect how decision makers deal with them?
4. Is the process of making strategic decisions different from making important decisions at lower levels of the organization?
5. Who are the participants in the strategic decision making process and how does their make-up change over time?

Formulation of strategies

1. How does the organization's ideology affect strategy formulation?
2. What are the stages of strategy formulation?
3. What are sources of influence on strategy formulation process?
4. Are there different styles of strategy formulation? If so, how do they differ?
5. How do organizations change their strategy to adapt to their environments?
6. What are the components of the planning process?
7. What are the stages—cycles of the planning process—and how do they change over time?

Strategy implementation

1. What are processes for effective strategy implementation?
2. How do strategic decision makers deal with resistance to implementation of their solutions?
3. How does organizational politics affect implementation?
4. What structural alterations are required to implement strategic decisions?
5. How are departures from current strategies initiated in the organization? Once an organization implements a new strategy how is that strategy revised?

formulation process? Initially, when the organization is created, strategy may in fact, as Chandler (1962) indicated, influence how the organization is structured. However, after the initial design is established, might not the structure of the organization in fact affect both strategic decision making and policy formulation? For instance, once an organization is highly decentralized with numerous decision makers, will it not be hard for that organization to pursue a stratgey that would require recentralization of decision making, etc.? The current decentralized units would strongly resist such a major shift in strategy. Also, it may be that the structure of the organization and the resulting management information system only allow decision makers to see certain things in their environment. If in fact organizations are rational, as Thompson (1967) has proposed, and thus structure themselves to buffer their technical core from uncertainty in the environment, then they may in fact "structure out uncertainty" and the key information associated with it. Thus, organizational decision makers may be assuming more certainty in their environment than there is and therefore do not identify the need to change their strategy.

An examination of the research questions identified regarding organization structure again indicates that in most instances we are trying to identify the processes involved. Thus our research strategy has to be qualitative.

Organizational Processes

Here the focus is on the power and communication processes in the organization. How do power relationships within the organization and between the organization and its environment affect the strategic decision making process and formulation process? What are the politics of organizational decision making? How do the dominant coalitions in the organization form? What is the basis for membership in the dominant coalition? What are the skills, expertise, etc., that qualify people to participate in this dominant source of influence inside the organization? How and why does the coalition change over time? How does the organization's ideology in terms of values and beliefs that the

dominant coalition subscribes to, get developed and modified over time?

Of particular interest here is how organizational politics affect strategy formulation. As the organization contemplates a shift in strategy, what are the political maneuverings that take place? For example, how does the chairman-CEO manage his board of directors to make sure changes in strategy get accepted? What are the influence processes involved here?

Here again, most of the research questions involved an identification of the processes involved, so a qualitative research strategy is indicated.

Environmental Analysis

Environmental analysis is concerned with diagnosing the nature of the organization's environment. What do organizational decision makers need to concern themselves with regarding the environment? Any organizational environment has the potential of being infinitely complex for decision makers. Thus, a key problem for organizations is one of defining the organization's domain. In defining domain, organizational decision makers determine the kinds of outputs the organization will produce and the components in the environment it will deal with. The interesting policy question is how do organizations define their domain? What is the process involved? Also how do organizations scan their environments? What are the behaviors of scanning units? Aguilar (1967) has addressed some of the latter questions, but more research is needed.

Once more, a qualitative research strategy is required since most of the research questions revolve around identifying the phenomena in question.

Making Strategic Decisions

Strategic decision making focuses on the fundamental decisions an organization makes that affect its operations. Examples of strategic decisions would be deciding to develop a new product, to change the CEO, or to implement a new computer based management information system. Once again, in studying this phenomenon, much of our effort is directed toward discovering just what the phenomena are and the processes by which they operate. What are the key stages of the strategic decision making process? Are the stages similar to or different from cognitive psychologists' studies of the decision making process? Just how do managers identify decisions as strategic? How do managers diagnose the strategic decision situation? What are key sources of information here? How does the strategic decision making process differ from making important decisions at lower levels in the organization? Are the mechanisms and processes the same and is it just the content of the decision that is different, or is the entire process different?

Again, a qualitative research approach is most appropriate as the major focus is on identifying the phenomena and their characteristics.

Strategy Formulation

Strategy formulation is concerned with the interrelationships of strategic decisions over time. What are the stages of the strategy formulation process? What are the key sources of influence on strategy formulation and how do they change over time? Are there different styles of strategy formulation and if so, what are they?

A particularly interesting issue in the strategy formulation process is how organizations develop a strategy to adapt to their environment. Just what is the adaptation process and how does strategy affect this? How do organizations develop a strategy whereby they take a proactive vs. reactive stance toward their environment? How does strategic planning activity take place? What are the cycles of the strategic planning process and how does it affect adaptation? What are the characteristics of successful strategic planning activities that lead to proactive adaptation to the environment? How do organizational decision makers learn to deal with their environment through the strategic planning process? How can organizations learn to anticipate the future in order that their strategic plans are future oriented rather than oriented to the past? As above, qualitative research designs are the most appropriate since the principal need is to identify the processes involved.

Strategy Implementation

Here the concern is with the process by which strategy is acted on in the organization. How do decision makers get their strategies implemented into the ongoing activities of the organization? Once a strategic decision is made, the focus shifts to making it work. What are the sources of resistance that strategic decision makers may encounter as they try to implement diversification strategy in an organization that has followed a very simple root strategy over a period of time? How can organizations implement diversification without encountering problems of control and integration of the new acquisitions? For example, Heublein acquired Kentucky Fried Chicken Corp., which had a radically different market than Heublein's liquor business. The result was that Heublein had problems adapting to and understanding the fast food business (*Business Week*, July 4, 1977). What can organizations do to more effectively implement diversification strategies? What are the processes involved? Again, qualitative methods are appropriate because the key research problem is one of identifying the phenomena involved.

Nature of Policy Theory and Research: Opportunity for Theory Building

Having discussed the above policy research questions, an attempt can be made to summarize the current nature of policy theory and thus make the argument for using qualitative methods.

1. Policy research questions are complex and involve a large number of variables that have been very difficult to measure. Thus, theory and research have been slow in developing (Mintzberg, 1977). For example, the components of strategy formulation are difficult to identify, let alone measure.

2. Policy research has been more concerned with asking questions about complex, relevant problems organizations face in terms of stra-

tegic decision making and policy formulation than with research rigor (Mintzberg, 1977). Policy questions in their relevant scope have tended to be ignored by organizational theorists who have been more concerned about rigor. Organizational theorists seem to learn more and more about less and less. Organizational theorists can tell us about the fact that organizations need less bureaucratic structures to deal with uncertain environments (Lawrence and Lorsch, 1967b; Duncan, 1974), but they cannot tell us how organizations change their structure in terms of the processes involved. Organization theorists, for the most part, have ignored studying strategy formulation processes because of methodological problems. Studying strategy formulation is hard to quantify and it is difficult to get a large enough sample of organizations for a sample size that would make the study legitimate to one's colleagues and the relevant journals. Organizational theorists have lost sight of the ultimate client of their work — the practicing manager. Their overconcern with rigor has caused them to write for one another and flee from studying important problems. Policy theorists are still grappling with the difficult issues with the hope of developing a theory for the practitioner. As a result, there is no common paradigm in policy theory and research. This really is not a shortcoming but in fact provides for more flexibility and potential creativity in policy as theorists/researchers continue to develop a body of knowledge.

3. Much of what policy researchers study deals with phenomena so complex that we still are not completely aware of the components involved. Thus, we first have to discover the phenomena and once they are discovered, we can then begin to explore relationships.

Given this brief assessment of the state of policy research, one can conclude that policy is a developing field where primary focus must be on theory building, as well as on theory testing. At this point, it is important to briefly discuss the theory building process and the role qualitative methods play in theory building.[2]

[2] This discussion on theory building is abbreviated and not meant to be a primer on "how to do it?" For a more complete discussion on theory

THE THEORY BUILDING PROCESS

In a well developed science, concepts are developed (see Exhibit 7.13) and are related to one another through logical relationships. The constructs have constitutive meaning in that they are related to one another and take part in the formation of laws and theories (Torgerson, 1958). In a well developed science, a sufficient number of these concepts possess operational definitions so that they can be linked to observable data. While all constructs should have constitutive meaning, they do not all have to possess direct operational definition, but they should all be linked to other concepts that do have operational definitions and can be tested empirically (Torgerson, 1958).

In less well developed sciences, like the social and behavioral sciences, there are gaps in the concepts that are defined and those that can be measured through operational definitions. Exhibit 7.14 indicates two sets of concepts, those on the right that are interconnected and linked through operational definitions to observable data and those on the left that are interconnected, but are not connected with the concepts that have operational definitions (Torgerson, 1958). What is required then is to link the complex concepts on the left to the ones on the right in Exhibit 7.14. This is the process of explication whereby concepts are more clearly defined so that they can be measured directly or linked to other concepts that can be operationally defined (Carnap, 1950). When concepts are more clearly defined and the explication process is complete, hypotheses can be developed and tested.

The most prevalent research paradigm in the social sciences is the deductive method. Here the researcher develops a set of hypotheses governing the phenomenon under investigation, tests these hypotheses and so confirms or disconfirms them, replacing them where necessary (Kaplan, 1964). This deductive method is preceded by the establishment of a body of theory.

However, in policy where much of the phe-

building, the reader is directed to Kuhn (1962), Kaplan (1964), Zetterberg (1965), and Dubin (1969).

Exhibit 7.13 The Structure of Well Developed Science

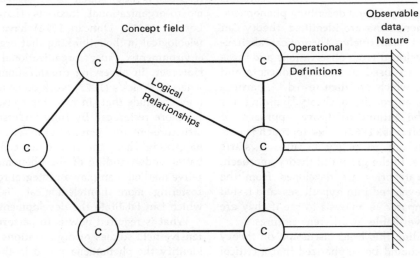

Exhibit 7.14 The Structure of Less Developed Sciences—Social and Behavioral

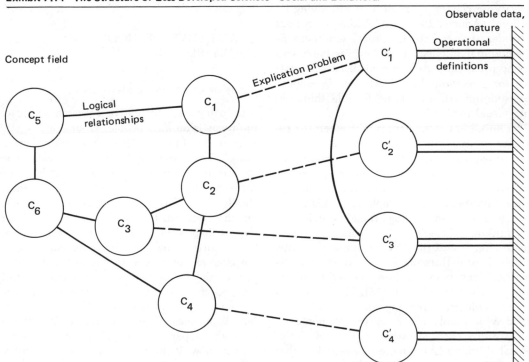

nomena are still to be discovered, research is geared at identifying and describing phenomena. Once the phenomena are identified, theory can be developed *inductively*. Theoretical abstractions are developed from observations and these abstractions are used to develop concepts and propositions, which are then tested. A particularly useful approach to theory building for policy is the grounded theory approach of Glaser and Strauss (1967). This approach is particularly relevant to policy because it starts with the data. In the grounded theory approach, conceptual categories are developed from the data, then developed into hypotheses, and tested through comparative analysis to see if they are empirically verifiable in different settings.

Before ending this brief discussion on theory building, it should be emphasized that a critical component of this entire process is creativity and openness on the part of the researcher to truly try to understand the phenomena under investigation. Adams points out that one of the key problems to problem solving and theory building is conceptual blocks, "... mental walls which block the problem-solver from correctly perceiving a problem or conceiving its solution" (Adams, 1974: 11). Adams then goes on to identify perceptual, cultural, environmental, emotional, intellectual, and expressive blocks to conceptualizing. Adams next discusses strategies for removing these blocks by developing a questioning attitude, using flexible thinking, using visual thinking, etc.

The important issue here is that when the researcher is studying new phenomena, he must be as open as possible to understanding the new phenomena and should not let prior notions create a narrowness in trying to conceptualize. Steinbeck (1962) emphasizes this in his distinction between teleological and nonteleological thinking. Teleological is concerned with causes, effects, and the purposiveness of events. Nonteleological thinking is concerned with "is thinking," the what or how, rather than the why (Steinbeck, 1962: 134–135). The usefulness of nonteleological thinking is that it is concerned with simply observing the phenomenon as it is and identifying what is going on. Teleological thinking is far more inferential in that it ascertains causes and in making causal in-

ferences is often open to error. For example, macro-organizational theorists (Lawrence and Lorsch, 1967b; Duncan 1974) have been very teleological in their thinking that organizational environments cause organizational structure. However, in observing organizations and considering Weick's (1977) work on enactment, one may conclude that, in fact, the causal links are far more reciprocal. By fully understanding the structure-environment fit in the sense of "what's happening" here the researcher can develop a better understanding of the phenomena. Qualitative methods can play an integral role, then, in fostering more nonteleological "is" thinking which can facilitate the development of theory.

What is required now is to perform more extensive field studies of organizations in order to identify the phenomena posed in the questions in Exhibit 7.12, which are primarily qualitative in their nature. What's going on here? What are the forms of the phenomena? What are the variations in the phenomena?

The next section of the paper will focus on the components of qualitative methods and the role these methods can play in policy research.

QUALITATIVE METHODS AND POLICY RESEARCH

FOCUS OF QUALITATIVE METHODS

In using the qualitative research approach, the focus is on *how* people, groups and organizations do things, rather than *why* they do things. The "how" and "why" are really a sequence of questions. Before researchers can focus on the "why" they first have to understand "how." The task, then, is one of describing the situation. It should be emphasized here that an important liability is that in observing, the researcher may be observing *bad* practice. For example, in observing how decision makers behave the researcher may have inadvertently selected an ineffective group. This is why after a theory or model is developed from data collected in one setting, it should be verified through comparative analysis in another setting to see how it holds up in another context. Whenever possible, measures should be sought to indicate whether the research has dealt with good or bad practice.

Qualitative methods produce descriptive data — people's own written and spoken words recorded, as much as possible, as *they* see it, rather than as abstracted or interpreted by the researcher. The concern is with how the actors in the situation see reality and deal with it. The problem with much behavioral science research is that the abstraction it uses distorts what common sense indicates was the actual day-to-day life of the actors involved. For example, a Markov chain analysis of decision making may be elegant mathematically, but it may not reflect the complexity and ill defined nature of the decision making process. The "elegance" of the mathematical model has lost the complexity of the decision making situation.

The recent work by Argyris and Schon (1974) and Weick (1977) has raised some important questions regarding the applicability of much of our current quantitative methodology in the behavioral sciences. In studying executive behavior, Argyris and Schon (1974) have distinguished between two theories that guide individual behavior. People have "espoused theories" and "theories-in-use." If the researcher asks a manager how he thinks he behaves, the manager may describe his espoused theory about his behavior. However, when actually faced with that situation and required to actually behave, the manager's behavior, or theory-in-use may not conform to his earlier espoused theory. For example, when asked, a manager may have indicated that he deals very openly with his subordinates, solicits their ideas and in general tries to create a climate in decision meetings where his subordinates feel free to disagree with him and challenge his ideas. Thus, the researcher has the manager's espoused theory as to how he thinks he behaves. However, upon observing how this manager actually behaves, the researcher may find that the manager's behavior is very different. He may cut off subordinates who disagree with him and generally dominate the conversation. Thus, the manager's actual behavior, his theory-in-use, is very different from what the manager described.

This phenomenon has important implications for researchers studying human behavior. Questionnaires ask people to provide their espoused theory — how they think they behave. Thus, if the researcher is trying to understand a complex phenomenon, the only real way to get an accurate understanding of it is to observe it happen, rather than to rely upon actors' reports of how they "think" it happened. The researcher has to, in fact, observe what's going on or at least interact with the subject to help define what's going on.

Weick's (1977) work on the enactment process also has important implications for the study of social phenomena. Enactment is the process whereby individuals define, structure, and put meaning on their environment. It is the process by which individuals make sense of and interpret their environment so that they can direct their behavior. There is no such thing, then, as "objective reality." The environment or situation only exists to the individual when he has put meaning into it through enactment processes. Given the enactment process, the researcher has to be aware that his mode of inquiry can enact on the part of the subject the very type of phenomena he is trying to study. The questionnaires used to ask about organization structure can "create" an organizational structure in the mind of the respondent that never before existed. By overstructuring data collection procedures, the researcher may be enacting contrived environments, environments that never existed before for the subject whose behavior the researcher is interested in understanding.

A particularly good example of the enactment problem occurs when researchers study how managers and organizations react to the environment. What is the environment and who defines it? A good example of this problem is Duncan's (1972) work examining how managers deal with the uncertainty in their environment. In this work, managers were asked to first define the factors in their environment. Once these factors were identified, a series of questions were asked about each factor. The factors were identified by providing a stimulus (Exhibit 7.15) to the respondents to help them describe their environment. They were asked to indicate which factors on this list they considered in decision making. The point here is that this methodology resulted in the method of questioning helping to enact the environment for the subject. In most cases, respondents indicated that, "I have never really thought that explicitly before about what my decision environment was. It now is much more complicated than I had thought it was."

Researchers must be aware of how their methods help the actor define reality and perhaps even create more structure and impose more rationality to the situation than actually exists. It is important that researchers thus be aware of the ethnomethodologist's concern for the examination of common sense and try to begin to understand *how* people see, describe and explain order in the world in which they live (Garfinkel, 1967; Turner, 1974; Mehan and Wood, 1975).

In summarizing the phases of understanding how people do things, Lofland (1976: 3) has indicated four areas:

1. Getting close-up to people actually acting someplace in the real world and developing *intimate familiarity*.

2. Focusing on and delineating the prime or basic *situation* the scrutinized people are dealing with or confronting.

3. Focusing on and delineating the interactional *strategies*, tactics, and so on, by means of which the scrutinized people are dealing with the situation confronted.

4. Assembling and analyzing an abundance of qualitative *episodes* into *disciplined abstractions* about the situation and strategies delineated.

In attempting to discover phenomena, researchers have to be sensitive to these four activities.

Exhibit 7.15 Environmental Components Used as Stimulus in Helping Managers Define Their Environments

Internal environment

ORGANIZATIONAL PERSONNEL COMPONENT

A. Educational and technological
   background and skills
B. Previous technological and managerial skill
C. Individual member's involvement and commitment to attaining system's goals
D. Interpersonal behavior styles
E. Availability of manpower for utilization
   within the system

ORGANIZATIONAL FUNCTIONAL AND STAFF UNITS COMPONENT

A. Technological characteristics of organizational
   units
B. Interdependence of organizational units in
   carrying out their objectives
C. Intraunit conflict among organizational
   functional and staff units
D. Interunit conflict among organizational
   functional and staff units

ORGANIZATIONAL LEVEL COMPONENT

A. Organizational objectives and goals
B. Integrative process integrating individuals and
   groups into contributing maximally to attaining
   organizational goals
C. Nature of the organization's product service

External environment

CUSTOMER COMPONENT

A. Distributors of product or service
B. Actual users of product or service

SUPPLIERS COMPONENT

A. New materials suppliers
B. Equipment suppliers
C. Product parts suppliers
D. Labor supply

COMPETITOR COMPONENT

A. Competitors for suppliers
B. Competitors for customers

SOCIO-POLITICAL COMPONENT

A. Government regulatory control over the industry
B. Public political attitude toward industry and its
   particular product
C. Relationship with trade unions with jurisdiction in
   the organization

TECHNOLOGICAL COMPONENT

A. Meeting new technological requirements of own
   industry and related industries in production of
   product or service
B. Improving and developing new products by implementing new technological advances in the industry

Exhibit 7.16 Analysis of Qualitative Researcher Techniques

	Strengths	Weaknesses
Case study	1. In depth analysis of the setting	1. Expensive for researcher
	2. Offers opportunity to develop history of the situation	2. Can be expensive for subjects to have in depth analysis
	3. Develops complete internal validity	3. External validity—problem of generalizing to other settings
	4. Adaptive—allows data collection on wide range of topics	4. Little opportunity for control of variables
		5. Little opportunity for comparative analysis in theory development
Interviews	1. In depth analysis of situation	1. Expensive for researcher
	2. Can follow and develop better understanding of "what's going on?"	2. Expensive in terms of time for interviewer
	3. Researcher can develop empathy and understanding with members in system	3. Problem of interviewer bias
	4. Allows data to be collected on real issues of concern as subjects can provide evidence to researcher	4. Requires rapport with interviewees
		5. Interviewee self-report bias
		6. Coding-interpretation problems
		7. Because of time, difficult to canvass entire organization
Observation	1. Collects data on behavior rather than self-reports	1. Costly in terms of time and money
	2. Provides opportunity to see how setting affects behavior	2. Can be disruptive to the system
	3. Allows researcher to identify unanticipated phenomena-variables that may be affecting behavior	3. Bias of observer
	4. Not retrospective, focuses on real situation as it happens	4. Problem of *what* behavior and *how* long to sample
		5. Problem of coding and interpretation

TYPES OF QUALITATIVE RESEARCH METHODS

In this section a very brief overview will be provided of several types of qualitative approaches that can be used to study policy questions such as those listed in Exhibit 7.12. These techniques are case studies, interviews, and observations. Exhibit 7.16 summarizes their general strengths and weaknesses. Their usefulness for policy research will be examined through a discussion of several recent policy research studies that have utilized them.

CASE STUDIES

Much more systematic and intensive case studies of organizations need to be done. Such intensive case studies can provide the setting in which various other qualitative techniques such as researcher observation, participant observation, unstructured interviewing, and personal documents can be used.

Levinson's (1972) work on organizational diagnosis provides a systematic outline of the case study approach and is presented here in a revised form as it provides an excellent framework for case study analysis.

Case Study Outline[3]

I. Genetic Data

    A. Identifying Information

        1. Name, location, organization type, size

    B. Historical Data

        1. Long and short range problems stated by key figures

        2. Background of organization in terms of developmental stages, major crises, product-service history

II. Description of the Organization

    A. Organization Structure

        1. Formal structure, financial structure, personnel (number, education

level, average tenure, range of skills, etc.) policies and procedures

    B. Process Data

        1. Communication systems, problem solving, decision making systems, and coordinating mechanisms

III. Interpretative Data

    A. Current Organizational Functioning

        1. Organizational perceptions from inside and outside the organization and the degree of accuracy of these

        2. Organizational Knowledge — how it's acquired and used

        3. Emotional atmosphere of the organization — prevailing mood and stability of this mood

    B. Attitudes and Relationships

        1. Attitudes toward customers, competition, employees, stockholders, etc.

        2. Attitudes toward the organization itself — who are we? Where are we headed? What are we trying to accomplish?

IV. Organization-Environment Relations

    A. Appraisal of impact of environment on organization

        1. Beneficial and harmful effects historically, contemporary, and anticipated

    B. Appraisal of the impact of the organization on the environment

        1. Beneficial and harmful effects historically, contemporary, and anticipated

The case study then has the potential of allowing the researcher to examine in depth the organization and the phenomena being studied. He thus can accomplish the phases of understanding *how* people do things as Lofland (1976) has pointed out. Thus in the case study, where the researcher gets in depth information on the system similar to that suggested in the above outline, he can attain intimate familiarity with the organization and can become aware of the situation in which people are behaving and of

[3] Revised and adapted from Harry Levinson, *Organizational Diagnosis*, copyright © 1972 by the President and Fellows of Harvard College, by permission of the publisher, Harvard University Press.

the strategies by which people deal with the situation.

The case study does have certain limitations that should be briefly mentioned. First, there is a problem of external validity. With a sample of $N = 1$ it becomes difficult to generalize to other situations. Second, the intensive case study is expensive in terms of the time of both the researcher and the subjects of the study. The researcher has to spend a large amount of time in the field to collect the necessary data. He does not have the luxury of the survey researcher who simply sends in several boxes of questionnaires and then picks them up, or the quantitative modeler who has in most cases no interactions with the research setting, but rather works with abstract formulations that often assume away as "externalities" most of the relevant phenomena. The case study approach is also expensive in terms of time for the subjects. The researchers will typically want to spend time interviewing and observing participants in the organization. Thus, they will have to invest a certain amount of time in the study.

Within the case study framework, a number of qualitative techniques can be used.

INTERVIEWING

Asking participants in the setting, "What's going on? What's happening?" is one way to begin to discover the phenomena. In using interviews, the researcher is relying on the respondents' ability to correctly describe the research setting, which makes an assumption that they know what is going on. While interviews are useful, we must always be aware that the respondents' descriptions of what's happening or what has happened may not always be accurate.

TYPES OF INTERVIEWS. Bouchard (1976) has identified four types of interviews, as indicated in Exhibit 7.17.

Type I interviews are totally structured with standard questions and standard answers. For example, the researcher may know a fair amount about work behavior so that he could use a Type I interview here.

Type II interviews are open ended. Questions

Exhibit 7.17 Four Types of Interviews Classified According to Type of Question and Type of Answer Required

Responses	Questions	
	Specified	Unspecified
Specified	I	III
Unspecified	II	IV

are specified, but answers are left open to the respondent. This type of interview might be more appropriate to policy research questions especially when one is trying to identify phenomena. It is also useful when the researcher simply does not know enough to identify specific responses for the respondent beforehand. For example, the researcher may have specific questions about the stages of strategic decision making, but he may not necessarily know enough about the process to specify appropriate response categories. At best, the researcher can ask the individual to try to describe the characteristics of the stages he sees.

Type III interviews do not specify the questions, but do specify the type of response desired. No one has used this type because it is a null set for research purposes.

Type IV interviews specify neither the question nor the response; this is the nondirective interview. Here the researcher is really carrying on a dialogue with the respondent, asking him to describe the situation and then simply probing the individual as he begins to explain the situation. For example, as one begins to try to identify the strategy formulation process, one may simply start out by asking respondents how the organization establishes strategy and then follow up with probes such as "How does this occur?" "What cycles do you go through?" In essence, the researcher is trying to clarify what the respondent is discussing. The specific questions are determined by the answers the respondent gives, i.e., the interview is an interactive process.

CYCLING OF INTERVIEWS. Bouchard (1976) indicates that in any research setting researchers may use several of the types of interviews mentioned above. The interviewing should begin with broad questions with unspecified response formats (Type IV). This helps the interviewer get an understanding of the setting and puts the respondent into the proper frame of reference. This format also gives the interviewer the opportunity to change the language of more specific questions which follow. If one were studying strategic decision making, one might start out by asking the respondent, "Could you tell me about your job and the kinds of decisions you make?" Once this part of the interview were done, questions could get much more specific with specified answers (Type I). Examples here would be the following: "How important are each of the following as a source of information for making decisions? Written communication from others in the organization, informal meetings with others in the organization, etc." If responses to these more structured questions contradict the earlier responses, the interviewer can then go back and ask why. In whatever format they take, interviewing can provide the basis for identifying the phenomena of interest to policy research.

SOME EXAMPLES OF INTERVIEW STUDIES. There are several key studies that have been done in the policy area that have used interviews to identify the phenomena of interest. Mintzberg, Raisinghani, and Theoret's (1976) study, Mumford and Pettigrew's (1975) study, and Zald's (1970) study, all on strategic decision making processes, are excellent examples of the qualitative approach of case studies using interviews as the primary data collection technique. As indicated in Exhibit 7.12, there are numerous questions that cannot be presently answered regarding strategic decision making processes. However, these studies begin to specify more precisely the process involved.

Zald (1970) was interested in how an organization, the Chicago YMCA, changed its orienta-

tion from an evangelical organization to a general service organization with particular concern for developing a new consciousness for inner city problems. Over a three-year period, several hundred interviews were carried out with members of the board, secretaries and other professionals. The following specific open ended (Type II) interviews were carried out:

1. 20 hours of interviews with the general secretary of the YMCA
2. 1½ hour interviews with thirteen executive secretaries and thirteen board chairmen from the Y
3. 1½–2 hour interviews with fourteen members of the executive committee of the board of managers
4. 1–10 hours of interviewing with nine assistant general secretaries in the Metropolitan office of the Chicago Y
5. Interviews with representatives of the Chicago Housing Authority, Chicago Welfare Council, etc.

From the above listing one can see the comprehensive approach Zald used in the study. From the interviews, Zald was able to abstract the process by which the YMCA was making its transition. Zald used the concept of political economy to explain the transition process. He was able to trace the interplay of power as the changes took place. The only way he could identify the processes involved was to ask the participants what was happening as the change took place.

Mintzberg, Raisinghani, and Theoret's (1976) study of 25 strategic decision processes is an excellent example of qualitative methods using the interview approach to identify the phenomena in question. Mintzberg et al. (1976: 246) were interested in identifying how organizations make strategic unstructured decisions — decision that have ". . . not been encountered in quite the same form and for which no predetermined and explicit set of ordered responses exist in the organization . . . and [which are] important in terms of the actions taken, the resources committed or the precedents set."

Student teams were used by Mintzberg et al. to collect the data. Each team studied a particular organization for 3–6 months and isolated one strategic decision made by that organization. The teams then were asked to describe the steps in the decision process in enough detail so that they could present a flow chart of the processes involved. A series of questions were developed to help define the decision process. Example questions were as follows:

1. What was the source of the initial stimulus?

2. Were stimuli frequent and/or intense?

3. Were specific constraints and objectives established early?

4. Where did management seek solutions?

5. Were many alternative solutions proposed, or did management "satisfice" by taking and testing alternatives one at a time?

Based on this procedure, Mintzberg, et al. were able to develop a general model of the strategic decision making process consisting of twelve elements. There are three central phases, three sets of supporting routines, and six sets of dynamic factors. The strategic decision process was thus shown to be exceedingly more complex than had initially been thought. This study is a particularly important one for two reasons: (1) the study examined how actual decisions were made and found that existing social psychological theories of decision making were oversimplified; and (2) based on the data collected, the authors developed a new theory of the strategic decision making process.

Mumford and Pettigrew (1975) have studied the process of implementing strategic decisions. They have examined the installation of large scale computer systems in four organizations over a period of 2–5 years from the decision to consider a new system, through the search for the system, the decision to go ahead with a particular manufacturer, and the difficulties encountered in putting the system into operation.[4]

In their study, Mumford and Pettigrew and the Computer Research Unit of the Manchester Business School interviewed managers, board members, computer specialists, as well as others, in the course of the study. They asked the following general questions in the course of their study.

1. How were innovation decisions started?

2. What role did innovating groups play in these decisions?

3. How do innovators define their roles? And how do these change over time?

4. What are the political processes that exert a major influence on technological decisions when the interests of a number of different groups have to be reconciled?

Based on the above data, Mumford and Pettigrew developed a theory regarding how organizations manage the uncertainty associated with the introduction of major innovations in organizations. They have found that as the organization tried to cope with the uncertainty in its environment by introducing computer based information systems, new uncertainties were generated inside the organization. These were caused by the abandonment of long established methods and procedures in favor of new ones. In addition, political behavior among different groups became very prevalent as each group tried to maintain its position in the organization. Once again, a qualitative approach identified the organizational phenomena to be more complex than initial theories had indicated.

The above studies indicate how interviews can help to identify the complex phenomena researchers are attempting to study in policy. The above studies had a common component to them that is essential in that the researchers used the data collected to construct a descriptive theory or model of the phenomena they were studying. That is, they went beyond the mere gathering of facts to provide a different view of reality than had existed before.

Interviews do have some liabilities. They are expensive both for the researcher in terms of time and money and for the interviewee in terms of investing the time to talk to the researcher. It is also difficult to canvas an entire organization because of costs and the result may be a nonrepresentative sample. There is also the

---

[4] The implementation of this new technology was a strategic decision for the organization in that they were able to develop more complex services and pursue different markets through the additional information and shorter processing times these systems provided.

problem of interviewer bias since the researcher may not pursue the same questions across all interviews. To get valid information, it is necessary that the interviewers have rapport with respondents and that they trust him, and this may be difficult to accomplish in some settings. There are also problems in coding and interpreting the data. Coding is costly and there is opportunity for coder bias to enter into the situation.

Observation Techniques

As indicated earlier, interview techniques rely on the individual's ability to accurately describe the phenomena the researcher is interested in studying. There are several problems we may encounter here. First, many of the phenomena of interest take place over a long period of time. Therefore, the researcher will frequently be asking individuals to "... think back when these strategic decisions were made and describe what happened." In some instances, it may simply be impossible for the individual to recollect what happened. Second, as Argyris and Schon's (1974) work has indicated, people's descriptions or theories about how they "think" they behave may be different from how they "actually" behave. Thus, self-reports are problematical. Third, much of a person's behavior is habitual and thus the individual is often not consciously aware of the exact process he is going through in performing the act. Duncan's (1972) work on how managers deal with uncertainty in decision making illustrates this problem. When managers were asked directly how much uncertainty they experience in decision making, they often indicated, "None, I am a good manager so I don't have any." However, after reviewing a number of very specific decisions, these managers would then begin to indicate that they experienced information deficiencies in a variety of areas, were unable to predict outcomes in decisions, etc. The problem was that they really had to relive past decision situations to respond to the questions.

Observation techniques put the researcher in the setting of the phenomena under investigation so that the researcher can actually observe how the individual behaves over time. According to Becker and Geer (1970: 133) the observation method is one in which:

> the observer participates in the daily life of the people under study, either openly in the role of the researcher or covertly in some disguised role, observing things that happen, listening to what is said, and questioning people, over some length of time.

In addition to overcoming the problems associated with interviews as discussed above, participant observation has two distinct advantages. First, it requires the researcher to analyze the behavior being observed from the perspective of the entire setting in which it is taking place. For example, in *observing* how managers make strategic decisions or formulate policy, the researcher is required to look not only at individual behavior but also at how the structure of the organization affects how managers interact. Thus, a broader perspective in examining the phenomenon in question is developed. A second major advantage is that observation gives the researcher the opportunity to observe unanticipated phenomena and thus learn about events that would otherwise go unobserved.

LEVELS OF PARTICIPANT OBSERVATION. Participation can occur at several levels (Gold, 1958; Junker, 1960). *Complete participation* occurs when the researcher becomes a member of the system and conceals this from others. This approach raises questions of ethics in the sense of not letting people in the system know they are being studied. Thus, because of the questionable ethics involved it should not be used. *Participant as an observer* exists when a participant in the system also acts as an observer. Here the individual is primarily a participant, but is doing some observation as to what is happening. *Observer as participant* occurs when the researcher becomes a member of the system and is publicly known as an observer. This is the most frequent example of observation techniques.

The participant as an observer might be particularly useful to the policy researcher. Training participants as observers can be a method to get a large amount of information on how things happen in the system. The participant is an "insider" and thus will not be viewed with suspicion, which might affect how people behave around him. He, in fact, can become a more unobtrusive measurer. Duncan et al. (1977) in studying problem solving in school systems provides a good example. The objective of this study was to see how the faculty groups in each school operated as a group during problem solving meetings. To do this, one teacher in each school was trained as a group facilitator to help the school's faculty use survey feedback for problem identification and problem solving. A second teacher from each school was then trained to be a monitor whose responsibility was to observe the problem solving meetings. The monitors received one day's training in how to observe group behavior and then used the form presented in Exhibit 7.18 to collect data on each meeting. In this way, participants were used as observers to help understand what happened in the meetings.

Policy researchers could use a similar approach to train managers on how to observe the policy processes. For example, now that Mintzberg et al. (1976) have developed a model of the strategic decision making process, managers could be trained in that framework so that they could then observe similar decisions over time to see if the framework was in fact an accurate reflection of reality.

There are several problems with using observation techniques. A major problem the researcher faces in observation is maintaining objectivity. Since the researcher becomes part of the situation, he could potentially lose his ability to accurately describe the situation. Several guidelines for maintaining objectivity are listed below (Bogdan and Taylor, 1975; Bouchard, 1976):

1. The researcher should be aware of his own biases and these might affect how he interprets the situation.
2. The researcher should be aware of the biases and motivations of subjects in terms of how this affects their behavior and interpretations.
3. The researcher should be aware of how the position he occupies might affect how he interprets the situation. (For example, observing the planning process from a planning department might cause one to see the potential usefulness of formal models. However, observing the planning process from a manufacturing department might cause one to take a much more pragmatic view toward planning.)
4. The researcher should support observational data with other data from interviews with others in the system, organizational records, etc.
5. The researcher should distinguish between data and his interpretations of it. Notes on what data base was used should be made and then he should later write up his interpretations of the data.
6. The researcher should observe subjects in as many different contexts as possible.
7. The researcher should not overly identify with subjects or be forced into roles in the system. On the other hand, it is important to win trust and confidence of subjects so that their behavior is not altered by observer.

In addition to objectivity-bias, there are several other problems with observation. It is expensive to the researcher because he has to be in the system for a period of time. Observation can be disruptive in the sense that when people know they are being observed they may alter their behavior to fit what they think the researcher is looking for (Rosenthal, 1966). There is a sampling problem in terms of what behavior to observe and how long to observe it. For example, in observing strategic decision making the researcher would have to decide when to start observing. Where does the process start — who defines the problem and where does this happen? Then the researcher has to be concerned about how long to observe. In strategic decision making the entire process might take months from initiation of the problem to implementation. Therefore, the researcher is faced with the problem of "how much" of the process to observe and also of being present when various key components of decision making occur. There is also the problem of coding and then interpreting the data. The unstructured nature of observation makes this particularly difficult to do, especially if standard observations are needed for statistical analysis.

442

Exhibit 7.18 Observer's Data Collection Form

Meeting of _____ group _____ School _____ Date _____

(program)
(review)
(etc.)

Number attending _____

	TOPIC I	TOPIC II

Short description of task(s)

Approximate timing of discussion: start ____ end ____   start ____ end ____

Survey data considered (category and/or items)

Origin of concern (e.g., survey data, principal, parents, etc.)

Stage of the decision and change process (e.g., evaluation, solution generation, etc.)

Climate (as related to topic)

Conflict: Low [_____] High   Low [_____] High

Cooperation: Low [_____] High   Low [_____] High

Level of dissatisfaction caused by topic: Low [_____] High   Low [_____] High

Openness: Low [_____] High   Low [_____] High

Discussion orientation:
  task: Low [_____] High   Low [_____] High

  personality: Low [_____] High   Low [_____] High

Exhibit 7.18 Observer's Data Collection Form (Continued)

Characteristics of the group session:

Degree of organization:

Degree of participation:

Unorganized	Moderately organized	Very organized
0%	50%	100%

	Frequency engaged in					Adequacy				
	Not at all	A few times			Very frequently	Not enough		Just right		Too much
Task functions										
1. Initiating	1	2	3	4	5	1	2	3	4	5
2. Information or opinion *seeking*	1	2	3	4	5	1	2	3	4	5
3. Information or opinion *giving*	1	2	3	4	5	1	2	3	4	5
4. Clarifying or elaborating	1	2	3	4	5	1	2	3	4	5
5. Summarizing	1	2	3	4	5	1	2	3	4	5
6. Consensus testing	1	2	3	4	5	1	2	3	4	5
Maintenance functions										
1. Encouraging	1	2	3	4	5	1	2	3	4	5
2. Expressing group feelings	1	2	3	4	5	1	2	3	4	5
3. Harmonizing	1	2	3	4	5	1	2	3	4	5
4. Compromising	1	2	3	4	5	1	2	3	4	5
5. Gate-keeping	1	2	3	4	5	1	2	3	4	5
6. Setting standards	1	2	3	4	5	1	2	3	4	5

SOME EXAMPLES OF OBSERVATIONAL STUDIES. Several major studies have been done recently in the policy area that have relied on observation as one of the major data gathering techniques. Here, we will focus on two such studies: the research by Mintzberg (1973) on managerial work, and the work by Pettigrew (1973) on strategic decision making.[5]

Mintzberg (1973) observed five managers one week each in his study on managerial work. Before the observation actually began, Mintzberg studied some background data on each manager. This background data covered three areas. One month of scheduled appointments from the manager's calendar was examined to get some initial understanding on how the managers spent their time. Organizational information — organization charts, annual reports, etc. — were collected to develop an understanding of the manager's environment. Managerial background information — education, working hours, analysis of his résumé, personal interview with manager, secretary and/or personal assistant — was collected.

During the actual observation, Mintzberg collected two types of data. Anecdotal data were collected on critical incidents and internal discussions with managers. Structured data were collected in three areas. The *chronology record* described how the manager spent his time. The *mail record* described each piece of incoming and outgoing mail. The *contact record* described each verbal contact the manager had. The data thus collected were used to inductively develop Mintzberg's theory of managerial work which focuses on various managerial roles (interpersonal, informational, decisional) and their variations. Exhibit 7.19 presents the outline of Mintzberg's analysis from raw data to his theory development.

The importance of Mintzberg's work is that through his extensive observation he has challenged prior assumptions that managers were

reflective, had no real duties to perform, and were very scientific and systematic in their behavior. Rather, his work indicated that managers work at an unrelenting pace, perform a number of very specific tasks, and rely a great deal on judgment and intuition.

Pettigrew (1973) was interested in the politics of organizational decision making in the adoption, installation, and use of new computer systems. Pettigrew entered the organization and was "housed" with the system's analysts as he began to observe the decision making process associated with the development of the new computer systems. This observation lasted for two years. Pettigrew points out quite vividly the initial distrust and antagonism that organizational participants had toward him. Pettigrew simply observed the decision process, used interviews, the content analysis of documents, questionnaires and the analysis of organizational documents, to develop a model of what he observed.

Pettigrew's study is important in that it identifies the sources of power, and the nature of power politics in an innovative decision making situation. Information gatekeepers — individuals able to provide information that could reduce uncertainty — had a lot of power within the organization. By observation, Pettigrew was able to see how these gatekeepers behaved, a complex phenomenon he could not have captured through the use of questionnaires.

POSSIBILITIES FOR FUTURE QUALITATIVE STUDIES IN POLICY

With the preceding discussion as background, some suggestions on how future studies might pursue the qualitative approach in the area of the formulation of strategy can now be offered. Hofer (1975, 1976) and Hatten and Schendel (1976) have emphasized the important role of the strategy concept in policy research. Hatten and Schendel have identified, quite correctly, that strategy formulation is a reconstructed logic when managers are asked to indicate what they did. In formulating strategy, managers have to deal with uncertainty, to try to predict and anticipate the future through a trial and error process. When managers are asked to describe

---

[5] Those interested in additional examples of the use of observational techniques, especially in different settings, are referred to the work of Selznick (1949), Gouldner (1954), Dalton (1959), and Blau (1963). Each of these is considered a classic in the organizational behavior field.

Exhibit 7.19 Outline of Analysis of Mintzberg Study on Managerial Work

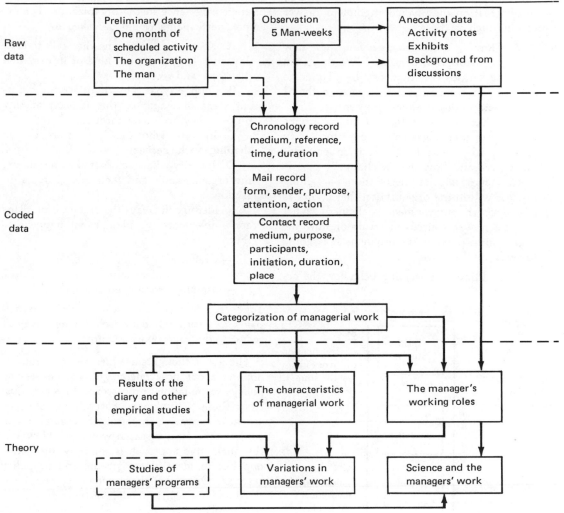

this process, they often overintellectualize on what they did, thus oversimplifying the complexity of the processes involved. Therefore, observation is needed to identify the actual processes involved.

The current energy crisis provides a useful setting in which such a study of strategic decision processes might be done. For example, given the current concerns over gasoline consumption, how will the automobile industry adapt to this serious threat from the environment? Observing the decision making process might help policy researchers' understanding of how organizations change their strategy. A study like this might proceed in the following fashion:

1. Observers might sit in on the key planning groups in the auto companies to observe just exactly how these groups decide to respond to

the current and proposed energy policy. Through such observation they would attempt to answer questions such as these:

A. How do these groups define these new energy consumption demands? Are they seen as being serious constraints to be adapted to or will the companies try to change them? What determines the outcome here?

B. What factors do these planning groups consider in their decision making process? In other words, what is the decision environment here and how does it change?

C. What is the negotiation/bargaining process within the organization that occurs as this decision environment is defined? What are the power sources in terms of how the organization defines the problems it is going to work on?

2. In addition to observing behavior, the actual participants could be asked to keep a diary of their experience in the organization. For example, participants would be asked to:

A. Keep a record of who they talk to each day, how long and what kind of information they seek and receive.

B. Outline what they think are the different steps or stages of the decision making process they are going through.

C. Indicate who the key actors are in shaping each decision.

D. Identify what factors lead to rethinking the organization's and their own group's direction.

E. Identify the ways the organization plans and implements the plan. What happens to the:

— structure,
— allocation of resources,
— use of personnel, etc?

Tape recorders could be used by the participants to record this data each day as a way of reducing the paper work required.

The above thoughts are just very preliminary notions about how one might start observing policy formulation processes. However, just from these preliminary observations, one can see how expensive in terms of researcher and subject time such research would be. However, the qualitative approach is the only alternative one has to identify the phenomena of policy research. Once such phenomena have been identified and descriptive models of them developed, policy researches can proceed through the various stages of the research process as McGrath (1964) has identified them (see Exhibit 7.20), including follow-up studies to test, refine, validate, and crossvalidate hypotheses. Qualitative methods need to play a key role in policy research at the present time as much of the field is still at the stage of identifying the phenomena.

Exhibit 7.20 Five-stage Path for Programmic Research

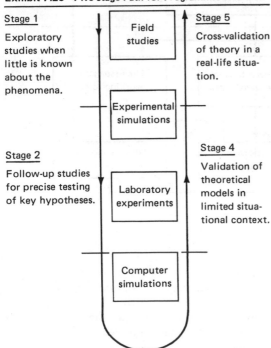

Stage 1

Exploratory studies when little is known about the phenomena.

Field studies

Stage 5

Cross-validation of theory in a real-life situation.

Experimental simulations

Stage 2

Follow-up studies for precise testing of key hypotheses.

Laboratory experiments

Stage 4

Validation of theoretical models in limited situational context.

Computer simulations

Stage 3

Elaboration and refinement of theoretical models.

SUMMARY

This paper's primary objective has been to provide a brief overview of qualitative research methods which might be utilized in policy research. Policy as a field is concerned with complex organizational phenomena that are difficult to identify, let alone measure and therefore qualitative research methods with their emphasis on identifying phenomena can often be very useful, especially in theory development. In doing such research, attempts should be made to study "best" practice so that both descriptive and normative conclusions are possible.

Quantitative Research Methods in Strategic Management

KENNETH J. HATTEN
Harvard University

INTRODUCTION

Quantitative research methods have had little impact on Business Policy, so far. This situation exists in spite of the potential for rigorous statistical testing of theory that quantitative methods offer, the availability of large-scale computing power, and the demonstrated applications of these methods and tools to business, e.g., in marketing research.[1]

Perhaps this is due to the nature of Policy itself: Policy is fascinating because it is concerned with divergent problems and speculations about the future, not with convergent problems (i.e., problems which have *demonstrable* solutions) which are easily formulated, amenable to quantitative analysis and easy testing. However, it is probably equally due to two other factors: a lack of familiarity of policy researchers with the available tools for statistical analysis, and a reluctance or inability (perhaps because of resource limitations) to pursue topics opened up by others. The field is so diverse and novelty so appealing, that outside of the well known Strategy and Structure research (e.g., Chandler, 1962; Scott, 1973; Rumelt, 1974), there are few other examples of any *continuous* and evolutionary streams of research which have begun with a new contribution to the theory of the field, and then been further developed.

The question this paper addresses is: "Is Policy amenable to quantitative research?" The paper suggests that, in fact, it is, within limits defined by the nature of the research process itself. The paper opens with a discussion of quantitative research in policy in terms of its use of data. Part of this discussion indicates how the nature of the data influences the choice of methods.

At this point, the paper asks the question: "What does the popularity of certain methods and, therefore, types of data, indicate about policy research?" Part of the answer is a suggestion that a set of unstated assumptions is being made about the nature of Policy with the result that the use of quantitative research techniques in the field is unnecessarily restrictive. Before widening the net, however, the discussion suggests further quantitative research possibilities for exploring a number of questions which lie unanswered in the existing body of quantitative policy research.

The paper then suggests an alternative research tack which would contribute to our knowledge of the strategy formulation process, rather than new information about the content of strategy (i.e., what strategy leads to what result). This section of the paper encompasses Factor Analysis, Conjoint Measurement and Perceptual Mapping (also known as Multidimensional Scaling). It suggests how these methods might complement the use of the more traditional quantitative research methods in the Policy field in the development of more rigorous and, therefore, more useful theories.

The paper concludes with a brief discussion of the inherent dilemma facing researchers in Business Policy. Policy of its nature necessitates a wide perspective and general applicability. Research by its nature necessitates a very narrow and particular focus, i.e., specialization. The dilemma is to determine the appropriate scope of inquiry into the problems of interest to Business Policy practitioners.

---

[1] Note that there will be no references to simulation and optimization methods, such as goal programming, in this paper — they are *primarily* tools for sensitivity analysis and planning, not research tools.

STRATEGY: A THEORY
FOR POLICY RESEARCH

There is no clear answer to the question, "How far can quantitative research advance Business Policy?" This is partly because managing the total enterprise involves both art and science, with art dominating the coalition for most practicing managers. In part, however, the uncertain role of quantitative research in Policy is due to a lack of rigorous theory and theoretical thinking in the field.

Policy is developing around the notion of corporate strategy, a construct which relates management's objectives to the choices it makes in the pursuit of those objectives. Corporate strategy encompasses both management's explicit and implicit decisions with respect to the products the firm makes and the markets it serves (product/market strategy), its decisions of how to compete in those markets and how to develop competitive advantage (business strategy), and its decisions intended to maintain and manage the firm's relationships with the wider society in which it operates. Chandler (1962) and other researchers have explored the relationship between (product/market) strategy and (organizational) structure.

In spite of the progress made in developing the rudiments of a common language to describe top management's role as the creator of an enduring and adaptive relationship between the firm and its environment, there is a question, is the strategy concept a good theory? Bower (1967) said:

> As its essence, good theory states its basic propositions in the form which makes abundantly clear the relationships among key assumptions and the manner in which the theory bears on evidence. Good theory cries for corroboration or refutation and beyond this, good theory stimulates experiments which extend the theory.

As a reconstructing descriptive logic for historical analysis, strategy seems to be without peer. In the classroom it provides a successful problem solving rubric. As a tool for top management, its value is uncertain — perhaps because of the way strategic analysis has been integrated into the formal planning process and because of the false expectation managers have of planning: that is, that the planning process, itself, will produce higher profits, of greater quality (e.g., stability and longevity) and, in addition, innovations of a substantial nature. But as a theory, the answer is not clear, nor is it so comfortable. The first sentence of Bower's "test" is a severe hurdle for the strategy concept — almost every book and paper in the field (including this one) offers a new definition of the concept; a situation which suggests that the propositions underlying the strategy concept are neither clear nor precise. This is one reason why research in the field has been slow in coalescing into distinctively recognizable streams. It suggests the need for more semantically rigorous concepts in the Policy field, i.e., more rigorous thinking.

In spite of these comments, however, the strategy concept has stimulated research. The problem, now, is how to extend the research already reported, for example, by refining the questions asked or by seeking better data to develop better theory. As the next section of the paper shows with respect to quantitative research, "students" of Policy appear to have a decided reluctance to build on Policy's existing research base.

QUANTITATIVE RESEARCH:
QUESTION, DATA, METHOD

At the outset of any research effort, there are a number of questions which must be answered:

1. What is the question to be answered, the hypothesis to be tested or the behavior or "object" to be described?
2. What data are likely to contain an answer?
3. What methodology will allow the researcher access to the data and the best chance of discovering an answer?
4. How are the data measured?

The last question is simplistic, but pertinent: It encompasses issues like, "May I have the data?," the bane of many Policy researchers.

Although the choice of a research topic is a personal one, the research process demands practicality (tempered with idealism, but not dominated by it). Consequently, one of the most important issues in the research process is to evaluate the data needs of the question to be addressed. In this evaluation, the researcher must determine how the data are to be obtained, measured and whether the measurements are adequate for the purpose in mind.

Measurement is central. It fundamentally involves establishing a one-to-one relationship between the properties or characteristics of objects or events, and symbols which have the same relevant relationships to each other as do the things which are represented. Measurement is concerned with: (1) the correspondence between empirical entities and a formal model consisting of abstract elements, for example, numbers; (2) the relationships among these elements; and (3) the operations which can be performed on them (Green and Tull, 1975).

The most important characteristic of a measurement is the information that particular measurement contains. The quality of the information contained in a measurement is determined by the characteristics of the scale used to make the measurement. This is because the assumptions underlying the scale restrict the statistical computations which can be made with measurements on that scale. The major scale classifications are: nominal, ordinal, interval, and ratio.

A nominal scale involves the simple correspondence of a unique name with a particular class of objects or events; for example, "profitable" and "unprofitable" firms. In an ordinal scale, the same firms which were classified nominally "profitable" or "unprofitable" might be ordered in terms of the profits they earned (Firm A greater than Firm B, but no information as to how much greater). Alternatively, more information about each firm could be used if an interval measure, such as dollar profits, was used for the research. There the differences in the dollars earned have meaning. However, if the research concerned three companies, respectively earning dollars, rupees and deutschmarks, the differences between the amounts would have meaning within each currency scale, but comparisons of differences in the amounts earned (in each currency) would have little meaning unless the ratio of value in one scale

to another was known. We could get around this problem if, instead of measuring profit in dollars, etc., we used "profitability" to further our research. The measure, return on assets, has meaning independent of the currency used and it allows meaningful comparisons of ratios. In this particular case, it is possible to measure one quantity (concept) on four scales; however, this kind of transference across scales is not always possible (e.g., because of differing accounting conventions and tax practices which have conveniently been assumed away here) or necessary (an issue which will come up later). It depends on what you are trying to measure and on the question being researched.[2]

What kinds of measurements have been used in Policy research to date? Exhibit 7.21 presents a classification of *some* recently published Policy research in terms of the kinds of data used in each study. For the most part, the kind of question the quantitative researcher in Policy has asked is: "How does Variable Y vary with Variable X_i where $i = 1 \ldots, n$?" i.e., the data used have been treated as Associative data.

Exhibit 7.21 has three sections. The top section of the Exhibit is concerned with associations between two variables, the second section is concerned with associations between a single criterion (or dependent) variable and multiple predictor (or independent) variables, and the last section is concerned with associations between multiple criterion variables and multiple predictor variables. The criterion and predictor variables are described by the scales on which they were measured: nominal, ordinal or interval.

Two research studies which fit into the top part of the Exhibit are the recently published paper on "Defining Corporate Strengths and Weaknesses" by Stevenson (1976) and work on acquisitions by Ansoff et al. (1970). Stevenson

---

[2] Green and Tull (1975) have a short, but clear discussion of measurement which references some of the more advanced works on measurement theory. Since the interval scale is sufficient for most conventional statistical computations and because the *ratio* scale allows all of the computations permissible on an interval scale, subsequently, this paper will discuss only nominal, ordinal and interval scaled data.

Exhibit 7.21 A Classification of Recent Quantitative Policy Research Studies in Terms of the Data They Used

Dependent variables		Independent variables		
		Single		
		Nominal (N)	Ordinal (O)	Interval (I)
Single	N	Stevenson, 1976		
	O			
	I	Ansoff, et al., 1970 Biggadike, 1976	PIMS (Schoeffler, et al., 1974; Buzzell, et al., 1975)	PIMS

		Multiple		
		N	O	I
Single	N			
	O			
	I	Rumelt, 1974		*Hatten, 1974; Stobaugh & Townsend, 1975; Fruhan, 1972; Tsurumi & Tsurumi, 1973; MacIntosh, Tsurumi & Tsurumi, 1973 PIMS, Hatten, Schendel and Cooper, 1978

		Multiple		
		N	O	I
Multiple	N			
	O			
	I			Schendel & Patton, 1976; Mueller, 1967; Grabowski & Mueller, 1972

*Most Industrial Organization research fits into this category — see Shepherd (1972), Vernon (1972), and Winn (1975).

examined the relationship between the types of criteria employed and the attributes examined by managers evaluating the strengths and weaknesses of their firm. His research fits into the category "nominal-nominal" in the first part of the Exhibit. The Ansoff, et al., work employed a series of interval criterion variables and examined the association between each variable mean and the presence or absence of formal planning systems. This work falls into the category "interval-nominal."

In the second section of Exhibit 7.21, it is difficult to find any Policy research where the criterion or dependent variable is measured on anything but an interval (or ratio) scale. Rumelt's research (1974) on the performance of diversified companies generally fits into the

category "interval-nominal"; he was looking at differences in performance between classes of diversified firms. Hatten's (1974) research on the beer industry substantially fits into the category "interval-interval" because virtually all the independent predictor variables used to explain profitability in the beer industry were measured on interval (or ratio) scales. The works of Fruhan (1972a), Macintosh, et al. (1973), and Tsurumi and Tsurumi (1973) also fit into this "interval-interval" category.

One of the most publicized but least understood research efforts, the PIMS project (Schoeffler, Buzzell, and Heany, 1974), uses interval criterion variables and for the most part interval predictor variables, and so fits into section two of Exhibit 7.21 as "interval-interval." However, many of the PIMS conclusions (Buzzell, Gale, and Sultan, 1975) appear to be based on cross-classification studies of interval and ordinal data (e.g., product quality) which puts PIMS in the first section of Exhibit 7.21 in both the "interval-interval" and the "interval-ordinal" categories (as well).

The last third of the Exhibit is sparsely populated. The only possible candidates for it are the industrial organization research of Mueller (1967), Grabowski and Mueller (1972), and Schendel's and Patton's (1976b) policy research in the beer industry. The two methodologies Schendel and Patton employed are types of simultaneous regression: (1) two-stage least squares (2SLS), which is substantially still a member of the second third of the Exhibit because the estimation process depends on single equation methods, and (2) three-stage least squares, 3SLS, which estimates all equations simultaneously and is therefore a valid member of the third section of Exhibit 7.21.

HOW ARE WE APPROACHING POLICY RESEARCH?

Exhibit 7.21 contains many empty cells. Some of these could be filled if examples were taken from the marketing and organizational behavior literature — and in terms of developing new research ideas and becoming familiar with a more comprehensive set of research tools, this is not a bad idea.[3] But, if we stay within the policy field the gaps left are substantial: Exhibit 7.22 creates an impression that there are many types

[3] There are a number of interesting collections of Marketing Research papers available in book form. One of the more useful for someone seeking applications of quantitative research techniques is Aaker's *Multivariate Analysis in Marketing* (1971). This book is organized around methods which have been grouped into sections: (1) on the analysis of dependence and (2) on the analysis of independence. Behavioral Researchers, to a far greater degree than recent Marketing Researchers, have employed bivariate methodologies. Lawrence's and Lorsch's *Organization and Environment* (1967b) illustrates the potential and limitations of ordinal data in Policy research.

of data which are not being used in quantitative policy research — nominal and ordinal data, for example. Why is this so (assuming the sample of research cited is representative)?

The most reasonable explanation is that there just has not been much of this type of quantitative research in Policy; perhaps because nominal and ordinal data are difficult to obtain — but this seems unlikely. It may be that researchers have been concerned about "Hawthorne" effects should they attempt to collect ordinal data in the field — i.e., that the researcher's presence and questions might alter management's perceptions of what is more and less important — but, although this may be a real problem in clinical studies which extend over a long period, such concerns seem unlikely in most quantitative research.

On the other hand, the reason may lie not in the costs and problems of collecting nominal and ordinal data, so much as in the apparent availability of interval data which allows the use of the most advanced analytical tools. It may even be because "higher" scaled data are considered more "respectable." If this is the case, it should be noted that usually, the more precise the measurement (of a concept), the less certain we can be of what it is we have in fact measured, as the Heisenberg principle warns us, e.g., "What single variable best measures scale of production?"

It is hard to say why Exhibit 7.21 looks the way it does but, as Exhibit 7.22 shows, it is not for want of statistical tools for data analysis. Exhibit 7.22 illustrates the large number of techniques available for the analysis of Associative data, i.e., data which are analyzed to determine the association of the level of a variable Y with the level of a series of variables X_i where $i = 1 \ldots, n$. And, the Exhibit is not exhaustive. Many quantitative research tools lie unused in the Policy field.

What does this mean? First, it is apparent that many types of data are not being used and that this is not due to a lack of statistical tools; second, a tendency to standardize our data treatment may be developing in the field, i.e., to partition the matrix into dependent and independent variables; and third, this partitioning suggests that Policy may become the *study of goal-*

Exhibit 7.22 Statistical Techniques for Analyzing Associative Data

Criteria or dependent variables

Single

		Nominal (N)	Ordinal (O)	Interval (I)
	N	Chi square; Contingency coefficient Phi correlation[1] Tetrachoric correlation[1]	Coefficient of differentiation	Correlation ratio Point biserial coefficient
Single	O	Coefficient of differentiation	Goodman-Kruskal gamma Spearman's rank correlation Kendall's tau	Coefficient of point multiserial correlation
	I	Correlation ratio Point biserial coefficient	Coefficient of point multi-serial correlation	Pearson's product moment correlation

Multiple

		N	O	I
	N[1]	Generalized regression AID	Kendall's nonparametric discriminant analysis	Two-group discriminant analysis
Single	O	Kruskal's monotone ANOVA	Guttman-Lingoes' CM-2 regression	Carroll's monotone regression
	I	Analysis of variance Dummy-variable regression AID	Transform ordinal scales of predictor variables followed by multiple regression	Multiple regression

Multiple

		N[2]	O	I
	N[2]	Canonical correlation with dummy variables	Transform ordinal scales, followed by canonical correlation with dummy variables	Multiple discriminant analysis Canonical correlation with dummy variables
Multiple	O	Transform ordinal scales, followed by multivariate analysis of variance	Transform ordinal scales, followed by canonical correlation	Transform ordinal scales, followed by canonical correlation
	I	Multivariate analysis of variance	Transform ordinal scales, followed by canonical correlation	Canonical correlation Full information simultaneous regression

[1] Restricted to binary-valued nominal variable(s), i.e., dichotomies.

[2] By nominal we mean here any single nominal variable that is multichotomous or any set of nominal variables, dichotomous or multichotomous.

seeking corporate behavior. I believe top management's role is more complex than this interpretation suggests and that other views can contribute to the unravelling of this complexity, but more about this later.

Now, the issue is how to extend the existing quantitative research base of the field and how to use the proven quantitative methodologies to develop and test new theories. Here, the focus will be on extending the research listed in the Interval-Interval cells of Exhibit 7.21.

SUGGESTIONS FOR FUTURE RESEARCH: PARTITIONED ASSOCIATIVE DATA

BUILDING ON PUBLISHED RESEARCH

Research is an evolutionary endeavor, for few research efforts terminate a line of inquiry. Good research should lead to sharper questions and more exact hypotheses, i.e., lead to new testable theory. What, then, is the most significant unresolved question in quantitative Policy research today?

The answer: *What is the practical significance of statistical homogeneity and heterogeneity?* Why is this so important? The explanation: Policy has been built on the premise that each industry has unique characteristics and that effective strategies for any firm in any industry should be based on *that* firm's distinctive competence or competitive advantages, i.e., on the firm's uniqueness.

Policy can be viewed as the study of the singular, unique competitive firm in a changing environment. In statistical terms, the implication of this premise is that data describing any one firm and how it is managed should be different from the data describing another. If this is so, as the industries involved become increasingly different, the differences between firms should become more pronounced.

Yet, and this is another reason why the heterogeneity/homogeneity issue is central to Policy, one of the major Policy studies, PIMS, is based on cross-sectional analyses of many dissimilar businesses, i.e., on data which may be heterogeneous. More importantly, conclusions based on this use of aggregative data are being passed on as "prescriptions" for managing businesses (Schoeffler, et al., 1974; Buzzell, et al., 1975). Such data usage is consistent with the usual practice of Industrial Organization, but it is at direct odds with the traditions of Policy.

VIVE LA DIFFERENCE? What does the difference mean? It is fundamentally an argument over the practical importance of the assumptions which *allow* statistical computations to produce *meaningful* results. In this case, it's a matter of how much heterogeneity is allowable in the data when methodologies which rest on the assumption of homogeneity are employed, e.g., cross-tabulations, regression[4] and the analysis of variance.

The argument can be made that all science advances by the use of cross-sectional data. But, the veracity of this statement depends upon knowing what the cross-sections used in any analysis are — so that only data on comparable objects or events are included in the analysis, i.e., so that only homogeneous data are used. If you were a fruit grower, for example, you might be interested in understanding what affects the growth of apples, pears, and watermelons. Yet, in spite of the fact that most of these are rounded objects and very often green at some point in their short lives, it would be unusual to treat them all as members of the one cate-

---

[4] This issue is discussed in detail in Hatten and Schendel (1976). In statistical terms it necessitates a trade-off:

An ideal sample space would include firms with very different strategies and resources. Where there are large differences between firms in the sample, the resulting estimates should represent the effects of changes in the independent variables on the dependent variable over a wide range. The quest for homogeneity forces the selection of more like firms reducing the sample space — a step which reduces the ability of the researcher to generalize from his results although it increases his confidence in the estimated parameters. This step reduces the degrees of freedom available for estimation and, therefore, exerts a pressure for parsimony in the range of variables included in the model — potentially threatening the representative quality of the model itself.

Exhibit 7.23   U.S. Brewing Industry: Industry vs. Group Estimates

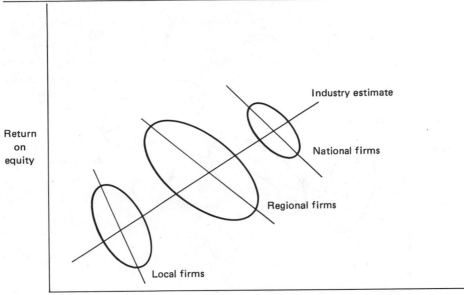

gory, "crops." It is hard to say how a conclusion reached on the analysis of pea data could help a farmer make his fortune in watermelons, which is not to say that the theory and practice of growing and selling peas might not suggest important elements of the theory and practice of growing and selling watermelons. What should concern Policy researchers is that even crude distinctions of this type are not being made when it comes to aerospace firms and cereal manufacturers in many cross-sectional studies of industries, firms and businesses.

Put the peas and watermelons aside and consider Exhibit 7.23. It shows the general relationship between Return on Equity (ROE) and Market Share, in the U.S. brewing industry. By pooling data on national, regional and local brewers, an industry estimate of the association between the two variables can be made (Hatten, 1974; Patton, 1976).

However, the same research has shown that for homogeneous groups of firms — let's call them Strategic groups (of firms) — the relationships are quite different to the industry-wide relationship, the two variables being negatively rather than positively correlated. For managers

in the brewing industry, this difference is important. The estimates suggest that at the firm level, efforts to increase market share may reduce ROE rather than increase it; yet, the managerial implication of the industry estimate is that increasing market share will increase ROE.

Exhibit 7.23 illustrates the market share profitability relationship for one industry. Exhibit 7.24 shows the hypothetical relationship between these variables for three industries: say, for breweries, railroads and electronics firms. Small railroads are profitable, large railroads are not. Many electronics firms seem to believe in the Experience Curve[5] and might be expected to have a ROE/Market Share relationship like the one Exhibit 7.24 shows — but electronics is a relatively young and technologically turbulent industry. Should each of these industries be lumped together into one class in any study of industries?

Note, the industry estimate of Exhibit 7.24 is consistent with the PIMS finding and with a

[5] The Boston Consulting Group, *Perspectives on Experience*, Boston, Mass., 1968.

Exhibit 7.24 Across Industry Estimate vs. Industry Estimates

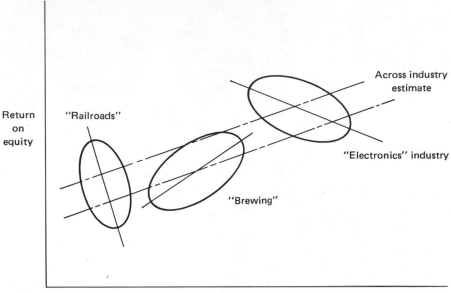

substantial body of Industrial Organization research (see Vernon, 1972). The association
which PIMS and many Industrial Organizations
economists have discovered between ROI and
Market Share (and concentration) is persistent
and strong and is based on analyses of data
on multiple businesses and industries. Hatten
(1974), and Patten (1976), and Hatten and
Schendel (1977) have shown, however, that
even within a single industry statistically significant differences can be found between firms
(i.e., between models of firms' strategic behaviors). And, there is other strong statistical evidence that the relationship for particular industries differs (Marcus, 1969; Rhoades, 1970;
Gale, 1972; Qualls, 1972; Bass, 1974). So where
are we? Quite simply, there must be truth on
each side of the story.

*The most important quantitative research
issue in policy is to establish just what the
different findings mean and to develop a rigorous theory describing how they are linked* because in researching this "difference" it should
be possible to expand our knowledge of how
businesses work and thereby make a major
contribution to practice, especially concerning

the management of strategic change and turnarounds.

Perhaps the explanation of the different findings lies in the questions being asked and the
purposes behind the questions. The users of
aggregated cross-sectional data seem to be interested in the identification of long-run, equilibrium relationships. Policy, on the other hand,
has always stressed the uniqueness of the individual company and, lately, the uniqueness of
the business defined by a particular product/
market. Policy researchers are more interested
in the dynamic short, intermediate and long-
term relationships which affect day-to-day operations and the long-run viability of the firm
than in the theoretical, ultimate, stable equilibrium state of an industry.

Why is market share sought? Experience suggests that building market share *costs*, but the
Boston Consulting Group suggests that this
experience applies in the short run only. If a
firm can climb the profitability ladder of Exhibit 7.23 by making the transitions between
"rungs," that is between groups, even the
within industry research shows that increased
market share is generally associated with higher

ROE. Of course, a useful question here is, "Share of which market?"[6]

THE STRATEGIC GROUP. One way to address the issues raised above is to exploit the construct "Strategic Group," groups of firms competing with similar resources to exploit similar opportunities.

Besides in the beer industry, Strategic Groups have been identified in the white goods industry (major appliances) (Hunt, 1972), the chemical process industry (Newman, 1973) and the consumer goods industry (Porter, 1973). Bass (1974) showed that, at least with respect to the profitability/marketing mix relationship, *groups of industries* exist (although because of sample size restrictions, he did not show that each group was internally homogeneous), and Rumelt (1974) established that distinct classes or groups of diversified firms exist. Moreover, the integrity of the group concept is supported by the fact that where statistical tests have been made for commonness of slope (using dummy variables), the null hypothesis has been rejected. This means that the ways and the effectiveness with which the members of the strategic groups compete are different (Bass, 1974; Hatten, 1974), i.e., the groups *are* different.

The discovery that within and between groups, firms employ *different* mixes of what are substantially the same strategic variables, gives us a sample space wider than the single firm in which we can test, *ex post*, the effectiveness of different mixes of those variables. This *ex post* test which is a quantitative and objective assessment of competitive strengths and weaknesses within the group, and between groups, can be used to create simulations to test new strategies *ex ante* and turn the experience of other companies to advantage.

For example, in preparing for a major change of strategy, management would have to know what group their business was in. Essentially, this means addressing not only the question of who their competitors are, but who they compete *like*. Management might next use their knowledge of strategic groups as a tool to address the *with* question, e.g., as a second step in preparing for a strategy change they might look at the membership of other strategic groups in their industry to determine what elements of the different companies' strategies have been successful or unsuccessful on a group-by-group basis. With an awareness of their own and their competitors' strategies, management could focus their attention on adapting the lessons of their competitors' experience to their own ends. A key issue in their deliberations would be cost.

KEY RESEARCH ISSUES. What can the Policy researcher do to help develop new theory and ultimately advise management? Strategic Groups might be identified *a priori* and then tested (Patton, 1976) or developed statistically (Hatten and Schendel, 1977). The key research topics relating to them are:

1. To determine why Strategic Groups exist and how they are distributed on an industry-by-industry basis.

2. To identify the most effective strategies and the key variables contributing to higher objective attainment on a group-by-group basis within and across industries.

3. To develop a more exact understanding of the role of market segments (which determine how we define market share) in the group structure of industries.

4. To determine how and when one objective should be sacrificed for another, i.e., objective trade-offs — see Hatten (1974) and more particularly Patton (1976) — as companies fight to maintain or improve their competitive position in an industry.

5. To determine what the barriers to a firm's changing its group are. By studying industries over an extended time period, it should be possible to identify companies which have (1) suffered a fall "down the ladder," or (2) have been able to climb the performance ladder to "join" a new more effective and efficient strategic group. By investigating these "switching"

---

[6] Although definition of market is an important and largely unexplored research issue in the policy field, it seems unlikely that market definition, alone, explains the existence of strategic groups. Market scope, corporate goals, and various resource capacities interact to determine how firms can and do compete.

firms we should be able to learn something more about Strategic change and its cost.

In the study of strategic groups and in the study of strategic change is the answer to the homogeneity/heterogeneity issue and the market share-concentration-profitability controversy. In pursuing this research the best "laboratories" may be those companies following strategies which have become ineffective, the failures, and those following new successful strategies, the turnarounds (Schendel and Patton, 1976a).

A Test for a Strategic Model

Aside from the drama of contrasting failures and turnarounds (i.e., the study of pathological firms), the high performer should provide another opportunity for useful research. Given existing theory, it is reasonable to expect that high performance could be partly attributed to more perceptively designed and efficiently implemented new strategies. If strategy is a viable concept, and if a series of major changes in a company's resource allocations and competitive practices have taken place, then *ex post* it should be possible to model the strategies used and statistically identify *when* a change was made.

Ideally, managers would like a model which could quickly alert them to changes in their competitors' strategic management practices, but models with this degree of sensitivity would be costly to maintain and are therefore unlikely to be developed. They would necessitate the use of quarterly, monthly or even weekly data.

On theoretical grounds, though, theory suggests a weak predictive test (Basmann, 1965).[7] If the strategy with which a company has operated has changed considerably and a new strategy has been in place for a substantial number of years, a sound statistical model, i.e., a correctly specified model, should be able to pick up this change.

With regard to a model's ability to identify a strategic change, there is a difference between

the findings of the two methodologies used to study the brewing industry (Hatten, 1974; Patton, 1976). In the single equation study (Hatten), different strategic models were found to apply over different time periods to the two largest brewers, Anheuser-Busch and Schlitz, and to the Associated-Falstaff group. A single model did not give a good description of the strategies of the two groups of firms over the full time period of the study, indicating that either changes in strategy had taken place or that the effectiveness of the strategies in use by these firms had changed over time. Patton's multiequation model (1976) did not establish any "difference over time" in the brewing industry.

The interesting question is why. The data shows that around 1958 and, again, about 1964, Anheuser-Busch and Schlitz shifted strategy (i.e., their resource allocations). In the first period, it was towards building plants, in the second it was with respect to advertising. At the same time, Associated's and Falstaff's fortunes began to wane.

Problems Likely to Be Met. What are the major research problems likely to be encountered in a quantitative pursuit of the homogeneity/heterogeneity issue and the study of strategic change? There are two. The first, besides the problem of specifying market share, is multicollinearity. The problem arises from the fact that market share is correlated with "every" managed variable,[8] e.g., size, advertising, number of plants, return on investment, average capacity, etc.

The key to understanding market share's role in the management of the firm is to identify the

---

[7] See Horsky (1977) for a recent and more sophisticated application of theory testing.

[8] Parsimony in the use of independent variables and careful model specification are probably the best ways to deal with multicollinearity. Johnston (1972) suggests statistical approaches for investigating the extent of the problem. Hatten (1974) used this approach in studying the brewing industry. One approach sometimes advocated is to use Factor Analysis to create new "independent" variables. This is statistically correct but the problem which develops is serious: what do the new variables mean? After all, they are a linear combination of many.

direction of causality, that is, does higher market share "cause" higher profits or do higher profits allow the firm to "buy" increased market share? Patton (1976) provides some substantial evidence suggesting that the latter explanation may be the case. This is an interesting issue for those interested in Policy, because of the anti-trust implications of large or dominant market shares and the advocacy of market share seizing strategies by some of the country's most respected consultants (who generally recognize the costs involved).

The second problem is to separate efficiency and effectiveness. This is really a more serious issue than multicollinearity because it is conceptual and it therefore must affect the research approach and the specification of any model. There are two ways around the problem (Hatten and Schendel, 1976):

> A strategic model should pay attention to the problem of separating the effect of operations and strategy on performance. Since the same accounting system provides the data for many independent and dependent variables, an apparently severe conceptual problem exists. Although efficiency and effectiveness are primary characteristics of successful management systems, the theory of Strategy suggests that efficiency alone, an operational attribute, cannot maintain success in the long run — that is, effectiveness dominates efficiency; and if the model is estimated over an extensive time period or over a broad cross-section of firms, the effects of strategic decisions will be revealed. . . .

There is another approach to the problem of separating the effects of strategy and operations on performance in a quantitative model. It is to acknowledge that these two components of the general management task are interdependent. Since one major use of strategy by the manager is to help him coordinate and integrate the functional operations of the business (it was the notion of integration which spawned the Policy course, itself the source of the concept of Strategy) this does not seem unreasonable. Following this train of thought, it makes sense to use a simultaneous equation model where the exogenous variables represent the environment and where the endogenous variables which are determined by the system of equations in-

clude firm performance on a number of objectives and various operational resource allocations. Grabowski's and Mueller's (1972) paper suggests how this might be done.

Patton (1976) followed the second of these two approaches when he developed a set of simultaneous models for the brewing industry. He used two "strategic objectives," ROE and market share, and an operational goal, "operating efficiency." Given that strategy is often concerned with multiple objectives, this is, on theoretical grounds, the better approach. Conceptually, it makes sense to seek an even better explanation of performance by increasing the number of operational equations and interdependencies in the model. Practically, such an approach might lead to a better understanding of the profitability/market share relationship. However, there are definite limits to how far one can go in this direction because, typically, the data available are limited in number or quality or both.

Conclusion: Associative Data

This brings the discussion of "research on the published quantitative policy research" to a close. The discussion has deliberately ignored "diversification" because that is a topic explicitly addressed by another author in this volume. However, many of the suggestions for studying strategic change are applicable to studies of diversifying strategies because strategic groups within industries are conceptually similar to Rumelt's (1974) clusters of similarly diversified firms.

So far, the discussion has focused on associative data. This is because, with some exceptions, for example, Stevenson's study, "Defining Corporate Strengths and Weaknesses" (1976), the bulk of policy's quantitative research effort has been focused on the *content* of strategy, i.e., we have been mostly interested in the variables a manager can influence or control to affect the performance of the firm.

In other words, quantitative policy researchers have been interested in goal achievement rather than in direction setting and the process of strategy making, and this has led us to collect and treat the data available to us in a particular way. We have partitioned it into two sets of variables, independent and dependent. In addition it has focused *research* attention almost exclusively on developing descriptions on the past rather than the future, which is the domain of Policy. As many glib sages have remarked, historic models of strategy have little value when major social, economic and technological discontinuities occur and change the mix of variables of concern to top management, e.g., the oil crisis. What they ignore is the value of understanding the firm's position vis-à-vis the "stable" part of its environment and the value of the strategy formulation process itself. Research could increase their understanding.

For us, there is another issue to address. Could an alternate quantitative research tack increase our understanding of the strategy formulation process? The answer, if we exploit *non-partitioned* data matrices to explore managerial judgment, is perhaps. It would open up a second front for quantitative research, by employing (non-partitioned) similarity and dominance data to explore the dimensions underlying top management decision making.

SUGGESTIONS FOR FUTURE RESEARCH: NON-PARTITIONED DATA

The suggestions offered so far have emphasized research on the content of Strategy. This section suggests how quantitative research could contribute to the stream of work on the process of *managing* strategy, e.g., Mintzberg (1977).

Consider the following, not unusual statements (Heenan and Addleman, 1976): [9]

---

[9] Heenan and Addleman provide an easy introduction to the use of many of the methods listed in Exhibit 7.22. A number of other references which discuss the use of these statistical methods are included in the references for this section, e.g., Dawes (1972); Green and Rao (1972); Green and Tull (1975), Green and Wind (1975), Johnston (1972); Kinnear and Taylor (1971); Morrison (1967, 1969); and Staelin (1971).

1. Many important issues seem to defy quantification and decision makers are forced to rely on their intuition and experience to a greater degree than is desirable.

2. There are no hard decisions, just insufficient facts. When you have the facts, the decisions come easy.

These statements describe many policy decisions. Policy is concerned with decisions where risk and uncertainty prevail and where intuition and experience have to be used to a greater degree than management scientists are comfortable with. When there are too few facts or, in spite of "2" above, too few principles to distinguish the relevant facts from the irrelevant, we are stuck with judgment and, as Vickers (1965) points out: ". . . there is no way in which any judgments made can be proved right or wrong, even after the event. Judgment seems to be an ultimate quantity or category which can only be approved or condemned by a further exercise of the same ability." Vickers further notes that good judgment can only be recognized over a long time period.

MANAGERIAL JUDGMENT AND POLICY RESEARCH

What is the nature of judgment? What kinds of data are used in judging whether to act or not act, and whether to act in a particular way or in some other way? Surely, judgment is an expression of preference and is based on perceptions of independence, dominance, indifference and likeness. For example, decisions to invest in a particular country or to acquire one of many companies are examples of decisions employing dominance or preference data.

Although quantitative policy research has mostly been descriptive, it has addressed strategic decision making from a preconceived notion of what should be done according to the normative dictates of our theory, i.e., strategy. But, is that what managers do? Why not work back from their judgment, explore strategic decision making[10] as a personal and group process and develop new theory?

---

[10] Mintzberg's work at times follows this tack, but it is nonquantitative. A very different, but important study in this context is Merton J. Peck's

Some years ago Wrapp (1967) suggested that "Good Managers Don't Make Policy Decisions." On close reading it turns out that Wrapp is not an iconoclast so much as a political realist. He really suggests that good managers should develop clearly thought out strategies but never publicly commit themselves to a specific set of organizational goals, because, in the interim, between investment and outcome, these goals will lead to inflexibility, and because once the outcome of resource allocation decisions is apparent the managers may appear unsuccessful. It is a sensitivity for political process such as Wrapp's that is missing from much normative writing in Policy today. For the researcher, however, he raises interesting questions: Are explicit goals at the top functional or dysfunctional? At what hierarchical level is what particular degree of goal specificity optimal? How does optimal goal specificity vary with organizational structure?

Not surprisingly, Wrapp was not alone in 1967. Vickers' (1965) [11] ideas seem consistent with Wrapp's concern over "goals," although Vickers' motivation is different. He describes Policy making as:

> ... the setting of governing relations or norms rather than the setting of goals, objectives or ends ... All course holding cannot be reduced to an endless succession of goals. Policy making takes the major variables into consideration as flows in the dimension of time.... Neglect of normholding leaves us with the purpose-ridden man whose only rational activity is to seek goals, but since each goal once attained,[12] disap-

pears, this leaves him purposeless and incapable of rational activity unless he finds another. . . .

Probably, the last thing policy needs is another set of words whose meanings overlap or encroach on the conceptual territory covered by strategy, strengths and weaknesses, posture, ... etc., but the ideas beneath the generalized language Vickers uses and Wrapp's warning are likely to be useful in developing a new research attack on the unknown in Policy.

What does Vickers mean by "Governing Relations or Course Holding Norms"? The most concise definition of a governing relationship is "a constraint." But this is only part of the picture. Vickers looks at the Policy making task as the art of abstracting solvable problems from reality. This reality is a web of relationships between controllable and noncontrollable variables *and* an accumulation of historical legacies, e.g., decision precedents and accumulated experience, which contain or limit the options available to management. The abstracting task is familiar to every planner, you have to envisage the "state" you want before you can plan a way to realize it.

In the Vickerian view, the Policy maker creates an "Ideal" which describes how he wants his organization situated vis-à-vis input sources, its outlets, and its competitors. In other words, the Ideal defines the kinds of *relationships* he wants between the organization and its environment. In this context, the Policy makers' goals are generalized and become aspirations; the optimization of specific objectives, *per se*, makes no sense. The Policy makers' job is to *balance* the desired relationships since these are likely to be mutually inconsistent. For the Policy maker, uncertainty and unpredictability are the order of the day, but the Policy maker can move or direct the organization towards the Ideal by redefining and changing the limits of lower level discretionary action. Hence, over time, or when new relationships are seen to be necessary, the organization can be moved towards a new Ideal. Vickers says: " ... the goals we [really] seek are changes in our relations and opportunities for relating, but the bulk of our activity consists in relating itself."

---

and Frederic M. Scherer's study, *The Weapons Acquisition Process: An Economic Analysis,* Boston: Division of Research, Graduate School of Business Administration, Harvard University, 1962. This is an example of a quantitative study exploring Policy decisions from a judgmental point of view.

[11] Vickers is a neglected contributor to the Policy field. The only reference I have seen to his work in the literature is in Ackoff's *A Concept of Corporate Planning,* (1970: 154). Ackoff recommends Vickers as a profound thinker in Policy matters.

[12] We can add, "the effect of not attaining his goals is often frustration."

Vickers and Wrapp offer an alternative view to what Policy is all about, that is, an alternative to the now orthodox goal-seeking view. They see the top manager's job as setting direction bounded by recognizable constraints which originate from desired and inevitable relationships between the organization and its environment, and from the organization's past.

What kinds of research could this different view lead us to? For a start, we could develop a new theory of planning. Policy is formed by managers playing an institutional role and this is well described by Vickers:

> The world in which Policy makers, like other people, effectively live is a mental artifact largely, but never wholly shared by its inhabitants whose main social function is to inherit it, preserve it, develop it and pass it on. . . . Policy is formed by men playing some institutional role. The structure and function of the organization within which they are acting, and its relations with other institutions, powerfully affect what they will regard as standards of success as well as defining the scope of their discretion and the extent of their power.

A theory of planning based on managerial perceptions, and the nature of consensus and conflict at the institutional level would be a natural outgrowth of the Vickers/Wrapp position. An important test for any such theory is to explain the observed gyrations and aberrations of planners and planning in an institutional context (Stevenson and Hatten, 1977), i.e., it must be researchable.

Other topics suggested by Vickers/Wrapp view of Policy research are:

1. What is the mental artifact managers use to describe the Policy makers' world, i.e., what are its dimensions and what is the *language* its inhabitants use to describe it? Do we manage through words?

2. How do institutional contexts affect the criteria managers use to judge their company's and their personal success and failure?

3. What is the *ideal* model of the firm sought by managers, at different firms, and at different institutional levels in a firm or different firms?

The next three subsections of this paper will suggest how quantitative techniques might contribute to an exploration of such issues. The discussion will suggest an important *link* between the suggested research on the ideal firm and research on strategic groups and strategic change.

SUGGESTIONS FOR QUANTITATIVE RESEARCH ON JUDGMENT

What is the mental artifact used to describe the Policy maker's world, i.e., what is its dimensionality and how are those dimensions described?

In making an investment in a new plant there is an implicit or explicit trade-off between: (1) realizing the efficiencies of scale and technological specialization, and (2) product flexibility, market responsiveness, and supply security. In decisions to change strategies for a whole corporation or even a substantial part of it, e.g., a division, it can be expected many factors are considered by the responsible managers.

It would be interesting to know just what dimensions (and how many) are necessary to adequately describe the decision spaces employed in situations like these. Already some qualitative work related to questions of this type has been reported by Carter (1971), who suggested eight hypotheses as to "how managers make decisions." The two which fit into the context of this paper are:

H_1 Submissions of projects for organizational approval are made on subordinates' prior estimates of the projects' likely chance of approval, "losers" are withheld, i.e., the precedents of past decisions constrain the possible rate of strategic change.

H_6 The greater the uncertainty of the outcome of a decision in the total environment of the organization, the greater the number of criteria which will be sought to guide the strategic decision, i.e., more relationships are tested against thresholds of indifference when uncertainty is greater. This implies increasing conservatism and risk aversion, which may explain why large companies have so much trouble innovating outside their traditional businesses.

Two quantitative techniques which could help us explore the dimensionality of the decision maker's space are Factor Analysis and Conjoint Measurement.[13] Factor Analysis might be helpful in defining the attributes necessary for discrimination among choices. Factor Analysis can be performed on data which are subjective ratings of objects, e.g., products or services or companies, on each of a set of attributes provided by the researcher. Table I of Exhibit 7.25 shows the results of a Factor Analysis of eight computer companies on each of fifteen attributes. The Table suggests that, *for the particular respondents* surveyed, one dimension dominates their view of computer companies. However, for the researcher, the problem is "What is that dimension?" In this case, it appears to be closely related to a service concept. Price flexibility, for example, appears to have little discriminating power.

As the illustration suggests, the central problem with Factor Analysis is to interpret its output. Unless the user can find a way to make sense of the output, the analysis has no value. Notwithstanding this problem, Table I, Exhibit 7.25, illustrates how Factor Analysis develops a picture of things being rated and the attributes which interested *the people surveyed*.[14] Here, we might suspect the people surveyed were business users, rather than scientists, because of the relative closeness of CDC, UNIVAC and NCR, a suspicion which should raise a warning flag about the output of all survey methods.

The results may depend on the population polled as much as on the explicit attributes used in the survey (providing another research opportunity).

Factor Analysis, nonetheless, provides a method whereby the critical dimensions underlying a decision might be revealed and then fed back into a Conjoint Measurement study to establish their relative importance to the decision maker. In this way, Factor Analysis might contribute to a more precise definition of the language used to describe strategy.

Conjoint Measurement starts with a subject's (say, a manager's) overall or global judgments about a set of complex alternatives. It then decomposes the original evaluation into separate and comparable utility scales by which the original judgment can be reconstituted.

The usual input to a Conjoint Measurement "survey" is a manager's ranking of a set of alternatives which differ on a set of *preselected* attributes. The output is a set of computed scale values for each attribute. In the data analysis the decomposition of the original judgment is constrained to preserve the manager's ranks for each alternative as closely as possible.

The output of a Conjoint Measurement study provides information about the relative importance of the various attributes in the decision maker's choices. The obvious limitation of the procedure is the "attributes selected for study" because "what goes in, comes out." However, the need for precise and parsimonious concept definitions would be a good thing for the policy field. It could ultimately force us to address the question: "Does our generalized language have meaning for practitioners?"

In the context of concept definition, and to further illustrate the opportunities for evolutionary research in the policy field which would allow us to develop new theory and test it, it should be possible to build on Stevenson's research on strengths and weaknesses and to link this to the industry study approach of Hatten and Patton. On the basis of the statistical modelling studies, membership of a Strategic Group can be characterized by patterns of variables which have positive and negative coefficients vis-à-vis some criterion variable, both within groups and between groups. The pattern of

[13] Paul E. Green and Yoram Wind in "New Way to Measure Consumers' Judgments," *Harvard Business Review*, July–August 1975, discuss the strengths and weaknesses of Conjoint Measurement techniques and their relationship to Factor Analysis, Perceptual Mapping and Cluster Analysis. The paper is a good "first" reading for those unfamiliar with these techniques.

[14] There is no reason to restrict the analysis to two dimensions. More can be handled and there are techniques available to guide the researcher in the task of structuring and simplifying data to discover its meaning.

Exhibit 7.25 **Applications of Factor Analyses and Perceptual Mapping**

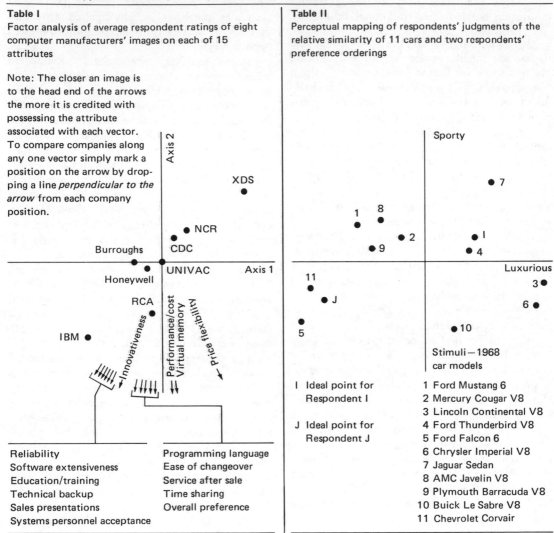

Table I

Factor analysis of average respondent ratings of eight computer manufacturers' images on each of 15 attributes

Note: The closer an image is to the head end of the arrows the more it is credited with possessing the attribute associated with each vector. To compare companies along any one vector simply mark a position on the arrow by dropping a line *perpendicular to the arrow* from each company position.

Reliability	Programming language
Software extensiveness	Ease of changeover
Education/training	Service after sale
Technical backup	Time sharing
Sales presentations	Overall preference
Systems personnel acceptance	

Table II

Perceptual mapping of respondents' judgments of the relative similarity of 11 cars and two respondents' preference orderings

I Ideal point for Respondent I

J Ideal point for Respondent J

Stimuli — 1968 car models

1 Ford Mustang 6
2 Mercury Cougar V8
3 Lincoln Continental V8
4 Ford Thunderbird V8
5 Ford Falcon 6
6 Chrysler Imperial V8
7 Jaguar Sedan
8 AMC Javelin V8
9 Plymouth Barracuda V8
10 Buick Le Sabre V8
11 Chevrolet Corvair

the coefficients indicates relative strengths and weaknesses, or perhaps opportunities and threats — it depends to an extent whether the manager's thinking is defensive (contingent) or aggressive (opportunistic). For the researcher it should be possible to contrast "what managers say," e.g., following Stevenson, beginning with "what the numbers say," and following Hat-ten's and Patton's approach, to identify key dimensions or comparable attributes for further study by Factor Analysis and Conjoint Measurement. By approaching the question, what are your strengths and weaknesses, from different research approaches it should be possible to refine the Strategy Concept and, ultimately, sharpen management's awareness of the relative strengths and weaknesses of their firm relative to its competitors.

How do institutional contexts affect the criteria used to judge success and failure?

Another technique which seems useful in policy research is Perceptual Mapping, which is also known as Multidimensional Scaling. The objective of Perceptual Mapping is to take a subject's (a manager's) overall judgments of similarity or preference and develop a picture in which objects, e.g., companies or products, plot near each other. The distinctive feature of these methods vis-à-vis Conjoint Measurement and Factor Analysis is that with Perceptual Mapping each respondent picks his or her own decision space — i.e., the attributes used to map the space and judge likeness or preference.

As with Factor Analysis, it is the researcher's job to discover the underlying dimensionality of the decision space. Table II of Exhibit 7.25 illustrates a perceptual mapping of 1968 model cars. The researcher has labelled the map "sporty-luxurious," an apparently useful labelling which may not be easily imitated for more complex issues, e.g., mapping the competitive space of an industry, which could be its major application in the Policy field.

However, look at Table II, Exhibit 7.25 again. Note the points marked "I" and "J." These are the "Ideal" points for two respondents. An ideal point corresponds to the respondent's most preferred attribute mix. Objects closer to this ideal point are more preferred; those at a distance are less preferred. The ideal point is an output of many mapping and scaling programs; its location, and the overall map, are calculated by algorithms which preserve preference orders between objects as they are placed, relative to each other, into a perceptual map. The ideal point represents a subject's optimal value in the decision space.

Perceptual Mapping should allow us to explore managers' views of corporate or personal success. It should be possible to design a within company or within industry survey to explore just how success or failure is perceived across hierarchies and across companies. Not only would the dimensionality of the perceptual space be of great interest, but so would the significance of any clusters of individual ideal

points. If they could be characterized, functionally or hierarchically, for example, we would have a quantitative tool which we could use to investigate the effect of institutional context on the decision maker's judgment.

What is the Ideal (model of the firm) sought by managers?

A more interesting application of perceptual mapping in Policy, however, is to use the ideal point to explore top managers' visions of the "Kinds of company they would like to lead." Earlier in this paper, this concept was described as the "Ideal" firm.

How do top managers set corporate direction? Adopting Vickers' thinking we could envision them moving their firms towards an Ideal. Imagine that the perceptual map of Table II, Exhibit 7.25 shows U.S. brewing companies instead of 1968 cars. Aside from sharpening our understanding of competition within an industry by challenging us to identify the key dimensions underlying management's view of its competitors, the perceptual map would allow us to test the validity of the Strategic Group Concept itself.

The imaginary version of the map in Table II, whose dimensions we will leave unlabelled, suggests that three clusters of firms exist: (5, 11); (1,2,8,9); and (3,6). Which firms belong to which clusters? Are the sets of judgedly similar firms the same as the sets of firms in the homogeneous strategic groups identified by Hatten (1974) and Patton (1976) (and illustrated in Exhibit 7.23)?

If they were substantially similar or identical, then the strategic group concept would gain further support. If they were not alike, then we would have a new question to research. We might argue that the model used to test for homogeneity was misspecified. Alternatively, we might argue that management did not know its own business and perhaps we might brand the strategic group concept a statistical curiosity.

Another question for study is, Where would the ideal points of the managers of each firm be located? For example, if manager "I" and manager "J" were respectively the managers of companies #5 and #11, "J's" aspirations would be more consistent with his firm's current position than manager "I's." The next question would be, how does "I's" divergent Ideal influence his strategic decisions? Similar analysis might be possible for managers at many levels and in many functions and further analysis of this data might let us discover how (or whether) "consensus" develops through a planning cycle, and to assess the underlying biases of different policy advisors. In addition, it might be possible to develop an appropriate measure of consensus and conflict and, thereby, relate process to output or performance, e.g., to *hard* goals like profitability and market share.

Among the interesting research possibilities using Perceptual Mapping (or Multidimensional Scaling) techniques is the study of corporate direction setting itself. If managers will allow us to study their perceptual maps of competition in their industries we could identify their respective ideal points, i.e., their ideal competitive positions in their industries.

Do they attempt to move their organizations towards their Ideal? What is the impact of the distance between the Ideal and current reality on their willingness to commit resources to change? Can they go beyond the Ideal and, if so, how and to what effect? More importantly, how do they think about moving the firm and changing direction?

Currently, policy research is anchored by the definition of strategy in product/market space. Common usage of these words and concepts relates to the management of *existing* product portfolios. Is it possible to help managers set a better corporate direction for future endeavors by exploiting different sets of words? Marketing theorists might advise us to consider "needs," operations managers might say "technologies," arguing that corporate aspirations tend to emerge from technologies. The marketers might argue that market segments emerge from unsatisfied needs and that it is the final product and its attributes which will determine or constrain the ultimate size of the market, i.e., the opportunity available.

Research on judgment, exploiting both conventional and nonconventional quantitative techniques as *part* of a total research attack using many methodologies, could help increase our understanding of corporate direction set-

ting. Survey dependent quantitative methods (non-parametric statistics) have capabilities which could open up complex managerial behavior, like direction setting, to forceful research. Significantly, unlike the quantitative methods which have been employed by Policy researchers to date, these are not restricted to historical analyses. They can explore the present, and the present pushing into the future.

THE ESSENTIAL DILEMMA

When theory is outstripped by facts, patterns of convergence in the data become important to practitioners and researchers alike. New theories have to be conceptualized, or alternatively, induced from the data. We have to work from the particular to the general before we can deduce from our accumulated experience what to do in new and different (particular) situations. Policy is in this situation today.

The essential dilemma we face is that, as an area, we are impatient for a wholistic theory of managing.[15] Individual research projects can never produce this type of theory. By its nature, research must be specialized and narrowly focused and its immediate conclusions can be only fragmentary contributions to an all-encompassing theory.

The key to productive quantitative research in Policy is to revise or modify our expectations of what it can produce. Quantitative methods have been "oversold" in too many fields already. Research including quantitative policy research, will advance faster if its focus is on generating questions and pursuing them, rather than on the quest for *the* all-encompassing answer. It's a matter of developing theory and finding ways to test it.

The standard model of the scientific method is hypothesize-test-hypothesize. In the policy field, there seems to be a push towards this form of research. However, a warning is in order. First, the scientific method, in spite of

---

[15] One skeptical and witty review commented: "Not the complete donut view which some functional areas claim to possess?"

its contribution to knowledge, is merely a huer- istic. It has no inherent value of itself.[16] Sec- ond, there is no particular reason why we have to partition every set of data examined into dependent and independent variables as a first or second step in the research process. As the discussion on non-partitioned data has argued, opportunities for valuable research lie in simply discovering the structure of judgment. Remem- ber, Francis Bacon's scientific method emerged about 1600 years after the birth of Christ. Before Bacon, science consisted of simply ob- serving patterns and discovering structure. Per- haps, in spite of the success of the scientific method, research or inquiry in the pre-Bacon

period has some useful lessons for researchers in policy today?

In the social sciences, hard tests on non- trivial issues are difficult to come by; more so, when we do not understand the meaning and structure of the data available to us. Today policy needs eclectic multidirectional research efforts to generate better descriptions, questions and hypotheses, so that we can increase our understanding of top management practice. As this paper has attempted to argue, our progress is likely to be greater if quantitative techniques are used (in conjunction with other approaches) to build upon the research base already es- tablished.

Commentary

WILLIAM NAUMES
Clark University

INTRODUCTION

This paper has two basic objectives. The first is to comment on the papers by Robert Duncan and Kenneth Hatten. The second is to present comments in areas not covered by these two papers. Included in the latter section will be research methodology dealing with simulations, Delphi technique, path analysis, Q sorts, and inductive reasoning.

SOME OBSERVATIONS ON THE DUNCAN AND HATTEN PAPERS

Duncan and Hatten have produced in-depth definitions of frameworks for classifying vari- ous pieces of research in the policy field. This, in itself, is a valuable addition to the literature and research thrust of the field.

Hatten quotes Bower (1967) as to the pre- requisite for good theory and then goes on to

adapt these prerequisites to strategy research. Particularly, the classification scheme presented in Exhibit 7.21 of his paper can be used as a guide for evaluating all forms of quantitative research in the field.

Duncan provides a complementary statement concerning qualitative research techniques. Ex- hibits 7.12, 7.16 and 7.20 present appropriate direction and questions for evaluating this form of research.

The major thrust of Hatten's argument is that the vast majority of the policy research that he reviews fails to take advantage of so- phisticated analytical data analysis techniques that are available. He concludes that this is apparently due to the tendency of most re- searchers to classify their data along classical dependent-independent variable lines, which fits a view of policy as a study of goal seeking organizational behavior. Hatten rejects both this view of policy and classification method as too narrow. He then explores some of the possi- bilities for using more sophisticated quantita- tive data analysis techniques if such constraints are relaxed.

[16] See Christenson (1976) for a brief and more technical exposition on alternate forms of inquiry.

Duncan also suggests that many policy research studies do not utilize the variety of qualitative research tools available to researchers. More importantly, however, Duncan suggests the need for a combination of qualitative and quantitative research techniques in most policy research. This point deserves greater emphasis. In the strategic management area, qualitative research frequently provides the theoretical and conceptual foundation upon which quantitative research is based. What we see then, is that the two forms of research share a symbiotic relationship. In strategic decision making terms, the combination provides synergistic results.

SOME ADDITIONAL OBSERVATIONS ON STRATEGIC MANAGEMENT RESEARCH

PROBLEMS OF STRATEGIC MANAGEMENT RESEARCH

It is interesting that the policy literature continually stresses the need for a wholistic theory of strategic management. Apparently there is the feeling that this is necessary to become a respectable part of the business research community. It is possible, however, that this is in response to practitioner requirements. It should be realized that the fields with which Duncan and Hatten compare strategic management (marketing, organization behavior, etc.) did not spring forth on the research scene with such a base. Typically, each researcher in these fields provided insights into a particular subtopic within his/her field.

The individual research studies were all, typically, reacting to some combination of internal and external stimuli. The external stimulus frequently takes the form of a stated theory or concept. The internal stimulus usually involves the desire of a researcher to either prove or disprove a portion of that theory.

The external theory that has been developed in the area of strategic management takes many forms. What should be noted here is that there is some consensus as to what forms the basis for strategic management, as Duncan and Hatten point out. It is not necessary to present yet another list of quotes and references to prove this point. Suffice it to say that the foundation for a theory of strategic management is present.

Many authors have developed their own frameworks for arriving at effective strategic decisions. Some of the earlier expositions of such frameworks were based on the author's intuitive feelings. Others, including the more enduring ones, were based on studies of one or more organizations that appeared to be "successful." The method for arriving at general, organization-wide decisions in such firms was then proposed as the definitive framework for strategic decision making. (See Chandler, 1962, Ansoff, 1965 and Holden et al., 1968.) The latter works are representative of some of the types of research described in Duncan's article. Moreover, many of the policy oriented case studies were the product of this type of research.

More recently, other authors have attempted to borrow concepts from other disciplines to provide the basis for such strategic decision making frameworks. For instance, Paine's and Naumes' 1974 text, *Strategy and Policy Formulation: An Integrated Approach,* is based on the premise that the strategic decision process is political and social as well as theoretical, and therefore incorporates concepts drawn from the organizational behavior literature.

Such behavioral frameworks present an answer to some of the problems described in Hatten's paper. That is, since strategic management deals with decisions that are made by people, such decisions are typically made by interacting power blocks, both inside and outside of the organization, as described by Mintzberg and Bower and Doz (see Section 2 and Section 3 respectively). As a result, the final strategic decision is more likely to present an acceptable solution than an optimal one.

Moreover, if strategic decisions are primarily heuristic in nature, as Paine and Naumes (1974) suggest, then it is not surprising that policy researchers have found it extremely difficult to test out their theories using anything but nominal data techniques. The results of such global, heuristic decision processes can usually only be quantified in a simplistic manner. The measurements are usually rank order in nature, if they are quantified at all. Consequently, part of the reason for the lack of sophistication in data analysis techniques in past policy research stems from the nature of the phenomena being investigated and not from a lack of knowledge on the part of the researchers as Hatten suggests.

In addition, strategic decision makers often rely on qualitative analysis of global problems in order to reach their conclusions, as Mintzberg (1972) suggests. It must be realized, however, that the top level managers who usually make such strategic decisions are frequently unfamiliar with the more sophisticated quantitative methods described by Hatten. These techniques are typically presented in publications not specifically aimed at the strategic decision maker. It is little wonder, therefore, that top managers fail to use complex quantitative methods in arriving at their strategic decisions. This lack of knowledge and limited use of quantitative tools adds still another dimension to the problem facing researchers who would like to rigorously analyze strategic decisions, since it is difficult to utilize sophisticated statistical methods to analyze qualitative global decision making processes because of the number of confounding variables associated with such processes. Emory (1976) describes the necessity for field studies for this form of research, a conclusion that supports Duncan's call for a combination of quantitative *and* qualitative research.

SOME AREAS WHERE QUANTITATIVE RESEARCH METHODS MAY BE EFFECTIVE

Although it may be necessary to use primarily qualitative research methods or to combine qualitative and quantitative research methods in most parts of the strategic management area, there may be some portions of the field in which it is possible to use primarily quantitative research methods such as those Hatten suggests, a point Hatten notes toward the end of his paper but does not explore sufficiently.

Thus, if the strategic decision making process is conceptualized as being divided into strategy formulation, evaluation, and implementation, one immediately notes that quantitative research methods have been used far more effectively in some of these areas than others. The evaluation phase, in particular, has lent itself both to quan-

titative research methods and to the use of optimization techniques in practice (Ferguson and Jones, 1969; Ricker, 1969; and Miller, 1971). These latter techniques are being used primarily at the middle level management however, not at the top level. That is, middle level managers and management consultants are using computer aided quantitative techniques to evaluate strategies that have been previously formed, often by top management.

In addition, quantitative research techniques can be used effectively in testing the use of such quantitative methods in strategic management decision making, since hard data is available for measurement. Typically, some form of simulation of the interactive effects of the strategy, the organization and the environment is used. Emory (1976) and Guetzkow et al. (1972) also note that simulation techniques are equally appropriate for qualitative research methods.

THE POTENTIAL FOR SIMULATIONS IN STRATEGIC MANAGEMENT RESEARCH AND PRACTICE

Both Duncan and Hatten neglect simulations as a viable tool for strategic management research and practice. For instance, qualitative research can be used to develop simulation models and quantitative techniques can then be used to test specific portions of the model in laboratory settings.

The computer can also be utilized to develop an analog of the real world, or at least some part of it. Thus, some of the research projects discussed in the Hatten paper are essentially a form of simulation. They are attempting to model an industry to determine the importance of various strategic variables. In effect, they have gone through the first iteration in developing a model for the industry. The next step would be to develop interactive effects and, through such iterations, to develop simulation coefficients for the industry or a firm within it.

The problem with utilizing such techniques in the research process, as elsewhere, is the difficulty in evaluating the validity of the basic simulation. The simulation has to be based on actual data which then require a test based on face validity. What the researcher is faced with is the problem we started with. Although the formulation of the simulation model may require sophisticated techniques, the testing of the model relies on simplistic and non-rigorous methods, such as individual case studies or other qualitative techniques described by Duncan.

The key point here, though, is that an attempt be made to break down the various components of the model for further research. Much as econometricians do not immediately attempt to model an entire economy, the researcher in strategic management should not necessarily attempt to include all interactions into his/her model at once.

The Potential of Computer Aided Decision Making in Strategic Management Research

The methods described above do not take full advantage of the resources of the computer, however. One of the real values of the computer is its ability to interact rapidly, if properly programmed. In this regard, several studies, including those of McKinney (1969), Naumes (1971), and Wynne and Newsted (1974), have attempted to simulate the strategy formulation process. In particular, they all examined various problems involved with use of computers during strategy formulation and evaluation although with varying degrees of sophistication in their statistical analysis. The key issue, however, is that they all attempted to simulate a portion of the strategic decision process on a responsive, interactive computer system.

Some Additional Methods of Quantitative Analysis Useful in Strategic Management Research

Whether looking at segments of the strategic decision making process or the entire process, what the policy researcher is typically studying is a flow of decisions. As Mintzberg (1972) states, "we define strategy as a pattern in a stream of significant decisions." Mintzberg uses this definition to focus on the development of a basic strategic decision making framework he uses in the intensive, qualitative analysis of two specific strategic decision processes. He

does not discuss, however, the potential for the application of advanced quantitative techniques that this definition of strategy provides the policy researcher, or the tools that can be used to analyze critically such decision flows.

Two such techniques involve the use of Q sorts and Path Analysis. Both of these techniques were developed to fill the needs of researchers in other areas. Since policy is supposed to be concerned with applied forms of decision processes, however, it is only fitting that it apply these techniques to its own needs.

An introduction into the use of Q sorts was presented in a paper by Miller (1975). The use of this technique allowed Miller to analyze patterns of decisions as presented in published sources such as *Fortune*. The principal difficulty he encountered involved the pre-determination of the variables to be considered. Since this tool is quite advanced and just beginning to be discussed in the research literature, it is quite likely that future applications will reveal other difficulties as well.

Path Analysis is another tool that can be used for analyzing streams of decision behavior. Anderson and Pfaffenberger (1974) have described one application of this tool to organizational theory research. Most of their conclusions would apply to strategic management research as well. The principal value of Path Analysis as their paper indicates is the ability to relax assumptions concerning interval scaling and linearity required by most other quantitative research methods. This is quite important for the strategic management area, since as we have stated, much strategic management research lends itself to nominal, ordinal data. Thus Path Analysis allows more rigor to be included in such studies when tracing and testing strategic decision patterns against an a priori set of hypotheses or expectations.

In short, Q sorts and Path Analysis are two more quantitative techniques that are available to the serious policy researcher who desires to use multivariate analysis of organization-wide issues and decisions, and because of the types of data they use they may prove more valuable than many of the techniques discussed by Hatten.

There is also a set of major qualitative research techniques appropriate for strategic management research that are not covered by Duncan. These are the various Delphi approaches that have been developed in the environmental forecasting literature. The value of these Delphi methods is that they allow decision makers to arrive at their own consensus rather than forcing the researcher to try to abstract conclusions (which are often biased) about the strategic decision making process.

Duncan also fails to explore the use of intuitive reasoning in the research process as fully as he might. He does discuss the use of such reasoning while trying to determine what should be studied. However, this method also provides one of the most frequently used methods of evaluating data once it has been gathered. Thus, while most quantitative research methods provide the researcher with some form of relationship, it is still up to the reasoning power of the researcher, frequently using inductive or deductive reasoning, to determine the potential reasons for the relationships. In short, initial research provides the model to be tested, relationships are tested, and finally, causation of relationships are determined and further tested.

CONCLUSIONS

Duncan and Hatten have primarily concerned themselves, especially at the beginning of their papers, with questions concerning global, or wholistic research issues in strategic management. There has been greater success in applying advanced research techniques to segments of the area than by trying to prove or disprove an entire theory, though, as Hatten eventually notes.

Together they consider a wide range of potential research methods and tools that may be used for strategic management research. However, they overlook others; for example, neither author explores the use of simulations and computer aided decision analysis as potential strategic management research tools or as aids to strategic management practice. Work has been done, however, on the application of these tools to policy research, as well as to management practice.

Methods such as Q sorts and Path Analysis also deserve to be included in any list of potential research methods for the strategic management area. One of the more interesting tools worth further discussion involves the application of Bayesian statistics to strategic management research. This is extremely appropriate since most strategic decisions are made as a result of estimates made by individuals with incomplete data.

Most research begins with a theoretical conceptualization of the topic in question. Intuitive reasoning, the Delphi method, or simply brainstorming can, therefore, often be used to define the direction and boundaries of the research project. Given the heuristic nature of the policy area, the development of an effective research design will usually include both qualitative and quantitative methods, as Duncan notes. In addition, it is often possible to utilize many of the more sophisticated quantitative research techniques, as Hatten suggests, since methods have been found to overcome many of the obstacles that once limited their use in the strategic management area. The relaxation of data constraints in the use of Path Analysis, as well as the development of inferential and non-parametric statistics, exemplifies these methods. Consequently, what is needed now is more research, using both qualitative and quantitative techniques, into the various segments of the strategic management field. The key is to develop the appropriate combination of qualitative and quantitative techniques for any given piece of research. If the research is conceptually based, the techniques used should usually be more qualitatively oriented. If the research involves hypotheses testing or data bases, quantitative research techniques would be more appropriate. Policy researchers should not feel compelled to use one form of research tool simply because they feel that they will gain acceptance by a particular academic group or add credibility to the research. Misuse of research tools adds nothing to the final outcome, and may cast doubt on the credibility of what might otherwise be significant findings.

Section 7 References

Aaker, David A. (editor). *Multivariate Analysis in Marketing: Theory and Application.* Belmont, Calif.: Wadsworth Publishing, 1971.

Ackerman, Robert W. *The Social Challenge to Business.* Cambridge, Mass.: Harvard University Press, 1975.

Ackoff, Russell L. *A Concept of Corporate Planning.* New York: Wiley–Interscience, 1970.

Adams, James. *Conceptual Blockbusting.* San Francisco: Freeman, 1974.

Aguilar, Francis. *Scanning the Business Environment.* New York: Macmillan, 1967.

Alchian, Armen A. "Uncertainty, Evolution, and Economic Theory." *Journal of Political Economy,* June 1950.

Allison, Graham T. *Essence of Decision: Explaining the Cuban Missile Crisis.* Boston: Little, Brown, 1971.

Altman, Edward. *Corporate Bankruptcy in America.* Lexington, Mass.: Lexington Books, 1971.

Anderson, Carl R. and Roger C. Pfaffenberger. "Path Analysis as a Research Tool." *Proceedings of the Eastern Academy of Management,* Maryland, 1974.

Anderson, Carl R. and Frank T. Paine. "Managerial Perceptions and Strategic Behavior." *Academy of Management Journal,* December 1975.

Ansoff, H. Igor. *Corporate Strategy: An Analytic Approach to Business Policy for Growth and Expansion.* New York: McGraw-Hill, 1965.

Ansoff, H. Igor (editor). *Business Strategy.* Baltimore, Md.: Penguin, 1969.

Ansoff, H. Igor. "Managing Strategic Surprise by Response to Weak Signals." *California Management Review,* Winter 1976.

Ansoff, H. Igor, Jay Avener, Richard G. Brandenburg, Fred E. Portner and Raymond Radosevich. "Does Planning Pay? The Effect of Planning on Success of Acquisitions in American Firms." *Long Range Planning,* December 1970.

Ansoff, H. Igor, R. P. Declerck and R. L. Hayes. *From Strategic Planning to Strategic Management.* New York: Wiley, 1976.

Ansoff, H. Igor and J. C. Leontiades. "Strategic Portfolio Management." *Journal of General Management,* Vol. 4, No. 1, 1976.

Ansoff, H. Igor and John Stewart. "Strategies for a Technology-Based Business." *Harvard Business Review,* November–December 1967.

Argenti, John. *Corporate Collapse: The Causes and Symptoms.* New York: Wiley, 1976.

Argyris, Chris and Donald Schon. *Theory and Practice.* San Francisco: Jossey-Bass, 1974.

Bakan, D. "The Test of Significance in Psychological Research." *Psychological Bulletin,* Vol. 66, No. 6, 1966.

Barton, A. "The Concept of Property-Space in Social Research," in Lazarsfeld, P. F. and Morris Rosenberg. *The Language of Social Research.* New York: The Free Press, 1955.

Basmann, R. L. "On the Application of the Identifiability Test Statistic in Predictive Testing of Explanatory Economic Models." *The Econometric Annual of the Indian Economic Journal,* Vol. 13, No. 3, 1965.

Bass, Frank M. "Profit and the A/S Ratio." *Journal of Advertising Research,* December 1974.

Becker, Howard and Blanche Geer. "Participant Observation and Interviewing: A Comparison," in Filstead, W. (editor), *Qualitative Methodology.* Chicago: Markham, 1970.

"Behind the Profit Plunge at Heublein." *Business Week,* July 4, 1977.

Berry, C. *Corporate Growth and Diversification.* Princeton, N.J.: Princeton University Press, 1975.

Biggadike, Ralph. "Entry, Strategy and Performance." Doctoral diss., Harvard University, 1976.

Blalock, H. *Theory Construction.* Englewood Cliffs, N.J.: Prentice-Hall, 1969.

Blau, Peter. *The Dynamics of Bureaucracy.* Chicago: University of Chicago Press, 1963.

Bogdan, Robert and Steven J. Taylor. *Introduction to Qualitative Research Methods.* New York: Wiley, 1975.

Boston Consulting Group. *Perspectives on Experience.* Boston: Boston Consulting Group, 1968.

Bouchard, Thomas, Jr. "Field Research Methods: Interviewing, Questionnaires, Participant Observation, Systematic Observation, Unobtrusive Measures," in Dunnette, M. (editor), *Handbook of Industrial and Organizational Psychology.* Chicago: Rand McNally, 1976.

Bower, Joseph L. "Strategy as a Problem Solving Theory of Business Planning." Boston, Mass.: Intercollegiate Case Clearing House #9-368-039, 1967.

Bower, Joseph L. *Managing the Resource Allocation Process: A Study of Corporate Planning and Investment.* Boston: Graduate School of Business Administration, Harvard University, 1970.

Braithwaite, R. *Scientific Explanation.* Cambridge: Cambridge University Press, 1953.

Burns, Tom and G. M. Stalker. *The Management of Innovation.* London: Tavistock Publications, 1961.

Buzzell, Robert D., Bradley T. Gale and Ralph

G. M. Sultan. "Market Share — Key to Profitability." *Harvard Business Review*, January–February 1975.

Cannon, J. Thomas. *Business Strategy and Policy.* New York: Harcourt, Brace and World, 1968.

Carnap, R. *The Logical Foundations of Probability.* Chicago: University of Chicago Press, 1950.

Carter, E. Eugene. "The Behavioral Theory of the Firm and Top-Level Corporate Decisions." *Administrative Science Quarterly*, December 1971.

Chandler, Alfred D. *Strategy and Structure: Chapters in the History of the American Industrial Enterprise.* Cambridge, Mass.: M.I.T. Press, 1962.

Channon, Derek F. *The Strategy and Structure of British Enterprise.* Boston: Graduate School of Business Administration, Harvard University, 1973.

Chevalier, Michel. "The Strategy Spectre Behind Your Market Share." *European Business*, Summer 1972.

Child, John. "Organization Structure, Environment and Performance — The Role of Strategic Choice." *Sociology*, January 1972.

Child, John, "What Determines Organization Performance? The Universals vs. the It-All-Depends." *Organization Dynamics*, Summer 1974.

Chin, Robert and Kenneth Benne. "General Strategies for Effecting Changes in Human Systems," in Bennis, W., et al. (editors). *The Planning of Change.* New York: Holt, Rinehart and Winston, 1976.

Christensen, C. Roland, Kenneth R. Andrews and Joseph L. Bower. *Business Policy: Text and Cases.* Homewood, Ill.: Richard D. Irwin, 1973.

Christenson, Charles. "Concepts, Theory and Techniques: Proposals for a Program of Empirical Research into the Properties of Triangles." *Decision Sciences*, October 1976.

Clifford, Donald K., Jr. *Managing the Threshold Company: The Making of Tomorrow's Leaders.* New York: McKinsey and Co., 1973.

Cole, A. *Numerical Taxonomy.* London: Academic Press, 1969.

Comte, Auguste. *The Positive Philosophy.* London: George Bell and Sons, 1816.

Cook, Curtis W. "Corporate Strategy Change Contingencies." *Academy of Management Proceedings*, August 1975.

Cooley, William W. and Paul R. Lohnes. *Multivariate Data Analysis.* New York: Wiley, 1971.

Cooper, Arnold C. and Dan E. Schendel. "Strategy Determination in Manufacturing Firms: Concepts and Research Findings." *Proceedings of the American Marketing Association Fall Conference*, August–September 1971.

Corey, E. Raymond and Steven H. Star. *Organization Strategy: A Marketing Approach.* Boston: Graduate School of Business Administration, Harvard University, 1971.

Crombie, A. C. and M. Hoskin. *The History of Science: Annual Review.* Cambridge: Heffers, 1969.

Dalton, M. *Men Who Manage.* New York: Wiley, 1959.

Dawes, Robyn M. *Fundamentals of Attitude Measurement.* New York: Wiley, 1972.

Day, George S. "A Strategic Perspective on Product Planning." *Journal of Contemporary Business*, Winter 1975.

Diesing, P. *Patterns of Discovery in the Social Sciences.* London: Routledge and Kegan Paul, 1972.

Drucker, Peter F. *The Practice of Management.* New York: Harper and Row, 1954.

Drucker, Peter F. *Management: Tasks, Responsibilities, Practices.* New York: Harper and Row, 1974.

Dubin, R. *Theory Building.* New York: The Free Press, 1969.

Duncan, Robert. "Characteristics of Organizational Environments and Perceived Environmental Uncertainty." *Administrative Science Quarterly*, September 1972.

Duncan, Robert. "Modifications in Decision Structure in Adapting to the Environment: Some Implications for Organizational Learning." *Decision Sciences*, October 1974.

Duncan, Robert, Robert Cooke, Gerald Zaltman, Allan Mohrman and Sue Mohrman. "Assessment of a Structural/Task Approach to Organizational Development in School Systems." Unpublished manuscript. Graduate School of Management, Northwestern University, 1977.

Durkheim, Emile. *The Rules of Sociological Method.* New York: The Free Press, 1938.

Egerton, Henry C. and James K. Brown. *Planning and the Chief Executive.* New York: The Conference Board, 1972.

Emery, F. E. and E. L. Trist. "The Causal Texture of Organizational Environments." *Human Relations*, February 1965.

Emery, F. E. and E. L. Trist. *Towards a Social Ecology.* London and New York: Plenum Press, 1973.

Emory, C. William. *Business Research Methods.* Homewood, Ill.: Richard D. Irwin, 1976.

Everitt, B. *Cluster Analysis.* London: Heinemann, 1974.

Farmer, Richard N. and Barry M. Richman. *Comparative Management and Economic Progress.* Homewood, Ill.: Richard D. Irwin, 1965.

Ferguson, Robert L. and Curtis H. Jones. "A Computer Aided Decision System." *Management Science*, June 1969.

Feyerabend, P. *Against Method.* London: New Left Books, 1975.

Fiedler, Fred E. *A Theory of Leadership Effectiveness.* New York: McGraw-Hill, 1967.

Filmer, Paul, et al. *New Directions in Sociological Theory.* New York: Collier-Macmillan, 1972.

Filstead, William J. (editor). *Qualitative Methodology.* Chicago: Markham, 1970.

Fruhan, William E. *The Fight for Competitive Advantage: A Study of the U.S. Domestic Truck Air Carriers.* Boston: Division of Research, Graduate School of Business Administration, Harvard University, 1972a.

Fruhan, William E. "Pyrrhic Victories in Fights for Market Share." *Harvard Business Review*, September–October 1972b.

Galbraith, Jay. *Organization Design.* Reading, Mass.: Addison-Wesley, 1977.

Gale, Bradley T. "Market Share and Rate of Return." *Review of Economics and Statistics*, November 1972.

Galtung, J. *Theory and Methods in Social Research.* London: Allen and Unwin, 1967.

Garfinkel, Harold. *Studies in Ethnomethodology.* Englewood Cliffs, N.J.: Prentice-Hall, 1967.

Gibbs, J. *Sociological Theory Construction.* Hinsdale, Ill.: Dryden Press, 1972.

Glaser, Barney and Anselm Strauss. *The Discovery of Grounded Theory.* Chicago: Aldine Publishing, 1967.

Glueck, William F. "Business Policy: Reality and Promise." *Academy of Management Proceedings*, August 1972.

Gold, R. L. "Roles in Sociological Field Observations." *Social Forces*, Vol. 36, 1958.

Gordon, R. "Rigor and Relevance in a Changing Institutional Setting." *American Economic Review*, March 1976.

Goronzy, F. "A Numerical Taxonomy on Business Enterprises," in Cole, A. *Numerical Taxonomy.* New York: Academic Press, 1969.

Gouldner, A. W. *Patterns of Industrial Bureaucracy.* New York: The Free Press, 1954.

Grabowski, Henry G. and Dennis C. Mueller. "Managerial and Stockholder Welfare Models of Firm Expenditures." *Review of Economics and Statistics*, Vol. 54, 1972.

Grant, D. A. "Testing the Null Hypothesis and the Strategy of Tactics of Investigating Theoretical Models." *Psychological Review*, January 1962.

Green, Paul E. and Vithala R. Rao. *Applied Multidimensional Scaling: A Comparison of Approaches and Algorithms.* New York: Holt, Rinehart and Winston, 1972.

Green, Paul E. and Donald S. Tull. *Research for Marketing Decisions.* Englewood Cliffs, N.J.: Prentice-Hall, 1975.

Green, Paul E. and Yoram Wind. "New Way to Measure Consumers' Judgments." *Harvard Business Review*, July–August 1975.

Guetzkow, Harold, Philip Kotler and Randall L. Schultz. *Simulation in Social and Administrative Science.* Englewood Cliffs, N.J.: Prentice-Hall, 1972.

Guth, William D. "The Growth and Profitability of the Firm: A Managerial Explanation." *Journal of Business Policy*, Spring 1972.

Gutmann, Peter M. "Strategies for Growth." *California Management Review*, Summer 1964.

Hanson, N. *Patterns of Discovery.* Cambridge: Cambridge University Press, 1965.

Harvey, D. *Explanation in Geography.* London: Edward Arnold, 1969.

Hatten, Kenneth J. "Strategic Models in the Brewing Industry." Doctoral diss., Purdue University, 1974.

Hatten, Kenneth J. "Strategy, Profits and Beer." Working Paper No. 75-14, Graduate School of Business Administration, Harvard University, 1975.

Hatten, Kenneth J. and Dan E. Schendel. "Strategy's Role in Policy Research." *Journal of Economics and Business*, Spring–Summer 1976.

Hatten, Kenneth J. and Dan E. Schendel. "Heterogeneity Within an Industry: Firm Conduct in the U.S. Brewing Industry 1952–1971." *Journal of Industrial Economics*, December 1977.

Hatten, Kenneth J., Dan E. Schendel and Arnold C. Cooper. "A Strategic Model of the U. S. Brewing Industry 1952–1971." *Academy of Management Journal*, December 1978.

Heenan, David A. and Robert Addleman. "Quantitative Techniques for Today's Decision Makers." *Harvard Business Review*, May–June 1976.

Hempel, C. *The Philosophy of Natural Science.* Englewood Cliffs, N.J.: Prentice-Hall, 1966.

Hofer, Charles W. "Some Preliminary Research Patterns of Strategic Behavior." *Academy of Management Proceedings*, August 1973.

Hofer, Charles W. "Toward a Contingency Theory of Business Strategy." *Academy of Management Journal*, December 1975.

Hofer, Charles W. "Research on Strategic Planning: A Survey of Past Studies and Suggestions for Future Efforts." *Journal of Economics and Business*, Spring–Summer 1976.

Holden, Paul, Carlton A. Pederson and Gayton E.

Germane. *Top Management.* New York: Mc-Graw-Hill, 1968.

Horsky, Dan. "Market Share Response to Advertising: An Example of Theory Testing." *Journal of Marketing Research,* February 1977.

Hunt, M. S. "Competition in the Major Home Appliance Industry, 1960–1970." Doctoral diss., Harvard University, 1972.

Hussey, David. *Corporate Planning: Theory and Practice.* New York: Pergamon Press, 1974.

Johnston, John. *Econometric Methods.* (2d ed.) New York: McGraw-Hill, 1972.

Junker, B. H. *Field Work: An Introduction to the Social Sciences.* Chicago: University of Chicago Press, 1960.

Kaplan, A. *The Conduct of Inquiry.* San Francisco: Chandler Publishing and Z. A. Malik, 1964.

Karger, Delmar W. "Long Range Planning and Organizational Performance." *Long Range Planning,* December 1975.

Kast, Fremont E. and James E. Rosenzweig. *Contingency Views of Organization and Management.* Chicago: Science Research Associates, 1973.

Khandwalla, Pradip N. "The Techno-Economic Ecology of Corporate Strategy." *Journal of Management Studies,* February 1976.

Khandwalla, Pradip N. *The Design of Organizations.* New York: Harcourt Brace Jovanovich, 1977.

Kinnear, Thomas C. and James R. Taylor. "Marketing Notes and Communications Multivariate Methods in Marketing Research: A Further Attempt at Classification." *Journal of Marketing,* October 1971.

Kitching, John. "Why Do Mergers Miscarry?" *Harvard Business Review,* November–December 1967.

Kuhn, Thomas. *The Structure of Scientific Revolutions.* Chicago: University of Chicago Press, 1962.

Lakatos, I. and A. E. Musgrave. *Criticism and the Growth of Knowledge.* Cambridge: Cambridge University Press, 1970.

Laudan, L. "Theories of Scientific Method from Plato to Mach," in Crombie, A. C. and M. Hoskin. *The History of Science: Annual Review.* Cambridge: Heffers, 1969.

Lawrence, Paul R. and Jay W. Lorsch. "Differentiation and Integration in Complex Organizations." *Administrative Science Quarterly,* June 1967a.

Lawrence, Paul R. and Jay W. Lorsch. *Organization and Environment: Managing Differentiation and Integration.* Boston: Graduate School of Business Administration, Harvard University, 1967b.

Lazarsfeld, P. F. and M. Rosenberg. *The Language of Social Research.* New York: The Free Press, 1955.

Levinson, Harry. *Organizational Diagnosis.* Cambridge, Mass.: Harvard University Press, 1972.

Lindsay, William M. and Leslie W. Rue. *Environmental Complexity in Long-Range Planning.* Oxford, Ohio: Planning Executives Institute, 1976.

Lofland, John. *Analyzing Social Settings.* Belmont, Calif.: Wadsworth Publishing, 1971.

Lofland, John. *Doing Social Life.* New York: Wiley, 1976.

Lorange, Peter. "Divisional Planning: Setting Effective Direction." *Sloan Management Review,* Fall 1975.

Lorange, Peter and Richard F. Vancil. *Strategic Planning Systems.* Englewood Cliffs, N.J.: Prentice-Hall, 1977.

Lorsch, Jay W. and Stephen A. Allen, III. *Managing Diversity and Interdependence: An Organizational Study of Multidivisional Firms.* Boston: Graduate School of Business Administration, Harvard University, 1973.

Lorsch, Jay W. and John J. Morse. *Organizations and Their Members: A Contingency Approach.* New York: Harper and Row, 1974.

Luck, David J. and Arthur E. Prell. *Market Strategy.* New York: Appleton-Century-Crofts, 1968.

Mace, Myles L. and George G. Montgomery. *Management Problems of Corporate Acquisition.* Boston: Graduate School of Business Administration, Harvard University, 1962.

Macintosh, N. B., H. Tsurumi and Y. Tsurumi. "Econometrics for Strategic Planning." *Journal of Business Policy,* Spring 1973.

Marcus, M. "Profitability and Size of Firm: Some Further Evidence." *Review of Economics and Statistics,* February 1969.

McCall, G. J. and J. L. Simmons. *Issues in Participant Observation.* Reading, Mass.: Addison-Wesley, 1969.

McGrath, Joseph. "Toward a 'Theory of Method' for Research on Organizations," in Cooper, W. W., H. J. Leavitt and M. Shelly (editors), *New Perspectives in Organizational Research.* New York: Wiley, 1964.

McKinney, George W. "An Experimental Study of Strategy Formulated on Systems." Doctoral diss., Stanford University, 1969.

Mehan, Hugh and Houston Wood. *The Reality of Ethnomethodology.* New York: Wiley, 1975.

Meltzer, B. N., et al. *Symbolic Interactionism: Varieties and Criticism.* London: Routledge and Kegan Paul, 1975.

Merton, R. *On Theoretical Sociology: Five Essays Old and New.* New York: Macmillan, 1967.

Metcalf, Henry C. and L. Urwick. *Dynamic Administration: The Collected Papers of Mary Par-*

ker Follett. New York: Harper and Brothers, 1940.

Meyer, J. and R. L. Glauber. *Investment Decisions, Economic Forecasting*. Boston: Graduate School of Business Administration, Harvard University, 1964.

Miles, Raymond E., Charles C. Snow and Jeffrey Pfeffer. "Organization Environment: Concepts and Issues." *Industrial Relations*, October 1974.

Miller, Danny. "Towards a Contingency Theory of Strategy Formulation." *Academy of Management Proceedings*, August 1975.

Miller, Ernest C. *Advanced Techniques for Strategic Planning*. New York: American Management Association, 1971.

Mills, C. Wright. *The Sociological Imagination*. New York: Oxford University Press, 1959.

Mintzberg, Henry. "Research on Strategy Making." *Academy of Management Proceedings*. Minneapolis, 1972.

Mintzberg, Henry. *The Nature of Managerial Work*. New York: Harper and Row, 1973.

Mintzberg, Henry. "The Manager's Job: Folklore and Fact." *Harvard Business Review*, July–August 1975.

Mintzberg, Henry. "Policy as a Field of Management Theory." *Academy of Management Review*, January 1977.

Mintzberg, Henry, D. Raisinghani and Andre Theoret. "The Structure of 'Unstructured' Decision Processes." *Administrative Science Quarterly*, June 1976.

Mitchell, Terence R. "Motivation and Participation: An Integration." *Academy of Management Journal*, December 1973.

Moberg, Dennis J. and James L. Koch. "A Critical Appraisal of Integrated Treatments of Contingency Findings." *Academy of Management Journal*, March 1975.

Mockler, Robert J. "Situational Theory of Management." *Harvard Business Review*, May–June 1971.

Morrison, Donald F. *Multivariate Statistical Methods*. New York: McGraw-Hill, 1967.

Morrison, Donald F. "On the Interpretation of Discriminant Analysis." *Journal of Marketing Research*, May 1969.

Mueller, Dennis C. "The Firm Decision Process: An Econometric Investigation." *Quarterly Journal of Economics*, February 1967.

Mumford, Enid and Andrew Pettigrew. *Implementing Strategic Decisions*. London: Longmans, 1975.

Nagashima, Yukinori. "Response of Japanese Companies to Environmental Changes." *Long Range Planning*, January 1976.

Nagel, E. "On the Method of Verstehen as the Sole Method," in Natanson, M., (editor). *Philosophy of the Social Sciences*. New York. Random House, 1963.

Natanson, M. *Philosophy of the Social Sciences*. New York: Random House, 1963.

Naumes, William. "Effects of Responsive Computer Interaction in the Strategic Planning Process." Doctoral diss., Stanford University, 1971.

Negandhi, Anant R. *Environmental Settings in Organizational Functioning*. Kent, Ohio: College of Business Administration, Kent State University, 1970.

Negandhi, Anant R. "Comparative Management and Organization Theory: A Marriage Needed." *Academy of Management Journal*, June 1975.

Newman, H. H. "Strategic Groups and the Structure Performance Relationship: A Study with Respect to the Chemical Process Industries." Doctoral diss., Harvard University, 1973.

Newman, William H. "Strategy and Management Structure." *Academy of Management Proceedings*, August, 1971.

Newman, William H. and James P. Logan. *Strategy, Policy, and Central Management*. Cincinnati, Ohio: South-Western, 1971.

Olson, S. *Ideas and Data: The Process and Practice of Social Research*. Homewood, Ill.: Dorsey Press, 1976.

Paine, Frank T. and Carl R. Anderson. "Contingencies Affecting Strategy Formulation and Effectiveness." *Journal of Management Studies*, May 1977.

Paine, Frank T. and William Naumes. *Strategy and Policy Formation: An Integrative Approach*. Philadelphia: Saunders, 1974.

Paine, Frank T. and William Naumes. *Organizational Strategy and Policy: Text, Cases, and Incidents*. Philadelphia: Saunders, 1975.

Parsons, Talcott. "Comment" on "Preface to a Metatheoretical Framework for Sociology." *American Journal of Sociology*, September 1961.

Patton, G. Richard. "A Simulation Equation Model of Corporate Strategy: The Case of the U.S. Brewing Industry." Doctoral diss., Purdue University, 1976.

Peck, Merton J. and Frederic M. Scherer. *The Weapons Acquisition Process: An Economic Analysis*. Boston: Division of Research, Graduate School of Business Administration, Harvard University, 1962.

Penrose, E. "Biological Analogies in the Theory of the Firm." *American Economic Review*, Vol. 42, 1952.

Perrow, Charles. *Organizational Analysis: A Sociological View*. Belmont, Calif.: Wadsworth Publishing, 1970.

Perrow, Charles. "The Short and Glorious History of Organizational Theory." *Organizational Dynamics*, Summer 1973.

Pettigrew, Andrew M. *The Politics of Organizational Decision-Making*. London: Tavistock Publications, 1973.

Popper, K. *The Logic of Scientific Discovery*. London: Hutchinson, 1959.

Porter, M. E. "Retailer Power, Manufacturing Strategy, and Performance in Consumer Goods Industries." Doctoral diss., Harvard University, 1973.

Pugh, D. S., D. J. Hickson, C. R. Hinings and C. Turner. "The Context of Organizational Structures." *Administrative Science Quarterly*, March 1969.

Qualls, David. "Concentration, Barriers to Entry, and Long Run Economic Profit Margins." *Journal of Industrial Economics*, April 1972.

Rhenman, Eric. *Organization Theory for Long Range Planning*. New York: Wiley, 1973.

Rhoades, S. A. "Concentration, Barriers and Rates of Return: A Note." *Journal of Industrial Economics*, November 1970.

Richman, Barry M. "Achieving Corporate Objectives: Significance of Cultural Variables." *Academy of Management Proceedings*, December 1964.

Ricker, Leon. "Using Computer Models for Short and Long Range Planning: A Case Study." *Business Quarterly*, Autumn 1969.

Rosenthal, Robert. *Experimenter Effects in Behavioral Research*. New York: Appleton-Century-Crofts, 1966.

Ross, Joel E. and Michael J. Kami. *Corporate Management in Crisis: Why the Mighty Fall*. Englewood Cliffs, N.J.: Prentice-Hall, 1973.

Rothschild, William E. *Putting It All Together*. New York: AMACOM, 1976.

Rumelt, Richard P. *Strategy, Structure, and Economic Performance*. Boston: Graduate School of Business Administration, Harvard University, 1974.

Schendel, Dan E. and G. Richard Patton. "Corporate Stagnation and Turnaround." *Journal of Economics and Business*, Spring–Summer 1976a.

Schendel, Dan E. and G. Richard Patton, "A Simultaneous Equation Model of Corporate Strategy." Paper No. 582, Institute for Research in the Behavioral, Economic, and Management Sciences, Purdue University, December 1976b.

Schoeffler, Sidney. "Key Impacts on Profitability." Address presented at E. I. DuPont De Nemours Auditorium, April 28, 1974. The Strategic Planning Institute, Cambridge, Mass., 1975.

Schoeffler, Sidney, Robert D. Buzzell and Donald F. Heany. "Impact of Strategic Planning on Profit Performance." *Harvard Business Review*, March–April 1974.

Schollhammer, Hans. "The Comparative Management Theory Jungle." *Academy of Management Journal*, March 1969.

Schon, D. *Displacement of Concepts*. London: Tavistock Publications, 1963.

Scott, Bruce R. "The Industrial State: Old Myths and New Realities." *Harvard Business Review*, March–April 1973.

Searfoss, D. Gerald and Robert M. Monczka. "Perceived Participation in the Budget Process and the Motivation to Achieve the Budget." *Academy of Management Journal*, December 1973.

Selznick, P. *TVA and the Grass Roots*. Berkeley, Calif.: University of California Press, 1949.

Shepard, R. N., A. K. Romney and S. B. Nerlove. *Multidimensional Scaling: Application in Behavioral Science*. New York: Seminar Press, 1972.

Shepherd, William G. "The Elements of Market Structure." *Review of Economics and Statistics*, February 1972.

Skidmore, W. *Theoretical Thinking in Sociology*. Cambridge: Cambridge University Press, 1975.

Sokal, R. R. and P. H. Sneath. *The Principles of Numerical Taxonomy*. New York: Freeman, 1963.

Staelin, Richard. "Another Look at A.I.C." *Journal of Advertising Research*, October 1971.

Steinbeck, John. *The Log of the Sea of Cortez*. New York: The Viking Press, 1962.

Steiner, George A. *Top Management Planning*. New York: Macmillan, 1969.

Steiner, George A. *Pitfalls in Comprehensive Long Range Planning*. Oxford, Ohio: Planning Executives Institute, 1972.

Steiner, George A. *Strategic Managerial Planning*. Oxford, Ohio: Planning Executives Institute, 1977.

Steiner, George A. and John B. Miner. *Management Policy and Strategy: Text, Readings, and Cases*. New York: Macmillan, 1977.

Steiner, George A. and Hans Schollhammer. "Pitfalls in Multi-National Long Range Planning." *Long Range Planning*, April 1975.

Stevens, S. "On the Theory of Scales of Measurement." *Science*, Vol. 103, 1966.

Stevenson, Howard H. "Defining Corporate Strengths and Weaknesses." *Sloan Management Review*, Spring 1976.

Stevenson, Howard H. and Kenneth J. Hatten. "A New Theory for Management Planning." Unpublished mimeo, Harvard University, 1977.

Stinchcombe, A. *Constructing Social Theories*. New York: Harcourt, Brace and World. 1968.

Stobaugh, Robert B. and Phillip L. Townsend. "Price Forecasting and Strategic Planning: The Case of Petrochemicals." *Journal of Marketing Research*, February 1975.

Terreberry, Shirley. "The Evolution of Organizational Environments." *Administrative Science Quarterly*, March 1968.

Thompson, James D. *Organizations in Action*. New York: McGraw-Hill, 1967.

Thune, Stanley S. and Robert J. House. "Where Long Range Planning Pays Off." *Business Horizons*, August 1970.

Torgerson, Warren. *Theory and Methods of Scaling*. New York: Wiley, 1958.

Tsurumi, H. and Y. Tsurumi. "An Oligopolistic Model of a Japanese Pharmaceutical Company," in Palda, K. (editor). *Readings in Managerial Economics*. Englewood Cliffs, N.J.: Prentice-Hall, 1973.

Turner, Roy (editor). *Ethnomethodology*. Middlesex, England: Penguin, 1974.

Utecht, R. E. and W. D. Heier. "The Contingency Model and Successful Military Leadership." *Academy of Management Journal*, December 1976.

Vernon, J. M. *Market Structure and Industrial Performance: A Review of Statistical Findings*. Boston: Allyn and Bacon, 1972.

Vickers, Sir Geoffrey. *The Art of Judgment: A Study of Policy Making*. New York: Basic Books, 1965.

Wallace, W. *Sociological Theory*. New York: Heinemann, 1969.

Wallace, W. *The Logic of Science in Sociology*. Chicago: Aldine Press, 1971.

Wasson, Chester R. *Dynamic Competitive Structure and Product Life Cycles*. St. Charles, Ill.: Challenge Books, 1974.

Weber, Max. *Essays in Sociology* (translated by H. H. Gerth and C. W. Mills). London: Oxford University Press, 1946.

Weber, Max. *Economy and Society*. Roth, G. and C. Wittich (editors). New York: Bedminster Press, 1968.

Weick, Karl. "Enactment Processes in Organizations," in Staw, B. and G. Salancik (editors), *New Directions in Organizational Behavior*. Chicago: St. Clair Press, 1977.

Weston, J. Fred and Eugene F. Brigham. *Essentials of Managerial Finance* (2d edition). New York: Holt, Rinehart and Winston, 1971.

Wilcox, Jarrod W. "The Gambler's Ruin Approach to Business Risk." *Sloan Management Review*, Fall 1976.

Winn, Daryl N. *Industrial Market Structure and Performance 1960–68*. Ann Arbor, Mich.: Division of Research, Graduate School of Business Administration, University of Michigan, 1975.

Woodward, Joan. *Industrial Organization: Theory and Practice*. London: Oxford University Press, 1965.

Wrapp, H. E. "Good Managers Don't Make Policy Decisions." *Harvard Business Review*, September–October 1967.

Wrigley, Leonard. "Division Autonomy and Diversification." Doctoral diss., Harvard University, 1970.

Wynne, Bayand and Peter R. Newsted. "Augmenting Man's Judgement with Inter-Active Computer Systems." Research Paper No. 74-2, Management Information Systems Laboratory, School of Business Administration, University of Wisconsin, Milwaukee, 1974.

Zald, Mayer N. *Organizational Change*. Chicago: University of Chicago Press, 1970.

Zetterberg, H. *On Theory and Verification in Sociology*. New York: Bedminster Press, 1965.

8

TEACHING IMPLICATIONS OF POLICY AND PLANNING RESEARCH

ISRAEL UNTERMAN
San Diego State University

W. HARVEY HEGARTY
Indiana University

To this point, research studies, needs, and methods in the various subfields of the strategic management/business policy field have been our major concern. But research results ultimately must be used to be of value. Therefore, teaching (technology transfer, if one prefers a term more applicable to nonacademic organizations) must enter to insure not only that students learning to become professional managers but that practicing managers and their organizations recognize and use the best available research findings to aid them in finding solutions to their problems.

While this volume is intended to review research findings and point out research needs in the strategic management area, it would be overlooking another kind of need if it were not to give some attention to the teaching problems and opportunities posed by the research findings. Teaching and learning take a variety of forms, ranging from small, in-house executive training programs, to formal courses at major universities. All of these forms are influenced by the new findings in the field.

The papers by Hegarty and Unterman deal mainly with teaching in formal degree programs. Before examining these two papers, a useful perspective can be gained by reviewing the evolution of the strategic management area.

EVOLUTION OF THE STRATEGIC MANAGEMENT AREA

Historically, the business policy area was regarded as a capstone integrative course, and not as an academic discipline, partly because this was the way the area came into being. When the first business schools were established in the United States, no separate course was established for the study of the functions of the general manager, as had been done in the various functional fields such as finance, marketing, and manufacturing. This may have been because most firms at the time had only one general manager (the president), so that there was little demand for such training; or because the major problems facing businesses at the time were of a financial, manufacturing, or marketing nature; or because no one was available who had the background and skills to teach such a course. Within a few years, however, most such schools felt the need for a course that integrated the student's various functional area training, and that exposed the student to "policy issues." As a result, business policy was created as a capstone course for the entire business curriculum.

Because of the high level of importance to the firm of integrating functional areas, and the breadth and wisdom that such integration demanded for effective resolution, most policy courses were taught by senior faculty. Most such faculty were chosen from different functional area departments in a procedure similar to that used for selecting general managers in business firms. However, these faculty usually kept their ties to their different functional area disciplines; and while they taught a policy course they did not devote all their research and teaching attentions to policy, partly because there were no advanced courses to teach, partly because the single course did not require full-time effort, and partly because most senior people maintained their research interests in their base disciplines.

For several decades, the capstone, integrative nature of the policy course and the age and experience of the typical policy faculty combined to make the course one of the most respected and highly rated of all the courses offered at most business schools.

However, in the first two decades after World War II, several pressures, including the growth in size and complexity of businesses, the application of quantitative and behavioral sciences to business problems, and the demand for more academic research on business problems (as reflected in the Gordon and Howell (1959) and Pierson (1959) reports), led to the transformation of most subject areas taught at business schools. Unfortunately, the two cornerstones of the earlier success of the policy course now became impediments to rapid progress. Because most policy teachers held allegiance to other fields, because no research tradition backed the discipline (some would claim it did not back other fields either), and because it was thought that age and experience were needed to teach policy, no doctoral programs had been established to train policy faculty. Moreover, doctoral programs, a traditional source of faculty supply, were aimed at meeting the needs of other, previously established functional areas. Where policy had once attracted the best and wisest minds from the various functional area faculties, it was now being used as a dumping ground for senior faculty who were no longer productive in their own areas. For obvious reasons, such faculty usually had little interest in either research or conceptual development in their new "discipline." Further, because policy was the capstone, or final course, it precluded the development of any "advanced courses" in the area in which junior or senior faculty could present the results of their research. The anecdotal, case orientation of the course also inhibited the development of the conceptual constructs necessary for such research (Hofer, 1975a).

The conceptual barrier was attacked with the development of the strategy concept by Chandler, Andrews, and Ansoff, as described in the Introduction. Strategy was used as an analytical construct both for integrating the firm with its external environment as well as for integrating the various functional areas within the firm. Initially, this construct led to the upgrading of the capstone policy course, to a variety of descriptive research studies in the area, and to the training of a limited number of first-generation junior faculty in the area. Such early developments were limited by the need for further development of the strategy concept; by failure to recognize the growth in complex business structures, which had to be integrated through the substantive content that underlies strategy; by the limited number of doctoral programs in the area (until 1967, Harvard was the only school with a formal doctoral program in business policy); and by the allocation of limited educational budgets to development of other areas.

Although each of these reasons was important in explaining the slow rise of the field, another damaging factor was the failure of the "policy sciences" approach to the area tried at schools such as Carnegie-Mellon, Berkeley, and Stanford. These, and some other schools tried to duplicate the operations research technique of combining specialists from a variety of disciplines into a single group that would then "solve" the problem. Unfortunately, this approach, which was successful in the solution of well-structured problems, proved incapable of handling most unstructured problems, at least in any rigorous way. Unfortunately, most of these schools blamed the area rather than the approach for the difficulties encountered. Thus, policy was eliminated at these schools as an area for scholarly investigation, although it was kept as a capstone course, usually taught by outside consultants, senior business executives, or elder statesmen drawn from the various functional disciplines. Even more unfortunately, a number of schools are still marching down this blind alley today!

At other schools, however, the strategy paradigm was elaborated and studied and used for the training of a second generation of Ph.D. students majoring in policy. These schools and their graduates have further added to both the strategy concept and policy research. As a result, enough has now been done so that we may suggest a new paradigm, that of strategic management, upon which a scholarly discipline can be founded, as the research surveyed in this text indicates. Unfortunately, this change in status has been more quickly recognized by practitioners than by our academic colleagues.

Nevertheless, at a few schools today, the strategic management field is healthy, vigorous, and growing. Such schools have added advanced courses in strategic management at the undergraduate and master's level and most provide doctoral training. Hence, in both practice and teaching the field is finally beginning to train its own specialists.

TEACHING IMPLICATIONS OF THE STRATEGIC MANAGEMENT PARADIGM

The most important teaching implication of the strategic management paradigm and the research based on it *is that business policy can no longer accurately be regarded merely as an integrative course that performs its function without substantive content of its own.* Rather, integration in the curriculum as in practice now rests on a new paradigm which forms the base for a new academic discipline which we have labeled strategic management. For the field to develop its full potential, further research and theory building will be required. Equally important to its development, however, will be changes in the nature of teaching in the area.

In his paper, Unterman describes more fully several of the implications that accompany the change in the status of the policy area from a "capstone, integrative course" to a scholarly, academic discipline. In particular, he elaborates the implications of this change in status: (1) for the types of concepts and models used in the area; (2) for curriculum development in the area; (3) for the objectives and design of the traditional business policy course; and (4) for pedagogy and teacher training in the area. The most extensive of Unterman's observations are on curriculum development and pedagogy. On these topics, he argues that the traditional policy course should be replaced with curricula in strategic management at the bachelor's, master's, and Ph.D. levels; that pedagogy other than the case method should be used for some of these courses; and that similar changes should also be made in executive program courses.

Hegarty's paper then elaborates on ways that the different research ideas and concepts discussed in this text can be incorporated into the traditional business policy course. More specifically, he discusses several ways that the key ideas of each of the invited papers may be built into the traditional policy course. Although Hegarty nevers says so explicitly, it seems clear that it would be impossible to incorporate all of his suggestions into a single course, a point that further suggests the need for a strategic management curriculum. Those uninterested in curriculum development can select from among Hegarty's various suggestions those that best fit their own course objectives and teaching skills.

Hegarty's discussion of cases and other teaching materials also highlights the real need that exists for the development of more extensive teaching materials that reflect our current state of knowledge about strategy and strategic management issues.

While supporting the observations made by Unterman and Hegarty, it should be noted that other curricula and course designs are possible besides those which they propose. Continued development of the strategic management field will also be enhanced by such broadened curricula and the opportunity they provide to use the research results developing in the field. This is particularly true at the Ph.D. level, as noted by Schendel (1975).

One further observation is necessary. Today there is a shortage of faculty to teach policy. As a result, "policy" faculty are still being sought from other functional fields, most prominently the organization theory and behavior areas, where an oversupply of new Ph.D.'s appears to exist. While there is a similarity between strategic management and organizational theory and behavior, there are also significant differences. Such incoming faculty can no longer be assumed to be fully prepared to teach in the field, any more than "outsiders" can in any other field. On the other hand, the strategic management area will be strengthened by newcomers, who can bring perspective and ideas, if they are willing to understand and learn the basis of this newly emerging and rapidly developing field.

The Teaching Implications of the Research in Policy and Planning: An Overview

ISRAEL UNTERMAN
San Diego State University

INTRODUCTION

In his commentary Hegarty provides a summation and identification of the teaching implications applicable to each of the research papers in this volume. Consequently, this commentary will deal with the combined impact of all the research reported herein and the possible effects of these studies upon the academic area of policy and planning. Hence, this discussion will focus on the following four topics:

1. The impetus provided by this body of papers for the evolution of the Business Policy Area, as well as new directions these papers suggest for teachers of Business Policy and Planning courses.
2. The implications of these papers for curricula development among undergraduate and graduate, as well as advanced management programs.
3. The implications and impact of this research upon the objectives and overall design of the Business Policy course.
4. The implications of this research for pedagogical methodology and teacher training in policy and planning.

NEW DIRECTIONS

In the concluding remarks of his paper, Steiner (Section 7) notes, "It has reached the point where management strategy is a *discipline* of its own and is reaching towards some maturity." This is an affirmation of the thoughts of other teachers of policy, including Schendel and Hatten (1972) and Hofer (1975a). If the area of Business Policy, or Strategic Management, is now emerging as a discipline, what are some of the teaching implications that stem from this fact and the body of research now developing?

Part of the answer would involve a change in our peer recognition of the area. When one studies the history of the curricula of schools of business, it is apparent that the identity and status of a subject area are evolutionary. For example, less than 30 years ago there was no defined academic area of Organization Behavior. Instead, the MBA programs included courses in Industrial Psychology and Industrial Engineering. Similarly, Operations Research evolved from areas such as Statistics and Business Mathematics. The evolution and maturation process of these and other academic areas have included conceptualizations and theories developed by researchers. *Similarly, the future Business Policy license and peer recognition of the area as a discipline will originate and be built upon the accumulation of Business Policy research.* Such research is our conceptual "raison d'être."

To enhance the development of the area as a discipline, it behooves the researchers (and teachers) of Business Policy to be distinctive and separate from other disciplines. Such distinction gives rise to an anomalistic process. By the nature of the breadth and depth of the subject area, policy researchers must "borrow" the techniques of research from others (Utterback, Section 3; Hatten and Duncan, Section 7). A critique made by discussants of these research papers is that Business Policy researchers do not borrow amply or eclectically from other disciplines. It would seem appropriate for Business Policy researchers to become familiar with additional applicable disciplines, such as anthropology and psychoanalytical theory. For example, Mintzberg (Section 2) constructs his skeletal theory of organizational power using concepts from sociology and political science.

Although policy researchers must borrow from others, an anomaly exists in that *the presentation of their research and the theories de-*

484

veloped therefrom must be accomplished in a manner which is measurably and discernibly different from the borrowed material, because wherever the policy researcher "over-borrows," the uniqueness of the policy area may be over-shadowed. Subject to this constraint, policy researchers and teachers must establish a position to convince university colleagues that there exists ample research of sufficient quality to support the creation of a discipline. Fortunately, the body of papers presented herein offers substantial evidence for the genesis and evolution of an academic discipline which is discernibly different from other disciplines.

As a result of this research, the status and identity of the area should change from that of an integrative, "capstone" course to that of *a distinctive academic area of study.* This change of status should constantly create the need and direction for a multi-course curriculum in the Business Policy area. Such an identity change should also influence the course objectives and design of the traditional Policy course, as well as the pedagogical methods used in the area.

IMPLICATIONS FOR CURRICULUM DEVELOPMENT IN THE POLICY AREA

With the establishment of a differentiated discipline, it follows that we can begin to design a sequential series of courses for teaching the sub-parts of the area, whether it is called Strategic Management, Business Policy, or Policy and Planning. As discussed by Rumelt (Section 4), the problems of semantics should not impede the progress of the work at hand. In the establishment of a discipline, it may be advisable and significant that advanced courses be created at all levels of instruction, that is, in the MBA and DBA programs, and in advanced management programs and other executive educational seminars, although such a series of advanced courses might create some unavoidable duplication among the different degree levels.

When one reads the literature related to the teaching of Business Policy (Starbuck, 1966; Hofer, 1969; Charan, 1975; Snow, 1976; Unterman, 1977a and 1977b), it is apparent that much of the writing is devoted to MBA students and their courses. The undergraduate Business Policy programs have, in good part, been neglected by such scholars. The sparseness of research and writing on undergraduate teaching may also reflect the omission of a Business Policy course in undergraduate schools of business. As a result, the examining committees of the AACSB (Stone, 1977) may be expected to emphasize Standard E in undergraduate programs. (Standard E refers to the need for a course defined as "a study of administrative processes under conditions of uncertainty, including integrative analysis and policy determination at the overall management level.") Although the AACSB does not specifically limit such a course to the policy and planning area, the effect of this criterion might be to compel, or at least motivate, the inclusion of Business Policy as a core course for business undergraduates. If so, this development would have major implications for the number of Policy teachers needed in the U.S.

For example, San Diego State University is changing the number of Business Policy sections from 3 to 15 or more per semester. The mere numbers of undergraduate and graduate students in universities offering an organized curriculum in business administration (609,745 undergraduates, and 100,721 MBA students, Delta Sigma Pi, 1976) could have an impact on the teaching of Business Policy at both degree levels. Such growth is also reflected in the growth of the number of faculty required as reflected in the expansion of the Business Policy and Planning Division of the Academy of Management from 50 members in 1971, to 457 in 1975, and 862 in 1977. These larger numbers of policy teachers are unlikely to be content teaching only one course. Instead, there may be a proliferation of different courses relating to policy. Further expansion in the number of courses could lead to a total policy curriculum. In addition, the accumulating policy research will provide the basic fundamentals and concepts for creating advanced courses at the undergraduate level and the graduate level. The differentiation between Policy courses at the two levels should become sharper with increasing knowledge.

How can this emerging body of research be used in the development and sequencing of courses in a Business Policy curriculum? The pedagogical concepts of Piaget (1957) and others offer some direction. *A basic pedagogical principle in teaching is to move from the general to the specific and then return to the general.* This concept is applicable to the sequence of a series of courses, as well as the sequencing of materials within a given course. This pedagogical concept requires classification of the current research into levels of complexity, especially as to concepts and fundamentals. Such classification could provide a basis for design of a series of courses, each with its own unique knowledge base. The policy course need not be served as the smorgasbord dessert course that always follows other functional area courses.

The start of such a series of courses could be in the Sophomore or Junior year of an undergraduate program. For example, current courses in basic management principles seldom describe the dynamics of business organizations in ever changing, uncertain environments. One might, therefore, ask whether or not a Fundamentals of Business Policy course better describes the overall functions of organizations. Such a course could be readily designed from the research material of Ansoff (Section 1), Mintzberg (Section 2), Steiner (1977), Berg and Pitts (Section 6), and Hofer (1975b), among others. Such materials are rich in descriptive material. For undergraduates, this theory and research may have to be abstracted and modified. However, when such material is presented in clear and simple terms, it could provide a starting point for business education, that is both more pragmatic and more conceptual than some of the "anecdotal" courses currently offered undergraduates. For example, in Mintzberg's Exhibit 2.5, the cast of players offers a total overview of the territory and environment of a business organization. Such an overview provides the undergraduate with a basic understanding of the many different factors and facets that the business curriculum will include, as well as the basic concepts of the role and responsibilities of the general manager.

Such an introductory course might be followed by a course which deals with the genesis

and evolution of new businesses. This might include an introduction to the concepts of leadership style and the evolution of an organization structure. This second course could be designed so as to restate and build upon the concepts taught in the Fundamentals course. Cooper, Susbauer, and Vesper (Section 6) provide ample material for such a follow-on course. Such a course could include the dynamics of the progression from the entrepreneurship to the managerial mode. Thus, progression could take in the psychology, sociology and economics of entrepreneurship and also trace the history of a firm from start-up through failure, merger, or significant growth.

These first two courses might then lead into a course on the Conceptual Foundations of Strategy. The content of this course could restate some of the basics taught in the first course, but with greater depth and detail. When such conceptualizations are taught, the techniques and models described by Hofer (1975a), Grant and King, Bower (Section 3), Rumelt (Section 4); Galbraith and Nathanson (Section 5), Berg and Pitts (Section 6), and Steiner (Section 7) provide the tools for understanding the varied and different approaches to the area of Strategic Management. Furthermore, such a course could provide the basics for the education and training of professional planners and strategists in the MBA program.

Finally, the undergraduate strategy cycle might be completed with a capstone course in Strategic Management. Different kinds of teaching methods, to be discussed later, could be used at this stage of the sequence. As part of such a course, skills in decision making in uncertain environments could be developed using the research, in modified form, of Utterback (Section 3), Rumelt (Section 4), Lorange, Galbraith, and Nathanson (Section 5).

It should be noted that these four courses constitute only one potential undergraduate sequence:

At the junior year level —
    Fundamentals of business policy
    Genesis of new enterprises
At the senior year level —
    Conceptual foundation of strategy
    Strategic management

Whether this particular sequence is used is not as important as developing a sequence to adequately expose students to the concepts in the area. Furthermore, there are additional courses that could be offered as electives at both the undergraduate and graduate levels.

The development and sequencing of advanced courses in a graduate program has been discussed by Schendel and Hatten (1972) and Hofer (1975a), as well as others. They have noted, but not stressed enough that the emergence of the policy discipline could lead to the development of a two-track curriculum at the graduate level.

The first track would be for non-policy majors. In it Business Policy would be offered as an integrative, capstone course near the end of the MBA program. This is the traditional approach. The usual sequencing involves two courses in the second year, e.g., The Formulation of Policy or Business Policy I, and Strategic Management or Business Policy II. Such courses could be required of all students in the MBA program.

A second track should be available to those students who wish to major in policy and planning. Such students aspire to become professional planners, generalists, and strategists. As a professional program, such a major, enhanced by differentiated applicable research, can now be offered. This could include in the first year:

Advanced management strategy
Formal planning systems
Strategic game simulations

In the second year, students would have the choice of electives such as the following:

Strategic negotiation
Strategic management of not-for-profit organizations
Seminar in the management of multi-national organizations —
Field studies or practicum in policy or planning.

This track could require a minimum of four or five courses. Depending upon the degree of interest, some of the courses such as Formal Plan-

ning Systems and Strategic Negotiation could be offered in the undergradate program as well.

Such a sequencing of courses would prepare the student for a variety of newly emerging positions, such as a professional planner. Such an academic major and profession has viability because of the demand emerging from today's more complex organizations.

It is pertinent to mention at least two additional course sequences. First, with the impetus of the AACSB recommendations at the undergraduate level, there will be a demand for teachers trained in Business Policy. Hence the doctoral programs will also be called upon for courses in Strategic Management. These could include:

Readings in policy and planning
Readings in policy related disciplines
Research methodologies in policy and planning
Seminar in pedagogical methods of teaching policy and planning.

In addition, some consideration should be given to inclusion of more policy research in advanced management programs and other executive programs. Such programs are usually practitioner oriented and it might seem that policy research would be alien to the objectives of such programs. A case for a contrasting viewpoint can be made however. Practitioners would appreciate and can use new methods, techniques, and tools for evaluating their strategic decisions prior to implementation. Therefore, a series of overlays, charts, and other screen projections could be extrapolated and developed from the research surveyed in this book. For example, after the practitioners discuss a case involving the formulation of strategy and have reached specific conclusions, their decisions could then be evaluated against the models such as PIMS and others discussed in the Grant and King (Section 3) and Rumelt (Section 4) papers. With the research evidence presented in experiential terms, the executives could then re-evaluate their decisions. Another use of the research would be in planning workshops for executives. Here, formal planning systems, designed by the executive participants, might be compared to the alternative models provided by the research summarized by Lorange (Section 5).

In summary, the body of research summarized in this text supplies a fountain of knowledge that is distinctive to policy and planning. Such knowledge enables policy faculty to offer a variety of interrelated courses. The sequencing of such courses should flow from the basic to the complex, from the undergraduate program through the MBA, and eventually into the doctoral and executive development programs.

IMPACT ON TEACHING OBJECTIVES

The sequencing of a series of courses to form a curriculum for Policy and Planning has implications for the pedagogical objectives and material contained within any individual course in that curriculum. Because of limited space, the discussion of such pedagogical impacts of policy research will be confined to the Business Policy course that is currently offered in most MBA programs. Typically, this course is identified as the capstone course of the MBA program. As such its prime objective is to integrate all of the student's previous functional courses (Hofer, 1975a). Such courses focus on the development of analytical skills under uncertainty (Christensen et al., 1978), and make extensive use of case histories (Gomolka and Steinhauer, 1977; Hegarty, 1977; Wolfe and Guth, 1975). Prior to the accumulation of a body of policy research, there were seemingly few academic objectives to achieve in this course other than the improvement of the student's analytical skills of integration. Now it is possible to reevaluate the objectives of the basic capstone policy course based on the research covered here. For instance, one might shift the basic focus of this course from one of skill development to one of knowledge acquisition. In this regard Mintzberg (1975) says:

> Knowledge must be put into the hands of the people who can change things. The main role of the teacher of Management Policy becomes that of providing the best descriptive theory to the practitioner or practitioner to be. . . . In effect, teaching in Management Policy be-

comes a "model building" exercise where exposure to theory builds in the students' heads models of the reality they will face.

Although a number of the conference participants were openly skeptical that there is yet a single universal concept or theory of strategic management, the papers of Ansoff, Grant and King, Bower and Doz, Steiner, and Mintzberg offer teachers a spectrum of concepts upon which such a Business Policy course might be built. The lack of academic agreement on concepts should not constrain us, as it has not constrained other disciplines such as economics and organization behavior. For example, the foundations of accounting principles are currently being seriously challenged. Yet this does not deter the teaching of such courses. In the same vein, each teacher of Business Policy now has available a body of research from which to extract those concepts which are amenable and compatible with his views of Business Policy.

This availability of acceptable concepts means that the primary emphasis on case teaching may no longer suffice. Furthermore, as teaching objectives change, different teaching methods may be useful in order to teach such concepts. For example, the course may start with a series of readings and discussions on topics, such as the definitions of strategy (Steiner and Miner, 1977; Hofer and Schendel, 1978; Christensen et al., 1978), or the territory of policy and planning (Ansoff, Mintzberg, and Steiner in this volume). Then additional conceptualizations and models could be discussed, such as suggested by Hofer (1975b) and in this volume by Berg and Pitts, Bower and Doz, Rumelt, and Lorange. Next a series of complex cases might be discussed and related to the discussions of the concepts and models. The finale of the course could be a field project, a complex management game, a negotiation simulation of policy implementation, or an extensive group or team report. Hegarty's paper offers a detailed analysis of the different cases and the ways they might be related to such conceptualizations.

At this stage, a word of caution is advisable. In the zeal and enthusiasm of creating a new discipline, it may be relevant to recall that teachers of Business Policy remain the only teachers who are charged with the integration of the entire MBA program. Although it is pertinent to teach theory and concepts, such teaching must add to, and not detract from, the integrative skills. Hence the sequencing of source materials becomes critical in attaining the traditional objective of integration, as well as such new objectives as imparting conceptual knowledge.

IMPLICATIONS FOR PEDAGOGICAL METHODS AND TEACHER TRAINING

Today most teachers of Business Policy use cases and/or simulations (Hofer, 1969; Charan, 1975; Wolfe and Guth, 1975; Unterman, 1977a; Gomolka and Steinhauer, 1977; and Hegarty, 1977) throughout most of a "capstone" Business Policy course. To reinforce such added teaching objectives as acquiring knowledge and developing concepts, while simultaneously developing skills of integration, it may be necessary to use pedagogical methods other than cases and game simulation.

The question of how to integrate such conceptualizations within a Business Policy course is not a simple one. Charan (1975) offers a clear picture of methodology useful for teaching the Policy course when integration is the prime objective. Appropriate methodologies vary by level of students (Unterman, 1977b) and teaching objectives (Hofer, 1969), however. In this regard, Dooley and Skinner (1977) identify eight different possible educational objectives:

1. Acquire knowledge
2. Develop concepts
3. Understand techniques
4. Acquire skill in use of technique
5. Acquire skill in analysis of business problems
6. Acquire skill in synthesis of action plans
7. Develop useful attitudes
8. Develop mature judgment and wisdom

Dooley and Skinner then evaluate and correlate case method teaching to each of these eight objectives. They suggest an inverse rela-

tionship, i.e., that the higher numbered objectives are best achieved through case teaching. They point out that skills of analysis, application of techniques, and synthesis of action plans cannot be taught by lecture or rote. They conclude that skills and attitudes are acquired through experiential learning, e.g., by the case method. In contrast, the lower numbered objectives are more efficiently achieved using other types of pedagogy. A review of pedagogical methods is given in Exhibit 8.1.

Hofer (1969) evaluated the effectiveness of five teaching methods — lectures, cases, role playing, games and in-basket against five teaching objectives — imparting substantive knowledge, developing conceptual understanding, developing behavioral skills, developing nonbehavioral skills, and changing attitudes and values (see Exhibit 8.2). He concluded,

we must first decide on the educational objectives we wish to achieve and the relative importance of each of these objectives and then select the teaching method best suited to achieve these objectives.

Gomolka and Steinhauer (1977), explored the pros and cons of eight pedagogical methods — cases, field projects, games, role playing, critical incidents, lectures, visual aids, and readings for teaching policy. Their data supported the hypothesis that there is a high degree of correlation between a specific teaching method used for business policy and its perceived effectiveness.

Unterman (1977b) discusses a number of additional methods for teaching policy, such as student teaching, group teaching, blackboard analysis, negotiation, and case writing. He borrowed pedagogical techniques from the fields of law, medicine and music. He concluded that many teachers do not learn, or experiment with, the variety of techniques available. One reason for such reluctance is the near lack of teacher training at the doctoral level. New teachers tend to emulate their mentors in the doctoral programs and fail to investigate additional pedagogical techniques. Although no hard data is available, few schools offer seminars or courses in the teaching development of their own professors. It would seem that the new body of research should inspire teachers of Business Policy

Exhibit 8.1   A Profile of Pedagogy in the Teaching of Business Administration

Category	Educational objective	Case description (example)	Application of a case	Teacher's role	Student's role	Class percentage teacher talks	Teacher's preparation	Teacher's skills and knowledge required	Problems and hazards frequently encountered	Requirements for success	Judging success of class
I	Acquire knowledge	Exposition of business practice	Very poor	Narrate Expose Enlighten Provide expertise	Listen	95%	Organize facts so as to be interesting, relevant and clear	Public speaking, Clarity of thinking and lucidity Organization of material	Student impatience, boredom	Student is concerned, feels problem exists and desires knowledge	Student interest, knowledge retention, ability to playback
II	Develop concepts	Exposition of problem or in business	Poor	Explain taxonomies and inter-relation-ships	Listen and question	85%	Organize facts to develop useful and meaningful inter-rela-tionships	Competence in theory and ability to explain it simply	Student unawareness, unconcern with prob-lems to which con-cept is addressed	Student hungers for concept after much wrestling with prob-lem with-out concep-tual scheme	Grasp of ability to playback and verbalize
III	Understand techniques	Problem-ette	Fair	Explain technique & its deriva-tion and application	Work prob-lem, examples Derive tech-nique	70%	Understand theory and derivation and impli-cations of technique	Ability to explain/ derive and demonstrate	Student failure to see useful-ness, prac-ticality, relevance of techniques Confusion	Student sees need for technique before he/ she gets it. Student derives technique himself/herself	Ability to work prob-lems correctly
IV	Acquire skill in use of technique	Short realistic business situation structured	Good	Question and probe to develop realism	Work out effective use of technique in business situation	33%	Understand applications and limita-tions and problems in use of tech-nique	Realistic recognition of problems in use of technique	"It seems too easy; it seems too hard; it seems too universal; it seems too limited"	Realistically demanding case. Teacher can restrain self from resolving problems	Practicality of student recommenda-tions

Exhibit 8.1   A Profile of Pedagogy in the Teaching of Business Administration (Continued)

Category	Educational objective	Case description (example)	Application of a case	Teacher's role	Student's role	Class percentage teacher talks	Teacher's preparation	Teacher's skills and knowledge required	Problems and hazards frequently encountered	Requirements for success	Judging success of class
V	Acquire skill in analysis of business problems	Complex unstructured slice of life	Excellent	Probe Clarify Inter-relate	Analyze Determine cause/effect relationships by analysis of facts and inferences	10%	Case analysis Develop many alternatives and predict possible student approaches	Questions to open up areas for discussion Careful listening Sense of realism	Teacher domination Teacher "telling" Teacher impatience, Teacher solving	Student willing to work, desires to analyze problem and feels competent	Thoroughness, variety, completeness of analysis in breadth and depth
VI	Acquire skill in synthesis of action plans	Problem with clear emphasis on action	Excellent	Challenge Question Extrapolate Role-play	Establish priorities, plan of action: Develop possible outcomes and implications	10%	Develop understanding of situation and possible approaches	Interpretation of student plan without domination	Teacher temptation to settle it with own ingenious analysis	Student feels he/she has necessary facts and is challenged to develop solution which he/she feels does exit	Creativity & realism of action plans
VII	Develop useful attitudes	V, VI, VII with emphasis on key executives	Excellent	Lift up the problem of executive attitudes	Discuss debate outcomes Personalize	10%	Consider variety of attitudes, present and possible	Seeing problem from its many sides	Teacher imposition of own attitudes/values	Teacher trusts that attitudes emerge as a long-term by-product of a demanding education	Changes in attitudes, increased confidence, humility, responsibility
VIII	Develop mature judgment/wisdom	Complex, realistic, unstructured problem	Excellent	Give feedback Restate Listen	Discuss/debate Develop alternatives and their implications	5%	Case analysis in all possible dimensions	Self-restraint Perception of student state of progress	Teacher impatience, teacher inability to tolerate student frustration	Teacher can tolerate student frustrations	Waiting & trusting

Exhibit 8.2 Evaluation of the Effectiveness of Various Teaching Methods in Achieving Different Educational Objectives

Teaching objectives / Teaching method	Impart substantive knowledge	Develop conceptual understanding	Develop skills		Change attitudes and values
			Behavioral	Non-behavioral	
1. Lecture method	good	fair	poor	poor	poor
2. Case method	fair	good	fair	good	fair
3. Role playing	poor	fair	good	poor–fair	good
4. Computer and other games	poor	poor–fair–good (depends on time allowed for analysis and caliber of feedback)	fair	fair–good	fair
5. "In-Basket Technique" and "Incident Method"	poor	poor–fair–good (depends on caliber of feedback)	poor	good	poor–fair

to explore different techniques, encourage pedagogical courses at the doctoral level, and motivate the continued development of teachers. A new, unique discipline should be nurtured and accompanied by a new, unique teacher.

CONCLUSION

The few examples cited above of ways in which current policy research may be applied to the teaching of Business Policy may or may not fit each individual's values or needs as a teacher. It is generally understood that teaching is an art and not a science. Yet, these papers offer such a wide range of findings, concepts and viewpoints that any teacher of strategy could find some sections which meet his needs as a teacher.

As Steiner (1976) says:

Improved curriculum [of General Management] is concerned with providing the skills for dealing with broad, messy unstructured problems. Students are entering an even more complex and interrelated world. Managerial problems are becoming more and more difficult to solve because they are less and less amenable to the present knowledge and problem-solving tools. . . . Nonetheless, somehow we must enable our future managers to deal with these unknowns.

Hence, the body of strategic management research surveyed in this book is critical to: (1) the need to establish a differentiated discipline; (2) the need to develop a Business Policy curriculum; (3) the need to change the teaching objectives of the traditional policy course; and (4) the needs of our students.

Research is like music to the deaf — until it is felt in the vibrations of touch. To some, successful research is that which can be used. . . . What better use is there than to use the research ideas in this volume as part of teaching?

Policy and Planning Research: Teaching Implications

W. Harvey Hegarty
Indiana University

In this paper, the major contributions of each of the invited papers will be discussed with respect to how these contributions might be used to enrich a policy course or curricula. Specifically, for each topic paper at least one teaching pedagogy will be suggested which can be employed to dramatize the central theme or major points expressed by the author.

The recommended teaching pedagogies are merely suggestions. Clearly, a different set of approaches could be developed which would be equally effective. Each of the approaches suggested has been used by the author. Each suggestion may not be equally successful across the variety of teaching situations that policy instructors face. These suggestions pragmatically illustrate policy concepts which are useful in most situations.

Finally, it should be noted that this paper has not incorporated the observations of the various commentaries. However, many ideas contained in these commentaries could be incorporated into policy courses in the same ways those of the topic papers were.

THE TEACHING IMPLICATIONS OF ANSOFF'S PAPER

The impact of environmental turbulence is quite profound and currently the research literature does not reflect this. Accordingly, we may not be giving enough classroom attention to this particular phenomenon. If we are only reflecting in the classroom what we as scholars know empirically about the environment, then the student may very well be not getting a full perspective of what the concept of strategy is all about. This has very important implications for those who place a great deal of importance on econometric models and extrapolation as the primary means in determining the strategic path(s) for business organizations.

A second and equally important theme presented by Ansoff centers around the legitimacy and acceptance of an organization's actions. Regulatory agencies and constituency groups are placing an increasing amount of pressure on organizations. To be sure, this is an area where a great deal of research needs to be done, but we cannot avoid the issue in the classroom because of a lack of an adequate research base. Selecting key external forces for more in-depth analysis is very appropriate. Whether this is a federal agency such as OSHA, or a public force such as the media, an in-depth analysis can help dramatize how critical environmental factors affect the strategic process.

A number of specific teaching suggestions can be made based on Ansoff's observations. Exhibits 1.1 through 1.8 in his paper capture many critical factors relevant to strategic management. There is evidence that these factors have significantly changed over the twentieth century. To dramatize these changes, one might develop a list of all such key environmental factors. One could then assign students two cases, one very current and one at least ten years old, e.g., Midway Foods (9–306–131 through 9–306–139) and Winnebago Industries (9–375–092).[1] The students could be asked to identify from the list of key environmental factors those which represent critical issues facing each company. Such a comparison would not only serve as a validation of Ansoff's thesis, but would make these points in a way that students could easily understand.

A second teaching recommendation from Ansoff's paper follows the theme of industrial development and its impact on the business frontier. Specifically, one could select an industry or organization rich in publicly available materials, present the students with five-year

[1] Numbers throughout this paper refer to Intercollegiate Case Clearing House numbers.

blocks of corporate data, request they lay out five-year plans for future strategic actions based on the available data, and then ask them to compare their strategic plans with the actual corporate posture that developed. After going through three or four such iterations, it will become quite obvious that each subsequent time period will incorporate many more decisions than can be dealt with effectively in a predictive mode.

THE TEACHING IMPLICATIONS OF MINTZBERG'S PAPER

Power configurations and how they operate is the central theme brought out by Mintzberg as he endeavors to build a contingency model of power which focuses on external forces and internal organizational structure. His thesis in many ways complements Ansoff's discussion of dealing with outside forces. He contends that the variable "power" has much to offer as a research concept because there are some sound theoretical underpinnings on which to base this particular type of research. Consequently, research in this area is sorely needed. He goes on to point out that traditional research on power does not consider information relationships or the moderating effects of organization culture and philosophy.

A truly excellent case that might be used to illustrate these points is the *Saturday Evening Post* (6–373–009). In this case, special emphasis is placed on both internal and external coalitions, central themes to Mintzberg's work. In particular, the case vividly describes how both the CEO and the Board relate to and, in many cases, fail to relate to various constituencies. Another case which focuses on internal coalitions and their effect on organizational performance is John Adams (6–373–157). The focal individual is a recent MBA graduate with whom the students can easily identify.

A recurring theme in Mintzberg's paper is the role of the PK (peak coordinator) both within the internal coalitions and in concert with the various forces in the external environment. The way these relationships develop and operate is shown quite nicely in the film, *The Corporation: A CBS Report*. This fifty-three minute color film about Phillips Petroleum focuses on the CEO position and its relationship to the Board of Directors, the federal government, foreign countries, and corporate competitors. Numerous examples of power relationships are clearly brought out by both the CEO (Mintzberg's PK), and the many individuals with whom he relates. Phillips, as described in this film, is very close to the closed system power configuration, one of six figurations Mintzberg presents at the end of his paper.

THE TEACHING IMPLICATIONS OF GRANT'S AND KING'S PAPER

The identification of key factors to be considered in developing a strategy and specifying a set of appropriate strategies are the two major themes in Grant's and King's paper. They point out that analytical aspects of the strategy formulation process are extremely important and then review numerous research efforts which attempt to isolate what key factors need to be addressed.

Once a strategist has completed the analytical phase of the process a set of viable strategies must be constructed to fulfill the organization's mission, given the environmental constraints and other controlling factors it faces. Several approaches to dealing with this problem are discussed including the PIMS model, Game Theory, the Delphi Method, and the GE Planning Matrix. Grant and King suggest that, among other things, the choice of an analytical framework depends on the aspirations and perspective of the organization as well as the time frame involved.

One approach to using this article would be to select two or three of the strategy formulation models and have students analyze different cases using the following models as frames of reference.

Strategic choice format	*Assigned case*
Delphi approach	Kampgrounds of America (9-374-343)
Scenarios	Prelude Corporation (6-373-052)
Strategic data base	Aerosol Techniques, Inc. (9-313-155)

The KOA case is an excellent vehicle for generating options concerning "where do we go from here." It also provides enough information to present some strong stands of disagreement for various options. The Delphi approach would be very appropriate for strategy formulation given the nature and ramifications of the problem situation faced by KOA.

Scenarios attempt to describe in some detail what events need to be considered if current options are undertaken and these paths meet with fruition. The Prelude Corporation offers such a challenge. At the end of the case, several options are outlined, but none are acceptable in their present state of development.

The strategic data base approach focuses on the generation of a set of statements isolating the most significant strategic factors in the situation under consideration. Based on these statements the organization's set of strategic choices are evaluated. Aerosol Techniques, Inc., presents a situation where a variety of product mixes are future options, but the environment is complex and filled with a great deal of uncertainty. Various constituency groups, historical precedents, and conflicting objectives make the generation of the most significant strategic factors very appropriate since any decision will be suboptimal for some group affected by the decision.

Using this approach the students will be exposed to more than one "way of thinking" in strategic management. This exposure should build on and enrich their appreciation for contingency theory management. It also will enable them to practice their integrative skills using a variety of perspectives.

THE TEACHING IMPLICATIONS OF UTTERBACK'S PAPER

According to Utterback, different approaches for environmental forecasting are needed for different environments. Unless one carefully examines the purpose of the forecasting exercise and the nature of the environment faced, a misuse of technique will be likely, resulting in the use of suboptimal information. Two key concerns in this area involve the integration of forecasting into the strategic planning process and knowing what should be forecast in the first place.

Utterback points out both the major flaws of current forecasting techniques and the necessary ingredients for success in the realm of environmental forecasting. One of the most important of these is the inconsistency and inability of currently known forecasting methods to predict the impact of several changes taken together. Also needed for success is an organization structure which supports the forecasting and planning functions. Finally, but perhaps most important of all, is the necessity for viable informal communication channels on the organization's boundary to maintain contact with key factors and individuals in the environment.

The Leisure Group, Inc. (9-376-204) provides a situation appropriate for the discussion and use of the environmental forecasting recommendations that Utterback makes. This Los Angles conglomerate experienced phenomenal growth in the late 60's, but faced a severe financial crisis in 1971. Poor and inappropriate forecasting techniques were in part responsible for this sudden decline. The company found itself in too many different environments to adequately monitor any of them. As a result, they were forced to divest themselves of a number of investments and now must decide where there is the greatest potential in their rebuilding effort.

THE TEACHING IMPLICATIONS OF BOWER'S AND DOZ'S PAPER

A comparison of the analytical versus incremental decision-making approaches to strategy formulation establishes the starting point for the discussion presented by these authors. They present the thesis of the analytical approach which basically involves setting objectives and moving from where you are now, to where the objective would have you be. In contrast to this approach is the idea that strategy is merely a set of disjointed decisions over a period of time made as reactions to problems as they arise.

The Peace Corps (6-371-282) and Carmen Company (6-372-338) are both excellent cases to illustrate these points. A common theme of the various approaches to strategy which the authors discuss is "How do you develop internal systems to deal with external demands?" The Peace Corps faces such a problem. Faced with changing demands from client countries and waning congressional support, the Peace Corps must develop some long-range plans to justify their existence, yet remain flexible enough to meet the needs of both volunteers and their host countries.

The Carmen Company would be a good case to use to discuss the analytical versus incremental decision-making theories of strategic management. The case traces the history of this sixty-two year old company primarily involved in the retail shoe business. Earlier periods of the case illustrate analytical concepts, while the recent decisions seem to have been made on political grounds.

THE TEACHING IMPLICATIONS OF RUMELT'S PAPER

The dimensions of strategy encompass the entire organization and for the most part focus on ill-structured problems with the major task being an attempt to reduce ambiguity. Rumelt suggests there are a number of models that each in its own way deals with this ambiguity.

Rumelt purports that there are four context free tests which need to be applied to evaluate any given strategy. First, the set of objectives and strategies embraced by the organization must be internally consistent (goal consistency test). Second, the areas and/or issues must be identified which are critical to the organization given its competitive position in the environment (frame test). Third, the organization must have the necessary resources to carry out the strategy (competence test). Finally, the proposed set of strategies embraced by the organization must be able to achieve the objectives set (workability test).

Deere and Company (9-313-124) and Massey-Ferguson Limited (9-313-123) can be used to illustrate these concepts quite well. Both Deere and Massey-Ferguson have strategies that are

unique to their organization and have as many differences as commonalities. Yet, both are in a very well defined industry and each must determine the most appropriate corporate strategy given the other's existence. A more in-depth analysis along these lines can be made by including in this sequence The Note on the Farm Equipment Industry (9–313–122) and J. I. Case (9–309–270).

THE TEACHING IMPLICATIONS OF LORANGE'S PAPER

The purpose Lorange attempts to fulfill in his paper is to give a survey of the state of the art regarding formal planning systems. First, he surveys various research studies that address the question of whether planning is worthwhile. Although the evidence indicates it is, the studies to date are not as strong as they might be. Lorange then discusses the pitfalls commonly associated with planning efforts that were identified in a number of studies. Next, he examines various studies of formal planning system design that may form the elements of a contingency theory of formal planning system design. Based on these studies, he concludes that formal planning systems can be used in a variety of different situations and they are important in both strategy formulation and implementation, with the extent of their use depending on a number of organizational and environmental characteristics.

Marlin Firearms (6–371–186) has a number of characteristics which are quite relevant to the issues Lorange emphasizes. The case can be examined over a period of time with particular regard to the nature of its planning system. One can assess whether it was effective in the past, and if it will continue to be effective in the future. There also is ample information to discuss whether major changes in its planning system would be accepted in this particular organization. This case also contains enough information about key decision makers that the key pitfalls to effective planning that Lorange reviews can be "tested."

Univis (9-313-132) is also recommended as a good companion case to Lorange's paper. The key issue in the case involves the development of a formal planning system. A detailed description of Univis' current planning process is also provided so the student has adequate information to support some concrete changes that would improve the functioning of this process and increase the likelihood that the objectives of the firm would be met.

THE TEACHING IMPLICATIONS OF GALBRAITH'S AND NATHANSON'S PAPER

Much of the work in the strategy/structure area is derived from Chandler's classic work. The essence of Chandler's thesis is that strategy follows structure, that there are stages of development in this sequence, and that structures are not changed unless organizations begin to recognize they have some inefficiencies.

Galbraith and Nathanson cover significant works which have built and elaborated on Chandler's propositions. For example, a significant number of studies have been conducted examining diversification strategies. Their conclusion still supports the theme that strategy follows structure and that there is a continuing adoption of the multidivisional form to deal with the problem of diversity.

Another stream of research explored by the authors focuses on the question: "How do you manage a complex diversified corporation once you have established its structural form?" Resource allocation, reward systems, and career development also deserve careful attention as there needs to be a matching of strategy and structure with people.

Galbraith and Nathanson conclude that, in general, strategy follows structure, but not always. In addition, they suggest that when a firm has a strategy/structure relationship that does not fit, performance is only adversely affected under adverse economic conditions or during a period of increased competition from rivals in the environment.

Much of what is brought out in this position statement involves how organizations develop and grow in the context of the strategy/structure phenomenon. However, while there is much research in this area, there are few cases that explore how the various changes that take place

are actually implemented. Many organizations went through a dramatic diversification phase in the last decade. Some were extremely successful, others were not. Consequently, one very fruitful way to explore these ideas in the classroom involves the use of top level executives from fairly large organizations. Banks who invested heavily in real-estate are another good example.

Blow-Mold Packers (9-372-239) incorporates many strategy/structure issues brought out in this paper. The case traces this organization from its inception to its current position of $33 million in sales. Strategy changes were made throughout the history of the organization with structural changes following that often did not provide a proper fit. At the end of the case, Blow Mold's current structure is not working well and they are contemplating a new strategy. Galbraith and Nathanson's section on integrating mechanisms is a very appropriate exposition to expose the students to before asking them to make future strategy/structure recommendations for this case.

THE TEACHING IMPLICATIONS OF COOPER'S PAPER

Including small businesses in the review of strategic management research is quite appropriate since they compose approximately 95% of all U.S. businesses. There is a tremendous amount of diversity among these businesses, however, and before inferences are made, one must be very careful to examine both the nature of the business as well as the motivation of the owners/proprietors. Cooper contends that the appropriate classification of strategies of small business is to look at their particular stage in development. In the early growth stage, the most important factors are flexibility and informality. To the degree that the firm establishes a niche early on and does not face heavy direct competition, it will be more likely to survive. A great amount of effort at this stage goes into "operating" the business, leaving little time for strategic planning, as such.

In the later growth stages, the employee base enlarges and more operating decisions are delegated giving the owner more time to plan. Many organizations which later experience success are very innovative during their growth stage.

One individual who is usually very familiar with success and failure stories of small businesses, and who could be brought into the classroom, is the local banker. To be sure, he may not be able to list in detail the reasons a particular business failed, but he certainly would be in a position to discuss factors that he has observed that appear to be associated with both success and failure. Other possible individuals who could serve the same purpose include a bankruptcy lawyer and a CPA whose principal clients are small businessmen.

A case that deals with the management of a new venture and incorporates examples of several of the key ideas discussed by Cooper is Fourwinds Marina (9-375-772). This organization found a niche with almost no competition, but failed to prosper due to a number of critical problems such as labor turnover, too much growth, too little delegation, weak controls, and a very short planning horizon. There is also a 24 minute color movie on the Fourwinds Marina in which the principal characters in the case discuss the problems of getting a small business started (BSC-177).

Tensor Lamp (9-370-041) is also an excellent case in the small business area. It clearly demonstrates the impact that the entrepreneur's values can have on shaping and molding company policy.

THE TEACHING IMPLICATIONS OF BERG'S AND PITTS' PAPER

Berg and Pitts argue that a great deal of effort should be spent studying the strategies of diversified companies since they control such a vast amount of corporate assets and account for approximately three-fourths of industrial profits.

In this regard, they identify several types of questions that are more or less unique to multi-industry firms such as: How and when to diversify? How do you deal with multiple levels of management and how do you undertake a successful divestiture?

Using second-year MBA students, case research projects on multi-industry firms could be designed where data bases of structured and unstructured questions could be developed. This effort can be much more than case writing. Case writing can serve as the foundation, with research questions being posed *prior* to the collection of data by the teams. (*Case Research* by Leenders and Erskine [1973] offers some good suggestions as a starting point. *Stages of Social Research* by Forcese and Richer [1970] also would be a good supplement to this assignment. The latter authors have included in their book a number of excellent articles pertaining to field research.)

Berg and Pitts also raise a number of questions that have yet to be sufficiently addressed regarding complex organizations in a complex environment. Many of the questions they raise are also brought out in the CML Group, Inc. (9-371-426). In CML, four acquired divisions must be operated in such a way that accountability is maintained, but owner-operators can enjoy sufficient autonomy. Conflicts between corporate and division objectives complicate the establishment of any long-term corporate mission.

THE TEACHING IMPLICATIONS OF WORTMAN'S PAPER

Not-for-profit organizations have received little attention from strategy researchers and offer a wide-open territory of inquiry. They often have ill-defined goals structures, are poorly managed, and rarely are efficient in an economic sense. Often, there are a number of constituent groups with different conceptions of the organization's mission, which means the organization attempts to serve several masters and consequently may serve none.

Although little has been done in assessing the strategies of not-for-profit organizations, this does not mean that the ideas applied to businesses can be directly applied to such organizations because there are some very real constraints on developing a long-term planning horizon. For instance, in such organizations, long-term financial commitments are uncertain and volunteer support is often sporadic. To permit students to fully appreciate the nature of the not-for-profit organization, one could bring an individual who has major responsibilities for managing such an organization into the classroom. Such people are present in most communities and they are generally very open concerning the problems they encounter in managing their organizations. Cases can also be used to explore some of these issues.

Monroe County United Ministries (9-376-697) describes an organization faced with many of the problems described by Wortman. The organization is a coalition of churches with the broad objective of meeting the social needs of the community. They must raise a budget of $140,000 from seven different sources including two federal agencies. Program development and evaluation are key areas of concern. Developing a viable structure for an organization that must mesh an employed staff of twenty with several hundred volunteers also presents a very difficult problem with which to deal.

Another excellent case in the not-for-profit area is the Boston Symphony (9-375-340). Maintaining fiscal responsibility and maximizing artistic freedom are two of the conflicting objectives for the Boston Symphony. Faced with declining ticket sales, the organization must develop a series to attract new subscribers. Their latitude, however, is somewhat limited by the traditional posture of the organization.

THE TEACHING IMPLICATIONS OF STEINER'S PAPER

Four main thrusts can be identified in the development of contingency theories as they relate to strategy. Steiner categorizes these areas as follows: case tradition theories, theories based on organization theory, those derived from empirical research and experience, and conceptual theories.

Case theories are very complex because they deal with such a large number of variables. However, some notable work has been done in this area such as the life cycle propositions developed by Hofer (1975b).

The area of empirical research and experience has recently been recognized as a fruitful avenue to pursue among the contingency components. Most notable among these are the PIMS studies. The Boston Consulting Group (1968) has also made a significant contribution in this area.

Ansoff's *Corporate Strategy* (1965) is the best known work among contingency conceptualization efforts. Glueck (1972) has developed a rather lengthy set of propositions which lay the framework for research that would fall into this category. This area for the most part, however, has not been as rich recently in substantive works.

It is difficult to develop an assignment where all four schools of thought described by Steiner could be encompassed in one teaching experience. Consequently my suggestions here will be directed at highlighting parts of the message which Steiner delivers. In this regard, Aerosol Techniques (9-313-155) is useful because it has a number of elements that directly and indirectly tie in with Steiner's paper. ATI has a diversified product line and is faced with increased competition, even though it remains an industry leader. Product line assessment and possible vertical integration are two strategic issues that must be addressed. The propositions developed by Hofer and Glueck, each of which Steiner discusses, would provide appropriate guidelines for this case analysis. Finally there is a considerable amount of effort spent describing the central figure in the strategy making process which Steiner points out as a key weakness of all the groups of contingency theories.

The Steiner paper would also be an appropriate foundation piece to develop conceptual skills among graduate students. One could ask such students to develop hypotheses or propositions for each of the four schools of thought. Then one could ask them to validate what they have generated by reviewing the cases already dealt with in the course. In this manner, Steiner's paper could be used toward the end of the course to tie together, from a conceptual point of view, the cases which have been used somewhat independently to dramatize various aspects of strategy.

THE TEACHING IMPLICATIONS OF DUNCAN'S PAPER

Duncan discusses several areas where qualitative data gathering methodologies can be used in the policy area. Among the more important of these are the use of organizational power and politics in the strategy formulation process and the design of structures and processes for the implementation of strategy. Others involve the leadership activities and skills of the chief executive officer. Duncan goes on to describe three qualitative data gathering methodologies that are particularly useful in the policy area: case studies, interview studies, and observation techniques.

The multiple uses of case studies for teaching purposes require no additional elaboration here. Some comments on how to use interviews and observations techniques for teaching policy are appropriate, however.

One way to use interviews for teaching policy would be to use the structured interview approach used by Mintzberg and others. Here students could be exposed to interviewing techniques while collecting data which could be used in the study of strategy. A study of the magnitude of Mintzberg's (1975) study would require a number of committed organizations within an accessible metropolitan area. For many, this would not be possible. A smaller sample with organizations of lesser complexity could provide the same types of information for class analysis and the same experience for the students, however.

An alternative project, which could be carried out on an individual, team, or class basis, would be to collect policy data using the observational technique. While the need for secrecy may foreclose the opportunity to observe strategy sessions in most business organizations, there are a number of other avenues worth pursuing. For example, town board meetings and public school meetings often deal with strategy and policy issues and are usually open to the public. Not only do they provide the scenario for policy study, they normally involve a number of key qualitative factors, such as organizational politics that need to be emphasized more extensively in policy courses.

THE TEACHING IMPLICATIONS OF HATTEN'S PAPER

To date quantitative research has had little impact on business policy. The question Hatten attempts to answer is: "Is policy research amenable to quantitative methods, and if so, what are their specific limitations?"

Hatten notes that distinct paths need to be followed in pursuing quantitative research. One stream involves the analysis of firms within an industry. Hatten argues that homogeneous groups need more in-depth quantitative analysis because the industry is an appropriate unit of analysis due to its homogeneity.

The second stream to be followed involves quantification of data relevant to the decision process of the strategist. Two of the more interesting topics in this area involve the dimensionality of the decision spaces employed in strategy formulation and the perceptual mappings of managers' judgments of priorities.

The aircraft cases, Piper (9-369-007), Beech (9-369-008), and the industry note (9-370-036), are very appropriately meshed with the approach advocated by Hatten. An even more intriguing analysis can be undertaken using perceptual mappings since four corporate officers for each company have ranked six factors they consider important in selling their products. These data are provided for five classes of aircraft where the companies are in direct competition and two classes where Piper alone is operating. Since there are notable differences as well as similarities across factors in various classes as seen by the executive, a perceptual map might be constructed to try to help understand how these managers' perceptions would affect the decisions they might make.

CONCLUSION

The purpose of this paper was to provide at least one teaching suggestion for each paper presented at the conference. For most papers, at least two and sometimes three suggestions were made. The majority of suggestions involve the use of proven Intercollegiate Case Clearing House cases. Most individuals who teach in the business policy area are familiar with case methodology, therefore incorporating these suggestions should present no serious problems. The selections were made using as a criterion: "What practical case best demonstrates a scenario that mirrors the author's theory or propositions?"

Numerous other recommendations were made which generally require more involvement by both the instructor and the students in successfully completing the activity. Sometimes these suggestions involve field work which obviously requires greater skills and time commitments. While these suggestions are more adventuresome and demanding, they are strongly recommended as the potential pay-offs are significant.

There are some other suggestions of merit that were not made in conjunction with any specific paper, but are worthy of note. One of these involves the use of the library to demonstrate the complexity and importance of both environmental variables and corporate strategic issues. One way to do this is to assign a general topic area to the class and ask them to find a specified number of articles over a five-year time period related to that topic. Then have the students do a content analysis of each article. This is an excellent way to demonstrate the nature and magnitude of changes over time in critical strategic factors and to dramatize the great need for strategic planning.

Another suggestion involves the use of individual board of director members. It is unlikely that one can get access to a full corporate board. However, in a university community, there usually are a large number of individuals who have had board experience. Bring a panel of these individuals into the classroom and have them discuss either the importance of strategic planning or the processes it involves. My experience has been that these persons are not hesitant to do so, but rather are honored by such a request.

Finally, top corporate executives can be brought into the classroom using the conference telephone system. This works particularly well if the call is made after a case analysis has been conducted on the executive's company. However, specific issues, such as "The Development of a National Energy Policy" using an oil company executive, work equally well.

Section 8 References

Ackerman, Robert W. "Marlin Firearms Co., Inc." Boston, Mass.: Intercollegiate Case Clearing House, #6-371-186, 1970a.

Ackerman, Robert W. "Peace Corps." Boston Mass.: Intercollegiate Case Clearing House, #6-371-282, 1970b.

Ackerman, Robert W. "Carman Co." Boston, Mass.: Intercollegiate Case Clearing House, #6-372-338, 1972.

Andrews, Kenneth R. *The Concept of Corporate Strategy*. Homewood, Ill.: Dow Jones–Irwin, 1971.

Andrews, Kenneth R. and R. G. C. Hanna. "Univis, Inc." Boston, Mass.: Intercollegiate Case Clearing House, #9-313-132, 1966.

Ansoff, H. Igor. *Corporate Strategy: An Analytic Approach to Business Policy for Growth and Expansion*. New York: McGraw-Hill, 1965.

Berg, Norman A. "John Adams." Boston, Mass.: Intercollegiate Case Clearing House, #6-373-157, 1965.

Berg, Norman A. and W. R. Boulton. "The Leisure Group, Inc. (A)." Boston, Mass.: Intercollegiate Case Clearing House, #9-376-204, 1976.

Berg, Norman and Charles W. Hofer. "Aerosol Techniques, Inc." Boston, Mass.: Intercollegiate Case Clearing House, #9-313-155, 1966a.

Berg, Norman and Charles W. Hofer. "Deere and Company." Boston, Mass.: Intercollegiate Case Clearing House, #9-313-124, 1966b.

Berg, Norman and Charles W. Hofer. "Massey-Ferguson, Ltd." Boston, Mass.: Intercollegiate Case Clearing House, #9-313-123, 1966c.

Berg, Norman and Charles W. Hofer. "Note on the Farm Equipment Industry." Boston, Mass.: Intercollegiate Case Clearing House, #9-313-122, 1966d.

Berg, Norman and Robert A. Pitts. "CML Group, Inc." Boston, Mass.: Intercollegiate Case Clearing House, #9-371-426, 1971.

Boston Consulting Group. *Perspectives on Experience*. Boston: Boston Consulting Group, 1968.

CBS News, Producer. *The Corporation: A CBS Report*. New York: Carousel Films. 1972.

Charan, Ram. "Classroom Techniques in Teaching by the Case Method." *Academy of Management Proceedings*, August 1975.

Christensen, C. Roland, Kenneth R. Andrews and Joseph L. Bower. *Business Policy: Text and Cases* (4th edition). Homewood, Ill.: Richard D. Irwin, 1978.

Christensen, C. Roland and E. L. Rachal. "Kampgrounds of America, Inc." Boston, Mass.: Intercollegiate Case Clearing House, #9-374-343, 1974.

Christensen, C. Roland, J. W. Rosenblum and C. B. Weigle. "Prelude Corp." Boston, Mass.: Intercollegiate Case Clearing House, #6-373-052, 1972.

Christensen, C. Roland and Bruce R. Scott. "Midway Foods. (A), (B₁), (B₂), (B₃), (B₄), (C), (D₁), (D₂), (D₃)." Boston, Mass.: Intercollegiate Case Clearing House, #9-306-131 to 139, 1959.

Christensen, C. Roland and A. T. Sproat. "Saturday Evening Post." Boston, Mass.: Intercollegiate Case Clearing House, #6-373-009, 1970.

Christensen, C. Roland, H. H. Stevenson and A. T. Sproat. "Blow-Mold Packers, Inc." Boston, Mass.: Intercollegiate Case Clearing House, #9-372-239, 1971.

Delta Sigma Pi. "25th Biennial Survey of Universities Offering an Organized Curriculum in Commerce and Business Administration." November 1976.

Dooley, Arch and Wickham Skinner. "Casing Case-Method Methods." *Academy of Management Review*, April 1977.

Forcese, D. P. and S. Richer. *Stages of Social Research*. Englewood Cliffs, N.J.: Prentice-Hall, 1970.

Glueck, William F. "Business Policy: Reality and Promise." *Academy of Management Proceedings*, August 1972.

Gomolka, Eugene C. and Ralph F. Steinhauer. "The Frequency and Perceived Effectiveness of Various Methods for Teaching Undergraduate and Graduate Business Policy." *Academy of Management Proceedings*, August 1977.

Gordon, Robert A. and James E. Howell. *Higher Education for Business*. New York: Columbia University Press, 1959.

Guth, William D. and A. T. Sproat. "J. I. Case Co." Boston, Mass.: Intercollegiate Case Clearing House, #9-309-270, 1962.

Hegarty, Harvey W. "The Use of Cases and Other Materials in Business Policy." Unpublished manuscript, 1977.

Hegarty, W. Harvey and H. Kelsey, Jr. "Fourwinds Marina." Boston, Mass.: Intercollegiate Case Clearing House, #9-375-772, 1974.

Hegarty, W. Harvey and H. Kelsey, Jr. "Fourwinds Marina Movie." Indiana University Audio-Visual Center. I.U.A.V. No. BSC-177. 1976a.

Hegarty, W. Harvey and H. Kelsey, Jr. "Monroe County United Ministries." Boston, Mass.: Intercollegiate Case Clearing House, #9-376-697, 1976b.

Hofer, Charles W. "Needed: The New Business Administration." *Singapore Manager*, December 1969.

Hofer, Charles W. "Policy as an Academic Discipline: Its Curricular Needs." *Academy of Management Proceedings*, August 1975a.

Hofer, Charles W. "Towards a Contingency Theory of Business Strategy." *Academy of Management Journal*, December 1975b.

Hofer, Charles W. and Dan Schendel. *Strategy Formulation: Analytical Concepts*. St. Paul: West Publishing, 1978.

Leenders, M. R. and J. A. Erskine. *Case Research: The Case Writing Process*. London, Ontario: School of Business Administration, the University of Western Ontario, 1973.

Lovdal, M. C. "Winnebago Industries, Inc." Boston, Mass.: Intercollegiate Case Clearing House, #9-375-092, 1973.

Mintzberg, Henry. "Policy Is a Field of Management Theory." *Academy of Management Review*, January 1975.

Piaget, Jean. *Logic and Psychology*. New York: Basic Books, 1957.

Pierson, Frank C. *The Education of American Businessmen: A Study of University-College Programs in Business Administration*. New York: McGraw-Hill, 1959.

Raymond, T. C. and N. H. Borden, Jr. "Consolidated Drugs, Inc." Boston, Mass.: Intercollegiate Case Clearing House, #9-554-006, 1952.

Salter, M. S. "Note on the Light Aircraft Industry." Boston, Mass.: Intercollegiate Case Clearing House, #9-370-036, 1969.

Salter, M. S. "Boston Symphony Orchestra." Boston, Mass.: Intercollegiate Case Clearing House, #9-375-340, 1970.

Salter, M. S. and T. N. Gearreald, Jr. "Beech Aircraft Corp." Boston, Mass.: Intercollegiate Case Clearing House #9-369-008, 1968.

Salter, M. S. and T. N. Gearreald, Jr. "Piper Aircraft Corp." Boston, Mass.: Intercollegiate Case Clearing House, #9-369-007, 1969a.

Salter, M. S. and T. N. Gearreald, Jr. "Tensor Corp. — Jay Monroe, President." Boston, Mass.: Intercollegiate Case Clearing House, #9-370-041, 1969b.

Schendel, Dan E. "Needs and Developments in Policy Curricula at the Ph.D. Level." Paper No. 521. Institute for Research in the Behavioral, Economic and Management Sciences. Purdue University, 1975.

Schendel, Dan E. and Kenneth J. Hatten. "Business Policy or Strategic Management: A Broader View for an Emerging Discipline." *Academy of Management Proceedings*, August 1972.

Snow, Charles. "A Comment on Business Policy Teaching Research." *Academy of Management Review*, October 1976.

Starbuck, William H. "On Teaching Business Policy." *Academy of Management Journal*, December 1966.

Steiner, George A. "Future Curricula in Schools of Management." *AACSB Bulletin*, October 1976.

Steiner, George A. and John B. Miner. *Management Policy and Strategy*. New York: Macmillan, 1977.

Stone, Ronald. "Standard E of the AACSB." Speech, Academy of Management, Division of Business Policy and Planning, August 1977.

Unterman, Israel. "An Experiment in the Acclimatization of Students to Business Case Learning." *Academy of Management Proceedings*, August 1977a.

Unterman, Israel. "A Note on Case Methodology Teaching." Boston, Mass.: Intercollegiate Case Clearing House, #9-377-633, 1977b.

Wolfe, Joseph and Gary Guth. "The Case Approach Versus Gaming in Teaching of Business Policy." *Journal of Business*, July 1975.

9

PRACTITIONERS' VIEWS: POLICY AND PLANNING RESEARCH

Ram Charan
Boston University

Ronald O. Aines
International Harvester Company

Benjamin C. Ball, Jr.
Gulf Oil Corporation

Rudolf W. Knoepfel
The Solvay American Corporation

Roderic C. Lancey
G. D. Searle & Company

Among the research conference attendees was a small, select group of practitioners most of whom head corporate planning at their respective companies or are consultants in the area. Four of these individuals, including a chief executive officer, were asked prior to the start of the conference to prepare remarks in reaction to the papers and discussions presented at the conference. Ram Charan served as a coordinator, catalyst, and leader of daily meetings among this group. He also acted as the coordinator in bringing their written remarks together for this volume.

LINK BETWEEN ACADEMICS AND PRACTITIONERS

In policy and planning, there has been no professional link between practitioners and academics as there has been, for example, in marketing or finance. To help forge such a link, or at least better understand why one is lacking, this practitioner panel was formed and included in the conference.

The lack of a practitioner/academic link stems from several sources in in our opinion. One is the relative newness of the policy field as an academic discipline. Thus, as noted in Section 8, most policy faculty had, until quite recently, entered the field from the various functional area disciplines. Such faculty were likely to attend professional meetings in their original disciplines if they attended any at all. Until the early 1960s, few staff specialists in business dealt with strategic issues and most of the line executives who tackled such problems had little time or interest in attending such meetings. Moreover, even if either group — academics or practicing managers — had such an interest, no professional societies existed prior to the late 1960s which focused their primary attention on such matters. So there was no organized way for such interactions to occur. Finally, even after such societies were established, the practitioners and academics went separate ways for several reasons. Among the most important of these were that: (1) until recently the methodology and knowledge that the academic has been able to offer the practitioner have been minimal since academic research in policy has lagged behind industry practice, and (2) practitioner meetings were scheduled at times and places that were both inconvenient and too expensive to attract large numbers of faculty. Such meetings also often focused on issues that academics found unsuitable for research, for either content or methodological reasons.

These conditions are now changing. First, most companies have increasingly begun to utilize professional planners to help design and operate the processes they will use to formulate their strategic plans and to help evaluate, monitor, and control these strategies. Such staff personnel are also more concerned with the abstract nature of the strategic management issues they face than are the line managers they serve. As a consequence, they are much more inclined to interact with academics than were yesterday's line managers. The interest in such interactions is also increased because academic research in the policy area has finally begun to catch up with the best business practice, so that academics have more to say that is of interest to practitioners. At the same time, such research has required sufficient amounts of complex, confidential data that academics have had to increase their personal contacts with industry just to obtain the data. Further, the dialogue between academic and practitioner has increased as they find more to say to one another about both their findings and their problems. Finally, the opportunities for such interactions between practitioners and academics are increasing as the professional societies of both groups are actively looking for ways to facilitate such interchange, although there is as yet no organization that has found a format equally attractive to both groups.

Still, the principal mechanisms for improving collaboration and knowledge acquisition and dissemination in the near future will be these professional societies and their meetings and publications. Here the pleas of Lancey and Knoepfel for academics to meet with planning practitioners in the North American Society for Corporate Planning (NASCP) or the International Affiliation of Planning Societies (IAPS) should be heeded.[1] At the same time, practitioners should join the relevant academic society, the Division of Business Policy and Planning of the Academy of Management. In the longer term what may be needed is a new superorganization capable of providing interchange of ideas, research, and experience through meetings and publications for both academics and practitioners.

OBSERVATIONS OF PRACTITIONER PANEL

The dialogue between practitioner and academic is just beginning and, judging by the remarks of both groups at the conference, it still has a long way to go. We hear complaints of excessive use of jargon in academic writing, a "semantic swamp" according to Lancey. The use of specialized language is owed perhaps not so much to the nature of the strategic management area, as to the disciplines in which the academic was originally trained, or to the firm in which the planner practices. To drain such a semantic swamp will require wide acceptance and further development of the strategic management paradigm on the part of both practitioners and academics.

Our practitioners further point out the need of strategic decision makers for much greater knowledge of what strategies work, that is, what constitutes better or preferably the best strategy in a given situation. While Ball questions whether we know enough even to suggest that better strategy leads to better results, let alone whether better (planning) processes lead to better strategy, there is enough evidence to indicate that the process–strategy–performance link can be made.

However, much more explicit knowledge is needed. It is only natural that the practitioner should be impatient to know more about strategies and processes that work. Results, after all, are their business. Strategic problems are complex, and difficult to resolve, but they appear to be yielding to rigorous concept definition and research, and that is where the academic tradition comes in. But as Knoepfel pointed out, it is time for much closer collaboration and coordination between the two parties to insure that the rate of knowledge acquisition is increased so that we can cope with the increasing complexity of both organizations and their environments.

The advice given by the practitioners is sound, not only because it is born of experience, but because it is in application where strategic management ideas and concepts must finally be tested. Strategic management is, after all, an applied field of knowledge, resting on still other basic dis-

---

[1] IAPS is a coalition of some fifteen separate practitioner planning groups around the world. Dr. Knoepfel and Mr. Lancey have both headed IAPS, and Dr. Knoepfel was instrumental in founding both NASCP and IAPS. A third major practitioner group is the Planning Executives Institute (PEI).

ciplines. So when Aines asks for whom the discipline is intended, one is tempted to answer, "It is intended for thee," and with due apologies to John Donne, Strategic Management is not an island, but a part of the managerial mainland, even though it seems to be newly discovered and incompletely charted. It is a field needed by all organizations and includes that class of decisions concerned with new direction, viability, growth, and even the choice of purpose. In fact, it is this important class of decisions, and all the tools that must be brought to bear on making them, that tells for whom the discipline is intended. It concerns us all, practitioner and academic alike.

Practitioners' Views of Policy and Planning Research

(Coordinated by RAM CHARAN, *Boston University)*

The following commentary was presented by "practitioners" from four multinational corporations. The commentators were: Mr. R. O. Aines, International Harvester; Mr. Ben C. Ball, Jr., Gulf Oil Corporation; Dr. Rudolf W. Knoepfel, The Solvay American Corp; and Mr. Roderic C. Lancey, G. D. Searle & Co. All are involved in Corporate Planning in their respective firms, Dr. Knoepfel as President of his firm. Their remarks were offered at the end of the conference as a response of practitioners to the ideas presented over the three days of the conference.

RONALD O. AINES
INTERNATIONAL HARVESTER COMPANY

My greatest single impression of business planning and policy research as presented at the conference is the imprecision of the terminology used. In comparison with other social science professional associations and research conferences, both national and international, the ways in which the same words were used at different times with different meanings was astonishing. This is a great weakness in the discipline of planning. The language and perhaps some of the concepts are not rigorous. Although planning and policy are not a mature area of study, this is no excuse. It is essential that we tighten up the way in which we communicate. An overly simplistic suggestion is to use *Webster's* for definitions of common words and to use those words consistently. Other new words that are needed can be coined, defined and then used consistently.

A second point deserving attention is a better definition and understanding of the mission and the customers of the discipline. Is the mission to explain the process of planning or is it to respond to the real world's problems? Is it to develop value judgments? Is it to provide tools for actual decision-making, or is it to facilitate decisions?

And the second important question — who are the customers? Are they the staff business analysts? ... Line operating management? ... Researchers? ... Teachers? ... or, Government and non-profit organization administrators? If all of these are the customers, what is the relative importance of these different groups as customers and consumers of the products and services provided by the discipline?

A third point is a concern for whether the full range of real-world variables, plus their interactions, have been acknowledged, accounted for, and utilized in research projects. Even the so-called soft variables need to be considered. There is no question that this does make research more problematical. These variables, however, do have an influence on the reality of the conclusions and generalizations of research projects. Omitting some of these variables is akin to only looking at some parts of the elephant and not the entire beast. Synthesizing the greatest number of variables usually does give the greatest payoff, as in the case of the chief executive officer who deals with the greatest number of variables and is the man who receives the highest salary.

A fourth point concerns whether sufficient attention is given to the human element in the various facets of the discussions, research, and application of results. This involves particular areas such as the process of planning, and the formal organizational structure versus the informal working organization. Some of the generalizations reached by policy research projects could well prove to be different if the human beings in the equation were shifted. For example, does it matter whether the individuals involved develop a strong dictatorial style of management or a flexible participative style of management?

A fifth point concerns whether policy research adequately considers all the components of a complete strategic planning system. These would include considerations such as:

1. Helping the individual manager plan for his job responsibility.
2. Providing the minimum information needed for strategic decisions.
3. The use of planning as a human resource development tool.
4. Planning the allocation of organizational resources to fit with society's values.
5. The use of planning as a management system for operating the business.
6. The communications functions of planning, both internal and external to the company.

A sixth point concerns the usefulness of various levels of abstraction. At the conference abstraction varied widely between the research papers. Some abstract or basic research is needed for the development of basic theory. A balance, however, is needed with attention given to some of the more specific strategic problems facing business today. Normally, the higher the level of abstraction, the greater amount of interpretation that is required before the research can actually be transferred, applied, and used in a real-world business situation.

Three suggestions I would make for further research work in the future are:

1. Research needs to be more futuristic oriented. That is, looking to situations, strategies, and relationships that represent what is coming in the future — helping to resolve business opportunities and problems that will have to be faced tomorrow.
2. More use of a multiple discipline approach promises great potential benefits and contributions. This should include areas such as economics, political science, behavioral sciences and/or psychology. The interests and influences of the various forces at work in our society and economy, should be considered and included in proportion to their anticipated impor-

tance in the future — such as organized labor, governmental/regulatory entities, the consumer and his advocates, etc. The input from these growing forces in our society must be considered as input to our business strategy.
3. How does an effective basic planning phenomenon take place and how should it take place to be more effective? A more explicit description and understanding of the strategy formulation process would help greatly in competitive analysis and analyzing the strategy being used in an industry as well as for the company itself. It should be of value to governmental control and regulatory entities (antitrust) and business in getting a more efficient allocation and pricing of resources and products.

To use some of International Harvester's terminology, there are some key vulnerabilities in the search for regularities and generalizations in strategic and policy research such as:

1. *Getting accurate, reliable, real-world data.* From outside of any company or business, it is very difficult to secure an accurate indication of the situation and where the power really lies. Confidentiality is a problem.
2. *The basic assumption of rationality.* Many times business decisions are made or are impacted significantly by forces which objectively and according to competitive theory are not rational (taxes, controls, restrictions, etc.).
3. *The human element.* This is a difficult element to include in research but it is very essential to do so if the conclusions are to approximate the real-world situation and be useful.
4. *Variability.* There are many sources of variability that significantly influence the generalizations drawn from research results. Differences in the environment and national characteristics between countries, for example, and differences in the business characteristics and structure of industries all give rise to differences requiring that contingent statements be made.

Thus the source, methods of research, and credibility of research generalizations must be considered in any attempt to make real-world business applications.

BENJAMIN C. BALL, JR.
GULF OIL CORPORATION

In being asked to present this paper, I am automatically cast in the role of a "professional planning practitioner," and I'm not sure such a role even exists. In the first place, it assumes that "planning" is some sort of specialty in and of itself, like doctoring or engineering, so that when you need that kind of thing done, you go to a "practitioner" and he practices his specialty. What I mean by "planning" is not that at all, but rather that it is one kind of decision-making process, the purposes of which are better understood than the process itself. It is more analogous to "health" than to doctoring. Everyone is a practitioner, consciously or unconsciously, although some of us put conscious effort into researching issues and methods, and some of us into applying those methods. It is really into this latter category that I fall. What we have come to call a professional planner can perhaps more accurately be described as a purveyor of planning methods among the decision makers of a firm.

In the second place, it is not at all clear that there is such a thing as a "professional" planner — or, at least, that a professional is better than an amateur. There is painfully little data to support the claim that more professional planning leads to better decisions or to better results. I, of course, believe it does, but this is largely an act of faith — or the results of deductive logic, if you prefer — not established fact. I trust we all share this faith, or we would not be here today.

An additional concern I have in presenting this paper is the classic concern about the management of any kind of research. Can research be managed? If so, how? These are poorly understood issues, and when they are applied to the emerging area of planning, their complexity is only magnified.

These reservations about my task today lead me to the feeling that it would be presumptuous for me to list for you the planning research issues I think you ought to be working on. And, worse than that, you might find it uniquely unhelpful to hear one man's opinion, regardless of how wise or qualified he may be. Therefore, I propose to approach my assignment by discussing issues which arise out of planning as it is practiced in the firm vis-à-vis the needs of the firm.

In the firm, "planning" is poorly defined and even more poorly understood. At the working level, its distinction from forecasting is still fuzzy. We still hear managers saying, "Tell me better what the future is going to be like, and then — and only then — will I do better planning." The other side of the coin is that we planners keep saying, "the chief planner is the CEO," thus confusing planning with management, decision-making, and execution.

In the long-term, the final test of planning in firms is a pragmatic one: Does it work? Is it useful in practical ways to the CEO? Dealing with these tests is difficult because of two perceptions. First, how often is a firm faced with a really strategic (i.e., life or death, history-making) decision? In fact, how often can a firm afford to make such a decision? Second, we speak of planning as a new, emerging field, and yet significant breakthroughs seem few and far between. With management science gaining acceptance along with BCG learning curves, GE SBU's, and Dow-Corning matrix organizations, is planning really emerging, or has it matured so that research is no longer where the action is? In fact, as planning gains acceptance and becomes institutionalized, it may become even more difficult for good research results to have an impact. For example, even if inflation accounting were all that good, it would probably face a tough battle simply because of the high degree of institutionalization of cost-based accounting.

It seems that these issues in the firm raise two relevant issues for planning researchers. But, let me be sure I communicate what I mean by "planning researchers." A mathematical analogy may help.

Suppose, x = operations   *or*   the management of operations

then, $\dfrac{dx}{dt}$ = planning   *or*   the management of the direction of operations (content)

and, $\dfrac{d^2x}{dt^2}$ = planning of planning   *or*   the management of the direction of planning (process)

and, $\dfrac{d^3x}{dt^3}$ = research on planning   *or*   direction of research on planning (meta process)

Research on planning processes provides the grist and the content of the second derivative. And now we are talking about the *direction* of planning research, which would put it somewhere in the range of the third derivative. If we can learn about this third derivative, then I believe we will have learned a great deal about the lower derivatives. Therefore, I would say our primary concern should be in developing quality controls for our research, which relates directly to performance measures. The question, "How do we know good research when we see it?" relates directly to the question, "How do we know good strategy when we see it?," the latter question being, I believe, a really pressing problem in the firm.

The second issue suggested is the implementation of the results of good research, which I believe corresponds to the issue of the implementation of planning (as opposed to the implementation of plans or strategies), which is the subject of most planning seminars today. In the same sense that a firm can become inoculated with "a little planning," and become therefore immune to the real thing, planners also are susceptible to preoccupation with operation of a planning system, with decreasing interest in planning the direction of that system.

To say the same thing another way, it seems to me that, among all others, planning researchers need to do some strategic planning with respect to the direction of planning research. That would, for instance, be the antithesis of asking me to suggest to you some areas in which research might be useful.

RUDOLF W. KNOEPFEL
THE SOLVAY AMERICAN CORPORATION

Being one of the ones who has, as the saying goes, "to hack it" in the real world of business, and has to make a profit, I am very pleased to be with you, who come mostly from the academic world. I have a kind of sinking feeling which I have not had since I passed my doctorate examination, because I am not in the least prepared and yet I had hoped to be the most thought-provoking. I have, unfortunately, due to poor planning, which may not come as a surprise since I have been a corporate planner, only been able to attend part of your sessions. I have, however, read, with the greatest interest, most of your papers which were distributed before this conference. They have, I must admit, disturbed me to a large extent. Yesterday evening I had a speaking engagement in Ottawa and in the early morning I was doing my usual thing running a few miles along the beautiful Rideau Canal and was wondering what on earth I was going to tell you. I decided to speak to you as a practitioner of planning, who, by June 1st, will have had thirty years of business experience in a multi-national corporation, with over two billion dollar sales in many countries. I was one of a small group of people who introduced corporate planning in the Solvay Group. Thinking back, I have talked about corporate planning, I have written about it and I am supposed to be fairly knowledgeable about it. Now Ladies and Gentlemen, fasten your seatbelts; here come my rather candid reactions to what I have read in your papers and heard in your discussions. I have listened to you and what I am about to say is not against academia *per se* because I have many good friends in academic circles. I correspond with them, I understand them — however, I read your papers and I have a hard time understanding what you are really talking about. From the viewpoint of a planner and CEO, I thought that the conference was about Business Policy and Planning Research. You have touched on about everything but the kitchen sink: there is sociology, societal criticism, you tear the corporation apart and so on and so forth. I have learned a few things and I have heard a few pretty good jokes, but I haven't found much substance in what I have heard and which taught me something basic. But, let me tell you briefly from a practitioner's viewpoint how we approach the problem of planning.

In an old-fashioned way, we still look back and make a *historical analysis* of what the corporation did in the past. Then we make some kind of fancy trend analysis and extrapolations, which are not too meaningful many times. Then we go and make what I call a *prospective analysis*, making some wild guesses as to what the world is going to be all about and how to cope with it. We have learned that this is a *continuous* and *iterative* process. None of you mentioned it, unfortunately, although you may know it, but plans are, bluntly speaking, strictly for the birds; once you have a written plan you may as well throw it out, because most of the time it is going to be absolutely wrong. The great importance of planning lies in the fact that it is a *continuous learning and decision making* process. As such, it is invaluable in any corporation worth its salt.

Now, many of the things that I have read in your papers and heard in your discussions do not relate to the business world I live in. My message to you is why don't you come and look a little closer at what we businessmen are doing. You are conceptualizing a world as you conceive it to be, but this is not the world business lives in. Maybe I am utterly wrong, but this is what I feel today.

I read your papers; some of them I understood and enjoyed, some of them I don't know what you are talking about. At the risk of being rude: very fancy language and "scientific jargon" do not cover up poor thinking. Second, if you want to do research, please focus on things that are new and relevant. As an example, I have heard here today that planning is a political thing as if this were an absolutely new concept. Well, I have, a long time ago, published a paper, "The Politics of Planning." ... So, why are you reinventing the wheel? Why don't you focus on the things that are important and urgent *today*, which are of interest to us (business managers/planners) and we will come and really listen to you.

Finally, what I really would like to see, and I speak as the past President of the North American Society of Corporate Planners and also as the former President of the International Affiliation of Planning Societies, is more real world research. Why don't you give it a try and do your research with us? I cannot help it, and I know you are not going to like this, but I have the impression that too many among you sit in an ivory tower, you look at some data, you analyze our annual reports, you interview us occasionally, but by and large you do research that is not very relevant for us. Therefore, I think that research, and we *do need* good research in policy making, strategic decisions, etc., should be done jointly. I think that most of us in business and industry are willing to work with you because we don't have much time to analyze, conceptualize and structure what we do while more or less "flying by the seat of our pants," which may be a poor way of doing things. There is more cooperation necessary among you, who are our intellectual peers, and us, who as I said, have to "hack it" every day.

I can think of at least four areas where joint research is most important:

1. What are the implications for business firms, especially in the U.S., of changing trends in social mores and expectations around the world?

2. How can we cope with the Third and Fourth World?

3. What to do with the growing maze of often unrealistic government regulations which seriously hamper and often threaten the very survival of companies and even industries?

4. How can we (i.e., business firms) live in a society which implicitly and sometimes explicitly condemns the free enterprise system, where, for example, anti-trust policy is no longer based on economic but more on socio/political considerations?

Thank you.

RODERIC C. LANCEY
G. D. SEARLE & COMPANY

I probably represent the essence of Peter Lorange's description of the "mundane" practitioner. I say that *not* as an intentional self-imposed put-down. On the contrary, I thoroughly enjoy the pragmatic (messy) aspects which are inherently wrapped into the role of managing a formalized corporate planning process.

Before offering my suggestions for research in business policy and planning, I'd like to share my reactions to this workshop. First of all, I've found it to be a stimulating and most enjoyable learning experience. In many ways, it has provided a unique opportunity to test some thoughts which have crossed my mind during the past two or three years in the field of formalized corporate planning. If anything, your papers and dialogue have opened up my awareness of several interrelated learning curves which every planning practitioner should be pursuing.

To help locate where I'm coming from as a planning process practitioner, permit me to comment on what this work typically involves within a diverse corporation. To do this, I'll draw upon the descriptive material which Peter Lorange shared with us, the administrative dimensions of a formalized planning system within a complex multi-business, multi-divisionalized firm.

In our planning system at G. D. Searle, we have defined eight separate steps which link, in a reasonably orderly fashion, the sequence of events in our annual corporate planning calendar. Without burdening you with a lot of specifics, I'll just confine my comments to the notion that each step is discrete, in terms of task assignments and expected results. In ag-

gregate, these eight steps enable the entire organization — both line and staff — to coordinate planning assignments throughout the year. Incidentally, I did not hear much discussion around, nor concern about, corporate staff involvement in the planning process or strategy formulation. There is, I believe, a role for staff groups to perform, and I would suggest some reconnaissance in this area.

Our sequential eight-step process explicitly recognizes corporate and divisional levels. (At Searle — "divisional" is the label we apply to top-level units, now know as Product Line Groups. We have four such Groups at this point in time, each operating within a global context.)

We're also reaching down one more tier to capture data and strategic plans around product/market segments (or SBU's, or if you prefer, Strategy Centers per Arthur D. Little, Inc.). It takes rather careful definitions to identify each segment, and we have at least 20 key ones. Additional fine-tuning may readily surface another ten or fifteen segments across the corporation. (Our sales, incidentally, are now in excess of $800 million world-wide, with approximately 65% in the U.S.)

We have rigorously adopted the top-down/bottom-up flow of dialogue which is described by Vancil and Lorange in their January/February, 1975, article in the *Harvard Business Review*, "Strategic Planning in Diversified Companies." Indeed, we distribute widely within the corporation an annual planning calendar diagram which features the hierarchical flow of information and decisions which are expected to occur as a consequence of implementing and practicing the eight-step sequence.

The annual cycle is launched with an environmental scan/issue identification step; it ends with top management's approval of next year's highly detailed Profit Plan. In between are six stages which address strategy formulation, management reviews, and action programming. It's the intent of the process to zero-in on taking decisions *now* to realize corporate objectives.

Our calendar diagram is closely related to the cycle described in Hekhuis' earlier discussion paper. In fact, we replicate precisely the timing of each event in his Exhibit 5.2. Incidentally, may I reinforce his comments around using the cycle architecture to capture, in advance, top-level managers' time and attention at key points during the year. That's a critical design parameter!

We track action plans during the year to determine if things are proceeding as committed in the Profit Plan. Feedback, on a continuing basis, is an important vehicle for sustaining meaningful participation and enthusiasm in our formalized planning effort.

I should also add that strategy formulation is explicitly addressed within Searle at both the corporate and Product Line Groups levels. It's the intent of the process to stimulate congruency of strategy formulation efforts throughout the firm. In slightly different terms, we view formalized planning primarily as a managerial communications system *and* process — and not as a separate functional exercise.

Here are my proposals for research:

First, I concur with those who urge in-depth field research. It's the only way I can perceive where one can learn about organizational culture, management style, and power brokerage. I submit every firm has a unique constellation of these factors; they revolve about the CEO's value system, and further that the manner of designing, installing, operating and renewing a planning process *will* reflect these values. The planning process must deal with the idiosyncratic features of the CEO's style of management.

And that brings up my next suggestion. I've been intrigued with the rather frequent mentions during this conference around organizational behavior. I personally believe that business leaders urgently need better descriptions of executive behavior, especially toward the pinnacle of an organization. Further, we need clarifying descriptions of managerial interaction throughout an annual planning cycle — not just during strategy formulation, but also during reviews of operational strategic responses to top-level targeting (i.e., goal setting) and during reviews of the specific content of next year's Profit Plans (where commitments and incentive compensation "packages" are detailed).

Bear in mind Hekhuis' comments concerning the limitations on GE's management of coping with 40 SBU's during their review sessions. So,

who really sets the ingredients of corporate strategy? I feel Bower's exposition on capital investment decision-making can be broadened to encompass most forms of strategy formulation within diversified firms. In particular, the role played by divisional (or SBU) managers *and* their functional subordinates needs further study.

There's also some evidence that a generation of managers is emerging who really "buy in" on *rigorous* formalized planning methodologies; indeed, they live it as a way of managing their businesses — they're "planner-doers." If this notion is reasonably descriptive, then let's borrow the concept of Good Manufacturing Practices (GMP's) from the pharmaceutical industry, and pose this question: What do we know about the impact of MBA educational experience during the past two decades on this new dynamic? What does the emergence of large numbers of MBA-trained executives mean for organizational behavioral norms in the future? Will staff planning professionals, per se, tend to disappear from organization charts? Some of us would like to know!

And then, we have heard discussion around various adjectives which leaves some of us in a "semantic swamp." Take, for example, a "robust" strategy. Does this suggest that only the highly unique and "stroke-of-genius" kinds of proposals should be examined? I hope not; most corporate strategy formulation tends to revolve around incremental situations associated with *today's* businesses. The complexities of making portfolio trade-off decisions among them represent, I feel, a rich lode for academic research.

Finally, may I suggest that you get to know the international corporate planner community through the various planning societies. There are a bundle of them here in the U.S. — in fact, too many! They draw together around 5,000 private-sector corporate planner/profit planner types. Perhaps we can aid your research efforts by providing access to formalized processes and experiences gained within our employer corporations. Beyond the U.S. and Canada are another 2,000 planners who belong to societies in the U.K., France, Belgium, Italy, Japan, and New Zealand. I think you'll agree — we need to talk to each other!

10

RESEARCH NEEDS AND ISSUES IN STRATEGIC MANAGEMENT

Dan Schendel
Purdue University

Charles W. Hofer
Columbia University

Careful review of the previous nine sections and our Introduction to this volume suggests many areas in which research needs and opportunities exist to modify, broaden, and test the strategic management paradigm. In this section, we will summarize, elaborate upon, and add to the research needs and opportunities that have already been identified and developed in the various papers. Many of these ideas are based on a modified, two-round Delphi study we undertook. The panel for the study was composed of the paper authors, discussants, and panel moderators, some fifty-six scholars in all, who attended the conference. The panel members were asked to provide their thoughts as they had developed during the summer immediately following the May 1977 conference. Hence, the observations that follow are based on: (1) the strategic management paradigm; (2) the papers and commentary in this volume; (3) the conference discussions, (4) the results of the Delphi study; and (5) our own experiences and biases.

In developing this section, we decided to follow the sequence of topics contained in the text, with the exception that we have added back topics such as Board of Directors and Social Responsibility that we were unable to include in the conference because of time constraints. In each area, our interest is not in casting up specific hypotheses, nor suggesting particular research methods and approaches that could be used in the given topic area, but rather, it is in pointing the way toward additional work that appears needed and would make useful contributions to the field. These views are offered both as a summary of the book and as a guide to those who want a better perspective on research in the field, or who are in search of ideas and issues that they might research themselves.

Research issues, needs and opportunities are offered in the following areas:

1. Strategy Concept
2. Strategic Management Process
3. Boards of Directors: The External-Internal Interface
4. General Management Roles in Strategic Management
5. Goal Formulation and Goal Structures
6. Social Responsibility
7. Strategy Formulation
8. Environmental Analysis
9. Strategy Evaluation
10. Strategy Content
11. Formal Planning Systems
12. Strategy Implementation
13. Strategic Control
14. Entrepreneurship and New Ventures
15. Multibusiness/Multicultural Firms
16. Strategic Management in Not-for-Profit Organizations
17. Public Policy and Strategic Management
18. Research Methods in Strategic Management

Clearly, there is room for overlap among these topics, as a review of the text will show. Our comments under each topic should not, therefore, be regarded as solely applicable to that area alone, even though such overlaps will not always be addressed explicitly. Nor can we elaborate each issue, idea, or comment so that the reader will be able to translate it directly into a research proposal. Our intention is to suggest and provoke further thought and ideas for others.

Under each topic, we will begin by briefly discussing what we include in that topic. While not everyone will agree with our classification system, we will at least make clearer what we believe the major content of each topic to be. Finally, the reader should note that these brief statements are not exhaustive descriptions of each topic area.

STRATEGY CONCEPT

Strategy is the key concept underlying the new direction of the strategic management field. The purpose of strategy is to provide directional cues to the organization that permit it to achieve its objectives, while responding to the opportunities and threats in its environment. Our strategy definition thus excludes goals, the processes by which goals are formulated, and the processes by which strategy itself is formulated.

Some issues relevant to the strategy construct are:

1. A definition of the strategy construct acceptable and usable by all is needed. In particular, a definition is needed that will lend itself to measurement, comparison among firms, and which can be related to goals and ob-

jectives, as well as to performance results. Above all, careless, imprecise use of this term should be avoided.

2. A distinction has been made in this text and elsewhere between corporate, business, and functional area strategies. All three levels seem to have the same overall purpose and components. However, the relationship between levels needs to be better understood.

3. Functional area strategies bear much more investigation and use than they normally receive in research or teaching. Such strategies should be regarded as necessary linkages between business strategy and the guidance that operating management requires for its day-to-day work.

4. The concept of strategy needs to be further tested empirically to provide more evidence that strategies differ among firms and that better strategies make a difference in performance results. Some support exists for this position, but more is needed.

5. The frequency with which an organization can significantly change its strategy is something we know little about. Can an organization afford frequent, and substantial changes in strategy? What happens to structure, processes, and behavior when strategy changes significantly?

STRATEGIC MANAGEMENT PROCESS

Our view of the strategic management process was developed in the Introduction to the book, and was depicted in Exhibit 2. That process includes more tasks than the traditional dual concerns of strategy formulation and implementation. As such, the process represents a new organizing paradigm for the field, and, we believe, breaks the field into component parts in such a way that research can proceed in each part without having to encompass the field's complexity, and yet in a way that permits the research to be effectively integrated back into the total strategic management process.

Issues that deserve further attention include:

1. The process proposed here bears critical examination and possible further development as to the tasks it includes and that appear separable, operational, and researchable.

2. The strategic management paradigm should be tested by using it as a taxonomy for research on a cross section of firms of all types (new ventures, medium-sized businesses, multi-industry firms, multinational firms, etc.) to identify how each organizes and performs the different tasks of the overall process.

3. The process should be examined and tested in terms of its value to not-for-profit organizations (churches, hospitals, government agencies, schools, etc.). Tests should also be made to see if the nature of the process is independent of organization type. Such tests might also be done on organizations in different cultures to learn how different societal values affect the process.

BOARDS OF DIRECTORS:
THE EXTERNAL-INTERNAL INTERFACE

In Section 2 some interesting hypotheses about the role of external environmental influences on internal organizational actions were developed. The board has been the traditional mechanism in businesses, and these days in third-sector, quasi-public/private organizations as well, for providing an intersection of external and internal influences. Some interesting research issues and opportunities in this area include:

1. A better understanding of the processes by which external environmental influences affect internal organizational decisions, including strategic decisions, is needed. For example, Mintzberg hypothesizes that: "Influencers have power in the external coalition to the extent that they are *concentrated* and to the extent that the organization is *dependent upon them.*" Is this true? He also speculates on the mechanisms by which the external coalition affects internal choice. Is he correct? If so, which of the mechanisms is most important?

2. In large, well-established, publicly held corporations, are boards captives of management until some crisis emerges that requires them to challenge managerial leadership? If so, is this bad? If true, what could be done to establish the board's independence when crises are not present?

3. Can board practices and roles as developed in businesses be used as models for the design of external governance mechanisms for not-for-profit organizations, and for third-sector organizations?

4. If boards are not considered suitably responsive to their environment and that of the firm, can this be corrected through changes in board structure and how it operates? If not, what other mechanisms for change exist?

5. What is the board's role in goal formulation? In strategy formulation? In the other tasks in the strategic management process?

GENERAL MANAGEMENT ROLES IN THE
STRATEGIC MANAGEMENT PROCESS

General managers have responsibilities in both strategic and operating management. A number of interesting issues and questions can be developed regarding the roles and behavior of general managers in the strategic management process, including:

1. How do (should) general managers allocate their efforts between strategic and operations management duties? What represents a full load of activity? How can performance measures be devised that adequately recognize responsibilities of general managers in each of these areas, and adequately balance short-term operating results and longer-term strategic results? What reward mechanisms are needed to balance long- and short-term considerations?

2. What is the impact of managerial style on strategic decisions?

3. Better descriptions of executive work and behavior at the uppermost levels of organizations are needed. There has been interesting work done here, but the sample size has been quite small and has not included *Fortune* 500 type firms. Much more needs to be done.

4. How do top executives form perceptions of their environments?

5. What will be the impact of increasing professionalism on the part of upper-level executives with respect to formal planning systems? Will such better trained managers take on more of the planning functions themselves, thereby reducing the need for staff help?

GOAL FORMULATION AND GOAL STRUCTURES

Organizations form and are maintained in order to achieve purpose. Such purposes or missions presumably give rise to goals, and these in turn to a hierarchy of objectives. It has been well established that personal goals can conflict within an organization, requiring some conflict resolution process for their settlement. There are a variety of goal formulation processes that can be proposed, some based on power and bargaining, some on competition and economic survival, and still others on a combination of these approaches. But whether the process is a rational/deductive one or a social/political one, goal structures do arise and are used to manage the affairs of organizations.

Some research issues and needs in this area include:

1. Most behavioral research that has been done on the usage of goals in organizations has been done at relatively low organizational levels. Research is needed at middle and upper levels of organizations to better understand the role of goals in top management behavior.

2. The influence of goal structures on the strategy formulation process needs further study at all levels of the organization, especially to identify whether and how goals and objectives are modified during the search for feasible strategies. In other words, what interrelationships exist between strategy formulation and goal formulation processes?

3. In business firms, growth versus profitability are advanced as two competing objectives. What is the trade-off between them and how is it made? Over what time horizon? What other common trade-offs are made? How do such trade-offs relate to life-cycle considerations?

4. The goal formulation models resting on power as developed in Section 2 should be considered as the basis for further study of goal formulation processes and goal content, especially because they are applicable at the highest organizational levels.

5. The role of goal structure in strategy evaluation and strategic control needs to be further developed. How are goals and objectives used to develop standards or criteria useful in evaluation and control?

6. How are goals and objectives factored within an organization to provide a hierarchy of consistent and usable targets for directing and evaluating organizational and managerial effort? Is this a process that begins at the top, bottom, or proceeds through the organization hierarchy in some other way? Is the concept of an interrelated, hierarchy of goals and objectives useful, and can one be developed in an organization? Do they occur naturally?

SOCIAL RESPONSIBILITY

Socially responsible firms are said to participate in many cost-incurring activities that are not required by competitive, legal, or regulatory requirements. Some issues in the social responsibility area that are relevant include:

1. Does being socially responsible mean the incurrence of costs not required by law and competitive factors? Does social responsibility have a role in management practice? Does it have a basis in economic theory? In formulating strategy should firms incur costs that go beyond a direct association with the basic goods and services they are providing?

2. How do (should) social concerns influence goals and strategy formation?

3. What are the trends in terms of the business/society/government interface? What mechanisms are needed to forecast, analyze, and otherwise prepare strategic managers for changes in this area?

4. Can (should) firms affect public sector decision-making? If so, how?

5. What will be the specific impact of "industrial democracy" on the firm? Should U.S. firms take a more active position on such trends?

6. What will be the impact of the increasing growth of government-owned business operations on privately owned firms? This is of particular relevance in international competition, where many barriers to competition exist in many foreign markets.

STRATEGY FORMULATION

Strategy formulation involves: (1) the identification of strategic issues and problems which suggest that strategy needs to be reformulated; (2) the creative process of generating alternative strategies; and (3) the identification and evaluation of the consequences of each alternative were it to be chosen. It is the creative aspect of problem-solving — defining the problem, and proposing and evaluating the consequences of solutions — that is at the heart of strategy formulation.

The issues that bear further investigation in this area include:

1. What events do (should) trigger the strategy formulation process? In

a reactive system this may be a more meaningful question than in an adaptive, cyclically repeating strategy formulation process.

2. Who decides and how do they decide that strategy needs to be changed? How do they determine the direction and nature of the changes needed? What processes and information are used to make such decisions?

3. An exhaustive description of strategy formulation processes has yet to be devised. Better descriptive work is necessary to try to create a taxonomy of such processes. In particular, the process types need to be studied and classified in terms of contingent variables such as organization size, rate of environmental change, competitive situation, effectiveness, etc. It may be possible to develop an evolutionary model of the strategy formulation process (and the strategic management process) in terms of one or more of these contingent variables.

4. How do entrepreneurs form the initial idea or strategy for forming a business? Is it related to the personal characteristics of entrepreneurs, or to other situational factors, or both?

5. If there exists a hierarchy of strategy, which seems to be the case, does (should) there exist alternative strategy formulation processes suited to each strategy and organizational level? If so, how do (should) these processes interrelate?

6. Who should be involved in strategy formulation? What kind of organizational relationships should exist and what types of organizational assignments need to be made to accomplish the strategy formulation task? How does this vary by organization type?

7. What is the role of analytical models in strategy formulation? What needs exist for better or different analytical models at the various levels at which strategy formulation must take place?

8. How do structural factors influence strategy formulation, that is, does strategy sometimes follow structure? What are the mechanisms by which this occurs?

ENVIRONMENTAL ANALYSIS

An organization's environment is composed of those noncontrollable variables that influence its strategy at each of the three strategy levels. Relevant environmental variables can be classified as technological; economic, including suppliers and competitive factors; social/cultural, including demographic factors; and political/legal in the broadest sense of those terms. Because these variables are noncontrollable, they must be forecast and assumptions made about them, and the organization's strategy adapted to them. Issues worth further investigation in this area are:

1. Perhaps the greatest need in this topic area is for better models of competitive market structures and the influence of such market structures

on strategy. Much better understanding of the influence of competition on strategies is also needed.

2. The effects of different rates of environmental change on strategy formulation should be further studied, because higher rates of change introduce greater uncertainty. For instance, does uncertainty cause substantial changes in the manner in which strategy is formulated? In the content of strategy?

3. What needs exist for better environmental forecasting methods, especially with respect to noneconomic environmental factors such as social/cultural and political/legal trends? Methodologies capable of analyzing and forecasting the interrelationships of large numbers of increasingly interdependent environmental variables are also required.

STRATEGY EVALUATION

Strategy evaluation deals with both the decision to reevaluate *existing* strategy to determine whether it should be changed, and with the evaluation of *proposed* strategies to help decide which should be chosen for implementation. The separation of this area from strategy formulation gives rise to a series of questions, including these:

1. What models can be used to evaluate strategy content? Of what value are firm (vs. industry) specific models of strategy developed from existing experience and data using mathematical statistics? (Are such mathematical models useful in other tasks in the strategic management process, e.g., strategy formulation?)

2. What is the relationship of strategy evaluation to the subsequent task of strategic control? These two processes are different, especially in their respective purposes, yet they both rely on goals and objectives for criteria development. What are the similarities and differences in the two tasks?

STRATEGY CONTENT AND PERFORMANCE RESULTS

Both theoretical arguments and recent empirical studies seem to indicate that good strategies produce superior results. Because of this, much attention has been given to developing various contingency theories of strategy content.

For a given set of environmental circumstances, such theories specify the types of strategies the firm should follow either: (1) to survive, or (2) to become a leader in the market. Most of the contingency theories developed from the business policy case tradition are of the former type. The findings of the PIMS program are the primary examples of the latter type. Few of these propositions about good strategy content have been tested empirically with data different from that used to develop them. Such evaluation is usually based on an assessment of the performance results, usually measured by profitability criteria, that the strategy produces. Research issues in the area of strategy content include these:

1. Strategy content studies depend upon developing an empirically measurable definition of strategy, which appears will have to be done in terms of components and variables within each component. Are there other ways of defining strategy? Which ways seem most useful for the enhancement of strategic management research?

2. How can the relative influence of strategic versus operating factors be separated in determining successful performance results? In other words, how can performance be attributed to doing the right things (effectiveness) versus doing things right (efficiency)?

3. How can success be measured in terms of performance results? If organizational objectives are to be used, how can multiple objectives be measured in composite and used? How can multiple criterion functions be established?

4. How valid are comparative, cross-sectional studies of strategy content, given that strategies are designed to create statistically nonhomogeneous groups of firms? Is there any purpose served by combining firms across industries into samples for study? What are the benefits and limitations of this approach?

5. Different strategies are required for different environmental circumstances. What do we know about, for example, capital management under inflationary conditions, high growth rate economies, public intervention? About other sets of conditions?

6. What can be learned about strategy content by studying samples of firms with unique performance results, for example, either no- or slow-growth rates, or exceptionally high growth rates?

7. There is a host of contingency strategies being offered as general solutions to strategic problems. For example, experience curve advocates argue that increasing experience leads to constantly decreasing constant dollar per unit costs. Competitive pressure requires that prices be constantly lowered if market share is to be maintained. Is it necessary to maintain market share leadership to be profitable and viable?

8. Are effective strategies transferable across cultures? If so, are there any limits to such transfers? If not, what causes the differences?

FORMAL PLANNING SYSTEMS

Formal planning systems include strategic planning systems. The latter are the manifestation of the strategic management process in most business firms. Traditionally, the purpose of strategic planning systems has been to provide the organizational context necessary for the formulation of strategy. In order to be effective, such systems require the support of top management. When such support is withdrawn, these systems are usually either disbanded or combined into the existing operations planning systems (including budgeting and control systems). In the latter cases, or where strategic planning systems have never been developed, the formal planning system is used more in implementation than formulation of strategy. Its function in such cases is to factor overall corporate goals and objectives into their subunit counterparts and to help develop operating plans for the achievement of these objectives. In the best strategic planning practice today, formulating, evaluating, implementing, and controlling strategy are all tasks performed by the formal planning system.

In this area, these issues bear further investigation:

1. It appears increasingly likely that a contingency approach needs to be taken to formal planning system design. What are the variables upon which such designs should be contingent? What is the nature of the contingency relationships themselves?

2. What roles should staff and line managers play in the formal planning system? What inputs should each have in the strategic management process?

3. How can the effectiveness of different formal planning system designs be evaluated in practice?

STRATEGY IMPLEMENTATION

Strategy implementation is better understood than most of the other tasks in the strategic management process. Implementation is an administrative task that uses the tools of structure, process, and behavior to achieve its ends. Its scope goes well beyond reporting relationships, delegation of authority, and information flow, to include such organizational systems and processes as resource allocations, measurement and evaluation, rewards and sanctions, management control, and personnel selection and development, and such behavioral considerations as leadership style, the acquisition and use of power, and interpersonal behavior. Some of the interesting questions and issues worth further attention include:

1. The strategy-structure-performance linkage deserves additional study. A series of studies has now been done, most of which corroborate the hypothesis in the opinion of the researchers involved. However, as Miner notes, their contentions are not always backed by the statistical data they have gathered. Is Miner correct when he argues that a structure/people fit is more important?

2. The stages of growth model needs to be broadened at both ends of the spectrum of organizational evolution. The start-up stage for small business could be a useful "stage" of development to study, even though it may be a transitory one. At the other end of the spectrum there may be

further organizational stages beyond the multidivisional business stage. What will be the nature of the next stages?

3. What structural, process, and behavioral problems occur under conditions of high growth rate strategies? Under no- and slow-growth rate strategies? What problems are created for using and changing strategy under such extreme conditions?

4. What influence do different organization structures have on resource allocation decisions made, not by capital markets, but by internal management decisions? (Theory would suggest that these allocations are not efficient in the sense of the efficient capital market hypothesis, although Williamson argues otherwise. Yet many such decisions have been removed from the capital market. What is at work in this seeming paradox?)

5. Better and more complete definitions of structure are required. Better means multivariate definitions, which can be measured and operationalized for use with statistical analysis techniques.

6. The role of measurement, evaluation, and reward systems as mediating variables capable of reconciling personal/organizational goals and short- versus long-range goals needs to be better understood, at all levels of complex organizations. In particular, the methods used to measure and compensate profit center and SBU general managers in multi-industry firms require attention.

7. The linkage between strategic and operating plans, and between strategic and operations management, needs further examination as to how it can be made. How can the implementation task be accomplished to most effectively link strategic and operating tasks?

8. How does the relative importance of structure, process, and behavior as tools for influencing task behavior change according to the stage of evolution of the organization?

STRATEGIC CONTROL

The essence of strategic control is to insure that the strategy selected is in fact being used, and if used, that it is producing the performance results that it was intended to achieve. Strategic control differs from financial controls and the budgetary controls used in operating management in terms of the scope and time horizon of its concerns. It is less interested in efficiency in an input/output sense than it is in assuring the proper direction and rate of progress of the organization toward its strategic goals and objectives.

These issues concerning strategic control seem worthy of attention:

1. The relationship of strategic control to strategy evaluation, the organization's goal structure, and to operational controls such as budgeting, needs to be further developed. The mechanisms for integrating the strategic control function into the organization's formal planning system also need to be studied.

2. What types of indices should be used to assess whether the strategy

selected is the strategy in use? What types of indices should be used to assess whether the strategy in use is producing the desired results? What tolerance limits should be established for each type of index? What time lags are reasonable? Will these factors vary with the degree of environmental uncertainty? With other factors?

ENTREPRENEURSHIP AND NEW VENTURES

All new firms, and perhaps all new organizations, owe their birth to the activities of entrepreneurs who undertake the risks and supply the ideas and strategy necessary to start them. New ventures are numerous. Relatively few survive, however, and even fewer grow into large organizations. Nevertheless, the birth process is necessary; and survival, regardless of size, requires a renewal of the key ideas on which the organization is built. In this overlooked field, these issues seem important:

1. What changes are demanded of the firm's entrepreneur/manager(s) as it grows in size and complexity, i.e., as it evolves through "stages of growth?" Can these changes be made by its founders, or must new generations of managers take over to move the firm to new stages of evolution?

2. How do entrepreneurs learn of noninstitutional sources of venture capital? What communications links exist in this area and how can these be expanded to geographic areas where the rates of new venture formation are low? What is role of capital versus new ideas and new strategies in enterprise formation? Which is more important?

3. What is the role of incubator organizations in starting new firms, especially new firms that are not in high technology industries? What are the sources of entrepreneurs?

4. Rates of new venture formation and the nature of entrepreneurship may differ by geographic region. Why are some geographic areas more prolific in spawning new ventures and entrepreneurs? If any causal factors are discovered (how can they be discovered?), can they be translated from one productive area to another? How?

5. How does entrepreneurship arise in large organizations and how can large firms retain the new ventures that they spawn? How can it be encouraged in such organizations? What are the strategic problems in managing new ventures within large organizations?

MULTIBUSINESS/MULTICULTURAL FIRMS

Large-scale, diversified firms are an organization form that has come into prominence during the last thirty years. The continuing growth of such organizations and their importance to the economy give rise to some very interesting questions that have not been satisfactorily investigated or answered, including these:

1. Why have diversified firms arisen generally? There are rational reasons to explain vertical and horizontal diversification, but the reasons for conglomerate diversification are less clear. Is the development of the latter due to synergies in capital formation, synergies in managerial skills, or is the need for power among top-level managers a better explanation? Why cannot financial institutions supply capital needs to individual businesses as cheaply as corporate-level agglomerations of businesses and managers can?

2. How are corporate-level strategies formed, and do such strategies integrate and provide guidance to business-level strategy? What is the content of corporate-level strategy, and in particular, are some corporate strategies better than others? Much more study on strategy content at the corporate level is needed.

3. What are the implications for structural design in transferring capital out of one stagnant or shrinking business and into a growing business? What behavior problems do such actions produce for the members of the harvested business? What are the public policy issues in allowing such capital reallocation? What public policies have encouraged such transfers?

4. What managerial problems are created by having businesses in the same corporation with different types of organization structures? How do such mixed-mode structures arise, and can they be managed as well as businesses with similar structures?

5. What are the problems in strategic control across organization level — as between corporate, business, and functional area strategies within the multibusiness firm?

6. What are the problems in multicultural environmental analysis? How can diverse inputs be made into a total environmental analysis useful in formulating corporate strategy?

7. What are the special problems in transferring manufacturing, marketing, and other technologies across geographic territories and different cultures?

8. Apparently there are differences in performance results, strategies, and other matters associated with internal diversification versus diversification through acquisition. What can be learned from replicating the early studies indicative of these differences? Is there a difference in profitability results between internal diversifiers and acquisitive diversifiers?

9. Are there corollaries to multibusiness, multicultural organizations in nonbusiness organizations? If so, what can be learned from comparative studies of such business and nonbusiness organization forms?

STRATEGIC MANAGEMENT IN THE NOT-FOR-PROFIT ORGANIZATION

Over the past decade or so, the highest growth rates in organization formation and development have been in not-for-profit organizations, particularly in U.S. federal agencies and other government organizations.

These organizations seem to have a short-term outlook, owed perhaps to their political nature, itself dependent upon the relatively short time period between elections. Overall, the United States has more than half of its work force engaged in service organizations, and while many of these are business firms, many more are not. A major consideration in the management of not-for-profit organizations is the primarily noneconomic character of their purposes and missions, and the impact this has on their goal and strategy formulation and implementation processes. While all of the ideas developed in this volume have some application in nonbusiness organizations, these issues seem particularly interesting:

1. Comparative studies of the strategic management process within for-profit and not-for-profit organizations would be most useful at this stage of development of the strategic management paradigm. Such research studies could proceed by breaking the process into the tasks outlined in this volume. Of particular importance to such comparative studies would be a focus on the differences in the basis of revenue generation and the influence of these differences on the strategy formulation process and the choice of strategic directions. Similar attention placed on the differences in implementation and control processes would also be of interest.

2. Businesses are concerned primarily with economic survival (and growth), while not-for-profit organizations seem to be concerned primarily with political survival (and growth). What are the implications of this fact for goal formulation and subsequent strategy development?

3. The planning horizons of nonprofit organizations seem abnormally short. Why? How can (should) they be lengthened?

4. Does the political nature of many not-for-profit organizations mean that rational, analytical processes cannot be employed in managing them? To what degree will the philosophy and techniques of the strategic management process transfer from for-profit to not-for-profit organizations?

5. Are there corollaries to the multi-business, multi-cultural organizational form among non-business organizations? If so, what can be learned from comparative studies of such business and non-business organizational forms?

PUBLIC POLICY AND STRATEGIC MANAGEMENT

Public policy issues abound in all of management, but they are of particular significance to the strategic management process because of its centrality and importance to the very essence of the organization. Some of the more interesting and important public policy issues that impact on strategic management are:

1. Regulatory policy rests on a model of market structure and competition that tends to run counter to the basic premise of strategy (i.e., that competitive advantage makes a difference and is the sine qua non of a good

strategy) and to the findings of recent strategic management research. The motivation for regulation rests on: (1) conventional economic theory, which assumes, among other things, perfectly competitive markets, no price differences among firms, and that the long-run average cost curve must rise within a relevant range; and (2) empirical studies of market structure done by economists in the field of industrial organization, most of which have used cross-sectional research designs and sector- or industry-level (rather than product/market segment level) data to relate firm profitability with factors such as industry concentration, advertising expenditures, and so on. Both these theoretical assumptions and empirical results are challenged by recent strategic management research, which shows that strategic groups of firms do exist within industries and that the inferences that one might draw from aggregated industry data are often quite different and sometimes even the direct opposite of those reached by studying the strategic group. Clearly, there needs to be a reconciliation made between empirical reality and economic theory, with appropriate changes in public policy. How can strategic management researchers help make this happen?

2. Do the disclosure rules that public companies must observe make public companies strategically weaker than their private counterparts, who do not have to publicly report their results? For example, because of these disclosure rules and the pressure of the stock market, there may be a short-term bias in public companies that favor greater, rather than lesser, current earnings. Does the efficient capital market hypothesis really take into account strategic issues and the necessity for trade-off of short-term earnings for long-term growth? Theoretically, it does, but as a practical matter does the market really have the necessary insight and technical information to do so? If not, what does this imply for the strategic management of our major publicly owned companies?

3. It has been traditional in the United States for corporate managers to remain aloof from political processes that affect them. Can they remain aloof under changing conditions that continue to make considerable inroads into their prerogatives? If not, what are the most effective mechanisms, from the viewpoint of both society and the firm, for corporate managers to become involved in such political processes?

RESEARCH METHODS IN STRATEGIC MANAGEMENT

Every field has unique requirements for the research methods it must use to study the problems peculiar to it. Strategic management is an exceptionally complex field because it requires so many different facets of the organization to be considered simultaneously and wholistically to have meaning. Needed are additional research methods that can cope with such complexity, and because the field is so young, it further requires research on the very methods it needs to use. Some important issues in this area include:

1. An understanding of the philosophy of science and the power of scientific method must be developed and appreciated by researchers in the field. There is a need for empiricism that goes beyond mere subjective description and interpretation. The field needs to accept and develop more rigorous research methodologies to continue its advancement. In particular, training of young researchers must be given careful attention.

2. Many variables of interest in the field are nominally and ordinally scaled. Much more work needs to be placed in using (and developing) methods capable of handling such measures more rigorously.

3. There is a need to create methodologies for testing the validity of what Rumelt calls "frame models" that go beyond the conventional wisdom offered by microeconomic theory and micro-organization theory. Trade-offs between tractability and mindless rigor and dogma will be necessary in this respect.

4. The field needs to go beyond profit measures as criteria for evaluating overall organizational performance. Such measures will also need to be adjusted for risk and must recognize differences in accounting policy. Multiple criterion measures capable of reflecting complex goal structures are needed. Research methods capable of handling multiple goals and objectives are also needed.

5. While useful starts have been made in developing quantitative strategic models, more attention is needed to insure that such models are based on strategically homogeneous sets of data, and that they recognize the emerging concept of a strategic group of firms. Especially required in such modeling efforts is much more attention to interactive affects of the various classes of variables contained in the model. Moreover, these classes of variables need to be expanded to simultaneously include strategic, operating, internal structure, and market structure variables.

6. Attempts need to be made to test the efficacy of the strategy and strategic management constructs wholistically. Tests are required that do not depend on organization type.

IN CLOSING

The topics above, and the research needs and issues developed under each one, considered collectively tell us a great deal about the state-of-the-art in the field of strategic management. One of the major purposes of the conference and this book was to define the field, to develop the state-of-the-art in it, and to suggest where the future research needs and opportunities lie. Our purpose has been well served. Now to the reader must go this challenge: Go out and make this material obsolete so some future set of authors and editors can do all of this again and help further establish the field of strategic management as a significant area of inquiry in managerial practice for all types of organizations.

Appendix 1 — Attendees

BUSINESS POLICY AND PLANNING RESEARCH:
THE STATE-OF-THE-ART

May 25–27, 1977

Pittsburgh, Pennsylvania

Ronald O. Aines
    International Harvester Company
Peter Alley
    York University
Benjamin C. Ball, Jr.
    Gulf Oil Corporation
Henry H. Beam
    Western Michigan University
Norman A. Berg
    Harvard University
Joseph L. Bower
    Harvard University
Edward H. Bowman
    Ohio State University
Louis K. Bragaw, Jr.
    U.S. Coast Guard Academy
Richard G. Brandenburg
    The Carborundum Company
Dorothy E. Brawley
    Georgia State University
Elmer Burack
    Illinois Institute of Technology
Derek Channon
    University of Manchester
Ram Charan
    Boston University
John Child
    Kent State University
H. Kurt Christensen
    Strategic Planning Institute
Patrick Conley
    Boston Consulting Group
Arnold C. Cooper
    Purdue University
Merrit J. Davoust
    A. T. Kearney, Inc.
William Dill
    New York University

Samuel I. Doctors
    University of Pittsburgh
John Doutt
    Kent State University
Yves L. Doz
    Harvard University
Robert Duncan
    Northwestern University
George Farris
    York University
Carl Fink
    ATCOR, Inc.
Jay Galbraith
    The Wharton School
John H. Grant
    University of Pittsburgh
Edmund R. Gray
    Louisiana State University
Patricia Haggerty
    Koppers Company, Inc.
Richard G. Hamermesh
    Harvard University
Kenneth J. Hatten
    Harvard University
Kichiro Hayaski
    McMaster University
W. Harvey Hegarty
    Indiana University
Dale Hekhuis
    General Electric Company
Harold Henry
    University of Tennessee
Charles W. Hofer
    Stanford University
George Jacobs
    Western Carolina University
Earl G. Johnson
    Loyola University

William R. King
  University of Pittsburgh
Raymond M. Kinnunen
  Northeastern University
Bruce A. Kirchhoff
  University of Nebraska at Omaha
Charles R. Klasson
  University of Iowa
Harold E. Klein
  Temple University
Walter H. Klein
  Boston College
Roberta E. Klemm
  The Wharton School
Rudolf W. Knoepfel
  The Solvay American Corporation
Roderic C. Lancey
  G. D. Searle and Company
Santa LaRocca
  Harvard University
Robert T. Lenz
  Indiana University
James P. Logan
  University of Arizona
Peter Lorange
  Massachusetts Institute of Technology
John F. Lubin
  The Wharton School
Michael McCaskey
  Harvard University
Ian MacMillan
  Columbia University
Renato Mazzolini
  Columbia University
Arlyn J. Melcher
  Kent State University
Richard D. Miller
  Southern Methodist University
John B. Miner
  Georgia State University
Henry Mintzberg
  McGill University
Edwin A. Murray, Jr.
  Northwestern University
Daniel Nathanson
  The Wharton School
William Naumes
  Temple University
William H. Newman
  Columbia University

Frank Paine
  University of Maryland
David J. Parker
  MacMillan Bloedel Limited
G. Richard Patton
  University of Pittsburgh
Robert Pavan
  Temple University
Robert Pitts
  Pennsylvania State University
Bernie C. Reimann
  Cleveland State University
Max Richards
  Pennsylvania State University
Richard Rumelt
  University of California at Los Angeles
David Rutenburg
  Carnegie-Mellon University
Charles B. Saunders
  University of Kansas
Dan E. Schendel
  Purdue University
Sidney Schoeffler
  Strategic Planning Institute
Robert W. Sexty
  Memorial University
J-C. Spender
  Gresham College
William Starbuck
  University of Wisconsin at Milwaukee
George Steiner
  University of California at Los Angeles
Jeffrey Susbauer
  Cleveland State University
Cedric L. Suzman
  Georgia Institute of Technology
William H. Tomlinson
  University of North Florida
Israel Unterman
  San Diego State University
James M. Utterback
  Massachusetts Institute of Technology
Karl H. Vesper
  University of Washington
Mitsuo Wada
  Keio University
John L. Ward
  Loyola University
Charles B. Weinberg
  Stanford University

James E. Weir
    Saint Louis University
William T. Whitely
    University of Kansas
William D. Wilsted
    University of Colorado

Max S. Wortman, Jr.
    University of Massachusetts
Leonard Wrigley
    University of Western Ontario

Appendix 2 — Program Schedule

BUSINESS POLICY AND PLANNING RESEARCH:
THE STATE-OF-THE-ART

May 25–27, 1977

Pittsburgh, Pennsylvania

Wednesday, May 25

8:00–8:15 A.M.
Introduction to Conference
John Grant
Dan Schendel

8:15–9:45 A.M.
"The Concept of Strategy and Strategic Management"
Author: H. Igor Ansoff (presented by Dan Schendel)
Moderator: Charles W. Hofer
Discussants: William Dill
             William Newman

10:00–11:30 A.M.
"Goal Structures and Rationality"
Author: Henry Mintzberg
Moderator: Cedric Suzman
Discussants: Max Richards
             Edwin A. Murray, Jr.

1:00–2:30 P.M.
"Strategy Formulation: Analytical and Normative Models"
Authors: John Grant
             William King
Moderator: Charles Weinberg
Discussants: Derek Channon
             David Rutenburg

2:45–4:15 P.M.
"Strategy Formulation: Behavioral and Political Models"
Authors: Joseph Bower
             Yves Doz
Moderator: Renato Mazzolini
Discussants: John Child
             Ian MacMillan

4:30–6:00 P.M.
"Environmental Analysis and Forecasting"
Author: James Utterback
Moderator: Elmer Burack
Discussants: Samuel Doctors
             Harold Klein

Thursday, May 26

8:00–9:30 A.M.   "Strategy Evaluation"
Author:	Richard Rumelt
Moderator:	Edward H. Bowman
Discussants:	Bruce Kirchhoff
	Sidney Schoeffler

10:00–11:30 A.M.   "Contingency Theories of Strategy"
Author:	George Steiner
Moderator:	Patrick Conley
Discussants:	Frank Paine
	G. Richard Patton

1:00–2:30 P.M.   "Strategy Implementation: The Role of Formal Planning Systems"
Author:	Peter Lorange
Moderator:	Charles Saunders
Discussants:	Dale Hekhuis
	Harold Henry

2:45–4:15 P.M.   "Strategy Implementation: The Role of Organizational Structure and Processes"
Authors:	Jay Galbraith
	Daniel Nathanson
Moderator:	Merrit J. Davoust
Discussants:	John Miner
	Leonard Wrigley

4:30–6:00 P.M.   "Strategic Management: New Ventures and Small Businesses"
Author:	Arnold Cooper
Moderator:	John Doutt
Discussants:	Karl Vesper
	Jeffrey Susbauer

Friday, May 27

8:00–9:15 A.M.   "Strategic Management: Multimission Business"
Author:	Norman Berg
Moderator:	Robert Pavan
Discussants:	Richard Brandenburg
	Robert Pitts

9:30–10:45 A.M.   "Research Methods: Quantitative"
Author:	Kenneth Hatten
Moderator:	Dan Schendel
Discussants:	John Lubin
	William Naumes

10:45–12:00 P.M. "Research Methods: Qualitative"
      Author: Robert Duncan
      Moderator: Charles Hofer
      Discussants: J-C. Spender
           William Starbuck

1:15–2:15 P.M. "Strategic Management: Not-for-profit Organizations"
      Author: Max Wortman
      Moderator: William Wilsted

2:15–3:30 P.M. "Policy and Planning Research: Practitioners' Views"
      Moderator: Ram Charan
      Discussants: Ronald Aines
           Ben Ball
           Rudolph Knoepfel
           Roderic Lancey

3:30–4:30 P.M. "Policy and Planning Research: Teaching Implications"
      Moderator: Charles Klasson
      Discussants: W. Harvey Hegarty
           Israel Unterman

4:30–5:00 P.M. Concluding Remarks
      Charles W. Hofer
      Dan E. Schendel

(continued from page iv)

Exhibit 7.18 Duncan, Robert; Cooke, Robert; Zaltman, Gerald; Mohrman, Allan; and Mohrman, Sue. "Assessment of a Structural/Task Approach to Organizational Development in Schools." Unpublished manuscript. Graduate School of Management, Northwestern University, 1977.

Exhibit 7.19 Fig. 19, "Outline of the Analysis" from *The Nature of Managerial Work* by Henry Mintzberg. Copyright © 1973 by Henry Mintzberg. Used by permission of Harper & Row, Publishers, Inc.

Exhibit 7.20 From Joseph McGrath, "Toward a 'Theory of Method' for Research on Organizations" in Cooper, Leavitt, and Shelly (eds.), *New Perspectives in Organizational Research*, (1964) p. 555. Reprinted by permission of John Wiley & Sons, Inc.

Exhibit 7.22 Paul E. Green, Donald S. Tull, *Research for Marketing Decisions*, 3rd edition, © 1975, pp. 325, 335, 340. Reprinted by permission of Prentice-Hall, Inc., Englewood Cliffs, New Jersey.

Exhibit 7.25 Paul E. Green and Yoram Wind, "New Ways to Measure Consumers' Judgments," *Harvard Business Review*, July–August 1975, copyright © 1975 by the President and Fellows of Harvard College; all rights reserved.

Exhibit 8.1 From Arch Dooley and Wickham Skinner, "Casing CaseMethod Methods," *Academy of Management Review*, April 1977. Reprinted by permission of the authors and the publisher.

Exhibit 8.2 From C. W. Hofer, "Needed the New Business Administration," *The Singapore Manager*, December 1969. Reprinted by permission.